SECOND EDITION

PROFESSIONAL

A RELATIONSHIP MANAGEMENT PROCESS

SELLING

JOHN I. COPPETT
University of Houston–Clear Lake

WILLIAM A. STAPLES
University of Houston–Clear Lake

COLLEGE DIVISION South-Western Publishing Co.

Cincinnati Ohio

To Mary

—John I. Coppett

To Darlene, Haley, and my parents,
Bonnie and John

—William A. Staples

Sponsoring Editor:	Randy G. Haubner
Production Editor:	Sharon L. Smith
Production House:	Custom Editorial Productions, Inc.
Cover Design:	Ben Ross
Interior Design:	John Odam Design Associates
Photo Research:	Carol Smith
Marketing Manager:	Scott D. Person

SD60BA
Copyright © 1994
by South-Western Publishing Co.
Cincinnati, Ohio

Library of Congress Cataloging-in-Publication Data

Coppett, John I.
    Professional selling : a relationship management process / John
I. Coppett, William A. Staples.
       p.   cm.
    Includes index.
    ISBN 0-538-82776-9
    1. Selling. 2. Customer relations. 3. Customer service—
Management. 4. Sales management. I. Staples, William A.
II. Title.
HF5438.25.C66 1993
658.8—dc20
                                                  93-1655
                                                CIP

1 2 3 4 5 6 7 D1 9 8 7 6 5 4 3

Printed in the United States of America

I(T)P
International Thomson Publishing

South-Western Publishing Co. is an ITP Company. The ITP Trademark is used under license.

Preface

Someone opening a textbook for the first time is usually curious about a number of things. Are the ideas communicated in an interesting and rational way? Are the examples current and consistent with the reader's perceptions of what is occurring in the real world? Is a unifying theme used throughout the book and is it communicated clearly? Although readers must delve into a book to evaluate its merit thoroughly, we believe, as authors, that we owe it to our readers explicitly to state the basic propositions that undergird this book and, furthermore, to offer them to you immediately. To that end, we have chosen to state our fundamental beliefs in this preface. The principles set forth in the following paragraphs establish the tone that we believe resonates throughout the book.

PRINCIPLE #1

People enjoy buying but they hate to be sold. It is unfortunate that the general public seems to have an impression that the basic responsibility of a salesperson is to make a potential buyer purchase the salesperson's products or services. We strongly oppose that idea. Instead, we assume that buyers are sufficiently intelligent to at least sense when they are being pressured, and their natural reaction will be to resist such pressure. We believe that today's professional sales representatives assist their customers in finding ways to secure the benefits that they are seeking. Discovering what these benefits are and how they can be attained via a particular product or service requires sensitivity and insight on the salesperson's part.

PRINCIPLE #2

Customers will purchase from you only after you have established a relationship with them. The formation of the relationship usually requires that the salesperson achieve two "sales" in addition to selling the primary product or service. First, the representative must sell himself or herself as a credible, trustworthy person whose message is worthwhile for the prospective buyer. In addition, the salesperson must present his or her company as the best supplier. How does one establish a relationship that will eventually lead to a purchase? The art of asking customer-oriented questions and of listening carefully to the response is prerequisite to establishing a relationship. Very specific guidance on questioning and listening is provided at several points in this book.

PRINCIPLE #3

Buyer-seller relationships are sufficiently varied to warrant an indepth examination of the *nature* of a particular relationship. Buyers purchasing for themselves or as agents for an organization reflect wide ranges of knowledge and experience in purchasing. A salesperson should analyze each potential relationship and respond to the circumstances appropriately. The insight required by the salesperson and the ability to adjust are two of the differences separating a professional salesperson from someone who is not.

PRINCIPLE #4

Much of a professional sales representative's success will depend on the ability to determine quickly whether a mutually beneficial relationship can be established with a prospective buyer. The salesperson's accurate appraisal of his or her capabilities and those of his or her company will permit the representative to identify more effectively prospective buyers whose needs and wants can be more effectively satisfied. Self-knowledge, an understanding of one's company and its capabilities, and insights into customers' needs will permit the salesperson to pursue customers who can be profitably served.

PRINCIPLE #5

What a salesperson says to a customer is not as important as how and when it is said. The careful nurturing of a relationship, whether in a sales situation or in another context, requires constant sensitivity to the other person's circumstances. Some people have greater skill in cultivating this sensitivity than others. All of us, however, given the motivation to become more aware of other people's feelings, can improve our abilities to empathize. We are confident that this book will help you improve in this important human relations area.

PRINCIPLE #6

Successful salespeople must be adept at selling both inside their company as well as outside to traditionally recognized customers. The representative whose customer needs to be billed in a certain way must persuade people in accounting to provide the customer with the bill in the desired form. Special shipping dates, credit terms, and packaging requirements are only some of the areas in which salespeople become involved with their peers in other departments of their company. Successful professional salespeople must be skilled boundary spanners capable of representing the customer's views to people in other departments and also of communicating with customers about what can and cannot be done by shipping, credit, or other departments.

PRINCIPLE #7

No one is ever transferred or promoted out of sales. Regardless of what your academic major is now or what your career aspirations are, you will remain "in sales." These statements reflect our belief that successful human interaction reflects the fundamentals of selling. The proposal and acceptance of ideas, whether or not they are associated with products or services, involves selling. Although the examples used in this book are sales-oriented in a conventional sense, you can easily translate the guidance given in various chapters to many other situations. A student seeking a job is selling. A professor presenting credentials to a tenure committee is also selling. Likewise a student asking that an examination answer be reviewed is selling. Examples of "sales" situations are everywhere anyone is attempting to persuade someone else.

Although these principles were reflected in the first edition, some changes differentiate this edition from its predecessor. The most significant changes are enumerated below:

1. Readers will find numerous updated examples of the various types of professional sales positions now available. A way of analyzing the variety of sales positions is provided. Students can engage in self-analysis to see which type of sales environment might be most satisfying to them personally.

2. More attention is paid in this edition to the use of high-tech means of finding prospective buyers. Databases, now plentiful and relatively inexpensive, are helping sales representatives search for new accounts.

3. The art of negotiation has been given considerably more attention. A complete chapter has been added that deals only with negotiation.

4. Twenty new cases have been inserted at the end of the chapters. This expanded case coverage permits students to improve their analytical skills over a broader range of realistic sales situations.

5. The theme of professionalism, which resonated throughout the first edition, has been strengthened in this edition. The authors are convinced that today's professional relationship managers, who bind customers closer to a company, are invaluable human resources. The skills needed to form and maintain strong relationships should be accorded the respect that skills required in other professions are accorded. In short, we want the readers of this textbook to aspire to be professional sales representatives.

*   *   *

The second edition of this book would not have been possible without the encouragement and assistance of many people. First, we owe a debt of gratitude to the students and instructors whose reactions to the first edition encouraged us to create this edition. Although there are too many to mention by name, we feel a deep sense of appreciation to them.

The personnel at South-Western Publishing Company have also been most supportive. Specifically, we wish to thank Jim Sitlington, whose experience makes him a consummate relationship manager in his work with authors. Sharon Smith, production editor, also exhibited great patience and skill in keeping the revision process moving smoothly

Two other skilled professionals also were of great help. Judy O'Neill served quite capably as the project manager. Joyce Rosinger provided expert guidance on rights and permissions, the securing of which can be a daunting task to authors.

Within our university we owe an enormous debt of gratitude to Becky Brand. Her ability to decipher our writing and turn out finished manuscript while performing in an unflappable manner characterizes her as a superb relationship manager.

Finally, authors cannot produce a book without support and understanding from family members. The hours spent in writing and revising this edition reduced the quality time that could have otherwise been spent with our families. Our gratitude for their support will linger long after this edition is completed.

Notwithstanding all of the support we received, we alone take full responsibility for the content of this book.

John I. Coppett
William A. Staples
University of Houston–Clear Lake

Brief Contents

Contents

PART ONE

Professional Selling, Marketing Communications, and Relationship Management

CHAPTER 1

What Is Professional Selling?

LEARNING OBJECTIVES

After studying this chapter, you should be able to:

1. Identify and describe several situations that illustrate how important the sales function is in many of the leading companies of the United States.

2. Explain how professional selling has evolved in the United States.

3. Describe three requirements a person must meet to be a successful professional salesperson.

4. Describe what salespeople do and why they must be good time managers.

5. Understand in a general way the compensation levels for salespeople.

6. Define the key terms used in this chapter.

KEY TERMS

- partnering
- strategic alliances
- professional
- boundary spanning
- Production Era
- Sales Era
- Marketing Era
- Strategic Marketing Era
- order taker
- order getter
- consultative selling
- sales cycle
- trade selling
- technical selling
- service selling
- inside selling
- missionary selling
- detail salespeople

JOHN CHARLESWORTH SLID the class schedule across the table to Nancy Kidd and said, "Here's a course I've been thinking about. It's called Professional Selling. I need an elective, and it's offered at a good time for me."

"Selling! No way!" said Nancy. "What're you going to learn, John? How to keep people from hanging up when you call them?"

"Well, I'm a marketing major, and I've heard that most of the job opportunities for new graduates are in sales," John said somewhat defensively.

"Yeah, I know. That's the main reason I'm thinking about switching my major to management," Nancy exclaimed. "I want to be treated like a professional person, and I don't believe selling is a profession."

"What gave you that impression, Nancy?" John asked.

"Well, you know, you see those obnoxious TV commercials where some loud-mouthed person is selling cars, or at dinnertime the phone rings and someone tries to sell you something. Even at the shopping malls you see the salespeople in stores. All they seem to ever say is 'Can I help you?' and 'Have a nice day.' No thanks, John, I don't want to take a course in selling."

"I hear you," said John as he dragged the schedule back and stood up to leave. I wonder, thought John as he walked away, is Nancy right? Will it be a waste of time?

All of us are curious as we start a course. We all have used the grapevine and asked other students such questions as: Was it a good course? What did you do in there? How can I use the course to get a job? Will it be beneficial later on in my career? These are very legitimate and practical questions. They deserve to be answered quickly. We do this now by illustrating how personal selling is regarded in some well-known Fortune 500 companies and how important selling is in managing one's career.

WHY STUDY PROFESSIONAL SELLING?

For those who are searching for some immediate job placement assistance, an excellent article appeared in the *Wall Street Journal* titled, "The Most Important Sale You'll Ever Make." A portion of it follows:

Out of work? Think again! You are really self-employed (with deferred income). Your new job is as a senior sales representative and chief marketing officer. You are selling personal services—yours. And it is one of the most difficult jobs you will ever know.

(from the "Manager's Journal" section of the *Wall Street Journal*, December 23, 1991, p. A8.)

The article states what a moment's reflection will tell you is true. Each of us must sell ourself. Through our education and life experiences, we "design" ourselves as "products." At various times we must sell our personal product to an employer. A course in professional selling will give you some useful insights about how to better package yourself as you engage in your personal sales campaigns.

We find a second reason for taking a course in selling by looking at what is happening at DuPont, an international manufacturer and marketer of chemicals. DuPont is sending to sales training those employees whose work routines bring them into occasional contact with customers.[1] DuPont's managers realize that whenever a customer comes in contact with a DuPont employee (a receptionist, a customer service person, and so forth), *that employee is DuPont* to the customer. DuPont wants the contact to be a positive experience; therefore, employees are going through sales training, learning how to "sell DuPont." In short, *everyone* whose job may bring them into contact with customers is "in sales." If this is occurring in some of the leading companies, why not get a head start by taking a course in college?

Another highly successful company, Ball Corporation, which manufactures packaging products, has this corporate philosophy:

Everybody sells. In addition to the sales force, people at every level of the organization, from accounting to quality control, are in touch with their counterparts at customer companies.[2]

In the Ball Corporation and in a growing number of firms, a trend called **partnering** or **strategic alliances** is occurring.[3] Two companies, one of which is a key supplier to the other, join together in a business venture. Their individual objectives are to achieve advantages over their respective competitors by forming a partnership or alliance. When this occurs, people in each company must work harmoniously with people in the other company. If you are in a shipping department, you may deal with personnel in the other company who are in production. Your ability to "sell solutions" to other people can make a contribution to the maintenance of a profitable partnership.

Finally, if someone with the same view as Nancy Kidd's is still not convinced, he or she might be persuaded by another *Wall Street Journal* article, "Chief Execu-

Figure 1-1 Whenever a customer comes in contact with an employee, that employee *is* the company to the customer.

tives Are Increasingly Chief Salesmen." Top managers in such companies as Xerox, Van Heusen, and Home Depot spend a significant amount of their time selling to their most important customers.[4] If Nancy ever advances to the executive level, do you think she will still have the same attitude toward selling?

Nancy Kidd's ambition to be a professional is admirable, however. You too are probably seeking a professional career. Based on the assumption that you are, this textbook has been written to portray successful salespeople in the 1990s as professionals. A tone of professionalism resonates throughout this book; you will not find suggestions on "how to disarm your negotiating opponent" or "how to break through a wall of objections." These obsolete practices and perspectives will not succeed in the 1990s. Let us turn our attention now to an analysis of professional selling and what *will* be required to succeed in these challenging times.

BASIC REQUIREMENTS OF A SALES PROFESSIONAL

Webster defines a **professional** as someone "participating for gain or livelihood in an activity or field of endeavor often engaged in by amateurs." All of us, unfortunately, have encountered people attempting to sell whom we have labelled amateurs. With luck you have encountered at least some people whom you judged to be professional in their demeanor. What were the differences between the professionals and the amateurs? Was it product knowledge and skillful service? Was it communication skill? Was it appearance? The answer to each of these questions might be yes, but more likely we based our judgments on whether the salesperson knew, or appeared to be interested in knowing, about us and our individual situations.

What are some of the basic things the professional sales representative needs to understand in order to know a customer or client? As you would expect, the range is quite broad.

Professionals Know Their Customers

Knowing the customer might seem so obvious that it would not require any specific mention. Unfortunately, the traditional approach to sales training has often emphasized product or service knowledge (knowing how the company's products worked, and learning their features and benefits) and largely ignored the need for a deeper understanding of customers. Who the best customers are in terms of their location, their buying power, and their size, and who they have purchased from in the past are just some of the areas of knowledge a sales rep needs if he or she is to understand a customer. Chapters 4 and 5 cover some of the things the well-prepared salesperson will need to know about a customer. Although we will stress it several times in later chapters, it is sufficiently important to mention here that one of the keys to successful selling is to know your customer well enough to understand how that customer can use your product or service to solve problems or achieve goals. If you are selling a product or service to an executive in another business and you want to communicate how your product can be used to help the executive's company make greater profits, you must *first know that customer's business.* That means knowing *its* competitors, *its* customers, and *its* operations.

Manuel Diaz, Director of Sales and Marketing at Hewlett-Packard, states, "The new salesperson will have to be able to understand customer requirements and explain solutions in terms the customer can understand."[5] Diaz's viewpoint is seconded by that of E. M. Cavalier, Vice President for Sales at Eli Lilly and Company: "Traditionally, our sales reps were the basic communicators of professional and technical information. But that's changing. Now they're going to have to demonstrate economic justification for buying our products."[6]

Professionals Know Their Own Companies

Another important quality of a professional salesperson is knowledge about his or her own company and the ability to get things accomplished within it. To the customer, *the sales representative is the company.* Often, customers are in contact primarily with the sales representative. Therefore, if merchandise is shipped late, if the bill is incorrect, or if customer service is poor, the customer expects the salesperson to fix things. The salesperson must be capable of interceding for the customer with people and departments who can expedite a shipment, correct a bill, and so forth. This calls for the salesperson to be adept at **boundary spanning**,[7] which means that a sales rep must be capable of "selling" customer responsiveness to fellow employees in departments such as accounting, shipping, and manufacturing.

One of the findings discovered in a research study conducted by Learning International Inc., a world-wide sales training firm based in Stamford, Connecticut, was that the most successful salespeople orchestrate all the internal resources of their firm to help solve customers' problems. They tap into a variety of different resources to add value to their products and services.[8]

Federal Express and Baxter Healthcare are two very successful companies that sell very different things (transportation service and pharmaceutical products). In both companies, salespeople are responsible for knowing when and on whom to call to help solve problems that exceed the salesperson's expertise. At Federal Express, engineering is regularly called upon to support sales.[9] Baxter Healthcare uses a team-selling approach to cement its relationships with hospitals. To maintain and strengthen relationships with a hospital, a Baxter salesperson can offer customers a "free" consultant from Baxter's organization who will work on a problem even if it does not directly involve a Baxter product.[10] Of course assistance like that cannot be offered to customers of all sizes, but judiciously used, such services are powerful inducements for a customer to continue to do business with a company. Who orchestrates these team sales? The salesperson who is ultimately responsible for retaining the customer's business. The key for the salesperson is bringing in the right technical person at the right time.[11]

Professionals Manage the Relationship

A third factor in defining a professional is more subtle, but no less important. The professional sales representative assumes responsibility for creating and nurturing lasting relationships with customers.[12] Rather than viewing the sales job as a series of transactions with a buyer, the successful salesperson views each customer as a partner in an ongoing relationship. A sale occurring during that relationship is but one event among many events involving the buyer and the salesperson. The sales rep acknowledges responsibility for managing the relationship and understands that repeat sales indicate the relationship is healthy.

Relationship management is one of the most important keys to successful professional sales, and therefore we will analyze it thoroughly in later chapters. The concept of relationship management and the idea of being a professional suggest a feature of relationships that is of paramount importance. That feature is integrity.[13] *Sales and Marketing Management* sponsored research among purchasing agents that revealed how highly they valued integrity in their most respected sales representatives (Exhibit 1-1).

Most Valued	Agents Responding (Percentage)
Reliability/credibility	98.6
Professionalism/integrity	93.7
Product knowledge	90.7
Innovativeness in problem solving	80.5
Presentation/preparation	69.7

Exhibit 1-1 Qualities Most Valued in Salespersons by Purchasing Agents

Source: "PAs Examine the People Who Sell to Them," *Sales and Marketing Management* (November 11, 1985): 39.

Coca-Cola's well-known formula change illustrates the necessity for integrity. McCann-Erickson, the advertising agency handling the Coca-Cola account, had to be confidentially apprised of the pending change so that it could prepare a suitable campaign. Although this particular circumstance is rarely duplicated in terms of drama, all successful salespeople who enjoy lengthy relationships with customers or clients become privy to information they must treat as extremely confidential. The client-attorney privilege has its counterpart in the world of the professional salesperson.

To summarize what it means to be a professional sales representative, we have identified and illustrated three key points:

1. The professional knows and exhibits an understanding of the key forces and factors that are relevant to a customer.

2. The professional understands how to get tasks accomplished within his or her company that will benefit the customer.

3. The professional views each customer or client as a partner in a relationship that, when managed correctly, yields sales.

ECONOMIC BENEFITS FROM INCREASED PROFESSIONALISM

Aside from the personal benefits of dealing with more professional sales personnel, what economic benefits could companies achieve? Let us examine how a company's net profits can be improved through the increased efficiency and effectiveness of its sales force. Most companies realize what the potential benefits are and, therefore, spend sizable amounts of money in sales training.

Reduced Sales Costs

Sales & Marketing Management revealed that the cost of making one sales call on an industrial customer was $250.54.[14] That was the average cost to make a sales call *regardless of the results of the call*. A realistic assumption is that for every new customer who buys a company's products for the first time, several sales calls were needed to close the sale. Indeed, research reveals the average number of calls needed to close a sale is four-and-one-half.[15] An executive from the Food Service Division of General Foods Corporation stated that General Foods sales representatives selling to the institutional food market (for example, factory cafeterias, university food services, and hospitals) usually called on a prospective buyer five to ten times before securing the first sale.[16] For purposes of this analysis, let's assume the four-and-one-half sales visit average is appropriate for industrial sales calls. At a sales call cost of $250.54, it would cost $1,127.43 to make one sale (regardless of what the revenue from the sale might be).

If the average number of sales calls can be reduced to three, the total cost of acquiring a customer becomes $751.62 ($3 \times \$250.54$). Costs have declined 33 percent! Conversely, the more sales calls made on people who aren't buying, the higher the total costs will be. Ultimately, the prices we pay as consumers must be raised.

One route to improved profitability is to retain the patronage of a customer for an extended period and permit the seller to reap the profits from repeat purchases. If a lasting relationship with a customer can be formed, it will reduce the costs of having to constantly replace one-time-purchase customers.

Developing a lasting relationship pays off in a wide variety of industries. Automobile industry studies reveal that a brand-loyal customer represents a lifetime average revenue of at least $140,000. Appliance manufacturers calculate that brand loyalty is worth $2,800 over a twenty-year span. Assuming you live in the same neighborhood for five years and patronize the same supermarket for the majority of your purchases, the average profitability to the supermarket will be $22,000.[17]

Implications for Productivity

As foreign competitors have penetrated U.S. markets, concern has grown over the productivity of United States workers. Marked improvements have been made in output per worker in the production areas of our businesses. Productivity improvements have been much more difficult to attain among white-collar or knowledge-industry workers, however. This latter group contains the vast number of salespeople that U.S. businesses employ. One important measure of productivity for sales representatives is the number of sales made relative to the number of sales calls.[18]

Although sales departments are adopting a variety of high-tech aids, such as lap-top computers and telemarketing (see Chapter 6), the sales activity cannot be "robotized." Significant productivity improvements can be achieved, however, through enhancing the level of professionalism in the sales forces of U.S. manufacturers and retaining customers by developing mutually profitable relationships for longer periods. By driving down the costs of acquiring new business and the costs of serving loyal customers, American businesses will have greater freedom to combat the lower prices of some foreign competitors.

THE EVOLUTION OF SALES TOWARD PROFESSIONAL STATURE

A study of selling would be incomplete without looking at the various periods or eras through which personal selling has progressed. Although all businesses, regardless of when or where they operated, have needed sales to survive, there have been periods in which the status of salespeople was different from what it is today in most companies. A brief description of the various eras in American marketing history illustrates some of the major changes in the evolution of selling. As you read and reflect on the changes that have occurred over the past 200 years, try to envision some of the different challenges that confronted salespeople who functioned in earlier days.

To structure this brief historical analysis, we have considered four primary eras or stages through which U.S. business has evolved (Exhibit 1-2). The first period, the **Production Era**, lasted from the beginning of our country until mass production began (roughly 1920). The second period, the **Sales Era**, spanned a much shorter period from approximately 1920 until 1950 (with the exception of the World War II years). The **Marketing Era** dawned in the early 1950s and was gradually replaced in the 1980s by the **Strategic Marketing Era**.

The Production Era (1776–1920)

The sales job during the Production Era was influenced by marketplace conditions. Generally, those conditions could be described as consisting of excess demand for goods. Production, in short, could not produce sufficient goods to satisfy the growing population. The job of salespersons was to take customers' orders and inform them about the availability of products. Salespeople were **order takers**. Under conditions of goods scarcity, the highest status in a company was usually accorded to individuals who could find ways to produce more of the products the

Exhibit 1-2 **The Evolution of the Professional Salesperson**

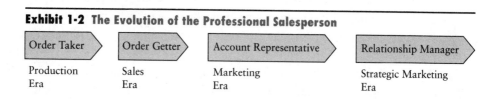

market was demanding. We should not conclude, however, that the sales job was easy. Communication was vastly different. Salespeople often had to personally perform the marketing communication tasks of finding customers, describing the products to them, taking their orders, carrying the orders back to headquarters, and perhaps even delivering the goods during the next trip to the customer. Often this involved laborious, time-consuming, and exhausting travel from one market to another. Many of the often-quoted traveling salesman jokes told during the early 1900s reflect selling during this time.

Truman E. Moore, author of *The Traveling Man*, recounts some of the jokes and anecdotes about the traveling salesperson.

A drummer went to the front desk to leave a wake-up call. "Never mind," said the clerk, "we get everybody up at 6, so we can use the sheets for tablecloths."

A hotel for commercial travelers in Oklahoma posted these rules:

1. *"Gents goin' to bed with their boots on will be charged extra."*
2. *"Three raps at the door means there is a murder in the house and you must get up."*
3. *"Please write your name on the wallpaper so we know you've been here."*

A salesman died while covering his territory. His office received a wire from the local sheriff asking for instructions. The home office wired back: "Search through his clothes and see if he had any orders."

Source: Truman E. Moore, *The Traveling Man: The Story of the American Traveling Salesman* (Garden City, N.Y.: Doubleday and Company, Inc., 1972), 58–59, 61. Reprinted with permission of Doubleday, a division of Bantam, Doubleday, Dell Publishing Group, Inc.

When these scenarios were occurring, there were no students majoring in marketing or taking college courses in sales. The only school in which salespeople enrolled was the proverbial "school of hard knocks."

The Sales Era (1920–1950)

As the Industrial Revolution quickened its pace in the U.S., and technological advancements permitted mass production, the supply-demand imbalance moved to the other extreme. More goods were now being produced than the marketplace could absorb. The role of salespeople shifted from order taker to **order getter**. The new competition for customers meant sales representatives were responsible for achieving a sales quota that, when attained by all the firm's salespersons, permitted the company to sell its output of goods. The philosophy of the Sales Era was captured in the statement, "Let's be sure we sell all we make." As an order getter, the sales representative faced the challenge of persuading buyers to purchase a specific brand from among a variety of competing brands. One of the unfortunate legacies of this era was the image of a sales representative as an individual who pressured customers into buying. Arthur Miller's famous play, *Death of a Sales-*

man, chronicled the life of Willy Loman, a pathetic figure who epitomized the salesman of that time.

Persons who sold during the Sales Era didn't need college degrees. What they required were psyches that could not be eroded by rejection or insults.

Although the late Henry Ford was a production genius, he is said to have made a comment that capsulizes perfectly the attitude of salespeople during this era: "I'll give them any color they want as long as it's black." Salespeople who have to talk people into buying black cars when they want something else do not lead a pleasant existence.

The Marketing Era (1950–1980)

Shortly after the end of World War II, a new age dawned in American business. Various marketing scholars have identified it as the Marketing Era.[19] In contrast to the Sales Era, the Marketing Era is reflected by the statement, "Let's be sure we make only what we can sell." The Marketing Era was characterized by businesses paying attention to what customers seemed to need or want *before* producing the goods. The idea was to discover customers' needs first and then develop a product or service to fill those needs. The discovery processes ushered in some profound changes in marketing and sales. In marketing, research activity became much more important in order to describe who might be a consumer of a particular product and what the consumer expected from the consumption experience. In sales, a new approach termed **consultative selling** emerged.[20] The emphasis changed from talking a prospective buyer into making a purchase to finding out what the prospect's problems were and trying to solve them.[21] Thus, the salesperson took a major step toward the ranks of sales professionals.[22]

The Strategic Marketing Era (1980–present)

The current strategic marketing stage has introduced some subtle and important differences. Managers are advised to manage their customers for profits, not just for sales.[23] Realizing that profitability is far more important than the number of sales, some firms are developing strategies to concentrate their marketing and sales efforts on the potentially most profitable customers.

An example of a company employing this strategic approach is MCI Communications Corporation. One percent of the nation's telephone customers account for about 40 percent of all long-distance dollars.[24] These huge corporate and institutional accounts are the target of MCI's strategy. "We have to show large customers that we have the right mix of services and depth of experience," states an MCI executive.[25]

When this cream-skimming strategy is employed, sales reps assigned to select accounts must be adept at developing and maintaining lasting relationships with customers.[26] Salespeople must become proficient at analyzing a major customer's environment and then proposing solutions to meet this customer's most significant problems. The company that truly is practicing strategic marketing is focusing on the relatively small percentage of customers who account for a disproportionate percentage of sales in an industry.[27] To be successful in executing such a strategy, a firm must have sales personnel who possess in-depth knowledge of the customer's situation and the skills to apply their firm's products or service to satisfying a customer's needs. Armed with a sales force capable of doing this, a firm can enjoy a strong differential advantage that competitors will find difficult to overcome.

In each of these various eras enormous changes were occurring in the U.S. economy. We shifted from an agricultural economy to a production-driven economy to a high-tech and service-oriented economy. As the country made these transitions, the variety of sales positions also grew. Now when someone states that he or she is "in sales," we must find out much more about his or her particular situation, since there are so many different types of sales positions. In the next section, we will briefly analyze some of the basic kinds of sales positions and use examples to illustrate the variety of opportunities for professional salespeople.

DIFFERENT KINDS OF SALES POSITIONS

Any observer of the business scene will quickly see that sales positions are quite diverse. For example, the Xerox sales representative can show his or her company's product, demonstrate its features, and actually provide instantaneous proof of what the machine can produce. A sales representative selling insurance for Northwestern Mutual Life, however, has no tangible product and cannot produce any tangible evidence of the immediate benefits a policy holder might enjoy. Aside from acknowledging that great diversity exists within the occupational field called "sales," of what importance is this variety to you as an individual? The answer to this question brings us to the very heart of the question many of you are asking— If I choose to become a professional sales representative, *what type of selling would be best for me?*

Analyzing Sales Positions

Exhibit 1-3 offers three criteria that can be applied to analyze any sales position. You may find these criteria useful as you evaluate specific sales positions and your particular background and interests. Let us describe each criterion in detail.

1. Amount and nature of technical or scientific training required.
2. Amount of structure involved in the daily performance of the work.
3. Length of the sales cycle.

Exhibit 1-3 Three Basic Criteria for Analyzing a Sales Position

Amount and Nature of Required Training

Why would some corporate recruiters interview biology or chemistry majors for sales work instead of business majors? Why would some companies send their recruits to expensive training programs while others train their personnel "in the field"? Because in some cases a salesperson could not be a credible spokesperson without extensive preparation, such as majoring in a certain field or developing advanced skills in a corporate training program.

Dow Chemical Company, for instance, has selected a group of about thirty-five colleges and universities from which it recruits almost all its new sales representatives. Each recruit spends one year in a structured training program. "We've calculated that after about four years with the company, our investment in a sales representative is in the hundreds of thousands of dollars," says Robert M. Baughman, Vice President of Human Resources at Dow.[28]

Degree of Structure Involved

Some people are comfortable only if they can predict what their daily work routine will be. In sales it might seem that this would be almost impossible. However, there are situations where a salesperson has a defined territory and calls on only several dozen customers or prospective customers who are relatively easy to identify.

For example, a pharmaceutical salesperson located in Houston, Texas knows where his or her geographical boundaries are. In addition, the rep realizes that only limited numbers and types of buyers exist for the pharmaceutical line. It would be ridiculous, for example, to call on retail clothing store buyers. Therefore, the pharmaceutical sales representative has a great deal more structure in his or her job than does a general-line insurance agent who may sell home, auto, and life insurance to both individuals and small businesses. In short, one is a specialist and the other is much more of a generalist. In which type of situation do think you would thrive?

Length of Sales Cycle

Generally, a **sales cycle** is defined as the period from the moment a contact is initiated with a prospective buyer until the moment when the salesperson knows

Figure 1-2 Structured training programs for sales representatives provide extensive preparation for new recruits.

definitely whether a sale is going to be made and the product or service is going to be installed. Cycles can range from minutes to years. A retail salesperson usually knows within a few minutes whether a shopper will make a purchase. A sales representative for IBM, on the other hand, may spend a year or more making many calls on one prospective buyer before selling a computer system.

Some people need frequent and rapid results for the efforts they expend. Usually such persons would function better if they were selling something that permitted them to know quickly whether they would be successful with a particular buyer. Patience is not an attribute that many U.S. business people have in abundance (a point on which we will elaborate in Chapter 17). Knowing yourself and your patience level can serve you well as you analyze various sales positions.

As you think about your particular interests, background, and personality, compare these factors with the different sales situations we now examine. Which one(s) do you think would be most satisfying to you?

Basic Types of Sales Positions

Interspersed throughout this text are examples of salespeople in action. You will read about professional salespeople from such companies as AT&T, Hewlett-Packard, IBM, American Hospital Supply, and many others. Some of their sales efforts involve products, while others involve services. Some require a great deal of technical expertise, whereas other situations depend more on the establishment

Type of Selling	Examples
Trade selling	Procter and Gamble, Levi's, General Motors
Technical selling	IBM, Boeing, DuPont
Service selling	Northwestern Mutual Life, CNN, J. Walter Thompson
Inside selling	Macy's, Access Biotechnology
Missionary selling	Merck, South-Western Publishing Co.

Exhibit 1-4 Basic Types of Selling

of interpersonal relationships. Sifting through the myriad sales positions and trying to focus on one or a few possible areas can be quite confusing. We have, therefore, broken down the general activity of selling into five basic categories (see Exhibit 1-4). As we describe each category, we provide some specific examples to illustrate what happens in each type of selling.

Trade Selling

Trade selling, also known as selling to the trade, means you are selling to a buyer who intends to resell your product for a profit. A salesperson from Procter and Gamble calling on a buyer at a Kroger store is selling to the trade. The Kroger purchaser is buying from Procter and Gamble and hundreds of other suppliers to provide within the Kroger store an assortment of products that will be attractive to shoppers. A sales representative from Levi's is also calling on the trade in such stores as The GAP and Sears. The buyers there are responsible for assembling attractive and profitable assortments of clothing that will be purchased by their customers.

Salespeople from the General Motors Corporation are calling on automobile dealers. The dealers, in turn, sell to the final consumers in the dealers' local markets. The GM sales reps ensure that their dealers are informed about GM's corporate promotion plans, rebate offers, pricing changes, and other details as well as encouraging the dealers to stock more cars and trucks.

It is very important that salespeople calling on resellers understand their customers' business conditions. If, for instance, the Levi's representative can keep buyers informed about the introduction of a new line of Levi's clothes, the profit potential available to the reseller, and Levi's national advertising plans, the buyer is much more likely to give the salesperson future orders for clothing.

Technical Selling

The phrase **technical selling** conveys the nature of another sales situation. Customers here are businesses or organizations using the seller's products or services as they, in turn, make and sell their products or conduct their operations. An IBM salesperson selling a new line of computers to a Disney Corporation purchasing agent will probably call on various people in the Disney Corporation many times before a sale is made. In this case, Disney engineers and computer programmers will probably be involved in the choice of a computer system. (We describe this kind of sale in Chapter 2.) People selling technical products or services usually must be adept at discussing their product or service with personnel in the prospective buyer's organization who are technically knowledgeable about that product or service.

A sales representative from Boeing Aircraft Corporation selling a multi-million dollar aircraft to Delta Airlines is obviously selling a highly technical product to a team of Delta personnel likely to be considering one or two other aircraft manufacturers' products. The length of the sales cycle can be two years or more, and the Boeing rep must know when and how to use other Boeing employees to help convince Delta's decision makers.

Likewise, a DuPont sales professional calling on someone at International Paper Company must not only be an expert on the DuPont product line but must also understand the technical challenges that confront a paper manufacturer trying to improve a competitive position. Many times this entails the use of a team approach to selling. Personnel from research, manufacturing, and sales may all go on an important customer call. (We discuss this kind of selling in Chapter 15.)

Service Selling

Service selling presents some formidable challenges! A salesperson usually has little or nothing of a tangible nature to show the prospective buyer. In contrast to the Levi's rep who can carry a sample into a buyer's office, a Prudential Life Insurance agent or a Merrill Lynch stockbroker has no such object to help him or her in making a sale.

Although credibility and trust are important in any type of sale, these traits are even more indispensable when selling a service. A Northwestern Mutual Life Insurance vice president summarizes what it takes to succeed in the sale of services: "We've always stressed the importance of people over product, and that's because the business we're in demands that we establish long-term relationships with our customers."[29]

Not only are services sold to private consumers, but other businesses are customers as well. A sales rep selling television advertising time for CNN calls on advertising agency media buyers to encourage them to recommend CNN to their agency's clients. What does the CNN rep have to sell? Basically, the seller has information about who is watching CNN at certain hours of the day. The ability of

CNN to deliver an audience is what a purchaser of television advertising time will look at. It is the salesperson's responsibility to show why a series of thirty-second time slots would be better for Ford Motor Company on CNN than on another channel. As we mentioned earlier, the successful salesperson must know not only his or her service, but also the customers' concerns as well.

We might not normally regard people in advertising as being in personal sales. However, ask an account executive with J. Walter Thompson, Ogilvy and Mather, or some other advertising agency what he or she does. Essentially, it is the responsibility of the account executive to keep his or her clients (like IBM, Ford, and General Foods) "sold" on their relationship with the agency. Advertising account executives are, in essence, professional salespeople.

Inside Selling

The term **inside selling** conveys to most people the idea that customers come to the salesperson. This can be accomplished in several ways. First, the prospective purchaser can come to the store or sales site and shop. Second, the customer can pick up the telephone and initiate contact with the salesperson. Third, the salesperson can initiate the contact by using the phone. In the case of The Home Shopping Club, the salespeople "come into" each potential shopper's home via television, make their presentation, and invite customers to call an 800 service number to place an order.

We will assume that you are sufficiently familiar with retail shopping that no explanations or descriptions of typical sales positions are necessary. What many readers may not know much about is another form of inside sales in the rapidly expanding field of telemarketing. (Chapter 15, "Emerging Trends and Technologies in Selling," provides much more detail about specific types of telemarketing applications.) In 1991, it was estimated that 481,000 U.S. companies were conducting all or part of their sales calls by telephone. The volume of sales has grown in the past ten years from $1 billion to an estimated $60 billion.[30]

An example of an inside sales position in a telemarketing operation is furnished by Access Biotechnology in San Francisco,[31] which sells doctors cancer drugs from fifteen different manufacturers. The benefit to a physician is that in one phone call he or she can purchase whatever drugs are needed; they are received the next day. Sales reps for Access Biotechnology are required to have a college degree, some sales experience, and some knowledge of medical products.[32]

Usually, the circumstances surrounding most inside sales positions will be characterized by short sales cycles. This is especially true if the customer initiates the call. If the inside sales representative serves several hundred identified customers, then there is likely to be a high degree of structure to the job.

Missionary Selling

People calling on individuals who decide what product someone else should buy are said to be engaged in **missionary selling**. Physicians and college professors are two types of professional people who decide what their patients and students, respectively, will purchase. Drugs that are prescribed and textbooks that are adopted are, of course, not purchased by the physicians or the college professors themselves.

Sales representatives calling on physicians are sometimes referred to as **detail salespeople**. The reps describe the purpose of a particular drug product, the recommended dosage, and its side effects (if any) and provide samples for the physician. This is done to encourage the physician to specify a particular drug brand on the prescription given to a patient.

Salespeople representing publishing companies engage in essentially the same kind of sales work when they call on professors. The rep informs the professor about new textbooks and the features that distinguish one text from others. In many cases, the representative makes arrangements for the professor to receive a free copy of a text so that he or she can examine the book and decide about adopting it for a future class.

Merck Pharmaceutical Company and South-Western Publishing Company employ salespeople to engage in missionary sales work. Merck spends millions of dollars training new salespeople and keeping experienced sales reps up to date on new products. South-Western's representatives meet as a group once a year to hear various editors describe the new textbooks they will be publishing. The sales reps are told how they can present their new texts to the professors, when the books will be available, and also what ancillary materials (videotapes, study guides, and so forth) will be provided.

In both cases, the sales forces call on professional people who are usually very well educated and knowledgeable about their field of specialization. The sales representatives themselves have to be comfortable interacting with other professionals.

HOW DO SALES PROFESSIONALS SPEND THEIR TIME?

As you read the brief descriptions of the various sales positions, you probably concluded that the way salespeople spend their time depends on the type of selling position. For instance, an inside sales representative using a telephone can spend almost all of his or her working day contacting customers. It is not uncommon for a salesperson to make twenty-five customer contacts per day by using the telephone.[33] Compare this to an outside field salesperson who calls on each of his or her customers face to face. In such cases, the average number of calls made per day is 4.5.[34]

Exhibit 1-5 is a breakdown of how salespeople in twenty-two industries spent their time. Several conditions revealed in this study conducted by the Dartnell Corporation, a research organization, are worthy of our attention. First, note the relatively small amount of time salespeople spend in face-to-face contact with their prospects and customers (30 percent). Even if you add the telephone time involved in selling (20 percent), actual selling time is still only half the total. Thus it is little wonder that sales managers are constantly seeking new ways and methods to increase the productivity of their sales personnel. (In Chapter 14 we look at time and territory management.)

Second, almost one-fourth the salesperson's time is spent "waiting and traveling." Travel activity can be very costly to a firm with salespeople who must fly a lot, stay in hotels, and be reimbursed for meals. *Sales & Marketing Management*, in a survey of sales managers, has found that the average annual reimbursement for salespersons' travel was $12,480.83.[35] This is another reason that telemarketing has become so widely used.

Exhibit 1-5 How Salespeople Spend Their Time

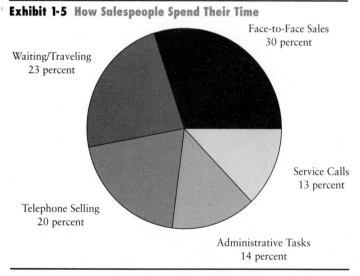

Face-to-Face Sales
30 percent

Waiting/Traveling
23 percent

Service Calls
13 percent

Telephone Selling
20 percent

Administrative Tasks
14 percent

Source: Dartnell Corporation, 26th Survey of Sales Force Compensation 1990, Dartnell Corporation, Chicago.

Year	Sales Trainee	Mid-Level Salesperson	Top-Level Salesperson
1987	24,046	36,469	55,418
1988	24,395	38,869	58,308
1989	25,079	37,073	58,981
1990	26,940	39,666	57,582
1991	26,036	40,194	59,955

Exhibit 1-6
Average Annual Compensation of Three Levels of Salespeople

Definitions of Sales Personnel

Sales Trainees: Persons at an entry level who are learning about the company and its products and services prior to being given an assignment.

Mid-level Salespersons: Persons ranging from newly assigned salespeople to more experienced people who possess a broad knowledge of their products and customers.

Top-level Salespersons: Persons considered to be capable of selling to a company's major customers.

Source: *Sales & Marketing Management, 1992 Sales Manager's Budget Planner,* June 22, 1992, p. 68. Reprinted by permission of *Sales & Marketing Management.* Copyright: *Sales Manager's Budget Planner,* June 22, 1992.

COMPENSATION

What do salespeople earn? It is all well and good to consider yourself a professional and, even better, to have the esteem of other people who also regard you as a professional. Nevertheless, most of us want to enjoy financial rewards as well as psychic satisfactions.

Exhibit 1-6 reflects findings gathered by *Sales & Marketing Management* over a five-year period. Three categories of salespeople are utilized to reflect the different levels of experience and expertise found in most sales forces. You may be curious about why the compensation figures for sales trainees show an increase each year whereas the figures for both the mid-level and top-level salespersons fluctuate up and down. Trainees usually are paid on a salary basis with no commissions or bonuses. As they "graduate" into the ranks of mid-level salespeople, however, they are usually put on a combination of salary plus commissions. In some companies, there may also be bonuses. Commissions and bonuses will be affected by several factors—not the least of which is general business conditions. Therefore, a salesperson selling in an industry or a part of the country in a recession might find that his or her sales volume decreased from the previous year, and, consequently, the total amount of commissions or bonuses granted would also decrease. One of the key points to be found in Chapter 7 is the importance for salespeople of managing their customer portfolios so that if one group of customers decreases its purchases, another group of customers may take up the slack. This is one way to minimize the "roller coaster effect" of making $65,000 one year and $55,000 the next.

PLAN OF THIS BOOK

Chapter 1 set the tone of professionalism we will reinforce throughout the book. You now have a broad overview of what a professional salesperson needs to know. In addition, you realize that there are many opportunities within professional selling. In Chapter 2 you will learn how (in well-managed marketing programs) personal sales efforts are coordinated with advertising and other forms of promotion to maximize a firm's marketing communications. Before focusing on the specific details of selling, it is important to understand the role of personal selling in the execution of marketing strategy. Chapter 3 concludes Part One with a description of relationship management. We explain various buyer-seller relationships and offer a description of the requirements a salesperson must meet to be successful in managing each type.

Part Two, "Why Customers Buy," examines the purchasing behavior of private consumers and industrial purchasers. Chapter 4 analyzes consumer behavior and the stages of the consumer's decision process. To effectively assist consumers as they make purchase decisions, a truly professional sales representative must understand each stage. Chapter 5 analyzes organizational buyer behavior and its unique challenges.

Part Three, "Relationship Management with the Customer," analyzes the sales process and the individual steps beginning with prospecting in Chapter 6. We provide descriptions and numerous examples of how prospecting is conducted so as to enhance the effectiveness of a salesperson meeting a customer for the first time. Chapter 7 reveals how the astute professional initiates and nurtures a relationship. Key activities for establishing relationships involve asking buyer-oriented questions and listening actively. We analyze both and provide specific guidance. Chapter 8 examines a variety of sales presentations, the dynamics involved in presentations, and specific information on how to plan an atmosphere in which you can deliver a professional presentation. Chapter 9 focuses on the importance of maintaining a positive attitude when negotiating. We cover how to analyze the buyer's environment, which influences his or her negotiating position. Strategies and tactics are described in the concluding section of this important chapter. Chapter 10, "Answering Objections, Closing, and Follow-Up Contacts," is the concluding chapter in Part Three. In this chapter, you will learn how successful relationship management-oriented salespeople perceive and handle objections. You will also gain an understanding of why sales are never really "closed," and finally, what should be done during follow-up calls to further cement relationships with a customer who has just purchased from you.

Part Four, "Relationship Management Inside the Organization," acknowledges the importance of the salesperson's achieving results inside his or her company. An obvious starting point is the representative's understanding of the sales department or organization. Chapter 11 covers a variety of sales organization structures, each of which has strengths and weaknesses regarding customer relations. Chapter 12 examines the relationship that sales and marketing have in many companies. Chapter 13 expands this analysis to cover the representative's relationship to a variety of nonmarketing functions in an organization. Ideally, all the departments or groups in an organization will be market-oriented, but realistically the salesperson will encounter fellow employees who pursue divergent goals. The cooperation of these people is frequently necessary to fulfill a commitment made to a customer. Sometimes the toughest sales are those to insiders.

Part Five, "Strategic Alternatives and Tactical Actions," contains two chapters describing some major technologically based influences that are affecting the way salespeople manage their operations. Chapter 14 reveals how salespeople manage their time and how they attempt to cope with stress in the busy world of professional selling. Chapter 15 explains the trend toward major account or key account sales and how telemarketing and personal computers are being used to execute sales strategies more effectively.

Part Six, "Professional Selling as a Career," begins with Chapter 16, "Ethical and Legal Issues in Professional Selling." With the need to establish and maintain long-lasting relationships with customers comes the necessity of examining a variety of ethical and legal questions and practices. The professional salesperson, to merit the title, must be sensitive to the pressures that can result in unethical or illegal practices. Chapter 17 moves into the international arena—an area promising increasing opportunities for sales professionals. Relationship management on a global scale is occurring with greater frequency, and many new salespeople will experience the differences and similarities of a variety of cultures. Chapter 18 concludes this section with an analysis of career progress. You will learn about various conditions that shape salespeople's careers and ways to manage the various stages of a career life cycle.

Two appendices are provided. Appendix A, Telemarketing, contains more detailed information on this growing field and gives specific guidance on the development of a script that could be used to sell a product or service via the telephone.

Appendix B, Resumé Preparation and Interviewing, may prove to be especially useful if you are seeking help preparing a resumé and wondering about what you may encounter as you interview for a job.

SUMMARY

1. Studying professional selling will be useful because (1) individuals must learn to sell to prospective employers, (2) most people, even though they may not be directly in sales, come into occasional contact with their company's customers, and (3) even top-level executives are realizing their need to sell to their company's best customers.

2. Professional salespeople have a thorough understanding of their customers or clients. They cultivate this understanding through careful research of the environment in which their customers live and work. Knowing customer needs is part of the level of understanding that a professional develops.

3. Successful salespeople accomplish things for their customers by getting other people or departments in the seller's organization to perform needed activities. Working effectively behind the scenes is a key ingredient to keeping a long-term relationship with a key customer intact.

4. A professional salesperson provides leadership in managing the customer relationship. An effective sales representative wants to be "the company" in the customer's or client's mind.

5. Firms successfully practicing relationship management can lower their selling costs, because there is less cost associated with maintaining a customer than with finding a new one.

6. As an occupation, sales has evolved over the past two centuries. As each economic era has passed, the importance of greater professionalism among salespeople has increased.

7. The various types of sales positions can be analyzed on the basis of the amount of technical expertise required, the extent of structure involved in the daily work routine, and the length of the sales cycle.

8. Professional selling opportunities exist in trade selling, technical selling, service selling, inside selling, and missionary selling.

9. The major activities that consume salespeoples' time were described. The implications of how a sales rep's time is spent were analyzed.

10. Compensation levels were identified for three levels of sales positions—trainees, mid-level, and top-level salespersons.

QUESTIONS FOR DISCUSSION AND REVIEW

1. Review the quotation taken from the article, "The Most Important Sale You'll Ever Make," which was used earlier in this chapter. Why do you think the author stated that "selling yourself" would be the most difficult job you will ever have?

2. How do you think an increased level of professionalism among salespersons can help overcome some non-U.S.-based manufacturers' cost advantages?

3. Why is it relatively difficult to measure a sales representative's productivity compared with a production worker's?

4. Are some companies and some salespeople still functioning as though the Sales Era were still in existence?

5. Why would it be appropriate to use the phrase "must be a self-starter" in a sales job advertisement when the job was one with little structure?

6. Give an example of how a salesperson could span several boundaries in his or her company.

7. What is the main difference between an order getter and an order taker?

8. Being an inside sales rep doesn't mean that customers must always come to the salesperson's place of business. Explain.

9. What is the major difference between a missionary sales representative and the other kinds of representatives described in this chapter?

10. Explain why the incomes of both the mid-level and top-level salespeople have fluctuated in the past while the sales trainee's income levels have steadily climbed.

CASE 1-1   ARE WE BEING PREPARED FOR THE 'REAL WORLD'?

Kelly Simmons and his friend Mac Craig were discussing the upcoming Career Day at State University. The annual event was sponsored by the university's Placement Center. Both young men were juniors majoring in marketing and had the following conversation:

Kelly: Professor Jackson announced today in class that we were going to have a chance to meet Lee Iacocca at Career Day. He's going to be the keynote speaker at the luncheon sponsored by the College of Business. Boy, there's a salesman! He really pulled the Chrysler Corporation back from the grave. Do you think he ever had to learn how to sell?

Mac: Yeah, if half his latest book is true, he's certainly led an exciting life. He's made millions, but I guess when you're that good, you're worth every cent.

Kelly: Do you suppose executives at that level ever really talk about some of the things we deal with in our marketing courses? Sometimes when we have a guest speaker in one of the classes, the person will drop phrases like, 'In the real world we do this and that' or, 'In the trenches this is what actually happens.'

Mac: I wonder about that too. When we get hired by a company like Xerox or Procter and Gamble, they train us for weeks or months before we actually sell anything. Are we really getting much of an education for what we want to do?

QUESTIONS

1. Can professional selling courses be taught in an atmosphere where no specific company's products or customers are studied in depth throughout the entire course?

2. What is the value to students like Kelly and Mac of courses such as professional selling?

3. What can these students do now to start becoming professionals even before being hired by a specific company?

CASE 1-2   WATCHING A PRO AT WORK

Marsha Smithson shook Paul Jarnigan's hand and said, "Paul, I hope today has given you an opportunity to see how we operate. You have my card and phone number, so don't hesitate to give me a call if you think of a question. I wish you the best in your career decision. As I mentioned this morning, I started with this company three years ago, and I've never regretted it."

Paul thought about this conversation and the events of the day as he walked toward his car. He had just finished spending the day with Ms. Smithson as she called on customers in her territory. Paul's visit with Marsha Smithson was a result of the invitation by Marsha's boss, who had interviewed Paul for a job with the Klaxon Company. The manager said he wanted Paul to experience first-hand the routine of a field sales representative.

The "typical" sales day started with a breakfast at 7:45 during which Marsha Smithson met with a buyer from one of her larger retail accounts. They discussed a new line of products Klaxon would be showing at a trade show in Atlanta within three weeks. Smithson found out when the buyer would be arriving at the trade show and made an appointment with the buyer so they could visit Klaxon's exhibit together. As Marsha later remarked to Paul, she wanted to be there in person to answer the buyer's questions and render assistance to the other Klaxon exhibit personnel as they showed the new line to visiting buyers. Marsha mentioned that she had gotten several good orders in the past by being present when a buyer's interest was at a peak.

By 8:50, Marsha and Paul were on their way to a new shopping mall where Marsha visited with the mall manager to find out which retailers would soon occupy space in the mall. Smithson said she wanted to contact people in these new shops before they actually opened for business. "If we can get our line of merchandise in, provide great service, and help with the start-up problems, our competitors will find it hard to overcome the head start we'll have," Marsha explained. "No matter how good you think your product is, you need all the advantages you can get."

By 10:30, Marsha and Paul were seated in a small room waiting to see another department store buyer. Marsha stated that this store had been a large customer in the past and now was interested in getting the Klaxon Company to manufacture products for it under the store's brand name. Private branding had never been done before by Klaxon, and while the corporate policy on this was being studied, Marsha's boss had instructed her to try to buy some time for the company. It was a ticklish business trying to keep a large customer happy while Klaxon's senior management looked at the advantages and disadvantages of producing products with a retailer's brand name on them.

After a fifteen-minute wait, the buyer emerged from his office with another person who Marsha later told Paul was a sales representative of a competitive company. When Marsha and Paul were seated in the buyer's office, he said to Marsha, "We're going to have to know within thirty days whether we can get private brand products from you. We've obviously been very satisfied with your goods, but our management wants to establish its own image in this area. When can you give us your answer?"

Marsha's response was that she had thought the decision would be made within two weeks, but production schedules were being reviewed and this, coupled with budget revisions, had delayed Klaxon's decision. She told the buyer the thirty-day deadline didn't seem unreasonable, and she would keep him informed as she became aware of news from her home office.

In the final stages of their meeting, the buyer mentioned that a consultant had been working with his company to establish a computerized ordering system. At a recent meeting, the buyers had been told there was a good possibility that by the first of the year there would be a computerized reorder system, which would react to instructions to automatically reorder some staple merchandise the store always carried. Marsha told the buyer the Klaxon Company had extensive experience in these systems and mentioned that she would be glad to arrange a visit to one of Klaxon's distribution centers to let the customer's buyers see the system at work. The buyer expressed his interest and said he would pass the offer on to his boss. Marsha, in turn, made a note to contact the Klaxon distribution center regional manager to see what dates would be suitable for the visit.

As Marsha and Paul drove out of the parking lot, Marsha picked up her mobile phone and called her boss. She informed him about the thirty-day deadline and mentioned her encounter with a competitive salesperson who could pose a threat if Klaxon couldn't supply the private brand merchandise. Marsha's manager said he had just finished a teleconference with the other district managers and the vice president of sales. They had been told the decision on this production policy would be announced within ten days.

After a short lunch, Marsha and Paul called on several small retailers whom Marsha said she visited about once or twice every four or five months. "Now," she said, "these mom-and-pop stores are handled routinely once a week by our Tell-Sell telemarketing program out of Kansas City. They get regular calls from someone there who covers this territory. About 95 percent of their business is handled entirely through the telemarketing center. The amounts such stores can buy individually can't justify regular personal sales calls and yet, collectively, their business is significant."

Shortly after 4:00 p.m., Marsha and Paul called on another one of Marsha's significant accounts. This time the focus was mainly on a new advertising campaign the Klaxon Company would soon be sponsoring on television. The ads would be starting in early November. Marsha used a small portable videotape machine, which allowed her to show the buyer some of the thirty-second ads that Klaxon would be featuring. They discussed the products that would be shown in the ads, and Marsha made an appointment for the following week to come back and discuss the possibility of increasing the buyer's recent order for the featured products. The buyer stated she needed to review her merchandising plan before she could purchase supplemental amounts.

After this call was finished at 5:15 p.m., Marsha drove Paul back to his car and wished him farewell.

QUESTIONS

1. What evidence in this case indicates that the Klaxon Company seems to be in the Strategic Marketing Era?

2. How does Marsha Smithson's behavior exhibit that she is a professional salesperson?

3. What are some questions Paul Jarnigan should ask himself as he contemplates whether Klaxon is a company he wants to work for?

CASE 1-3   A ROOKIE GETS SOME ADVICE

Frank Brower, a recent college graduate, was in his third month of employment with the Apex Corporation. Apex, a chemical manufacturer, offered Frank a job as a sales trainee when he graduated. As soon as he reported to work, Frank was enrolled in a six-week training program followed by a two-week course at one of Apex's refineries. After completing his training, he was assigned to a territory in the Chicago market. Frank's territory included several large meat packing and food processing companies. These large customers had purchasing departments staffed with personnel who specialized in buying different categories of products or services for their respective companies. As a result of this specialization, the purchasing agents were extremely knowledgeable in their particular product/service specialty. In addition to their extensive purchasing knowledge, the buyers usually relied on close-knit relationships with a few principal suppliers to keep their firms stocked with the necessary supplies. For instance, the sales rep Frank was replacing had been calling on the same buyers for twelve years. When the rep retired, it opened up the territory to which Frank had been assigned.

Frank was aware of the challenging environment he faced. When his boss, Carla Adams, met with him to brief him on his customers, Frank was intent on absorbing as much of her advice as possible. Two things in particular that Carla said became embedded in Frank's memory as he prepared for his first sales calls. First, Carla told Frank the most important thing to remember was that salespeoples' credibility was Apex's most important asset. "Credibility with our customers is even more important than product quality," Carla said.

The second piece of advice she imparted to Frank was, "These people don't care how much you know until they know how much you care."

Frank was pondering his conversation with Carla as he studied his product manuals during the evening preceding his first day alone in his new territory.

QUESTIONS

1. How do you think a position that rates sales reps' credibility over product quality can be justified?

2. Other than not misrepresenting his products, what can Frank Brower do to protect his credibility with these very astute buyers?

3. How can Frank convey to his customers that he is genuinely concerned about their business needs?

NOTES

1. "America's Best Sales Forces," *Sales & Marketing Management* (June 1989): 39–40.

2. Ibid., 42.

3. William F. Schoell and Joseph P. Guiltinan, *Marketing: Contemporary Concepts and Practices*, 5th ed. (Boston, Mass.: Allyn and Bacon, 1992), 718.

4. Gabriella Stern, "Chief Executives Are Increasingly Chief Salesmen," *Wall Street Journal* (August 6, 1991): B1.

5. William Keenan, "Power Selling: America's Best Sales Forces," *Sales & Marketing Management* (September 1991): 48.

6. Ibid., 56.

7. Michael A. Hitt, R. Dennis Middlemist, and Robert L. Mathis, *Management Concepts and Effective Practice* (St. Paul, Minn.: West Publishing Company, 1983).

8. Kate Bertrand, "What Makes a Winning Sales Rep," *Business Marketing* (March 1989): 42.

9. Jane Fitz, "Selling with Technical Support," *Sales Training* (February 1990): S7.

10. Beverly Geber, "The Whys and Wherefores of Team Selling," *Training* (January 1991): 72–78.

11. Fitz, "Selling with Technical Support," S7.

12. Paul H. Schurr, "Evolutionary Approaches to Effective Selling," ed. Arch G. Woodside, *Advances in Business Marketing* (Greenwich, Conn.: JAI Press, 1987), 50–80. See also Theodore Levitt, "After the Sale Is Over . . .," *Harvard Business Review* (September–October 1983): 87–93.

13. "PAs Examine the People Who Sell to Them," *Sales & Marketing Management* (November 11, 1985): 39.

14. "Compensation & Expenses," *Sales & Marketing Management* (June 17, 1991): 72.

15. Richard Cardozo and Shannon Shipp, "New Selling Methods Are Changing Industrial Sales Management," *Business Horizons* (September–October 1987): 24.

16. Alan Plassche, vice president of General Foods Corporation, in remarks made to the American Telemarketing Association 1987 Annual Convention, November 3, 1987, in Monterey, California.

17. Karl Allrecht and Ron Zemke, *Service America! Doing Business in the New Economy* (Homewood, Ill.: Dow Jones-Irwin, 1986).

18. William J. Stanton and Richard H. Buskirk, *Management of the Sales Force*, 7th ed. (Homewood, Ill.: Irwin, 1987), 626.

19. E. Jerome McCarthy and William D. Perreault, Jr., *Basic Marketing*, 9th ed. (Homewood, Ill.: Irwin, 1987), 27.

20. Gilbert A. Churchill, Jr., Neil M. Ford, and Orville C. Walker, Jr., *Sales Force Management* (Homewood, Ill.: Irwin, 1985).

21. Mack Hanan, James Cribbin, and Howard Berrian, *Sales Negotiation Strategies* (New York: AMACOM, 1977).

22. Carl Rieser, "The Salesman Isn't Dead: He's Different," *Fortune* (November 1962): 124.

23. B. P. Shapiro et al., "Manage Customers for Profits (Not Just Sales)," *Harvard Business Review* (September–October 1987): 101.

24. "The Long-Distance Warrior," *Business Week* (February 17, 1986): 86–94.

25. Ibid.

26. Theodore Levitt, "Relationship Management," ed. Theodore Levitt, *The Marketing Imagination* (New York: The Free Press, 1983), 111–26.

27. Richard T. Hise and Stanley H. Kratchman, "Developing and Managing a 20/80 Program," *Business Horizons* (September–October 1987): 66–73.

28. Keenan, "Power Selling: America's Best Sales Forces," 46.

29. "America's Best Sales Forces," *Sales & Marketing Management* (June 1989): 41.

30. Aimee L. Stern, "Telemarketing Polishes Its Image," *Sales & Marketing Management* (June 1991): 107–110.

31. Ibid.

32. Ibid.

33. Rudy Oetting and Geri Gantman, "Dial 'M' for Maximize," *Sales & Marketing Management* (June 1991): 102.

34. "Compensation & Expenses," *Sales & Marketing Management* (June 17, 1991): 76.

35. Ibid., 72.

CHAPTER 2

Personal Sales as a Marketing Communications Tool

LEARNING OBJECTIVES

After studying this chapter, you should be able to:

1. Identify the basic elements of the marketing mix and explain why, when combined, they are called a mix.

2. Identify the basic elements of the promotional mix and explain why the word *mix* is appropriate.

3. Reconstruct a communications model and explain how different promotional tools are used to attract a customer's attention, arouse interest, stimulate desire, and generate action.

4. Explain why salespeople must analyze a buying center to identify key people and the various roles they may be playing in the center.

5. Define the key terms used in this chapter.

KEY TERMS

- marketing mix
- promotion
- promotional mix
- source
- receiver
- encode
- decode
- noise
- AIDA model
- buying center
- trade show

N A MEMO TO Carl Stewart, vice president of marketing communications Sheila McKernery, director of the consumer products division, and John Danforth, director of the industrial products division, Frank Folkes, executive vice president of marketing, asks each of his top marketing professionals to submit proposed plans for new product launches: Please submit your proposed plans for supporting the new products that will be launched in the second half of this year. These plans should specifically address the following questions: (1) What types of promotion will be used during the first three months after a product is introduced to the market? (2) What is the purpose of each of the promotion methods you intend to use? (3) When and how will the field sales forces be notified about their roles in the promotional efforts and how will the sales personnel be kept informed about such things as distributor contests, advertising theme changes, and consumer sweepstakes? Plans are due in my office on April 15.

Year after year, Procter and Gamble (P&G) ranks among the top five companies in advertising expenditures. What may not be as widely recognized is that P&G also has an excellent field sales force.[1] The massive expenditures on advertising coupled with a world-class sales force and high quality products makes P&G a formidable competitor. Coordinating the sales department, advertising personnel, and brand managers with advertising agencies that serve the P&G account requires tremendous executive skill. One of the essential factors for success is that individuals in sales must understand their particular roles and responsibilities and how they coordinate with other professionals who may be specializing in other marketing communication efforts such as advertising. The memo from Frank Folkes to his subordinate managers is attempting to ensure that the necessary coordination occurs. The purpose of this chapter is to provide you with an understanding of how personal sales contributes to a firm's marketing communications efforts.

In Chapter 1, a brief description was given of the shift from the Sales Era to the Marketing Era and, more recently, the dawning of the Strategic Marketing Era. No one should interpret that transition to mean that the role or importance of personal selling has been diminished. In this chapter, we will describe the fundamental role of personal selling and the sales function's relationships with other marketing-related areas such as products/services, channels of distribution, and prices. We define personal selling as an element in the promotional mix.

This chapter will provide an in-depth analysis of how personal sales must be coordinated with a variety of promotional methods such as advertising, sales promotion, and publicity. We will clarify the roles different communication tools play with a widely used marketing communication objectives model. Finally, the last section of this chapter will describe a situation that demands the highest skills of the professional salesperson.

A FIRM'S MARKETING ACTIVITY: THE SETTING FOR THE SALES FUNCTION

In the early 1960s, a noted marketing scholar, E. Jerome McCarthy, introduced the four P's of marketing—product, price, place, and promotion.[2] In addition to identifying the basic ingredients of the **marketing mix**, McCarthy advised that marketing planning should be based on a customer orientation. Exhibit 2-1 shows product, price, place, and promotion surrounding the target customer, which,

Exhibit 2-1 The Marketing Mix and the Promotion Mix

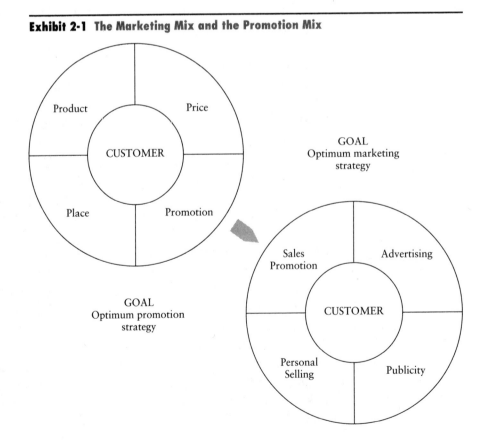

of course, suggests that the goal of the firm's marketing program is customer satisfaction.

Promotion consists of advertising, personal sales, sales promotion, and publicity. The promotion activities of a business are the various ways the business uses to communicate the virtues of its products, the prices of those products, and, in some cases, their location. Exhibit 2-1 also shows the relationship of the promotional activities to the marketing mix elements. Thus, personal selling is a subset of the promotion marketing mix element. What does this mean to the sales representative?

It means that sales personnel must understand how their role (involving personal contact with customers/clients) supports and is supported by the other promotion efforts exerted by their firm. The truly professional salesperson understands what his or her firm is attempting to do to successfully market its wares.

Consider the example of a sales representative for Perdue Farms calling on a buyer for Roche Supermarkets, a large chain of stores in the northeastern United States. The sales representative, as he convinces the buyer of the profit potential available in a new line of chicken frankfurters, reveals Perdue's plans for widespread media advertising for the product. The buyer, aware that consumers will soon see these advertisements, decides to stock the new item so the stores can capitalize on this opportunity. Without knowing about the upcoming advertising campaign, its duration, and some of the media that will carry the ads, the salesperson might not be able to convince the chain store buyer to carry the new item. On the other hand, if the salesperson had not been there to ask for the order, the advertising campaign could have been conducted but sales would not have occurred if the product had not been available in the local stores. Together, each of the major forms of promotion—advertising and personal sales—establish the synergy that is necessary to effectively promote the new poultry product. This "one-two punch" is only one example of how advertising and personal selling work together to contribute to marketing success.

Observers of the business scene, who have studied the interaction of the various forms of promotion such as personal sales and advertising, have concluded that McCarthy's term *mix* aptly conveys what the skillful promoter does when planning promotional campaigns.[3] All of the means of promotion listed in Exhibit 2-2 are ingredients that can be employed in the promotion of a product or service. They form the **promotional mix** of a firm. The efforts of the firm's sales representatives are one vital ingredient in the promotional mix.

As we analyze the various forms of advertising, sales promotion, publicity, and personal selling, we see that many combinations of promotional mixes are possible. Managers who create and implement a promotional program must know the

Exhibit 2-2 Characteristics of the Promotional Mix

Communication Mode	**Personal Selling** *Direct and* *Face-to-Face*	**Advertising** *Indirect* *and Nonpersonal*	**Publicity** *Usually Indirect* *and Nonpersonal*	**Sales Promotion** *Usually Indirect* *and Nonpersonal*
Communicator's control over situation	High	Low	Moderate to low	Moderate to low
Amount of feedback	Much	Little	Little	Little to moderate
Speed of feedback	Immediate	Delayed	Delayed	Varies
Message flow	Two-way	One-way	One-way	Mostly one-way
Control over message content	Yes	Yes	No	Yes
Sponsor identified	Yes	Yes	No	Yes
Speed in reaching large audiences	Slow	Fast	Usually fast	Fast
Message flexibility	Tailored to prospect	Uniform and unvaried	No direct control over message	Uniform and varied

Source: Charles W. Lamb, Jr., Joseph E. Hain, Jr., and Carl McDaniel, *Principles of Marketing* (Cincinnati, Oh.: South-Western Publishing Co., 1992), 437.

particular strengths and weaknesses of each promotional tool. By recognizing the inherent strengths and weaknesses of a particular promotional tool, such as advertising, an effective mix can be developed. Exhibit 2-2 lists the strengths and weaknesses of the four basic promotional tools.

It is not enough, however, to just identify the promotional mix tools if you are an executive planning a promotion program. Each element in the mix must be coordinated with the other parts of the mix. This need is reflected in the opening vignette in which Frank Folkes, executive vice president of marketing, is requesting his subordinates to tell him what their plans are for promoting new products. This is an important management responsibility. It may cost a firm millions of dollars to use each promotional tool, such as sales promotion, to promote one or more products. To achieve maximum effectiveness, each ingredient in the promotional mix must be coordinated with all the other ingredients. If this is achieved, a synergy results (that is, a situation where the result is greater than the mere sum of the individual parts).

To further explain this situation, let's imagine how one of Mr. Folkes's managers will respond to his memo. Ms. Shela McKernery, director of the consumer products division, will perhaps use TV and newspaper advertising to stimulate the target consumer audience's awareness and interest in one of her new products. She will know when and for how long each advertisement will run in a particular

Figure 2-1 Each ingredient in the promotional mix must be coordinated with all other ingredients to achieve synergy.

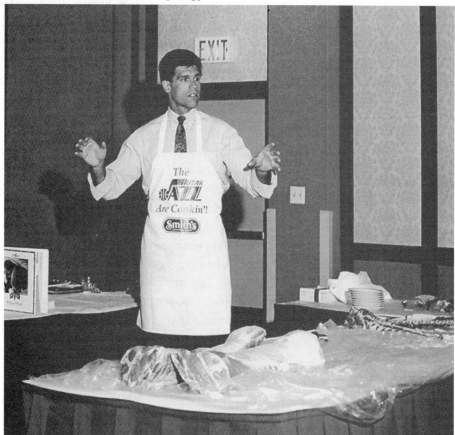

market area. The new product may also be supported by cents-off coupons printed in the Sunday supplements. Regardless of what combination of other promotional mix elements is used, her company's sales force will be utilized. That is why in question 3 of Folkes's memo he asks each manager to indicate how the sales force personnel will be informed of the anticipated roles they will play.

It is essential that a salesperson be well informed about the company's marketing activities. To be "blind-sided" by a promotional activity, which a customer knows about but a visiting salesperson does not know about, is an embarrassment. Therefore, the sales force should be kept informed well in advance of the introduction of new promotional offers to customers. The sales reps can revise their presentations in concert with the promotional plans of the company.

THE RELATIONSHIP OF PERSONAL SALES TO PRODUCT, PRICE, AND PLACE

Personal selling has been depicted as one of the mainstays in a firm's promotional efforts. In addition, we have stated the importance of the individual salesperson's having knowledge of how his or her role contributes to overall promotional success. To increase your understanding of how important a skilled sales force can be, we will now examine the relationship of personal sales to the remaining three P's—product, price, and place.

Product

Most products are multifaceted, as Exhibit 2-3 shows. For example, a potential new car buyer is likely to view the warranty conditions of seven years or 70,000 miles as an integral part of the car purchase package. Safety features or a reputation for safe handling are another part of the "bundle of satisfactions" the buyer considers. The relationship of personal sales to the total product is that the salesperson is responsible for clearly and persuasively communicating to the buyer those features of the total product that are most meaningful to that individual buyer.

Personal selling is the only marketing communication tool with the ability to probe the customer's mind, reveal which of the components of the total product are of the greatest importance to the buyer, and then focus interpersonal communication on them. The skilled sales professional, by using some well-timed ques-

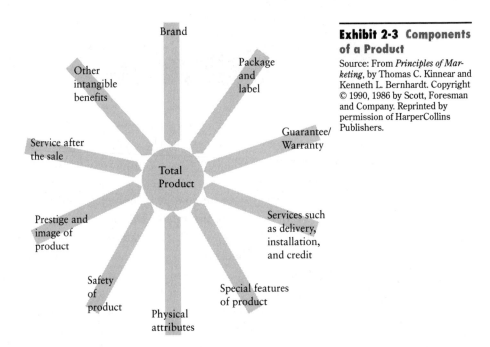

Exhibit 2-3 Components of a Product

Source: From *Principles of Marketing*, by Thomas C. Kinnear and Kenneth L. Bernhardt. Copyright © 1990, 1986 by Scott, Foresman and Company. Reprinted by permission of HarperCollins Publishers.

tions and careful listening (a skill covered in Chapter 7), can direct the prospective buyer's attention so that a product is shown to its best advantage.

Price

How is the personal sales activity related to price? In many discussions between a salesperson and a customer, there is considerable negotiation over price. Two major opportunities exist for salespersons to enhance the possibilities for making a sale by skillfully handling the price-related questions or concerns of buyers. First, a skilled professional salesperson will detect the situation in which a buyer sees the price as a barrier to making the purchase (perhaps without even hearing the prospective buyer say it). By pointing out the durability, or some other positive features of the product, the sales representative can turn what seems to be an initially high price into a veritable bargain.

A sales representative selling a Mercedes Benz costing $75,000 is an example. By comparing the cost of operating the car for its probable lifetime (perhaps twelve years) to the total costs of acquiring and operating two initially less expensive cars during the same period, the salesperson can provide an economic rationale that might otherwise escape many buyers.

Second, the sales professional's skill is exhibited during negotiation over the terms of a sale—payment of freight charges, discounts for cash payments, trade-in allowances, and other factors that can affect the total delivered price of a product. These situations are frequently encountered in industrial marketing and, to a lesser extent, in selling big-ticket items to consumers. Real estate sales professionals negotiate with buyers and sellers on closing costs, points, and other factors that can have an impact on the price of buying a home.

A salesperson's negotiating skills would also be important when a purchasing agent buys steel from a supplier located in the same city as the purchasing agent's company. When a sales representative from another company located outside the city calls on the agent, the sales representative is confronted with the challenge of negotiating the base price of the steel plus the shipping costs. You will learn about negotiations and receive some guidance on how to negotiate in Chapter 9.

The most important point to be grasped now is that prices, in many situations where salespeople are involved, are not static. Prices are frequently the central point for negotiations with a potential buyer, and the sales representative is the spokesperson for the selling company.

Place

In the marketing mix, "place" refers to the channels of distribution the marketer employs to reach the targeted market(s). Distribution channels for some companies sometimes contain thousands of resellers—the individuals and organizations that acquire goods for the purpose of reselling or renting them to others at a profit.[4] A&P and Sears are two well-known resellers.

A manufacturer or a wholesaler selling to another firm that, in turn, will resell the product should regard the relationship with the reseller as very important. Who from the seller's organization is most frequently in contact with the personnel of the reseller? If your answer is the sales representative, you are absolutely correct. Thus, the important task of maintaining relations with a network of resellers is the sales representative's responsibility.

A specific example is Armstrong Cork Company's sales force and its interactions with distributors.[5] The Armstrong sales representatives do not sell just to distributors of Armstrong products. Rather, they work on selling to the distributors' key accounts as well. By also selling "downstream" in the channel, the flow of Armstrong products through the distributors is increased.

A COMMUNICATION MODEL

We have made an assumption in the preceding explanations of how the salesperson relates to the product or service being sold, its price, and the distributors or dealers. That assumption has been that communication is occurring. Communication between the sales rep and the potential buyer as the rep describes and demonstrates a product is one of the bedrocks of successful sales. Communication between salespeople and retailers and various wholesalers is no less important, however.

A model of the communication process will strengthen your understanding of this vital activity. By analyzing the fundamental components of communications, you can gain a better grasp of the material covered in later chapters, which deal with sales presentations, negotiating, and handling objections.

Exhibit 2-4 shows a frequently used model that identifies the basic components of the communications process.

Source and Receiver

Although this model can be used in any interpersonal setting (for example, student–teacher, friend–friend, husband–wife), here it depicts communications between a salesperson and a customer. The **source** and the **receiver** in this model are the salesperson and the customer. As communication occurs, the roles of source and receiver will switch back and forth between the sales rep and the customer. One of the most important skills a salesperson can possess is knowing when to be a receiver rather than a source. The art of listening (becoming a skilled receiver) will be covered in Chapter 8.

Encoding and Decoding

When a person **encodes** a message, he or she arranges ideas into symbols such as words, gestures, and even facial expressions. These words, gestures, and expressions are meant to convey a message from someone whom (in this model) we call a source to another party called a receiver. The receiver **decodes** or interprets the message(s). Sometimes the message that was sent is decoded correctly and sometimes it is not. One purpose for asking questions is to determine if an intended message has been received and interpreted, or decoded, correctly.

Sometimes the code is quite simple and requires very little intellectual effort to decode (for example, "Get out of this office and don't ever come back again!"). The point will be made again later, but it is so central to successful selling that it cannot be made too often. *The key to successful decoding and the creation of successful answers or responses is good listening habits.*

A final condition that should be acknowledged before concluding our discussion of the encoding-decoding activity involves body language. Communication also occurs in a variety of nonverbal ways. The alert salesperson learns to detect signals from his or her customer that are telltale signs of interest, fear, boredom, disbelief, excitement, or anger. Chapter 10 offers guidance on how to detect signals from a customer and respond appropriately.

Common Ground

The amount of overlap between the two circles in the communication model (Exhibit 2-4) signifies the two communicators' common areas. If the communicating

Exhibit 2-4 A Model of the Communication Process

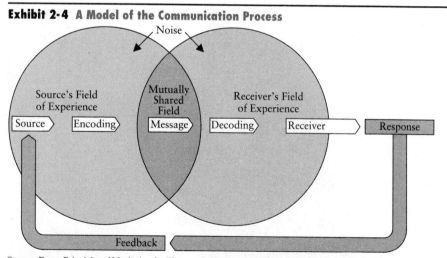

Source: From *Principles of Marketing*, by Thomas C. Kinnear and Kenneth L. Bernhardt. Copyright © 1990, 1986 by Scott, Foresman and Company. Reprinted by permission of HarperCollins Publishers.

parties know a lot about each other, the area of overlap will be large. In the sales context, if the sales rep knows a lot about the buyer's situation and the buyer knows the sales rep, the product or service being sold, and the rep's company, then the overlap will be large. These circumstances will probably make it much easier for the people to understand one another. It does not mean, however, that the two parties will agree. Excellent communication can occur in situations where the communicators understand each other but cannot accept each other's propositions.

Noise

Noise is anything that may detract from or diminish the effectiveness of the communication. It may be a telephone call interrupting a conversation between the salesperson and the prospective buyer. It could be a distracting mannerism by either person or the pressure of a work schedule that causes either of the communicators to misinterpret the other person's statements. Because of the many possibilities for noise to occur, the professional salesperson spends much time and thought honing skills to minimize the negative impacts of noise. More specific examples of how to combat and handle noise will be provided in Chapters 8 and 9.

Although this model has been enormously useful to convey the basics of the communications process, it does not provide any guidance on the nature or dura-

Figure 2-2 Finding a quiet area in which to hold a meeting with a prospective buyer is Important to the eventual success of the communication.

tion of the communication. You can easily envision a conversation between a sales representative and a buyer in which the dialogue is focused on a point-by-point comparison of the salesperson's product with competitive products. A less obvious but still important example of communication is the postsale telephone call from a sales representative to see if the buyer is experiencing any problems with a new purchase. The communication model's versatility in providing a framework permitting the illustration of so many communication situations requires us to spend some time identifying the mental conditions a salesperson attempts to establish in his or her customer.

A SEQUENCE OF CONDITIONS

During the communication process, the salesperson attempts to achieve various objectives. The most obvious objective is the prospective buyer's agreement to purchase the product. Knowledgeable salespeople know, however, that for the buying objective to be reached it will be necessary to establish several conditions in the mind of the prospective buyer. The conditions have been described in several ways (some of which will be described in Chapters 4 and 5). One frequently cited analysis is the **AIDA model**.[6] AIDA comprises the first letters of the words *attention, interest, desire,* and *action*. Each of these conditions must occur if a sale is to be made. The astute salesperson is constantly aware of the need to cultivate these conditions in the prospect's mind so that a sale can eventually be made. Indeed, one of the themes of this book is that if a strong relationship can be formed between the buyer and the seller, the stimulation and maintenance of these conditions within the buyer can be made easier and quicker.

A sales representative contemplating a customer contact should think about how to attract the customer's attention, stimulate interest, cultivate a desire for the product, and evoke a buying action. The professional salesperson will realize that other marketing communication tools (for example, direct mail or newspaper, magazine, or television advertising) may have acquainted a prospect with the salesperson's company.[7]

An example is the statement many marketing professors (who are potential adopters of a text) hear a sales representative make. It usually runs something like this: "Professor Jones, you may have seen our new marketing management text advertised in the recent issue of *Marketing News*." In this very commonplace situation, the publishers and their sales representatives are counting on media advertising to alert the professor to the presence of the new book. A favorable review of the text in the *Journal of Marketing* would, perhaps, serve to stimulate some professors' interest in the text. The publicity provided by this favorable review could

Exhibit 2-5 **The Impact of Promotional Tools on Consumer Response**

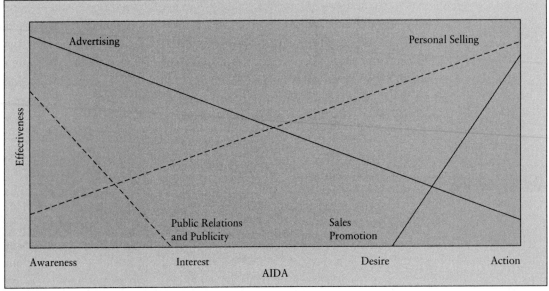

Source: Larry J. Rosenberg, *Marketing*, © 1977, p. 407. Adapted by permission of Prentice Hall, Englewood Cliffs, New Jersey.

also serve to accelerate the creation of a sufficiently strong desire to see an examination copy. The professor, assuming these conditions had occurred, might be much more likely to request a copy of the text and, ultimately, adopt it for classroom use.

Exhibit 2-5 shows how some of the various marketing communication tools can be used to stimulate the conditions identified in the AIDA model. The slopes of the lines indicate the increase or decrease in a promotional tool's effectiveness in stimulating a particular condition. For example, advertising is most effective at arousing the attention of a large number of people compared with some of the other marketing communication tools. Personal sales is, on the other hand, relatively ineffective. How many people can a salesperson contact in face-to-face encounters in one day? At the action end of the axis in Exhibit 2-5, however, personal selling is vastly superior to advertising at getting the buyer to take action. Action, in this case, is defined as agreeing to make a purchase or actually making a purchase. Exhibit 2-5 thus shows how a well-orchestrated use of marketing communication tools can be employed to effectively move a prospective buyer through the various stages of attention, interest, desire, and action.

Of the four marketing communication tools depicted in Exhibit 2-5, personal sales has some unique characteristics, which should be noted. These characteristics are so important that in some situations personal selling is the primary means of promoting a product or service. One generalization is that personal sales is a more prominent factor in the sale of industrial products and services compared with consumer goods and services.[8]

"Why," you might ask, "are industrial goods more likely to be promoted via personal sales efforts?" A response must take into account a number of conditions that are commonly found in the sales of industrial goods. First, industrial goods are more likely to require some degree of customization to the buyer's situation compared with a consumer good. A lubricant for a high-speed drill is, for example, more likely to need some special chemical properties than a lubricant for a consumer's lawnmower. The complexities of the industrial product and the circumstances under which the product will be used frequently require a salesperson to do a lot of homework before meeting with a purchasing agent. The salesperson must be ready to answer questions that have been asked of a purchasing agent by floor supervisors or engineers to ensure that the lubricant can protect expensive industrial equipment. None of the other promotional tools permits information collection and interpretation to be conducted as well as the personal sales representative can.

In addition, none of the other promotional methods identified in Exhibit 2-5 can, in comparison, so precisely tailor the promotional message to an industrial buyer's needs. The skilled professional salesperson can produce a tailored sales message and respond to questions from buyers by listening carefully to the buyer's descriptions of his or her needs.

Another strength of personal sales (when it is performed skillfully) is its unique ability to create and maintain a relationship with a buyer. Media advertising, creative as it may be, cannot establish a relationship. Neither can cleverly crafted publicity or sales promotion campaigns. The establishment of these relationships, of course, is costly compared to the cost-per-thousand figures for persons who have seen a television ad (for example, $675,000 for a thirty-second spot on Super Bowl Sunday divided by 45 million viewers creates a cost-per-viewer of one and one-half cents—$0.015).

Another reason for using personal sales as the primary marketing communication tool in some situations is the ability of the sales representative to detect a buying center. The **buying center** as defined by McCarthy and Perreault comprises "all the people who participate in or influence a purchase."[9] The buying center phenomenon is of sufficient significance to warrant some explanation about its composition and how salespeople must adjust to the varying values and needs of people who comprise a buying center.[10] As a result of the analysis of a buying center, you will gain a better understanding of personal selling's power as a marketing communication tool.

BUYING CENTER

A sales representative for Apex Aircraft Company, calling on a purchasing agent at Cougar Chemical Company, is informed that Cougar's corporate pilot and chief financial officer will both meet with the Apex sales representative. If these separate meetings result in a recommendation to Cougar's president, a recommendation to purchase a plane will be forwarded to the Board of Directors for its approval. This is an illustration of a buying center at work. If the product or service had been typewriters or janitorial service, the participants in the center would, of course, have been different individuals. Such centers are not formally recognized on an organization chart, and the composition of a center will change depending upon the product or service being considered for purchase. Research studies have revealed that participants in a buying center play one or more of the following roles:[11]

1. *Users*. Although users do not make the decision about whether or not to buy a product, a user will often initiate a request ("We're running low on half-inch casters"). They also, in some cases, define or identify the specifications that the new product or service must meet. In the corporate aircraft purchase situation, the company pilot would be the most obvious (and knowledgeable) user.

2. *Influencers*. Any person whose evaluation of the product will be used by the ultimate decision maker or someone in the chain of command to pass on approval is an influencer. The chief financial officer, the pilot, and the president all serve as influencers to the Board of Directors in the corporate aircraft purchase example.

3. *Buyers*. These individuals have been vested with the formal authority to make purchases for the organization. Often they will be called purchasing agents or purchasing managers.

4. *Decision makers*. In the corporate aircraft purchase situation, the decision makers will be the Board of Directors for Cougar Chemical Company. Occasionally, some of these persons (assuming the aircraft is purchased) will also be users.

5. *Gatekeepers*. A gatekeeper serves to protect a decision maker or others in an organization from being harassed by unwanted communication with persons who wish to sway the decision makers, influencers, buyers, or users. The gatekeeper is, in the aircraft scenario, the purchasing agent. The purchasing agent is telling the sales representative that permission is granted to contact the pilot and the chief financial officer to set up appointments. Some companies have policies that require all vendors to first gain clearance through the Purchasing Department.

To be successful, a sales representative would have to first determine who in the customer's organization is participating in some capacity in the buying center.

Second, the sales representative must gain access to the participants (or at least the influencers and the decision makers). Finally, information must be gleaned from them so that the product or service can be described and/or demonstrated in such a way that it will comply with their responsibilities, interests, and levels of understanding.

Returning to the AIDA analysis, we know that attracting attention, arousing interest, and so on, will require different methods depending on whether the salesperson is trying to communicate with a user, an influencer, or a decision maker. Getting the attention of the president of Cougar Chemical Company might best be achieved via an advertisement in the *Wall Street Journal*. The corporate pilot, on the other hand, might best be made aware of Apex's aircraft through an exhibit at a trade show, which is another alternative in the array of marketing communication methods. A **trade show** is an event where a seller (usually a manufacturer) exhibits products with other sellers. The products are ordinarily not for sale; orders, however, can be placed.

Because of differing responsibilities, each participant in the center will probably require a different message to stimulate his or her interest. Once again, the sales representative and other persons responsible for a company's marketing communications program must develop ways and means of appealing to the variety of interests represented in the buying center for a particular product.

Space will not permit a detailed description of how a salesperson might use one or more marketing communication tools to arouse the attention of each role player in the buying center, stimulate individual interests, cultivate desire for the product, and get him or her to take the appropriate action. However, in every encounter with a different person, the sales professional will be striving to move the person closer to action. Also, in every encounter, the salesperson will be encoding and decoding information in the manner depicted in Exhibit 2-4. The orchestration of the variety of marketing communication tools presents a formidable challenge to each salesperson and to the managers who are responsible for designing and implementing a firm's marketing communications or promotion programs.

So far, the examples provided have focused on selling in an industrial marketing setting. Although the buying center concept is associated with industrial marketing, is there any similarity between selling an aircraft to a corporation and selling an automobile to a family? The answer is yes, since the family can also be viewed as a buying center that reflects the activities and influences of the individuals who make up the family.[11] The same five roles have been used to describe family consumption decisions. These roles may be assumed by the husband, wife, or children, and multiple roles and multiple actors are normal. Marketing communication programs in general and personal sales efforts in particular must be designed and executed with the same types of questions in mind—What will attract the attention of the kids and cause them to become interested in the automobile? What will need to be said to satisfy a mother's interest in, for example, providing for a child's safety in a car? How will it be communicated to the family decision makers that they can afford the car?

The marketer, therefore, is asking questions about the availability of various promotional tools and the timing of when to most effectively use the tools to move a prospective buyer (whether a consumer or a business) toward consenting to make a purchase. The sales representatives are, of course, among the most powerful (and costly) promotional tools to which most companies have access. How skillfully the executives identified in the memorandum that opened the chapter utilize their promotional tools will have a major effect on the sales of their products during the next year. Case 2-2 provides a glimpse of how one of these managers plans to do this.

SUMMARY

1. Sales representatives are but one of the ways a company has of communicating with customers and potential customers. The other ways (advertising, sales promotion, and publicity), when combined with personal sales, form a promotional mix.

2. The promotional mix is part of a larger mix, the marketing mix, that comprises the product, the price charged for the product, the distribution channels through which the product moves, and promotion.

3. Promotional messages are delivered to a receiver (a customer, potential customer, or the public) who translates or interprets the messages and responds (perhaps) in a way that causes the sender of the message to vary the content of the message.

4. A sales representative or anyone responsible for creating and presenting a promotional message needs to be aware of the state-of-mind of the receiver of the message. The AIDA model provides a description of four conditions believed to be necessary prior to a person's buying a product or service. These conditions are attention, interest, desire, and a readiness for action.

5. Marketing communicators in general and salespeople in particular must be aware that the decision to purchase is often made in the context of a buying center. People playing different roles—users, influencers, gatekeepers, purchasers, and decision makers—comprise the center.

QUESTIONS FOR DISCUSSION AND REVIEW

1. Why is the term *mix* so appropriate when one envisions the relationships among the four P's (product, price, place, and promotion)?

2. What is personal selling's biggest advantage compared to media advertising? What is personal selling's greatest weakness compared to media advertising?

3. Why do marketers of industrial products or services rely so heavily on personal sales force efforts to promote their goods and services?

4. What does the AIDA model suggest to the salesperson who is planning a meeting with a prospective buyer?

5. What is a buying center and why does this phenomenon present such a challenge to a salesperson?

6. Using the marketing communication model in your answer, explain why it is so important for a salesperson to have good listening skills.

7. Explain how a sales representative might engage in unsuccessful communication with a prospective buyer if the salesperson was guilty of a Production Era mentality.

8. How would the salesperson's communications efforts be conducted if a Marketing Era outlook was used by the sales representative?

9. If a salesperson knows who the decision maker is in an organization or a family, why would the salesperson spend time with users or other persons in an organization?

10. How would the communication model be changed to show a greater degree of understanding between the source and the receiver of communication?

CASE 2-1   FILLING TWO SALES POSITIONS

Ms. Catherine Magee is calling Professor Hector Gomez to inform him about two sales positions she is trying to fill. Ms. Magee is the owner of Sales Resources, a personnel search firm whose clients are companies located in the Houston, Texas area. Most of their hiring needs are for salespeople. The clients asked Ms. Magee to help them find the needed talent to staff their sales forces.

Magee: Hector, I'm calling to find out if you know of any recent graduates whom you would recommend for sales.

Gomez: Well, thanks, Cathy, for thinking of us. Our semester just ended two weeks ago, and I'm sure there are some people who would be interested. What type of work is involved?

Magee: One position is inside sales. All the contacts the salesperson will make will be on the telephone selling electrical connectors to purchasing agents. The company would like to hire someone who has one or two years of sales experience, but it doesn't have to be with this type of product. The other job is outside selling here in Houston with a company that is an IBM office equipment distributor. The company, in this case, will train the person and no prior sales experience is required.

QUESTIONS

1. If you were an inside sales rep, and your only contact with customers was through the telephone, how do you think the encoding-decoding activities would be affected?

2. If you were selling electrical connectors to be used as parts in manufacturers' products, how would the buying center differ from a situation where you were selling office equipment?

3. What other types of promotion would a manufacturer of this product find useful to supplement the personal sales efforts?

4. If you were a sales manager what would you do in the initial contact with an applicant to determine whether the applicant would be suitable for an inside sales position?

5. In terms of encoding and decoding, what advantages does selling IBM equipment offer?

CASE 2-2   LAUNCHING PRODUCT 60

To: Mr. Carl Stewart, Vice President, Marketing Communications
From: Mr. John Danforth, Director, Industrial Products Division
Subject: Promotion support needed for Product 60

Carl, as we discussed yesterday, Product 60 will be launched in July, and I will require extensive support from your group as this new product is introduced. The following timetable and the activities I am planning are submitted for your group's guidance as it schedules time and allocates resources:

April–May: Visits to each regional sales manager's meeting to acquaint the sales force with Product 60, its features, its benefits, and how customers can apply the product. Sales reps will also be told when they can expect promotional brochures for distribution in their respective territories. Information on suggested retail prices, quantity purchase discounts, and case and promotional allowances will be communicated to sales personnel.

June 1:   Trade show in Montreal. My staff and I will have an exhibit at the show. We will need posters and brochures from your shop by May 20.

June 15:   Full-page, four-color advertisement appearing on inside front cover of *Industrial Equipment News*.

June 20:   Full-page, four-color ad in *Iron Age*.

July 1:   Exhibit booth at National Association of Purchasing Agents in Las Vegas. Same arrangements as those for Montreal show.

Sept. 1:   Sales representatives get information about distributor contests. Distributors are given brochures and information allowing them to participate in a Super Bowl sales contest that lasts from October through December.

As your personnel work with the advertising agency, please impress upon the agency people to include an 800 number in each advertisement so that interested readers can get more information on Product 60. We will be coordinating this through our telemarketing group. They will get information about the caller's business and then send this to the appropriate field salesperson for follow-up. In addition, this will give us some idea of the effectiveness of our print advertisements to stimulate responses.

When we participate in the Montreal and Las Vegas trade shows, my people will take the names, addresses, and other relevant information about people who come by our booth. We'll be sending these leads to the field sales force for follow-up.

QUESTIONS

1. What evidence reveals the marketing mix in this case?

2. What evidence reveals the promotional mix?

3. What should sales reps be told about Product 60 that would involve the buying center concept?

4. Put yourself in the place of a salesperson who will be selling Product 60. How do you think you would personally benefit from the activities planned to launch Product 60?

CASE 2-3   CREME CONDITIONER CAPER

Frank Stidwell was making his first call on a department store buyer after having returned from the Apex Corporation's annual sales meeting. At the meeting, the brand manager for personal grooming products had unveiled plans for a new type of hair conditioner that was to be available in leading department stores within three months.

Apex had high hopes for this new hair conditioner. The brand manager in her presentation to the sales force covered product and promotion information. She explained to the group that Apex's R&D laboratories had run extensive tests on the conditioner and found it superior to other conditioners in that the conditioner's effects lasted longer on the user's hair than other conditioners. Another feature that supposedly made it superior was that it was "self-adjusting." In other words, the conditioner worked harder in those areas of the user's hair most needing the conditioner.

The brand manager also informed the sales force that Creme Conditioner would be advertised in time slots during prime time television, in *Cosmopolitan* and *Seventeen* magazines, and by a former Miss USA making a national tour to promote the new product.

The following comments are excerpts taken from the conversation that occurred between the sales representative, Frank Stidwell, and Carolyn Rundell, the Forley Company buyer:

Stidwell: . . . so the person using this conditioner can be assured that only that part of her hair that needs conditioning is actually being conditioned. That's the reason for the "self-adjusting" claim.

Rundell: Uh huh, I see. Tell me about your company's plans for co-op advertising. If I feature this product in, let's say, the Sunday paper advertising, what percent of the advertising cost will you pay?

Stidwell: I don't, uh, think we covered that but let me, before I forget it, tell you this conditioner has a protein base that stimulates the hair follicles much more thoroughly than any of the competitive products.

Rundell: Very interesting. What is your discount on a purchase of fifty cases?

Stidwell: I'll have to get back to you on that. Incidentally, I'm sure you would like to have the chance to sign up your stores for visits from Miss USA. She'll be touring the country and she should draw the crowds.

Rundell: Well, of course, that depends on whether we decide to stock the product. Why don't you leave me that sample and the brochures, and my assistant will contact you if we decide we want to carry the product.

As Stidwell departed the buyer's office, he felt sure he would not be getting an order. He was puzzled because he still was convinced he had the best product on the market.

QUESTIONS

1. Which element in the marketing mix (the four P's) is the sales rep emphasizing in his presentation?

2. Which element(s) does the buyer wish to discuss?

3. Why do you suppose Carolyn Rundell, the department store buyer, appears to be uninterested in Frank Stidwell's sales presentation?

4. Draw a version of the communication process model (see Exhibit 2-4) that symbolizes the situation occurring in this case. If the sales rep had made a presentation that provided information the buyer valued, what would the model look like?

5. At what stage of AIDA is this sale stuck? What could Stidwell have done differently to move it forward toward a favorable action by the buyer?

NOTES

1. "America's Best Sales Forces: Six at the Summit," *Sales and Marketing Management* (June 1990): 62–82.

2. E. Jerome McCarthy and William D. Perreault, Jr., *Basic Marketing*, 10th ed. (Homewood, Ill.: Irwin, 1990), 37–42.

3. Philip Kotler, *Marketing Management: Analysis, Planning, Implementation, and Control*, 7th ed. (Englewood Cliffs, N.J.: Prentice-Hall, 1991), 68–70.

4. Ibid., 70.

5. Michael M. Pearson, "Ten Distribution Myths," *Business Horizons* (May–June 1981): 194.

6. Allan L. Reid, *Modern Applied Selling* (Englewood Cliffs, N.J.: Prentice Hall, 1990), 175–77.

7. Benson P. Shapiro and John Wyman, "New Ways to Reach Your Customers," *Harvard Business Review* (July–August 1981): 103–10.

8. Carl McDaniel, Jr., and William R. Darden, *Marketing* (Newton, Mass.: Allyn and Bacon, 1987), 525.

9. McCarthy and Perreault, *Basic Marketing*, 202.

10. McDaniel and Darden, *Marketing*, 168. See also "How to Master Major Account Sales," *Personal Selling Power* (Jan./Feb. 1991): 34–35.

11. James F. Engel, Roger D. Blackwell, and Paul W. Miniard, *Consumer Behavior*, 5th ed. (New York: Dryden Press, 1986), 272.

CHAPTER 3

Relationship Management: Strategic Implications

LEARNING OBJECTIVES

After studying this chapter, you should be able to:

1. Define relationship management and describe the relationship life cycle.

2. Explain the differences among the different types of buyer-seller relationships.

3. Explain how relationship management is supportive of the three business strategies: differentiation, low-cost producer, and focused.

4. Describe what management needs to do to permit relationship management to succeed.

5. Define the key terms used in this chapter.

KEY TERMS

- relationship management
- product life cycle
- relationship life cycle
- patience-pays-off model
- flash-in-the-pan model
- recycled model
- penetration model
- counselor relationship
- supplier relationship
- systems designer relationship
- differentiation strategy
- low-cost producer strategy
- focus or niche strategy

ALESPEOPLE MUST FORGE partnerships with their customers if they want to succeed in the future, according to three panelists at a recent colloquium sponsored by Max Sacks International, Segundo, Calif.

William Cahill, David Barone, and Richard Hodgetts all agreed with Max Sacks' president, Roy Chitwood, that "partnership selling" is the wave of the future.

In the 21st century, nonmanipulative selling techniques will be key to survival, because increasingly sophisticated clients will not fall for gimmicks or deception, said Cahill, director of undergraduate behavioral science programs at Nova University, Fort Lauderdale.

Salespeople must assume the role of lifelong learner so they can assist customers in solving their problems, he said. And they must become skilled listeners to better recognize the customer's needs.

Effective salespeople will need to display empathy and warmth to develop deep relationships with clients. Cahill said salespeople will have to take on the role of counselor to clients who need solutions to problems. "Salespersons will need to learn to do things for their clients rather than to them."

In the future, he said, sales will become almost incidental—a natural outgrowth of a long-term relationship—and salespeople will have to develop dual loyalties to both the customer and the company.

The salesperson may benefit from innovative ways of changing customers' attitudes, said Barone, associate professor of psychology at Nova. Tomorrow's salesperson may become more involved in offering customers free try-outs of the company's product or service.

The whole company will have to be involved in building customers, he said. This can be done by demonstrating trustworthiness, pointing out similarities in attitudes and interests between the two parties, having repeated pleasant visits, and performing favors for the customer, he said.

Increased international selling by U.S. firms will force salespeople to become familiar with foreign languages, cultures, and politics, said Hodgetts, professor of management at Florida International University, Miami.

The abundance of new product introductions in upcoming decades will require continuous training, focused on selling value benefits, payoffs, and results rather than individual products.

There also will be more individualized training using technological advances such as interactive video. Salespeople will receive more teleconference training, Hodgetts said, supplemented by telephone/electronic mail hook up and workbooks.

Other trends Hodgetts said will affect the salesperson's role in the future are: a greater emphasis on developing a "sustainable advantage," a movement toward market-driven enterprises, changing organizational cultures, and shifting employee values.

Source: Reprinted from "Partnership Selling: The Wave of the Future," *Marketing News*, December 19, 1988, p. 17.

In Chapter 2 we emphasized that personal sales is but one of the marketing communication tools at the disposal of a firm's marketing management. The use of the tools is, or should be, directed toward the successful execution of the firm's strategy. In this chapter, we will explore how relationship management as an approach or perspective toward sales can contribute to successful strategic execution. This leads to the very logical question, "What is relationship management?"

THE DEFINITION AND NATURE OF RELATIONSHIP MANAGEMENT

Relationship management, as it is employed in a personal sales context, is the planned, goal-oriented interaction between a buyer and seller designed to render mutually beneficial results and thereby foster subsequent interactions between the buyer and the seller. Several characteristics of relationship management must be analyzed to truly understand this key perspective. First, relationship management is not a buzzword to replace or glamorize sales activity. It is a fundamentally different perspective influencing the interactions between a salesperson and his or her customers or prospective customers.

Unfortunately, the principles of personal selling as they have been taught in the past have been *transaction-oriented*. The salesperson's performance, when transaction-oriented, is focused on making a sale. Philip Kotler, a marketing scholar, summarizes the differences between the transaction-oriented salesperson and a salesperson who is practicing relationship management:

The principles of personal selling and negotiation are transaction-oriented; that is, their aim is to help marketers close a specific sale with a customer. There is a larger concept, however, that should guide the seller's dealings with customers, namely, that of relationship management. The seller who knows how to build and manage strong relationships with key customers will have plenty of future sales from these customers. [1]

To enhance your understanding of relationship management, we will analyze how the term *management* is used in its definition. Who, you may wonder, is the manager in the relationship management situation? It is not the salesperson's boss or the vice president of marketing. It is the salesperson. If you aspire to move into the ranks of management as soon after graduation as possible, you can more quickly satisfy that ambition by becoming a professional salesperson and practicing relationship management with your customers. Indeed, the activities expected of you as a manager of relationships form the basis for the majority of the remaining chapters in this book. One further note to correct any misconceptions of what is meant by managing the relationship with customers: we do not mean manipulating customers. Manipulation tactics tend to be associated with transaction-oriented sales practices. The sales representative who is only slightly removed from the ranks of the con artist is likely to be a manipulator. That unprofessional individual not only has no desire to form a relationship with a customer but, in fact, hopes never to encounter the unlucky or gullible person who has bought something and later regretted it.

A second characteristic in our definition of management is that the encounter between the salesperson and the customer is planned. The professional sales representative understands that the customer's time is valuable. Successful salespeople don't, by either word or action, imply that the customer's time has little value. For instance, the remark made unwittingly by some salespeople, "I was in your area and thought I would just drop by," is taboo. Such statements leave the impression with the customer that the sales representative has little regard for the customer's time. On every occasion that a truly professional salesperson makes a contact with a customer, there should be a specific and immediately recognizable reason for the contact. It is vitally important that the *customer* recognizes the reason and has confidence that granting the salesperson an appointment will be beneficial to the customer. The benefit may be new information about upcoming products or additional services, an invitation to a seminar, or even tickets to a ball game or other social event. The key question for the salesperson to ask when reviewing a customer contact is, "Did my meeting with that customer leave the customer in a better condition than before the meeting occurred?" If the salesperson

Salespeople who regard themselves as relationship managers strive to build strong relationships with their customers.

cannot confidently say yes to that question, then more attention should be paid to preparing for future meetings.

Perhaps the most important, yet least obvious, feature of relationship management is that a successful relationship has a quality of *durability*. Some writers have drawn an analogy between relationship management in sales and the institution of marriage.[2] If both parties—the buyer and the salesperson—are experiencing benefits from the relationship, there is a higher probability that the relationship will not only continue but will grow stronger over time. One manifestation of increased strength in a relationship is the level of sales a customer may award to a salesperson. Thus, we have a time factor and a sales-level factor. Both factors will be described in more detail in the next section of this chapter.

THE RELATIONSHIP LIFE CYCLE

One of the most important concepts in marketing is the **product life cycle** (PLC). The PLC depicts a product's sales history through four stages: (1) introduction, (2) growth, (3) maturity, and (4) decline (see Exhibit 3-1). The product life cycle concept has proven quite versatile and can also be used to depict the entry, growth, maturation, and eventual decline of celebrities, ideas, concepts, practices, places, and social concerns.[3] Some celebrities enjoy long life cycles (for example, Bob Hope); others enjoy only brief popularity and then quickly fade. Jogging is an ex-

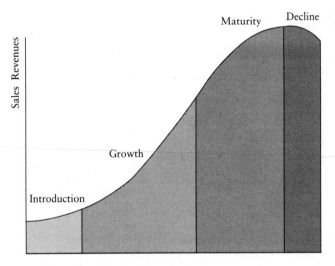

Exhibit 3-1 Product Life Cycle (PLC)

ample of an activity that grew in popularity, matured, and experienced decline. Resort locations also come and go in popularity.

You will see strong similarities between Exhibit 3-1 (PLC) and the **relationship life cycle** (Exhibit 3-2). You can find the first point of similarity between the two life cycles by looking at the axes. The axes in both the PLC and the relationship life cycle (RLC) are labeled the same—the vertical axes measure sales revenues (not profits), and the horizontal axes measure the passage of time. Also, the RLC and the PLC both curve upward to a peak or plateau that signals a significant point in the "life" of a product or a buyer-seller relationship. There are, in reality, many possible shapes to the PLC and the RLC—some of which will be described in this chapter. Before we examine these variations, we need to gain a better understanding of the basic relationship life cycle model.

One of the most important points for you to grasp as you study the RLC is the absolute necessity of managing a relationship with a customer so that it does not deteriorate (a condition illustrated in Exhibit 3-2 by the dotted lines descending after any sale). The situation is aptly described by Theodore Levitt:

> *The seller has made a sale, which he expects directly to yield a profit. The buyer has bought a tool with which to produce things to yield a profit. For the seller it is the end of the process; for the buyer the beginning.[4]*

In the time prior to the first sale, the pre-first-sale effort period in Exhibit 3-2, the salesperson engages in efforts such as finding prospects, analyzing the prospect's needs, and making presentations to the prospect. These activities are described in Chapters 6 through 9. In many cases, this set of activities is the major focus of salespeople. Important as each activity is, the experienced sales professional realizes a successful relationship comprises much more than prospecting, approaching the prospect, and making presentations. As an example, while the pre-sale activity is occurring, the sales representative may be working with a variety of personnel from other departments in his or her company. Shipping may need to be consulted to determine how rapidly that department could respond to reorders from a customer. The prepared sales representative needs this information *before* making a promise to a customer about delivery arrangements. Billing is another department the sales representative may turn to for necessary information. If, for instance, an industrial buyer wanted to be billed to accommodate its particular accounting system, the sales representative would be well advised to know what his or her company could do to meet such a request. To avoid an embarrassing situation later, the credit department should be consulted, too, to determine what, if any, credit limitations would be imposed on the customer. These situations require skill in internal relationship management—an area explored in Chapters 10 to 12. The need for intracompany support exists throughout a sales relationship, and the skilled professional must know how to get things done *for* the customer (rather than *to* the customer).

The first sale identified in Exhibit 3-2 may be a trial purchase by the customer. Prior to this, the buyer may have acquired the product or service from other sources and may still regard other sellers as the primary source(s). Regardless of whether the situation involves an industrial or a consumer sale, the time immediately following the first sale is crucial. Providing total consumption satisfaction by

Exhibit 3-2 Buyer-Seller Relationship Life Cycle (RLC)

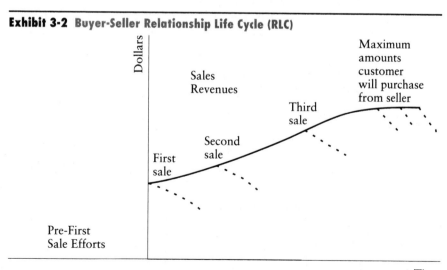

attending to delivery, installation, training, credit arrangements, and other such matters are examples of follow-up postsale activities that, if performed smoothly, can go a long way toward cementing a lasting relationship.

The second sale depicted in the RLC model reflects a slightly larger dollar sales volume, which indicates the buyer's growing confidence in the seller. There still may be, however, a lack of total purchasing commitment by the buyer. In many cases, it would be unrealistic and unproductive to believe that total purchasing commitment to a single supplier can ever be attained. One writer has termed this situation "always a share," meaning that a seller must always share the buyer's business with some (hopefully, only a few) other vendors.[5] Realistically, of course, this makes sense. You cannot reasonably expect a customer to become too dependent on any one source of supply, especially if the buyer-seller relationship is in the industrial world.

The third sale reveals a significantly larger amount of revenue coming from this relationship with a customer. One possibility, among many, is that the buyer has decided to purchase other complementary products or services from the seller. Once again, vigilance in the follow-up activity is as necessary as it was in previous sales efforts. The penalty of complacency by the salesperson is the loss of the business to other sales representatives who are hungry to achieve a foothold and who will not approach their postsale responsibilities in a lax manner.

The peak of the revenue curve signals the maximum amount of revenue the relationship between this particular customer and the salesperson will yield. Each selling organization should analyze the amount that can realistically be sold to a particular customer. The management of customer accounts, which vary in the revenues and profits they generate (that is, from blue-chip to marginal accounts), is causing many firms to search for more cost-effective ways to maintain communications with their customers.[6]

The model of the relationship illustrated in Exhibit 3-2 might be considered an idealized version of a relationship. In other words, there is a steady progression of increased revenues from the first through the third sales. In this greatly simplified illustration, the sales curve increases at a positive rate until it peaks out. Several other versions of the relationship life cycle model give a more realistic picture of what can happen in relationships between buyers and sellers.

The Management Science Institute found only 17 percent of product classes and 20 percent of individual brands have the modified S shape depicted in Exhibit 3-1. Many different shapes of the product life cycle exist.[7] It is also thought that many different shapes of the relationship life cycle can exist. Exhibit 3-3 contains diagrams of four variations of the general RLC model. Let us look at each of these variations.

Exhibit 3-3 Various Relationship Life Cycles

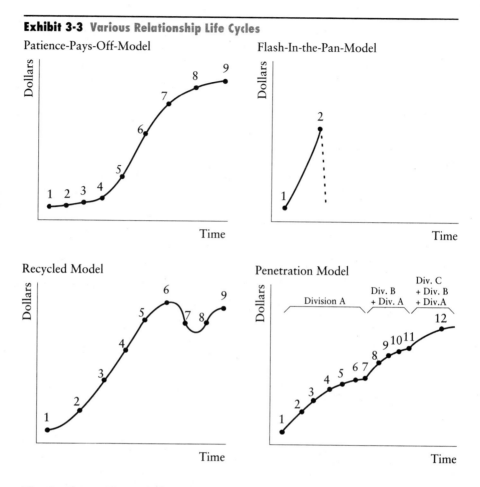

Patience-Pays-Off-Model

Flash-In-the-Pan-Model

Recycled Model

Penetration Model

The Patience-Pays-Off Model

The **patience-pays-off model** shows very slow progress in the early stages of the relationship. The gain in sales revenues between the first and fourth sales is relatively small. Of course, many factors could account for this slow revenue growth. One of the more obvious factors is that the buyer in the early periods might not need much of the product or service. Aside from the external causes, there are some conditions a sales representative can affect. One of the reasons sales may not be increasing much between the early sales is because the buyer may simply be cautious in these early stages. The customer may be testing the salesperson, the salesperson's company, and/or the products or services. Once this rather long trial period has ended, however, the sales curve turns sharply upward. The lesson to be gained is that the sales representative shouldn't be too quick to assign this customer to a category of low-volume purchasers (or worse yet, stop calling on the customer altogether).

Another reason is that perhaps the customer's other supplier(s) have neglected to maintain the relationship with the customer and, seeing the lack of service, the customer awards business to the persistent and high-quality seller. One executive states:

> All that matters is that your salespeople have the perseverance and patience to position your company as Number Two to enough prospects. If they're standing second in line in enough lines, sooner or later they will move up to Number One.[8]

The final reason offered for the slowly climbing sales volume is that the buyer may be taking a long time to learn how to use the product or service and, until the buyer has some confidence in the ability to use it, the amount of the product or service purchased will be low. Salespeople confronted with such situations may need to pay more attention to helping train the customer or customer's personnel on how to properly use the product so the buyer will feel justified in accelerating purchases. An example would be a firm buying personal computers for its employees. Until the work force becomes computer literate, the purchase rate of PCs might be low. After the salesperson or a technical representative conducts a seminar on personal computer use, the requests for additional computers may cause sales levels to rise.

The Flash-in-the-Pan Model

The **flash-in-the-pan model** has an extremely short life span. As shown in Exhibit 3-3, it is over after two sales have been made. What is the reason for this sudden demise? Once again, many reasons could be offered, but the major reason is that the customer failed to see any value in continuing the relationship with the sales representative. The salesperson may have lied about delivery schedules, product quality, postsale service, or any number of things. Another possibility is that the sales representative didn't even realize he or she was involved in a potential relationship with the customer. Treating the situation as a one- or two-time transaction, the salesperson didn't follow up and a salesperson who had been waiting in the wings (similar to the circumstances in the patience-pays-off situation) won the customer away.

Managers of salespeople whose performance is characterized by this model should become very concerned. The total costs of acquiring those few sales from this customer may overshadow the total revenue obtained. Although more detailed information about the costs of prospecting will be provided in Chapter 4, suffice it to say that it costs a lot to replace a lost customer. Increasingly, management must be asking the question, "When does a customer become profitable to us?"

The Recycled Model

Through sales event 6 in the **recycled model**, the situation looks very much like the basic relationship life cycle model in Exhibit 3-2. Apparently something happened to cause sales revenues to slump from the high point represented by event 6. Once again, there could be a vast number of reasons for the momentary downturn, but two circumstances are worth analyzing now. First, a competitor may have made the buyer a deal that seemed too good to turn down. The buyer, therefore, switched a portion of the business to the competitive supplier. This accounts for the downturn in sales volume in sales events 7 and 8. After this slump, the sales revenues depicted by sales event 9 returned to the level in sales event 6. What caused this? The explanation could be that the presumed advantages forthcoming from the new competitor did not materialize—that is, the products or services weren't what were represented, the deliveries weren't made on time, and so on.

Another possible explanation of the dip in sales revenues might be that the relationship suffered a temporary lapse because the sales representative who originally established the relationship was transferred, left the company, or was promoted. The replacement, not enjoying the same rapport with the customer, experienced a momentary decline but, after a time, restored the purchaser's confidence and sales returned to the previous level.

In a highly competitive market, such situations as depicted in the recycled RLC model are inevitable. You want, however, to minimize the amount of time between the twin peaks represented here by points 6 and 9. You want to minimize lost business. Someone said, "The price of freedom is eternal vigilance." That statement, when modified to fit the world of competitive sales, might be, "The price of good customer relationships is eternal vigilance." Any salesperson who starts to take a customer's patronage for granted will shortly discover that other representatives from other companies will move in swiftly.

The Penetration Model

The **penetration model** of the RLC, as shown in Exhibit 3-3, is the optimal situation. The title "penetration" describes a situation in which a sales representative cultivates additional business within the buying unit (which can be a firm, an organization, or a family). The additional sales are forthcoming from other departments or people in the buying center. In the model, the added revenues from sales to other groups first become apparent at points 8 through 11. At point 12, still another gain has been made. This is a very healthy situation from the sales representative's standpoint, because he or she is finding more ways to serve the buying center. In this model, other divisions are being added to the sales representative's source of revenue from this one customer.

An office supply sales representative might commence the relationship with Division A of a large firm. This situation, as a result of excellent management by the salesperson, led to adding Division B to the sales representative's penetration of the account. Division C was eventually added. If the purchasing agents for these three divisions function independently, then the representative will have basically three relationships—one with each of the purchasing agents.

Another common example is the insurance company (for example, Sears' Allstate) that advertises total protection—home, life, and auto. In effect, the insurance agent who eventually gets a client to insure a home, an automobile, and obtain life insurance has fully penetrated the individual consumer's insurance needs.

Banking services are another example. Most banks would like to develop a relationship with a depositor that causes the depositor to open a checking account and, subsequently, a savings account, a money market fund, a safety deposit box, and a credit card. A financial institution that can penetrate a customer's need for financial service to that extent is likely to have a long-lasting relationship with the depositor.

Although various relationships—business as well as social—tend to have finite time spans, there is also another aspect of this subject that we must address. We need to analyze the *types* of relationships buyers and sellers form.

TYPES OF RELATIONSHIPS

The basic types of relationships described in this section indicate what a customer or client expects from the relationship (see Exhibit 3-4). One must never forget that buyer expectations are crucial to the formation and continuation of a buyer-seller relationship. An in-depth analysis of buyer behavior appears in Chapters 4 and 5. Three types of relationships will be described here: the counselor relationship, the supplier relationship, and the systems designer relationship.

The Counselor Relationship

Counselor relationships are frequently found, for example, in sales of insurance, real estate, and financial services (see Exhibit 3-5) and exist in both consumer and industrial markets. Although most consumers need assistance making choices in real estate investments, insurance, and financial services, such as trading stocks and bonds, so also do many corporate executives. Executives responsible for buying and selling commercial real estate, evaluating health plans, or managing their firm's stock portfolios need the best advice available.

Exhibit 3-4 **Basic Types of Relationships**

Type	Customer Circumstances	Sales Rep's Responsibilities
Counselor	Knows general objective or desired condition, but doesn't know how to implement a solution. Places high value on personalized attention and easy access to the salesperson.	In-depth understanding of the customer's desired goals and objectives. Extensive expertise in various solutions to customer's problems and objectives. Keeps solutions matched to changing needs and goals of customers in a dynamic environment.
Supplier	Knows the objective he/she wants to attain. Knows what type of product/service will be needed to achieve objective. Needs assistance in procuring specific product or service.	Secures specific brands of goods and services the customer has indicated are needed. Solves any logistical problems that occur such as shipping, billing, or replacing damaged goods. Keeps buyer informed of new offerings and their availability.
Systems Designer	Unaware of ways to perform an activity or function in a more efficient way. Expects total solution to a problem once it has been established that a better approach exists.	Conceptualizes a better system for performing a function the customer is now performing. Implements the new system in the customer's environment. Upgrades the system to optimize its efficiency, when necessary.

Customers or clients have certain expectations and goals that influence the type of interaction occurring between the buyer and the seller. First, even if not actively seeking a solution to a problem at the time the sales representative approaches, the customer usually has a vague idea of what condition he or she wants to exist in the future. For example, the parents of a six-month-old baby may not have started a financial program that enables their child to have funds available for college. They do, however, often express the goal of giving their child a college education. They also realize that tuition costs will rise and will present a formidable budget challenge. Under these circumstances, this family becomes a prospect for a financial services sales representative who can provide them with the counseling they need to permit them to achieve their long-term goals.

Second, such customers also expect extensive personalized attention. This is logical in view of the wide array of possible solutions to the customer's problem(s).

Figure 3-1 In a counselor relationship, the sales representative acts as an adviser to the buyer.

To present the customer with an optimum choice, the sales representative needs an in-depth understanding of the customer's circumstances. Such a situation requires close personal contact.

A third feature of the counselor relationship is the customer's access to the salesperson. This is particularly important in counselor relationships involving investment services. Customers expect salespeople to keep them informed of conditions in the dynamic investment environment. The customer also wants to be able to initiate contact with the counselor salesperson and to have questions answered or anxieties calmed.

Customers may have relatively little time or talent to study the details of the various solutions the professional sales representative is expected to know. For instance, a college professor whose field is American history may not know much about the best investments to achieve financial security at retirement. A manager responsible for finding office space in a new area cannot be as knowledgeable about opportunities in the new environment as a local commercial real estate salesperson. Relying upon the expertise of the sales representative and the advice about office space conditions in the new city causes a relationship to develop between the manager and the real estate salesperson. If this opportunity is managed successfully by the sales professional, it could lead to other opportunities with this firm.

One of the most important expectations the customer or client has in this type of relationship is the integrity of the salesperson. As you can understand from reading these examples, the salesperson needs, and is expected to possess, an in-depth

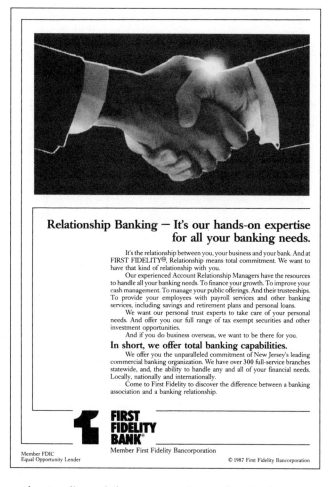

Exhibit 3-5 A Counselor Relationship in Banking

First Fidelity Bancorporation. Reprinted with permission.

understanding of the customer's or client's circumstances. Frequently, this includes the customer's financial situation and other very personal and confidential matters. Sensitive information, whether it involves a person or a corporation, requires the salesperson to be discreet.

The commercial real estate example illustrates this point. A salesperson's insider knowledge about the client corporation's expansion plans must be handled discreetly to avoid tipping off competitors. In many cases, salespeople involved in counselor relationships will possess information that, if divulged, could jeopardize a client's operations or embarrass an individual.

So far, we have described the customer's expectations in a counselor relationship. Now we can ask about what requirements a successful salesperson must meet when functioning in sales situations characterized by the counselor relationship circumstances.

Sales representatives serving as counselors to their customers can benefit from analyzing other professional people's efforts to establish relationships with clients where a great deal of trust must exist between the counselor and the client. One particular trait that is a prerequisite to success is *patience*. When the salesperson needs to have information normally regarded as personal (for example, a customer's financial conditions, health problems, domestic circumstances), the successful sales representative will spend more time *listening* to the customer than talking about details of the product or service. This is an extremely important requirement, whether the sale is to a homeowner or a corporate benefits manager. The advice to "always be closing" is definitely not appropriate in the counselor relationship.

Second, the representative must also earn the trust and confidence of the customer or client. Some companies have conducted research on what types of salespersons should be matched with various customer types in an effort to better cultivate that trust. Generally, the effort to match salespeople with customers on the basis of age, education, and experience seems to be worthwhile. The underlying rationale is that most people tend to trust and regard with favor those people who are most like themselves.[9]

A third requirement for successful selling as a counselor is the quick access to accurate and up-to-date information on the products or services that can be the solutions to the customer's problems. One reason for a customer's trust and confidence is the level of expertise the customer perceives in the sales representative. Customized investment programs, real estate transactions, insurance programs, and other business relationships such as these require the mixing and matching of a combination of services, which demand a deep knowledge of the availability of services that could fit the customer's "needs."[10] The realization of how critical this is to a salesperson's success has caused some innovative companies to provide computerized information retrieval systems for the use of the sales force.[11] One such example is the lap-top computers Integrated Resources Life Insurance Company provides its salespeople to help them get information on-the-screen when the field sales rep is working with a client.

The rapport between a counselor-type sales professional and a customer or client is further facilitated by the image the salesperson's company has established. Millions of dollars are spent each year by banks and insurance firms, real estate companies, and stock brokers to position their respective firms in the mind of the target customer. The messages are designed to convey an impression of impeccable honesty and integrity and to establish an initial impression that, when coupled with the professional demeanor of the salesperson, can create faster and stronger bonding between the salesperson and the customer.

The Supplier Relationship

The major difference between the **supplier relationship** and the counselor relationship is the amount of knowledge customers have about the products or services that will meet their needs. Whereas customers in a counselor relationship need help in finding a "solution," buyers in a supplier relationship not only know their needs but also are confident about how to fulfill those needs.

Most experienced industrial purchasing agents have the responsibility of procuring supplies that will be consumed in the daily operations of their companies. Purchasing agents frequently know when certain supplies will be needed as well as who will need them. Also, the purchaser usually has several potential sources of supply for any given product or service.

Whirlpool Corporation is an example of a well-known company that engages in thousands of supplier relationships. Whirlpool, in its manufacture of appliances, relies on a supplier base of approximately 1,200 companies. One of the commodities Whirlpool requires is steel. Whirlpool uses 500,000 tons of steel a year and secures most of its steel from three major companies. The sales reps who are responsible for maintaining the relationship between their company and a customer like Whirlpool have a major responsibility!

For a potential vendor, being selected by Whirlpool means making a major commitment to the relationship. The ultimate goal of Whirlpool's procurement department is to select suppliers who can develop into strategic partners, allowing them to become extensions of the company.

How does Whirlpool choose the companies with which it will develop a supplier relationship? Bill Agnew, a Regional Procurement Director, outlines four specific areas judged by Whirlpool:

1. *Quality.* Whirlpool is moving toward a supplier certification program. All suppliers in this program will certify that all parts in their shipments conform to specification.

2. *Technology.* Suppliers are expected to provide innovative materials, processes, and product features and to become involved in the design of Whirlpool's new products.

3. *Service.* Suppliers are expected to ship on time and to be flexible in changing schedules.

4. *Price.* Whirlpool measures the cost of materials worldwide. Sales reps for companies selling to Whirlpool must be aware that, in effect, they are competing against "the world."[12]

A salesperson functioning in a supplier relationship should possess no illusions about the basic nature of this type of relationship. Rather than having an exclusive arrangement in which the buyer purchases only from one company, the purchaser's job demands that multiple sources be used to at least provide the buyer with some security if a strike or disaster hits a particular supplier. Also, the salesperson should understand that, with an abundance of potential suppliers, the buyer can and probably will frequently reevaluate all vendor relationships.[13] Rather than producing anxiety for the salesperson, competition should be welcomed as an opportunity to prove why a continuation of the relationship makes good sense for the purchaser.

We should not conclude from this discussion that the counselor relationship is superior to the supplier relationship or vice versa. The purchasing experience and superior knowledge of the buyer in the supplier relationship simply make these totally different situations. The successful salesperson in the supplier relationship must be just as professionally and socially skilled as sales representatives responsible for managing counselor relationships or *systems designer* relationships, which we turn to next.

The Systems Designer Relationship

The **systems designer relationship** is based on the customer-oriented premise that purchasers need and want solutions to problems that may require several products and services working compatibly to solve the problem. Systems designer relationships range from those in which a sales representative helps a customer design a home entertainment system to those involving the design and installation of a desk-top publishing system linked to several offices (see Exhibit 3-6).

At the beginning of this relationship, customers may not be aware of a better way to perform an activity until the sales representative educates them. AT&T is an example of a company that devotes considerable resources to teaching businesspeople how to solve some of their problems through the use of telecommunications. AT&T's Knowledge Plus seminar series addresses a number of problems seminar attendees may be experiencing (for example, expensive sales visits with too many nonprospects; poor or unresponsive customer service; and selling to small, unprofitable accounts). The seminars suggest ways of solving these problems through the adoption of various telecommunications systems.

Once alerted to the possibilities for improvement, the customer is usually receptive to the suggestion that the sales representative design and present a system for the customer's approval. For instance, the design of an AT&T telemarketing system will usually include specifications of the recommended size of the center (for example, number of employees, number of square feet, and amount of telephone equipment needed).

Exhibit 3-6 Advertisement Suggesting a Systems Designer Relationship

©1988 Entré Computer Centers, Inc. Entré Computer Centers are independently owned and operated.

In many system designs, the salesperson will require the help of technical support personnel. Indeed, the availability of such expertise is, in some cases, the determining factor in deciding which competing vendor may be granted the business. Therefore, the company must provide its sales force with extensive technical support resources.

Because of the complexity of many systems and the speed of technological improvements, the customer expects a sales representative to assist in monitoring the system's operation after it has been installed. This is, of course, a great opportunity for the salesperson to further cement the relationship by being a valuable consultant. As technological improvements occur, the sales representative and the rep's technical support personnel can recommend upgrading equipment and services, thereby improving the system's efficiency.

When a sales representative works in an environment that requires system design and maintenance, great opportunities exist to apply the success in one department, unit, or family to other groups that are closely associated with the original user of the system. Because systems are usually significant elements in a customer's operations or life-style, they are likely to be discussed and shown to other people who also may need and desire a similar system. Thus, a favorable climate can be established for the enterprising salesperson to penetrate other sectors of an organization or even a neighborhood and make additional systems sales—home security systems, farmland drainage systems, robotized production line systems, and electronic order-entry systems. Experienced sales professionals realize that word-of-mouth promotion from one satisfied party to other interested potential buyers can be a powerful way to leverage one success into many successes. This situation is illustrated in the penetration model of the relationship life cycle.

What qualities are required for a salesperson to succeed in this sales environment? First, the *ability to conceptualize a systems solution* to a customer's problems is indispensable. This quality (presumably possessed by their salespeople) is so crucial to success that Hewlett-Packard uses it as a theme in some of their advertisements (see Exhibit 3-7). Before beginning the actual system design, the salesperson must envision how the array of available equipment and services could be configured into a system that would address the specific customer's needs.

Another example is the sale of a user-friendly computer system to Dayton's Department Store in Minneapolis for use in the bridal gift department. A sales representative became aware that people purchasing bridal gifts might inadvertently select a gift that duplicated another gift already purchased for the same couple. The solution was the design of a computerized data base listing the array of gifts the bridal couple desired. By keying in the bride's and groom's names, a customer could receive a computer printout of the gifts remaining on the wish list. The system solved a problem for shoppers, gave them greater confidence in their gift selections, and increased store sales. As a result, the same type of system was designed for the infant department. Initially, however, the salesperson had to conceptualize how the system would work.

Another important quality is the salesperson's ability to describe the proposed system and implementation steps to the customer. This, of course, requires a high order of communication skills. The ability to encode (see Chapter 2) information so it can be understood (that is, decoded) by the customer is crucial to the successful establishment of the system designer relationship. The challenge is increased when a number of people are involved, such as previously described in the buying center.

For example, a sales representative promoting a computer system might deal with a data processing manager who is concerned with keeping downtime to a min-

Exhibit 3-7 An Example of a Systems Designer

Ad ran during 1987. Courtesy Hewlett-Packard Company.

Figure 3-2 Services to in-store buyers represent areas where the systems designer relationship can be effectively utilized.

imum. The manager's peer in personnel might not be concerned at all with that situation but wants assurances that memory storage would permit more information to be kept on file for each employee. Still another participant in the buying decision might be someone from the finance department who is primarily interested in the payment plans available for the proposed system. Members from other functional areas affected by this computer system would have different concerns—all of which require the sales representative's attention.

Thus, the salesperson must be able to orchestrate a variety of specialists from the sales representative's company. As talented and energetic as the salesperson might be, usually there are questions in each new system design that go beyond the salesperson's depth of knowledge. The amount and quality of support on which the salesperson can rely are crucial in the successful installation and maintenance of technical systems.

After a system of products and services has been purchased by a customer, the good sales representative will realize that the relationship has reached a crucial point. The purchaser, whether a demanding professional purchasing agent or an anxious consumer, wants affirmation that expectations will be met.[14] The professional salesperson realizes this and makes certain that the purchaser's expectations are fulfilled.

Periodically, the opportunity arises for the sales representative to suggest a review or audit of the system to determine how or whether it can be improved. This can be an occasion to further demonstrate to the purchaser why the purchase decision was a wise one, and, equally important, why the sales representative merits future business.

RELATIONSHIP MANAGEMENT AND BUSINESS STRATEGY

If a firm's business strategy is to serve as a guide for how the firm intends to achieve its goals and objectives, then every activity must positively contribute toward the successful execution of this strategy. Thus, if relationship management is to be the guiding theme used by the firm's sales force, it must be compatible with the seller's selected business strategy. Fortunately, relationship management is not wedded to any particular strategy. As we will demonstrate in the remainder of this section, it can be used successfully with any of the generic strategies. We will briefly describe three popular strategies: differentiation, low-cost producer, and focus or niche.[15]

Differentiation

The essence of a **differentiation strategy** is to create something buyers perceive to be unique and of sufficient value so that the seller can receive a higher price for the product. Differentiation provides insulation against competitive rivalry because of brand loyalty by customers and resulting lower sensitivity to price. The resulting customer loyalty and the need for a competitor to overcome uniqueness provide entry barriers.[16]

Increasingly, educated and demanding buyers realize the "product" they are seeking from a vendor is not just the core or basic product or service. The product buyers seek is really a package of anticipated satisfactions.[17] As mentioned earlier, part of the package includes such things as speed of delivery, extended warranty, efficient installation, and other customer service items. The relationship between the buyer and seller is an important part of the composite that buyers are seeking.[18] One bit of evidence to support this claim is found in the research exploring vendor selection systems and decisions. This research found three crucial factors in the choice of a vendor: (1) the ability to meet quality standards, (2) the ability to deliver the product on time, and (3) performance on previous contracts.[19]

The implications of these findings for relationship management are very important. It is the primary responsibility of the sales representative serving a buyer to see that the contract performance is above reproach, thereby setting up a favorable atmosphere for the next sales event with the customer.

When a relationship has matured to the degree (that is, reached the peak of the relationship life cycle) that the buyer is purchasing more (or entirely) from one vendor than others, the relationship has then produced a differential advantage for the favored seller. Thus, an entry barrier has been developed that may cost would-be competitors more than they are willing to pay. Cynics have said there is no brand loyalty that two cents off can't overcome.[20] The assumption, which is frequently false, is that competitors would be willing to "buy" the business by reducing their price. The cost to them of cutting a price may be prohibitive even if the buyer could be enticed to switch. Strong relationships make this circumstance less likely to occur. Management in a firm wanting to use relationship management to differentiate itself cannot just wish this will occur. In this case, actions speak louder than words.

How does a professional sales representative help his or her company achieve a differential advantage over competing firms? The rep does so by realizing that the buyer, in most situations, will be evaluating many things in addition to the basic product or service. Was the product installed on time? Were the service people knowledgeable, courteous, and concerned about customer service? Did the salesperson resolve any problems that arose without delay? These are only a few of the questions customers ask themselves as they compare potential suppliers. In some situations, the major factor in the differentiation effort is the sales representative. The statement has been made previously but it is sufficiently important to repeat—since the salesperson is the individual with whom the customer is in contact, the salesperson *is* the company in the estimation of the customer. Thus, if the salesperson is judged by a customer to be superior to the other salespeople vying for that customer's business, a potent differential advantage has been established. When the sales representative approaches a customer from a relationship management perspective rather than a transaction-oriented perspective, a differential advantage is more likely to be the result.

Low-Cost Producer

A low-cost producer has found a way to create products or render services more economically than any of the other competitors in the industry. Usually this low-cost condition results from a combination of economically sound practices involving all of the functions in a business—production, marketing, finance, and other functions.

No doubt, some of you will have difficulties reconciling relationship management and the **low-cost producer strategy**. Relationship management, after all, might be perceived to be associated with three-martini lunches, executive visits, and other high-cost activities. The truth, however, is that it is generally less expensive to maintain a customer relationship than to start and develop a new one. This claim is supported by three research studies. The Technical Assistance Research Program found that it cost five times more to find a customer than to maintain an account.[21] This is further supported by Cardozo and Shipp's study that revealed it required four and one-half field sales calls to close the typical order.[22] McGraw-Hill discovered that each of these sales calls cost approximately $230.[23] One can readily see that it is expensive to search for and secure customers.

Firms intent on lowering their operating costs can, by practicing relationship management, retain their customers and thereby avoid spending time and money constantly having to win new ones. This opportunity tends to be overlooked largely because the term *low-cost producer* focuses executive attention on production rather than on the firm's total operations.

An explanation of how a manufacturer could lower costs via the practice of relationship management can be given. Let us return momentarily to the penetration model identified in Exhibit 3-3. In that situation, the salesperson, over a period of time, has won the confidence and business of several divisions in the customer's organization. In the latter stages of the relationship life cycle, the sales rep is selling to Divisions A, B, and also C. By developing such a favorable relationship, the astute salesperson is helping his or her company to lower costs in several ways.

One way to lower business costs is to enjoy the benefits of economies of scale. It may be cheaper on a per unit of product basis to sell 500 units of product than 50. By increasing the amount of total product sold to a single customer, the seller might reduce the unit cost. The maxim "cheaper by the dozen" applies in many purchasing situations. Other factors can reduce total costs. The sales rep may be able to make one sales call on the customer and see the buyers for Divisions A, B, and C. This could lower travel costs compared with three sales trips to call on three different customers. Another factor working to lower costs is shipping. By having to pay for only one large shipment to a customer rather than many separate shipments, the seller can usually save money. Thus, relationship management can, in some cases, become a strong contributor to the successful execution of a low-cost producer strategy.

Focus

The **focus or niche strategy** rests on the premise that a firm can serve a narrow strategic target more effectively or efficiently than competitors who are selling more broadly.[24] Relationship management not only is compatible with this strategic approach, but also is necessary to such a firm's success. There are two reasons for this. First, the firm that focuses on a narrow target group of customers must not lose the relatively few customers it has. The seller has selected its market niche because it believes better service and a higher quality product will be recognized and purchased by customers in the selected niche. After carefully selecting the customer group, designing the product, and delivering it, the seller must retain the customers' loyalty to make an adequate return on investment.

Second, many customers' needs are such that they can be well served only by a vendor who renders a specialized product or service. Those firms willing and able to meet customers' special needs can enjoy a relationship with customers that will be advantageous to both the buyers and the seller. Relationship management permits the seller to learn the customer's requirements and develop ways to meet these needs. By discovering ways in which the seller can aid a buyer, the rep cements relationships. Crown Cork and Seal, for example, successfully practices a focused strategy.[25] Its customers are firms producing products that require special cans and containers. Although such customers do not form a massive market for Crown Cork and Seal, its ability to satisfy these special container needs has put Crown Cork and Seal's profitability above the industry average.

MANAGEMENT'S RESPONSIBILITIES

What can management do to enhance the possibilities that relationship management will succeed in a firm? Senior management cannot rely only on exhortations to the sales force to implement and maintain durable relationships with customers or clients. If this fundamental sales perspective is to become a successful reality in a company, management must fulfill certain responsibilities.

First, managers must give considerable thought to the characteristics of the relationships the firm wishes to create with its customers.[26] For example, after analyzing its industry and its competitors' behavior, management must realistically determine how much patronage a particular customer is likely to award to any single vendor or supplier. This appraisal is as necessary for an independent insurance agency as it is for IBM in analyzing its chances of being the sole supplier of computers for customers who can select from among Apple, DEC, and many other brands.

An analysis of the type of relationship desired (counselor, supplier, or systems designer) is necessary so that the sales force can be given specific guidance on what activities it is expected to perform. Management will gain from this analysis needed insights about the time and money required to establish the desired relations.[27]

Second, management must develop internal systems responsive to customers and to salespeople as they serve their customers. When we examine the relationship models and envision the challenges confronting a sales representative who must interact with many sources of information within the firm, we can readily see that user-friendly information systems are a must.[28] Salespeople (particularly when they are in the presence of the customer) can enhance their status by getting quick and accurate answers for a customer. One example of this is a company that established an 800 number for its sales personnel to use as a hotline to headquarters where specialists were available to answer product questions.

A company that has benefited greatly in creating relationships featuring information systems is American Hospital Supply.[29] The company's ASAP (as soon as possible) ordering system permits customers to transmit an order through a computerized system and quickly determine the order's cost and arrival time. This system facilitated the formation of relationships to the extent that the average order size placed with American Hospital Supply is approximately three times as great as the industry average.

Third, management must impress upon *all* company employees the need for a *total* company effort to effectively execute relationship management.[30] The sales force needs to call on various departments for help in shipping, credit arrangements, training, maintenance, and so forth. These diverse groups of specialists must understand their roles in supporting the relationship management concept.

Fourth, management at the executive level must realize (and welcome) the responsibility of participating from time to time in sales situations. Sometimes a customer's or client's top-ranking executives want a vendor's executives to be present at a meeting where important matters will be discussed. Matching the buyer's executive levels with the same levels of executives from the seller's firm may be necessary to cater to executive egos. In addition, it provides the seller's executives with first-hand knowledge of the challenges and opportunities confronting the sales force.

SUMMARY

1. Relationship management is a fundamental perspective requiring sales representatives to plan and pursue goals when interacting with buyers so that both the buyer and the seller will experience benefits and thereby seek subsequent interactions with each other.

2. Relationships between buyers and sellers have life cycles that reflect the condition of the relationship.

3. There are three fundamental types of relationships—counselor, supplier, and systems designer—each characterized by different expectations from the buyer and requiring different skills on the part of the sales representative.

4. Relationship management is compatible with three generic business strategies: differentiation, low-cost producer, and focused or niche marketing. All can be executed more effectively if a firm's sales force employs relationship management in its dealings with customers.

5. A firm's senior management cannot mandate relationship management as the firm's course of action and then forget about it. All management levels must work to see that the appropriate conditions exist and take an active role in meeting with customers when such action is desirable.

QUESTIONS FOR DISCUSSION AND REVIEW

1. What is the essential difference between the relationship management approach and the transaction-oriented approach to sales?

2. What are the three basic types of buyer-seller relationships? Which one requires the salesperson to possess or have access to technical expertise?

3. In the patience-pays-off relationship life cycle, what are some possible causes for the modest level of purchases a new customer might make at the beginning of the relationship?

4. In industrial sales, what does "always a share" mean?

5. What could a successful relationship management sales program do to assist a firm in becoming a low-cost producer? a differentiator? a focused or niche marketer?

6. What are some possible causes of the recycled model of the relationship life cycle? the flash-in-the-pan model?

7. An executive said, "Relationship management can't be the sole responsibility of our sales department." What did the executive mean?

CASE 3-1   AKROID PRODUCTS EVALUATES ITS VENDORS

Tom Franklin, a sales representative for Berry Rubber Products, was asked to meet with his customer, the chief purchasing manager for Akroid Products, Bernie Roberts. Tom Franklin has been selling to Akroid Products, a very large account, for three years. In the past twelve months, for instance, Franklin had sold Akroid $1.5 million dollars worth of products.

The two men are meeting in Roberts's office at Akroid headquarters.

Roberts: I'm glad you could come by, Tom. I'm sure you've heard rumors about all sorts of changes we're making around here.

Franklin: Sure, Bernie. The word on the street is that you are going to review all of your suppliers and cut down the number of suppliers you are buying from. Our company, of course, is very concerned because you've been and, we trust, will continue to be one of our best customers. We want this relationship to continue indefinitely.

Roberts: That's what I wanted to discuss with you, Tom. I wanted to describe what we are going to do. We're presently buying our supplies from over 2,500 different vendors. We want to cut this number by 50 percent in the next nine months. And then, within eighteen months we want to be buying from no more than 1,000 suppliers. This will mean that we will have a much closer relationship with the remaining vendors we do business with.

Franklin: I see.

Roberts: There are a lot of advantages for us and, I might add, for those suppliers we eventually select. Let's say we only use your company and two other vendors for all the rubber molding component parts we use in our kitchen appliances and dental/medical equipment. That means we "lop-off" 15 other suppliers from whom we have bought various amounts of rubber moldings.

Franklin: How do you intend to make the choice among the vendors?

Roberts: We've worked out a vendor evaluation system for every group of products and services we purchase.

Franklin: Is that evaluation system confidential or can I get some information on how you will conduct the evaluation?

Roberts: Oh, it's not secret. We'll be telling all of our vendors how we're going to make the evaluation. These are some of the points that are related to your product category (shoving a paper toward Franklin who starts to scan it).

As Franklin read the list, he saw the first four requirements:

1. Agreement by vendor to participate in Akroid's Zero Defects Program.
2. Compliance with delivery schedule with the objective of reducing rubber molding supplies in Akroid's inventory by 50 percent.
3. Permission granted by a supplier authorizing Akroid's new product planners to be informed about the supplier's R&D programs.
4. Willingness by the supplier to sign a five year contract during which Points One, Two, and Three will govern the relationship between Akroid and the supplier.

Franklin: Bernie, I don't see any mention of prices in here.

Roberts: Well, as I mentioned, this is only the beginning of the evaluation list. I will say, however, that we are concerned with *value*—not necessarily price.

Franklin: What do you mean by value? That's a pretty subjective term.

Roberts: I know. We want, above all, to know that whatever we are buying will lower our total costs of operation. For example, let's say one of your rubber gaskets is 2 cents a unit higher than the competition. If you can guarantee through the Zero Defects Program that we don't have to have a quality control operation, which is costly, our overall costs can be reduced. We should, obviously, be better off buying from you, even though you had a higher priced product. That's just one example of how we will determine value.

Franklin: Okay, I see.

QUESTIONS

1. How does this case reflect the central points in the chapter's opening vignette, "Partnership Selling: The Wave of the Future"?

2. If Tom Franklin's company, Berry Rubber, is pursuing a differential advantage strategy, how can Tom Franklin's approach to a relationship with Akroid reinforce Berry Rubber's strategy?

3. What kind of strategy does it seem that Akroid is pursuing? What effect is that strategy having on Akroid's relationship with vendors?

CASE 3-2   RELATIONSHIP MANAGEMENT ON THE COLLEGE CAMPUS

Marie Gillespie shook hands with Dr. Tom Peters and said, "Welcome to Iowa, Dr. Peters. I hope you'll be very happy here!"

Gillespie was a young sales representative for IMF Corporation, a company that managed professional people's investments. Marie was assigned the Drake University faculty and part of the Iowa State University faculty. She was responsible for establishing and retaining the accounts of investors who were college teachers and administrators.

If a university professor decided to use the IMF investment program, Marie notified the appropriate office at the university, and an automatic monthly payroll deduction was initiated. The university, depending upon its personal benefit policy, also contributed monthly to the individual's investment program. The contributed monies were invested by IMF and, eventually, when the person retired, IMF disbursed the principal and its earnings to the investor.

A variety of investment programs are available to academic professionals throughout the nation. Each investment program offers various options to prospective investors. The options permit the investment companies to differentiate themselves from each other and thus be competitive.

Gillespie had many clients among the faculties at Drake and Iowa State. She met each new faculty member shortly after the academician arrived. Gillespie gathered as much information as she could about the person, his or her family, and his or her career goals. Only then did she start to describe IMF's investment opportunities. Part of the service Marie offered was a financial analysis that included the projected retirement payments an investor would receive from IMF plus projected Social Security benefits and any other income the professor believed he or she might receive. This permitted Marie to show how a customized program could be developed for each potential client.

Gillespie was calling on Tom Peters, who had recently joined the Computer Science Department at Iowa State. This was Tom's first full-time academic assignment after completing his doctoral degree at Michigan State University. Gillespie's objective was to get Peters started on one of IMF's investment programs.

In the seven years Marie Gillespie had worked for IMF, she had observed several things about the college market and the professional people whose investments she managed. First, there was a lot of turnover. It was not uncommon for a new Ph.D. to change universities two or three times in the first ten years of his or her career. This was especially true of people in fields where there was a shortage of faculty (for example, engineering, business, and computer science). Second, most university professors were not skilled investors and, in many cases, were not especially interested in investments. Their dedication to their chosen field left them little time to examine financial opportunities.

Perhaps the most important thing Gillespie had learned was that the longer she advised a professor the more investments the professor was likely to make. As the professor was promoted from assistant to associate to full professor, his or her income and general financial well-being improved. Therefore, in addition to investments in a basic retirement plan, professors would invest in tax-sheltered annuities and other financial plans. With a client base of approximately 200 university professors, Marie had to keep careful records to alert her to changes in the career of each of her clients. She knew the best time to counsel with a client was within thirty to sixty days after a promotion had been announced. Marie believed an individual's standard of living would not change too drastically in that period. Increasing an investment or starting a new investment program would be a logical step for a newly promoted person to take.

QUESTIONS

1. If Professor Peters invests with IMF, which type of relationship life cycle will Marie Gillespie attempt to create?

2. What type of relationship seems most likely to be formed if Peters becomes a client of Marie Gillespie? What evidence is there to support your conclusion?

3. What problem(s) does personnel turnover pose in this situation? What should IMF do to minimize the problem?

4. Is there any evidence in this case that leads you to believe Marie Gillespie is a skilled professional?

CASE 3-3   KABCO OFFICE DESIGN

"We're not selling office furniture anymore. We're helping our clients create more productive work environments. Our success depends on all of us in this company realizing this. This is especially true of you sales consultants." With these comments, Kabco CEO Frank Sharp ended his annual presentation to the assembled Kabco sales force at its meeting in Tarpon Springs, Florida.

Kabco Office Design Corporation was formed in 1950. Its growth had been largely attributable to the expansion of the office staffs of many companies. Such staffs comprise the people sometimes referred to as "knowledge workers." Kabco had grown from a start-up company with three sales reps to a corporation with an annual sales volume of $100 million and thirty salespeople. Each salesperson had some expertise in interior design but was primarily paid to sell office furniture. Now that situation was going to have to change.

Several factors were influencing top management's thinking about Kabco's future approach to sales. Clients who purchased office design consultation and office furnishings were becoming much more interested in how their offices could be designed and equipped to improve worker productivity. Most of Kabco's clients were large companies employing 500 or more office workers. These firms were interested in decreasing worker turnover, "burnout" absenteeism, and worker disabilities caused by unsatisfying workplace environments.

Another significant factor was the trend among competitive office design companies to conduct detailed studies of each client's environment before making a sales proposal. These studies usually involved the measurement of noise and light levels in a work environment. Other analyses involved measuring work flow patterns as well as intra- and interdepartmental communication patterns. In short, the office design and furnishings industry approached sales much more scientifically compared to when offices were furnished as inexpensively as possible.

As a result, some of Kabco's competitors were specializing in different kinds of office environments. Some firms had become specialists in designing and equipping workstations for telemarketing clients. The telemarketers' workstations had unique requirements because of people's need to handle as many as 150 calls per day, check on inventory availability and credit status, and answer callers' questions. Other design firms were specializing in work environments housing large numbers of computer programmers, who required a specific environment.

As a result of the studies conducted before a sale was proposed, salespeople required more time to gather and analyze data and develop their proposals. Some very large clients were asking vendors to conduct presale tests in one or two office spaces to see how well the vendor's equipment and office furniture performed. The setting-up and monitoring of these tests required more time from the sales rep responsible for the account.

QUESTIONS

1. What kind of buyer-seller relationships are apparently being formed by Kabco's competitors?

2. What skills will the "new" sales reps at Kabco need to effectively manage relationships with more demanding clients?

3. If you were a consultant to Kabco, what would you recommend to that company's management to better prepare its sales reps to function in the new environment?

4. What basic business strategy are some of Kabco's competitors using? How does skillful relationship management aid the execution of the basic business strategy?

NOTES

1. Philip Kotler, *Marketing Management: Analysis, Planning, and Control*, 7th ed. (Englewood Cliffs, N.J.: Prentice-Hall, 1991), 678–81.

2. Theodore Levitt, "After the Sale Is Over. . . ," *Harvard Business Review* (September–October 1983): 87. See also Harvey B. Mackay, "Humanize Your Selling Strategy," *Harvard Business Review* (March–April 1988): 44.

3. William F. Schoell and Joseph P. Guiltinan, *Marketing: Contemporary Concepts and Practices*, 4th ed. (Boston, Mass.: Allyn and Bacon, 1990), 305.

4. Theodore Levitt, "Relationship Management," *The Marketing Imagination* (New York: The Free Press), 111.

5. Barbara Bund Jackson, "Build Customer Relationships That Last," *Harvard Business Review* (November–December 1985): 120–28.

6. Benson P. Shapiro and John Wyman, "New Ways to Reach Your Customers," *Harvard Business Review* (July–August 1981): 103–10.

7. William A. Cohen, *Marketing Management: Analysis, Planning, and Implementation* (New York: Macmillan, 1988), 351–52.

8. Harvey B. Mackay, "Humanize Your Selling Strategy," *Harvard Business Review* (March–April 1988): 46.

9. Thomas R. Wotruba and Edwin K. Simpson, *Sales Management: Text and Cases* (Boston, Mass.: PWS-Kent Publishing Co., 1989), 304. See also Donald J. Moine, "To Trust, Perchance to Buy," in *Sales and Sales Management Today: A Readings Book,* ed. Barry L. Reece and Gerald L. Manning (Boston, Mass.: Allyn and Bacon, 1991), 133–35.

10. John I. Coppett and William A. Staples, "Product Profile Analysis: A Tool for Industrial Selling," *Industrial Marketing Management* 9 (1980): 151–57.

11. "Laptop Computers Aid Sales Productivity," *Marketing News* 21, no. 5 (February 27, 1987): 6.

12. Shirley Cayer, "Building a World-Class Supplier Base Is the Number-One Priority," *Purchasing* (April 14, 1988): 52–55.

13. Jackson, "Build Customer Relationships That Last," 120–28.

14. Levitt, "After the Sale Is Over. . . ," 87–98.

15. Michael E. Porter, *Competitive Strategy: Techniques for Analyzing Industries and Competitors* (New York: The Free Press, 1980).

16. Theodore Levitt, "Marketing Success Through Differentiation of Anything," *Harvard Business Review* (January–February 1980): 83–91.

17. Ibid.

18. Levitt, "After the Sale Is Over. . . ," 89.

19. Gary W. Dickson, "An Analysis of Vendor Selection Systems and Decisions," *Journal of Purchasing* (February 1986): 5–17.

20. Kotler, *Marketing Management*, 473.

21. John A. Goodman and Arlene R. Malech, "How an 800 Number Can Expand Your Marketing Power and Turn Service into Profits," *Telemarketing* (December 1984): 30–33.

22. Richard Cardozo and Shannon Shipp, "New Selling Methods Are Changing Industrial Sales Management," *Business Horizons* (September–October 1987): 24.

23. *LAP Report #8013.8* (New York: Laboratory of Advertising Performances, McGraw-Hill Research, 1986).

24. Porter, *Competitive Strategy*.

25. Jackson, "Build Customer Relationships That Last," 120–28.

26. Ibid.

27. Steven R. Isaac, "Worksheet for Determining the 'Life-Worth' of a Customer," *Telemarketing Insider's Report* (October 1985): 13–16.

28. John I. Coppett and Cornelius H. Sullivan, "Marketing in the Information Age," *Business* 36, no. 3 (April–June 1986): 13–18.

29. Robert I. Benjamin et al., "Information Technology: A Strategic Opportunity," *Sloan Management Review* 25, no. 3 (Spring 1984): 3–10.

30. Buck Rodgers and Robert L. Shook, *The IBM Way: Insights into the World's Most Successful Marketing Organization* (New York: Harper and Row, 1986).

PART TWO

Why Consumers Buy

CHAPTER 4

Consumer Buying Behavior

LEARNING OBJECTIVES

After studying this chapter, you should be able to:

1. Identify the steps in the consumer's decision-making process.
2. Describe the major psychological influences on a consumer's behavior.
3. Describe the major social influences on a consumer's behavior.
4. Explain the different types of consumer decision processes.
5. Explain the relationship between the types of consumer goods and consumer decision processes.
6. Define the key terms used in this chapter.

KEY TERMS

- problem or need recognition
- information search
- alternative evaluation
- evoked set
- purchase decision
- postpurchase evaluation
- cognitive dissonance
- motivation
- motive
- perception
- learning
- hierarchy of effects
- attitudes
- opinions
- personality
- life style
- perceived risk
- culture
- subculture
- social class
- reference group
- opinion leader
- family life cycle
- consumer goods

STEPHANIE MASKAS was trying to decide what to do about buying a car. She would soon return to college for her second year and needed transportation to get between her college dorm and her part-time job as a waitress at a restaurant. Her father had gone with her to Murphy Motors, a car dealership where Mr. Maskas had bought his two automobiles. Stephanie was also interested in another dealership which sold some other brands. One of Stephanie's friends had recently bought a car from this other dealership. Before visiting Murphy Motors, Stephanie and her father had discussed such issues as car models, colors, options, warranties, and price. While Stephanie would be making the down payment for a car from her savings, her father would assist her with the monthly car payments, and he alone would pay for the insurance. As they entered the dealership, they were met by Jay Dugas, the sales representative from Murphy Motors who had sold cars to Mr. Maskas previously.

The adoption by many firms of the marketing concept as a business operating philosophy has placed the customer or buyer in the spotlight. The primary focus is on understanding the customer's wants, needs, or problems rather than on the product or the salesperson. More precisely, the challenge is to determine what customers want and how their needs might be fulfilled. According to the marketing concept, the attention devoted to the customer should result in profits *and* customer satisfaction.

Customer satisfaction will ideally lead to repeat purchases by the customer and positive word-of-mouth communication by the satisfied customer to others. If the customer engages in repeat buying, the possibility exists that the salesperson-customer relationship will develop even further beyond the one-time or transaction exchange. It must be remembered, however, that for an exchange to lead to a long-term relationship, the buyer and seller must view the process as mutually beneficial.

The field of buyer behavior has grown dramatically in the past twenty years. Today, almost every undergraduate program in marketing has one or more courses devoted to buyer behavior. In Chapters 4 and 5, we will discuss the field of buyer behavior from both the consumer and industrial or organizational perspectives. Whether the salesperson is selling consumer or industrial products, or both, he or she must know as much as possible about the customer. A thorough understanding of the process of, and influences on, buyer behavior should enable the salesperson to better adapt and respond to each customer he or she encounters.

A MODEL OF CONSUMER BUYER BEHAVIOR

The field of buyer behavior is extremely complex, due to the number of issues, concepts, and terms associated with it. To simplify the discussion, Exhibit 4-1 presents a generalized model of consumer buyer behavior that will guide our discussion of the topic.

Although a variety of books deal with consumer buyer behavior, almost all of the texts have some major aspects of buyer behavior in common. The three common elements include the decision-making process, psychological influences, and social influences. As shown in Exhibit 4-1, each of these three elements includes a number of concepts that affect the buyer's behavior. The salesperson should be aware of all these factors as well as the decision-making process the consumer engages in when contemplating whether or not to purchase a product or service.

In many respects, the salesperson's task is to discover the what, when, where, who, how, and why of consumer behavior. All these questions are important, but the real challenge is to uncover why people select one brand or type of product or service over another. A starting point for the salesperson is to fully understand the decision process a consumer goes through every time he or she initiates buying behavior (see Exhibit 4-1). Once the decision process is understood, the relevant psychological and social influences can be assessed as to their effect on the buyer's decision.

THE DECISION-MAKING PROCESS

The starting point for understanding a customer's behavior is the decision-making process a person engages in when involved in a buying or purchasing activity. Whether the customer realizes it or not, he or she normally goes through a series of steps that cover activities before, during, and after the purchase. The salesperson must be able to assume the role of the customer to better understand what that person is going through. This ability is referred to as empathizing with the customer.

Problem or Need Recognition

As shown in Exhibit 4-1, the first step in the customer's decision-making process is **problem or need recognition**. In essence, individuals will engage in buying behavior when they recognize a problem or need. More precisely, a problem or

Exhibit 4-1 A Model of Consumer Buying Behavior

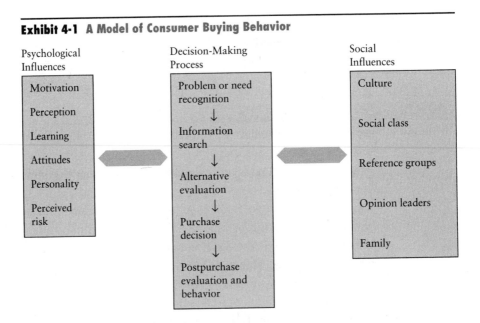

need must not only be recognized, but must be of sufficient importance and urgency to warrant action. For example, the number of individuals and families that would like a new automobile or house normally far exceeds the number that are in the active process of buying.

The discovery of the problem or need underlying a potential purchase is a critical activity for the professional salesperson. It has often been said that people do not buy products or services, but that they buy solutions to their problems or needs. Consumers can often verbalize the problem or need they are experiencing and how the problem could have a negative impact on them. A person who has an automobile that is difficult to start may readily be able to describe not only the problem (a hard-to-start car), but also the solution (a new battery).

In other situations, the problem may be apparent to consumers, but not the solution. If salespeople have a thorough understanding of how the products or services they have available match up with different types of problems, they have an opportunity to guide their customers to select one of their products. In the rapidly growing field of financial planning services, there is a segment of the market whose members realize they need to get more out of their savings, but aren't really sure how to do it and what alternatives are available. A salesperson who can offer information on product alternatives such as stocks, bonds, individual retirement accounts, and certificates of deposit, among other items, may be able to have a significant effect on what action the customer takes to satisfy a need or solve a problem.

At the other end of the continuum from the situation in which the customer knows the problem and the solution (or at least thinks he or she does) is the situation in which the customer does not realize either the problem or the solution. This may well be the most difficult challenge faced by the salesperson, because the potential customer has not engaged in the first step of the decision-making process. For example, salespeople selling life insurance may find this situation with many customers. The head of a family with one or two children may believe, due to his or her young age or income level, that life insurance is not a need. The failure to realize the dilemma that his or her spouse and children would face if he or she were to die may not be something that the person recognizes or even wants to recognize at this time.

Whether the problem-solution relationship is apparent, partially recognized, or not acknowledged, the professional salesperson must be constantly aware of what underlies a customer's behavior. Too much focus on one's products or services and a lack of understanding of the underlying problem or need will likely cause the salesperson to miss or underestimate the why behind the customer's actions.

Information Search

The salesperson who understands the problem or need faced by the customer will also want to know what information sources the customer uses to assess what products or services might solve the problem or satisfy the need. **Information search** is the collection and use of information provided by personal and non-personal sources in the decision-making process. The consumer may rely on past experience, advice from friends and relatives, publications such as *Consumer Reports*, or information offered by salespersons. For example, Stephanie Maskas had discussed her car purchase with her father prior to visiting Murphy Motors.

A challenge for the salesperson is to uncover how much information the consumer already has since customers may have none, a little, or a great deal of information before they encounter a salesperson. In fact, some purchases of consumer goods are probably made with little or no input from a salesperson. Personal care products such as toothpaste and deodorants are purchased based primarily on information gained from previous experience and from magazine, newspaper, radio, and television advertising.

Salespersons should expect customers to see them as a primary source of information about the product or service in question. The extent to which the salesperson is able to play this role increases the likelihood of a sale. Since every customer is unique, the professional salesperson must be able to respond to different customers with varying levels of product or service information. For example, a salesperson who sells houses will need to assess whether or not the consumer is a first-time buyer whose knowledge of housing is limited or an experienced home purchaser who may be trading up after owning several previous houses. Although both customers need housing, their frames of reference in terms of information about housing may be vastly different. Exhibit 4-2 shows some information sources purchasers use for various home-buying decisions.

Alternative Evaluation

In the third step of the decision-making process, **alternative evaluation**, the consumer compares various products or services as to whether they would satisfy the problem or need. As a result of the information search, the prospective purchaser will most likely have located some alternatives for further consideration. In most cases, a problem or need may be satisfied by numerous products. In the earlier example, Stephanie Maskas was trying to decide which model of car to buy and from which dealership. The consumer's task is to decide which, if any, of the available alternatives is the best. In some respects, alternative evaluation represents alternative elimination until the best solution to the problem or need remains.

The salesperson obviously hopes her or his product will be one of the items the customer believes could satisfy the problem or need. The range of product brands or service groups assembled by consumers, which can be considered their real alternatives for consideration, is called the **evoked set**.[1] Failure to have one's product included in the customer's evoked set usually means the purchase probability is zero or negligible unless the salesperson can change the customer's mind regarding the product's applicability.

If the salesperson's product is in the customer's evoked set, the salesperson must still attempt to understand what criteria the customer will use to decide which product to purchase. Studies of buyer behavior indicate consumers have

Exhibit 4-2 Information Sources in the Purchase of a House

Types of Information Needed	Possible Sources of Information
Location Alternatives	Friends, Relatives, Business Associates
Price Ranges	Builders
Reputations of Builders and Housing Styles	Real Estate Agents
Mortgage Loan Sources	Bank or Savings and Loan Personnel and Newspapers, Brochures, and Magazines
Property Insurance Sources	Insurance Agents
Real Estate Firms and Agents	Observation and Experience

from one to nine criteria by which they judge product or service alternatives.[2] In the purchase of a washer-dryer combination, a potential buyer may compare each product alternative on the basis of price, brand reputation, color availability, washing and drying options (normal, permanent press, delicate), energy efficiency, and product warranty.

Knowledge of the customer's criteria is valuable for the salesperson, but he or she should also determine if the customer places equal or differing weight on various criteria. Frequently, not all of the customer's criteria are of equal importance. In the washer-dryer example, the prospective buyer may place the most importance on price, followed by washing and drying options and product warranty, with much less emphasis on brand reputation, color availability, and energy efficiency.

The salesperson must always remember that although customers are similar, they are also different. Thus, some customers may have the same purchasing criteria for a product category, but the weights or level of importance attached to each criterion may vary. And some customers may have entirely different criteria.

Purchase Decision

The consumer's decision-making process may or may not result in a purchase decision depending on whether or not the customer's information search and alternative evaluation have been successful. The **purchase decision** is the determination by the individual(s) that the exchange process with the seller will be completed. As noted in Chapter 2, the actual purchase of a product or service may be the result of the behavior or input of various individuals who may be labeled gatekeepers, influencers, deciders, buyers, and users according to the different roles they occupy in the buying process.

The challenge for the salesperson is to understand the roles different individuals may play in the decision-making or buying processes. When selling to just one individual, this is not a problem. When selling to a husband and wife or a family, however, the roles in the buying process take on major significance. In purchasing a major consumer product, such as a house, each member of the household or family may have a varying impact on the house selected. The actual influence of the wife, the husband, and the children, individually and collectively, varies from one family to another. The characteristics of alternative houses—such as wood or brick exterior, size of yard, proximity to schools, family room, type of kitchen, and number of bedrooms—may be perceived and evaluated differently by each member of the family.

Perceptive salespeople are constantly alert to uncover the different likes and dislikes of each customer who is a party to the purchase decision. Identification of the gatekeepers, influencers, deciders, buyers, and users could mean the difference between making or losing a sale. The purchase decision is thus a series of decisions made by various participants in the buying process.

Postpurchase Evaluation and Behavior

If the customer makes the decision to purchase, he or she will then undergo some type of **postpurchase evaluation**. Regardless of the amount of money spent, every purchase involves a certain degree of assessment of whether or not a good purchase was made. It should be recognized, however, that the more money a consumer spends, the more likely the postpurchase evaluation stage of the decision-making process will be extensive. Thus, in the purchase of major consumer durables such as houses and automobiles, the postpurchase evaluation will be more extensive than in smaller purchases.

This stage of the consumer's decision-making process is critical for the salesperson for a number of reasons. First, a positive postpurchase evaluation tends to lead to additional purchases of the same product or service by the consumer. Also, very satisfied or very dissatisfied customers are more prone to tell other people about their experience. This word-of-mouth advertising can have a positive or negative effect on other consumers who might be potential customers of the salesperson.

If the customer has purchased a product, but not the one offered by the salesperson, the postpurchase evaluation stage is still critical, since the customer may decide that he or she made the wrong decision or question whether or not the right decision or selection was made. This assessment of the negative aspects of the product bought and the positive features of the items considered but not purchased, is called **cognitive dissonance**. The greater the level of cognitive dissonance, the more likely the consumer will select a different brand or type of product in the future. Thus, postpurchase evaluation may have a positive or negative effect on the consumer's future buying behavior. Exhibit 4-3 presents a comprehensive view of the purchase decision process for an automobile from problem or need recognition to postpurchase evaluation and behavior.

PSYCHOLOGICAL INFLUENCES ON CONSUMER BUYING BEHAVIOR

The consumer's decision-making process is only the starting point for the salesperson's attempt to understand why the customer behaves in a certain way. As shown in Exhibit 4-1, a customer's behavior is also affected by psychological influences, including motivation, perception, learning, attitudes, personality, and perceived risk. A knowledge of these should enable the salesperson to better adapt to each individual customer.

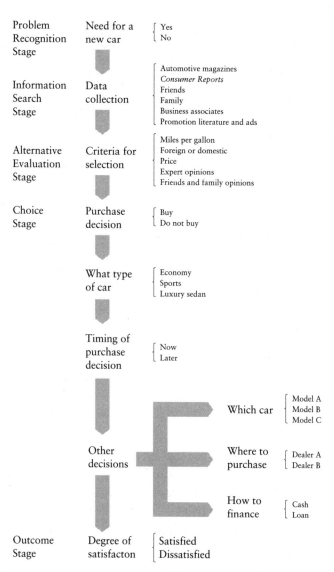

**Exhibit 4-3 Automo-
bile Purchase Decision
Process**

Source: William H. Cunningham, Isabella C. M. Cunningham, and Christopher Swift,
*Marketing: A Managerial Ap-
proach* (Cincinnati, Ohio:
South-Western Publishing,
1987), p. 153.

Motivation

The major force underlying a consumer's behavior is **motivation**. The problem or
need, which a customer in the decision-making process recognizes, is based on
one or more motives he or she has acknowledged. A **motive** can be viewed as a
force that leads a person to act in a certain way in response to a need.[3] According
to Maslow's hierarchy of needs, an individual has a number of needs that vary in
strength.[4] As shown in Exhibit 4-4, the first level revolves around basic physiological needs such as food and shelter. Once this level of needs is satisfied, a person

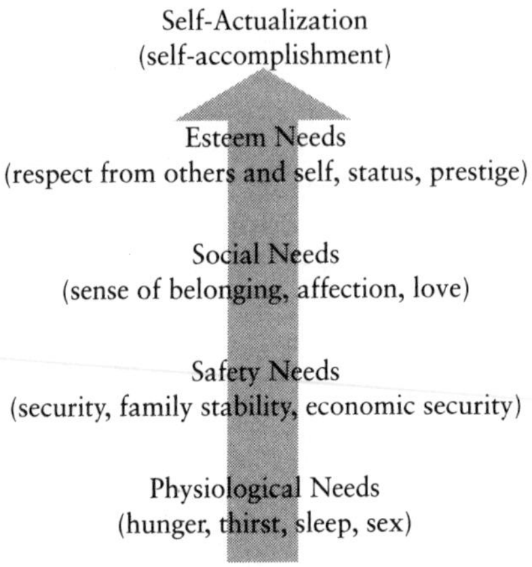

Self-Actualization
(self-accomplishment)

Esteem Needs
(respect from others and self, status, prestige)

Social Needs
(sense of belonging, affection, love)

Safety Needs
(security, family stability, economic security)

Physiological Needs
(hunger, thirst, sleep, sex)

Exhibit 4-4 Maslow's Hierarchy of Needs

Source: William H. Cunningham, Isabella C. M. Cunningham, and Christopher Swift, *Marketing: A Managerial Approach* (Cincinnati, Ohio: South-Western Publishing, 1987), p. 174.

will move to higher-level needs. In order of occurrence, these needs include safety and security, belongingness, self-esteem, and self-actualization.

It is important for the salesperson to recognize what needs are motivating a consumer's purchase decision. A person selling insurance may be offering a service directed at the safety and security need while a product such as an automobile, house, or clothing may affect social, self-esteem, and self-actualization needs. Most consumers focus their attention on satisfying needs beyond the physiological and security needs.

Perception

A problem for the salesperson is that each consumer's response to his or her motives and needs will be also influenced by his or her perception of potential solutions for the problem or need. **Perception** is the way in which individuals collect, process, and interpret information from their environment.[5] A salesperson should realize that consumers will vary in the extent they experience products, services, salespersons, and other things going on around them. Within the area of perception, a consumer will experience selective exposure, attention, comprehension or understanding, and retention of advertisements, sales presentations, and other marketing or promotional communications.

Thus, the professional salesperson must face a number of challenges to get the sales message across to the consumer. Not only must consumers be exposed to the message, they must be willing to pay attention, understand, and retain the ideas, concepts, or benefits presented by the salesperson. The more complex the product or service offered, the more likely that less than optimal perception will occur. For example, a retail salesperson selling a video camera or personal computer must be careful to ensure that the customer does not get lost during the presentation. Even if the customer is paying attention, the salesperson cannot be certain that understanding or comprehension, let alone retention, is occurring. The key word for the salesperson to remember is that the influence of perception on a customer's behavior is a very *selective* process.

Learning

Customers' decision making and behavior will also be greatly influenced by learning that has taken place over a long period of time before a given purchase. **Learning** refers to a change in behavior that is a result of past experience.[6] Previous learning through experience affects consumers' behavior with respect to the extent of information search and alternative evaluation in which they will engage. This learning or experience base is something the salesperson should attempt to discover, since, due to prior experience, the customer may have a great deal of knowledge about the product or service in question. For example, an individual who uses a personal computer at the office and is considering a computer for the home may have already developed a level of knowledge, based on experience, that is far beyond that of a first-time computer buyer. In essence, the salesperson must determine what level of knowledge the prospective customer already has about the product or service. Failure to do so may cause the salesperson to overestimate or patronize the customer—either of which may result in a lost opportunity.

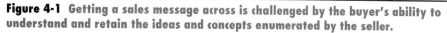

Figure 4-1 Getting a sales message across is challenged by the buyer's ability to understand and retain the ideas and concepts enumerated by the seller.

In all forms of promotion, including personal selling and advertising, the **hierarchy of effects** hypothesis suggests that a consumer moves through a series of stages leading up to the purchase act. These steps include going from unawareness to awareness and then knowledge about a company, product, or service. Although a new product or service may be at the unawareness stage for many consumers, the salesperson should not assume that because his or her product has been on the market for a considerable period of time the consumer's knowledge of it is high.

Attitudes

The effects of perception and learning result in a consumer forming attitudes and opinions. **Attitudes** or **opinions** are a person's positive, neutral, or negative feelings about products, services, companies, or salespersons.[7] Salespeople must be careful to discover whether the prospective customer has a positive or negative attitude toward their company and products.

As noted in the decision-making process, the customer may consider only a few products or services in the alternative evaluation stage. The consumer may or may not include a salesperson's offering based on already formed attitudes and opinions. Whether the consumer holds a positive or negative attitude about the product, it is critical that the sales representative understand what underlies this assessment or feeling. The challenge to maintain positive attitudes, overcome negative attitudes, and positively influence neutral attitudes is an ongoing task for the professional salesperson.

Although the task of overcoming a customer's negative attitude may seem insurmountable, an understanding of consumer behavior may enable the salesperson to uncover the basis for the negative attitude. Due to selective perception or incomplete knowledge about a product or service, the customer may have formed an incorrect perception that led to an inaccurate attitude, which should not be the case. A salesperson who takes over a territory or account that was mishandled by his or her predecessor should be aware that some degree of attitude change will be required before the desired buyer behavior change will occur.

Personality

Some consumers will be affected by similar motives or needs, learning, and attitudes, and other consumers will not. This difference among consumers can be attributed in part to what is known as personality. **Personality** has been defined as the sum total of an individual's traits that make that individual unique.[8] To some degree, every consumer is unique, but the salesperson should also remember

Figure 4-2 A consumer's value system and personality contribute to the decision to buy. For example, some consumers are more image conscious than other consumers, a factor often reflected in their choice of clothing.

there are groups of consumers who have similar personalities. For example, certain consumers are more compulsive, gregarious, independent, or ambitious than other consumers.

Although the role of personality in consumer behavior has been studied for some time, a new development has been the focus on what is known as life style. **Life style** refers to how people live and how they spend time and money.[9] A consumer's personal value system and personality determine the manner in which he or she lives or acts. The outward expression of personality and life style is a person's activities, interests, and opinions. For example, an individual may believe strongly in "saving for a rainy day" while another individual may adopt a "live for today" attitude and life style. The resulting behavior for the first individual may be very different from the behavior of the second. In the financial services field, some banks and savings and loans have distinguished different customer segments based on their behavior toward saving money. Two important and attractive market segments are referred to as "involved investors" and "solid savers"; a third and less attractive segment is called "self-indulgent spenders." These differences would be of major importance to the professional salesperson in adapting to different customer types.

Perceived Risk

A major influence on a consumer's decision-making process is also the amount, if any, of perceived risk associated with the purchase of a particular product or service. **Perceived risk** is the belief that negative outcomes may result from engaging in specific types of behavior. Normally the greater the level of perceived or actual risk experienced by the consumer, the greater the propensity to engage in information search to reduce the level of risk. From a sales perspective, the consumer sees various drawbacks to making a given purchase.

The salesperson should be aware that the customer's perceived risk may include functional, physical, financial, social, and psychological risks. Functional risk is the possibility that a product will not perform in the manner that it should; physical risk is the possibility that use of the product may cause injury to the individual. For example, recent problems with three-wheel, all-terrain recreation vehicles eventually led to a ban on the product. Even before the product ban, many consumers had major concerns about the safety of this product.

Another type of perceived risk, financial, can be seen in the purchase of a house, which is normally the major purchase for a family or individual. The financial risk is not only the major cost involved, but also the length of the time commitment associated with this purchase. Again, the greater the financial and time commitment to a product or service, the greater the likelihood of extensive information search and alternative evaluation by the consumer.

Last, the purchase of a product may also involve a level of social or psychological risk. Social risk refers to the risk that a product or service may cause embarrassment before others, such as friends or associates. In contrast, psychological risk is the risk associated with an individual's ego such that the person would feel less about himself or herself.[10] Items such as clothing often are purchased with an assessment of not only how the consumer feels about the item, but also how the consumer believes friends and associates will judge the items. Whether the perceived risk is real or imaginary, the salesperson should be prepared to deal with it. Failure to do so will inhibit, if not block, the purchase process.

SOCIAL INFLUENCES ON CONSUMER BUYING BEHAVIOR

Although the psychological influences on consumer behavior are extremely important for the salesperson to understand, he or she must also be aware of the social influences that affect the consumer. Psychological influences might be categorized as individual influences, while the social influences are more focused on how groups affect a person's behavior. Social influences may be exerted by large groups, such as a culture, as well as small and intimate groups, such as the family. In the following sections, the social influences of culture, social class, reference groups, opinion leaders, and the family will be discussed.

Culture

Because they live in the United States, consumers are part of the U.S. culture. **Culture** is defined as that set of values, ideas, attitudes, and other symbols and objects created by people that shape human behavior.[11] Culture has two main characteristics—it exists to satisfy needs and it is learned. In the United States, cultural values, ideas, and attitudes include beliefs about achievement and success, material comfort, individualism, and freedom of choice, among others. Such values also serve as a basis for buying decisions that save time and money, provide convenience, express who we are or want to be, or enable us to have a range of choices to satisfy our needs. The marketing of lawn care, financial planning, tax preparation, and physical fitness services is a partial response to cultural values that focus on the importance of time, convenience, and personal appearance.

Culture should serve only as the starting point for the professional salesperson in gaining a better understanding of why consumers behave as they do. A breakdown of the U.S. culture into subcultures based on ethnic, religious, regional, racial, economic, and social differences may help pinpoint various behaviors and opportunities. A **subculture** is a distinct social group existing as an identifiable segment within a larger culture. The knowledge of buyer behavior differences among whites, blacks, and Hispanics, or southerners and westerners, helps the salesperson adapt to individual and group attitude and behavior differences. Important opportunities may be uncovered by studying specific population changes and subgroups. For example, as shown in Exhibit 4-5, major changes will occur from 1990 to 2000 in the growth of certain age groups, including those 45 to 54 years old (baby boomers) and those 75 years old and over.[12] Likewise, since 1980, the Hispanic population has grown four times faster than the U.S. total. Over the next 25 years, the Hispanic population in the United States is expected to almost double, reaching 40 million people.[13] In addition, cultural differences are important for those sales personnel selling to international customers, and this topic will be covered in Chapter 17.

Social Class

Several social classes may exist within a culture or a subculture. **Social class** is defined as a somewhat permanent and homogeneous group of people with similar behavioral patterns, interests, and life styles.[14] The major determinant of social

Exhibit 4-5 Population Projections: 1990–2000

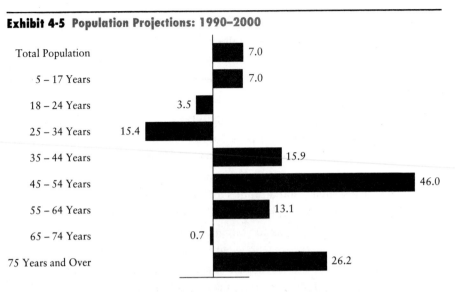

Total Population	7.0
5 – 17 Years	7.0
18 – 24 Years	3.5
25 – 34 Years	15.4
35 – 44 Years	15.9
45 – 54 Years	46.0
55 – 64 Years	13.1
65 – 74 Years	0.7
75 Years and Over	26.2

Source: *Statistical Abstract of the United States*, Bureau of the Census, 1988, Table 16.

class is the consumer's occupation, but there are other important determinants including level of personal achievement or success in one's occupation, social interaction patterns, possession of material goods, and value orientation. Individuals in the same social class exhibit similar behavior and engage in similar activities or life styles.

Social class is a critical variable for a salesperson to understand since studies have shown that social class may have a significant impact on a consumer's behavior. For example, members of higher versus lower social classes vary in magazine and newspaper readership, leisure activities pursued, and saving and spending habits.[15] With respect to saving, higher social classes are more likely to invest in common stock and life insurance policies, while lower social classes place their money in savings accounts and land. With respect to credit card usage, higher social classes view the credit card as a convenient alternative to checks and cash while lower social classes see their cards as providing instant installment credit. Although the concept of social class covers large groups of people, there are major buying behavior differences among the upper, middle, and lower classes.

Reference Groups

A much smaller group than social class, but no less influential, is the reference group. A **reference group** refers to any group of people that has an influence on a person's attitudes, behavior, or decisions.[16] A person may belong to several groups, such as various professional associations or organizations, yet he or she may or may not be affected by being a member of a particular group.

The major relationship between reference groups and consumer behavior is how a reference group can influence product choice and brand choice.[17] A salesperson who sells items such as clothing and furniture should understand that reference groups may affect the brand purchased, but not whether or not the product is purchased. In contrast, the purchase of an air conditioner is one of high reference group influence on the product, but little, if any, influence on the brand purchased. A common thread that runs throughout studies relating reference groups to buyer behavior is that products or services that are highly conspicuous from a social viewpoint tend to be affected significantly by reference groups. The challenge for the salesperson is to discover what reference groups the consumer is using as a frame of reference in deciding whether or not to purchase a particular product or a specific brand.

Opinion Leaders

A concept related to the effect of reference groups on consumer behavior is opinion leadership. An **opinion leader** is the individual who influences the purchasing behavior of another individual. In this situation, the consumer or person being influenced is referred to as the "follower."[18] Research shows that opinion leaders often display various product-related characteristics such as being:

1. more knowledgeable about the product category;

2. more interested in the product category;

3. more active in receiving communications about the product from personal sources; and

4. more likely to read magazines and other print media relevant to their area of product interest.[19]

Word-of-mouth communication, such as that between the opinion leader and opinion follower, may not be the major influence in every product category, but it may be important when reference group influence is a strong source of information and influence. Research suggests this will occur when:

1. the product is visible and therefore behavior is apparent;

2. the product is distinctive and can more easily be identified with style, taste, and other personal norms;

3. the product has just been introduced;

4. the product is important to the norms and belief systems of the reference group;

5. the purchase of the product is likely to be seen as risky, encouraging a search for additional information; or

6. the consumer is involved in the purchase decision.[20]

The opinion leader is thus seen to be an individual who is highly involved with a product category. Due to active information seeking about the product or being one of the first to purchase the product, the opinion leader becomes a source of information or a product expert for other consumers seeking advice about the purchase of the product. A salesperson will want to identify opinion leaders due to their influence on other consumers. Opinion leaders are also a major target for the salesperson since they are most likely to be early adopters of new products and services. Consumers frequently ask others who have already purchased a product or service for their assessment of it. A positive or negative response by an opinion leader may be enough for the consumer to purchase or reject the product as a viable alternative to satisfy his or her need or problem. The salesperson may be able to identify opinion leaders by analyzing product purchase records or orders to see who were the early purchasers. In addition, individuals who have asked for more product information, by responding to such things as an inquiry card in a magazine, are likely to have high product interest and involvement.

Family

Although the concepts of culture, social class, reference group, and opinion leader refer mostly to influences on the consumer's decision-making process, the family unit may not only be an influence factor, but also a decision-making group. As noted in Chapter 2 in the discussion of the buying center, individuals may occupy various roles in group decision making, whether in consumer or industrial buying behavior. In the family unit, different family members may occupy one or more of the influencer, gatekeeper, decision maker, buyer, and user roles. The purchase of major consumer durable products, such as houses and automobiles, which represent significant family investments, may mean that different members of the family unit will play active roles in problem or need recognition, information search, alternative evaluation, and the purchase decision. One challenge for the salesperson, with respect to family decision making, is to uncover which family members are playing which roles in the buying process. Studies of family decision making have indicated that husbands dominate decisions regarding automobiles, and wives dominate decisions for food, toiletries, and small appliances.[21] Joint decision making by the husband and wife is likely for decisions on housing, vacations, and furniture.[22]

The following buying situations are ones in which joint decision making is more likely:

1. when the level of perceived risk is high;

2. when the purchase decision is important to the family;

3. when there are few time pressures;

4. when middle income groups are involved;

5. when families are younger (during the first years of marriage);

6. when only one of the parents is working outside the home; or

7. when there are no children in the family.[23]

Major social changes in the past twenty years, such as more women working outside the home and married couples having fewer children, are likely to have increased the occurrence of joint decision making. For example, the high number of married mothers who are now in the labor force has contributed to more husbands assuming household roles previously associated with wives. Role sharing is more likely in families with young, well-educated, and affluent husbands and wives. A recent study of young working parents found that men spend an average of 12 hours a week on home chores and 15 hours a week on child care.[24] However, a salesperson should also be aware that as women work outside the home, not only does their influence on buying decisions rise, but due to time demands on working couples, each spouse often takes responsibility for certain product categories with only major items such as housing, major appliances, and vacations left to joint decision making. In other words, the wife will be responsible or mostly responsible for some decisions while the husband will carry most of the responsibility for other decisions. A few major decisions will continue to involve joint decision making.

In addition to the importance of the roles of family members in decision making and the occurrence of individual or joint decision making, the salesperson should also take into consideration the effect of the family life cycle. The **family life cycle** includes the stages involved in the formation, growth, change, and dissolution of a typical two-parent family.[25] The stages of the typical family life cycle include young single, young married without children, young married with children, middle-aged married with children, middle-aged married without dependent children, older married, and older unmarried (see Exhibit 4-6).

The salesperson must realize that as a family moves from one stage of the family life cycle to the next, its needs, experience, income, and family composition may change. Failure to recognize these changes and adapt to them will hinder the salesperson's success. For example, a young married couple without children will be in a different situation than one with children. Although both couples may have similar needs and past experiences and may be making their first purchases of major

Exhibit 4-6 Family Life Cycle

Family Life Cycle Flows

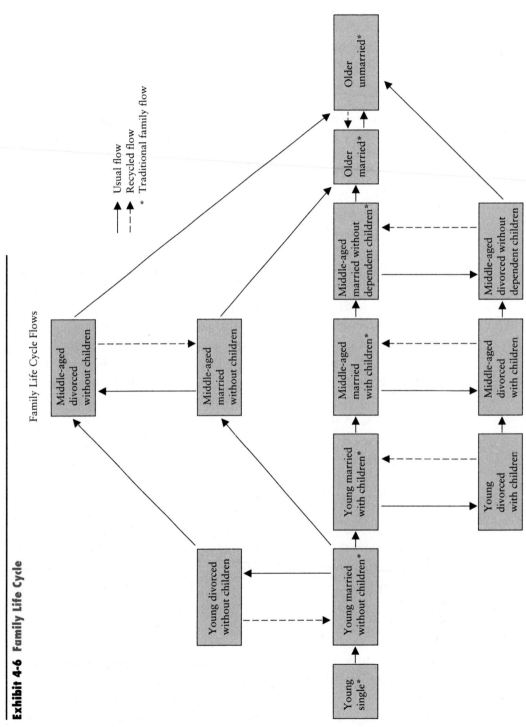

Source: Patrick E. Murphy and William A. Staples, "A Modernized Family Life Cycle," *Journal of Consumer Research* (June, 1979), p. 17. © 1979 by the *Journal of Consumer Research*. All rights reserved.

consumer products, such as appliances and home furnishings, the married couple with children may be in a more limited buying situation due to differences in family composition and discretionary income. In contrast, a middle-aged married couple without dependent children may be in a much better financial position to purchase a variety of products and services, including more discretionary items such as vacations and second automobiles. This group would also have more experience and information dealing with buying situations. Think of how the financial situations of Stephanie Maskas and her father were going to impact the purchase of a car and car insurance.

Recent changes in the social environment have also affected traditional family life cycle stages. In the past twenty years, later marriages, fewer children, and divorce have changed the family life cycle for many families. For example, three fifths of U.S. adults aged 18 and older are married. Yet, one third of all children born in the last ten years will probably live in a step-family before they are 18 years old, and a quarter of all children are now being raised by a single parent.[26] As shown in Exhibit 4-6, families are affected by divorce whether the head of household is young or middle-aged. These changes result in a married person's returning to single status or becoming a single parent. The decision making of a married couple, a single person, and a divorced parent with a child or children may vary significantly, since the needs, income, and family composition have undergone one or more major changes. Besides the higher divorce rate, the tendency to marry at an older age means the importance of the "singles" market is likely to increase. Exhibit 4-7 shows changes in marital status from 1970 to 1986. In addition, those married couples who have fewer or no children differ from more traditional married couples in their needs and income. The decrease in family sizes means that marketers who appeal to large families with products like station wagons, four- or five-bedroom homes, and large size packages of consumer products may need to reassess their sales efforts. Changes in the family life cycle for both traditional and nontraditional families are a social phenomenon each salesperson should be aware of and respond to effectively. Failure to recognize different market segments with different needs, experience levels, and incomes will limit the salesperson's success.

Marital Status	1970	1986
Married	75.3%	65.5%
Single	18.9%	25.3%
Widowed	3.3%	2.6%
Divorced	2.5%	6.6%

Exhibit 4-7 *Marital Status: 1970 Versus 1986*

Source: *Statistical Abstract of the United States*, Bureau of the Census, 1988, Table 46.

Exhibit 4-8 Types of Consumer Decision Processes

Type of Consumer Decision Making	Amount of Search	Amount of Time Required	Level of Perceived Risk	Prior Experience	Purchase Frequency
Extended	High	High	High	Low	Low
Limited	Medium	Medium	Medium	Medium	Medium
Routine	Low	Low	Low	High	High

TYPES OF CONSUMER DECISION PROCESSES

The consumer's decision-making process, as discussed previously, includes a number of steps that an individual or group goes through in deciding whether or not to buy a given product or service. Due to the effect of psychological and social influences, each individual's behavior is unique. Although it is difficult to classify the various consumer decision processes, a three-way classification of decision processes may help the salesperson analyze the situations she or he faces. Exhibit 4-8 shows three types of consumer decision making: extended, limited, and routine.

Extended consumer decision making is characterized by a high degree of search activity and often a high level of perceived risk. The amount of search activity and perceived risk are due, in part, to the relatively low levels of prior experience with the product or service because of infrequent purchase or possibly no previous purchase whatsoever. For many products and services in extended decision making, the time pressure to purchase is also relatively low. A salesperson would expect this particular consumer to spend a great amount of time in information search and alternative evaluation. Major purchases such as houses, automobiles, and some household furnishings would likely be in this category.

At the other extreme is routine consumer decision making. With a high level of prior experience in frequent purchases of the product, the consumer will engage in little or no search since the level of perceived risk is low and the time pressure to satisfy the need is high. In an extreme case, the consumer will skip the information search and alternative evaluation stages and proceed directly from problem or need recognition to the purchase decision. If the consumer is buying the salesperson's product or service, he or she has developed brand loyalty, which should be guarded with care. On the other hand, if the salesperson's brand is not the one presently purchased by the consumer, the salesperson should realize the magnitude of the task confronting him or her in attempting to get the consumer to switch from an existing brand to the salesperson's brand.

Between extended and routine consumer decision making is the limited category showing only a medium amount of search, time pressure, perceived risk, prior experience, and purchase frequency. Even though the consumer has previously purchased the item, he or she is still willing to engage in a moderate amount of information search and alternative evaluation before deciding whether or not to purchase a particular product or service. The time spent before purchase will not be as long as under extended decision making, but not as short as under routine decision making. In limited decision-making situations, the salesperson should realize the consumer is willing to spend some time and effort comparing products, but not a great deal of time. The consumer's known product alternatives are likely to get much more consideration than unknown alternatives for which additional information is needed. However, the opportunity to gain or lose a customer engaged in limited decision making should not be taken lightly. The ability of the salesperson to "size up" the customer's decision process may be crucial in retaining or gaining a customer's purchase.

CONSUMER GOODS AND CONSUMER BEHAVIOR

The consumer's decision process is also related to the type of consumer good that he or she is contemplating purchasing. **Consumer goods** are those products and services destined for personal, family, or household use. Exhibit 4-9 shows the three major types of consumer goods: convenience, shopping, and specialty. Products may be classified into one of the three categories by assessing a product in terms of the consumer's knowledge prior to purchase, effort expended to acquire the product, willingness to accept substitutes, frequency of purchase, information search, and the product's distinguishing characteristics.[27]

A salesperson should expect most consumers to use routine decision making for most convenience products due to low information search, high frequency of

Exhibit 4-9 Types of Consumer Goods

	Convenience	Shopping	Specialty
Consumer Behavior	Little time and effort to get the product. High product knowledge due to frequent purchase.	Considerable time and effort to get the product. Low product knowledge due to infrequent purchase.	Considerable time and effort to get the product. High product knowledge due to brand loyalty.
Distinguishing Characteristics	Wants immediate availability and convenience.	Shops and compares for the best buy.	Has high brand loyalty and will not accept substitutes.

purchase, and high level of knowledge prior to the purchase. In contrast, extended decision making, or at least limited decision making, would be expected for most shopping goods. The desire to shop and compare various products or brands may be very important to the consumer to ensure that the best choice is made. Specialty products have some characteristics of both convenience and shopping goods. The key distinguishing feature is that the consumer has developed a degree of brand loyalty to the extent that he or she will not accept substitutes, but will expend time and effort to get a particular brand.

Although Exhibit 4-9 looks very precise in separating one product type from another, the salesperson must realize that for one consumer a product may be a convenience good, while for another the product may be a shopping good; for yet another, it may be a specialty product. A shirt purchased by a business executive may be a convenience product with little attention paid to brand or store, a specialty good where only one brand, such as Arrow, is acceptable, or a shopping good where brands are compared and contrasted due to infrequent purchasing.

The definition of consumer products includes services as well as goods. Due to their increasing importance in the U.S. economy, services deserve special mention with respect to consumer behavior. The major difference between goods and services is the tangibility of the former and the intangibility of the latter. The ability of the consumer to see and touch some goods while only hearing about a service makes the task for the salesperson selling services that much more difficult. In addition, services are inseparable from the seller, since the seller provides the service. Two other qualities make services unique: (1) their perishability or the inability to inventory services for future sale and (2) the variability in quality of service from one offering to the next.

Selling professional services, such as accounting, legal, financial planning, or consulting, highlights some of the difficulties confronted by a salesperson who sells services. The replacement of a tangible product such as a house or automobile, with an intangible product, such as expert advice, places a greater requirement on the salesperson's selling skills. Since the service and the salesperson are inseparable, the salesperson is called upon to sell himself or herself much more than he or she would in marketing consumer goods. Also, the salesperson is challenged not to lose the sales opportunity, since the service cannot be inventoried for future use; thus, lost time is a lost sale. The salesperson must also strive to be consistent in the service offering from one customer to the next to maintain the level of service quality. Although the challenge is great, successful sales of services can be attained by paying careful attention to the unique characteristics of services and the differences between the selling of goods and services.

SUMMARY

1. The effective salesperson must have a thorough understanding of the consumer's decision-making process and activities before, during, and after the purchase.

2. A knowledge of the various psychological and social factors that influence a consumer's decision making and behavior enable the salesperson to better understand and respond to the consumer.

3. Sales representatives should realize that the extent of the consumer's decision-making process will vary from extended to routine decision making.

4. The salesperson should understand that there is a relationship between the type of consumer product and the type of decision process used by the consumer.

5. Sales personnel should be aware of the differences between the selling of goods and services and the unique characteristics of services.

QUESTIONS FOR DISCUSSION AND REVIEW

1. How does the study of buyer behavior advance the practice of the marketing concept?

2. The most important thing for a salesperson to determine is why a consumer selects one product over another. Why or why not?

3. Why is it often said that people buy solutions to problems or needs rather than buying a product or service?

4. In the purchase of a stereo system, what personal and non-personal sources might be used during the information search?

5. If the purchase of a product or service involves a decision by a family, what should the salesperson pay particular attention to in assessing buyer behavior?

6. Why is the postpurchase evaluation and behavior stage so important to the salesperson?

7. What is meant by the term *selective perception*?

8. Explain the possible risks associated with the purchase of a chain saw, a wedding dress, and a personal computer.

9. Why is the family life cycle such an important concept for the salesperson to understand?

10. Explain the differences among extended, limited, and routine decision making.

11. What would be some of the differences in selling services as compared to products?

12. Which do you think would be easier to sell—a product or a service?

CASE 4-1 PURCHASING A HOME COMPUTER

Judy and Rick Sherman are discussing whether they should purchase a computer for use at home. Rick, a human resources manager, is already a user of computers, since his employer implemented a computer system that links all the company's managers and secretarial staff. He has been using a computer for the past five years at work. Judy, a homemaker, has not used any type of computer, but sees the need for a home computer for use by the three Sherman children, Sarah, Rebecca, and Jay. Since their high school has developed a computer-intensive curriculum, Sarah and Rebecca will be frequent users of a computer, especially for word-processing applications. All the Sherman children are also interested in computer games. On the other hand, Rick Sherman sees a home computer as a link to his company, enabling him to do his work during evenings and on the weekend, if needed, without going to the office.

Based on the recommendation of a friend who recently purchased a computer for home use, Rick and Judy Sherman are about to visit Computer Resources, Inc. Prior to this visit, Rick reviewed an analysis of various computer brands that appeared in *Consumer Reports*. Of all the brands reviewed, no single brand was a clear winner. Rick realizes that the type of computer he uses at the office is not the same type used by his children at their schools. Judy is also concerned about whether they can afford a home computer at this time, given their other obligations.

At Computer Resources, Inc., Rick and Judy Sherman are met by sales representative, Mack Smith, who has been with the company for a number of years. As a successful salesperson, Mack Smith knows that he has to ask appropriate questions as well as be a good listener.

QUESTIONS

1. With respect to the Shermans, what stage of the decision-making process are they in at the present time?

2. How have social influences affected this situation?

3. In terms of perceived risk, what potential problems does the purchase of a home computer present?

4. What questions could Mack Smith ask to uncover some of the information described in the case?

CASE 4-2 MILLER REALTORS

Miller Realtors is one of the top three real estate companies in Center City. For the past three years, the firm has had the most listings of any realtor in the city, was the overall sales leader for one year, and was second and third the other two years. Ms. Darlene Gray has been employed by Miller Realtors for six years. She has consistently been one of the two top listing and sales agents for the company.

A current client of Ms. Gray is the Tompkins family. Jim and Betty Tompkins are moving to Center City from out of state. Jim has been transferred by his company to the new location after a recent promotion. The Tompkinses have two children—Amy, age sixteen, and Alex, age twelve.

Darlene Gray is planning for her initial meeting with Jim and Betty Tompkins, who are visiting Center City on a house-hunting mission. They are attempting to sell their existing house; but, if they are unsuccessful by the time they are to move to Center City, Mr. Tompkins's company will buy their house.

Ms. Gray did know, based on a telephone conversation with Mr. Tompkins, that the family is interested in a house that is close to his work and the schools the children will attend. She also knows that although Mr. Tompkins has visited Center City twice for business purposes, Mrs. Tompkins and the children have never been to Center City.

Because she has sold numerous houses to many families, Ms. Gray realizes that each family has unique personal interests and tastes in housing. She always strives to do her best to meet the needs of each and every client. She tries to empathize with buyers by placing herself in their position. She is particularly excited about the opportunity to help the Tompkinses since, in his new position, Mr. Tompkins will be the manager of human resources, which will handle the relocation of all company employees. The expansion plans of the company are critical to Ms. Gray.

In preparing for the meeting, Ms. Gray is assessing which questions she will ask to better aid the Tompkinses in their house hunting. She realizes she will need to do a great deal of listening, and she wants to obtain a sufficient amount of information to expedite their purchase of a home.

QUESTIONS

1. What will Ms. Gray need to consider in terms of the roles of the various family members in the buying process?

2. Although the Tompkinses have indicated that they want a house close to work and school, what additional buying criteria information should Ms. Gray uncover?

3. How will the Tompkins's consumer decision process affect their relationship with Ms. Gray?

CASE 4-3 NASH AND ASSOCIATES, INC.

Jim and Sylvia Nash are finally fulfilling a desire to operate a business of their own. They selected the finanical planning services field due to their business backgrounds. Jim, the older of the two siblings, majored in finance in college, while Sylvia concentrated on marketing. They thought financial services would be an appropriate area to take advantage of their college degrees. Through seminars, workshops, and self-study programs, Jim and Sylvia attained the status of certified financial planners.

Prior to entering financial planning, Jim worked for a local savings and loan association where he concentrated primarily on residential and commercial real estate loans. Sylvia previously held a position as sales representative for a manufacturer of air conditioning and heating equipment. In this position, she called on architects and building contractors who designed and built commercial buildings, including office buildings and shopping centers.

Based on Jim's experience with the savings and loan industry, Jim and Sylvia believe they have a good understanding of what market segments will be the best target markets for their company. The problem from their point-of-view is how to best approach each target market. They realize the same approach cannot be used effectively for each market segment.

Due to her sales and marketing experience, Sylvia knows the importance of understanding the consumer's decision-making process. Although she does not know the financial services industry as well as Jim, Sylvia does have a keen sense of how to adapt to the buyer despite the fact that her experience has been mostly in industrial selling.

Sylvia and Jim have decided they should conduct a formal assessment of the similarities and differences they will face in selling a service to both individuals and families. The decision-making process and the factors that will influence the consumer need to be reviewed and studied.

QUESTIONS

1. What should Sylvia and Jim expect with respect to the problem or need recognition stage of the consumer's decision-making process?

2. What are their customers' motives likely to be in purchasing financial planning services?

3. What impact will the family life cycle have on Sylvia's and Jim's selling of financial planning services?

NOTES

1. Carl E. Block and Kenneth J. Roering, *Essentials of Consumer Behavior* (Hinsdale, Ill.: Dryden Press, 1976), 405.

2. Martin Fishbein, "Attitude, Attitude Change, and Behavior: A Theoretical Overview," ed. Philip Levine, *Attitude Research Bridges the Atlantic* (Chicago, Ill.: American Marketing Association, 1975), 3–16.

3. Gerald Zaltman and Melanie Wallendorf, *Consumer Behavior: Basic Findings and Management Implications* (New York: John Wiley and Sons, 1979), 340.

4. Abraham H. Maslow, "A Theory of Motivation," *Psychological Review* (July 1943): 370–96.

5. Harold W. Berkman and Christopher Gilson, *Consumer Behavior: Concepts and Strategies* (Boston, Mass.: Kent Publishing, 1981), 235.

6. Henry Assael, *Consumer Behavior and Marketing Action* (Boston, Mass.: Kent Publishing, 1984), 61.

7. Joel R. Evans and Barry Berman, *Marketing* (New York: Macmillan, 1987), 144.

8. Ibid.

9. Ibid., A37.

10. Ibid., 146.

11. William H. Cunningham, Isabella C. M. Cunningham, and Christopher M. Swift, *Marketing: A Managerial Approach* (Cincinnati, Ohio: South-Western Publishing, 1987), 154.

12. Judith Lynne Zaichkowsky, "Consumer Behavior: Yesterday, Today, and Tomorrow," *Business Horizons* (May–June 1991): 51–58. See also Charles D. Schewe, "Strategically Positioning Your Way Into the Aging Marketplace," *Business Horizons* (May–June 1991): 59–66.

13. Barry Berman, "The Changing U.S. Consumer: Implications for Retailing Strategies," *Retail Strategist* (1991): 19.

14. Cunningham et al., *Marketing: A Managerial Approach*, 160.

15. Sidney J. Levy, "Social Class and Consumer Behavior," ed. Joseph W. Newman, *On Knowing the Consumer* (New York: John Wiley and Sons, 1966), 155; James M. Carman, *The Application of Social Class in Market Segmentation* (Berkeley: Institute of Business and Economic Research, University of California Graduate School of Business Administration, 1965), 31; Pierre Martineau, "Social Classes and Spending Behavior," ed. Louis E. Boone, *Classics in Consumer Behavior* (Tulsa, Okla.: Petroleum Publishing, 1977), 310–11; H. Lee Mathews and John W. Slocum, Jr., "Social Class and Commercial Bank Credit Card Usage," *Journal of Marketing* (January 1969): 71–78.

16. Cunningham et al., *Marketing: A Managerial Approach*, 166.

17. Francis S. Bourne, "Group Influence in Marketing," ed. Louis E. Boone, *Classics in Consumer Behavior* (Tulsa, Okla.: Petroleum Publishing, 1977), 211–25.

18. Assael, *Consumer Behavior and Marketing Action*, 370.

19. Ibid., 382.

20. Ibid., 372.

21. Harry L. Davis, "Dimensions of Marital Roles in Consumer Decision Making," *Journal of Marketing Research* (May 1970): 168–77; Haley, Overholser and Associates, Inc., *Purchase Influence: Measures of Husband/Wife Influence on Buying Decisions* (New Canaan, Conn.: Haley, Overholser, 1975).

22. G. M. Munsinger, J. E. Weber, and R. W. Hansen, "Joint Home Purchasing Decisions by Husbands and Wives," *Journal of Consumer Research* (March 1975): 60–66; H. L. Davis and Benny P. Rigaux, "Perception of Marital Roles in Decision Processes," *Journal of Consumer Research* (June 1974): 51–62.

23. Jagdish N. Sheth, "A Theory of Family Buying Decisions," ed. Jagdish N. Sheth, *Models of Buyer Behavior* (New York: Harper and Row, 1974), 17–33.

24. Cathy Trost, "Men, Too, Wrestle with Career-Family Stress," *Wall Street Journal* (November 1, 1988), B1.

25. Cunningham et al., *Marketing: A Managerial Approach*, 171.

26. Berman, "The Changing U.S. Consumer," 20.

27. Evans and Berman, *Marketing*, 239.

CHAPTER 5

Organizational Buying Behavior

LEARNING OBJECTIVES

After studying this chapter, you should be able to:

1. Explain the similarities and differences between organizational and consumer buyer behavior.

2. Identify the steps in organizational decision making.

3. Identify the major environmental, organizational, group, individual, and product influences on an organization's buying behavior.

4. Describe the different types of organizational buying decision processes.

5. Explain the relationship between the types of industrial goods and organizational buying decision processes.

6. Define the key terms used in this chapter.

KEY TERMS

- organizational buying
- new task
- straight rebuy
- in supplier
- out supplier
- modified rebuy

DAVE BURK HAD just completed three months of sales training with his new employer, Healthcare Systems, which sold medical and dental insurance to a variety of organizations, including businesses, government agencies, and nonprofit organizations. Dave was preparing to make his second sales call on Steve Thomas, human resources manager for Hawkeye Pipe and Valve, Inc., which was a company of almost five hundred employees. Steve had told Dave that at this second meeting other company representatives would be present to hear Dave's formal presentation, namely the president, the vice president of finance, and the purchasing manager for Hawkeye Pipe and Valve, Inc. Dave realized he knew almost nothing about the other participants and had only met Steve Thomas for the first time at their earlier meeting. Dave was encouraged by the fact that the top management of Hawkeye Pipe and Valve, Inc., would be present at the meeting. Dave began to assess what he wanted to present at this upcoming meeting, along with the things he needed to uncover during the meeting.

Although consumer buyers may be classified as individuals, households and families, organizational buyers encompass a more diverse group of customer types such as manufacturers, industrial distributors, wholesalers, and retailers. These categories include large companies such as General Motors, IBM, Sears, K-Mart, and Xerox as well as a variety of medium- and smaller-sized companies.

Governmental institutions are another major classification of organizational buyers. The largest of these is the federal government with its numerous agencies, such as NASA, Department of Defense, General Services Administration, and others. In addition to the federal government, states, counties, and cities are buyers. The products and services they purchase can include everything from airplanes, computers, and mass transit vehicles to stationery, pens, pencils, and paper clips.

A third type of organizational customer is nonprofit organizations who buy products and services to maintain their operations—for example, churches, museums, and universities. The efforts of companies such as Apple Computer and Steelcase to sell computers and furniture, respectively, to nonprofit organizations, the government, manufacturers, wholesalers, and retailers represent the diversity of organizational buyers and sales situations that are available to the professional salesperson.

CONSUMER VERSUS ORGANIZATIONAL BUYER BEHAVIOR

The field of buyer behavior includes not only consumer behavior, but also organizational buyer behavior. The professional salesperson must have an understanding of both behaviors when his or her company sells products or services to each market. Even if one's company is presently marketing a product to either the consumer or the organizational market, knowledge of each type of buyer behavior is helpful, particularly if there is a likelihood that existing or new products or services could be sold to the market that is not presently served.

Even though there are differences between consumer and organizational buying behavior, there are also a number of similarities. First, the buyer in both situations engages in a decision-making process marked by a number of identifiable steps. Second, the buyer is affected by individual (psychological) and group (social) influences on his or her behavior. Third, the decision processes associated with consumer behavior (discussed in Chapter 4) also exist in organizational buying behavior.

A good understanding of organizational buyer behavior should include a keen awareness of some of its major differences from consumer buyer behavior. Exhibit 5-1 summarizes a number of differences between consumer and organizational buyer behavior. Organizational buying uses the product or service in the production of another product, in operations, or for resale. In contrast, consumer buying is normally for personal, family, or household use. These characteristics also influence the buyer's motivation from personal in consumer buying to both personal and organizational in organizational buying. Because there is a formal buyer in many organizations—commonly referred to as the buyer, purchasing manager, or purchasing agent—he or she is more knowledgeable about the products and services being purchased, since that is this individual's job responsibility. Just as a salesperson is responsible for selling, the buyer or purchasing agent is responsible for buying. Since sales personnel will interact with this person regularly and continually, it is critical that they understand his or her responsibilities and authority.

In organizational buying, there is also a greater likelihood of group decision making. In other than routine purchases, a number of individuals from such areas as engineering, manufacturing, and finance may be involved, while for consumer buying, individual decision making is more common than group decision making. The major reasons for group decision making in organizations are the large dollar

---

Exhibit 5-1 **Consumer Versus Organizational Buyer Behavior**

Aspect of the Purchase	Consumer Buyer	Organizational Buyer
Use	Personal, family or household	Production, operations or resale
Buyer motivation	Personal	Personal and organizational
Buyer knowledge of product or service	Lower	Higher
Likelihood of group decision making	Lower	Higher
Dollar amount of purchases	Lower	Higher
Quantity of purchase or order size	Smaller	Larger
Frequency of purchase	More	Less
Number of cyclical purchases	Lower	Higher
Amount of negotiation and competitive bidding	Little	Much

amount and the order size or quantity of the purchase. The purchase of a computer system for the entire network of Sears stores compared with a single personal computer for home use presents a very different buying situation due to the number of units and dollars involved. Because the orders from organizations are larger in both dollars and units, the frequency of purchase is normally less than that of consumers. Rather than purchasing weekly, an organization may place orders only monthly, quarterly, semiannually, or annually. The purchasing frequency for some products and services may be even more infrequent if changes in the economy cause cyclical fluctuations that affect an organization's business.

Two other relatively major differences between consumer and organizational buying behavior are the widespread use of negotiation and competitive bidding in organizational buying. Consumers make minimal use of these buying techniques. For some organizations such as the federal government, however, the process of competitive bidding is the norm, not the exception. Even nongovernmental organizations frequently have a seller or vendor list of companies that may place a bid for the buying organization.

Failure to acknowledge and understand the differences, as well as the similarities, between consumer and organizational buyer behavior places the professional salesperson at a severe disadvantage. The ability to respond effectively to the needs and problems of each individual buyer is mandatory for effective relationships to be developed between the seller and buyer. Let's look more closely at buyer behavior in the organizational setting.

ORGANIZATIONAL BUYING AND DECISION MAKING

Organizational buying is defined as "the decision-making process by which formal organizations establish the need for purchased products and services, and identify, evaluate, and choose among alternative brands and suppliers."[1] Although the organizational and consumer buying decision-making processes are similar, the actual steps vary slightly. In contrast to consumer decision making, which has five steps, the organizational buying process has eight steps.[2]

Step 1: Anticipation or Recognition of a Problem or Need

The first step is the anticipation or recognition of a problem or need. The underlying cause for this initial step may be a variety of situations, including running out of the existing product, a growing level of dissatisfaction with the brand of product being used, or a new opportunity that creates the need for a product or service not previously purchased by the organization. It is extremely important for the salesperson to understand the problem or need underlying the prospective purchasing decision of the organizational buyer because of the large quantity, dollar value, and infrequency of purchase of some products.

Step 2: Determination of the Characteristics and Quantity of the Needed Item

Once the problem or need has been recognized, a determination must be made as to how to best deal with the specific situation. If the product or service is frequently purchased and the existing product has performed well in the past, this step in the organizational buying process may be routine and may occur quickly. On the other hand, if this is a first-time problem or the purchase is a major financial investment, the second step may be time-consuming and involve a number of company personnel. For example, the purchase of a company's first computer system may be seen as a major decision, while the purchase of an additional forklift for the receiving and shipping department may be seen as a routine purchase.

Step 3: Description of the Characteristics and Quantity of the Needed Item

The shift from Step 2 to Step 3 means a translation from a general to a specific description of the product or service desired. This step is needed in order to effectively communicate to potential suppliers the nature of the item desired. Depending on the product's or service's use and cost, one, a few, or a large number of individuals may be involved in this step. The setting of product or service specifications may present an opportunity for the salesperson to provide valuable information to the company personnel charged with this activity. Because of his or her expertise and relationship with the company's personnel, the salesperson may sometimes serve not only as an information source, but also as a participant in the process.

Step 4: Search for and Qualification of Potential Sources

Once Steps 2 and 3 of the organizational buying process have been completed, the focus of the organizational buyer moves to the search for and qualification of potential suppliers of the product or service desired.[3] Again, this step may be completed very quickly for products that are purchased frequently and for which there are a number of suppliers. In contrast, for nonstandard products, this step may involve a considerable amount of time.

Many firms are emphasizing proactive evaluation, which is front-end loaded by shifting the focus to prescreening and selection. More time is spent on prequalification. For example, at Honda of America, a team including representatives from purchasing, quality, and engineering is sent to a supplier's plant to perform a quality assessment valuation. This assessment includes not only quality of the part or component needed by Honda, but also worker attitudes, management systems, safety compliance, and potential environmental problems, among other factors of the supplier's operation. The team then rates each supplier visited.[4]

Frequently, there may be a number of vendors or suppliers offering the needed product or service. This step determines which of the potential suppliers should be given further consideration or an opportunity to submit a formal proposal. As noted in Exhibit 5-2, key attributes evaluated by personnel in the buying organization with regard to suppliers might include product availability, financial stability, business reputation, and customer service.[5] The suppliers who pass this initial evaluation are given an opportunity to be considered further.

In addition to the attributes listed in Exhibit 5-2, buyers for companies who are resellers of products, such as Sears and Target, may have some additional attributes or criteria in selecting suppliers. For example, key attributes in a reseller's evaluation of suppliers might also include services offered by the supplier or manufacturer, such as promotional allowances, training of retail sales personnel, restocking shelves, and setting up displays. An even more important attribute for the reseller will be the profit potential of doing business with a particular supplier. Specifically, quantity discounts, trade discounts, and mark-up potential (that is, the difference between the selling price and the cost of the item) would be very important. Finally,

Criterion	Indicators	
Product availability	Delivery date compliance Inventory levels Out-of-stock occurrences	**Exhibit 5-2** Buyer Evaluation of Supplier Attributes
Financial stability	Credit rating Years in business	
Business reputation	Current customers Former customers	
Customer service	Exchange and refund policies Complaint-handling procedures Response time to service request	

resellers might also be interested in whether they could be the exclusive distributor of the supplier's product or service in a designated geographical area.

Step 5: Acquisition and Analysis of Proposals

In relatively routine purchases of standard items, Steps 4 and 5 occur almost simultaneously, with little information search, since existing suppliers would continue to be used. However, when the problem or need is new to the buying organization or when the buyer's information about the item in question is incomplete, the acquisition and analysis of proposals from suppliers or vendors may require a considerable amount of time before any decision can be made. For example, a company may spend as long as a year considering which proposal to accept (if any) for a telecommunications system. During this time, proposals may be analyzed, questioned, partially rejected, rewritten, and resubmitted for review before a final decision is made by the organizational buyer. The salesperson should expect a considerable investment of time and effort under conditions of uncertainty. At this stage, the salesperson should know his or her major competitors and the advantages and disadvantages of each competitor's product or service offerings.

Step 6: Evaluation of Proposals and Selection of Suppliers

Once the supplier proposals have been received, a more formal proposal evaluation stage occurs. This may entail not only a review of a written proposal by the buying organization, but formal, in-person presentations by the sales personnel of the supplier organizations that have passed earlier hurdles to reach this stage. A key aspect of this stage for the salesperson is a knowledge of the major participants in the selection decision. Just as in consumer buying, individuals in a buying organization may occupy one or more roles as decision makers, buyers, users, influencers, and gatekeepers. Knowledge of the decision criteria and the criteria

Figure 5-1 Solicitation of formal and informal performance feedback should be standard operating procedure.

weights is critical for the salesperson as he or she interacts with the buying organization. Once the formal evaluation of the various suppliers or vendors has been completed, one or more of the suppliers may be selected by the company to provide the product or service in question.

Step 7: Selection of an Order Routine

Discussion of an order routine between the buying and selling organizations includes the timing for sending the purchase order to the supplier, submission of status reports by the supplier on the delivery dates, and a determination of the inventory levels that will be carried by both the buying and the selling organizations. Thus, when a supplier is selected, the salesperson must pay careful attention to a number of details regarding the actual production or supply, shipping, and inventory of the product so an effective order routine that is satisfactory to the buying organization can be established. The order routine may be especially important to a retailer such as a local pharmacy, which must depend on timely delivery of needed medical supplies.

Step 8: Performance Feedback and Evaluation

The last step of the organizational buying process is similar to the postpurchase evaluation and behavior stage of the consumer buying process. Based on the performance of the supplier, the buying organization will assess how well the supplier performed in supplying and servicing the company's need or solving the company's problem. An example of how a buying organization is involved in performance feedback and evaluation is the case of the d-Con company, which holds a "supplier day" during which meetings take place between the company's personnel (machine operators, production supervisors, and quality assurance personnel) and packaging component suppliers. The individuals meet face-to-face to discuss current problems and possible solutions. At the end of the day, d-Con's purchasing personnel review with each supplier their current status with d-Con. Suppliers are asked to write up a summary of the day and what actions they plan to take to solve problems identified.[6]

The salesperson must make every effort to ensure that the buying organization is satisfied. Solicitation of formal and informal feedback should be normal operating procedure. It will, in large part, be up to the salesperson to maintain his or her company as the current supplier. A positive postpurchase performance evaluation by the personnel in the buying organization will go a long way toward developing a long-term buyer-seller relationship. The type of feedback involved in the organizational buying process is shown in Exhibit 5-3.

FACTORS INFLUENCING ORGANIZATIONAL BUYING BEHAVIOR

Five major factors influence organizational buying behavior: the environment, organization, group, individual, and product. The professional salesperson must understand that these factors are more complex and extensive than those found in consumer buying behavior.

Exhibit 5-3 **A Model of Supplier Evaluation in Organizational Buying**

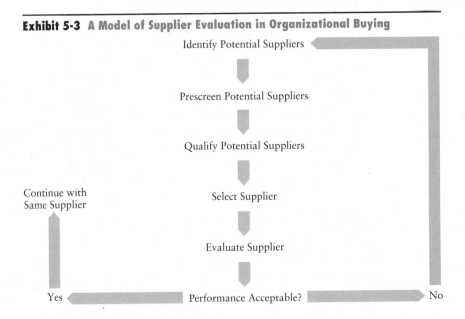

Identify Potential Suppliers

Prescreen Potential Suppliers

Qualify Potential Suppliers

Select Supplier

Evaluate Supplier

Continue with Same Supplier

Yes   Performance Acceptable?   No

The Environment

Major environmental influences—economic, legal, political, technological, cultural, and physical—surround each organization or company.[7] These forces may present opportunities, problems, or constraints. General economic conditions such as interest rates, inflation, unemployment, and wholesale and retail price indexes may have major effects on an organization's buying activity. For example, when interest rates are high, the residential and commercial building industries suffer due to the high cost of financing faced by purchasers of houses and office buildings. This buying slowdown then causes the building firms to purchase fewer materials, such as lumber and paint for construction projects.

Legal and political influences on organizational buying behavior are often closely related. Legal statutes define accepted ways of doing business. For example, products may need to conform to certain safety standards or must disclose to prospective customers certain types of information when use of the product may affect a person's health or safety. Political influences on buying behavior are important because the policies enacted by federal, state, or local governments often result in legislation on such issues as deceptive trade practices, which may affect the buyer-seller relationship.

Technology may also have a significant impact. The development of new ways or methods of doing business often means that some process or method is upgraded or replaced by something better. Thus, changing technology may be a problem and an opportunity at the same time. For example, rapid advancement in computer technology has changed the computer hardware and software available to business customers. The same could be said for telecommunications systems, which changed from a regulated to a deregulated market. Although technological influences may be the most difficult to predict, the salesperson must be able to adapt to new situations and the related needs of buying organizations.

Besides the legal aspects of business relationships, cultural influences also shape the buyer-seller interaction. The professional salesperson must be aware of the cultural influences that may affect this relationship. Two particular aspects deserve special mention. One is the development of values and norms of expected behavior. Ethical behavior by both the buyer and seller is a major ingredient in developing a long-term business relationship. In contrast, failure to do business ethically will almost always result in a failed business relationship. A second major cultural influence affects those who sell multinationally. Each salesperson must ensure that he or she exhibits conduct appropriate to the buyer's culture. For example, differences between customers in the United States and Japan must be acknowledged if the salesperson is to be effective. In Japan, buyers are less likely to say no in a face-to-face situation and often want to develop a social relationship before conducting business.

A final environmental influence on organizational buying behavior is the physical environment: the geography, climate, and ecology of an area. Certain industrial organizations have to buy products or services that comply with environmental standards. Companies, such as steel mills, must effectively deal with air and water pollution. In essence, a political issue (concern for the environment) has led to legal statutes that are enforced by the Environmental Protection Agency and affect the economic and physical environment of steel mills. New product developments due to advances in technology turned a problem situation into one that offered new opportunities for companies which sell emission control equipment. This one example shows the interrelationships between environmental influences and organizational buying behavior.

The Organization

Three major characteristics of the buyer's organization—its orientation, size, and degree of centralization—influence an organization's buying behavior.[8] A salesperson must be aware of the buying organization's overall orientation, what might be referred to as the organization's culture. Based on an organization's development over time and the backgrounds of its top management, organizations often take on a culture marked by the dominance of a particular business function. An

Figure 5-2 Cues regarding an organization's culture may be ascertained during the course of a routine business lunch.

organization may view itself as primarily a technology, production, or marketing company. Depending on the organization's culture, key personnel in the buying organization may be, among others, engineering, research and development, manufacturing, or marketing personnel. This information is crucial for the professional salesperson preparing to sell to a given organization.

Two additional factors, an organization's size and degree of centralization, are also important for the salesperson to assess. There is a tendency for larger companies to use group or joint decision making more than smaller organizations. Knowledge of who are the key decision makers is critical in assessing the extent of group or joint decision making in the buyer's organization. In addition to the size of the organization, the more decentralized an organization, the more likely that decisions will be made by a group. Knowledge of the buyer's organizational structure may shed additional light on whether group or joint decision making or individual or autonomous decisions will be dominant.

The Group

As already indicated, the purchase of products and services is either a group or an individual decision. In those situations marked by group or joint decision making, the professional salesperson must address three key questions:

1. Who are the organizational members who will take part in the buying process?
2. What is each member's relative influence in the decision?
3. What criteria are important to each member of the group in evaluating prospective suppliers?[9]

The concept of the buying center (introduced in Chapter 2) may play a major role in organizational buying behavior. Individuals in the buying organization may serve in the roles of influencer, decider, buyer, user, or gatekeeper. It is critical that the salesperson know who is involved in the purchase and the extent of each person's involvement relative to the first two questions above.[10] Group or joint decision making may take a rather informal structure, such as a buying center, or be a more formal unit known as a buying committee. An example of the participants in a buying center and their influence at various stages of the buying process is given in Exhibit 5-4.

In assessing the pattern of group decision making in the buyer's organization, the salesperson must realize the situation will be dynamic or changing as opposed to static or unchanging. The composition of the buying center may evolve during the purchasing or buying process, vary from one organization to another, and vary from one purchasing situation to another.[11] The salesperson must continu-

Exhibit 5-4 Buying Center Participants at Different Stages of the Buying Process—Purchase of a Computer System by a Large Manufacturer

Stages of the Buying Process		Influence of Buying Center Participants		
	Purchasing	Information Systems	Finance	Top Management
Recognition of problem or need	Moderate	High	Moderate	Moderate
Determination and description of the needed item	Moderate	High	Low	Moderate
Search for and qualification of potential sources	High	High	Moderate	Low
Aquisition and analysis of proposals	Moderate	High	Moderate	Low
Selection of suppliers	Low	High	Moderate	High
Selection of an order routine	High	Moderate	Low	Low
Performance feed-back and evaluation	Moderate	High	Moderate	Moderate

ally monitor changes in personnel and procedures occurring in each buying organization.

The Individual

The importance of the individual in organizational buying behavior, whether in joint or autonomous decisions, should not be underestimated. In those situations involving routine and recurring purchases, the purchasing manager or agent may play the dominant role. However, for first-time purchases of major equipment requiring a high financial commitment, purchasing personnel may be only one part of a rather complex buying structure. Whether the buying situation is relatively simple or complex, the professional salesperson should strive to better understand individual influences on the buying decision.

Some traits affecting individuals involved in the buying process are their professional and personal backgrounds, the information sources they use, and their previous experience with the product or service.[12] The salesperson should learn as much as possible about each individual's position in the buying organization, including his or her responsibility and authority. The formal organizational chart may be a starting point, but often it is just as important for the salesperson to understand the informal relationships. As the salesperson gains information on the professional backgrounds of personnel in the buying organization, he or she may also seek to know the individual better from a personal perspective. Do the person's interests outside the work environment include golf, tennis, jogging, or some other activity?

In addition to an individual's background, the salesperson will want to gain a clearer picture of what information sources each key buying center member uses. Information sources may include salespersons, word-of-mouth, exhibitions and trade shows, direct mail, journal advertising, and professional and technical conferences. Sources may vary significantly from one product category to another. An individual in the buying organization may place greater or lesser emphasis on an information source, depending on whether the purchase is routine or complex. Also, for a given purchase, an individual may use only a few sources or as many information sources as possible.

The salesperson must also consider the individual buyer's previous experience with the product or service, the salesperson, and the salesperson's company. Just as in consumer buying behavior, previous use of a product or service has resulted in some postpurchase evaluation and behavior. Favorable attitudes about the product, the salesperson, and the salesperson's company may pave the way for future sales. However, dissatisfaction with any of these three may present an obstacle in gaining future sales. Information about the individual's experience with the salesperson's product should be supplemented with information about the buyer's experience and level of satisfaction with competitive products.

The Product

A final factor that influences organizational buying behavior is represented by the product itself. The three major product influences are the type of purchase, the perceived risk, and the time pressure to make the purchase.[13] The type of purchase—routine and recurring versus a first-time purchase or one requiring a major financial expenditure—is likely to have a significant effect on whether or not the decision to buy is delegated to one individual, such as the purchasing manager, or is made by a group, such as a buying center or committee.

Similarly, the buyer's level of perceived risk affects the likelihood of the occurrence of individual versus group decision making. The salesperson should expect that the greater the uncertainty or perceived risk of the buying organization, the more likely that group or joint decision making will occur.

A third influence, the time pressure to make the purchase, suggests that the shorter the time available to make a decision, the more likely that an individual decision will occur. The desire to have a buying committee meet to discuss the various product or service alternatives may be ideal, but it may not be feasible, due to the urgency of the buying decision, the product's or service's importance to the operations of the company, or an emergency beyond the company's control.

In summary, when the buying situation is marked by the purchase of a routine, low-priced product or service involving low-level risk under conditions of limited time, a salesperson should expect to find individual rather than joint decision making. When the opposite is true, group or joint decision making is more likely.

TYPES OF ORGANIZATIONAL BUYING DECISIONS

As discussed earlier, the organizational buying process includes eight steps from anticipation or recognition of a problem or need to performance feedback and evaluation. While an industrial buyer goes through each step, the salesperson must have a keen awareness of not only the step that the buyer is in, but also the situation confronting the buyer. Organizational buyers may be faced with one of three situations: new task, straight rebuy, or modified rebuy.[14] Failure to recognize the buyer's situation will probably cause the sales representative to misread the buyer's needs initially, or worse, to lose a sale.

New Task

For many reasons, the **new task** may present the greatest opportunity and challenge for the professional salesperson. Buyers in this situation often have little or no prior experience dealing with the particular problem or need. Due to this lack of experience, the buyer may experience a high level of risk that he or she handles with a more lengthy search process. Buyers will actively seek information on alternative ways of solving the problem. With little, if any, existing supplier loyalty, extended decision making is required. The salesperson has the opportunity to become the buyer's supplier when the buyer purchases the product or service for the first time. The benefit of being in on the ground floor with a buyer may pay not only short-run dividends, but also may be the first step in building a long-term relationship with the buyer and his or her organization. An example of new-task buying might be a company that was buying its first computer system, selecting its first advertising agency, or hiring its first accounting firm. The new-task situation is one in which each supplier has a relatively equal footing in the competition for the customer's business, since this is a first-time problem or need.

Straight Rebuy

The opposite of the new task is the straight rebuy. The **straight rebuy** occurs when the buyer is engaging in behavior centered on a continuing or recurring purchase.[15] The desire for new information and for additional suppliers is low. Due to prior experience, the buyer perceives relatively little risk. Since a straight rebuy is marked by routine decision making, the purchasing department plays the major role. The salesperson's view of the straight rebuy depends on whether his or her company is the in supplier or the out supplier. If the salesperson's company is the **in supplier**, extreme care must be taken to nurture the buyer-seller relationship. Attention to the buyer's changing needs, problems, or expectations must receive a high priority. The time and financial cost to the seller of gaining, losing, and then trying to regain a customer should not be underestimated. In contrast, the salesperson whose company is the **out supplier** will face a major challenge in getting the buyer to reassess the existing situation. Although a customer in a straight rebuy relationship with a competitor is not necessarily a lost cause for the salesperson, he or she must acknowledge the differences from a new-task customer.

Modified Rebuy

An organizational buyer's middle ground between the new task and the straight rebuy is the modified rebuy. In a **modified rebuy**, the buyer has made the purchase one or more times before and thus has already undergone a certain amount of information search about suppliers and their products or services. A buyer, however, may feel the need to seek more information and to reevaluate the product alternatives or suppliers. The buyer's change from a straight rebuy to a modified rebuy posture may be due to a number of factors, including personnel changes in the buying organization's purchasing department, some dissatisfaction with the current or in supplier, a change in the supplier's sales representative, or a directive from top management to reassess the appropriateness of existing buyer-seller relationships. This type of limited decision making means the in supplier must reinforce the buyer's belief that the seller's company should remain the supplying organization. In contrast, the out supplier may have a new opportunity due to an organization's shift from the straight rebuy to the modified rebuy.

The professional salesperson must be continually aware of the status of each of his or her customers and prospects. Different buying situations call for different strategies and actions or reactions by the salesperson. The opportunity to further strengthen existing buyer-seller relationships or to initiate new relationships must be seized by the salesperson. Exhibit 5-5 presents the three major buying situations and the appropriate salesperson responses.

INDUSTRIAL GOODS AND ORGANIZATIONAL BUYER BEHAVIOR

As with consumer goods, the types of industrial goods also play a major role in organizational buying behavior. As shown in Exhibit 5-6, the six major classifications

Exhibit 5-5 **Salesperson Responses in Buying Situations**

Buying Situation	Customer Situation	Salesperson Responses
New Task	Uncertainty as to how to handle a new problem or need	Aid customer to identify problem or need. Provide customer with references to similar situations and how the problem or need was resolved.
Modified rebuy	Uncertainty as to whether or not to retain current supplier	If current or in supplier, uncover reasons why the customer might consider other suppliers and respond to the problem or issue. If out supplier, uncover the weakness of the in supplier and capitalize on it.
Straight rebuy	Relatively certain the current supplier is the most appropriate	If current or in supplier, reinforce the customer's supplier selection by attention to problems and acknowledgement that the relationship with the customer is highly valued. If out supplier, present product or service as a viable backup, alternative, or replacement to the current supplier. Arouse concern or uncertainty in order to gain customer's reevaluation of suppliers.

of industrial goods include installations, accessory equipment, raw materials, component materials, fabricated parts, and supplies. The range of products included as industrial goods covers the spectrum from generators, forklift trucks, coal, and steel to thermostats and light bulbs. In contrast to the types of consumer goods discussed in Chapter 4, industrial goods are normally only in one category, since most industrial purchasers view a given product similarly.

Industrial goods can be compared and contrasted on a number of different dimensions. For example, on the characteristic of per-unit costs, installations would be high, accessory equipment would be moderate, and the remaining types of industrial goods would be low to very low. A similar comparison exists for the degree of organizational decision making from high on installations to very low on

Exhibit 5-6 Classification of Industrial Goods

		Type of Good				
Characteristics	*Installations*	*Accessory Equipment*	*Raw Materials*	*Component Materials*	*Fabricated Parts*	*Supplies*
Degree of organizational decision making	High	Moderate	Low	Low	Low	Very Low
Per-unit costs	High	Moderate	Low	Low	Low	Very Low
Rate of consumption	Very Low	Low	High	High	High	High
Item becomes part of final product	No	No	Sometimes	Yes	Yes	No
Item undergoes changes in form	No	No	Yes	Yes	No	No
Major consumer desire	Long-term facilities	Modern equipment	Continuous, cost-efficient, graded materials	Continuous, cost-efficient, specified materials	Continuous, cost-efficient, fabricated materials	Continuous, cost-efficient, supplies
Examples	Production plant	Forklift truck	Coal	Steel	Thermostat	Light bulb

Source: Reprinted with permission of Macmillan Publishing Company from *Marketing* by Joel R. Evans and Barry Berman, Copyright © 1987 by Macmillan Publishing Company.

routinely ordered supplies. The opposite holds true for the rate of consumption, with installations the lowest and materials, parts, and supplies the highest.

The diversity of industrial products presents a number of challenges for the professional salesperson. First, the salesperson who sells high-cost items, such as installations and accessory equipment, should expect the length of the presale stage to be longer than for other industrial goods. In addition, the number of individuals in the buyer's organization who are involved in the purchase decision is likely to be greater. Due to the diverse interests of multiple buying influences in the customer's organization, lengthy negotiation may occur with each buyer or buying influence interested in the same or different aspects of the product in question. Because these product categories are major capital assets of the buyer, economic factors such as the cost, reliability, and return-on-investment may receive high priority from one or more members of the buying organization. Contact with not only purchasing but also manufacturing, engineering, and top management may be the norm rather than the exception when selling installations and accessory equipment.

The salesperson will encounter a different selling situation with raw materials, component materials, and fabricated parts than he or she would with installations and accessory equipment. The key differences would be the lower per-unit costs of materials and parts, the use of materials and parts in the buying organization's product, the quantity purchased, and the rapidity with which they are repurchased and restocked. Although the primary decision makers or influencers will be production and engineering personnel, the salesperson will deal mostly with the purchasing manager or agent. Some materials and parts may be standard, but others may be custom-made or designed for a given buyer, which gives the salesperson a differentiated product to sell.

Selling supplies provides a major contrast to marketing installations and accessory equipment. These relatively routine purchases, which are low-priced and rapidly used, primarily involve the purchasing department of the buying organization. Although production and engineering personnel may have been the key decision makers in other industrial product categories, the purchasing manager will be the primary decision maker in buying supplies. Just as the salesperson must be careful to adapt to the needs and desires of other personnel in the buyer's organization, purchasing personnel now come front and center and must not be taken for granted in the selling process. The salesperson must remember that, just as with different buying situations, different types of industrial products influence the organizational buying and selling process.

SUMMARY

1. The salesperson should understand the similarities and differences between organizational buying behavior and consumer buying behavior.

2. The professional salesperson should know the eight steps of the organizational decision-making process, from the anticipation or recognition of a problem or need to performance feedback and evaluation.

3. The salesperson should study the interrelationships among the environmental, organizational, group, individual, and product influences on organizational buying behavior to better adapt to the buying organization.

4. The new task, straight rebuy, and modified rebuy situations are important to the salesperson, and he or she must assess them from the position of the in supplier or out supplier unless the situation involves a first-time buyer.

5. Just as different customers engage in different buying patterns, different types of industrial goods call for alternative selling perspectives by the professional salesperson.

QUESTIONS FOR DISCUSSION AND REVIEW

1. What are three of the major differences between consumer and organizational buying behavior? What are three similarities?

2. Identify two attributes that might be used by the buyer to assess supplier capability.

3. Explain how different environmental influences on organizational buying behavior may affect each other. Give an example.

4. In terms of organizational influences on buying, what is an example of an organization's orientation?

5. What are three important questions the salesperson should attempt to answer when dealing with members of a buying center or buying committee?

6. Why is it important to know a buyer's personal interests as well as his or her professional background?

7. Explain what is meant by the terms new task, modified rebuy, and straight rebuy.

8. What is the difference between an in supplier and an out supplier?

9. Compare and contrast the organizational buying behavior for the purchase of a company's first computer system with the purchase of a new copier for use by office personnel.

10. Is selling to an organizational customer more difficult than selling to individual consumers or households? Why?

11. In terms of various buying situations, is the new task situation always the most difficult for the salesperson?

12. If you were in Dave Burk's situation, which was described at the beginning of this chapter, what would you try to uncover during the upcoming meeting?

CASE 5-1 TYLER CLOTHIERS

Virginia Nichols was the Sales Representative for Fashions Unlimited, a manufacturer of clothing for women, men, and children. She had been in sales with this company for three years after being employed with one of Fashion Unlimited's competitors for the previous four years. Ms. Nichols' territory included Arkansas, Louisiana, and eastern Texas. Her primary customers were retail clothing chains of three or more stores or outlets.

One of Virginia's customers was Tyler Clothiers, owned by Robert and Marleen Adler. After opening their first store in Tyler, Texas, Mr. and Mrs. Adler opened three additional stores in Beaumont, Dallas, and Houston, Texas. Each of the stores did well especially the two in Tyler and Beaumont, which had less competition. Two members of the management team of Tyler Clothiers were Ed Easley, Vice F Finance, and Lou Ann Simpson, Vice President of Merchandising.

The challenge confronting Ms. Nichols was to get Tyler Clothiers to purchase clothing for women and children for resale, in addition to clothing for men, which they already purchased from Fashions Unlimited. In each of these three product lines, Tyler Clothiers did business with a number of current suppliers. However, there were more suppliers competing in the market for men's clothing than in women's or children's, although these latter two markets offered greater profit potential.

After two recent sales calls in which she met with Robert and Marleen Adler plus Ed Easley and Lou Ann Simpson, Virginia Nichols reviewed the notes she had taken in summarizing the meetings. Based on conversations with Robert and Marleen, Virginia had taken note of their interest in being exclusive distributors for clothing lines in a particular geographic area, especially around Tyler and Beaumont. Both Robert and Marleen were bottom-line managers, and the profit potential of any clothing line was important to them. In sizing up Ed Easley, who had been with Tyler Clothiers for fifteen years, Virginia remembered that he was very interested in the availability of discounts and potential markups for women's and children's clothing, while Lou Ann Simpson, who had just joined Tyler Clothiers last year, had commented to Virginia about the importance of the availability of promotional allowances and training for retail sales personnel in any new clothing line added by the company.

Prior to visiting Tyler Clothiers again to discuss Fashion Unlimited's women's and children's clothing lines further, Virginia Nichols pondered what other information she needed to gain this new business.

QUESTIONS

1. What advantage might Virginia Nichols have with Tyler Clothiers that competing suppliers would not have?

2. With respect to Robert and Marleen Adler, Ed Easley, and Lou Ann Simpson, what questions should Virginia Nichols be asking herself?

3. What would Virginia Nichols want to know about Tyler Clothiers' present suppliers of women's and children's clothes?

CASE 5-2 OFFICE SUPPLY, INC.

Haley Allison is a recent graduate of Central State University with an undergraduate degree in marketing. She has been employed by Office Supply, Inc., for almost six months. Although most of this time has been devoted to training, she has been calling on her own accounts for about one month.

Office Supply, Inc., is a twenty-year-old company that sells office furniture and supplies. The company's product mix includes tables, chairs, desks, computer stands, typewriters, and file cabinets. The company has built a solid reputation in the office supply and equipment field.

Ms. Allison has called on Reed Manufacturing twice during the past month. On her first visit, she met Harve Hade, Reed's Purchasing Manager. Ms. Allison also met Mr. Hade's Administrative Assistant, Ms. Jennifer Bentley, who has worked for Mr. Hade for over seven years.

In response to Ms. Allison's questions, Mr. Hade indicated that his company is in the market for new office furniture, since the existing furniture is over ten years old. Reed

Manufacturing's previous supplier is no longer in business. All the administrative offices are to be refurnished, and the total dollar expenditure will be about $50,000.

Harve Hade said that he is interested in an established supplier who stands behind the products it sells. He also mentioned prompt delivery and service after the sale. He did signify, however, that since the purchase is likely to be around $50,000, other key personnel in Reed Manufacturing would also have input into what furniture is purchased and from which supplier.

In concluding his third meeting with Haley Allison, Harve Hade suggested Ms. Allison should feel free to contact Ms. Bentley about the specific types of furniture Reed Manufacturing is currently using. Mr. Hade suggested that Ms. Allison should develop a proposal for his review, which could then be presented by Ms. Allison to some of Reed's managers.

QUESTIONS

1. Given the information in this case, what type of organizational buying decision process does Reed Manufacturing have? Also, what are the implications of its decision process?

2. What key pieces of information does Ms. Allison already have after three visits to Reed Manufacturing?

3. Before developing her proposal for Mr. Hade, what additional information should Ms. Allison obtain?

CASE 5-3   WASTE DISPOSAL SYSTEMS

Denise Alfaro is a Sales Representative for Waste Disposal Systems and has been with the company for the past ten years. Prior to her current position, she earned an undergraduate degree in industrial engineering and a graduate degree in business administration. She has been the leading salesperson for Waste Disposal Systems for the past three years in terms of dollar sales volume.

Waste Disposal Systems provides disposal removal services for business, government, and nonprofit organizations, including hospitals. The company handles everything from routine waste, such as paper and cans, to toxic wastes generated by hospitals and medical centers. Waste Disposal Systems is one of three major companies in the waste disposal business.

Denise Alfaro has been trying to gain the business of Memorial Hospital for the past year or so. Currently, Memorial Hospital's waste disposal is handled by Waste Reduction, Inc., one of Waste Disposal Systems' major competitors. Since it is the largest hospital system in the metropolitan area, Memorial Hospital is a very attractive customer. In addition, the hospital's annual cost for waste disposal is almost $200,000.

In talking with Joey Burton, Purchasing Manager for Memorial Hospital, whom she has known for about three years, Denise discovered that Mr. Burton is not totally satisfied with the performance of Waste Reduction, Inc. According to Mr. Burton, Waste Reduction has indicated to him that they anticipate a major price increase for the next calendar year. Mr. Burton also indicated that other individuals on the hospital's management team want to reevaluate the suppliers the hospital does business with if the contract is for $150,000 or more in a given year.

Denise also discovered that Memorial Hospital's administration is interested in awarding a five-year contract to one company for a comprehensive waste disposal process. Currently, the hospital has only a two-year disposal contract. Ms. Alfaro realizes the situation presented by Memorial Hospital is a major opportunity for both immediate and long-term business.

QUESTIONS

1. If you were in Denise Alfaro's position, what questions would you want to ask Joey Burton?

2. What information should Denise Alfaro attempt to uncover about Waste Reduction, Inc.?

3. Why would an account like Memorial Hospital be so important to Denise Alfaro and Waste Disposal Systems?

NOTES

1. Frederick W. Webster, Jr. and Yoram Wind, *Organizational Buying Behavior* (Englewood Cliffs, N.J.: Prentice-Hall, 1972), 2.

2. Patrick J. Robinson, Charles W. Faris, and Yoram Wind, *Industrial Buying and Creative Marketing* (Boston: Allyn and Bacon, 1967), 12–18.

3. Richard E. Plank and Valerie Kijewski, "The Use of Approved Supplier Lists," *International Journal of Purchasing and Materials Management* (April 1991): 37–41.

4. Larry C. Giunipero, "Supplier Evaluation Methods," *NAPM Insights* (June 1990): 21–22.

5. Kenneth N. Thompson, "Scaling Evaluative Criteria and Supplier Performance Estimates in Weighted Point Prepurchase Decision Models," *International Journal of Purchasing and Materials Management* (January 1991): 27–36.

6. Julie Murphree, "A Scorecard for Supplier Day," *NAPM Insights* (June 1990): 23.

7. Webster and Wind, *Organizational Buying Behavior*, 40–46.

8. Jagdish N. Sheth, "A Model of Industrial Buyer Behavior," *Journal of Marketing*, Vol. 37 (1973): 50–56.

9. Michael D. Hutt and Thomas W. Speh, *Industrial Marketing Management* (New York: Dryden Press, 1981), 80.

10. Martin Everett, "This Is the Ultimate in Selling," *Sales and Marketing Management* (August 1989): 28–38.

11. Hutt and Speh, *Industrial Marketing Management*, 80.

12. Sheth, "A Model of Industrial Buyer Behavior," 50–56.

13. Ibid.

14. Robinson, Faris, and Wind, *Industrial Buying*, Chapter 1.

15. Ven Sriram and Venkatapparao Mummalaneni, "Determinants of Source Loyalty in Buyer-Seller Relationships," *Journal of Purchasing and Materials Management* (October 1990): 21–26.

PART THREE

Relationship Management with the Customer

CHAPTER 6

Beginning the Relationship

LEARNING OBJECTIVES

After studying this chapter, you should be able to:

1. Explain the difference between a sales lead and a prospect.

2. Describe how a marketing plan can be used to guide a salesperson's prospecting activities.

3. Identify several ways a sales rep can maintain a stream of sales leads.

4. Describe how direct mail, media advertising, directories, and trade shows can be used to generate leads.

5. Explain how sales leads can be qualified by using the telephone.

6. Identify several sources of information a sales rep can use to learn more about a prospect before actually meeting the prospect.

7. Explain the who, what, and where questions a rep should answer when planning the initial meeting with the customer or client.

8. Define the key terms used in this chapter.

KEY TERMS

- prospecting
- sales leads
- prospect
- marketing concept
- endless chain
- center of influence method
- networking

- direct mail
- bingo card
- subject-oriented directory
- general industrial directory
- trade show
- tight lead
- loose lead

HEWLETT-PACKARD in Palo Alto, California, has aggressively attacked the problem of generating sales opportunities for its reps. The company created a Customer Information Center, which takes a coordinated approach to the company's direct mail advertising and the subsequent responses from potential customers. Their efforts are illustrated in Exhibit 6-1. The five major sales support activities performed in Hewlett-Packard's center are lead generation, inquiry management, lead qualification, lead distribution and feedback, and promotion campaign measurement and market analysis.[1]

Chapter 2 emphasized the need for a company to integrate its promotional efforts to achieve maximum effectiveness. In this chapter, we will show how integrated, targeted promotion programs such as Hewlett-Packard's assist sales reps in initiating and developing customer relationships. Marketing communication programs designed to produce faster, more economical matching of salesperson to customer are becoming commonplace.

First, we will define leads and prospects. Second, we will compare the nature of prospecting to the marketing concept to show how prospecting is (or should be)

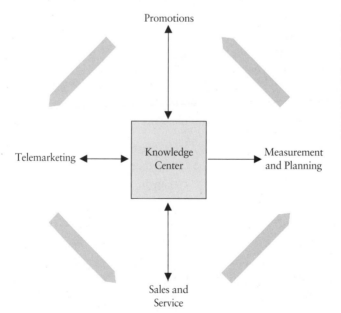

Exhibit 6-1 Sales and Marketing Closed-Loop System

Source: Karen Blue, "Closing the Loop: Hewlett-Packard's New Lead Management System," *Business Marketing* (October 1987): 74. Reprinted with permission from *Business Marketing*.

related to the target market of the salesperson's company. Third, we will describe some of the most popular methods of generating names of potential buyers. Fourth, we will explore how telemarketing can be used to determine whether a face-to-face sales call is advisable. The chapter concludes with descriptions of how sales reps should plan their approaches prior to actually meeting a prospect.

LEADS AND PROSPECTS

Leads

Prospecting is the activity involved in generating names and addresses of people or businesses that may be in the market for the salesperson's products or services. This effort, however, does not directly generate prospects. In the initial stages, prospecting does generate what are generally referred to as *sales leads*. Leads are, in a sense, the raw material that is mined from the environment(s) or markets in which the salesperson or his or her company is operating. **Sales leads** are the names of people or organizations that possess some characteristic believed to be an indicator of demand for the product or service.

Two of the most crucial steps in professional selling are (1) getting a sufficient supply of leads and (2) developing an economical method for screening or qualifying the leads so that bona fide prospects can be identified. Notice that in the previous sentence the word *prospects* is treated differently from the term *leads*. This is no minor distinction.

Prospects

When a lead has been screened or qualified (that is, judged to be worthy of the sales rep's further attention), a **prospect** has been found. Therefore, prospects are derived from leads. One writer has clarified this distinction by stating that a sales lead is a suspect (not a prospect) until the lead has been checked on or qualified. Those leads that have sufficient potential to warrant further sales efforts then become prospects (see Exhibit 6-2).

Is this a mere play on words? No indeed; not when one considers that, like many other professional people, a salesperson's time is an expensive and scarce resource. Therefore, the amount of time devoted to prospecting (securing leads and qualification of the leads) plus the accuracy in judging whether a lead is "hot or not" frequently determines whether a salesperson can reach his or her objectives.

Exhibit 6-2 Lists, Leads, and Prospects

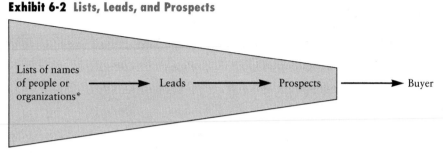

*Tradeshow attendees, residents of subdivisions, membership directories, etc.

Given the importance of prospecting, it is not surprising that some firms spend millions of dollars annually to generate leads for their sales forces and, in some cases, expend additional monies to qualify these leads. This is what Hewlett-Packard is doing in its Customer Information Center with the hope of turning over the highest quality prospects to its sales force, which usually results in increased sales force productivity.

PROSPECTING AND THE MARKETING CONCEPT

The **marketing concept**, which was created during the Marketing Era (see Chapter 1), has become an important business philosophy. Fundamentally, the marketing concept is based on the idea that, for long-range success, a firm should orient its products, prices, promotions, and distribution efforts to the needs and wants of an identified target group of customers. The number of potential customers may be in the millions for a consumer product or service or, for expensive industrial products, there may be a few dozen potential buyers. The important point is that the identification of the target market and an understanding of its buying and consumption behavior are vital to success.

The rationales underlying prospecting activity and market targeting are basically the same. The sales representative engaged in prospecting is attempting to determine on whom to call (that is, worthy targets). In Figure 6-1 the rows of people symbolize the mass market. The individual with a target on her back symbolizes the target market that might be suitable for a particular firm's products or services.

The salesperson who wants to spend his or her time efficiently wants to (1) identify those individuals or businesses that are most likely to need and want a product or service, and (2) concentrate on those "targets" or prospects.

Although there is nothing new about wanting to spend time with potential buyers who are most likely to make a purchase, an abundance of high-tech sales aids are now available to assist in identifying a "target" customer.

Figure 6-1 Prospecting is the process of determining worthy targets.

More information will be provided in this chapter about companies' efforts to assist their sales representatives in the efficient use of their time. Chapter 15, Emerging Trends and Technologies in Selling, describes how technology-based sales aids are being used to save time in prospecting as well as other sales activities.

ANSWERING THE QUESTION "WHO IS THE PROSPECT?"

Sales representatives, familiar as they are with their respective markets or territories, should not have to answer this question without assistance. The answer to "Who is the prospect?" should be one of the key elements in a firm's product, brand, or market plans.[2] The salesperson's efforts to locate consumers or businesses possessing the characteristics of a prospect should be a natural extension of the product plan or other similar plans developed by marketing.

This is not to suggest that the sales representative who finds eager buyers whose characteristics don't coincide with the company's marketing plan should not pursue the business opportunity. When sales personnel discover buyers who aren't part of a firm's target market, it may be that the planners have overlooked an important market segment.

The marketing plan must, therefore, be taken as a guide, not an infallible answer that will invariably point the sales representative to prospects. On the other hand, the sales force that ignores the market plan's descriptions of a target market is likely to waste time and energy calling on people who are not optimum prospects.

Exhibit 6-3 Key Questions for Consumer Salespeople

1. How would I describe my best customers/clients in terms of
   - economic bracket,
   - marital status,
   - children (number, if any, and their age groups),
   - occupations, education, hobbies, homeownership,
   - club or organization membership,
   - addresses?
2. How did I first make the acquaintance of my 20 best customers?
3. Who are some of my other customers whom I *don't* consider to be my best customers? How did I meet them?
4. Using the criteria in Question 1, what are the major differences between my best customers and those I have just identified in Question 3?

Unfortunately, not all companies have a detailed marketing plan. In other cases, the salespeople do not have access to the plan. When those situations arise, the sales rep must create his or her own target customer profile. Exhibit 6-3 provides a list of useful questions for targeting prospects for a consumer product or service.

After analyzing the existing customer group an insightful salesperson will have a fairly accurate answer to the question "Who is the prospect?" The reason for analyzing *both* the "best customer" and "not so good" group is that usually some worthwhile distinctions will start to emerge. These differences, when noted, can be useful guides for the salesperson as he or she searches for new prospects.

The industrial salesperson is, of course, in no less need of answering the question about who his or her prospects are. Exhibit 6-4 offers a series of questions to guide an analysis which would be relevant to the industrial sales rep.

Customer profiles need not be cumbersome things to create and store. A growing number of relatively inexpensive software packages are now on the market which can be used in a variety of ways to help salespeople. The following list of software packages are a few examples:

Advanced Micro Link Systems, Inc.
DOMINO
Sales lead tracking and management with call back reminders, scripting, note pad, mail merge, literature fulfillment, and shipping/order entry. Over 20 customizable fields, optional SQL and query report writer available. 1989; IBM/compatible; DOS/NOVELL; 512K; Multiple User; $299.

Exhibit 6-4 Key Questions for Industrial Salespeople

1. How would I describe my best customers in terms of
   - the products or services they produce and sell,
   - their location(s),
   - the size of their workforce,
   - the way they use my product or service in their operation,
   - the way they purchase from me — is it from a centralized purchasing office or are they decentralized?
2. For each of the individual customers I have identified in Question 1, how did I first become aware of the possibility of selling to them?
3. What is the average number of different products I am selling to these customers?
4. If I am selling several items in my product line to each of these customers, what product item did they purchase first?
5. Who are some of my other customers whom I *don't* consider to be my best customers?
6. Using the criteria in Question 1, what are the major differences between my best customers and those I have just identified in Question 5?

Dynamic Software
GSAM (General Sales Activity Manager)

A lead tracking and contact management program that allows users to track sales leads and manage all sales activity contacts. New release; IBM/compatible; MS-DOS 3.1 or higher; 640K w/HD; Multiple User; $395.

Commercial Micro, Inc.
SCEO Sales

Client/prospect tracking, event/media tracking, tickler, appointment, purchase, forecasting, scripts, custom files, import/export, on-line instant and batch letters, labels, envelopes, instant on-line reporting, single key operation, multi-file/salesmen, optional dialer hardware. Multiple-user signer profiles, brilliant color, windows, graphics. 1982; IBM/compatible; LAN; MS-DOS; 640K; Multiple User; $395.

InterActive Micro, Inc.
The Front Office

A marketing and sales productivity system for lead tracking, call reporting, telemarketing, sales follow-up, sales performance, sales orders, job costing, salesman commissions, forecasting. 1984; IBM/compatible; MS-DOS; 640K; Multiple User; $295.

GENERATING NAMES AND LOCATIONS OF SALES LEADS

Sales management, when contemplating how to generate leads, should ask two questions: (1) How do we want our salespeople to spend their time? and (2) Can systems be developed to produce high quality sales leads at less expense than using field sales personnel?

To answer the first question, management usually wants its salespeople to spend as much time as possible performing revenue-producing activities. Chapter 1 revealed that, in most cases, there is a need for improved efficiency here. Reducing paperwork and managing time and territory better (see Chapter 14) are two common goals for improving a salesperson's efficiency.

Increasingly, firms such as Hewlett-Packard are answering the second question by turning to technology. A study of 160 U.S. companies revealed that many are using computerized systems to help sales staffs select more promising prospects and develop useful information about their needs and requirements.[3] Notwithstanding the increased reliance on high-tech systems, there is still a place for the individual salesperson's efforts to generate names and other information concerning leads. In the next section, we will describe some of the main methods employed by sales representatives as they generate their own leads. Then we will discuss company-sponsored efforts directed at lead generation.

INDIVIDUAL SALESPERSON'S EFFORTS

Textbooks written ten or more years ago featured long lists of ways in which salespeople generated leads. Some sales reps are still responsible for the entire spectrum of sales activity from sales lead generation through closing and follow-up on postsale activities. The frequency of this, however, is diminishing. The reason is traceable to the realization that sales personnel's time is very expensive. Therefore, whenever possible, the rep should be producing revenue. Notwithstanding the fact that more companies are generating and then qualifying those leads for their sales forces, there are occasions, several of which will be covered in this section, in which an alert sales rep can obtain sales leads without relying on the company.

Present Customers

Present customers can usually identify several other people who could, in their opinion, use the same product or service. These names can often be excellent leads, because the current customer has talked to the person about the product and has expressed satisfaction. Favorable word-of-mouth advertising establishes a positive image that can increase the probability of a sale. This prospecting system is sometimes called the **endless chain**.[4] Supplied with new leads, the sales representative contacts them, eventually sells to one or more of them, and then gets names from them—hence the chain continues. This method works well when it is important for the sales representative to quickly establish legitimacy and credibility with a prospective purchaser. Even if the person has never heard of the sales representative's company, the sales representative may still get a hearing by using the name of a friend or relative. The endless chain approach is used frequently in the sale of consumer goods or services.

Len D'Innocenzo, author and consultant, offers some sound advice to sales reps who have been selling to medium- or large-sized departmentalized organizations. He recommends that salespeople think of their contacts in one department as *internal advocates* who can be valuable allies in meeting people in other departments of the organization.[5] This situation can greatly facilitate the creation of a penetration buyer-seller life cycle (depicted in Exhibit 3-3). By skillfully using internal advocates in one or more departments or divisions, a sales rep can gain entry to other potential areas of the organization.

Influential People

Research has revealed that people consistently look to a trusted source who, at least for certain types of products or services, is considered an expert. For example, one person in an office might have established a reputation for extensive knowledge about stereo equipment. Others in the office, when contemplating the purchase of a stereo system, would probably seek that individual's advice. This situation is sometimes called the **center of influence method**, and the sales representative attempts to cultivate the person who is considered an expert in that field of consumption. Another example is the sale of athletic shoes. Many successful college coaches have contracts with the manufacturers of athletic shoes such as Nike, Adidas, Pony, and Converse. A sales rep who can persuade a coach to outfit a team in shoes seen on television and by fans in a stadium is performing a valuable feat. Other college and high-school coaches (and individual consumers) are apt to buy a particular shoe as a result of an "expert's" adoption of it. Nike believes Michael Jordan's endorsement was worth several million dollars!

Two questions should be addressed here: (1) In what circumstances do experts or well-known persons' endorsements have the most influence? and (2) How does the sales rep find the relevant expert and, hopefully, get his or her endorsement?

Figure 6-2 An influential person's endorsement of a product can be worth millions.

The answer to the first question depends on the nature and complexity of the product or service being sold. If the average buyer cannot inspect a product and reach a conclusion about it, then other trusted sources of information can be used. Twenty-five years ago, sneakers were generally regarded as similar in quality. Today, the scene is vastly different. Each manufacturer has a particular characteristic it is touting. The buyer looks to a respected source of information to help solve the purchase dilemma.

In addition to potential buyers' inability to inspect a product and judge it, other conditions make an expert's opinion valuable to a buyer. One of these conditions is if the product will be displayed where many of the owner's friends and acquaintances will see it (termed conspicuous consumption). Another condition is the expenditure of a significant amount of money that forces the buyer to live with his or her decision for a lengthy period.

How do you find experts or influential people if you are a sales rep? The officers of clubs, trade associations, and fraternal organizations, who have usually been elected by their members, have earned the respect of the members. Thus, it usually would be worthwhile for a sales rep to cultivate these influential people. The identities of people who are being elected to officer positions or who are being promoted into key jobs can be acquired by scanning the business and society sections of most newspapers. Trade association newsletters also give space to such matters. By obtaining a membership in the American Telemarketing Association, salespeople who, for example, sell telemarketing equipment or services can acquire newsletters that keep them posted on customers' or potential customers' job promotions or changes.

Networking

Networking has become a popular word. People are frequently advised to network to solve a host of problems. Executives searching for employment, people needing emotional support because of divorce or loss of a spouse, and newcomers to a community are some situations in which networking is recommended. **Networking** involves using one's contacts with other people to achieve a particular goal. People involved in a network often are persons who have experienced the problem themselves and can thus appreciate the challenges confronting the individual. Others comprise a network of people whose contacts allow them to, collectively, have a wider circle of acquaintances than any one individual could.

This latter group is, of course, very important to a sales rep. By participating in a network of people willing to share names and information about other people, a salesperson can expand the number of leads. Some firms pay the membership dues to country clubs for their salespeople to provide them with a desirable place to take clients or customers. A less obvious but no less useful reason is to engage in networking. A professional salesperson will, while participating with other club members, develop friendships with a wide range of people. During the social interaction, names and information about people or organizations that may be prospects will be exchanged. When done discreetly and effectively, networking is not unethical or in poor taste. Each one of us, whether we realize it or not, is involved in several networks (friends, workplace associates, clubs, classes, and so on). Salespeople consciously develop a number of networks (alumni associations, professional associations), which can provide them with names of potential customers or clients. Of course, participating in a network is not a one-way street. The sales rep must provide input to the network by sharing information that will be useful to other network members. Good judgment and a great deal of professional discretion are required. In Chapter 3, we described various types of relationships. One of the points we emphasized about the counselor relationship was the critical need for trust between the salesperson and the client or customer. Given this need, the salesperson must be very careful about sharing information concerning clients with other sales reps.

Networking is an art which takes time, patience, and some insight into what one is attempting to accomplish. The skillful networker understands that just meeting a lot of people is not sufficient. It's not so much how many people you know, but *whom you know* that is important.

The skillful network builder will seize upon appropriate opportunities to expand and strengthen a network of friends and business associates. One prime opportunity to network is provided by parties. An individual who knows how to "work" a party can come away from such occasions with sales leads and/or referrals which can be turned into leads. Exhibit 6-5 contains some guidelines that can enhance your skill in making the most of a social occasion.

In the prospecting methods described so far, the sales rep is presumed to conduct all or the majority of the prospecting activity. One of the natural consequences

---

Exhibit 6-5 Seven Deadly Sins of Party Working

1. Don't have any goals. An efficient networker will have at least one or two people in mind that he or she wants to meet. If possible, the salesperson will have arranged to have someone make the introductions.

2. Stay with someone you know throughout the party. This may be the most comfortable thing to do if you are shy but it isn't profitable.

3. Find a corner of the room and stay there. Adroit party workers suggest positioning oneself just to the left of the door inside the room. The reason is that people tend to drift to their left as they enter a room when a social function is underway.

4. Don't approach your targeted contact unless you have another person there to introduce you to that contact. If you don't have anyone to help you, don't waste the occasion. Position yourself close to your contact, wait for a break in a conversation, and then introduce yourself.

5. As soon as you meet someone, start eyeing other people to spot your next contact. This lack of attentiveness is a real "turn-off." Give the person with whom you are conversing your undivided attention and then, when it is appropriate, move on.

6. Keep working until the last guest has left. Know when to leave. You don't have to be the first person to leave, but you shouldn't be the last to leave.

7. Don't worry about following up—it was only "party talk." If you indicated you would send an article or report to someone you met, be sure to do it. Your credibility is just as much at risk in these circumstances as it is if you are making commitments to someone in an office visit.

Source: Adapted from David Dworski, "Social Selling," *Sales & Marketing Management*, December 1990, 41.

of a sale and the subsequent contacts with a satisfied customer is the collection of names and information about other possible buyers. This is time-consuming, even when successful. Also, there are obvious limits to networks. When a salesperson "runs dry," it presents serious problems. As a result of these limitations, as well as the benefits derived from using expensive salespersons to spend more time with customers, more companies are turning to a variety of methods to stimulate and qualify sales leads. The next section will describe what companies are doing to support their salespeople in lead stimulation and qualification.

COMPANY EFFORTS TO SUPPORT FIELD STAFFS

In this and previous chapters, points have been made about the cost of making sales calls and the number of calls it takes, in many cases, to actually make a sale. Realizing there is a serious erosion of profits as sales call costs escalate, more businesses are asking what can be done to use the salesperson more efficiently. Circumstances are forcing companies to analyze their marketing communications programs to determine ways to cope with the problem of rising personal sales costs. In general, the solutions have been to substitute other methods of generating and qualifying leads. The more frequently used methods of generating leads are direct mail, media advertising, directories, and trade shows.

Computer Specialists, Inc., a $5 million computer-service company in Monroeville, Pa., makes it profitable for all of its employees to be concerned about leads for its sales force. If an employee passes on a name that eventually becomes a customer, the employee may receive a bonus of as much as $1,000, depending on the size of the sale to the customer. The president of Computer Specialists, Inc., stated, "We can't afford to have 50 salespeople scouting around for new business. This way, everybody who works here is a salesperson."[6]

Direct Mail

Direct mail is letters, cards, and advertisements sent directly to potential customers.[7] Ryder Truck Rental is an example of a firm with a regionalized approach to its direct mail program; it uses twenty-one direct mail pieces—one for each sales district.[8]

Exhibit 6-6 is another example of a direct mail piece: a card mailed to homeowners around the 2222 Purple Plum Lane address. The rationale was that homeowners who might be thinking about selling their homes would, on seeing the salesperson's success in selling the Purple Plum home, contact the sales rep or the

Exhibit 6-6   Direct Mail Piece to Solicit Business for a Realtor

> *BMS Realty*
> *12345 El Camino Real, #201*
> *Houston, Texas 77058*
> *Office: (713) 555-1900*
> *Res: (713) 555-7039*
>
> We just sold another home in your area at
>
> 2222 PURPLE PLUM LANE   .
>
> We also have other buyers interested in your
> neighborhood. If you would like a market analysis of
> your property, please give me a call. I would be
> happy to show you what your home is worth now.*
>
> *If your property is currently listed, disregard this solicitation.
>
> *Bob M. Smith*
> *Certified Marketing Specialist*

rep's agency identified in the direct mail piece. This form of direct mail would probably be noticed by more people than the word "sold" added to the realtor's sign on the front lawn.

Frequently, the direct mail piece gives a toll-free telephone number for the recipient to call to express interest in the product or service. When the caller inquires about the product or service advertised in the direct mail piece, the person answering the call collects some information to determine whether a visit by a sales rep is justified. More detail about how this is actually done will be provided later in this chapter under Sales Lead Qualification.

Media Advertising

McGraw-Hill, publisher of a wide range of general business and specialized industrial periodicals, conducts extensive research on the various ways and costs of contacting potential customers. It estimates that the cost of getting someone to see an ad in a business publication averages nineteen cents per reader.[9]

One of the most frequently used forms of lead stimulation is the **bingo card** or reader service card (see Exhibit 6-7). The reader is asked to circle a number that has been assigned to a particular advertiser whose ad appears on another page in that issue. With the bingo card in Exhibit 6-7, the reader can obtain information

Exhibit 6-7 Reader Service Card

FREE INFORMATION FOR READERS OF BUSINESS WEEK!

The advertisers listed here are making information available, with their compliments, to readers of Business Week. For type of information available, see categories below. To obtain information, see adjoining page.

Annual Reports

1. Anritsu Corporation
2. Komatsu Ltd.

Financial Products and Services Information

3. Continental Illinois
4. Fred S. James & Co., Inc.

Products/Services Information

5. Allied-Signal Inc.
6. American Gas Association
7. Andersen Corporation—Andersen Windows
8. Avis Rent A Car Systems, Inc.
9. Belgium Tourist Office
10. Budget Rent-a-Car
11. CSX Transportation
12. Canon Faxphone 10
13. Canon Typewriters
14. CAST
15. Cricketeer Clothing
16. Dale Carnegie & Associates, Inc.
17. Dictaphone's Connexions™ Voice Processing systems
18. Embassy Suites
19. Freightliner Trucks
20. General Electric Mobile Communications
21. Gould Inc.
22. Hammermill Papers Group
23. Hewlett-Packard
24. Hilton International Kensington
25. Industrial Development & Investment Center
26. International Conference Center Vienna
27. Fred S. James & Co., Inc.
28. Konica's Royal Copiers
29. Mitsubishi Motor Sales of America
30. NCR Tower General Purpose Systems
31. Nikko Hotels International (Hotel Beijing Toronto)
32. Northwestern National Life Insurance
33. Pitney Bowes Facsimile
34. Qume
35. Radio Shack
36. Standard Register
37. Steelcase Incorporated
38. Texaco Industrial Lubricants
39. Toshiba America, Inc.—Facsimile Products Group
40. Toshiba America, Inc.—Information Systems Division
41. UNISYS
42. Wausau Insurance Companies
43. Western Union Telegraph Co.

Area Development Information

44. Cincinnati Gas & Electric
45. Greater Raleigh Chamber of Commerce
46. Louisianna Dept. of Commerce
47. Michigan Department of Commerce Office of Economic Development

---

FREE INFORMATION FOR READERS OF BUSINESS WEEK!

Business Week has made it possible for you to send for further information simply by filling out one of the cards below. There is no charge for this service. *Please note:* Only those requests which have been *completely filled out,* including company name, will be honored.

The advertisers listed on the adjoining page are waiting to hear from you.

Do not use the card for change of address.
Please write to: Business Week, P.O. Box 430, Hightstown, N.J. 08520.

Please type or print (in ink) all information. Allow sufficient time for processing your requests. Note expiration date. Cards received after this date cannot be processed.

BusinessWeek

This card must be received by July 31

For more information about annual reports, financial products and services, products/services or area development, consult the page adjoining this card and circle the corresponding numbers below. There is no charge for this service. Please only circle items for which you have specific interest.

1	2	3	4	5	6	7	8	9	10
11	12	13	14	15	16	17	18	19	20
21	22	23	24	25	26	27	28	29	30
31	32	33	34	35	36	37	38	39	40
41	42	43	44	45	46	47			

PLEASE CHECK ONE ITEM FOR EACH CATEGORY:

1. Are you currently a Business Week subscriber?:
   A ☐ Yes B ☐ No
2. Type of firm:
   1 ☐ Agriculture 2 ☐ Mining, Construction 3 ☐ Manufacturing, Processing
   4 ☐ Wholesale, Retail Trade 5 ☐ Finance, Insurance, Real Estate
   6 ☐ Government 7 ☐ Transportation, Public Utilities 8 ☐ Service Industries
   9 ☐ Other (Please Fill In)
3. Title:
   A ☐ Chairman of the Board B ☐ President C ☐ Vice President
   D ☐ Treasurer, Secretary E ☐ General Manager F ☐ Division Manager
   G ☐ Department Manager H ☐ Other Manager
   I ☐ Other (Please Fill In)
4. Number of employees in your company worldwide:
   1 ☐ Under 100 2 ☐ 100-2,499 3 ☐ 1,000-2,499
   4 ☐ 2,500 to 4,999 5 ☐ 5,000 to 9,999 6 ☐ 10,000 or more

Name _____
Company _____
Address _____
City _____
State _____ Zip _____
Telephone AREA CODE _____ NUMBER _____ EXTENSION _____

BusinessWeek

This card must be received by July 31

For more information about annual reports, financial products and services, products/services or area development, consult the page adjoining this card and circle the corresponding numbers below. There is no charge for this service. Please only circle items for which you have specific interest.

1	2	3	4	5	6	7	8	9	10
11	12	13	14	15	16	17	18	19	20
21	22	23	24	25	26	27	28	29	30
31	32	33	34	35	36	37	38	39	40
41	42	43	44	45	46	47			

PLEASE CHECK ONE ITEM FOR EACH CATEGORY:

1. Are you currently a Business Week subscriber?:
   A ☐ Yes B ☐ No
2. Type of firm:
   1 ☐ Agriculture 2 ☐ Mining, Construction 3 ☐ Manufacturing, Processing
   4 ☐ Wholesale, Retail Trade 5 ☐ Finance, Insurance, Real Estate
   6 ☐ Government 7 ☐ Transportation, Public Utilities 8 ☐ Service Industries
   9 ☐ Other (Please Fill In)
3. Title:
   A ☐ Chairman of the Board B ☐ President C ☐ Vice President
   D ☐ Treasurer, Secretary E ☐ General Manager F ☐ Division Manager
   G ☐ Department Manager H ☐ Other Manager
   I ☐ Other (Please Fill In)
4. Number of employees in your company worldwide:
   1 ☐ Under 100 2 ☐ 100-2,499 3 ☐ 1,000-2,499
   4 ☐ 2,500 to 4,999 5 ☐ 5,000 to 9,999 6 ☐ 10,000 or more

Name _____
Company _____
Address _____
City _____
State _____ Zip _____
Telephone AREA CODE _____ NUMBER _____ EXTENSION _____

about Hewlett-Packard by circling number 23. The inquiry by the reader is a sales lead insofar as Hewlett-Packard is concerned. Individuals send in the bingo cards to *Business Week,* which then turns the leads over to the Hewlett-Packard Company. Persons inquiring about Hewlett-Packard will be contacted by the company's Customer Information Center to determine the inquirer's specific interests and whether or not a salesperson should make a face-to-face call.

Respondents to a *Business Marketing* survey indicated that publication reader service or bingo cards generated more leads than any other advertising method. The survey further revealed that companies using magazine advertising viewed it as the primary source of their leads, followed in efficiency by direct mail pieces.[10]

A large number of ads now feature an 800 number for readers to call rather than sending a bingo card or some other printed inquiry (see Exhibit 6-8). This, of course, saves the time of all concerned. The prospective customer can initiate an inquiry and by talking to someone, get additional information beyond what was contained in the advertisement. At the same time, the recipient of the call can collect information from the caller and determine whether or not a personal sales visit is warranted.

Directories

There are two major types of directories: subject-oriented and general industrial.[11] An example of a **subject-oriented directory** is the *Buyer's Guide* published annually by *Telemarketing* magazine. Readers and subscribers to *Telemarketing* are usually people who are in the market for telemarketing equipment and services. By looking in the *Buyer's Guide* and contacting a vendor listed in the guide, the inquirer can obtain information in a fast, convenient manner while the vendor obtains a lead that will possibly materialize into a sale.

An example of a **general industrial directory**, which is much broader in scope, is *Thomas Register of American Manufacturers.* Approximately 60,000 manufacturers are listed in this publication and prospective purchasers can easily find the information to expedite their search for a supplier.

Perhaps the broadest-scoped directory is the Yellow Pages. Among all of the more glamorous and dramatic forms of marketing communications, this medium has been called the "plumbing" in the architectural structure of marketing communications. It is the fifth-largest advertising medium with ad revenue of $4.6 billion annually.[12]

The Yellow Pages are becoming computerized and have the potential to help salespeople find sales leads more rapidly than ever before. American Business

These aren't vacation snapshots to pass around. These color pictures from Kodak mean business. They are, in fact, digitized images transmitted quickly and accurately over ordinary phone lines from one Kodak SV9600 still video transceiver to another, displayed within seconds on a monitor, with quality prints made by a Kodak SV6500 color video printer.

The transceiver and printer are members of a family of new Kodak products that capture, store, display, and transmit high-quality still video images in continuous-tone color.

Individually, linked together, or integrated into existing communications and imaging systems, they can enhance the efficiency of image handling in the workplace.

For more information about Kodak still video products and the name of a dealer who can arrange a demonstration, call **1 800 44KODAK (1 800 445-6325), Ext 110.** Or, send the coupon below.

Imaging Innovations For The Workplace.

Exhibit 6-8 Advertisement with a Toll-Free Number

Reprinted courtesy of Eastman Kodak Company.

NOW, TELEPHONE FOR THE LATEST PICTURES FROM KODAK

The new vision of Kodak

Send me information on the products I have checked.

☐ *KODAK SV9600 Still Video Transceiver*
☐ *KODAK SV7500 Still Video Multidisk Recorder*
☐ *KODAK SV7400 Still Video Recorder*
☐ *KODAK SV6500 Color Video Printer*
☐ *KODAK SV5035 Slide/Video Transfer Unit*
☐ *KODAK SV5000 Video Transfer Stand*
☐ *KODAK SV1300 Color Monitor*

Eastman Kodak Company
Dept 412-L
Rochester, NY 14650

☐ *Please have a sales representative contact me.*

Name _____ *Title* _____

Organization _____

Nature of Business _____

Address _____ *Phone No.* (____) _____

City _____ *State* _____ *ZIP* _____

Lists, Inc., (ABL) in Omaha, Nebraska, recently introduced Instant Yellow Page Service, which allows on-line access to a data base of more than 6 million U.S. businesses.[13] This service permits a salesperson to determine, for example, how many doctors are in Ames, Iowa, or the names, addresses, and phone numbers of all office supply stores in Clear Lake City, Texas.

The advantages of Yellow Page directories are:

1. Leads are available in a compact, easy-to-handle package.

2. Almost every business, organization, and professional in a given location is listed with phone numbers.

3. The leads are relatively inexpensive.

The disadvantages are:

1. The categories are broad, and some entries are listed twice.
2. The names may be poorly qualified, and a high call-per-sale ratio may result.

Business directories listing businesses alphabetically, geographically, by market segment, or all three are published for most major industries. City directories list consumers and businesses in a given city. They are usually ordered alphabetically by street names; each entry on a given street is listed by street number.

The advantages of using city directories to generate sales leads are:

1. Leads are inexpensive per name.
2. Detailed information is often provided on each listed business or organization.
3. Some directories, because their distribution is more limited than telephone books, will have phone numbers that are unlisted elsewhere.

The major disadvantage is that many directories are updated rather infrequently and may be several years old.

Figure 6-3 Trade shows offer salespersons valuable opportunities to identify leads.

Trade Shows

A **trade show** is an industry convention where manufacturers, resellers, and sometimes consumers meet to discuss, study, and observe industry trends.[14] The primary purpose of trade shows is not necessarily to book orders, but to identify leads.[15]

Trade shows, if managed properly, can be a cost-effective means of generating new business leads. One estimate of costs associated with reaching prospects puts the figure at approximately $90 per lead,[16] which is less than half the cost of a personal sales call.

The trade show atmosphere demands that people representing a firm's products to visitors be well organized. Mr. Joe Nedder, Field Communication Manager for Wright Line, Inc., manufacturers of office furniture, states, "Within fifteen minutes you have to qualify the customer, give a product demo, and make arrangements for follow-up."[17]

One device to assist the people working at a trade show is a lead card or form (see Exhibit 6-9). This permits the exhibitor's representative to capture the necessary information while carrying on a conversation with an exhibit visitor. The lead card should be divided into two sections—one for at-show data and the other for postshow data.

At-show data begin with the contact's name, the date, and information on the contact's company or organization. The salesperson lists the product or service the visitor is inquiring about and the application(s) to which the product or service would be put. It is also important to know what product or service the trade show contact is now using and any information about it that the person will provide. After this, the buying time frame is noted (buying now, in one to three months, and so on). Also important are the names and titles of other people in the prospective buyer's organization who may be involved in the purchase decision.

The other side of the card is devoted to follow-up information gathered in the postshow period. It's important that contacts made at the trade show be reached as soon as possible after the show has ended.

Sales Lead Qualification

The cost of generating leads, in whatever manner, requires that considerable thought and effort be expended in following up on the leads to qualify them. Robert Hood, General Manager at CUSTOMTEL in Minneapolis, categorizes sales leads as follows:

1. *Hot lead.* Intends to buy within three months

2. *Warm lead.* Intends to buy in three to twelve months

Exhibit 6-9 Trade Show Lead Card, XYZ Trade Show, July 12–14, 1993

At-Show Data

Contact Name _____

Date _____

Company _____

Division _____

Address _____

City, State_____ Zip_____

Telephone (_____)_____

Product Interest

A _____

B _____

Application _____

_____

Product Now Using_____

Comments _____

Buying Time Frame _____

Budget Allocated_____

Other Buying Influences

Name _____

Title _____

Name _____

Title _____

Requests Personal Call_____

Requests Literature_____

Post-Show Data

Mail Date _____

Enclosures _____

Telephone Date _____

Comments _____

_____

Field Sales Visit Date _____

Sales Rep's Name _____

Comments _____

_____

_____

_____

Outcome Report

_____

_____

_____

_____

_____

_____

_____

_____

_____

_____

3. *Long-term potential.* No purchase intent in the next twelve months, but is a definite prospect

4. *No potential.* Has no application for the product or is not a decision maker or influencer

5. *Unusable.* Not a business, no longer in business, etc.[18]

Obviously, sales reps want as many hot leads as possible. These leads are also sometimes referred to as **tight leads**. The less-likely-to-buy leads are **loose leads**.

Hewlett-Packard provides its sales reps with hot leads through its Customer Information Center. Another well-known company that is using telemarketing in qualifying leads is 3M in St. Paul, Minnesota. The company's system takes the qualification burden off its distributors and direct salespeople, who previously received unqualified leads.[19]

An increasing number of firms are either conducting lead qualification through their telemarketing group or encouraging their salespeople to qualify their leads over the telephone.[20] An example of the extent to which telemarketing enhances sales force productivity can be seen when one analyzes an advertising campaign that generates 1,000 leads. If the leads were sent directly to the sales force, it would take the equivalent of twenty-five weeks to call on all the leads (assuming five to eight customer calls per day as the norm for one salesperson's efforts).

A telemarketing sales support person can call fifty contacts per day, thereby covering the 1,000 leads in the equivalent of twenty person-days of work. The advantages are that the leads have been qualified faster while prospective customer interest was higher, and, of course, the telephone contact is much more economical ($10 to $15 per contact) compared to a face-to-face contact, which may cost more than $200.

The qualified leads are then sent to the sales force. Sales representatives are much more likely to pursue the qualified leads because of the higher quality of the lead. Transamerica Insurance Group, a major writer of property and casualty coverages, is another company providing its independent agents with this support.[21]

Earlier we mentioned that not all salespeople have their company's assistance in generating and qualifying sales leads. In situations where the sales rep must do this himself or herself, it is important for the rep to conserve time and energy while producing a steady stream of prospects. Joseph Stumpf, an expert on the use of the telephone for prospecting, advocates the following six steps to gain prospects:

1. *Punch the dial.* By this he means to set a goal of a certain number of calls to make daily. After setting the goal, let no other activities sidetrack you from meeting the goal. Stumpf cites the example of a rep making a six-figure income selling com-

puter training products who makes at least 100 call attempts per day. The rep states, "I take care of the call attempts and the call attempts take care of sales."

2. *Develop a list of good prospects.* Stumpf's position is that it is important to get a list of names to call that is not the same list your competitors have. One way to do this is ask yourself the question, "What other product or service might a prospect have purchased *prior to* becoming interested in my product?" For instance, we would expect a new car buyer to be interested in shopping around for the best car insurance after purchasing a new car. Lists of new car registrations can be obtained by the sales rep. From such lists, the sales rep makes prospecting calls.

3. *Concentrate on the first ten seconds of the call.* Try to sound like you know the people you call and cause them to search their minds to remember who you are. By doing this, the recipient of the call tends to keep an open mind and to listen to you. Otherwise, the tendency is for the prospect to say, at least mentally, "I'm being contacted by someone who wants to sell me something. I must be on guard against this."

4. *Ask smart questions.* The following three very important questions must be posed if an effective sales lead generation and qualification call campaign is to be conducted:

   - Are the prospects interested in finding out more about your product or service?
   - When would they like to take some action?
   - If they have previously purchased the product or service, what did they look for in the brands they considered? What were the criteria they used?

5. *Try to build rapport.* Rapport-building can be enhanced by trying to become a mirror image of the person to whom you are talking. This is one of the cornerstones of neurolinguistic programming (NLP). According to NLP theory, rapport is more likely to be developed with someone when the rhythm, tone, and volume of the conversation between the two communicating parties are the same.

6. *Use a script.* "In my company," states Stumpf, "as we studied the high achievers in telephone sales, we consistently noted that the use of written scripts played an integral part in their overall success."[22]

Scripting for telephone selling should follow several basic guidelines. Although the guidelines are simple, any script that does not follow them is likely to sound artificial. Scripts should be based on the spoken, not the written word. In other words, write like people talk. Also, never develop a script in which you talk for more than thirty seconds without asking a question. In addition, a good script seeks to get a definite commitment. When a sales rep uses the phone to generate prospects, the commitment (if the rep has determined that it is appropriate) will be to set up an appointment for a face-to-face visit.

Regardless of how or who performs the prospecting activity, the salesperson will emerge with a list of prospects. These are the consumers or businesses that the rep has judged to be worth a face-to-face sales call. If the prospect was generated from a trade show, the per-prospect cost may have been approximately $100 to the trade show exhibitor. If the prospect saw an ad in *Business Week*, called a toll-free 800 number, and talked to someone in a telemarketing center, the cost to the firm for that prospect may have been $10 to $15. The time has arrived, however, for the sales rep to prepare to meet the prospect. In most cases, if the rep does not capture the attention and stimulate the prospect's interest in this first meeting, there will not be a second opportunity. The cost of generating and qualifying the prospect will have been wasted. The professional salesperson, knowing this, will work diligently on this next step of the sales process.

PREVISIT PREPARATION

The adage "You never get another chance to make a first impression" is very appropriate in the world of professional sales. The sales representative who is content to consistently "wing it" will soon find that most prospects have little tolerance for unprepared salespeople.

The question that looms after the salesperson acknowledges a need to prepare is "Where can I get information that will permit me to be prepared?" The five sources of information are customer files; trade papers, journals, and newspapers; credit reports; annual reports; and other sales representatives.

Customer Files

One of the most obvious ways to prepare to meet a new prospect is to determine whether the prospect has ever purchased from the company before. If so, what were the circumstances? Did the former customer switch to a competitor and, if so, how long ago was this? Were there any credit problems associated with the previous relationship? These are just a few of the areas that, when checked prior to approaching the prospect, can save the salesperson and the customer embarrassment.

Trade Papers, Journals, and Newspapers

Some companies have information resource centers staffed with personnel who can conduct a library search for data pertaining to a prospective customer. Their search may uncover information about key figures in a buyer's organization, competitive circumstances confronting the buyer, or new products or services that may cause the prospect to become interested in the sales representative's offerings.

Knowing a firm is confronted with price competition from foreign manufacturers may permit a sales representative to tailor the approach so that the purchasing agent becomes immediately interested in the sales presentation. This pre-approach "intelligence" work can pay dividends and alert the prospect to the knowledgeable attention this salesperson can provide in the future.

Credit Reports

Knowing the creditworthiness of a prospect is very important in the sale of many big-ticket products. By understanding how a person or business has handled previous financial obligations, the sales representative can make some plans on what products might best fit the prospect's budget and what financial arrangements would be most acceptable to the prospect. It is recommended that you consult with your credit manager *before* contacting a prospective customer (see Exhibit 6-10).

Annual Reports

Information contained in annual reports can identify new strategic directions, new markets, new types of products, and other significant changes in a company. Usually a firm attempts to project its most favorable image in its annual reports, and an alert salesperson can determine where the most significant developments are occurring in a firm.

A more detailed and perhaps more useful annual report is a Form 10-K. This report must be filed with the Securities and Exchange Commission within ninety days of the end of a company's fiscal year. The major advantage of using a 10-K report is its more detailed description of the firm's business that is contained in Item 1. The annual report to stockholders is a summary for the investors and does

> "If I stick my neck out too far,
> we lose money. If I'm too cautious,
> we lose customers.

> "Some people think managing
> credit is a thankless situation.
> "I disagree. The tougher the game,
> the better it feels when you win."

In the delicate balance of risk and reward, credit managers live where it's liveliest. In the middle.

They must be careful, but not cowardly. Be risk-takers, but not gamblers. Which means, to keep their footing, they need information that's equally well-balanced.

And they get it from Dun & Bradstreet. We not only have more information than anyone else, we get it from more kinds of sources. As a result, our reports offer a depth that makes credit decisions more realistic.

The fact is, more credit managers rely on D&B than any other source. They make tough decisions every day. But deciding where to go for information isn't one of them.

To put D&B to work for you, call us at 1-800-234-DUNS.

Dun & Bradstreet
The fine art of managing risk.

Dun & Bradstreet Business Credit Services
A company of The Dun & Bradstreet Corporation

Exhibit 6-10 Knowing the creditworthiness of a prospect lets the salesperson gauge what products and financial arrangements best fit a prospect's budget.

not generally present a lengthy discussion of the firm's business.[23] All companies required to register with the SEC must provide 10-K reports.

Other Sales Representatives

Perhaps the most useful intelligence sources are the peers of the sales representative who is preparing for the contact. In firms where the sales force is organized along product lines, a salesperson specializing in one product line may have peers who are also calling on the same customer. In many cases, their contacts in a company will be different, but they still can exchange useful information. Details on billing requirements and purchase limitations for certain levels of managers are examples of the areas where salespeople from the same company can help each other understand and prepare to function in a customer's environment. An exchange of information between salespersons who have contacted people in a customer's purchasing department may accelerate a new salesperson's knowledge of how to penetrate a prospective buyer's purchasing department.

Planning the Who, What, and Where of the Approach

Armed with information, the sales representative can now proceed to plan the actual approach. The salesperson should consider three key questions as plans are established:

1. What is the objective of this first meeting?
2. Who should participate in the approach meeting?
3. Where should the approach meeting occur?

The Objectives

The objectives largely depend on the type of relationship the salesperson perceives to be desirable. We described the three types of relationships—counselor, supplier, and systems designer—in Chapter 3. The counselor relationship is based on the customer's perception of the salesperson's expertise and his or her confidence in the credibility and trustworthiness of the representative. Given this, the objective of the first meeting could be to learn as much as possible about what the prospect's objectives or goals are as they relate to the product or service the salesperson is representing. In addition, the salesperson also probably wants to learn as much as possible about the prospect's background to determine the prospect's readiness to accept counseling. An example is the sales representative for an investment firm who wants to know about the investment philosophy of a prospective client. Is the client conservative or more interested in reaping the rewards associated with riskier investments? The investment program ultimately offered would depend on the client's tendencies plus, of course, other considerations such as financial resources.

The objectives for the first meeting in a supplier relationship could be to discover three things: (1) Who is supplying the prospect's needs now? (2) What are the criteria the purchaser uses for analyzing a supplier—from a fairly formal system to an extremely subjective one—and how are those weighted? (3) How satisfied is the purchaser now with the present supplier and how vulnerable is that relationship to a new vendor-customer relationship?[24]

The objectives in the first meeting in a potential systems designer relationship are to discover what (if any) system is presently being used and who is the user group. Because this particular relationship is usually more complex than the others, the sales representative is more likely to be dealing with the buying center.[25] It is important to determine who will be involved in making the decision as well as the nature of their informational input on a new or additional system.

As an example, consider a representative from AT&T who is attempting to get a prospective customer to replace long-distance telephone service now provided by MCI. In the first meeting with the telecommunications manager, the salesperson attempts to determine the specifications of the prospect's long-distance network. In addition, the salesperson needs to determine whether the telecommunications system is used primarily for voice or data communications and what departments or divisions are the major users. The salesperson may also need to ascertain how the manager would react to the sales representative's contacting some of the users of the present system. It is not uncommon for the gatekeeper (in this case, the telecommunications manager) to be reluctant to have salespeople contacting anyone on the matters for which the gatekeeper is responsible. This is one of the delicate but important nuances of the systems designer relationship.

Participants in the Approach Meeting

Who, in addition to the salesperson, should participate in the approach meeting with the prospect? This question is relevant primarily when the sale is targeted at a business. There may be times, especially in system-design sales situations, where the sales representative may find it desirable to have a technically sophisticated specialist accompany him or her. If it is deemed important to immediately establish the image in the prospect's mind that the salesperson represents a firm with strong technical expertise that can be made available to customers, the sales representative may wish to use a technical person in the approach meeting. When the prospect is a private citizen, the sales representative will usually conduct the approach on a one-on-one basis.

Another consideration that sometimes is important is the *level* of the manager or executive who is the salesperson's initial contact. If a sales vice president is the person to whom the approach will be made, the sales representative may find it helpful to have a vice president from the salesperson's firm present in this first meeting. The momentum established by a favorable climate in such a meeting can help the sales representative open doors to lower-level executives at later stages of the sales cycle.

Location of the Approach Meeting

The answer to the question about where the approach should occur is not as obvious as it might seem. Although the majority of meetings involving prospects and salespeople occur in the home or office of the prospect, there are opportunities to stage an approach meeting at trade shows and company-sponsored seminars. The business luncheon and golf course are other sites that are sometimes used to bring the sales representative together with the prospect.

In some situations, the location will be obvious; but if the sales representative has an opportunity to choose a location, he or she should consider the following questions in selecting the optimum site:

1. Where can I have the maximum amount of the prospect's undivided attention?

2. Who else from my company or the prospect's family or firm should participate in this first meeting? Do they need to be present during the entire meeting or should they come in after the meeting gets started?

3. How necessary is it for the prospect to experience the product or service in action to make the meeting successful?

4. How do rival salespeople approach this prospect and what can I do to positively differentiate myself and my company?

SUMMARY

1. Prospecting is basically finding individuals or organizations that are members of the selling firm's targeted market.

2. To assist in the prospecting activity, sales representatives and sales managers should use their firm's marketing plan and, specifically, the portion that identifies the anticipated target market.

3. Many companies have systematized the generation of sales leads and the qualification of those leads. Increasingly, firms are using information technology such as computerized Yellow Pages and telemarketing to perform lead identification and qualification tasks more cost effectively.

4. Professional salespeople engage in considerable planning before they make contact with a prospect. The skillful use of information sources such as trade papers, credit reports, annual reports or, in some cases, other salespeople can pay dividends later when the representative actually contacts the prospect.

5. Other considerations a professional salesperson will give attention to are the objectives, the participants, and the location of the approach meeting with a prospect.

QUESTIONS FOR DISCUSSION AND REVIEW

1. How is prospecting related to sales force productivity?

2. How would the prospecting by salespeople who work for a production-oriented company differ from the actions of people working for a company that practices the marketing concept?

3. What is the endless chain form of prospecting and what is the logic behind this approach?

4. What is an internal advocate?

5. "Prospecting is too important to be left to the salespeople." Comment on this statement.

6. Examine Exhibit 6-7. Why is bingo card an appropriate name?

7. If all other factors are equal, which lead—a mailed-in card or a call on a toll-free 800 number—is likely to be the best? Why?

8. How can telemarketing improve the efficiency of sales lead qualification?

9. Describe the guidelines for establishing an effective sales lead qualification program that uses the telephone.

10. What are the major sources of information a salesperson might use to prepare for a meeting with a prospective customer?

11. How do the objectives of the first meeting with a prospect differ if the representative is attempting to establish a (1) counselor relationship (2) supplier relationship (3) systems designer relationship?

12. The location of the first meeting between a prospect and the sales representative is an important factor for the salesperson to consider. Explain.

CASE 6-1   AZTEC CORPORATION'S PARTICIPATION IN SUPER SHOW '92

Marina Garza is preparing to leave her office in Houston, Texas, to attend Super Show '92, the sporting-goods industry's premier exhibition. Super Show is conducted annually and attracts exhibitors from all over the world. This is Marina's first experience in leading a staff of people for her company as it participates in the huge event.

Each year Super Show is sponsored by the National Association of Sporting Goods Manufacturers. Association members use the show to exhibit their latest products to prospective wholesale and retail buyers. In the past three years, the average attendance at each year's shows has grown to approximately 20,000 attendees. By providing this four-day event, the manufacturers' association creates a convenient opportunity for buyers to inspect a wide variety of goods and establish their purchasing plans.

The Aztec Corporation is a leading manufacturer of athletic footwear whose sales volume for the most recent year was $825 million. The company manufactures and sells four lines of athletic footwear—basketball, football, running/track, and baseball shoes—each containing many different models and levels of quality. The intent is to have a shoe for every purpose the many different types of consumers might have. In the U.S., Aztec sells its products via 50 independent sales reps who not only sell the Aztec shoes but also represent other manufacturers of complementary sporting products such as athletic equipment (e.g., rowing machines, weights, treadmills, and so forth) and athletic clothing. Because these independent sales reps are not Aztec employees, Aztec makes a constant effort to get them to spend more time and attention on the sale of Aztec's products. One way to stimulate the reps' efforts on behalf of Aztec is to pay them competitive commissions on their sale of Aztec products. Several salespeople selling the Aztec product lines receive commission checks of $100,000 annually. Another way of holding the reps' attention is to help them get more business by providing them with leads.

When Marina Garza was hired she was told that her major responsibilities would be to serve as a liaison with the salespeople and to coordinate all Aztec's appearances at various trade shows. The show she is preparing to attend is by far the largest and most important of all the shows conducted each year. Not only will thousands of buyers be there, but all the salespeople Aztec utilizes will be in attendance. Marina perceives that she has two important constituencies: the wholesale/retail buyers and the salespeople.

One of Marina's major responsibilities while at Super Show '92 is to ensure that Aztec's exhibit space is set up and maintained properly. The expandable panels, carpeting, shelving, and lights and furniture have been shipped from Houston to Atlanta. One hundred of Aztec's many models of shoes, point-of-purchase displays, brochures, and other "props" have to be attractively arranged in the 50′x40′ exhibit area.

Marina also has to supervise preparations for the three large cocktail parties Aztec is going to sponsor on Tuesday, Wednesday, and Thursday evenings. One month prior to the show, Marina's staff mailed 2,500 invitations to people inviting them to attend one of the two-hour parties. Marina anticipates that each party will attract approximately 500 people.

To assist her, Marina has a staff of six people. They will take turns in the Aztec exhibit area, analyze competitors' lines of merchandise, work out last minute arrangements for the cocktail parties, and be "on duty" during the parties, circulating among the guests. The typical day for an Aztec employee at the show is sixteen hours long. The costs and the impact on business relations, however, make such personal efforts worthwhile.

Marina calculates the costs of attending and participating as an exhibitor at about $150,000. The Atlanta Trade Mart is charging Aztec $10,000 for the 2,000 square feet of exhibit space for five days (one day is consumed in setting up the exhibit). Transportation and set-up costs are $5,000. Celebrity appearance fees for famous athletes who endorse Aztec footwear total $100,000. Six superstars representing the different sports will be present at various times in the Aztec exhibit area. Hotel and catering costs are also significant. Each cocktail party, for instance, will cost about $10,000.

Marina's staff has been meeting regularly for the past three months going over the details of the show. Marina is very concerned that Aztec glean all the benefits it can from this very expensive event. Marina is aware that Aztec's senior management has wondered what benefits Aztec is reaping from its participation. "This year," Marina vows to herself, "we have to show our management what we got for $150,000."

QUESTIONS

1. Describe how the "funneling process" illustrated in Exhibit 6-2 can occur before, during, and after Aztec participates in Super Show '92.

2. Given the Super Show atmosphere described in the case, what item illustrated and described in the chapter will be indispensable if Marina is to succeed in proving that Aztec's participation was worthwhile? Why?

3. Considering the type of sales force Aztec uses, why it is very desirable for Aztec to not only get large numbers of leads but also engage in qualifying the leads?

4. What type of buyer-seller relationship seems most likely to be formed between the salespeople and the wholesaler/retailer buyers?

5. If you were a consultant and someone from Aztec approached you with the problem of justifying Aztec's participation in the Super Show, how would you approach the justification problem?

CASE 6-2 TICKER PUBLISHING COMPANY

During a sales meeting in Orlando, Florida, the Ticker Publishing Company is introducing its sales force to a new line of books it will soon be launching. Gil Bell, the manager at Ticker's headquarters who is primarily responsible for the new line, has a session to explain the plans for launching the new books.

"The company is attempting to capitalize on two trends," says Gil Bell. "One is the wave of enthusiasm for owning your own businesses—in other words, the entrepreneurial trend. The other is people's desire to know more about the financial markets. We now have a line of inexpensive paperback books dealing with these two subjects."

Gil Bell has overseen the three test markets Ticker has used in Grosse Point, Michigan; Saddlebrook, New Jersey; and Mill Valley, California. Gil's presentation to the assembled sales personnel reveals that the people most likely to read these books are those he calls the "up-scale market": college-educated, suburban homeowners, earning more than $30,000 a year. Most of them are in lower- to middle-level management jobs. Discretionary time is in short supply for many of them.

The Ticker Publishing Company's sales force has previously been selling to bookstores in suburban malls and in central city locations. Although these locations will continue to be outlets for the new line of books, there is a market, Gil Bell contends, in a growing variety of other places. Bell's research reveals that consumers purchase new books as impulse items. Because of this consumer behavior, the books are priced to permit consumers to indulge their impulsive desires.

At the conclusion of Bell's presentation, Sam Riddell, Vice President of Sales, says to the sales representatives, "This new line of product signals the beginning of an expansion at Ticker. We're looking at opening up some new distribution channels for our products. As I understand Gil's comments about the targeted consumer for these books, we're going to need to find new outlets. We're going to have to develop a new prospecting system that will provide you with leads. Many places where these books can be sold are going to be totally new customers to most of you. I want each of you during the next few days, as you go back to your territories, to think about where we can sell these new books."

QUESTIONS

1. Assuming these books will be purchased more on impulse than after careful shopping, what are some outlets that seem suitable for this product?

2. If you were a Ticker sales representative, after you had answered the previous question, which one(s) of the sources of information revealed in the chapter would be useful to you in your prospecting efforts?

3. What kinds of assistance can the Ticker Publishing Company headquarters group provide its sales personnel to help them generate and qualify leads?

CASE 6-3 IMAGE MASTER

Pam Beneke was preparing to make her initial call on Margaret Cannon, a manager in the Centaur Telephone Company. Beneke is a Sales Representative for Image Master, manufacturers of hardware and software that permit a user to make customized 35mm slides. The ability to make slides for corporate meetings, using their new desk-top publishing capabilities, has been welcomed by many organizations that, in the past, had to send printed material to graphics designers. These designers usually required three to five working days to complete an order for twenty or thirty slides. In some situations when an executive wanted overnight service the cost of providing slides was significant ($30 per slide). Technological advancements are rapidly making this practice obsolete, and Pam's company, Image Master, has the equipment to permit a company to make its own 35mm slides in a more timely and cost-effective way.

Margaret Cannon, Pam's prospective customer, manages the Customer Presentation Center, which provides support for Centaur's sales force. The telephone salespeople bring customers to Centaur's Presentation Center for demonstrations of new telecommunications equipment and services. Cannon's group at the center conducts hundreds of presentations during the year. They use extensive amounts of audio-visual support, such as slides, overhead transparencies, and videotape.

At a trade show in Dallas in April, Cannon visited the Image Master booth and watched a brief demonstration. She was sufficiently impressed with the possibilities of cutting her department's costs and saving time to fill out a card requesting a sales visit. Since Margaret's office is in Pam's territory, the trade show personnel passed her request to Pam for a follow-up call.

As Pam thought about her first call on Cannon, she concluded that it would be beneficial to know what type of slides her prospect's group was presently using. Pam called the Customer Presentation Center and made arrangements with one of the staff members to attend a demo. During the presentation, Pam made notes about the number of slides used, and the number and types of colors used in the slides. She wrote down some of the text used in the slides so that she could match the quality of her system's slides against those the Cannon group was presently using.

In addition, Pam took several paper copies of slides she had seen and visited three graphic arts shops in the city. Posing as a customer, she asked for price quotations for various quantities of slides. She determined that it cost approximately 175 percent more, on average, to have slides made by the graphics shops than what it would cost to make them using the Image Master unit.

Anticipating questions about training, Pam called her Dallas office to obtain the dates of classes to be conducted during the next three months. She also found out how much advance notice was required to ensure a reservation for one of the training sessions.

One question Pam had been asked on other occasions was, "Who else in this area uses this system?" Picking out three of the companies in town who use Image Master, Pam called her contacts in each of the businesses and asked permission to use them as references.

QUESTIONS

1. How does this case illustrate the marketing concept in action?

2. What type of relationship does this situation suggest will be formed between buyer and seller?

3. What else should Pam Beneke do to prepare for her first sales call on Margaret Cannon?

NOTES

1. Karen Blue, "Closing the Loop: Hewlett-Packard's New Lead Management System," *Business Marketing* (October 1987): 74–78.

2. F. Beaven Ennis, "Make Your Annual Marketing Plan Must Reading," in *Marketing Management and Strategy: A Reader*, 3rd ed., ed. Philip Kotler and Keith Cox, (Englewood Cliffs, N.J.: Prentice-Hall, 1984), 236–43.

3. "Computer Sales Support Gaining Grip," *Marketing News* (October 24, 1986): 1.

4. Frederic A. Russell, Frank H. Beach, and Richard H. Buskirk, *Selling: Principles and Practices*, 11th ed. (New York: McGraw-Hill, 1982), 53.

5. "A Company of Lead Generators," *Inc.* (September 1987): 111.

6. Len D'Innocenzo, "How to Discover New Prospects from Within Your Established Accounts," *Personal Selling Power* (April 1990): 60.

7. Christine Amer and Dean S. Amer, *Dictionary of Business and Economics*, rev. ed. (New York: The Free Press, 1984), 131.

8. Terry W. Kennedy, "Boost Productivity with Computer-Enhanced Selling," *Marketing News* 18, no. 23 (November 8, 1984): 20.

9. "Advertising in Business Publications Supports Personal Selling at Only 19¢ per Contact," *LAP Report #7020.7* (New York: Laboratory of Advertising Performance, McGraw-Hill Research, 1986).

10. Bob Donath, "Survey on Sales Lead Handling," *Business Marketing* (October 1984): 16.

11. Gerald Posner and Eil J. Walcek, "Implement Lead Follow-up System for More Business-Marketing Sales," *Marketing News* 19, no. 22 (October 25, 1985): 22.

12. Ralph D. Rose, "Yellow Pages: Vital Marketing Tool Is Changing Rapidly," *Marketing News* 19, no. 11 (May 24, 1985): 39.

13. Ibid.

14. Robert Lusch and Virginia Lusch, *Principles of Marketing* (Boston, Mass: Kent Publishing, 1987), 473.

15. Richard Koenig, "More Cities Rush to Host Trade Shows," *Wall Street Journal* (May 24, 1984): 35.

16. "How To Win at the Show," *Sales and Marketing Management* (February 4, 1985): 48.

17. Ibid.

18. Robert Hood, "Increase Sales by Decreasing Number of Bad Leads," *Marketing News* 20, no. 11 (May 23, 1986): 18.

19. Kate Bertrand, "You Can 'Lead' a Rep to Prospects," *Business Marketing* (April 1987): 56.

20. "Qualifying Prospects is Best Left to Telemarketing," *Marketing News* (July 31, 1987): 10.

21. John I. Coppett and Roy Dale Voorhees, "Telemarketing: Supplement to Field Sales," *Industrial Marketing Management* 14 (1985): 213–16.

22. Joseph Stumpf, "The Six Keys to Powerful Telephone Prospecting," *Telemarketing* (January 1988): 60–62.

23. K. Fred Skousen, *An Introduction to the SEC*, 2d ed. (Cincinnati, Ohio: South-Western Publishing, 1980), 86.

24. John I. Coppett and William A. Staples, "Product Profile Analysis: A Tool for Industrial Selling," *Industrial Marketing Management* 9 (1980): 151–57.

25. Thomas B. Bonoma, "Major Sales: Who *Really* Does the Buying?" *Harvard Business Review* (May–June 1982): 111–19.

CHAPTER 7

Customer Contacts

LEARNING OBJECTIVES

After studying this chapter, you should be able to:

1. Understand the differences among the three contact stages of the multistage communication model.

2. Explain why the arts of effective questioning and active listening are so important.

3. Describe the effect that time between contacts has on cementing or eroding buyer-seller relationships.

4. Understand the categories of contact situations depicted in the contact matrix.

5. Analyze the benefits to salespersons who understand and actively manage their customer contacts as though they were managing a portfolio of assets.

6. Define the key terms used in this chapter.

KEY TERMS

- channeling question
- clarifying question
- verification question
- active listening
- contact matrix
- clean slate contact
- brand-switching contact
- resupply contact
- exit barrier
- supplementary sales contact
- portfolio management concept

A RESEARCH REPORT summarized in an issue of *Sales & Marketing Management* revealed what 432 buyers in small and large companies liked and didn't like about salespeople who were contacting them. Some of the most noteworthy findings were:

- Buyers overwhelmingly prefer a soft sell. Only 5% indicated they liked salespeople to be aggressive.

- A major reason for switching from one supplier to another was that the salesperson lost contact with the customer. Twenty-seven percent cited this as the reason for giving their business to another sales rep.

- Qualities that the buyers liked to see in the salesperson calling on them were confidence, enthusiasm, intelligence, personality, and persistence.

Source: Adapted from "Listen Up," *Sales & Marketing Management* (February 1990): 10.

Chapter 6 described methods used to generate leads and the ensuing efforts to qualify the leads to determine which ones were prospects. This chapter builds on Chapter 6 and analyzes a variety of contacts or meetings that occur between a salesperson and prospective customers. Because we are emphasizing the relationship management responsibilities confronting the sales professional, we will examine more than the initial contact between the salesperson and the prospective buyer. In a transaction-oriented approach to selling, the emphasis is almost entirely on the first (and perhaps only) meeting between the involved parties. Relationship management, however, takes a longer view. Over the course of a successful buyer-seller relationship, there will be many contacts with a customer, and the professional salesperson will not take success for granted. Each contact with a customer will be important to the maintenance and growth of the relationship. To facilitate our description and analysis of the various contacts, we use two new tools: the *contact matrix* and the *customer portfolio model.*

Regardless of what type of contact is occurring—a first-time meeting with a customer or some subsequent meeting—there is communication. Thus, this chapter will also modify the communication model introduced in Chapter 2. The modification, the *multistage communication model*, will illustrate some important conditions that occur as a salesperson and a customer establish a relationship.

Before beginning an in-depth analysis of the actual contact, the salesperson needs to do several things. First, the rep needs to consciously ask himself or herself "What is the purpose of this contact?" If this is the first time the two parties have been in communication, the salesperson should review the information he or she has collected (see "Planning the Who, What, and Where of the Approach" in Chapter 6).

Second, the salesperson should recognize that in the opening seconds of the contact, he or she is making a claim on the customer's time and attention.[1] What "signals" can be transmitted to the other person that will gain the person's attention and begin to stimulate interest? Research studies indicate that although the actual words a person uses are important in the communication process, a tremendous amount of nonverbal communicating also takes place. Therefore, image is important.[2] Readers interested in improving their personal image can consult a number of excellent books, some of which are listed at the end of the chapter.

In the Business Etiquette section of a recent *Sales & Marketing Management,* a writer asked a business etiquette expert, Ann Marie Sabath, for advice on how salespeople could make a better first impression. Her answer was:

In order to make a better first impression, why not encourage your employees to use the business etiquette "Rule of Twelve":

Figure 7-1 A tremendous amount of nonverbal communication takes place during the opening seconds of a salesperson-buyer interaction.

- *The first 12 words they speak to customers should include a form of thanks, if appropriate. (For example: "Thank you for agreeing to see me today." "It's a pleasure meeting you.")*
- *The first 12 inches from their shoulders up should include impeccable grooming. Their hair, collar, tie, scarf, etc. should reflect that they are high-quality individuals.*
- *The first 12 steps your marketing reps take should be [taken with] confidence. Whether they're walking from the parking lot to a customer's office or just down the hall, encourage them to walk with vim, vigor, and vitality.*[3]

THE MULTISTAGE COMMUNICATION MODEL

Exhibit 7-1 is a useful starting point in examining what happens when two individuals attempt to communicate, whether by phone, through correspondence, or in person. The essential elements are the source and receiver, and encoding and decoding. The obvious indicator of success is the increased overlap between the circles in Stage 3. Before enjoying the benefits of good communication, the rep must successfully manage the circumstances associated with Stage 1.

Stage 1

This stage occurs when the salesperson first makes contact with someone. Depending on whether the salesperson is qualifying his or her own leads or has assistance, the individual can be considered either a lead or a prospect. If the sales representative has to furnish and then qualify his or her own leads, the nature of the first contact will be different from what it would have been had the sales rep known the lead was qualified and the individual was a definite prospect. The significant feature of Stage 1 is the absence of any mutually shared field (absence of common interests). It is crucial to the successful establishment of a relationship that this absence of a mutually shared field be eliminated as soon as possible. Numerous examples exist of efforts to quickly establish something in common with a prospective customer. For instance, a comment by an auto insurance salesperson might be, "Ms. Jones, would you be interested in possibly lowering your auto insurance costs by 15 to 20 percent?" Another opening gambit, one that is related to the endless-chain method of prospecting described in Chapter 6, is to use the name of someone known to both the salesperson and the potential buyer: "Ms. Jones, I was just talking to Fred Smith, your neighbor, who suggested I visit with you." The purpose, once again, is to develop something in common with the contact as rapidly as possible.

Exhibit 7-1 Multistage Communication Model

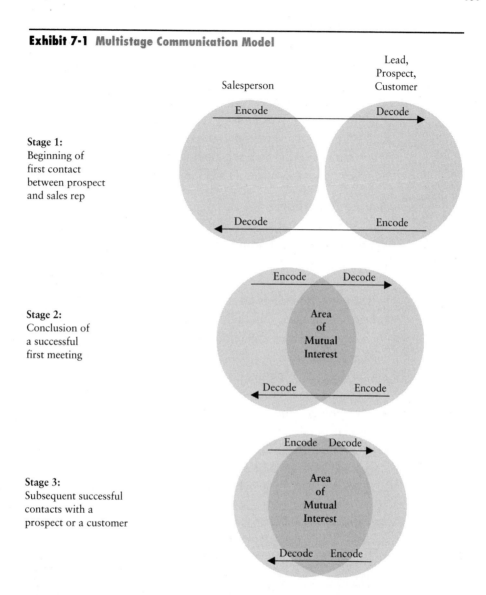

Stage 1:
Beginning of
first contact
between prospect
and sales rep

Stage 2:
Conclusion of
a successful
first meeting

Stage 3:
Subsequent successful
contacts with a
prospect or a customer

A factor at work in the initial stages of a first meeting is the natural defense mechanism many people have when they think someone is going to try to sell them something. For most people, it is not that they do not want to buy anything. Indeed, *most of us do enjoy buying things.* Conversely, *most of us do not want to be sold anything.* How do we know (or think we know) when someone is trying to sell us something? Primarily, we analyze the communication occurring between ourselves and the salesperson. If the salesperson is *telling* us what we need without exhibiting any knowledge of our specific circumstances or making any effort to learn about our specific needs, then we are almost certain we are being sold. The tendency is to withhold or diminish our trust in the person (and perhaps the company the person represents). Customer trust is a key factor that influences the ability of a salesperson to influence a prospect.[4]

Allesandra and Wexler say, "People buy because they feel understood, not because they are made to understand."[5] The salesperson should pose the question, "How can I develop an 'understanding' of my customers?" The answer is by *asking questions* about the customer's circumstances and *listening*.

Asking Questions

Most of us have not spent much time or effort analyzing the questions we ask to get more information from other people. The professional sales representative, however, takes a more than casual interest in how to use questions to his or her best advantage.

Exhibit 7-2 identifies three common types of questions, lists their purpose, and provides examples. Although the range of situations involving salespersons and their customers is so great that it would be impossible to cover all of them, we can look at the purpose for each of the questions and draw some conclusions about a successful sales rep's question-asking strategy.

First, the salesperson might ask a **channeling question** to begin the serious discussion (after the social amenities are over). For example, to determine the expansion plans of a customer, he or she might say, "I saw a lot of construction equipment at work on the north side of your plant. What's happening?"

Second, in listening to the response to this question the salesperson will probably need to ask a **clarifying question** such as, "When the expansion has been

Exhibit 7-2 Three Basic Types of Questions, Their Purposes, and Examples

Type	Purpose	Example
Channeling	To direct or redirect the conversation to subjects pertinent to the sales visit, the customer's circumstances, the products or services, or other relevant matters	"You've told me about your previous home, but now, if you would, can you tell me what you are seeking in your new home?"
Clarification	To gain more specific information and a better understanding of the buyer's situation	"You mentioned that one of your requirements is prompt delivery. What specific day do you need delivery?"
Verification	To see whether or not the buyer agrees/disagrees with the salesperson	"If we can find you a car with these options, may we proceed to write the order?"

completed how much will that increase your daily production of Product A?" Clarification questions may be more frequent during the conversation than the broader-scoped channeling questions.

Finally, from time to time the sales representative will want to verify whether he or she and the customer are understanding each other—hence, a **verification question**. This does not mean the parties are agreeing on every point; however, it is just as necessary to the eventual goal of successful communication that they realize where they disagree. A verification question might be, "What I believe I hear you telling me is that your purchasing responsibilities are going to be about triple what they are now. Is that right?"

In the real world of actual conversation, each party listens to the other. Thus, questioning and listening to the answer(s) permits the salesperson to formulate other questions that elicit more information.

Listening

Some consultants advocate "active listening," which is not the same as simply keeping quiet while the other person talks.[6] **Active listening** involves paying attention to what the other person is saying, decoding the message, and then stating your interpretation of his or her feelings.[7] By feeding back what you believe you have heard, you can prove or correct your understanding. Feedback also signals to the other party that you are genuinely interested. A realtor might ask, for example, "When you move to Clear Lake, what will be your most important concerns?" The person responding will describe job locations and, perhaps, a need for easy access to schools, church, shopping, and other facilities. If the realtor actively listens, there will probably be some indication of the relative priorities the person is placing on living close to each of these sites. The salesperson can then feed back a summarized version of what the client has said by asking a verification question such as, "What I'm hearing you say is you place a great deal of value on not spending more than fifteen minutes driving to work, your children's school, and a supermarket. Is that right?"

The active listener who also observes the following common sense rules of good listening etiquette is building an information bank while also projecting an image of concern about the prospective customer's needs:

1. Don't interrupt people when they are talking, even if you know what they are going to say next.

2. Look at the person when you are talking to him or her or when he or she is talking to you, but don't stare.

3. Don't toy with pencils, paper, or rubber bands while listening.

Figure 7-2 Active listening involves paying attention to what the other person is saying, decoding the message, and relating your interpretation of the message back to speaker.

4. Although some reaction to the other person's statements is desirable, don't overemphasize this with too many nods or other expressions.

5. Be careful to avoid looking at your watch or clock. Do so only if it is necessary and then explain why you must do so.

6. Don't use the opportunity to recount too many situations in which you were "the hero."

One writer summarized what every sales representative fresh from a recent training program should keep in mind: "People don't care how much you know until they know how much you care."[8]

Questioning and listening skills are part of Stage 1 of the multistage communication model, but the perceptive reader will recognize that good listening habits and perceptive questions are no less essential to the salesperson at all stages of the buyer-seller relationship. To reinforce this, we will again refer to the importance of questioning and listening in Chapter 9 when we describe how to negotiate and meet objections.

Asked to identify the No. 1 problem of salespeople, nearly half of 432 corporate buyers surveyed recently said salespeople are "too talky." Indeed, the survey by Communispond Inc., a New York consulting firm, suggests that an inability to communicate is souring many buyers on the salespeople who call on them. Only 1% said the salespeople they deal with have "excellent" sales skills, while 69% rated them as poor or merely fair at their job.

The latest corporate slogan may be "listen to the customer," but many salespeople apparently need to listen up. At least customers think so.

Sure-Fire Skills	Percent of Buyers Impressed By
Salespeople who really listen	28%
Salespeople who answer questions well	25%
Salespeople who don't waste their time	19%
Salespeople who have good presentation skills	18%

Exhibit 7-3 Talk, Talk, Talk, Talk: Try a Little Listening

Source: *Wall Street Journal,* March 22, 1990, p. B1. Reprinted by permission of the *Wall Street Journal,* © 1990 Dow Jones & Company, Inc. All Rights Reserved Worldwide.

Seven of eight buyers said most salespeople don't know how to ask the right questions about their companies' needs and 95% said they prefer the soft sell to the hard-driving sales pitch.

Does a mediocre sales rep make much difference? Apparently. When asked which reason for switching vendors was most familiar to them, 27% of buyers cited an out-of-touch sales rep.

Stage 2

At this point, as a result of the salesperson's questions about the buyer's situation and the information provided by the buyer, the two communicating parties have formed impressions of each other. The sales representative has a good idea about whether the person is a strong prospect or not. The customer has also formed some impressions about the quality and the intent of the salesperson's questions. Other perceptions the client or customer is forming (and verifying) as Stage 1 evolves into Stage 2 may include the following:

1. The congruence between the salesperson's personal image and the corporate image held by the prospect. For instance, did the IBM rep look and act the way the customer thought an IBM rep would look and act?

2. The degree to which the sales representative appears to want the business. There is usually a fine line between our impressions of people who want us to do business with them and those individuals who seem desperate to get an order. In most cases, our business goes to people who want us to say yes but who don't seem to be personally or professionally desperate.

3. The sincerity and integrity of the salesperson. Most of us decode a wide range of signals to determine whether another person can be trusted: eye contact or lack of it, evasive answers to questions about other people or businesses who

have bought the product, and jargon or acronyms, which may mean something to the salesperson and his or her peers but are unknown to us. These indications of sincerity, integrity, and other character qualities are, of course, not always accurate. Most of us, however, think we can judge another person's character, and the foregoing signals are illustrations of what we use.

As the initial meeting between the salesperson and the prospect progresses, the area of intersection in Stage 2 of the multistage communication model should be growing if the two parties are finding areas of mutual interest. If the salesperson appears to be knowledgeable, buyer-oriented and capable of helping the customer or client, and the prospect seems capable of making a decision, then the atmosphere is favorable for a continuation of the contact. If no common ground can be found, the relationship will probably not develop, and no sale will occur. This is what makes cold calling (making calls without the benefit of any prior knowledge about the customer) so difficult. With no friends or acquaintances or other information in common, the two parties may find it extremely difficult to establish rapport in the time each party is willing to devote to the contact.

Stage 3

If the area of mutual interest between the salesperson and the potential buyer is great enough, there will be more contacts between the salesperson and the customer or client. We should mention here that no sale (in the traditional sense) has yet been made. Indeed, if the sales representative is responsible for qualifying his or her own sales leads, the salesperson may, at the end of Stage 2, merely be satisfied that the person is a bona fide prospect. On the other hand, if the newly found prospect *also* concludes that the sales representative has something that may be worth considering, the prospect may grant approval for another meeting. The essential point is that both parties must perceive some value to another meeting.

Especially in the beginning stages of what the rep hopes will be a relationship, *time is of the essence.* Salespeople need to be attentive to the dangers that come with allowing too much time to elapse between contacts with a prospect and after a sale with a customer. Three examples illustrate the importance of timely contacts between the salesperson and the customer.

First, imagine that the potential buyer sees or hears an advertisement offering more information to interested parties (for example, the bingo card in Chapter 6), or has visited a vendor's booth at a trade show. In either situation, the person has exhibited a degree of interest in the product, service, or company. It is important to follow up to determine whether the lead is a prospect or just a "literature picker." The sales representative usually has only a relatively short time to capitalize on the expressed interest. If the person is a prospect, it is safe to assume he or she will soon give competitors an opportunity to meet his or her needs.

Recognizing the need to expeditiously and economically handle these opportunities, many firms are now inviting people to call toll-free 800 numbers to ask for information they have seen in an advertisement. This not only permits the company to swiftly initiate the fulfillment process by sending the catalog, brochure, or other information, but also gives the telemarketer who receives the calls the chance to ask a few questions that can be used to qualify the callers as strong or weak sales prospects. The telemarketing group then turns over the strong prospects' names and addresses and other information to the appropriate field salespersons.

A second moment at which time is of the essence is *after* the first sale to a customer. Theodore Levitt states, "The seller has made a sale, which he expects directly to yield a profit. The buyer has bought a tool with which to produce things to yield a profit. For the seller it is the end of the process; for the buyer the beginning."[9]

If the seller acts as if it is the "end of the process," says Levitt, the situation will deteriorate and the potential for a growing and probably mutually profitable relationship will wither and die. Thus, it becomes crucial for the professional salesperson to support earlier claims about customer satisfaction with a caring attitude and, if necessary, action on behalf of the customer. The salesperson's ability to take not only swift but effective action on behalf of the customer will greatly strengthen the relationship.

Finally, time is important virtually *whenever* a customer or client has a question or a postsale need. Although the first sale is a particularly important event in most relationships, it is nevertheless important to emphasize that *all* signals of need or interest from customers merit expeditious responses to keep the bonds between buyer and seller strong. Recognizing this responsibility to keep giving a superior grade of service to accounts has led some companies to implement *national* or *key account management structures.*[10] Others use telemarketing to give customers twenty-four-hour-a-day, seven-day-a-week access to the seller's personnel.[11]

Federal Express stresses the importance of attending to its customers' signals of need or interest with its "sundown rule." Any customer inquiry must be answered on the same day Federal Express receives it (before the sun sets). On the rare occasions when a Federal Express employee can't give an answer, he or she contacts the customer that day and acknowledges the customer's inquiry. In addition, the employee makes a commitment to the customer to contact him or her as soon as an answer can be provided. This attention to maintaining communications is one of the major reasons customers repeatedly re-use Federal Express services.

So far, we have stressed that the professional salesperson does not view contacts or meetings with a customer as culminating in a sale and then abruptly ending (this is the transaction orientation). We have emphasized instead the need to build a growing number of mutually beneficial experiences between the salesperson and the prospect who, eventually, will become a customer. This philosophy sets the stage for us to examine the different contacts that occur between professional salespeople, prospective customers, and established customers.

THE CONTACT MATRIX

The **contact matrix** (Exhibit 7-4) is a two-dimensional model that illustrates some basic types of customer contacts a sales representative makes. The vertical axis represents the range of experience a particular customer has had with a specific sales representative. One extreme is that in which the salesperson has never before called on the person. At the other extreme, the sales rep has had numerous meetings with the customer and their relationship has resulted in many sales. On the horizontal axis, circumstances range from situations in which a customer has had no product experience to situations in which the customer has had extensive experience.

Note the important distinction between a product and a brand. Product is defined as a general class of goods or services such as a personal computer product or a car rental service. A *brand*, however, is a specifically identified kind of product—Compaq's personal computer or Hertz's car rental. A sales representative from Budget Car Rental calling on the travel arrangements manager at company X might discover that the manager has extensive experience purchasing car

| | Experience with Product | |
	None	Extensive
Experience with Sales Rep — None	Clean Slate	Brand Switching
Experience with Sales Rep — Extensive	Supplementary Sales	Resupply

Exhibit 7-4 Customer Contact Matrix

rental services, but only from Avis and Hertz. In contrast, another travel manager's experience might be confined to purchasing airline services with no car rental services of any kind. Each circumstance poses a different challenge to the Budget rep; we will analyze these kinds of challenges below.

There are four major types of customer contacts: clean slate, brand switching, resupply, and supplementary sales. Quite obviously, no simple four-celled matrix can capture the rich variety of all possible types of customer-salesperson contacts; however, the important point to be grasped from the following analysis is that sales professionals must be flexible and versatile in managing a variety of customer contacts.

Clean Slate Contact

There has been no previous interpersonal experience between the salesperson and the potential buyer in a **clean slate contact**, and the potential buyer has had no experience with any other brand of the product or service. Examples of such circumstances are abundant, but we will use only two. One is a person who has never owned a VCR; the other is a person who has never purchased a tax-sheltered annuity.

The prospective purchaser of the VCR may have heard about the convenience of videotaped programs and movies. The prospective buyer is sufficiently curious to seek some information, and he or she goes to the home entertainment department at a local department store. There the prospect encounters a salesperson who is presented with an opportunity. If this contact is managed correctly, it may lead not only to the sale of a VCR but also, perhaps, to other purchases of home entertainment equipment over an extended period.

As we envision the two individuals meeting in the store and commencing a dialogue, we should keep in mind what we have stressed about the establishment of successful communication: both parties must share a mutual field of interest. Thus, it would be a serious mistake for the salesperson to launch immediately into a bewildering description of the features of VCRs on the shelves. By getting information about such things as the brand and size of the buyer's television set as well as the buyer's programming desires (for example, does the buyer want to tape programs that occur when he or she is working?), the salesperson can begin to formulate a solution to offer the prospective buyer. It will probably become apparent to the salesperson that the prospect has never owned a VCR and may not even be convinced that the purchase of *any* particular brand is desirable. Knowledgeable about the product as the salesperson may be, he or she should resist the temptation to start comparing the VCRs feature-by-feature. Otherwise, the salesperson's descriptions will probably just be confusing and result in a dampening of whatever interest the customer had. The salesperson should also take care to avoid using jargon and acronyms as the conversation proceeds. Manufacturers have spent millions of dollars making high-tech products user-friendly, but the component parts inside the equipment are mysterious and forbidding to many persons. Therefore, salespeople should strive to develop the ability to talk to the customer in understandable terms without giving an impression of being forced to simplify their descriptions.

This particular situation may be the beginning stage of what we described in Chapter 3 as the systems designer relationship. The individual seeking information about VCRs is probably unaware of the various brands of VCRs and their differences. The salesperson thus has the responsibility to determine the customer's television programming needs, verify them by asking questions and listening, and help the customer implement the optimal solution.

In the example of tax-sheltered annuities, we will assume the prospect has little knowledge of available annuities but does have some interest in his or her future financial condition. In contrast to the VCR example, the initial contact with a salesperson is much less likely to be started by the prospect. The sales representative may have obtained the name of the prospect from company headquarters, which may have recently mailed a brochure to the prospect at his or her request. After setting up an appointment, the sales representative will go to the prospect's home or office. The same need exists for fact-finding and careful listening as in the previous example. Once again, it would be a serious blunder for the salesperson to attempt to sell a tax-sheltered annuity before verifying that this financial service is really the best solution to the person's financial needs. Because of the large sums of money that may be involved, the astute salesperson realizes that, in reality, there are two sales to be made *before* the annuity can be sold. The first sale is the sales representative as a person. The professional salesperson should occasionally ask himself or herself, "If I were a prospective customer, would I want to do business with me?" The second sale, which you may have anticipated, is the salesperson's company. Serious investors will demand evidence of how well the company has performed to give them confidence that their investments will be secure and that the company will be responsive to requests for beneficiary changes, loans, or other matters.

This initial contact will, if properly managed by the salesperson, eventually become a counselor relationship (described in Chapter 3). The prospective client has at least a vague idea of the financial condition he or she desires to be in twenty years hence but has no ideas about the best ways to attain that goal. Thus, the sales representative will become a trusted advisor who, supported by a sound, well-managed company, can provide the solution to the client's needs.

Brand-Switching Contact

In a **brand-switching contact**, the prospective customer has experience with the type of product or service the sales representative is selling. That experience, however, does not include the salesperson's brand. Thus, the salesperson will attempt to persuade the potential customer to engage in brand switching. The other major factor in this contact is the customer's lack of experience with this specific sales representative. As you can see, this is a challenging situation!

The sales representative may have found the individual's name in a wide variety of ways. If this is a consumer product or service, the sales representative may have a clipping service that gathers names of people whose promotions or new job announcements appear in the business section of a daily paper. If a person is a newcomer to a community, the sales representative may have acquired the name from a Welcome Wagon organization that calls on people shortly after they move into a new residence. Still another method, which has been previously mentioned, is the endless chain that generates names as a result of recommendations from people who have just bought from the salesperson. In the case of an industrial product or service (discussed in Chapter 6), the salesperson may have been given a list of companies from an analysis of the Standard Industrial Classification. Or the rep may have used directories.

In this scenario, sales representatives will find two formidable challenges awaiting them. One challenge is to sell themselves and the company they represent. The second challenge is to get the prospective purchaser to agree to switch brands and at least give the representative's brand a trial. Obviously, the salesperson will find prospective buyers in various conditions of readiness to switch. Some people (probably because another sales representative has been negligent in handling the

Exhibit 7-5 What Counts Is Trust

In selling, nice guys can finish last, product knowledge isn't all that vital.

What counts is trust, asserts Jack Snader, president of Systema Corp., a Northbrook, Ill., consultant. "Don't automatically teach 'people-chemistry' skills. Don't spend countless hours having your salespeople learn every technical gizmo. Rather, ask customers how they want to be treated, and do it that way," he says.

Salespeople rated tops in technical proficiency by their managers can be seen as technical incompetents by their clients. Similarly, great personalities often are bested by people with fewer social skills. But "over 200,000 customers say they must be able to trust the salesperson to do what he says he will do," he advises.

"There can be little trust, he says, if customers believe sales reps are just trying to meet a quota."

Source: *Wall Street Journal*, December 27, 1990, p. A1. Reprinted by permission of the *Wall Street Journal*, © 1990 Dow Jones & Company, Inc. All Rights Reserved Worldwide.

relationship) will be very receptive to a switch. In other cases, the time, effort, and expense involved in getting the person to switch allegiance would not be justified.

In brand switching, one of the major objectives in the first contact meeting with potential customers is to find out how satisfied they are with their present brand. As we envision the communication occurring between a salesperson and the prospective buyer, we can gain an appreciation for the art of asking questions that plant a seed of doubt about whether the customer is being well served by his or her present brand. In keeping with our earlier advice to avoid immediately describing product features without first determining the customer's needs, it would also be a mistake to directly attack the features of the competitive brand the prospect is using. Such a clumsy tactic is likely to arouse the buyer to defend the other brand even if what the sales representative has said is true. The best policy to keep in mind when attempting to achieve a brand switch is to *sell positively*. The rep should find out what the customer's present needs are and show how his or her brand meets those needs and even exceeds the expectations of the user.

Gaining the prospect's trust is vital in brand switching contacts. Sales professionals realize, however, that trust between the parties in a business relationship takes *time to develop*. Swan, Trawick, and Silva, all of whom are marketing scholars, found that the average number of calls required before a salesperson was trusted was 5.6.[12] Only three of the forty-two respondents in this study felt they could trust a salesperson after one sales call. We must keep in mind several factors as we think about the 5.6 calls that are, on average, needed to establish buyer trust. First, this finding was obtained from a study of industrial products whose purchasing agents are professional buyers and, for the most part, more cautious than many consumers are in their evaluation of a salesperson's trustworthiness. Second, the calls necessary to establish the trust condition are an investment. There are the direct costs of transportation to the customer's location, the salary of the salesperson, and brochures and other sales aids used during the visits. Even more significant, however, is the indirect cost of these visits. While the sales representative is spending time and money attempting to develop the relationship with the new customer, other sales opportunities must be forgone. Thus, there is an opportunity cost that probably can't be calculated but should at least be acknowledged.

After this emphasis on trust building you may be asking how one builds trust. Exhibit 7-6 is a composite of responses by pharmaceutical salespeople that reveals what they think they must do to establish trust. Basically, their advice boils down to this: "Do what you say you will do."

It is little wonder many sales managers complain that their sales personnel get in a rut of calling only on their established customers and neglect to go after new business. When the new business must be generated by persuading the prospect

---

Exhibit 7-6 Behaviors That Convey Trust Attributes

Dependable/ Reliable	Honest/Candid	Competent	Customer-Oriented	Likeable/ Friendly
Set expectations, demonstrate	Be honest	Use technical knowledge	Stress benefits, availability	Be likeable, friendly
Use proof sources	Use proof sources	Use proof sources	Use proof sources	Establish common ground
Be candid	Be business-like, establish a common ground	Demonstrate competence, honesty	Tell disadvantages	Be business-like, polite, courteous
Show interest in customer needs	Tell pros/cons	Assert availability		
	Give merits of company product, etc.			

Source: Reprinted by permission of the publisher from "How Industrial Salespeople Gain Customer Trust," by John E. Swan, I. Fredrick Trawick, and David W. Silva, *Industrial Marketing Management* 14, p. 206. Copyright 1985 by Elsevier Science Publishing Co., Inc.

to switch from one brand to another, or expand the number of brands purchased, many salespeople cringe at the effort. When the salesperson is working on straight commission (that is, without any base salary), the time needed to make contacts with a prospect that *may* lead to a brand switch can appear too costly.

There are also ethical implications to be considered when one analyzes this type of contact. Chapter 15 is devoted to an analysis of ethical behavior in professional selling, but you can probably already recognize some of the potential ethical problems that can arise when a salesperson is attempting to cause another person to decide to purchase a different brand.

Resupply Contact

In Chapter 5 we referred to a resupply contact as a straight rebuy, which is a familiar term in industrial purchasing circles. In a **resupply contact** the sales rep regards the customer as a well-established buyer of the salesperson's brand of product. A relationship has developed between the customer and the salesperson, and both parties are reaping the benefits of their mutual efforts to establish a supplier relationship (see Chapter 3). The customer in the resupply contact knows what product and brand will satisfy his or her needs, and, fortunately, it is the brand represented by the sales representative. The major responsibilities of the salesperson when making contacts with these established customers are to keep the customer informed about logistical circumstances, such as the company's new overnight order fulfillment service, and about new models or varieties of the products or services. To maintain the relationship's strength, the salesperson must give top priority to any problems the customer has had with billing, delivery, or other matters. The purpose of this diligence is to render such good service that an **exit barrier** is created to minimize the possibility of a customer's being enticed to exit the relationship and switch to a competitive brand.

The major danger to avoid in resupply contacts is leaving an impression with customers that their business is taken for granted. Although many firms have strict codes of conduct limiting the gifts or services their purchasing managers can receive, this should not excuse a sales representative from providing the mementos a customer can accept. Of course, these limitations are not placed on private citizens in their role as customers. Real estate salespeople as well as insurance agents sometimes express their thanks for a customer's business by taking the customer's family to dinner or a sporting event.

To avoid any impression that the two vital skills of questioning and listening are less used in resupply contacts, let us examine some of the most salient areas the sales representative should probe. Although the number of areas into which a sales representative could beneficially inquire is almost limitless, the following four examples illustrate some essential things about which the alert salesperson should seek information. Two examples pertain to industrial sales and two are applicable to consumer sales.

Industrial Sales

Because the demand for many industrial products is *derived* (that is, the demand for Product A, used in creating Product B, is derived from the demand for Product B), the sales representative needs the purchasing manager's views on any anticipated changes the manager would be willing to share that will affect the products or markets of the purchasing manager's company. A salesperson who can help a purchasing manager acquire the amount of supplies to meet a new just-in-time (JIT) inventory management program will greatly enhance the relationship with the buyer. Gathering information in advance of such a change will permit the salesperson to give better service and probably reduce the crises that such a changeover might precipitate in the salesperson's company as it strives to revise shipping schedules to accommodate a customer.

Another area to probe involves personnel changes. In previous chapters, we have mentioned the buying center concept. Changes in the personnel involved in the buying center signal a need for the salesperson to contact the new person(s) and keep them sold on the brand(s).

Consumer Sales

If the product or service is a consumer product, the sales representative's conversations with the customer or client can focus on a family's or individual's plans for such things as a new job, a pending promotion, a new birth, graduation, or retirement. These significant events affect expenditure patterns and pose either a threat or an opportunity to the salesperson's continuation and expansion of service to the consumer.

Another checkpoint for the salesperson to consider in consumer sales is looking for signs of boredom with the product or lack of knowledge about what benefits the customer is receiving from the products or services.

For example, customers tend to forget some of the provisions that insurance policies or other financial management services offer. Smart sales representatives will tactfully keep the product or service sold and will make a note of the benefits mentioned at a particular meeting so they can reinforce other benefits the next time.

Supplementary Sales Contact

In a **supplementary sales contact**, the salesperson and the customer have had previous purchasing experiences with each other, but the sales representative has additional products or services to sell that supplement the products the buyer is already purchasing from the salesperson. A family who last year purchased a sedan might now be considering the purchase of a van as a recreational vehicle. Or a company that purchased its telephone service from AT&T might now consider buying personal computers for its employees from AT&T.

When the sales representative hopes to expand the customer's purchases into additional product lines, there is at least one obviously significant advantage compared to the clean slate contact. The sales representative has the benefit of a track record with the customer.

Thus, the salesperson will not need to cope with the problem of gaining the customer's trust. These contacts occur in either the counselor relationship or the systems designer relationship. The salesperson managing a counselor relationship with a customer and seeing a need to supplement what the customer is now purchasing must take care to prove the benefits that will accrue to the customer from making this additional purchase. By stressing the benefits of having, for instance, both homeowners' insurance and auto insurance with the same agency, the salesperson can strengthen the relationship.

As we conclude this analysis of the four types of customer contacts a professional sales rep makes, we should note that a rep is constantly confronted with competition. In the resupply customer contact, although the rep has sold many times before to a customer, competitors' salespeople are contacting the account. They regard it as a brand-switching opportunity. The same circumstances exist insofar as a supplementary sales contact is concerned. If, for instance, an AT&T rep is attempting to get a long-time customer not only to continue using AT&T long-distance service but also to purchase personal computers, the possibility exists that an IBM rep is also trying to sell PCs to the customer.

It is this dynamic atmosphere in which the professional sales rep functions that tests the skill of the true professional. One way to understand this environment is to regard customers as assets (which in reality they are). These individual assets, however, as a result of their power to purchase or withhold their patronage, have varying amounts of value. Thus, it is useful for salespersons to regard their customers as a portfolio that must be managed much like financial assets.

MANAGING A CUSTOMER PORTFOLIO

In 1977, the Boston Consulting Group introduced the **portfolio management concept**.[13] The essence of the concept was that a business had within its product line(s) groups of products that were experiencing various stages of growth. Some were providing cash resources to the firm while others were using more cash than they returned. One of the recommendations to senior management was to analyze its business ventures and products to determine whether the firm had an adequate supply of cash providers ("cash cows") and products or business divisions that would eventually become future cash cows.

There is a close parallel to this reasoning if a salesperson analyzes the range of customers that he or she is contacting.[14] Exhibit 7-7 identifies three customer categories representing different stages of maturity and calling for different management by the salesperson. Those customers who have never purchased from the sales representative (Category 1) represent the new business opportunities of the future. The prudent sales representative will perceive the need to have a supply of these potential customers to at least replace the inevitable losses occurring in the ranks of the established customers (Category 3). Unfortunately, even the best sales personnel have customers who move out of the territory, die, or go out of business. Just as some products in the original portfolio concept were considered cash users, so also are some of these customers net users of resources. In

Customer Categories	Maturity Conditions of Customers in a Salesperson's Portfolio
Category 1	Prospects and those upon whom the sales rep has called to gather information about their needs and uses of the products/services
Category 2	Those to whom the sales rep is making a formal presentation *and* new purchasers of the sales rep's products or services
Category 3	Established repeat purchasers of all or part of the sales rep's product or service line

Exhibit 7-7 Customer Portfolio Mix

this situation, the resource the customer is using that is valuable to the salesperson is *time*. The professional sales representative realizes that time is one of the most important resources he or she has to manage (see Chapter 13). Sufficient but not excessive amounts of time must be allocated to groom potential customers so that eventually a large percentage of them will become established accounts. You may recall that in Chapter 1 we cited the statistic that, on average, 4.5 sales calls were used before an industrial product was sold. The accounts in Category 1 are those that are probably receiving the first, second, or third visits. At any rate, these potential customers are being cultivated and trust building is under way.

The second category of accounts in the sales professional's portfolio includes those potential buyers who have been targeted for a formal presentation. Obviously, the sales representative hopes to receive an order from these persons. Other accounts in Category 2 are those customers who have just purchased something from the representative. These customers could be symbolized by a ?, one of the symbols used in the Boston Consulting Group's model. A question mark is appropriate because the formation of the relationship has reached a crucial stage. When the sales representative is preparing for the closing presentation to make the first sale to the account, it is not unusual for the salesperson to devote a considerable amount of time preparing customized visual aids, readying a meeting site, and asking other people from the salesperson's company to attend the presentation. Obviously, under these circumstances, a lot is at stake. If the sale has just been made, the delivery and/or installation is occurring or has been completed, and the customer is just starting to use the product. There are definite customer expectations that the salesperson must make sure are satisfied. For instance, the customer expects the product to perform as the sales rep said it would. Also, the customer expects safety and, in most cases, simplicity of use. The professional salesperson realizes that this is a crucial point in the establishment of a firm, lasting relationship.

The third category of customers are those who are now using the product or service and are regarded by the salesperson as satisfied, established accounts. These customers are the sales representative's foundation for present success. The attention and effort he or she has devoted to them are now providing rewards. It is to these customers that the sales representative is aiming his or her efforts at resupplying or supplementing their purchases with other products or services.

By managing all of the contacts with potential customers, new customers, and established customers as though a portfolio of financial assets were involved, the salesperson can maintain growth and vitality among the accounts for which he or she is responsible. Viewed from this perspective, the sales representative is definitely an important manager in the context of a business.

SUMMARY

1. As the salesperson makes the first contact with a prospective customer, one of the most important objectives is to establish and expand the mutually shared field or the area of common interests between the two people.

2. Salespeople must realize that, in many situations, they are actually attempting to make three sales to a prospect. First, sales professionals must, especially in the initial contact stages, sell themselves. Second, they must sell their company. And, third, they must sell the products or services.

3. Skillful questioning and active listening are indispensable to the successful establishment and maintenance of a relationship with a customer.

4. The amount of time between contacts with a prospect or an established customer can play a decisive role in relationship management.

5. The contact matrix illustrates some basic contacts occurring between salespeople, prospects, and established customers.

6. Contacts range from prospective customers who have never dealt with the salesperson and have never purchased the type of product the sales representative is selling to those customers who are experienced in dealing both with the salesperson and the product.

7. There are four major categories of seller-buyer contacts: clean slate, brand-switching, resupply, and supplementary sale.

8. As they analyze the time, effort, and expense incurred in making contacts with customers and prospective customers, salespeople should manage their customers as they would manage a portfolio of financial assets.

QUESTIONS FOR DISCUSSION AND REVIEW

1. Why is it necessary to modify the basic communication model?

2. What would be wrong with a salesperson approaching a prospective customer and starting to tell the customer about the product features?

3. What are some of the first impressions people are likely to form as a result of the initial contact they have with a particular salesperson?

4. What makes the brand-switching contact sometimes more challenging than the clean slate contact?

5. Describe three practices people should avoid when they are listening to someone.

6. What is the major benefit to the salesperson who perceives his or her group of customers as a portfolio to be managed over an extended time period?

7. What is the signal salespeople send when, after making the first sale to a customer, they don't recontact the buyer until they think the buyer is ready to purchase additional goods or services?

8. Review the Multistage Communication Model (Exhibit 7-1) and the Customer Contact Matrix (Exhibit 7-4). In which type of customer contact would the area of mutual interest be the greatest? the least? Why?

9. If a salesperson truly practices the marketing concept, good listening habits are indispensable. Discuss.

10. Face-to-face sales visits with customers are very expensive. How do you justify the expense of sales visits with customers if you don't intend to try to sell them something on each visit?

RECOMMENDED READING

In the February 1991 issue of *Sales & Marketing Management,* a very interesting and useful article was published. The article, "Building a Better Image," details how CEOs and business executives feel about projecting a professional image. Not only does the article convey information about the importance of image, it also provides excellent advice on how to improve your image. At the conclusion of the article, the authors have thoughtfully provided a list of sources which can be consulted for more detailed information. The sources are listed below.

Career Chic, Carol Ann Pearch

The Eternally Successful Organization, Philip B. Crosby

John T. Malloy's New Dress for Success, John T. Malloy

Leadership Development, George Shinn

More Like Us, James Fallows

The Professional Image. . .On Women Only, Susan Bixler

Self-Esteem, McKay and Fanning

Smart Moves, Sam Deep and Lyle Sussman

The Total Executive, Herbert E. Knoll Jr.

You Are the Message, Jon Kraushar

CASE 7–1   PRODUCT KNOWLEDGE IS NOT ENOUGH

Frank Bobbitt was preparing to call on Jose Molinas, owner of Amigos Auto Repair Shop located in Laredo, Texas. Frank sold grinding and sanding equipment and supplies used in repairing automobile bodies. Frank had been calling on Molinas for the past year, but in the four visits he had made he still had not made any sales. Because the Amigos account was potentially a large one—Frank's estimate of its purchases was approximately $100,000 a year—there was no reason to discontinue the sales calls.

As Frank considered his next call on Jose, he recalled their previous contacts. Jose always seemed to be interested in discussing only one thing: price. Many times, Frank remembered, his presentation was cut short by Jose's question, "What's your price?" When that occurred Frank would respond with what he knew to be a very competitive price. Jose invariably answered, "That's too high," and would usually mention that his shop was far too small and unprofitable to afford such costly equipment and supplies. Frank knew, however, that in reality Amigos Auto Repair Shop was financially successful and fully capable of purchasing any item he could offer. He suspected that the price objection was just a convenient excuse.

"This visit," thought Frank, "I'm going to have the most impressive evidence I have ever had that shows how superior our products really are. When I show Jose these charts and the samples we picked up at last week's training sessions that'll be the clincher. Now I can get this account away from that guy at Lone Star. He's had the business long enough."

* * * * * * * * * *

Jose Molinas looked at his desk calendar and noticed that tomorrow afternoon Frank Bobbitt was scheduled to call on him at 2:00 p.m. Frank, in Jose's opinion, was a serious, well-intentioned young man. He always had a lot of information about his products. "Frank just doesn't know me, though," thought Jose. "If he did, he would change his approach. Bart Owens, from the Lone Star Company, is my kind of guy. He really knows the car repair business. Over the years I've learned a lot of good techniques for preparing car surfaces from him. One time last year Bart spent all day working in the shop on a really tough job. Thanks to him we kept a customer satisfied. Bart seems to want to talk more about my business than he does about his products."

QUESTIONS

1. What type of contact is Frank Bobbitt going to make when he meets with Jose Molinas? When Bart Owens meets with Jose what type of contact is it?

2. Examine Exhibit 7-6 and pay particular attention to the headings (dependable/reliable, and so forth). From the information in this case, in what category does Bart Owens seem to have a big advantage over Frank Bobbitt? What evidence is there in the case to support your answer?

3. What is your prediction of Frank's chances of getting Jose to switch suppliers? Why?

4. If you believe that Frank should change his sales tactics to have a chance at getting some of Jose's business, what would you suggest that he needs to do?

CASE 7–2   THE "CLASSIC" APPROACH

Liz Jones pulled a copy of the St. Louis Yellow Pages off the shelf and began to leaf through it to the Men's Clothing and Furnishings-Retail section. She was looking for one kind of ad. Liz was not thinking about buying clothes from a store in St. Louis. As a matter of fact, she was more than a thousand miles away from St. Louis. Her office was in San Francisco.

Liz was a Sales Representative for the San Francisco Yellow Pages telephone directory, responsible for selling advertising space in the directory. Her job was to get businesses that were not listed in the directory to purchase an advertisement and those that were listed to increase the size of their advertisements. Another important responsibility was to retain the business once it had been secured. What Liz and her colleagues did not like to see happen was advertisers reducing the size of their ads or, worse still, dropping them completely.

The reason Liz looked in the St. Louis directory (she had already looked in the Denver, Minneapolis, and Seattle directories) was to find ads for particular types of men's retail clothing stores that would serve as examples. Liz was preparing to contact a customer, Oscar Torres, who owned a men's clothing store.

Oscar's store, The Classic, featured two highly advertised lines of men's suits: Hickey Freeman and Southwick. In addition, The Classic carried a wide variety of shirts made by manufacturers such as Hathaway. For the extremely demanding customer, Oscar offered custom-tailored shirts. He rounded out his inventory with several brands of conservative ties, socks, and other apparel worn by men in professional or managerial careers.

On previous visits she had made to The Classic, Liz had formed the opinion that Oscar's approach to promotion was as conservative as the clothing he sold. Oscar said that the customers to whom he sold never seemed interested in semiannual clearance sales. Therefore, he had not featured that form of sales promotion for over five years. When the typical Classic customer wanted or needed a new suit or other clothing, he purchased what he wanted without shopping for bargains. In addition, the executives who frequented the store were busy people who required instant attention when they came in. Quick alterations and suit pressing were necessities, because often the customer wanted the new garment before he left on a business trip within a day or two after the purchase. To accommodate these customers, Oscar provided same-day alterations if the purchase was made before 1 p.m. If the suit was bought in the afternoon, the alterations were made overnight, and it was ready the next day. Free delivery was available if the purchaser's office was within five miles of the store; 87 percent of the store's customers had offices within seven blocks of the store.

Oscar's present advertisement in the Yellow Pages was a one-line ad containing the name of the store and the telephone number. Jones believed a one-and-one-quarter by two-inch advertisement would allow enough space to identify the best known brands in the store and to indicate the services available to customers.

QUESTIONS

1. Liz is preparing for what kind of contact?

2. Do you think Liz should be looking for ads sponsored by stores similar to The Classic in other cities, or should she be trying to find ads of other San Francisco stores that have merchandising approaches different from that of The Classic?

3. The cost of the ad Liz wants to propose will be significantly higher than for the present one-line ad. What reasoning do you think she should be prepared to use to justify the higher cost?

4. Because of the nature of Oscar Torres's business, should Liz Jones be particularly careful about her personal appearance? How would her appearance affect the interpersonal communications between Liz and Oscar?

CASE 7-3   NANCY FRANKLIN'S WEEK

Nancy Franklin looked at her appointment schedule for the coming week and saw that it appeared to be a typical week full of customer contacts. Nancy worked for Productivity, Inc., a company that marketed products to firms that had or were establishing employee service recognition programs. The Productivity product line consisted of lapel pins, pen and pencil sets, plaques, cups, trophies, wristwatches, and clocks.

Companies with employee recognition programs usually give a gift to an employee as he or she passes a certain milestone, such as an employment anniversary with the company. In some firms, recognition commences with an employee's tenth year of service and continues at five- or ten-year intervals until the employee retires.

Most of the people Nancy contacted were managers of human resources or personnel departments. They were interested in products that were tastefully designed and could be used for many years by the employees. For instance, one of the products Nancy offered was a handsome clock that could be displayed on a mantle or credenza. Usually such an item was given by a company to employees who had been with the company for twenty-five years. Another gift was a ballpoint pen set upright in a walnut block with the company logo attached to the wooden stand. This was sometimes awarded to employees for ten years of service.

Among the contacts Nancy would be making during the week were ten sales leads that had been forwarded to her. The leads came from a trade show in which Productivity had participated. The cards on which the information was recorded contained the name of the person to contact, his or her address and phone number, the person's job title, and a question about whether or not the company was presently engaged in a formal employee service recognition program. Only one of the firms appeared to have a current program.

Aside from contacting the ten people who had filled out the cards at the trade show, Nancy also had five meetings scheduled with managers of several human resources departments. Each of these five managers represented business that Nancy had been attempting to acquire for over two months. She now was ready to present, in each case, an employee recognition program that would utilize her product line. Two of these prospective accounts had employee recognition programs, but the programs recognized only people who were retiring.

To round out her week of planned contacts, Nancy had eight accounts to call on that had been buying from her for more than a year. Three of these now purchased her complete line, but the remaining five were using only two or three of her products in their recognition programs.

QUESTIONS

1. Develop a channeling question Nancy could use to get the meeting started with one of the sales leads she is pursuing.

2. As she makes each contact with the managers who filled out cards at the trade show, what information does Nancy need to provide and what information does she need to collect?

3. When you analyze carefully what type of presentations Nancy will be giving to the various managers, what tells you that she probably represents a marketing-oriented instead of a sales-oriented firm?

4. Using the contact matrix, analyze the contacts Nancy will be making during the week.

5. How does this case illustrate the portfolio management concept?

NOTES

1. Saul W. Gellerman, "The Tests of a Good Salesperson," *Harvard Business Review* (May–June 1990): 64–69.

2. "It's Not What You Say. . . ," *Sales & Marketing Management* (March 1989): 19.

3. Ann Marie Sabath, "When Your Salespeople Are Rough Around the Edges," *Sales & Marketing Management* (February 1991): 88.

4. Robin Peterson, *Personal Selling: An Introduction* (Santa Barbara, Calif.: Wiley/Hamilton, 1978).

5. Anthony Alessandra and Phil Wexler, "The Professionalization of Selling," *Sales and Marketing Training* (February 1988): 38.

6. Diane Gage and Noonie Benford, "Active Listening," *American Way* (October 15, 1987): 17–23. See also Abner Littel, ". . . Look at Who's Talking," *Personal Selling Power* (October 1990): 31.

7. Ibid., 19.

8. Harvey B. Mackay, "Humanize Your Selling Strategy," *Harvard Business Review* (March–April 1988): 36–47.

9. Theodore Levitt, "Relationship Management," *The Marketing Imagination* (New York: The Free Press, 1983), 115.

10. John I. Coppett and William A. Staples, "Managing a National Account Sales Team," *Business* (April–June 1983): 41–44.

11. John I. Coppett and Dale Voorhees, "Telemarketing," in Arch G. Woodside, ed., *Advances in Business Marketing* (Greenwich, Conn.: JAI Press, 1987), 1–15.

12. John E. Swan, I. Fredrick Trawick, and David W. Silva, "How Industrial Salespeople Gain Customer Trust," *Industrial Marketing Management* 14 (1985): 203–11.

13. Derek F. Abell and John S. Hammond, *Strategic Marketing Planning* (Englewood Cliffs, N.J.: Prentice-Hall, 1979), 178, as adapted from "The Product Portfolio" (Boston, Mass.: The Boston Consulting Group, 1970), Perspectives No. 66.

14. See Renato Fiocca, "Account Portfolio Analysis for Strategy Development, *Industrial Marketing Management* 11 (1982): 53–62; see also Alan J. Dubinsky and Thomas N. Ingram, "A Portfolio Approach to Account Profitability," *Industrial Marketing Management* 13 (1984): 33–41.

CHAPTER 8

Sales Presentations

LEARNING OBJECTIVES

After studying this chapter, you should be able to:

1. Describe the fundamental differences among the five basic sales presentations.
2. Explain the circumstances that make structured presentations more appropriate than unstructured presentations.
3. List the variables a salesperson can manipulate to affect the dynamics of a presentation and explain why each variable is important to the quality of a specific presentation.
4. Describe what a salesperson should do to prepare for and deliver an effective product demonstration.
5. Explain the guidelines a rep should use when preparing visual aids for a presentation.
6. Correlate the various presentation openings to the appropriate types of customer contacts.
7. Explain why the salesperson in some customer contacts has to make presentations that sell not only the product or service, but also the salesperson's company and the salesperson as an individual.
8. Describe the points a salesperson should cover as the salesperson prepares for a group presentation.
9. Define the key terms used in this chapter.

KEY TERMS

- canned presentation
- stimulus-response presentation
- benefitizing
- threshold
- chain of logic presentation
- constant affirmation
- barrier theory
- need-satisfaction presentation
- problem-solution presentation
- presentation pace
- drivers
- analyticals
- amiables
- expressives
- presentation scope
- depth of inquiry
- two-way communication
- 2:1 ratio
- introductory approach
- curiosity approach
- benefit approach
- referral approach
- business case

"Y OU SOUNDED LIKE A SALESMAN, Joe," Bill Jackson said as he held the door open for Joe Brickman. They were leaving the Flores Corporation building after a sales call.

"What's wrong with that, Bill? After all, that's what we are. I don't follow you," Brickman responded with a note of irritation in his voice.

Jackson was a District Sales Manager for the Quality Paper Company and Brickman was a rep who worked in Jackson's district. Jackson spent at least one day with each of his salespeople every two months.

"I know. I know. Up until a couple of weeks ago, I would have said the same things the same way you just did. But last month I went to an interesting seminar that changed my thinking about presentations. Rather than making presentations to people, they said we should concentrate on having conversations with our customers. Essentially, the guy I listened to said, 'forget all the stuff you heard about linking features with benefits and other salesmanship techniques that make you sound unnatural! All that really does,' he said, 'is make the customer think about ways to resist the sales talk'."

"I gather that you don't buy into what Tom Walsh, the company sales trainer, teaches us at SMIC?" Brickman asked. SMIC was the Sales and Marketing Instruction Center for Quality Paper Company.

"No, I don't, and the more I've thought about it, I think our presentation training is at the root of some other problems."

"What do you mean?" Brickman asked.

"Well, O.K. Do you remember what it was like the first few months in the company when you had your first territory?"

"Sure, I was scared to death on every sales call. I was glad I had a memorized presentation. As soon as I shook hands I was into my spiel."

"You didn't sell much either, did you?" said Jackson.

"No, I didn't. Actually I started to do better when I got up enough courage to just keep my mouth shut and not try to answer every objection as soon as I heard it. Just let the customer talk instead of trying to control everything. I found the more I relaxed and let things happen naturally, the more sales I made and that, in turn, increased my confidence."

"So why were you sounding like a company-programmed robot back there at Flores?" Jackson asked as they walked to their car.

Brickman laughed and said, "Well, Bill, you *are* the boss, and I thought you believed in the company-approved sales presentation. I was selling to you more than I was to the customer. When someone from the company isn't with me I let the real me come through."

"Great, on our next call just forget about me and do it your way. From the results you've been producing, that must be working," Jackson said as he patted Brickman on the back.

WHAT IS A PRESENTATION?

One author has stated that the sales presentation bridges the gap between the customer's needs and the salesperson's product.[1] Extending the metaphor of a bridge even further, we can ask the question: Who is going to design and build this verbal bridge? Will the salesperson build the kind of "bridge" he or she has been taught to build, or will the sales rep *and* the customer work together to build the bridge?

The answer given to this question will make an enormous difference in the interactions occurring between the salesperson and customers. A significant portion of this chapter will be devoted to describing various presentation methods. In some cases, the salesperson will, by using various methods, attempt to dominate the interaction with the buyer and thereby "win" a sale. In other situations, the presentation will not resemble a monologue at all. It will seem like a conversation which, in an almost incidental way, results in a sale.

Another way of viewing the variety of presentations is to see them arrayed on a continuum (see Exhibit 8-1). At one end, we see a situation where the verbal output is heavily skewed toward the customer. At the other end, we see a situation where the verbal output is heavily skewed toward the salesperson. It is important

Salesperson   Customer
Dominates   Dominates

Exhibit 8-1 Amount of Verbal Output Between Salesperson and Customer

to note that the person doing most of the talking *does not necessarily have control over the conversation.*

At a later point in this chapter, we will describe the 2:1 ratio. Suffice it to say now, however, that in some situations, it is very desirable for the customer to talk twice as much as the sales rep. As one very successful executive once said, "I can't learn anything as long as I'm doing the talking."

All students of professional selling should understand (1) the basic models or types of presentations, (2) the dynamics involved in all kinds of presentations, and (3) ways to create an atmosphere that will permit the best quality presentation. This chapter will address each of these three points as well as other factors relevant to professional selling. We will begin by analyzing two fundamentally different perspectives. One view regards presentations as something that salespeople produce.[2] Adherents to this position view presentations as something a salesperson creates and delivers to customers. The phrase "making a presentation" illustrates this position. Another perspective views presentations as something the rep and the customer create *together.*

Presentations as Products a Salesperson Creates

Many years ago, a group of National Cash Register's best sales reps were studied to determine what made them successful. Analysis of their presentations revealed striking similarities. Following the discovery, a standardized presentation was prepared at corporate headquarters. Contained in it were the phrases and demonstration techniques that had been successfully used by the best NCR sales reps. Senior management then ordered all NCR sales personnel to learn and use the same presentation.[3]

Such standardization of what an entire sales force says and does parallels the manufacturing process. More specific information will be provided when we describe the stimulus-response method of selling, but it is interesting to note that standardized presentations are frequently called **canned presentations**. One relatively new method of selling frequently uses standardized presentations. Large numbers of telemarketing firms provide scripts to guide their telephone salespersons. Chapter 14 will examine in depth telemarketing's growing role in sales.

Presentations as Jointly Produced Products

Sales personnel who perceive the presentation as something that both buyer and seller create believe that joint input is indispensable to a successful presentation. To try to maximize the customer's participation, the rep relies heavily on questions to initiate and encourage dialogue. You may wish to refresh your memory by returning to Chapter 7 where the three basic types of questions were described— channeling, clarifying, and verifying.

Viewing a sales presentation as something all participants create has much to recommend it in most sales situations. By acknowledging the necessity of customer participation, the sales rep immediately starts to think of *us* (the customer and me) instead of being inwardly focused (me). Subtle indicators are seen in such statements as, "We have analyzed your need together this afternoon and reached the conclusion that we need to take some action." By contrast, the inwardly focused salesperson who has finished making a presentation might say, "I think I have clearly demonstrated that you need to take some action."

Does the adoption of this perspective diminish the need to plan and prepare for a presentation? Quite the contrary; sales reps who intend to work with customers and jointly create a mutually beneficial sales presentation must be better prepared than those reps who use a canned presentation. Why?

If the presentation has been produced at company headquarters or at the salesperson's office and then used time after time with each customer, the rep believes he or she is prepared by just knowing what to say. After memorizing the statements that have been designed to elicit favorable customer responses, the rep thinks all that is needed is the customer's name, address, and appointment time.

In contrast, a salesperson who views presentations as joint creations will not have preconceived notions about what to tell the customer. Good, incisive questions to draw out information from a customer require an understanding of the customer's industry, neighborhood, and profession. Mayer and Greenberg have stated that empathy (the ability to understand what another person is experiencing) is indispensable to success.[4] The salesperson cannot understand or empathize, however, without knowing a great deal about the circumstances in which the buyer functions. The customer's questions or concerns can be understood only if the salesperson knows about the customer's environment. It takes a confident and well-prepared salesperson to invite a customer to ask any questions he or she can think of pertaining to the product, service, or the company.

BASIC TYPES OF PRESENTATIONS

Numerous titles or labels describe the basic presentations. Many sales consultants who conduct seminars and workshops to teach their particular approaches to more effective selling have coined titles to distinguish their sales methods. The five presentations described here—stimulus-response, formula-based, chain of logic, need-satisfaction, and problem-solution—have all been successful in various circumstances. Let us analyze the situation in which a particular presentation seems to be the most efficient.

Stimulus-Response Presentations

Psychologists conducting research in learning behavior have probed extensively into stimuli and the responses to stimuli. A classic example is the application of an electric shock to a white rat to stimulate the rat to learn an activity, such as running through a maze. Humans also respond to stimuli, and because of humans' higher capacity to reason, the stimuli (fortunately) do not always have to be as obvious as electrical shocks. In most sales situations, the stimuli are words.

In the **stimulus-response presentation**, a series of statements about the customer, the salesperson, the salesperson's company, and the product are created, and words and phrases that are believed to be stimulating are inserted. The presenter believes that these stimuli will evoke positive responses from the customer. Examples of words that tend to elicit a positive response are user-friendly, satisfaction guaranteed, profit, productivity improvement, no money down, easy terms, exclusive, maximum protection, and the person's name. Of course, these are only a few of the words and phrases we frequently see and hear in sales presentations, printed advertisements, direct mail pieces, and television and radio commercials. The theory underlying the stimulus-response presentation is that the customer's reaction to the salesperson and the opportunity to buy will be favorable if enough positive stimuli are directed at the prospective buyer.

To reinforce the benefits of buying the videotapes, a sales presentation might also include sample advertisements for expensive training courses that had been featured in the customer's local newspapers. The salesperson could show the customer how much it would cost the organization to use the "other guy's approach" versus the videotaped method. In addition, the sales representative can mention that once the videotapes are purchased, they can by played over and over as needed, whereas training sessions conducted by an instructor must be scheduled several days or weeks in advance and are much more costly in the long run.

The stimulus-response method has definite strengths in certain situations.[5] When a product or service is standardized and cannot be changed to fit a specific

Exhibit 8-2 How to Create a Stimulus-Response Presentation

1. **Benefitize** your product or service by translating the features of the product or service into benefits you believe to be valuable to the customer.

   Example: The product in this example is a video-tape training film which could be used to train people on how to use personal computers.

   Features
   a. Pictures show close-up shots of the keyboard.
   b. Freeze-frame situations stop the action at key points in the presentation.
   c. Pictures illustrate what each key-stroke should produce on the CRT in front of the student.
   d. Video-tape series is broken up into beginning, intermediary, and advanced stages.

   Benefits
   a. Students get to see and hear the instruction they are receiving, so they learn faster.
   b. Freeze-frame shots permit the instructor to keep everyone moving at the same pace—no one gets "left behind."
   c. Trainees can quickly verify whether they are getting the instructions right.
   d. Three different classes can be conducted jointly, thus achieving greater productivity.

2. Identify words and phrases that will stimulate a positive reaction toward the feature/benefits: easy-to-understand, learner oriented, eliminate computer phobia, more cost-effective training, faster learning, scientifically proven instruction techniques, satisfaction guaranteed, flexible.

3. Develop pictures and/or other visual aids which a salesperson can use to illustrate what he or she is saying during the presentation. One such visual aid would be a large picture of a computer keyboard with the appropriate key circled to show how easy it will be for a learner to follow the instructions.

4. Develop a script containing statements and questions which can be used by the salesperson which utilize the feature and benefits that have been linked together. Employ the words and phrases identified in Step 2 in the script.

   Here is part of a script: "Ms. Jones I really appreciate your giving me a few minutes of your time to describe one of the most economical, easy-to-understand ways of training people to use personal computers. Would you be interested in introducing a training program that has been scientifically designed to teach people how to use a PC in as little as two hours of economical instruction?"

customer, or if the desired benefits are generally the same from one instance to another, then such a presentation may be appropriate. Advocates are attracted to this method because it is efficient in the time it takes to deliver the presentation. The developers of the sales points can link them together using visual aids when necessary. During sales training, the presentation can be taught to an entire sales force. Sales force management then has the assurance that all the reps are delivering a uniform, quality presentation. This may be important in circumstances where the sales force is inexperienced, employee turnover is high, or management cannot or does not want to spend much time or money training sales personnel before they are given a territory and assigned sales responsibilities.

The biggest drawback to the stimulus-response, canned form of presentation is that it tends to make the salesperson sound artificial. Rather than carrying on a give-and-take conversation with all of the normal asides and explorations of minor points, the sales rep who sticks closely to the "script" will cover a broad range of features and benefits in a very short time. In fact, the coverage may seem so broad it will tend to overwhelm the listener. The listener (i.e., prospective customer) will in turn become more defensive and, in some cases, even hostile. The tendency is to dismiss canned presentations as "sales talk."

Formula-Based Presentations

First of all, there is no formula, real or imaginary, that can always be used to achieve a successful sale. However, sales trainers working with salespeople find that the use of a "formula" will help the trainees remember some important points or circumstances that should occur in a sales presentation. The two formulas described in the following material are the AIDA formula and the FUN-FAB OPTIC formula.

The AIDA Formula

The AIDA acronym is comprised of the first letters of various mental conditions a purchaser is believed to go through as he or she decides about making a transaction. The salesperson, as he or she makes a presentation, tries to present information in such a manner that will cause a sale to be made.

The first element in the formula is *attention*. Second, after gaining the prospect's attention, the sales rep attempts to arouse the *interest* of the individual to whom the presentation is being made. The third condition the rep hopes to stimulate is the *desire* of the prospect for the product or service. Fourth, the salesperson wants the prospect to be willing to take *action* (namely, agree to a purchase).

How the transition from one mental state to the next will be accomplished is of course largely influenced by such factors as (1) the degree of perceived need for the product in the mind of the prospect before the salesperson even approaches the prospective buyer, (2) the nature of the product or service—generally, tangible products are easier to sell than intangible services because of demonstration possibilities, (3) the lack of interruptions that will distract a buyer's attention, and

(4) the perceptiveness of the salesperson who must detect when the prospect is sufficiently interested in the proposed offering to move to the next step in the sale.

In some cases, prepared sales presentations which are to be memorized and delivered verbatim by sales reps are created with the AIDA formula as the foundation. A script will be written which contains statements for the sales rep to use which are expected to get the attention of a prospect.

> *Here is an example of an opening statement meant to arouse a person's attention: "A recent survey by AARP indicates that less than 50 percent of all retired people are financially self-sufficient."*

Additional statements—and perhaps questions—will then be created which are aimed at stimulating a strong interest, fostering the desire to purchase the product or service, and moving the prospect to take action.

The AIDA formula should be viewed as a helpful, easy-to-remember reminder. Taken too literally by inexperienced salespeople, it can produce confusion and discouragement among the sales reps who believe that customers always behave in exactly the way the formula suggests. For example, attention can be disrupted at any time during a presentation. One of the worst things to happen is for the customer to receive a telephone call between the time the salesperson has asked the question "How many of these do you need?" and the customer's response. Distracted by other matters and perhaps reminded of factors not previously considered, the customer's intention to purchase may vanish. This situation tests the poise of a professional salesperson who must then try to revive the sale.

How customers function according to the AIDA model is illustrated in Exhibit 8-3. Attention is its foundation. The salesperson must keep the customer's attention while the other psychological conditions are being developed. Interest grows into desire that, in turn, causes action. Ultimately, satisfaction is achieved if the customer's expectations have been or are being met.

In much the same way that individuals have varying amounts of tolerance for pain, heat, cold, and so on, so also do they have varying amounts of interest and desire in a particular product or service. This, in turn, affects their individual desires to know more. The strength of a person's desire will affect his or her readiness to take action. As an example, an avid photographer, because of his or her interest, might be attentive to a salesperson who offers to demonstrate a new camera. Capitalizing on the initial interest, the astute salesperson attempts to make statements and provide credible evidence supporting the camera and, thereby, strengthen the desire of the camera buff to take action and purchase it.

Psychology offers a useful concept called *thresholds* to anyone interested in influencing other people's behavior. A **threshold** is the level of awareness a person

EXHIBIT 8-3 Stages of the AIDAS Model*

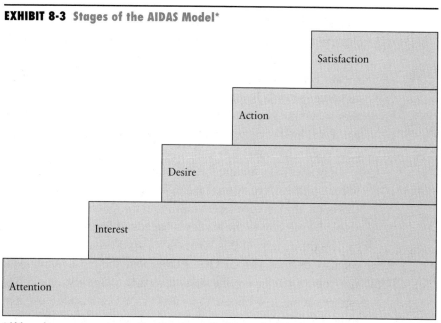

*Although current communication theory usually does not include the "S" stage, Kinnear and Bernhardt have wisely added an additional level. The "S" level or stage takes into account the outcome of the purchase—to what degree the consumer is satisfied—which is important in establishing and maintaining lasting customer relationships.

[Thomas C. Kinnear and Kenneth L. Bernhardt, *Principles of Marketing*, 2nd ed. (Glenview, Ill.: Scott, Foresman, 1986), p. 445].

experiences that causes the person to realize some condition exists (for example, hunger or cold).

What does this have to do with personal selling? The salesperson has to stimulate enough interest and desire to get a customer to take action and make the commitment to purchase. In other words, each of the steps in Exhibit 8-3 represents a threshold. The salesperson obviously has to rapidly evaluate the most effective way to help move a customer over a threshold into a condition closer to the action step.

Another challenge is to determine how much time and what kind of effort to expend before testing whether the customer is ready for action. Asking whether the customer is ready to take action is what salespeople refer to as a *trial close*. How does the salesperson detect that the customer has crossed one of these thresholds? Usually, by asking questions and listening carefully. Another, less direct, route is observation of body language.[6] As a relationship grows between salesperson and customer, an alert sales professional will learn which reactions are most revealing about a particular customer's thoughts. More information on trial closes and reading customers' reactions appears in Chapter 9.

The FUN-FAB OPTIC Formula

Professor Stan Kossen in *Creative Selling Today* explains the three stages of the FUN-FAB OPTIC formula in an easy-to-remember way.[7] He begins with the statement, "Let's have some FUN." This cautions the salesperson to *f*irst *u*ncover the customer's *n*eeds before starting to describe the product or service. Kossen further recommends that the rep discover these by asking probing questions such as, "What kind of car are you now driving? When are you planning to move? What kind of jobs have you had in the past?"

Only after determining the specific needs should the rep begin to move into the second phase. Here again, Kossen has a short memory-jogger: "Make it FAB." At this point, the rep can start to talk about the *f*eatures, *a*dvantages, and *b*enefits that would be relevant to the particular needs of the customer.

The third stage of this formula is easy to remember by using Kossen's statement, "Convince with OPTIC." At this point the rep is reminded that most prospective buyers will have some *o*bjections that will require the rep to *p*rove his or her earlier claims. In addition, the salesperson is advised to use a *t*rial close to determine whether the customer is now ready to buy. If not, there will be a need to provide more *i*nformation to insure that all questions or objections have been resolved. Finally, the rep who uses this formula will be reminded to gain *c*losure for the sale.

This particular formula is instructive in that it initially reminds the salesperson to zero in on the concerns of the customer. Why waste time describing features, advantages, and benefits that are not of interest to the prospect? A second advantage is that the formula takes into account the distinct possibility that a customer will have objections, or at least questions that must be answered, and the desire to see proof and be assured that the product will do what the salesperson claims it will.

The FUN-FAB OPTIC memory jogger, while useful, does not guarantee success. Considerable skill, for instance, is required on the part of the salesperson to comply with the first stage of the formula and uncover the prospect's needs. As we will see, this method of structuring a sales presentation has much in common with the need-satisfaction method described later in this chapter.

Chain of Logic Presentations

A **chain of logic presentation** assumes (1) the agreement to purchase the offered product or service is a logical solution to a customer's problem or potential problem, and (2) the customer will recognize that it is the logical answer. Based on these assumptions, the sales rep develops a presentation that begins with statements and questions designed to get the customer to agree with the salesperson. For example, a sales representative is talking to a purchasing agent about paint spraying equipment for use on an assembly line. The dialogue might run something like this:

Sales rep:	Top management seems to be interested in increasing productivity in any way it can, don't you think?
Purchasing agent:	Yeah, we hear about it all the time.
Sales rep:	One way to increase productivity is to use machines to replace people when the tasks are repetitive. Have you seen evidence of that in your operations?
Purchasing agent:	Sure, we find that automation provides us with a lot of benefits.
Sales rep:	I certainly agree with that. Several of my customers have found that a piece of equipment we sell increases their productivity by an average of 5 to 10 percent a day. Would you be interested in such an improvement in this plant?
Purchasing agent:	What do you have in mind? If you can prove that it can do that much for us, we surely would be interested.

Obviously, space will not permit more than a glimpse at the sequence of steps or stages in this presentation. The sales rep's objective is to build a series of logical arguments so that, finally, the customer feels the purchase agreement seems to be the logical step to take. Sometimes this form of presenting a product or service is called **constant affirmation** because the sales rep wants the customer to agree with each point he or she mentions. When disagreement does occur, the sales rep must tactfully explore why the customer cannot accept the next logical point. For instance, if the purchasing agent had not agreed that automation would improve productivity in a manufacturing operation, the sales rep should not attempt to move to the next level of logic until agreement was obtained.

The **barrier theory** is another term used to describe such presentations. The rationale for the term barrier is that once a person has agreed to a proposition, the agreement forms a mental barrier. For example, if a customer had previously agreed that he or she was interested in saving money and that the product in question would save money, those two agreements would logically block the person from saying he or she was not interested in the product. If the customer did express a lack of interest, it would signal the sales rep that there was some other obstacle barring the path to a sale. In Chapter 9, we will describe ways to handle objections—direct as well as hidden ones.

It is not recommended that salespeople view their presentations as characterized by barriers or logic traps. To do so puts the interaction occurring between the salesperson and customer in an adversarial light. Lasting relationships are not developed in situations where the customer feels trapped or manipulated into making a purchase.

There is definitely nothing wrong, however, with salespeople analyzing the information they intend to convey and the sequence in which they intend to use it, and then testing it for logical flow. This is very important in the counselor and systems designer relationships (see Chapter 3). As you recall, the customer or client in these relationships may initially have very little idea about how to achieve a goal. The purpose of a presentation, therefore, would be to educate the customer or client and build and reaffirm trust in the salesperson. Starting with some mutually agreed upon position, the salesperson would then present information in a logical manner to guide the customer or client to conclude that the recommended solution is appropriate.

Need-Satisfaction Presentations

The sales rep making a **need-satisfaction presentation** is oriented toward discovering and meeting a customer's needs. To make the discovery, the salesperson must ask questions very skillfully. This is especially true in the first meeting with a new customer. A word of caution, however. If the questions are too intrusive or blunt (for example, "How much money do you make?"), the customer may become irritated.

In the description of the stimulus-response presentation, we mentioned identifying the benefits of a product or service and developing a standardized sales talk. These steps are taken in the absence of a customer. Contrast this to the need-satisfaction presentation, in which the process occurs in the presence of the individual customer, and the salesperson finds out for that specific customer what the most important benefits are. Thus, each presentation is truly customized to the particular customer or client.

For example, a Xerox salesperson selling a copier to an office manager in an architectural firm would not use the same sales presentation in a school superintendent's office. The reproduction requirements for architectural drawings dictate that the salesperson learn all he or she could about the nature of the material the architect would want to reproduce. The same need exists to explore the document-copying activities in the school superintendent's office so that an appropriate presentation could be made.

One sales consultant states that questioning and analyzing customer needs have replaced the traditional (canned) presentation as the most important step in the selling process.[8] Because of the value most companies place on being customer-oriented, the need-satisfaction presentation method would seem to be vastly superior to the three presentation methods mentioned earlier (especially stimulus-response). It *will* be superior if the following conditions exist:

1. Salespeople can be trained to ask the right questions to discover customer needs.

2. There is significant difference among customers to warrant an in-depth examination of individual needs.

3. The revenue from making a sale is large enough to permit a salesperson to spend a lot of time with an individual customer to learn about his or her circumstances.

If these conditions don't exist, the sales rep would be better advised to use one of the more traditional, structured presentations. More customers or prospective customers can then be contacted at less cost.

Problem-Solution Presentations

The **problem-solution presentation** has strong similarities to the need-satisfaction method. Both are considered in-depth analyses of a specific customer's circumstances. Problem-solution presentations differ primarily in that they are based on more formal studies of the customer's operations. Several sales visits are usually required. One of the first tasks of salespeople using this approach is to get the customer's permission to allow the sales rep to conduct a study. The sales rep will then conduct the study and meet again with the customer to discuss the findings and determine whether a significant problem exists to warrant some action. In most cases, the salesperson submits a proposal, which is frequently accompanied by a formal presentation during which several of the customer's personnel may be

Figure 8-1 Salespeople can be trained to ask the right questions in order to discover customer needs.

present. Some technical support people from the sales rep's company may also be present. Usually, this situation involves a very significant dollar expenditure, and the elapsed time from the start of a formal study or analysis to the presentation of a proposal may consume several months. The types of products and services being sold are very expensive industrial goods and services: computer systems, advertising campaigns, telecommunications systems for entire companies or office buildings, and commercial banking services are a few examples.

Of the three basic relationships described in Chapter 3, this selling presentation method is most likely to be used in conjunction with the systems designer relationship. Professional salespeople functioning in this kind of environment must be highly proficient in analyzing problems and communicating persuasively with a wide range of people in the customer's organization. The sales rep must also be able to solicit technical support personnel's help from within his or her own firm. The costs of preparing and giving a presentation of this nature can be enormous. AT&T paid $100,000 to each of the four advertising agencies that were finalists for the American Bell account.[9] This was considered to be the cost of researching and preparing proposed advertising campaigns and presenting them to a committee of American Bell managers. When one considers, however, that a $60 million advertising account was at stake, the costs were not exorbitant (0.17 percent).

Another well-known company whose salespeople are engaged in the problem-solving method is the Mobil Corporation. Salespeople in the Plastics Division of Mobil use the problem solving approach when selling disposable food service items to hospitals.[10] The alternatives to Mobil's plastic utensils are glass and stainless steel. Mobil's sales reps acquire cost figures from the hospital which they use to analyze how much it is costing a hospital to conduct its food service operation. Using this data in an accounting model, Mobil reps can compare the hospital's operating costs if it continues to use the glass and stainless steel utensils rather than the plastics which Mobil could provide. The acquisition and verification of data takes time. When a decision is made, however, the quality of the purchasing decision is likely to be much better because of the various costs and the total benefits that have been painstakingly studied.

Which Presentation Is Best?

There is no unequivocal answer. In today's sales environment, where consumers and organization buyers are generally better educated and more demanding, the need-satisfaction and problem-solution presentations would seem to be favored. The skilled professional salesperson can reap some beneficial insights, however, from analyzing and judiciously using portions of the other three presentations.

From the stimulus-response method, a salesperson can learn that each person has special interests to which the sales rep can appeal by using words that signal the customer, "This salesperson has something of value for me." The AIDA formula can make a contribution by sensitizing salespeople to the various behavioral states or conditions through which a customer moves. The chain of logic can reveal the need to analyze the logical flow of the dialogue between a salesperson and a customer. And as noted earlier, that should not mean that logic will be used to trap or ensnare the customer.

The successful salesperson will become a student of each presentation method and will search for ways in which each method's strengths can be employed. One way to analyze and improve presentations is to study the dynamics of a good presentation.

PRESENTATION DYNAMICS

Dynamics deal with the forces and factors that drive and govern an object or an event. We sometimes compliment a speaker by saying "What a dynamic presentation!" In such cases, we have been impressed with the vigor and clarity with which the speaker has made the presentation. Unfortunately, not all speakers or salespersons make dynamic presentations. All presentations, regardless of whether they are dynamic, are influenced by certain forces or dynamics.

Exhibit 8-4 depicts factors that affect a sales presentation. The figure has the customer at the center, which symbolizes the customer's importance as the target of the presentation. Surrounding the prospective customer are variables the sales representative should use to ensure the most effective presentation for an individual customer. It is important to understand the term *variable* as we study sales presentation dynamics. The salesperson has an opportunity to vary, as he or she sees fit, each of the elements that surround the prospective customer in Exhibit 8-4. As each variable is explained, the opportunities available to the sales rep to modify it in some way will be described.

Presentation Pace

Presentation pace is the speed with which an attempt is made to move a presentation toward its conclusion. The pace of a stimulus-response presentation is usually much faster compared to a need-satisfaction presentation. When a sales rep will have only one contact with a customer to either make a sale or determine that one cannot be made, the pace is rapid because the salesperson wants to know as quickly as possible whether he or she is wasting time with the prospect. The rep who doesn't have to work under such severe time constraints can take several

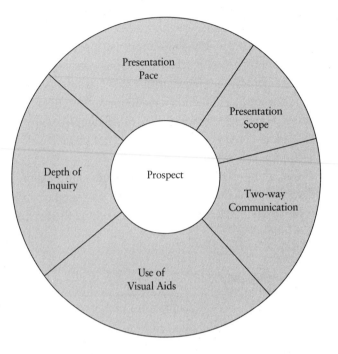

Exhibit 8-4 Factors
Affecting Sales
Presentations

factors into account to find the optimum pace for an individual customer. One factor is the ability of the customer to intellectually grasp the content of the presentation. One of the biggest problems with canned, memorized presentations is that the salesperson usually has no knowledge of the customer's abilities (or lack of abilities) to understand the information. The salesperson starts peppering the customer with facts, figures, features, and benefits that may escape the customer's understanding.

The optimum pace of a sales presentation is affected by the customer's communication style. Various communication styles have been analyzed, and one widely used analysis identifies individuals as being either drivers, analyticals, amiables, or expressives.[11]

Drivers tend to want information that will permit them to make rapid but accurate decisions. Presentations to such people must be fast-paced. The logic used by the salesperson should be quickly apparent to the driver. He or she is likely to be very goal-oriented and, to be satisfied, wants to know that these goals are being attained.

Analyticals typically want information in great detail. The pace of a presentation to such a person will be much slower as the analytical digests the facts and requests more information.

Amiables want presentations that are lengthy enough to contain information on how the proposed product or service will affect people. Because amiables tend to be sensitive about how people feel, they want details that would be considered irrelevant by drivers. Amiables may also take a long time to decide because they want other people's approval before making a decision. They don't want to feel they are being pushed; therefore, the presentation should be slower-paced to accommodate this type of people.

Expressives, on the other hand, seem to be impulsive. A presentation to them can be fast-paced if it contains the right material. Expressives regard products as symbols or indicators of status. They use products and symbols to communicate. If they can be assured that buying and using a particular product is the "in" thing to do, the presentation pace can be rapid.

In addition to the customer's communication style, three other factors govern the speed with which a presentation should move. One is the customer's previous experience in purchasing the product or service; closely related is the buyer's experience in purchasing from the sales representative and from the rep's company. The optimal situation is for the rep to be a trusted information source and to be backed up by a company that, in the mind of the buyer, is a reliable supplier.

Another factor is the complexity and future significance of the product or service to the buyer. The greater the number of features the customer considers important, the slower-paced the presentation should be.

The third factor is the clarity with which the customer perceives a need for the product or service. In the supplier relationship described in Chapter 3, you will recall that customers were aware of their needs and what it would take to satisfy them. When this situation exists, the pace of the presentation may be extremely quick ("Yes, we have the product available and it can be shipped immediately"). In contrast, an unsought good such as business interruption insurance will require that the pace be slowed to permit the sales rep to (1) educate the client to the need for such insurance and (2) persuade the prospect that a specific policy is the best buy.

Presentation Scope

Presentation scope is defined as the range of features, benefits, and sales terms covered in one presentation. Basically, there are three factors to take into account when planning the scope of a single presentation or a series of presentations. First, how much does the sales rep know about the customer's priorities or values? Probably one of the most frequently used phrases in sales is "Find the prospect's 'hot button.'" In the typical stimulus-response presentation, a broad-scoped presentation is used. Such presentations are designed to have appeals for as many people as possible. In contrast, many highly successful salespeople find that after listening to the customer's responses to questions, they are able to focus the presentation on the one most important benefit to the customer. In the complex environments of large businesses, a number of decision makers (each of whom have different interests) are likely to confront the salesperson. In such cases, the sales rep will need to differentiate the scope and content of presentations, depending on the management level and the specialty of the persons attending the presentation.[12]

A second factor is the approach the sales rep takes when dealing with competitors' claims. Some reps may choose to counter potential competitor claims explicitly and point-by-point. This can lead to a very broad-scoped presentation. If the sales rep knows what benefit or small group of benefits competitors are focusing their efforts on, he or she can narrow the scope of the presentations accordingly.

The third factor is the salesperson's perception of the time span in which the customer will probably make a decision. The insightful salesperson can determine fairly accurately a customer's sense of urgency. Some salespeople attempt to stimulate the buyer's sense of urgency by using a technique called the standing-room-only (SRO) close.[13] The SRO close threatens future nonavailability of the product unless the buyer makes a quick decision to purchase. When effective, this tactic serves to curtail additional searching by a buyer and the attendant risk that the buyer will purchase from someone else. It can be counterproductive, however, if buyers suspect they are being pressured or that the salesperson is lying about the pending nonavailability of the product.

Depth of Inquiry

Depth of inquiry is the extent of effort put forth by the sales rep to learn the details of the buyer's decision-making process. One of the most obvious factors influencing the depth of inquiry is the amount of information the salesperson has from previous contacts with the customer. A second factor is the extent to which multiple decision makers or influencers will figure in the sale. This is especially important in the early stages of the systems designer relationship, when the sales rep must learn the roles of various executives in a buyer's organization. A third factor influencing a sales rep's depth of inquiry is the degree of precision with which a potential buyer cites a goal or lodges an objection. Vague objections (see Chapter 9) should be clarified, usually with a question, such as "Thank you, Mr. Smith, for mentioning your concern over reliability. Can you give me an example of reliability problems you have had with other similar products?"

The final factor influencing depth of inquiry is the extent to which the prospect is favorably predisposed toward the product prior to the presentation. On some occasions, sales reps have endangered the sale by attempting to conduct an in-depth inquiry when all that was needed was to provide an order blank. More frequently, however, it is necessary to elicit information from the prospective buyer to determine how positive or negative he or she is toward the product and the salesperson's company. After a relationship has been established, this will not be as necessary as it was in the initial stage of a buyer-seller relationship.

Two-way Communication

The sales rep can provide ample opportunities for the customer to engage in **two-way communication**. The more intelligent and assertive the buyer is, the more the buyer will demand a participative role in the presentation. If the salesperson, to retain control over the meeting, ignores a customer's questions or brushes aside objections, he or she runs the risk of alienating the customer.

Another reason for the rep to actively encourage two-way communication with the buyer is that it gives the salesperson an opportunity to modify some point that will make the sale more attractive to the customer. For example, prices and delivery dates can be changed or modified in many industrial purchasing situations.

As you think about seller-buyer communication, a good rule-of-thumb to remember is the **2:1 ratio**. If the salesperson doesn't voice twice as many questions as statements about the product, then the salesperson needs to examine whether he or she is attempting to control the presentation too much. James Lorenzen, writing in *Marketing News*, states, "If the rep's ratio of questions to statements is 2:1, you have a top producer."[14]

Use of Visual Aids

Psychologists specializing in learning theory advocate the use of aids that will activate as many of the learner's senses as possible (sight, sound, taste, and feeling). As reps prepare for a presentation, they should devote thought to how various aids could be used.

One obvious aid, which many sales reps use effectively in their presentations, is the product itself. Getting hands-on experience with the product can involve otherwise bored or disinterested customers in the salesperson's presentation. Skilled professionals use several guidelines (see Exhibit 8-5) to improve their preparation prior to making a product demonstration.

Desk-top publishing has the capability to produce charts, graphs, and slides, permitting almost everyone to improve presentations. Just having visual aids, however, is insufficient. The rep should know how to use them correctly. The Audio Visual Division of 3M Corporation publishes a booklet, *Six Secrets to Holding A Good Meeting . . . Every Time*, that contains many helpful suggestions, some of which are contained in Exhibit 8-6.

EXHIBIT 8-5   A Checklist for Preparing and Rendering Effective Demonstrations

1. Has the product been checked to see that it is working correctly before the presentation? Have all the functions that will be demonstrated been checked?

2. When was the last preventive maintenance check? Are back-up parts available for components that might need replacing, such as batteries and bulbs?

3. If the demonstration will occur on the customer's premises, will any special conditions be required (lighting, power sources, and so on), and are they already available at the customer's site?

4. Will anyone be present who has had any experience using the product? If so, what were his or her reactions? If generally positive, could that person help demonstrate the effectiveness of the product? If generally negative, how does the product overcome the problems that were experienced earlier?

5. If the product performs a range of functions, which functions will be of most interest to those at the demonstration?

6. Will the customer use the product during the demonstration? If so, in a group? Are there some people who are more skilled who can participate in the demonstration? Is anyone likely to be present whose ineptitude or lack of knowledge might cause embarrassment?

7. Avoid jargon unless the audience understands it.

8. Has a competitor already demonstrated his or her product? If so, what were the features he or she emphasized?

9. If the product can be left with the customer for a trial period, has the customer had hands-on experience with it in addition to the demonstration? Names and telephone numbers the customer can call to get help should be provided.

10. If the product requires a warm-up period before it will work to its best advantage, pre-demonstration set-up time should be planned for.

We now have some understanding of the characteristics of a good sales presentation. We know that even though to a casual observer the presentation given by a skilled professional may seem as though it "just happened," in fact, it did not. An effective presentation is correctly paced for the customer, the scope is appropriate, all parties have an opportunity for two-way communication, and the appropriate visual aids are used. Now our attention will turn to approaching the customer.

APPROACHES: GETTING STARTED

By this stage in our examination of professional selling, you should not be surprised to learn that there is no universally accepted best way to approach a customer and commence a sales presentation. For instance, a sales rep who works for an internationally known company with a very good reputation probably has a dif-

---

Exhibit 8-6   A Checklist for Designing and Using Visual Aids

1. A slide or transparency should usually contain no more than four or five short phrases. Too many phrases cause the audience to focus more on the visual aid than on the speaker.
2. The presenter should speak directly to the audience (whether one other person or many people), rather than talking to the screen or the overhead projector.
3. Each visual aid should be tested to ensure it is clearly legible from any seat in the room.
4. Visual aids should be in the order in which they are needed and unpacked before the presentation starts.
5. If the customer might need the information, there should be copies to leave with him or her. This avoids having the customer copying down the information and not listening to the presenter.

---

ferent approach than the salesperson with a company that is just getting started. Four approaches, which were introduced in Chapter 7, will now be discussed and related to the customer contact situations (clean slate, brand-switching, resupply, supplementary sale).

Introductory Approach

The **introductory approach** is the most straightforward and frequently used approach. Here is an example of the approach:

Sales rep: Good morning, Mr. Jones. I'm Bill Carter from the Systems Division of IBM. We talked on the phone last week. I appreciate your giving me an opportunity to see you. (As Carter shakes hands, he extends his business card.)

The two sales situations for which this approach is best suited are the clean slate and the brand-switching contacts. As you recall from Chapter 7, in each of these contact situations the customer had had no experience dealing with the salesperson. Therefore, the sales rep not only has to sell the product but also has to sell himself or herself and his or her company.

Curiosity Approach

The **curiosity approach** requires imagination and a thorough knowledge of the customer's typical reactions to surprises. Checks written for extravagant sums, piles of real-looking "money," and pictures of the customer in the company of celebrities are some of the gimmicks salespeople have used to attract curiosity and hold customers' attention. The curiosity approach must be quickly followed up with statements revealing that the sales rep has a product or service that merits the customer's continued attention and interest.

Generally speaking, the curiosity approach should be used when the sales rep has previously established rapport with the customer. Otherwise, the salesperson may appear to be a huckster who uses gimmicks and can't be trusted. As a rule, sales reps should remember that their value to a customer is usually not based on their ability to entertain.

The curiosity approach is most likely to be effective in supplementary sales contact situations. If the customer has not previously purchased some particular item in the sales rep's line of products or services, the curiosity approach may be an effective way to introduce the customer to other products or services.

In another example of the curiosity approach, a salesperson encouraged dealers to stock a full line of his company's office supplies before the start of a dealer contest. All dealers who stocked the full line would be entered in a sweepstakes that had three expensive sports cars as grand prizes. The sales rep had sets of keys made with the sports cars' brand medallions attached to the key chains. As the rep met each of the dealers in their offices, he handed them a set of keys with the sports car medallion conspicuously dangling from the key chain. This provided a natural lead into an explanation of the upcoming contest and what the dealers needed to do to be eligible.

Benefit Approach

The **benefit approach** to launching a sales presentation is frequently used at the beginning of stimulus-response and formula-based presentations. The benefit cited by the salesperson is usually one that is expected to appeal to a broad range of people. Examples of such benefits include lower premiums for auto insurance coverage, higher interest rates on investments, more durable equipment, and faster, more versatile computer systems. A salesperson who uses the benefit approach might start a conversation with a customer in the following way:

Sales rep: Thank you, Ms. Smith, for permitting me to explain how the Acme Company can annually increase the value of your investment by at least 10 percent more than the company you are now using.

A benefit approach can also be employed on the second or subsequent contact a rep makes with a particular customer. In an initial meeting with a customer, the sales representative may have engaged in fact-finding, revealing the benefits the customer is seeking from a particular product or service. Armed with knowledge of what the customer's desires are, the sales rep finds a way in which his or her product will satisfy the customer. When the rep revisits the customer, the benefit approach communicates the result to the customer.

Sales rep: Frank, after discussing your business expansion plans, we have found a way
for you to handle your telephone service needs for the next three years at the
same monthly rate you are now paying.

In this situation, the salesperson is using a benefit (low telephone service costs)
that is known to be important to the customer. When the benefit approach is used
in conjunction with the stimulus-response or formula-based presentations, the
salesperson can only hope that the benefit is meaningful to the customer.

The benefit approach will work in three of the four customer contact situations:
the clean slate, brand-switching, and supplementary sales contacts. Of course, if
the customer is already buying the product or service (the resupply contact circumstances), it would be ridiculous to start the conversation with a recitation of
the benefits the customer is already receiving.

Referral Approach

Starting the interaction with a new contact can sometimes be done more effectively if the salesperson can mention the name of someone the customer knows
and respects. Although using the name of someone who has recommended that
the salesperson contact a customer—the **referral approach**—is effective in both
consumer and industrial selling, it has added significance in industrial selling. In
the industrial sales environment, it is important to know who has the authority to
make significant decisions.[15] When the salesperson can find and contact such a
decision maker, then the purchasing agents can be informed about the meeting
and the referral.

Sales rep: Good morning, Mr. Bellows. I am Janet Smith with Goodmonth Manfacturing
Company. Your Vice President of Operations, Ms. Francis, said I should talk
with you about a new pollution monitoring system in which Ms. Francis expressed some interest. I believe your department handles the purchasing
even though Ms. Francis has budget responsibility. Is that right?

The referral approach will work in either clean slate or brand-switching contacts. If the sales rep is attempting to get a customer to switch brands, it will help
if the person who has referred the sales rep is a well-known and trusted figure in
the eyes of the customer.

Sales rep: Ms. Rose, Sally Johnson, a friend of yours who is also one of my clients, suggested that I call you. She said you had a conversation the other day about single parent life insurance programs, and Sally thought you would be interested
in talking about our company's program.

This approach will work well if the endless-chain system (described in Chapter
6) is utilized. This approach alerts the customer that a friend or acquaintance has

enough confidence in the salesperson to make such a referral. By using the name of someone the customer knows, this approach also answers some questions about how he or she was discovered by the salesperson.

PRESENTATION CONTENT

What the rep has to sell forms the basis of the actual presentation content. A sales presentation should address three key questions to which a prospective buyer wants answers:

1. Is the proposed product or service a solution to my needs?
2. Is this company the best source of supply of the product or service?
3. Is this salesperson knowledgeable and truthful?

As we've already discussed, salespeople find that sometimes there will be three sales in one (the product or service, the company, and the sales rep). Getting the sale will mean (1) convincing the prospect that purchasing the product or service will benefit the prospect, (2) persuading the prospect that the firm will stand behind its wares, and (3) instilling confidence in the prospect that the sales rep is knowledgeable and trustworthy. Not every customer contact will result in presentations that explicitly sell all three. Exhibit 8-7 reflects the way the content of a presentation will differ for each type of basic customer contact across the three points described above, and we discuss the content in more detail below.

Selling the Product and the Brand

Salespeople sometimes encounter prospective customers who have never used any brand of a particular product. For example, a sales rep for a FAX equipment vendor may encounter a prospective customer who does not have a FAX machine in his or her office and has never used one. Rush deliveries of outgoing mail have always been turned over to Federal Express. Naturally, the sales rep would like to convince the customer to use FAX instead. In such situations, the first objective in the sales presentation is to convince the customer that FAX equipment and its benefits are superior to overnight delivery service.

A sales rep can use questions to draw out information from the customer about his or her mail transmission schedules and determine whether there is a need for a FAX. When the customer has had no experience with this product, it is important to take time to first establish the need in the customer's mind. In this particular case, the rep would want to know (1) what type of letters or documents the customer's office sent via overnight delivery, (2) how frequently these letters or documents were mailed, and (3) whether the volume of outgoing mail was ex-

Exhibit 8-7 Presentation Content by Type of Customer Contact

Type of Contact	Presentation Content			
	Product or Service *	*Brand* **	*Company*	*Salesperson*
Clean slate	✓	✓	✓	✓
Brand switching		✓	✓	✓
Resupply		✓		
Supplementary sale	✓	✓		

*Product or service is defined as the general category or object bearing a name that identifies it—personal computers, cable TV, bottled water, etc.

**Brand is defined as a specific member of a product group—IBM Personal Computer, Storer Company Cable TV, Perrier bottled water, etc.

pected to increase or decrease. This information would be needed to develop a **business case**.

A business case is a quantitative justification for making a purchase decision. The salesperson selling FAX equipment would use the data supplied by the customer to determine an average month's costs using Federal Express for all rapid deliveries of mail. If an anticipated increase in outgoing mail were significant, the associated costs would also rise. With information revealing the comparative advantage of using FAX, the salesperson would make a presentation in which at least the first portion would be devoted to explaining why a FAX is a more cost-effective solution to the rapid delivery problem. The business case created by the salesperson could also be used by the buyer to explain to his or her superiors why the purchase of FAX equipment was justified.

Assuming that the business case successfully persuaded the customer to use a FAX, the next stage would be to sell the customer on the sales rep's particular brand of FAX equipment. Since any potential buyer has a wide variety of brands from which to choose, the sales rep must develop a differential advantage for a brand in the customer's mind.

If the customer thinks the purchase will involve a significant outlay of money, reflect on the purchaser's judgment, or otherwise be an important decision, he or she is likely to want to compare various brands of FAX equipment. The sales rep who has asked the right questions and gathered relevant information through questions and skillful listening can match the features of his or her brand to the relevant benefits sought by the buyer. With his or her analysis of the brand's features and benefits the rep will make statements about the company. These statements can convince a buyer that the rep not only has a good brand, but equally important for many people, also has an excellent company to back the brand. This in-depth description of the product and the company's reputation for service is very important in selling industrial products and services. Professional purchasing agents are especially interested in knowing about the vendors to whom they award business.

Selling the Company

One easily understandable attribute of a vendor is size. For instance, the Gannett Company, a diversified national news and information company, owns ninety daily newspapers including *USA Today*, thirty-five nondailies, and *USA Weekend*, a weekly magazine.[16] A Gannett sales rep, calling on an advertising agency or a potential advertiser, could cite some of these facts to give a potential customer an appreciation of the company's stability and influence.

Financial strength is another important attribute to potential investors and clients. A sales rep for Shearson Lehman Hutton (owned by American Express Company) could tell a client about Shearson's $4.2 billion in capital, its $95 billion in asset management funds, and the nearly three million U.S. households that are served by its network of almost 12,000 financial consultants.[17]

A frequent question in industrial selling is, "Who else is buying from you?" A well-prepared sales rep should be able to describe as impressive a list of customers as possible. When the salesperson can reel off a number of well-known companies that are using the rep's products or services, it usually enhances the selling firm's image.

Another potentially useful bit of information to use in selling a customer on the company is any awards or seals of approval granted by a trade or professional association. Prestigious groups, such as the American Medical Association and the American Dental Association, occasionally issue awards or endorsements to companies. The receipt of an award can be used to good effect by sales personnel.

Testimonials by satisfied customers are one of the most powerful and efficient ways to sell a company. When a salesperson is attempting to establish a systems designer relationship, a visit by the prospective customer to other satisfied customers' plants or offices often has a strong impact. Not only can the prospect see the product or service operating in someone else's business, but also the old customer and potential customer can discuss the seller's abilities to provide pre- and postsale service.

Selling Yourself

How does a salesperson convince another person to do business with him or her when other products and other firms have similar offerings? When the competition is intense, the individual sales representative can be the decisive factor. When addressing a class of IBM marketing trainees, F.G. "Buck" Rodgers, former Vice President of Marketing at IBM, said, "Part of the beauty and excitement of selling comes with the knowledge that you—one person—can make a profound difference."[18]

Salespeople cannot overtly sell themselves as individuals. The former boxing champ, Muhammad Ali, could say, "I am the greatest," but that is not acceptable coming from a professional salesperson. Therefore, the sales rep sells himself or herself covertly by being packaged professionally: clean, businesslike attire, unobtrusive hair style, and an alert but pleasant manner. Next, the salesperson sends powerful messages about his or her competency by asking incisive questions and responding with truthful and accurate answers. And finally, the successful salesperson conveys that he or she adds value to the product or service by getting things accomplished for the customer (for example, quickly correcting billing or shipping problems with a minimum of inconvenience to the customer, or getting repairs made as fast as possible). Perhaps in no other area of business are actions more convincing than words. The sales rep cannot rely on words to sell himself or herself. Just as the product or service must ultimately perform, so must the salesperson.

GROUP PRESENTATIONS

Most of the time when we think of sales presentations, we envision a one-on-one situation (a salesperson talking to another party). Frequently, if the product or service is very expensive and/or complex, the rep will need to make presentations to a buying committee or a task force of people appointed to study the purchase. In Chapter 2 and also in Chapter 5, the buying center situation was mentioned. Occasionally, the members of a buying center will be participants on a committee. This offers a sales rep an opportunity to speak to each member and also to address them as a group. When such opportunities arise, the salesperson needs to realize that his or her preparation for a group presentation requires some different preparations compared with presentations to individuals. Exhibit 8-8 provides a checklist to be used in getting ready to deliver a presentation to a buying committee.

Know the Power Structure

In most buying committees, some person will outrank the other members. This person is called "the decisionmaker" in earlier descriptions of the buying center (see Chapters 2 and 5). When you are informed of your presentation opportunity, you should ask about the people who are most likely to attend the meeting. Gen-

Exhibit 8-8 A Checklist for Preparing a Buying Committee Presentation

1. What is the power structure among the attendees?
2. How much time has been allotted?
3. What types of visual aids or other sales aids are available for use?
4. What is most likely to be important to the group?
5. Will the group members be actively involved?
6. What is the most important point for the group to remember twenty-four hours after the presentation?
7. Would it be permissible and/or desirable for someone from the selling firm to accompany the rep?
8. What type of "leave behind" material would be effective?
9. Can a rehearsal be arranged?
10. What will occur after the presentation?

erally, your contact will indicate what positions are held by the probable attendees. The titles will normally indicate the ranking of the people.

Knowing the responsibilities of the meeting participants will permit you to start narrowing the scope of the material you could employ in your presentation. For instance, if the committee is chaired by the company controller you will certainly want to think about incorporating pay-back periods, start-up costs, and other financial data that would be significant to the controller.

A note of caution, however, is merited. After you know the ranks and the job responsibilities of people, don't neglect to have at least some information for each person's specialty. Even if it cannot be as much material as you plan to use for the decision maker, you don't want to ignore other members who may be quite influential. At the very least, be prepared to field questions from the other people.

Time Available

The committee may be hearing other presentations during their meeting. One extreme example involved two executives from Pilot Air Freight who made a presentation to GTE's traffic council.[19] The GTE council had allocated three days to hearing proposals from more than a dozen competitors who were seeking the GTE account. Each competitor was given four *minutes* to make a presentation and then was expected to answer council members' questions.

Fortunately, most salespeople don't have to squeeze their presentations into such time frames but, nevertheless, you should not plan on much more than ten minutes for your comments. It is far better to keep your prepared comments brief and spend most of the time answering questions the committee members will have. This will permit you to provide information that is important to them and that, after all, is what is most important.

Visual Aids

Your wise selection of visual aids is very important when you have a limited time to tell your story. Earlier in this chapter, guidance was given on the design and clarity of the visuals. Don't try to pack too much onto slides or overheads. Pick out key words or phrases and try to use terminology that is meaningful and important to your audience.

Content That Is Relevant

It would seem unnecessary to remind anyone preparing a presentation to evaluate it on the basis of its relevance to the listeners. Time and again, however, presentations are made using a litany of features and benefits which have been lifted out of a mass distributed sales brochure. Sometimes some of the features and benefits are relevant to a given group and other times not. The sales rep who can visit with the individuals prior to making a presentation to them as a group can avoid the dangers of a "shotgun" approach. As plans are being made, the presenter should be analyzing what could be presented in terms of the power structure situation. (Now that I know Ms. Franks is going to be there, will product delivery date information be more important than warranty date?) Using this type of evaluation can help zero in on what information should be included in your presentation.

Group Member Involvement

Think about ways to get your product, a mock-up of it, or even some key component part into the hands of the participants. In addition, giving them opportunities to ask questions or make comments will enhance the individual attendee's participation. The greater the involvement, both psychologically as well as physically, the more likely you are to make an impression on your audience.

Making a "Durable" Presentation

How many times have you heard a presentation (lecture, sermon, etc.), and within fifteen minutes after leaving the meeting, you couldn't recall the topic? This information "overload" is especially dangerous if your presentation is going to be just one of a number of other presentations or subjects which a buying committee will consider. Creating and delivering a presentation that will linger in the committee members' minds is a function of several things such as relevance, involvement, and the clarity with which you deliver your central points. Pick out one or two points you want your audience to remember and build your presentation around those points.

Using Other People from Your Company

If you are selling a complex, highly technical product or service, if your audience will contain technically oriented people, and if you are permitted to bring someone with you, a team presentation approach can be very useful. Reps are increasingly being asked by purchasers to assure the purchaser that pre- and post-sale installation and maintenance services are available. By having a representative to answer questions and exhibit your company's commitment to customer service, the buying committee can see tangible proof of what it is seeking.

"Leave-Behinds"

Brochures, models, samples, and letters of endorsement are some of the things that reps find useful to put in the hands of a committee for their scrutiny after the rep has departed. This is one more point to check on in your effort to be remembered and positively considered during the post-presentation evaluation session.

Figure 8-2 It is useful for sales reps to leave behind brochures so that buyers and buying committees have something to scrutinize after the rep has departed.

Rehearsal Plans

Even if you are only allotted four minutes, such as the Pilot Air Freight executives were, several "dry runs" before the presentation are very important. If you can get a person from the customer's organization to critique your rehearsal(s), so much the better. Ask your "audience" to think of some questions to ask you so you can practice your responses. If a staged rehearsal cannot be arranged, take time to rehearse your remarks on your own. One salesperson who makes many group presentations stands in front of a mirror in his hotel room the night before and practices his "lines." It is very useful to hear yourself saying the words you will eventually use. The more times you rehearse, the smoother and more professional your presentation will be.

Beyond the Presentation?

Will you know before you leave the group's presence what the next step is going to be? Perhaps the group will hear other presentations after yours and then convene for a final decision. Knowing when that might occur could present you with an opportunity to contact individual members of the group to see if they had thought of questions since your presentation.

SUMMARY

1. There are two fundamentally different views of sales presentations. One perspective is that salespeople make and deliver presentations in which they tell the customers about their products and services and their companies. The other is that a presentation is a participative process that heavily involves the customer. In the latter, the salesperson and the customer co-create the presentation so that each party has a stake in it.

2. The two perspectives are reflected in the five basic types of presentations covered in the chapter: stimulus-response, chain of logic, formula-based, need-satisfaction, and problem-solution.

3. Regardless of the basic presentation type used, each is characterized by various dynamics: speed or pace, scope, depth of inquiry, opportunity for two-way communication, and use of visual aids.

4. There are several ways to start a presentation: the introductory, curiosity, benefit, and referral approaches. The selection should be governed by the type of contact the sales rep will be making, whether the clean slate, brand-switching, supplementary sale, or resupply contacts.

5. Before a customer makes the first purchase from a salesperson, three sales have to be made. The prospect must be convinced that the product or service will satisfy a need, that the company represented by the salesperson is reliable, and that the salesperson is knowledgeable and trustworthy.

6. Presentations to a group of people in the buyer's organization must be planned carefully. By learning as much as possible about who will attend the presentation, the time allotted for the presentation, and other relevant circumstances, a salesperson can make the most of the opportunity.

QUESTIONS FOR DISCUSSION AND REVIEW

1. Do you think NCR still uses stimulus-response presentations among its salespeople who are selling expensive equipment to retailers? Why? What form of presentation do you think would be most suitable for NCR's salespeople under present business conditions?

2. What circumstances would make each of the following types of presentations appropriate?
   a. Stimulus-response
   b. Need-satisfaction
   c. Problem-solution

3. Even if a salesperson did not use the formula-based or chain of logic types of presentation, what could he or she learn from them that might be useful?

4. What is the difference between a dynamic presentation and presentation dynamics?

5. Why are the sales presentation variables clustered around the prospect in Exhibit 8-4?

6. What factors affect the pace of a sales presentation?

7. Of the presentation types listed in question 2, which one would probably allow the least amount of two-way communication between the sales rep and the customer?

8. Which of the presentations would require the greatest depth of inquiry by the sales rep? What circumstances would justify an extensive in-depth inquiry?

9. Why would it be risky to try the curiosity approach with a customer in a clean slate contact situation?

10. How would the benefit approach differ in a canned presentation compared with a need-satisfaction presentation? (Note: Assume the need-satisfaction presentation is occurring on the sales rep's second visit.)

11. Discuss the use of the referral approach as it would relate to the AIDA presentation.

12. What type of prospecting would permit the use of the referral approach?

13. Describe three ways a salesperson might persuade the customer that the salesperson's company is the best one with which to do business.

14. If you thought you were going to be making a presentation to a "driver," what approach would you use if you knew you had fifteen minutes and would not have another chance to meet with the person unless you succeeded in presenting something interesting to him or her?

15. What types of products or services would seem to involve groups of people to whom presentations can be made?

16. What are "leave behinds" and why are they frequently used?

CASE 8–1   PREPARING FOR AN IMPORTANT GROUP PRESENTATION

Phyllis Flood, a National Account Manager for International Communications, hung up the telephone. She had just finished making reservations for her company's Customer Presentation Center. The meeting she had scheduled would be conducted at 10:00 a.m. on the twelfth of April, which was two weeks away. Phyllis' group was getting ready to make a two hour presentation to the Physical Facilities Committee of ZENOR Petroleum Company, one of International's largest customers.

The ZENOR corporation annually purchased approximately $10 million in telecommunication services from International. ZENOR's operations were dispersed around the world in fifteen different countries, with headquarters in Dallas, Texas.

Phyllis' responsibility as the National Account Manager was to ensure that ZENOR continued to rely on International for its telecommunications services. To assist her, Phyllis had five people dedicated to the ZENOR account. Other resources Phyllis could utilize were product managers in International's headquarters in Basking Ridge, New Jersey, and technical experts in the R&D facility who could describe new product research. On the local scene, Phyllis could utilize people in the Customer Presentation Center, who would assist her in creating audio-visual materials and preparing any equipment and services to demonstrate International's vast array of telecommunications products and services.

Phyllis was now attempting to sell ZENOR a teleconferencing system that could link all its major offices around the world with ZENOR'S headquarters. She and her subordinates had been calling on various ZENOR executives for the past six months. One of the key people was Mark Fitzpatrick, ZENOR's Telecommunications Manager. Phyllis was grateful that Mark had expressed a keen interest in creating the teleconferencing network. He had shared with Phyllis several stories about the enormous travel costs ZENOR paid each year as a result of executives traveling to meetings. ZENOR's organization now contained an office devoted exclusively to making travel arrangements for people who were planning to make business trips.

During the six months Phyllis' group had worked on this project, they had taken Mark to visit three other customers who had adopted teleconferencing within the past three years. They toured the customers' office spaces and, in one case, watched an actual meeting in which five locations were linked together (New York City, Los Angeles, Honolulu, London, and Madrid). In addition, Phyllis had escorted Mark and his boss, Wanda Mercer, to Edloe, New Jersey, where they toured International Laboratories, the R&D facility that International used to create new products and services. There they saw an array of new products that would soon be available to make international teleconferencing even easier to use.

Shortly after the trip to New Jersey, Phyllis and Mark had a meeting to discuss how to proceed in the next stage of the sale. Mark had said that Wanda Mercer, the VP of Facilities Management, was enthusiastic about the teleconferencing concept and wanted to see a formal proposal. Wanda had ten managers reporting to her who were located in ZENOR's largest office buildings in the U.S. and in other countries. These would be key people in the successful creation and implementation of the teleconferencing network. The group met twice a year at ZENOR headquarters to discuss facilities maintenance plans, budgets, and other new developments in physical facilities. They would be meeting during the week of April 10, and Phyllis had been invited to make a presentation to the group on April 12.

As Phyllis hung up the phone, she immediately realized the need to call her people together to tell them about the scheduled group presentation. They had two weeks to prepare for this very important event.

QUESTIONS

1. If you were in Phyllis' position, what would you want to ask Mark Fitzpatrick that would permit you to develop a good plan for the upcoming meeting?

2. If you were one of the physical facilities managers who would be attending this meeting, what would be the most beneficial and impressive thing that could be done to convince you of the virtues of teleconferencing?

3. Will Phyllis' major obstacle to a successful sale be eliminated if she and her group succeed in persuading the facilities managers that they need teleconferencing services in their respective office buildings?

4. Use the guidelines provided in Exhibit 8-8 to help analyze Phyllis' information needs as she prepares her group for this important customer presentation.

CASE 8-2 COFFEE AND CUSTOMER ANALYSIS

Frank Turk, Amelia Decker, and Joe Johnson are having coffee in the hotel restaurant before starting their semiannual sales meeting. All three are sales reps for Danton Supply, an office supply wholesaler. Each has covered a sales territory for at least three years.

Johnson: I'm telling you, this is a funny business. I called on a prospect the other day who I have never been able to sell to before. Every time I have tried in the past, I haven't gotten to first base. This time I said, "What the hell, I'm just going to go straight for his throat." So when I went into his office I didn't even introduce myself again, hold out a card, or anything. I just said, "I can ship you twenty cartons of data processing paper at a price 20 percent below our normal price if you order within the next three days!" The guy slapped his hand on the desk and said, "Now you're talking my language. You got a deal!"

Turk: I have one or two customers like that, but I have several others that are like fly-paper. You're almost certain they're going to buy from you, but they want you to explain every last detail even though you know they've heard it before. When I know I'm going to call on one of them, I don't plan any more calls for that part of the day. One sales call can take practically all morning or all afternoon. When I come out of the office, I feel I've been grilled!

Decker: At least you guys sound like you've been selling something. I called on a fellow yesterday who said he was going to switch suppliers because a study he recently conducted among the secretaries revealed they like the other company's stationery better than ours. When I showed him our new price list for quantity purchases, he said we were 10 percent cheaper than the competition, but he still wouldn't give me an order until he checked with his boss.

QUESTIONS

1. Each of these sales reps described a customer with a distinctly different communication style. What is the communication style in each of the three situations?

2. What advice can you give these salespeople on how to present information to these different customers?

3. The statement "It's not what you say, but how you say it" seems especially true in this case. Comment.

CASE 8–3   SELLING TO A SALES EXECUTIVE

Jane Donnelly, a sales representative for Austin, Inc., was making an important presentation to Martin Bruce, Vice President of Sales for Bayton Industries, producers of pollution control equipment. The presentation was the third time the two had met, and Donnelly had now completed a two-month study of Bayton Industries' sales lead generation and qualification activities. Bayton Industries, like many other firms, used some of its media advertising to stimulate interest and inquiries from readers who might be sales prospects.

Bayton's print advertisements featured a coupon that could be clipped out and mailed to Bayton's headquarters. The person returning the coupon filled in his or her name, address, name of business, and type of products the business manufactured. Bayton would then send a brochure to each inquirer explaining more about its equipment. The coupon was also sent to the sales rep located closest to the person who had made the inquiry. Thus, it became a sales lead that the sales rep was supposed to follow up.

Jane Donnelly's company specialized in telemarketing services. The particular service that Donnelly wanted to sell Bruce was sales lead qualification, which would be conducted by telephone. Donnelly was going to propose that Bayton Industries (1) permit Austin telemarketers to call each person who had responded, (2) discuss the person's business situation, using Bayton's guidelines, to determine whether the sales lead warranted a personal sales call by a Bayton rep, and (3) allow Austin telemarketers to call the appropriate Bayton sales office and relay the information.

The following dialogue is a part of the presentation conducted by Donnelly, the sales rep, and Bruce, Bayton's Vice President of Sales:

Donnelly: As we agreed in January, I conducted a study of the sales lead generation activities your company uses. I'm here to report what I found and also to make a proposal that, when adopted, will increase your efficiency. I think we can save Bayton Industries at least $50,000 a year on this activity.

Bruce: Okay, let's hear it.

Donnelly: To expedite this, let me use a simple diagram on this flip chart [see Exhibit 1]. Let's start with stage 1. During the two months I studied this, there were 326 sales leads generated as a result of responses to your advertisements. The average time between mailing the request and your headquarters receiving the inquiry was two days. From that time until the leads were subdivided and sent to the proper sales offices, another day elapsed. Each sales office indicated it received its leads in about two days, so the total elapsed time was six days just to get a lead to the appropriate sales office. Does that concern you, Mr. Bruce?

Bruce: Not too much. After all, we're not selling an impulse item here. Our buyers don't rush out and purchase pollution control systems overnight, you know. But, go on.

Donnelly: Of the 326 sales leads that were sent to the field offices, 150 were actually followed up during the time of the study. I talked to three of the branch sales managers and they told me that only about one of ten inquiries they received ever produced any sales. Therefore, the sales force was not particularly eager to pursue this type of lead.

Bruce: I know, but since one sale is usually worth at least $250,000 . . . .

Donnelly: When we first met, you told me that the average cost of your sales calls was about $100. The 150 calls your salespeople made cost you $15,000 for a two-month period. Of the 150 calls, twelve sales apparently will be made.

Bruce: How do you know that?

Donnelly: I asked each of the branch managers to give me their estimates and, as of yesterday, their salespeople had twelve proposals accepted that were traceable back to this group of leads.

Bruce: Okay. That seems to jibe with my figures.

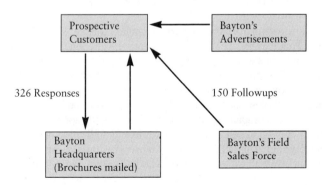

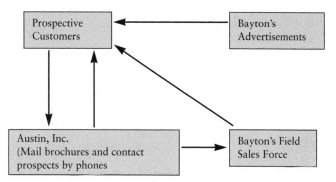

Donnelly: What if we could continue to deliver sales leads that would produce that rate of sales yet cut down on the amount of wasted sales calls your people are now making?

Bruce: I'd be very interested.

Donnelly: Let me show you a modification of the schematic we looked at earlier. Here we have inserted Austin's telemarketing service [see Exhibit 2]. The sales leads are sent to the telemarketing group, each lead is qualified by telephone, and then those that justify a field sales visit are transmitted to the appropriate sales office. Does that seem like a workable arrangement?

Bruce: Maybe, but how would your group know what constitutes a good sales lead for our salespeople?

Donnelly: The telemarketing personnel would use the guidelines your salespeople would give them to qualify each lead. We have found that getting our client's salespeople to tell us how they determine hot prospects builds the confidence of the client's salespeople. If the field sales reps know these leads have been qualified by using their recommendations, the reps are a lot more likely to follow up on them.

Bruce: Okay, tell me how I'm going to save $50,000 a year.

Donnelly: All right. First of all, to simplify our calculations, let's assume there were 300 leads instead of 326. Let's also say that each lead *had* been followed up by your field sales reps. That would have cost you $30,000. However, it would have cost approximately $7.50 per contact to telephone each lead, or a total cost of $2,250. At first, it would seem that this would have been a savings of $27,250 for the two-month period. However, your reps didn't visit all 300 leads. They actually called on only 150 of them, so the cost savings for the two months would have been $12,750. Remember this was for a two-month period, so if that was a typical stretch of time, you could have saved $76,500 in a year. And, perhaps best of all, the entire 300 leads could have been contacted, not just half of them.

Bruce: That's pretty impressive.

Donnelly: Good, but that's not all, Mr. Bruce. [Continues the presentation.]

QUESTIONS

1. What type of presentation is this? Explain.

2. How does this case illustrate various sales presentation dynamics?

3. What type of relationship appears to be forming here between Donnelly, the Austin sales rep, and Bruce, the Bayton executive?

4. Does Donnelly appear to have a good grasp of this sales situation? What evidence indicates she does or does not?

5. What are some additional inducements Donnelly could offer to Bruce to make this sale?

NOTES

1. Patrick O'Connor, *Personal Selling* (New York: Macmillan Publishing Company, 1990), 233.

2. Marvin A. Jolson, "The Underestimated Potential of the Canned Sales Presentation," *Journal of Marketing* 39 (January 1975): 75–78.

3. Truman E. Moore, *The Traveling Man* (New York: Doubleday, 1972), 58–61.

4. David Mayer and Herbert M. Greenberg, "What Makes a Good Salesman?" *Harvard Business Review* (July–August 1964): 119–25.

5. Jolson, ". . . Canned Sales Presentation," 75–78.

6. Nathan J. Muller, "Taking Care of Business Means Taking Care of People," *Business Marketing* (June 1987): 78–84.

7. Stan Kossen, *Creative Selling Today*, Second Edition (New York: Harper & Row, Publishers, 1982), 180–85.

8. James Lorenzen, "Needs Analysis Replacing Product Presentation," *Marketing News* (April 25, 1986): 8.IP0,5

9. "The Changing Identity of AT&T After Deregulation," *Corporate Marketing Videos* (New York: Macmillan, 1987, in cooperation with RCC Reeves Corporate Services).

10. Thomas N. Ingram and Raymond W. LaForge, *Sales Management: Analysis and Decision Making* (Hinsdale, Illinois: The Dryden Press, 1989), 30.

11. Hugh J. Ingraci, "How to Reach Buyers in Their Psychological 'Comfort Zone,'" *Industrial Marketing* (July 1981): 60–64.

12. William A. Staples and John I. Coppett, "Sales Presentations at Three Company Levels," *Industrial Marketing Management* 10, no. 2 (April 1981): 125–28.

13. John I. Coppett and William A. Staples, "A Sales Mix Model for Effective Industrial Selling," *Industrial Marketing Management* 9 (February 1980): 31–36.

14. Lorenzen, "Needs Analysis Replacing Product," 8.

15. Thomas V. Bonoma, "Major Sales: Who Really Does the Buying?" *Harvard Business Review* (May–June 1982): 111–17.

16. Gannett Co., Inc., 1987 Annual Report, 1.

17. American Express Company, 1987 Annual Report, 3.

18. Buck Rodgers and Robert L. Shook, *The IBM Way: Insights into the World's Most Successful Marketing Organization* (New York: Harper & Row, 1986), 80.

19. Martin Everett, "This Is the Ultimate in Selling" *Sales and Marketing Management* (August 1989): 100.

CHAPTER 9

Negotiation

LEARNING OBJECTIVES

After studying this chapter, you should be able to:

1. Explain why it is becoming more important for professional salespeople to be better negotiators.

2. Understand why a negotiator's attitude is important.

3. Analyze the three levels of the environment that confront all negotiators regardless of whether the negotiator is a buyer or a seller.

4. Explain two basic negotiation strategies and identify tactics used with the strategies.

5. Describe the guidelines a negotiator needs to keep in mind to be more effective.

6. Define the key terms used in the chapter.

KEY TERMS

- negotiation
- negotiation strategy
- problem-solving negotiation strategy
- aggressive bargaining negotiation strategy
- bogey tactic
- unbundling
- crunch tactic
- walking away point
- take-it-or-leave-it tactic
- psychological currency

HANK CLEMENS, Vice President of Sales for KABCO, Inc., studied carefully the curriculum description he had been handed by Sushila Morshad. Sushila, or Sue as she was called by her friends, was the Training Director for KABCO, a large manufacturer of magnetic resonance imaging (MRI) equipment. MRI equipment permitted physicians to diagnose illnesses and injuries much more effectively than standard x-ray equipment. KABCO had profited from the sale of this sophisticated medical technology to large hospitals. The total price for the equipment, installation, and training of personnel ranged between $1 million and $1.5 million per unit sold.

"I see some major additions to the sales training program, Sue. You've added a subject we used to not cover very much—negotiations. I'm all for this!" Clemens exclaimed.

"Good, I'm glad you approve," Sue said. "Our sales people told us through the surveys we conducted that negotiation was an area in which they felt they needed some help."

"Yeah, I know," said Clemens; "MRI equipment takes a long time to sell—10 months to a year. A salesperson has to negotiate dozens of things in addition to the price. Sometimes you wonder if you'll ever answer all the questions and satisfy all the people in a hospital who have to approve of a purchase like this."

When you first think about negotiating, you may envision political leaders or union and management executives seated at a table with each side represented by several people. That is only one scenario in which negotiations occur. All of us negotiate something every day and in places that are anything but formal. For example, perhaps you have met with an instructor to discuss what you believed to be a correct response to an exam question. Your intent was to try to negotiate a better grade. In another situation, a husband may desire to vacation at a resort where he can play golf. The wife wants to go to a city where she can enjoy the opera. Their differences can be resolved through negotiation. As these brief examples illustrate, **negotiation** is basically a conference between two parties so as to arrive at the settlement of some matter.[1] This chapter will focus on analyzing negotiating activities between salespeople and buyers. Negotiations can last only a few minutes or, as in the opening vignette, they can consume months and involve many people from the buyer's and the seller's organizations.

First, this chapter will explain why negotiation skills are becoming more important as salespeople and buyers increase their professional skills. We discuss the importance of creating and maintaining a positive attitude toward negotiating activities. Then we present guidance on how to analyze the environment that influences the parties involved in negotiations. Understanding each negotiating party's strengths and weaknesses is very important whether you are a seller or a buyer. The chapter will cover strategies and tactics and will conclude with some guidelines useful in increasing a negotiator's effectiveness.

NEGOTIATION SKILLS: WHY ARE THEY BECOMING MORE IMPORTANT?

Purchasing managers are approaching their responsibilities with greater skill than ever before.[2] Many purchasing agents have obtained a college degree with a major in purchasing. The National Association of Purchasing Management, an organization dedicated to its members' professional development, offers seminars and courses in negotiation. Salespeople, consequently, must also improve their negotiating abilities in order to avoid being at a disadvantage with those customers who are purchasing professionals.

One of the conditions that salespeople must recognize and be prepared to deal with is that an astute purchaser (whether a professional purchasing agent or a private consumer) is likely to have a wide range of concerns. Today, smart buyers realize that not just prices but many other conditions are subjects for negotiations. Delivery dates, service before and after the sale, training assistance, and transportation costs are just some of the things that can be negotiated to add value to a product or service. As the scope of issues broadens, salespeople must be better prepared. Obviously, when conducting business with prepared buyers who are capable of negotiating over a wide range of buying conditions, a sales representative cannot depend on a canned or memorized sales presentation to successfully conclude a sale.

The well-trained salesperson must have an understanding of and be prepared to negotiate in those areas which are most important to a particular customer. For example, a purchasing agent for Dow Chemical Company may want to negotiate the delivery schedule for supplies, whereas the AJAY Chemical purchaser might only be concerned with credit terms. Such diversity requires well prepared, flexible negotiators capable of making significant decisions quickly. In the opening vignette, mention was made of the price tag associated with the sale of MRI medical

Figure 9-1 Negotiating skills are of paramount importance to successful salespeople. Today, smart buyers realize that other conditions besides price are subjects for negotiation.

equipment. Salespeople responsible for a single sale that brings in over a million dollars of revenue must be capable of interacting with various levels of personnel in a customer's organization. Usually, at each level, different issues will require some negotiation. The sales rep, to maintain the customer's confidence, must be capable of responding quickly while staying within the boundaries of the rep's authority. For example, if the AJAY Chemical Company purchasing manager had requested that the normal payment schedule of thirty days be extended to ninety days, an informed sales representative would know whether he or she had the authority to grant such a concession.

One of the most interesting topics in sales and marketing is the increasing globalization of markets. The needs of people from different countries and cultures to do business with each other places a premium on negotiation skills. Negotiation styles, like many other business activities, vary among cultures. What happens before, during, and after negotiations is crucial to the success of a sale in some countries.[3] Salespeople, if they are not sensitive to a customer's cultural practices, can lose a sale and never understand why.[4]

A final reason for the increased significance of negotiating skills is the theme of this book: relationship management. Buyers and sellers both are attempting in more and more cases to establish significant relationships with each other.[5] Such relationships, once created, can be costly to sever. The potential partners usually spend much time and effort making sure there is a good fit. This requires extensive negotiation. Recently, announcements have been made about such well-known companies as Procter and Gamble and Wal-Mart, and also IBM and Apple, entering into alliances or relationships that will ultimately involve millions of dollars and have far-reaching effects on these companies' product lines and merchandise. You don't have to be an experienced business executive to envision the complex negotiations that preceded the formation of these relationships. In such cases, the negotiations were conducted by teams of people who ranged in rank from senior executives to lower levels of staff support personnel.

Regardless of your rank in an organization, it is important to develop and maintain a positive attitude as you approach negotiations. That challenge is analyzed next.

"The Cool Dudes Win"

Most of us have started a conversation with someone, hoping to get him or her to accept our viewpoint, only to discover that we have become emotional. Perhaps the conversation ended on an angry note, and after you analyzed it, you discovered that a lot of grievances had been aired. Consider a conversation like this:

Figure 9-2 A significant relationship between buyer and seller, once established, can be costly to sever.

Salesperson:	(entering a purchasing agent's office) Good morning, Mr. Smith. I'm glad to see you after your vacation. I hope it was a good one.
Purchasing Agent:	(who is in a foul mood) Yeah, it was O.K. Say, have you folks improved your on-time delivery performance to conform to our contract?
Salesperson:	Mr. Smith, that's the first thing I wanted to talk to you about today. As you know, we were hit by a strike last month . . .
Purchasing Agent:	(breaking in angrily) Here we go again! Another set of excuses for late deliveries. I don't know why our engineers keep insisting we buy from you guys. Personally, I think you have lousy products and you never keep your word!
Salesperson:	(now becomes angry at being attacked) Well, it's good that someone in your organization has enough intelligence to recognize quality! Your finished products wouldn't be as good as they are if you weren't using our supplies!

This angry exchange probably hides a large backlog of frustrations and disappointments that have built up over weeks or months. Regardless of the cause, we cannot be optimistic about the eventual outcome. Both people were lashing out in anger. One person's response fueled the other's. Notice how in this very brief dialogue the scope of conversation broadened from a delivery problem to other problems involving quality and price.

It is important to realize that most successful negotiations begin with the participants possessing positive "we-can-solve-our-problems" attitudes. Of equal importance is the capability of a good negotiator to *monitor his or her attitude* as interaction between the parties occurs.[6] There are several advantages to maintaining one's composure and remaining positive about the possibilities of resolving problems in a mutually satisfying way. What are they?

Focusing on the Problem

As a result of a positive outlook, one's thoughts are devoted to making progress on solving the immediate problem or issue. If a rep becomes distracted from the issue and moves to another subject area, after a short time in which nothing is solved, the negotiating parties may become so aware of the growing list of issues and differences that they break off all efforts to negotiate.

Attitudes are Contagious

A calm, focused, confident attitude can spread. Positive as well as negative attitudes are contagious. We tend to respond to others in the same way we think they are treating us. This is the well known "tit for tat" situation.[7] People who are optimistic and up-beat tend to evoke positive reactions in others. This does not mean, however, that a salesperson should act in a submissive manner or immediately make an important concession in hopes that a demanding buyer will reciprocate.[8] This is likely only to cause an aggressive negotiator to become even more belligerent and demanding. A strong, mentally tough person who stays composed and self-controlled can usually cause a less controlled negotiator to wonder why his or her opposition is not caving in. As we will see in a later section, an emotional outburst by another negotiator may be a deliberate test to see whether the salesperson can be baited or coerced into making unwise concessions.

All this advice may seem easy to agree with and implement. As you read this, you are not confronted with the actual challenge of keeping your composure. In the real-world of professional selling, however, most salespeople have to consciously work on maintaining a positive attitude. What is it about the professional sales environment that makes this easier said than done?

THE CHALLENGES OF MAINTAINING A POSITIVE ATTITUDE

Even very successful professional salespeople hear the word *no*. Rejection "goes with the territory;" that doesn't mean you have to like it, but you do need to keep it in perspective. Some sales consultants state that true sales skills first become evident when the customer starts to raise objections. (Chapter 10 will provide more specific information about objections.) For those who are not mentally tough, the cumulative effect of being rejected starts to affect behavior. The salesperson who allows previous rejections to adversely affect his or her present-day contacts will be at a big disadvantage. Dr. Fran Pirozzolo, Chief of Neuropsychology at the Baylor College of Medicine, states that great athletes such as Nolan Ryan and Evander Holyfield have had to overcome adversities in their careers.[9] Unless people can work through momentary rejections or defeats, the negative attitudes accumulate and affect performance.

Potential Buyers Sometimes Seem Irrational

To the salesperson who has worked hard to determine the buyer's needs and problems and has presented what appeared to be an ideal solution, hearing that the buyer was really not serious can be demoralizing. Particularly frustrating is the buyer's stating one criterion for making a decision and then changing it. For example, a buyer in the first meeting states that ease-of-use is the most important feature of a personal computer. Later, however, the same buyer states that price is the most important concern. Dealing with people who seem to be irrational can have a detrimental impact on the sales rep's attitude unless the rep acquires mental toughness.

Intra-Firm Hassles

Surprising as it may seem, another reason that salespeople must occasionally be their own cheerleaders has to do with the salesperson's company. Unfortunately, all salespeople don't work for companies in which customer satisfaction is stressed. A relationship with a customer that a salesperson has worked to establish can be jeopardized by careless, indifferent responses from people in other departments in the rep's firm. If a salesperson doesn't consciously work on maintaining a positive attitude, such problems can result in frustration and a loss of confidence, diminishing the rep's performance as an effective negotiator.

How does the salesperson keep from falling into the trap of pessimism? The next section provides some guidance.

Developing and Keeping a Positive Attitude

Your mood as you approach a negotiation session is very important. Recognizing that, what can you do to try to maintain a positive attitude and the mental toughness an effective salesperson needs?

Prepare, Prepare, Prepare

If retailers stress location as the most important factor for success, the successful salesperson can, with equal confidence, emphasize the direct and indirect benefits of thorough preparation. The person who is thoroughly prepared *and knows he or she is prepared* is usually confident. Self-confidence promotes calmness, which is vital to clear, objective thinking. Also, keep in mind that no preparation is wasted. Even if you cannot sell to today's prospective buyer, you will eventually be able to use your preparation on another customer.

Yesterday Is Gone; Tomorrow Is a Dream

Every day is both literally and figuratively a new day. You need to keep in mind that you cannot do anything about yesterday. Whatever successes or failures you experienced are passed. If you experienced success or failure, do you have any ideas *why* you were successful or unsuccessful? Analyze those occasions where you experienced a less than stunning victory to learn from them, and then vow to avoid making the same mistakes. Don't let a momentary set-back hamper your future effectiveness. On the other hand, if you enjoyed a success, don't assume you can continue your winning streak without preparing for the next sales effort.

Your Associates Do Make a Difference

People who are successful tend to attract other successful people. In some sense, this situation creates its own momentum. The person who gets things accomplished and is a high achiever is invited to participate with other persons who are accustomed to success. As a result of their network, they tend to know about opportunities and exploit their advantages quicker than other people. On the other hand, those people who are "losers" welcome other people to their crowd. Such individuals usually spend their time thinking of all the reasons something can't be done: bad timing, lack of resources, lack of management support, and so forth. None of their justifications are worth listening to.

Stress Management Is Important

Schedule your activities prior to a key customer presentation or negotiating session so that you are physically and mentally sharp. Professional sales work is physically and mentally taxing, and a sixty hour week is not unusual. Eventually, the body rebels, resulting in fatigue or illness. Maintaining the proper frame of mind is impossible when you are exhausted or ill. Leading a balanced life with adequate rest and exercise can do wonders to restore your psyche.

You Have Plenty of Help

Today, every salesperson has available a wide range of resources to help him or her master the profession of selling. Books, cassette tapes, videos, seminars, and professional organizations are abundant. Any salesperson can walk into most bookstores and find several paperbacks written by experts on all phases of selling. Engaging in a continual self-study program will not only enhance your understanding of your profession, but will also boost your confidence.

Keep Track of Your Growth

Maintain a diary or log. Every day, write down what you are doing and how you feel about what is happening in your life. Don't be self-conscious or timid. This is your highly personal record. Be honest and identify those areas of selling you know need improving. After every perceived problem, indicate what you can do to eliminate the problem. Psychologists tell us that acknowledging and confronting our difficulties is vitally important. Don't write it down and forget it, however. By indicating what action you are taking, you are making a commitment to improve. Once a month or so, look back in the diary and honestly appraise the progress you are making. If you are sincerely attempting to improve, you will have followed through on your commitments. The satisfaction you will experience from this personal growth will bolster your confidence. Progress is a self-perpetuating phenomenon. When you sense your progress, you will become even more dedicated to improve so you can continue to enjoy the positive feeling of accomplishment. As the momentum increases, so will your feelings of self-worth and confidence.

ANALYZING NEGOTIATING ENVIRONMENTS

Earlier, we stressed the importance of being prepared. A fundamentally important step in your preparation involves analyzing your environment and the environment of your negotiating counterpart.

This section provides a way of analyzing both the buyer's and the seller's circumstances. Exhibit 9-1 is divided into two sections: first, the market conditions confronting the buyer and the conditions affecting the seller; second, an analysis of the individuals who will be involved in negotiations.

The assumption being made is that negotiations will be affected by both the market conditions in which the buyers/sellers are operating and also by the skills of the individuals participating in negotiations. To be prepared, you should analyze the market from the buyer's perspective as well as your own perspective. Next, you should attempt to understand the specific individual participants who will be active in the negotiating process.

Buyer-Seller Market Conditions

Exhibit 9-1 provides a brief but by no means exhaustive list of factors that can give a salesperson a realistic, informed appraisal of conditions likely to affect negotiations with a particular customer.

Space limitations prohibit us from examining each of the factors listed under the Buyer's Situation and Seller's Situation sub-sections. As you analyze the individual entries, you will see that there are many possible points you could use as you engage in negotiations. For example, using the factor "potential for future sales if buyer can be satisfied now," a salesperson may decide to be more liberal in granting certain concessions to a buyer (e.g., provide free training to fifty employees rather than the usual twenty-five) if the buyer will sign a three-year contract promising to buy all its supplies from the sales rep's company. The greater the potential future sales to this customer, the more attractive it may be for the rep to negotiate over an immediate sale.

One factor listed under the Seller's Situation is very important in the case of high-tech products and services. That factor is *expertise*. In many cases, exhibited expertise is the crucial factor a buyer uses in choosing a supplier. In short, expertise can provide the seller with an edge. Chapter 3 described several types of relationships between buyers and sellers. The seller's expertise is a particularly important factor in both the counselor relationship and the systems designer relationship.

An example is provided by the National Association of Purchasing Management in their *Guide To Purchasing* designed for assisting professional buyers. One sec-

Exhibit 9-1 Analyzing Negotiating Environments

Buyer/Seller Market Conditions	Possible Impact on Negotiations
Buyer's Situation:	
Percent of seller's output now being purchased (e.g., 1%, 15%, etc.)	The higher the percentage, the more power the buyer will have.
Reputation and visibility of buyer	Better known buyers can be valuable to sellers as they deal with other potential customers. Buyers such as Sears and Wal-Mart know this.
Potential for large future sales *if* buyer can be satisfied now	Lure of greater future reward is hard for many sellers to ignore.
Ability of buyer to make the product/ service instead of buying	Buyers with such capabilities are more powerful than organizations that can't furnish their own supplies.
Financial condition	Buyers needing financial aid are less powerful if the financial support is furnished by the seller.
Seller's Situation:	
Percent of seller's production capacity being utilized	Seller with unused production capacity needs business and may make liberal concessions to get additional sales.
Percent of seller's output now consumed by the buyer	Seller can become the buyer's captive if a significant percent of seller's production is devoted to one buyer.
Opportunities to sell product/service elsewhere	The greater the diversity a seller has, the more power the seller enjoys.
Importance of seller's product to buyer's product quality	If seller furnishes an important component part, seller is likely to have more power (e.g., Briggs-Stratton engines in lawn mower manufacturer's products).
Expertise	Seller's power can be enhanced by possessing needed expertise that buyer doesn't have.

Individuals Involved In The Negotiations	Possible Impact on Negotiations
Experience:	
1. In negotiations *per se*	The more experienced negotiators are likely to have a strategy and variety of tactics.
2. With Product/Service Involved	Inexperienced buyer for a particular product/service may welcome a trusted expert salesperson.
Interpersonal Skills	Participants with greater interpersonal skills (whether acting as buyer or seller) are likely to be powerful negotiators because they know "what is happening."
Level of Authority to Make Decisions	A negotiator who can make decisions without having to consult with higher authority has more flexibility and more power.
Access to Expertise	Knowledge is power—this is why teams of people are sometimes used in complex negotiations.

tion of "Choosing a Third-Party Computer Maintenance Vendor" illustrates the importance of the seller's ability to exploit its technological expertise. The following statement was intended to guide purchasing agents as they selected a computer maintenance vendor:

> *. . . check the level of skills and training expected of field engineers and technicians being hired by the vendor. For example, find out how much schooling is required and how much prior experience.*[10]

Individuals Participating in Negotiations

Most salespeople are sufficiently acquainted with those with whom they will be negotiating to make it worthwhile to analyze those individuals. By evaluating the experience (or lack of it) someone has had in negotiating and the experience he or she has had with the purchase of the product or service, a salesperson can gain some insights and be better prepared for upcoming negotiation sessions. Other check-points are such factors as the perceived interpersonal skills of the negotiators, the authority the negotiators possess to make significant purchasing decisions, and the level of expertise the buyers have access to within their company.

Although at first glance the many factors listed in Exhibit 9-1 seem to require enormous amounts of preparation, an experienced sales rep who has had contact with a buyer in pre-negotiation meetings will have already collected a considerable amount of information. The exhibit provides an orderly way of analyzing the many points that should be considered.

NEGOTIATING STRATEGIES AND TACTICS

Understanding the environment in which your customer is functioning (the general market conditions, the amount of power the negotiator possesses, and so forth) is an essential beginning to effective negotiations. Beyond that, however, is the need to understand the particular strategy and tactics a negotiating buyer may use.

Negotiation strategy is defined as the general approach a negotiator takes to achieve his or her objectives and can be identified as falling into one of two general categories. One of these is "problem solving" and the other "aggressive bargaining."[11] **Problem-solving negotiation strategy** primarily involves discovering ways to increase the benefits available to *both* the buyer and the seller.[12] Negotiators using this strategy are said to employ a collaborating style as they approach a conflict situation.[13] In the past, the aggressive bargaining strategy predominated. **Aggressive bargaining negotiation strategy** takes the position that the negotiators are adversaries who should not reveal any more information than necessary.[14] In such an atmosphere one side basically "wins" and the other "loses." Foreign competition mentioned earlier in the chapter is now exerting an increasing influence on negotiating strategies.[15] Buyers and sellers are realizing that *both* can "win" if there is more cooperation between negotiators. On the other hand, in the face of increasing foreign competition in many markets, both the domestic buyer and the seller could lose a lot if either were forced out of business. For example, Wal-Mart has worked with a number of domestic manufacturers to help the manufacturers stay in business. As a result of this enormously powerful buyer's purchases, the manufacturers now supply products to Wal-Mart under conditions that are favorable to Wal-Mart as it competes with such retailers as Sears.

Aggressive Bargaining Tactics

There are still some buyers who believe that information about costs, budgets, competition, and technical matters should be concealed from the other negotiator.[16] How can you detect the general strategy a particular agent or buyer is employing? Recently, research on interpersonal communications between salespeople and buyers has revealed several cues or verbal signals that can tell whether your customer is using a win-lose (aggressive bargaining) strategy or a win-win (problem solving) strategy.[17] Exhibit 9-2 contains a list of several tactics, the definition of the tactics, and some example statements that someone using the aggressive bargaining approach might use.

Exhibit 9-2 Some Aggressive Bargaining Tactics

Tactics	Definition	Example
Promises and Threats	A prediction by a negotiator that he or she will provide reward or punishment	"If you can deliver within 10 days, I can guarantee an order immediately."
Derogation	Negotiator disparages the other negotiator, his or her product, organization, or offer	"Your products are not built to standard and are inferior to other products we are considering."
Nonconcessional Offers	Negotiator makes a statement that indicates no flexibility	"We never do business with a supplier who won't permit our engineers to first inspect the supplier's quality control department."
Charge Fault	Negotiator attributes to an opponent such things as incompetence or lack of good faith	"The reason we don't buy from you anymore is that your accounting system won't bill us the way we asked you to."

Source: *Academy of Marketing Journal,* Volume No. 19, Issue No. 2, Spring 1991, JAI Press Inc. Greenwich, CT, Reprinted with Permission.

Gary Karrass in his book, *Negotiate to Close: How to Make More Successful Deals*, identifies three basic tactics an aggressive negotiator may use. They are the *bogey*, the *crunch*, and *take-it-or-leave-it*. The first two tactics seem very reasonable and will usually be delivered by a negotiator in a very pleasant manner. The take-it-or-leave-it tactic, however, may be delivered in a hostile, belligerent manner.

The Bogey

The **bogey** is what some people would call a form of a promise and threat situation.[18] An example is a statement such as, "I really think the product is great, but my budget for this type of product is $100 lower than your price." Within this short statement is an implicit promise and, tactfully worded, also a threat. The "promise" is that the prospective purchaser will be an eager buyer (after all, didn't the purchaser say he liked the product?). The "threat" is that the sale can't be made unless the price is lowered by $100.

How can a salesperson respond to a bogey? Mainly by informing the other person of the value he or she will receive that will make the $100 difference in price seem like a bargain. Another approach is to help the potential buyer "unbundle" the product. **Unbundling** is the breaking down of the price of a product into parts, so that each part or component service has a price. The total price for a product that requires shipping and handling, installation, training the buyer's personnel, and warranty is based on the cost of the basic product plus the costs of providing the other services. The sales rep, by asking questions about other budgets such as training, equipment maintenance, and so forth, may be able to suggest ways a purchaser can buy the product and charge part of the purchase to other budgets.

The "Crunch"

The **crunch** is usually played out in the following way. A prospective purchaser starts negotiating by describing a product or service characterized by easy-to-provide specifications or qualities. It may be essentially a stripped-down version of an existing product or service. As the conversation between buyer and seller progresses, the buyer starts to add features or ask for concessions that were not available in the original set of specifications. When the sales rep concedes or agrees to add the features (usually there has been some preliminary talk about the potential size of future orders), the negotiator slowly builds up to his or her next demand. If the sales rep starts to increase the price to adjust for the add-ons, the negotiator may then attempt to "crunch" the deal by either referring to competitors' offers or reminding the sales rep of the potential for future business.

When you are confronted with this situation you can respond in several ways. One way is to carefully take notes detailing the original description of the purchaser's request. When it becomes apparent that a power play is being attempted, you can let the buyer know that you know what is happening by describing what was initially considered to be an acceptable product. This puts the buyer on notice that you are in control of the situation and not as succeptible to this tactic as he or she may believe.

At the very least, you should have in mind your **walking away point**. This is the point in the sales negotiation situation when it becomes unprofitable for your firm *if you make the sale.* You need to know how much profit you will be giving up each time you concede something, such as agreeing to pay for more training, reduced shipping charges, and especially a lower unit price. At some point, your firm would actually be financially better off if you did not make the sale.

Do not be reluctant to state that you need time to consider the proposal or demand the other party is making. You should be very careful not to be pressured into spur-of-the-moment decisions.[19] This is much more likely to be a danger for young, inexperienced salespeople who may think, "If I don't make a decision now, I'll never get back in here again and I'll lose the sale." If you are selling a good product or service, develop the mental toughness to not be railroaded or goaded into a hasty decision.[20]

Take-It-Or-Leave-It

"Ten dollars a unit is the price I will pay. That's it. No more than that if you want the business." In some cases, the purchaser may even say such words in a hostile way that reveals apparent disgust with you. This is the ultimate coercive power tactic, designed to test your confidence and courage. There appears to be no room for maneuvering. The price the buyer has just mentioned seems to be set in concrete. It is, apparently, a price that is set *forever for now.*[21] Why forever for now? At this particular moment, the price is based on the perceptions of the buyer and how badly he or she thinks the product is needed. Later, however, as circumstances change, so will the buyer's perceptions of need. If you can withstand the temptation and wait, what seemed like a fixed, irreducible price may be modified. This is especially true if you can get the buyer to tell you how he or she arrived at that "final offer." A conversation like the following one reveals what can happen:

Purchasing agent: We have decided to make you our very best offer of $96.53 per unit. This is our final offer, and if you want to sell to us at that price we will buy from you right now. Do you want our business?

Sales rep: Of course I want your business. Before I can say yes or no to that price, however, I believe it would be helpful to both of us if you would tell me what you expect to get for $96.53 per unit.

Purchasing agent: I expect to get your standard Grade A product which you have sold us before at $98.00 per unit. That's it. Very simple.

Sales rep: I see. Well we could do that but, incidently, did you know that the $98.00 product now has some added post-sale service visits that are going to be available after 1 November? Those are worth, by themselves, at least $25.00 each.

Purchasing agent: Do you mean the $98.00 buys us the product plus more service?

At this point, the purchaser's perceptions are beginning to alter, and what was once a hard and fast situation seems already to be in the process of changing. As the rep injects new information about the total product offering, there is a strong possibility that what shortly before was a firm price will be modified.

The essence of all effective negotiations in an adversarial atmosphere is patience and knowledge—patience with the other negotiator who may from time to time display some hostile or less than professional behavior. Patience is also needed in listening and cataloging the various tactics the negotiator is using. Knowledge is required of your own circumstances to understand the cost of your product and the various ancillary services associated with the delivery and installation of the product. With these resources you need not fear negotiating in an atmosphere where the other party wants to use an adversarial strategy.

As we mentioned earlier, the other major form of negotiating strategy is the problem solving approach.[22] What are some indicators you can use to detect it as you talk to a customer?

Problem-Solving Negotiating Tactics

As "partnering" between buyers and sellers has become more commonplace, the problem solving or collaborative approach to negotiating has increased.[23] Why has buyer-seller partnering become something that we commonly read and hear about in the business press? Because both parties are realizing that cooperation works. Cooperation is a far more powerful strategy for making both buyers and sellers more profitable in the long term than any adversarial approach yet devised.[24]

What specific companies have realized the value of collaborating with their suppliers rather than viewing them as adversaries? Motorola, Tektronix, Xerox, Honeywell, Ford, and Chrysler are some of the well-known corporations.[25] Carlisle and Parker in their book, *Beyond Negotiation: Redeeming Customer-Supplier Relationships*, have identified four conditions that must exist if a workable collaborative buyer-seller relationship is to develop:

1. A trust that both parties will perform as they promised.

2. A willingness to be vulnerable to the other party based on the confidence that the vulnerability will not be exploited.

3. An awareness of the other party's needs and a desire to see that both the buyer's and the seller's needs are satisfied.

4. Extensive communication between the relationship partners to keep each other informed.[26]

It should be clear from this description that collaborative negotiating is fundamentally different from negotiations occurring between buyers and sellers who perceive each other as adversaries.

What are some key indicators you can look for if you think your prospective buyer is willing to collaborate or become a partner in the negotiating process? Here are three.

Concessions Offered

If a negotiator is willing to collaborate, there must, at least on occasion, be some "give" in his or her position. By fully examining the description of products and *all* the purchasing conditions, you can determine whether the purchaser is willing to work *with* you rather than work you over. For example, the purchasing agent might offer to forego any training program you would routinely offer, if your firm could extend the warranty from three years to four years.

More Information Offered Than Absolutely Necessary

If partners are to work together over an extended period and mutually benefit from the relationship, they cannot be constrained by a lack of trust. Secrecy has no place in a strong buyer-seller relationship. Providing information that will be useful to the other negotiating party is a solid indicator that there is trust between the negotiators. An example is a statement such as, "If we sold this part to you at ninety-five cents a unit our profits on the sale would be only two cents per unit. We have experienced a ten cent rise in our costs over the past year."

Questions with Accompanying Explanations

The negotiator who asks questions and explains the reason(s) for the questions, rather than announcing hard and fast positions (the take-it-or-leave-it tactic), is seeking understanding. Such a negotiator is stating implicitly, "I want to know your circumstances, your perspective." An example is a buyer who states a question in the following way:

Can you tell me what other companies are using your telecommunications systems? I'll have to be able to sell this proposal to my upper management.

GUIDELINES FOR EFFECTIVE NEGOTIATIONS

Regardless of what style or strategy the other negotiator may use, there are some useful guidelines for anyone attempting to reach an agreement. The renowned writer and consultant, Mark McCormack, author of *What They Don't Teach You At Harvard Business School*, offers some advice to negotiators:

1. Don't get hung up on "how much."
2. Don't deal in round numbers.
3. Deal in psychological currency.
4. Avoid showdowns.
5. Trade places.
6. Deflect with a question.
7. Question positions but don't ignore them.
8. Use candor.[27]

Let's look at each in more detail.

The How-Much Roadblock

A sales rep can use many variables to justify a particular price; delivery dates, discounts for purchasing quantities of product, warranty terms, and installation service are only a few that add total value to a product. Focusing on one or more of these variables makes the how-much problem less important. McCormack's advice is, "Don't deal with numbers in isolation. Numbers are just one piece—no bigger and no smaller than the other pieces—of the negotiating pie."[28]

Round Numbers Are Taboo

The next time you visit an automobile agency, look at the sticker prices. You won't see $12,000, $14,000, or $20,000. Round numbers beg to be negotiated, usually by a counteroffer in round numbers. Odd numbers sound harder, firmer, and less negotiable.[29] State prices or cost figures such as $109.63.

Deal in Psychological Currency

The sports world is definitely big business. Almost every professional athlete has an agent to handle negotiations with team management and companies that seek the athlete's endorsements. As we read the sports and business pages, we see terms such as no-cut contracts, contract extensions, and right-to-refuse-trade clauses. The agents representing the athlete sometimes trade actual dollars for greater job security or **psychological currency**. An example is a college football player drafted by the National Football League. The player's agent might choose to negotiate a $150,000 contract containing a guarantee that the player will not be cut from the team, which could be preferable to a $200,000 contract enforceable only if the athlete makes the team.

Examples of psychological currency are frequently found in personal sales. A sales rep whose product is priced higher than competitors' frequently counters such a disadvantage by reminding the buyer of the feeling of security that can be experienced when purchasing a product backed by extended warranties.[30]

Avoid Showdowns

This bit of advice would seem superfluous in situations where salespersons are practicing relationship management. After all, lasting relationships can hardly be based on shows of bravado. Nowadays, successful bargaining is win-win negotiation, in which both sides win—or at least no one loses.[31] Don't use phrases like "Take it or leave it," or "That's nonnegotiable," or anything that sounds like a dare to the other person.[32]

On the other hand, if you encounter a prospective customer who uses the showdown, remember that it is usually a tactic to test the other negotiating party. Keep your poise and tactfully remind the customer of other benefits the product or service provides that compensate for the point upon which the buyer's attention has been focused.

Trade Places

McCormack recommends that a negotiator run through a series of questions and answer them as if he or she were the other person in the bargaining session. He offers the following sample questions to get the negotiating party's perspective:

1. What are "my" real limitations?
2. How badly do "I" want this deal to happen?
3. What are "my" options if it falls through?
4. Will "I" look good, or will "I" have to always be defending this internally?
5. And what trade-offs can "I" get to assure that this doesn't happen?[33]

By attempting to view the buying situation through the buyer's eyes, a sales rep can more quickly detect potential barriers to a sale.

Deflect with a Question

Ask a question if you don't like what you are hearing.[34] Chapter 7 described various types of questions—channeling, clarification, and verification. A clarification or verification question would be suitable in most negotiation sessions if the other party has proposed something you don't want to happen.

Let's look at how clarification and verification questions could be used in a negotiation session. In the following example, a buyer for a manufacturer wants a written guarantee that the buyer will be permitted to specify the transportation company that will handle all the shipments from a supplier. In addition, the buyer wants the supplier to pay 50 percent of all shipping costs.

Sales rep:	(using a clarification question) Are you requesting the right to name the shipper because you believe you can get more economical rates that way?
Buyer:	Yeah, of course. We have dozens of suppliers we do business with in your plant's area. We can consolidate the shipments from all these suppliers with a shipper, and the shipper will give us a good deal.
Sales rep:	(using another clarification question) What if you let us pick the shipper but we guarantee the shipping costs with our selected shipper will never exceed those costs charged by the outfit you would have used?
Buyer:	If we can work out arrangements to determine that the costs are the lowest, then that would be acceptable.
Sales rep:	(using a verification question) Okay, do I understand our arrangements? One, my company will choose the shipper. Two, we split the transportation charges fifty-fifty. Three, we show you the quotes we received from all the shippers to prove we got you the best deal. Is that right?
Buyer:	Fair enough.

Don't Ignore the Other Side's Position

Even though you may think the other side's position is totally unreasonable, and you hope the other party will eventually recognize this, don't try to pretend it doesn't exist. That will cause the buyer to push even harder. Usually, the first reaction when someone seems not to acknowledge our statements is to believe we need to restate our position. Restating a position tends to entrench it even more. Soon the two parties, as they try to ignore each other's positions, are just talking at each other. A simple statement such as "I hear what you are saying" may be sufficient.

Use Candor

Especially when negotiations seem to have gotten tense and a sale seems to be in jeopardy, statements like "I really want this to be successful," or "We both are, essentially, looking for the same thing," reflect a more human side of the negotiations.[35] This may be an effective signal to the other party that even though you are firm, you still want the negotiations to succeed.

SUMMARY

1. Negotiation skills are becoming more important for salespeople, because as purchasers become better educated, sales are decided on a greater variety of factors. Salespeople are also increasingly being required to communicate their company's policies. Global competition is causing negotiations to be viewed as more important.

2. Salespeople must maintain a positive attitude to meet the challenges involved in negotiating with shrewd buyers. This can be accomplished by thorough preparation, analyzing successes *and* failures, associating with successful people, managing stress, and using the many resources available to salespeople.

3. The well-prepared salesperson analyzes the buyer's environment at two levels: (1) the buyer's organization and (2) the individuals who will actually participate in or influence the purchase decision.

4. Negotiating strategies fall into two broad categories: problem solving and aggressive bargaining. The aggressive bargainer tends to view the other negotiating party as an adversary, whereas the negotiator, using a problem-solving strategy, perceives the other party as a collaborator or partner.

5. Guidelines to follow are: don't be too focused on price, avoid the use of round numbers, employ psychological currency, avoid showdowns, trade places psychologically with the buyer, use questions to deflect unwanted proposals, and be candid.

QUESTIONS FOR DISCUSSION AND REVIEW

1. Identify three products consumers purchase that usually involve negotiations with a salesperson. Describe the features of each of these products that you believe are most frequently discussed in negotiations between the buyer and the seller.

2. Why are industrial products and services more likely to involve negotiations than consumer products?

3. Explain why the price of a product is sometimes not the most important thing involved in negotiations.

4. Why is a negotiator's attitude important, and why is it a challenge sometimes for a salesperson to maintain a positive attitude?

5. If you were a salesperson preparing to negotiate with a purchasing agent employed by a college or university, what five pieces of information do you think would be helpful as you negotiated with that purchasing agent? Why?

6. For each of the following situations, which one of the two basic negotiating strategies seems to be the most reasonable to use:

   a. a used car salesperson who never expects to sell the buyer another car,

   b. an insurance sales rep is selling life insurance to a couple who have a young family,

   c. a building supply manufacturing sales rep is calling on a construction contractor.

7. Develop a dialogue between a sales rep and a customer that illustrates unbundling.

8. How does the knowledge and expertise of a sales rep help the rep avoid the problems associated with the low balling tactic? Is all business "good business?" Explain.

9. Explain the phrase *forever for now*. With what tactic is this phrase associated?

10. Which broad negotiating strategy seems to be most closely associated with long-term buyer-seller relationships? Why?

11. If you analyzed the circumstances of your customer's purchasing agent and found that he or she had very little experience in making purchases of your equipment, what kind of "psychological currency" might you offer him or her that might be more valuable than a lower price?

CASE 9–1 PREPARING TO NEGOTIATE WITH A POWERFUL CUSTOMER

Jim Garrett had been working for Timberlake Manufacturing Company for approximately six months. Before assuming his territory, he had completed a two-month training program, learning about Timberlake's rubber gasket product line and other details of his selling responsibilities.

The largest customer Jim had in his territory, Federal Motors Corporation (FMC), was near the end of a two-year contract with Timberlake. The contract expired in ninety days, and Garrett had been preparing for negotiations that would, he hoped, lead to a renewal. FMC was a very large and influential automotive manufacturer that purchased almost $5 million of rubber products annually from Timberlake. The two companies had a ten-year relationship. Jim Garrett realized that successfully renegotiating the contract with FMC was very important to Timberlake and to his career.

The purchasing manager at FMC who was Jim's contact was Lisa Gibbons. Jim had met twice with Lisa since he had assumed his new responsibilities. He had learned in their first meeting that she was an experienced purchasing agent who prided herself on her knowledge of the automotive manufacturing business and the suppliers with whom she did business. As a result of Lisa's fifteen years of experience, she was well acquainted with other purchasing managers in other automotive companies.

When Jim Garrett checked in with his office one afternoon he received a message that his boss, Terry Paul, wanted to meet with him and discuss the upcoming FMC contract negotiations. When the two men met Terry gave Jim the following advice:

Terry: One of the first things Lisa will tell you as you begin your meeting is that she has been approached by at least a half dozen other vendors who have basically the same product as ours. She will also hint strongly that some of them are offering extremely attractive prices on their products. Don't try to defend our prices or even exhibit any interest in price. We don't want to start off playing the price game. You may, eventually, have to play the price card, but we don't want it to be a major issue. The main thing to do in the first meeting is to let Lisa talk as much as she will. We want to find out whether FMC is thinking about instituting a vendor evaluation program. I heard that GM is starting to do that and they plan to reduce the number of vendors they are purchasing from to only 500 in the next three years. That means over 3,000 vendors will be cut. If FMC does that too, we sure want to be among the chosen few.

Jim: What can I talk about then, if I can't talk price?

Terry: Talk high-quality customer service. We've tracked that business closely for the past four years, and we have a 95 percent on-time delivery record. We also have a less than 2 percent reject record. No other vendor that I know of has a better record of delivering unblemished products on time.

Jim: What else? Do you have any suggestions about the best type of questions?

Terry: Yeah, try to find out what Lisa thinks will be her customers' major problems for the next three years. See whether FMC is going to be pursuing any major programs. You know, like Ford's "Quality is Job One." Stuff like that. If they are in a second or third meeting, we'll come back with a proposal that will tie in with the FMC program. Don't make any concessions of any kind. Lisa knows you're new at this and she'll try to get you to give our product away, but don't do it. She'll try to throw her weight around as a buyer for FMC, but it is largely a show. We have a good product and she knows it.

QUESTIONS

1. Using Exhibit 9-1, identify ten questions that Jim Garrett might create and then attempt to answer *before* he meets with purchasing manager Lisa Gibbons.

2. What general strategy is Terry Paul expecting Lisa to use in the first meeting with Jim?

3. Develop some points Jim could use that would be "psychological currency" for the negotiations.

4. Create a dialogue you think could logically occur between Lisa and Jim that would illustrate the use of (a) a bogey tactic, and (b) unbundling.

5. What type of buyer-seller relationship seems to be most likely when you analyze the case and compare it with the basic relationships identified in Chapter 3? Explain your answer.

CASE 9–2 NEGOTIATING WITH A TOUGH BUYER

The following dialogue is taken from a session between Mary Hart and Bob Barrett. Mary is a sales representative for Sharpe Hospital Supply. Bob purchases for a group of twenty hospitals that have created a centralized purchasing organization called the Affiliated Buying Group (ABG). By purchasing in very large quantities, ABG can get quantity discounts from suppliers, which would not be possible if each hospital purchased for its own needs. ABG's purchasing managers collectively buy thousands of different kinds of products and services used by the hospitals.

Mary's company is a leading supplier of blood collection products such as needles, test tubes, and so forth. Sharpe has captured a very large share of the market (approximately 40 percent). It is known as a vendor of state-of-the-art products and has a very efficient distribution system.

Bob and Mary have been doing business with each other for approximately three years. Both take pride in their respective negotiation skills.

Bob: I know your MEDIVAC product is the best in the field. I'm very well informed about all its features. The fact remains, however, that my budget is the same size it was last year. I can't spend a penny more per unit this year than I did last year.

Mary: I hear you, Bob, but I also have some information that will show you how you can reduce your total costs of purchasing blood sample collection tubes.

Bob: What is it?

Mary: Bob, for the past three years you have been buying, I would estimate, not more than twenty percent of all your total blood collection tubes from us. Am I right?

Bob: It's true, you aren't our sole source of supply for these products. You will never be the only supplier we use for tubes. I might add that if you can't lower these prices I'll probably purchase a smaller percent of my needs from you.

Mary: Bob, how many days' supply of tubes do you think you carry in stock?

Bob: We think it is necessary to carry around sixty days' worth of that item.

Mary: In the study we made, which you authorized, we found the average was around seventy-five days' worth of supplies.

Bob: O.K. What's your point?

Mary: Bob, for every ten days' worth of supply you carry, the cost of money or interest rates that finance that stock adds two percent to the price of the product. In other words, if you are carrying fifty days worth of inventory, the total cost of the inventory is ten percent higher than it would be if you didn't have that inventory on hand.

Bob: Yeah, I know that, but that's an unavoidable cost of doing business. What if we had an emergency, or a supplier went on strike?

Mary: We can, under certain conditions, guarantee you two-day delivery on all your orders. That's because of our new electronic order entry and delivery system called READYLINE. That will permit you to reduce your order cycle from us from two weeks to two days. In other words, you can reduce your safety stock and save your hospitals a lot of money.

Bob: O.K., that's fine but I still can't pay any more per product than I did last year. I want the new service that READYLINE provides, but I also want your products at last year's prices.

Mary: You remember I said a minute ago that under certain circumstances we could give you the two-day delivery. We can give you that at last year's prices if you agree to purchase eighty percent of all your supplies from us for the next three years. We estimate that that arrangement will save you three million dollars over the life of the contract in the form of reduced inventory finance charges.

Bob: That's pretty interesting. Let me think about it.

1. What negotiating strategy does Bob Barrett appear to be using?

2. What tactics are illustrated in Bob's comments?

3. What strategy does Mary Hart seem to be using?

4. Assuming Bob agrees to Mary's proposition, who "won" in the negotiation? Why?

CASE 9–3   CREATING A TRAINING PROGRAM TO IMPROVE NEGOTIATION SKILLS

Sue Morshad had asked three KABCO Company salespeople to help her design a training program emphasizing negotiation strategies and tactics. She had discussed the need for adding this to KABCO's sales training program with Hank Clemens, Vice President of Sales.

Sue was meeting with the three sales reps, Tony Anthony, Michelle Smith, and Michael Warner, in her office in KABCO headquarters. Sue planned to use their suggestions as she fashioned the two-day training program that would become a required course in all of KABCO's sales training programs.

The following dialogue was occurring among the four people:

Sue:	All of you have been with KABCO for at least three years and, according to Mr. Clemens, you have had a lot of experience in negotiating with important customers. As you and other salespeople have told us, the buyers in hospitals and clinics are getting much more sophisticated, and the challenges you confront in selling to these buyers are becoming more difficult. We have decided to create a two-day training module on negotiations. To make it realistic and helpful to the field sales force, we need your help, and that's why I asked you to come to this meeting.
Tony:	I think some training in this area is an excellent idea! One thing I would like to see stressed is how to prepare for negotiating sessions. I've just kind of learned through the 'school of hard knocks.'
Sue:	O.K., how do you the rest of you feel about that?
Michelle:	I think that's a good idea. One of the things that surprised me when I was just starting was how people's behavior seemed to change. People who normally seemed very cordial became absolute tigers in some cases when you started negotiating.
Michael:	One thing that needs to be emphasized is the idea that price is one of the last things a sales rep should start tinkering with. A new sales rep probably thinks about dropping prices first thing in a negotiation.
Michelle:	That's true. Let me suggest that before we start identifying all the cards you can play such as shipping dates, payment schedules, and so forth, we better have arrangements worked out with other departments. You don't want salespeople negotiating delivery dates and then have the shipping people screaming that we have agreed to an impossible schedule.
Sue:	That's a good point. We must know what the negotiation boundaries are for each thing such as payment schedules. Otherwise, the salespeople will be in danger of making commitments that can't be fulfilled, or, if they are fulfilled, will make the business unprofitable for KABCO.
Tony:	How about role playing sessions in negotiating? I would think that actually participating in some mock sessions would be beneficial. It is beneficial to read and talk about negotiating, but some actual practice would really help.

Michelle: I remember the first time someone tried the take-it-or-leave-it routine on me. I knew about that approach, but actually sitting across the desk from someone who could sign an order for a million dollar sale and having to respond to an ultimatum—you have to be able to think on your feet. That takes some experience.

Sue: One thing along those lines which I've been thinking about is to get a negotiations expert such as Dr. White to help us. We would have each trainee engage in a mock negotiation, and the session would be videotaped. We would get Dr. White to view the tapes and give his suggestions about how the sales rep could improve. After getting feedback, the rep would then participate in another negotiation training session and attempt to incorporate Dr. White's suggestions. How does that sound?

Tony: That's great! Could each rep keep the tapes to review later on? That would be a big help to keep the training "edge."

Sue: Good suggestion, Tony. What I would like to propose to you is that I put together a tentative schedule of the subjects, time of coverage devoted to each subject, and other details. I'll have the proposal in your hands by Friday and then I'll ask each of you to give me your evaluations by the following Wednesday. Is that acceptable?

Group: O.K.

QUESTIONS

Before answering the following questions read the opening vignette at the beginning of the chapter. This information will be helpful in refreshing your memory about the nature of KABCO's business.

1. How could the negotiation tactic of unbundling be used if the sale were focused on a piece of highly sophisticated medical equipment such as KABCO sells?

2. Who else in the KABCO company needs to have input into the content of Sue Morshad's proposed negotiation training program?

3. Create scenarios and dialogues that could occur between a sales rep and a hospital purchasing department representative that illustrate: (a) the use of the bogey tactic, (b) the use of the crunch tactic, and (c) the use of psychological currency.

NOTES

1. *Webster's New Students Dictionary*, (Springfield, Massachusetts: G.&C. Merriam Company, 1991).

2. Traci Goings Gorny, "Predicting the '90s in Purchasing," *NAPM Insights,* Vol. 2, Number 1 (Tempe, Arizona: National Association of Purchasing Management, Inc., 1991): 22–23.

3. Karen L. Christ and Jon M. Hawes, "International Sales Negotiations: A Review of Graham's Theory Contributions," in *Professional Sales and Sales Management Practices Leading Toward the 21st Century*, ed. James B. DeConinck, (Dallas: National Conference in Sales Management, 1990), 104–06.

4. John L. Graham and Roy A. Herberger, "Negotiators Abroad—Don't Shoot From the Hip," *Harvard Business Review* (July–August 1983): 160–68.

5. Robert E. Spekman, "Strategic Supplier Selection: Understanding Long-Term Buyer Relationships," *Business Horizons* (July–August 1988): 75–81.

6. Roger Fisher and Scott Brown, *Getting Together: Building Relationships As We Negotiate* (New York: Penguin Books, 1989), 48.

7. Ibid., 197.

8. Roger Fisher and William Ury, *Getting to Yes: Negotiating Without Giving In* (New York: Penguin Books, 1983), 8.

9. Dr. Fran Pirozzolo, "A Strong Case for Debunking Mental Toughness Images," *Houston Post* (July 18, 1991): C-10.

10. "Choosing a Third-Party Maintenance Vendor," *Guide To Purchasing,* (National Association of Purchasing Management, 1988): 4.

11. Barbara C. Perdue and John O. Summers, "Purchasing Agents' Use of Negotiation Strategies," *Journal of Marketing Research* (May 1991): 175–89.

12. Ibid.

13. Ralph L. Day, Ronald E. Michaels, and Barbara C. Perdue, "How Buyers Handle Conflicts," *Industrial Marketing Management* (May 1988): 153–60.

14. Paul A. Rubin and Joseph R. Carter, "Joint Optimality in Buyer-Supplier Negotiations," *Journal of Purchasing and Materials Management* (Spring 1990): 20–26.

15. Robert E. Spekman, "Strategic Supplier Selection: Understanding Long-Term Buyer Relationships," *Business Horizons* (July–August 1988): 75–81.

16. Rubin and Carter, "Joint Optimality," 20–26.

17. Joe F. Alexander, Patrick L. Schul, and Emin Babakus, "Analyzing Interpersonal Communications in Industrial Marketing Negotiations," *Journal of the Academy of Marketing Science* (Spring 1991).

18. Gary Karrass, *Negotiate to Close: How to Make More Successful Deals* (New York: Simon & Schuster, Inc.), 95.

19. Fisher and Ury, *Getting to Yes*, 129.

20. Karrass, *Negotiate to Close,* 117.

21. Ibid., 108.

22. Perdue and Summers, "Purchasing Agents," 175–89.

23. Barbara C. Perdue, Ralph L. Day, and Ronald E. Michaels, "Negotiation Styles of Industrial Buyers," *Industrial Marketing Management* (August 1986): 171–76.

24. John A. Carlisle and Robert C. Parker, *Beyond Negotiation: Redeeming Customer-Supplier Relationships* (New York: John Wiley & Sons, 1989), 5.

25. Ibid., 10.

26. Ibid.

27. Mark H. McCormack, *What They Don't Teach You at Harvard Business School: Notes from a Street-Smart Executive* (New York: Bantam Books, 1984), 144.

28. Ibid.

29. Ibid., 146.

30. "Advertisers Put Fear into the Hearts of Their Prospects," *Marketing News* (August 15, 1988): 1.

31. Michele Willens, "The Manly Art of Win-Win Negotiations," *Money*, no. 16 (1987): 199–202.

32. McCormack, *What They Don't Teach,* 148.

33. Ibid., 149.

34. Ibid., 150.

35. Ibid., 154.

CHAPTER 10

Answering Objections, Closing, and Follow-Up Contacts

LEARNING OBJECTIVES

After studying this chapter, you should be able to:

1. Explain how a successful salesperson regards his or her customers' objections.

2. Analyze four common sales objections and explain how the salesperson can meet each objection.

3. Explain some common body language signals that indicate the need for an abrupt change by the sales rep. Explain some signals that should encourage the rep to offer the customer an opportunity to buy.

4. Describe the difference between a trial close and a close.

5. Describe various ways to close a sale.

6. Explain why it is important for the salesperson to maintain contact with the customer after a sale.

7. Define the key terms used in this chapter.

KEY TERMS

- third-party method
- body language
- red, yellow, and green signals
- closing
- trial close
- assumptive close
- closing on a minor point
- summary close
- physical action close
- standing-room-only close
- single objection close
- limited choice close
- direct appeal close
- follow-up contacts

SUCCESS   SUCCESS   SUCCESS

Learn 23 different responses to "Your price is too high,". . . 17 for "I have to think this over,". . . 14 for "I am too busy to talk with you," plus much, much more!

Detach and mail to:
SUCCESSFUL SELLING
P.O. Box 1234
Anywhere, USA 56789

- -

YES! Send me your fantastic new selling tool, *Successful Selling Power*, for only $127 today!

[ ] Check enclosed   [ ] Charge my credit card

VISA or Mastercard # _____

Expiration Date: _____ Signature: _____

Telephone: (____)_____ Date: _____

For faster service call TOLL-FREE 1-800-GET-RICH

IMA FAILURE
2700 Bay Area
Houston, Texas 77058

Each day, thousands of people's mail boxes are stuffed with direct mail pieces advertising seminars, videotapes, and books. Some of them are similar to the one above. They claim people who buy and use these training programs can improve their skills in negotiating, handling objections, and closing sales. Phrases such as "overcoming resistance," "winning the battle of the minds," and "countering objections" frequently appear in these direct mail pieces. The implication is that what is occurring between buyers and salespeople is a battle of wits. Armed with new, more powerful psychological weapons after having attended such seminars or having read the advertised book, the salesperson can, it is claimed, be a victor in the battle with reluctant buyers.

Such techniques are far removed from true relationship management. Professional salespersons don't "batter down" customer opposition. Trust and respect between buyer and seller cannot be fostered when salespeople perceive themselves as engaged in efforts to overcome the customer's resistance. Customer objections must be successfully answered and sales must be closed. (We will make the point later that the term *closed* may be misinterpreted by people who are learning how to become professional salespersons. For the time being, however, we use the traditional term because of its widespread acceptance.)

The purposes of this chapter are threefold. First, we will describe how successful relationship management-oriented salespeople perceive and handle objections. Second, we will explain why, in a healthy buyer-seller relationship, sales are never closed. Finally, this chapter contains advice on what can and should be done during follow-up calls to maximize the possibilities for a continuing profitable relationship with a buyer who has recently purchased from you.

OBJECTIONS

Before we analyze some specific objections customers frequently voice, it is important to have an understanding of what objections actually are. Refer back to the communication model (see Exhibit 2-4) in Chapter 2. As you examine the model, you will notice a "feedback loop." Buyers' objections are one of the most important forms of feedback a sales representative can receive. Imagine how difficult it would be for a salesperson to make a sale if the buyer could not or would not say anything that would indicate a readiness or reluctance to make a purchase commitment.

Exhibit 10-1 provides some guidelines to help a salesperson develop and maintain a proper perspective involving objections. A brief analysis of each point made in Exhibit 10-1 follows.

Objections Signal Customer Interest

One authority in the sales field states that the sales objection should always be seen for what it really is—a plea for more information.[1] Another well-known sales consultant, Tom Hopkins, author of *How to Master the Art of Selling*, states, "Objections are the rungs of the ladder to sales success . . . you'll learn to love objections—because they announce buying intention and point the way to closing the sale."[2]

Opportunities to Learn More

Every time someone objects to purchasing a product or service the prospective buyer is saying, at least implicitly, "What you've told me isn't what I'm interested in. Here is what interests me." This provides you with an insight on how to redirect your presentation. You have, if you will grasp it, an opportunity to immediately tailor your message to meet the needs that are relevant to that individual. Obviously,

DO regard objections as:

1. indications that the customer is interested.
2. opportunities to learn more about your prospect's interests and needs.
3. stages in a buyer-seller dialogue at which it is possible to gain buyer commitment and make a sale.
4. opportunities for you to demonstrate your professional skills and enhance your credibility.

DON'T regard objections as:

1. indications that you are not performing satisfactorily.
2. signals that the prospect is not interested, uninformed, or even hostile to you.
3. reasons why a customer may not be agreeable to make a purchase.

Exhibit 10-1 Objections—Guidance Toward a Proper Perspective

not all your customers will be so helpful that they will tell you precisely what their needs and interests are. We have described in Chapter 7 the different kinds of questions a good salesperson can use, as well as the need to be an effective listener. If the reason for the customer's resistance is not clear, the salesperson can ask questions and learn more about the buyer's needs and then modify the sales presentation accordingly.

Opportunity to Gain Buyer's Commitment

Every time you successfully answer a buyer's objection, there is at least a momentary opportunity to see whether the buyer is ready to commit himself or herself to making a purchase. Later in this chapter, you will read about a closing technique called "closing on an objection." If you are aware of this opportunity, you will look forward to hearing an objection. After you deliver your answer, you then can move the conversation in a direction that permits you to get the customer's approval.

Opportunity to Exhibit Professional Skill and Integrity

The responses a salesperson gives to a buyer's objections will reveal a lot about the salesperson (his or her preparation, integrity, poise, and so forth). Some buyers in the early, formative stages of a buyer-seller relationship will offer objections for the primary purpose of testing the sales rep.[3] The observant buyer may be testing for one or more of the following:

Figure 10-1 Successfully answering a buyer's objection provides an opportunity to explore her readiness to commit herself to making the purchase.

1. Does the salesperson empathize with me, or does he or she try to minimize the importance of my objection?

2. Does the rep maintain a confident and poised demeanor? If not, what is the reason?

3. Does the rep lie or make inaccurate claims to try to answer the objection?

It is also important to keep in mind what objections are *not*, as stated in Exhibit 10-1. Unfortunately, all too many times we wish to avoid any signal that conveys the idea that a buyer is not ready to make a purchase commitment. Because salespeople are usually up-beat and positive in their attitudes, some of them overreact and/or distort the meaning of objections. Most salespeople, like all of us, want to be rewarded for effort and rewarded *quickly*. Objections are indicators or signals that the buyer is, at that moment, not yet ready to reward the salesperson. The important thing to remember is not to fear objections and draw conclusions that are unwarranted. Just as it is important for a salesperson to know what objections *are*, it is also important to understand what objections are *not*.

Reflections on a Sales Rep's Performance

Inexperienced salespersons might think that a perfect sales visit consists of making a presentation in which there were no objections, based on the erroneous belief that objections are barriers to the completion of a sale. Following that line of reasoning, the more objections voiced by the buyer, the less skillfully it might seem the salesperson is performing. At this point, after having learned what objections truly are, you should not feel that the presence or absence of customer objections is a reflection on a rep's performance. *How the objections are handled is what is important.* A salesperson dealing with a seasoned buyer may encounter a situation in which the buyer tests the rep by raising objections. If the salesperson gives up or exhibits a lack of conviction in what he or she is selling, the buyer will note it and probably lose respect for the salesperson.[4]

A Signal That a Sale Cannot Be Made

As long as the prospective buyer is talking, even if it is to raise objections, there is a chance to make a sale. Prospects who care or are interested enough to voice an objection can be sold. The time to be concerned as a salesperson is when the prospective buyer stops the dialogue with you. As long as you know (or believe you know) what the concerns of the buyer are, you can still address them.

An Infallible Indication of the Buyer's Reluctance

Customers do not always reveal the true concerns or anxieties that may be holding up a sale. This situation is so important that a special section will be devoted to it later in this chapter. Suffice it now to say, however, that some objections are actually "hidden." For instance, a statement such as, "I'm waiting several months for the price to go down," *may* be a reasonable and socially acceptable way of saying, "I can't afford this product right now." There are several ways an astute salesperson can deal with the hidden objection. (We discuss these methods later, but first, the salesperson must remember that not *all* objections can be taken at face value.)

RESPONDING TO OBJECTIONS

Now that you have a deeper understanding of the nature of objections, it is appropriate for us to analyze some of the specific objections customers frequently use. In each case, we will give specific examples of how the objection is typically voiced and also show how the skillful salesperson can respond.

High Price

When a prospective buyer says, "Your price is too high," what is he or she actually saying? In many cases there are several interpretations the salesperson could make. First, and most obvious, is that the price being asked is more than the buyer is willing to pay. Second, the buyer believes he or she cannot afford the offering. A third is that the price is higher than the customer would have to pay if the product were purchased from a competitor. Fourth, the price objection is being used to discourage the sales rep; the prospect wants to break off the contact.

Your first objective after the price objection has been raised is to identify the real reason for it. Does the prospect believe he or she can't afford the product or service you are selling? Has a competitor undercut your price? In other words, you can't truly address the objection until you understand the rationale being used by the customer.

A research study of highly effective salespeople sought to discover how successful reps handled the price objection.[5] It found three methods of dealing with the price objection. One approach focused on providing the customer with more information about the economic benefits he or she would enjoy by purchasing the product. Here is an example in the form of a dialogue between a hotel sales rep and a person making arrangements for a convention site:

Buyer: That's more than we can ask our members to spend; $110 a night for a double occupancy room is just too high.

Rep: Let's take a look at what $110 gets you. First, there's a free buffet breakfast for all our registered guests. That's not a continental breakfast, either. That's a full breakfast, which is at least a $7.50 value in most coffee shops in the area. Second, we have a free airport shuttle bus that departs from the hotel on the hour. That's another $5 value right there. Third, there's a Happy Hour from 3 until 5 p.m. every day except Sunday. For some, that may save $5 or $10. Also, from your association's standpoint, the cost of the ten different meeting rooms is lower, so you don't need to charge your members as much for conference registration.

Another approach taken by other highly successful sales reps is to break down total cost over a reasonable period of time.[6] This approach is frequently used in advertising as well as personal sales (see Exhibit 10-2). Rather than quoting a price of $58.50 for thirteen weeks, *The New York Times* cites a weekly price of $4.50.

The third approach identified in the study revealed that some salespeople want to know the customer's basis for comparison in making the objection.[7] The sales rep uses a clarifying question, such as, "In relationship to what other product is my price too high?" or "What do you consider a fair price?"

Successful salespersons tend to search for the underlying causes of a prospect's objection. The sales rep who can isolate the reasons for a price objection can take one of the three approaches just described.

One of the few things many sales consultants agree on is that the rep should not resort to lowering the price of the products or service. One result of decreasing

Exhibit 10-2 **An Example of Total Cost Expressed as a Weekly Price**

Please deliver the National Edition of The New York Times at the introductory price of just $4.50 a week for the first 13 weeks.

Name _____

Address _____ Apt. (or office) _____

City _____

State & Zip _____

Telephone: Home (___) _____Office (___) _____

For service less than seven days a week, please check here:
☐ Monday — Friday at $2 a week for the first 13 weeks.
☐ Saturday and Sunday at $3 a week.

(This introductory offer is for readers who have not had seven-day home delivery of The New York Times within the last 90 days. After the first 13 weeks, service will continue at our low regular rate of $5.50 a week for seven-day delivery or $2.50 a week for Monday-Friday home or office delivery. Delivery is not available in some areas.)   *Source CA*

Source: *New York Times*, Home Delivery Dept., 7800 West 95th St., Suite 201, Hickory Hills, IL 60457.

price in response to an objection is to cast doubt on previous claims of quality. After a presentation or demonstration that includes statements about product or service quality, a retreat by the sales rep on his or her prices can undo earlier efforts.[8]

Buyer Indecision

Virtually every salesperson has heard these objections: "I'm not ready yet," or "I don't know." This is called buyer indecision. An effective salesperson should seek to find the underlying reasons, address the reasons, and create a plan with the buyer for finalizing the sale. On the other hand, ineffective salespersons tend to repeat the sales presentation, create a sense of urgency, and press for immediate decisions, without understanding the reasons for buyer reluctance.[9]

In Chapter 8, we gave a description of various communication styles (driver, analytical, amiable, expressive). A perceptive salesperson should factor in his or her customer's communication style before responding to the "not ready yet" objection. Remember, amiables like to check things out with other people. Analyticals, on the other hand, seem to crave details and data. Pressuring such people can backfire.

The sales rep's best resource—good questions—should be used when the customer is indecisive. One expert salesperson said he probes for the reasons behind indecision by asking such questions as, "Is there anything I haven't told you about the product? How do you feel about the price—are we in the ballpark? Do you feel that it's the proper offering in terms of the function of the machine versus the cost?"

Buyer Disinterest or Lack of Need

Buyer disinterest or lack of need for the product can indicate several things. One, it may signal that the sales rep's prospecting system is not working very well, or that the salesperson is doing a lot of cold calling (calling on people or businesses that haven't expressed any interest in the product or service). Two, the objection could signal that the sales rep's presentation hasn't identified the customer's need and explained how the product or service could satisfy it. Three, this objection is being stated rather than the real one, which may be an uncomfortable one for the prospect to voice. Some people are reluctant to flatly say they cannot afford a product or service. In other business-to-business sales, an individual may be reluctant to acknowledge that he or she lacks authority to make a purchase.

How should these objections be handled? Obviously, the several possibilities just described should not all be handled the same way. If the sales rep suspects that he or she is the victim of a poor or nonexistent prospecting system, that is a problem for the sales rep's management. However, if all signs initially indicated that the potential customer was a good prospect, but the "I don't need it" objection was still raised, then the rep needs to evaluate what he or she is doing (or not doing). One of the first things to examine is the sales presentation. Were there any questions posed by the rep at the beginning of the presentation to determine the prospect's needs? If it was a canned presentation involving little two-way communication (see Chapter 8), the problem may be *insufficient opportunity for the prospect to tell you how to sell to him or her.* One of the interesting facts about sales rep/customer interaction is that when the sales rep provides the customer with the right opportunities (through questions), the customer will frequently guide the sales rep to a sale. Once again, timely, appropriate questions can unlock numerous sales opportunities.

When the salesperson is sure his or her presentation has sufficiently explored the customer's needs, something else is wrong. When the customer has indicated a need but still objects with "I don't need it," there is a hidden objection. Hidden objections can be handled by using the **third-party method**. This technique uses another customer as an example. The other customer, according to the sales rep, had a problem similar to that of the present customer. The sales rep then goes on to describe how the problem was resolved. The rationale underlying this method is that by taking the spotlight momentarily off the present customer and focusing on another customer, the rep allows the prospective buyer to open up and reveal what is causing him or her to reject the sale. For example, a sales rep for an auto manfacturer is attempting to sell to the fleet manager of a company that purchases 200 cars per year for its sales and sales management personnel. The automotive manufacturer's rep would like the fleet manager to purchase air bags that would enhance the safety of the cars. The fleet manager has said she doesn't think this feature is needed, since the cars already have standard seat belts.

Sales rep: I was talking to another auto fleet manager the other day who told me he couldn't afford to put air bags in his cars. He said his budget had just been cut by 20 percent.

Buyer: That happens here, also. I'm sure these bags are the wave of the future, but until the manufacturers make them standard equipment I just can't afford them. (Reveals the real problem.)

Sales rep: I understand your concern, but if you can save $150 per car by spending $100 wouldn't that be a pretty good deal? Let me show you how we can do that. (Now starts to address the problem.)

In this scenario, the sales rep has tactfully used an example of another buyer who had an objection that was similar to the real objection of this prospect.

Competition

Satisfaction with a competing firm is an objection to the sales rep's company and could easily be one of the first things a rep hears when making a brand-switching contact call (see Chapter 7). This situation is one in which all the sales rep's pre-call preparation pays off. The information about the prospect's circumstances should have been analyzed by the rep in anticipation of this objection. Based on the facts and some safe assumptions, the rep must formulate several customer-oriented questions that can be asked immediately:

Rep to prospective industrial customer: Haven't you just announced the acquisition of the XYZ Company? Its production plants are all in the northwestern part of the country. Wouldn't you be interested in another supplier whose distribution center is closer to those plants?

Rep to individual consumer: Isn't your daughter, Helen, about to enter college? Would you like to just look at our young adult medical insurance plan and compare the rate with your present carrier?

The goal here is to reveal, as quickly as possible, that you have done your homework on the individual customer. Customer-oriented questions reveal your preparation and, in many cases, will make a prospect curious to find out what else you know about him or her. Fortunately (for the truly professional sales rep), there are many other salespeople who will not have exhibited any sensitivity to the customer. When a well-prepared rep does make a contact, it can open up an opportunity that initially seemed nonexistent.

Reading the Customer

Research studies have revealed that people don't communicate their feelings and attitudes by relying only on words. More than half our communication is conveyed through nonverbal signals. Most people refer to this form of communication as **body language**, defined as any movement of our bodies that communicates something to other people.[10]

Shifts in posture (crossing one's legs, slumping in a chair, leaning forward) are some of the ways we communicate. It is very important that a salesperson become adept at "reading" or interpreting the nonverbal signals a prospective buyer is sending.

One authority has categorized various body language signals into three groups—red, green, and yellow.[11] **Red signals** tell a sales rep to stop doing or saying what he or she is now using to communicate with the customer. **Yellow signals** reveal customer doubts or boredom. **Green signals**, as you might imagine, indicate agreement. What, specifically, are some of the body language signals? (See Exhibit 10-3)

Figure 10-2 The ability to read the customer's body language can improve the rep's communication with the buyer.

Exhibit 10-3
Some Common Body Language Signals

RED (STAND ON THE BRAKES)
Customer clenches hands into fists
    compresses his/her lips
    leans away from salesperson
    roughly handles sample or other material
    glances at watch or clock

YELLOW (SLOW DOWN)
Customer folds or crosses arms
    clasps hands together
    rests head on one hand
    rubs or massages forehead

GREEN (GO-FOR-THE-GOLD)
Customer sits on the edge of chair
    leans toward the salesperson
    open, relaxed hands
    nodding head affirmatively
    posture the same as sales rep's
    handles sample or other material carefully

Red Signals

Some of the most obvious signals are such things as looking at a watch or clock, picking up the telephone and making a call, or drumming one's fingers on the desk. Most of the time, the person who signals (see Exhibit 10-3) "I don't want to continue" has probably sent less obvious signals *several minutes earlier.* When you see your customer giving one or more of the red signals, stop your presentation immediately and ask a question to find out what is bothering the buyer. At this point, you need not worry about bringing your presentation to a graceful conclusion. The prospect is on the verge of ending the meeting; therefore, you may as well take a chance on uncovering the problem and attempt to regain the buyer's acceptance.

An example is a textbook publisher's sales representative calling on a college professor for the purpose of encouraging the professor to adopt a particular book for classroom use. The salesperson seated across the desk from the professor opens the textbook to a chapter and hands the book across the desk to the professor. A "red signal" might consist of the professor's quickly glancing at the page and then closing the book and handing it back. If the salesperson is aware of what is happening, it would be appropriate to ask a question such as, "Is there another textbook that covers this subject more effectively, in your opinion?"

In summary, the wise salesperson must be prepared to make a fundamental change in whatever he or she is doing because the sale is in jeopardy. It is better to take the initiative by asking a question than to continue on and let the customer build up a growing resentment to your efforts.

Yellow Signals

Exhibit 10-3 identifies several behaviors that reveal the prospective buyer is in doubt. Perhaps the buyer is questioning the accuracy of the rep's statements.

Sales rep:	(selling tires to Mr. Thompson) "Mr. Thompson, there is no reason why a driver who takes care of his car and keeps these tires properly inflated can't get 100,000 miles out of them."
Mr. Thompson:	(folding his arms across his chest) "I've bought a lot of tires before and I've never heard anyone say that."

In this example, Mr. Thompson is really helping the salesperson by exhibiting an "I doubt that" signal *and* verbalizing his disbelief. The salesperson can handle this in different ways. First, he or she can acknowledge the customer's doubts with a statement such as: "I hear you, Mr. Thompson. That is an incredible claim, isn't it? I wouldn't say that, however, if I didn't have several people who could back me up on this. Do you know any of them?" (shows Thompson a list of people who have been very satisfied with the same tires Thompson is being shown).

Another approach is to ask the prospective buyer how much driving he or she normally expects to do on a set of tires. Depending on the customer's answer and the rep's assessment of the customer's ability to understand technical descriptions, the sales rep might then proceed to show the customer a cut-away portion of a sales demonstration tire. The rep could talk about the materials in the tire and explain how technological improvements could permit such a claim to be credibly made. This product-feature oriented approach to removing doubt should not be used unless the customer is judged to be capable of understanding and interested in hearing a somewhat technical presentation.

Yellow signals in a sales situation should caution the rep that doubts or concerns are beginning to distract the listening customer. Some sales consultants advise reps to attempt to get the buyer to reveal what is causing doubt by asking a question such as, "Is there a question I could answer for you concerning this feature?" Other consultants recommend a less direct method—the **third party method**. In such cases, the rep, sensing the customer's doubt, might handle the case in the following way:

Sales rep:	"Jane, when I have said this about our product, many people have wondered about whether it can truly do these things. As a matter of fact, when we first heard about this at our annual sales meeting I told my boss, 'My customers will never believe this.' She quieted my doubts, however, when she provided

me with the latest study conducted by *Consumer Reports* magazine. Since then I've seen reports provided by United Consumers League and other groups. If you would care to have copies of these reports I would be glad to give them to you."

Yellow signals left unanswered or ignored can turn into red signals, so watch closely for the symptoms identified in Exhibit 10-3.

Green Signals

Green signals tell you that your prospect is ready to make a commitment. The customer is symbolically saying, "I'm ready to buy. Let's do it." Some of the classic signals of approval are nodding one's head, sitting forward in the seat, leaning toward the sales rep, and handling a sample of the product carefully (perhaps even giving signs of wanting to keep the sample). When the alert salesperson sees one or more of these positive signals, it is time to get the customer to make a purchase commitment.

Some sales reps who detect their prospects' green signals mistakenly interpret this behavior to mean that the prospect is enjoying the rep's performance and wants it to continue.[12] The verbose salesperson continues on, the prospect starts to get bored, and negative thoughts start to surface in his or her mind. In a sense, the unwary salesperson starts buying his or her product back from the prospect who a moment ago had bought the salesperson's proposition. Even if you have much more you could tell the customer about a product or service, when you see the "I'm ready to buy" green signals, give the customer an opportunity to make the purchase.

CLOSING A SALE

The most casual student of business is aware of words and phrases that are traditional in business conversation: *share of market, bottom line,* and *prospecting* are examples. *Closing* is also a word that is widely recognized and has for many decades been the focal point for intense study by salespeople.

Although various writers' definitions differ, the common theme in their explanations is that the **closing** is the culmination of the salesperson's efforts to acquire an order. In short, when a sales rep closes, he or she asks for the order. The techniques used to get the customer's agreement to purchase are called *closes*.[13]

Closing should be analyzed in the context of the basic theme of relationship management. The sales rep who is making a first-time sale to a new customer is not closing anything. *He or she is making a beginning.* If the sale is to an established customer, the agreement to purchase is a *continuation.* Emphasis on developing the proper perspective for this activity, which we refer to as closing, is a key to building successful relations between buyers and sellers.

Allessandra and his colleagues prefer not to use the word *closing*. They use *confirming the purchase* instead and state, "To maintain a profitable relationship with your customer, you will have to follow up, service, promote, satisfy, and continually communicate with him."[14]

Although in this text we will continue to use *close* and *closing*, you should keep in mind that when an agreement to purchase is secured for the first time, the only thing this signals is that *one phase* in the buyer-seller relationship is closed or finished. The buyer is now a customer—not just a prospective customer.

Attitudes Toward Closing

The salesperson who would order *Successful Selling Power*, mentioned at the beginning of this chapter, probably fears closing. As a result of a lack of success in selling, he or she is likely to be in the market for a quick fix. What many unsuccessful salespeople don't realize is that there are no magical formulas, no catchy phrases or power moves, that can remedy their problems. Usually their fears of closing are a result of not understanding what they have been doing wrong. Several circumstances can account for this problem.

First, there is the possibility that the people upon whom the rep is calling are simply not good prospects for the product or service being sold. Some sales managers from the old school would say, "You have to *make* them want what you are selling." This philosophy, of course, gives rise to high-pressure sales behavior, which is a far cry from the level of professionalism most successful companies want their salespeople to attain today. Unfortunately, there are still companies and sales managers who believe that if you call on enough people and make a sales pitch to enough people, you will attain your sales volume goals. Using such strong-arm tactics makes it seem as though the success of a sale comes down to a sales rep's ability to close. As President Bush said about an interview he had with Dan Rather of CBS during the 1988 presidential campaign, "It was tension city." When a sales rep is calling on the wrong people, every sales visit and every encounter is tension city.

Another reason for some reps' fears at closing time is their ineptitude at finding the customer's wants or needs that can be fulfilled by the product or service. This is a particularly big problem when the sales rep is using a canned presentation featuring a generalized approach to describing how the product or service satisfies a wide variety of needs. If the rep doesn't know whether he or she has appealed to a particular prospect's needs, then the customer's response to the rep's closing effort may be the first, and belated, indication of success or failure.

When to Close

If the salesperson is using a canned, prepared sales presentation, the answer is obvious. The close effort will be exerted at the point in the presentation where the designer of the presentation has decided it should occur.

An example is the sales pitch made by a part-time employee of a company that uses the telephone to contact prospective customers. The portion of the sales presentation containing the close might run something like this:

Sales rep: Ms. Jones, I'm pleased to inform you that you have been selected as a winner in our Clear Lake Properties contest! We have some fabulous prizes that we want to give you if you would be willing to spend a short time looking at the wonderful lots and weekend retreats located at Clear Lake. Some of the prizes are diamond dust earrings, fur coats, and many other outstanding gifts. You can select your winnings on any of the next three weekends by showing up at the guest quarters offices of our company at Clear Lake. Which one of the next three weekends would be most convenient for you?

What is being sold is an appointment to get people to go and inspect vacant lots upon which houses can be built. Property development companies sometimes find it difficult to get sufficient numbers of clients to come without any inducement. To ensure a flow of investors, the development company will hire a company that specializes in telephone selling and solicitation to canvass a market. The telephone sales company, in turn, will create a sales presentation that its employees will memorize and use. The canned presentation is given over and over again by the telephone sales reps to thousands of people. Several hundred of the recipients of these calls will be persuaded to make an appointment and pick up their "fabulous prize." The close in this example was the question, "Which one of the next three weekends would be most convenient for you?" Some analysts may say this is not a true sale situation and, therefore, no real close is occurring. Granted, no real property in the form of building lots is being sold. What the telephone sales company is really selling is the prize. The price the lucky winner will have to pay is the time and effort exerted to go to this property on a weekend (and be subjected to sales efforts to purchase a lot).

When the rep does not use a canned presentation with a built-in close, the answer to the time-to-close question becomes much different. A perceptive sales rep will detect, by analyzing the customer's reactions, when it seems appropriate to use a closing technique. Sometimes this may occur before a rep has described more than one or two benefits of the product or service (remember the communication style described in Chapter 8 involving people who were identified as drivers). Other times, especially with analyticals, the time to close may occur only after the prospective buyer has thoroughly analyzed all the benefits.

When it is left to the salesperson's discretion to determine when to try to close a sale, the rep may try a trial close. A **trial close** is an attempt to determine the prospect's attitude toward the product and the sales presentation.[15] One of the most common trial close methods is asking questions. For example, "When will we need to deliver these products?" or "How many of your employees should we plan on training?" By asking questions that focus on postpurchase details, the rep can determine whether it seems that the prospect has already mentally resolved the fundamental issue and is now considering relatively minor details. Some experts call this an **assumptive close** (see page 287) or **closing on a minor point**.[16] If the buyer answers in a manner that indicates he or she is thinking about the details that would follow the purchase, then the rep may proceed to finalize the sale. If the buyer says, "I haven't even made up my mind whether I want to buy this yet" (or words to that effect), then the sales rep has gained insights about the need to continue the selling effort.

In addition to questions, other trial closes are based on the sales rep's physical movements or verbal pattern. Reaching into a briefcase for an order book or contract, placing them on a buyer's desk or table with a pen, or in a retail store moving toward the cash register, are all subtle messages. If the buyer doesn't stop the rep with a statement or question that signals, "I'm not ready yet," then the rep may couple his or her efforts with questions similar to those above.

Occasionally, salespeople will make a trial close by pausing after making what they believe is a point important to the customer. The pause permits the buyer to respond and thereby provides the salesperson with an opportunity to see how the buyer is accepting the proposition. The pause or planned silence technique is also used in connection with the final closing efforts. Some sales consultants advise that when a closing effort has been made, such as "May we write the order?" the rep should pause and not say anything else until the other person speaks. A long silence should not unnerve the rep. He or she should wait patiently and permit the customer to think. Nervous salespeople, lacking confidence in their abilities or their products or services, can convey their unease to otherwise unsuspecting buyers. If the conversation reaches a logical point where it is time for the buyer's response but the sales rep seems reluctant to permit the response, the following might occur:

Sales rep: We've covered a lot of reasons why this product makes good sense for your business, Ms. Brown. May I call my office and tell them to ship this to you tomorrow? But before you give me your answer, let me remind you of just one last thing. . . (Continues talking.)

Trial closes, if smoothly handled, can be conducted several times during a presentation, but there should be enough flexibility so that if the prospect is not yet convinced the sales presentation can continue.

CLOSING TECHNIQUES

Coverage of closing techniques varies in textbooks on personal selling. Although terminology differs from one textbook to another, there seem to be six common closing techniques: summary, assumptive, special deal, single objection, limited choice, and direct appeal.

Summary Closes

During the presentation, the salesperson has described and verified a series of benefits that would be meaningful to the customer. The **summary closing** technique consists of a *brief* summary of the benefits and then a request for the order. The summary close is a useful approach to take when several benefits have been demonstrated or the product or service under consideration is relatively complex.

An example of a summary close occurs when a sales rep has been describing the benefits of a home security system to a buyer for a housing development company. If the buyer agrees to purchase the system, each new home the developer is constructing will have the security system installed.

Seller: Joe, you said you needed a system endorsed by a well-known consumer protection agency, one that prospective homeowners would recognize. We showed you what *Consumer Reports* said about this system. You also wanted a system that was durable, and we showed you letters from other developers that revealed this was a very trouble-free system. Then, you also wanted a system that had options that could be chosen by new homeowners as they planned their new home. We described our four-option system. Are we ready to do business?

When using the summary close, the rep must be careful to *make it a summary*. Otherwise, this could be a launching pad to simply going over the presentation another time. That would be a disaster if the sales rep were selling to a driver-type customer who might welcome a summary but become irked at a time-wasting rehash of the presentation. The sales rep who uses this approach should keep the summary crisp and fast-paced.

Assumptive Closes

An **assumptive close** is based on the assumption that the buyer wants or needs the product or service and that a sale is going to be made. Behaving as though the sale is a foregone conclusion, the rep asks a question or makes a statement that tactfully conveys the message "I know you are going to make a purchase." The following statements are examples of how this can be conveyed to a buyer:

1. "How do you wish to pay for this, Ms. Smith, by cash or credit card?"

2. "When will it be most convenient for you to take delivery?"

3. "How many different colors would you need, Ms. Jones?"

Questions such as these can be asked while the sales rep is completing an order form. Filling out the form is another easily decoded signal to the buyer that the sales rep is confident of the sale. Such behavior is sometimes called a **physical action close**.

Special Deal Closes

Everyone is familiar with advertisements that emphasize "for a limited time only" and imply the price of a product or service will eventually be higher. Such efforts to close a deal in personal selling are sometimes referred to as a **standing-room-only** (SRO) close, which describes how (the rep hopes) buyers will respond to the attractive offer the seller is making. So many potential buyers will be attracted by the seller's special deal that there will be, figuratively speaking, standing room only.

A salesperson using the special deal, special concession, or SRO close will tell the buyer that what is being offered is, in effect, something that is not going to be available much longer. The idea, of course, is to make the sale now rather than later. SRO closes are frequently used to try to keep buyers from engaging in further search and alternative comparisons.

Salespeople must be careful how they employ this closing tactic. It has been used so often that some buyers are likely to be cynical. A special note of caution should be sounded to reps selling industrial products and services (the business-to-business market). Special concessions, inducements, or promotional offers that are made to induce a sale may be illegal under some conditions. Chapter 16 will cover the ethical and legal issues confronting salespeople. Suffice it to say at this point that a rep whose company is selling to competing businesses must make the same special concessions to each competitor to be safe from legal action.

Single Objection Closes

In the **single objection close**, the customer has raised an objection, and the sales rep uses this as an opportunity to close. After resolving the objection, especially if it is the only objection, there is a logical point for a closing effort. Some sales reps use the opportunity to see how close they are to achieving a sale. Consider this example of a dialogue between a rep and a customer.

Customer: (examining a sample of men's and women's swimwear) You realize that swimwear goes through fashion cycles, also. Your line needs some more exciting styles.

Sales rep: (using a clarifying question) What I think I hear you telling me is that I need to provide you with something other than these traditional fashion garments. Is that right?

Customer: Yeah, that's right. My customers like the latest styles in all clothing, and that includes swimwear.

Sales rep: (using a verifying question) If I can provide the styles being advertised now in *Seventeen* and *Esquire*, can you think of any other reason that this line shouldn't be in your store?

Customer: No, I think your quality and prices are okay.

Sales rep: Good! In that case, let me show you these high-fashion items that will be available for shipment in thirty days. I'm sure we can write you an order today and have them in your store well before the peak buying season starts.

By realizing that the buyer has only one objection to be overcome, the rep has isolated the problem and can concentrate fully on resolving it without worrying that other problems, such as price, will arise. Note again the important role that questions have played in the sales rep/customer interaction.

Limited Choice Closes

Even though the customer may be strongly attracted to the basic product, he or she may find it very confusing to make a choice from among a wide range of different versions. Because the customer is sometimes psychologically overwhelmed by the models, sizes, or colors presented, the sales rep, by watching the customer's responses, should determine which options or product models are of greatest appeal. The rep then simply takes away the products or materials that seem to evoke little customer interest.

By narrowing the choices to a few—the **limited choice close**—the rep has set up a situation in which it is natural to ask the customer, "Which version would you like?" You will notice that, here again, a question is used. The way in which the question is posed is similar to the assumptive close discussed earlier. The assumption made by the salesperson is that the customer has already decided to buy the product—the only dilemma is the selection of one or more of the different versions of the product.

A salesperson confronted with this fortunate situation must be tactful, however, as he or she narrows the choices to aid the customer. The sales rep must exert care not to leave the impression that he or she is trying to hurry the customer. A comment by the sales rep, such as, "May I assume that you are less interested in this style (color, option, model) than in this one?" is a way to get the customer's permission while achieving the sales rep's objectives.

Direct Appeal Closes

In the **direct appeal close**, the rep simply asks in a straightforward way, "Are you interested in making this purchase?" Although the words may vary, the direct appeal is very simple. Direct appeal questions, such as "May I write this order for you?" or "Can I get your signature here?" are appropriate when coupled with three of the previously described techniques: the summary, special deal, and single objection closes.

As you recall from the description and illustration of the summary close, the sales rep reminds the prospective buyer in a sentence or two how each of the buyer's needs or interests have been met. It is appropriate at the end of the summary to ask directly for the order. When the close is built on resolving the customer's objection, the rep can move to a direct appeal after answering or demonstrating how the objection can be resolved.

Organizational buyers see many different sales presentations and closing efforts. It is particularly refreshing to do business with a salesperson representing an excellent company and selling good value products or services who comes straight to the point. The confidence the salesperson must have to use the direct appeal close sends a positive message to a buyer. Even if the buyer is not currently in the market for the product or service, the impression of the sales rep's forthrightness and honesty may set the stage for future sales to that buyer.

FOLLOW-UP CONTACTS

Regardless of the sales rep's techniques, when the customer consents to the sale, the rep's responsibilities to that customer have just begun—**follow-up contacts** are vital. A successful clothing store owner paved the way for repeat sales and long-standing relationships with customers when he stated at the conclusion of every TV advertisement, "No sale is ever closed. If you should become dissatisfied at any time after you make a purchase, bring the item back. You have my word on it, and I own the store." Whether the item being sold is blazers or boilers, such a philosophy is the foundation for durable, profitable customer relationships.

Now that the customer has committed to make a purchase, some short-sighted salespeople believe their responsibilities have ended. That is a very dangerous belief. Until the product or service is consumed by the buyer, all the buyer has are expectations about the benefits obtainable from the product or service. After the sale has been made and the goods are in the hands of the buyer, *reality either confirms or disproves the buyer's expectations.* In your role as a salesperson, you have an obligation to ensure that your product or service is fulfilling the customer's expectations.

One sales consultant and author states, " . . . closing the sale may be only 50 percent of the total selling process. After making a sale, you must *make it happen* in order to create a satisfied customer. The professional salesperson excels at delivering on promises made during the selling process; it is the key to generating more business. Satisfied customers sell; unhappy customers kill sales."[17]

A Xerox Company sales representative has said that the three most important moments in a sales cycle are the first time you meet a prospective customer, the presentation that entails closing the deal, and ten days after the product is installed. After ten days the customer has had the product long enough for the novelty to have worn off and is much more capable of determining whether true satisfaction is going to be obtained.

Exhibit 10-4 provides several important reminders for salespeople. Before briefly analyzing each of these points, it is important to remember that as far as the customer is concerned, *you are the company.* The customer is normally not acquainted with your company's personnel in delivery, billing, or other departments. Therefore, the customer expects you to either solve directly or participate in solving any problems associated with the purchase. This is a great opportunity! In addition to delivering the benefits your product or service is providing to the customer, by acting as the representative for the customer, you can resolve any difficulties that may be detracting from the customer's total satisfaction.

Make It Easy to Communicate with You

Do your customers feel that they have easy access to you, their salesperson? One of the purposes of business cards is to provide the recipient with a phone number he or she can use. Be sure all the people in your customer's organization or family have cards with your name and phone number. Better yet, if your product is one that permits it, put a copy of your card on or in the product so that a user can contact you easily if necessary.

Give Customer Complaints or Questions the Highest Priority

Customer service delayed is customer service denied. Just remember that the longer customers feel neglected, the more negative word-of-mouth advertising they produce. This can be devastating to you in your territory when potential future customers hear complaints. On the other hand, a responsive salesperson who is attentive to customers will have no difficulty in getting referrals from satisfied customers.

KISS (Keep It Simple, Stupid)

Unfortunately, most people (in their roles as either consumers or employees) feel that their lives are too complex even under the best conditions. When they purchase a product or service, find it necessary to have a problem solved, and then experience the frustrations of a complicated bureaucratic "run-around," customers may vow never to purchase the product again. Don't expect customers to be interested in an explanation of the proper routine to make contact with some

1. Make yourself accessible to your customers. Don't make a sale and then hide from them.
2. Customer complaints or questions must receive prompt attention. Do your best to simplify things for your customers. Don't bend their ears with tiresome explanations of administrative routines.
3. Do your utmost to protect your credibility with your customers. It is your most valuable asset.
4. Make sure you have an objective that will be beneficial to you *and* to your customers each time you contact them.

Exhibit 10-4 Guidelines for Improving Post-Sale Contacts with Customers

distant and anonymous person or department. In Chapters 11 and 12, we will describe the many relationships a skilled professional salesperson must cultivate within his or her own company. Suffice it to say now that the customer should expect a one-point-of-contact arrangement with a seller's organization. The logical point of contact is, of course, the sales rep.

The Cornerstone Of Successful Relationship Management Is Salesperson Credibility

By this point the importance of credibility should be no revelation. A salesperson's credibility is probably tested more frequently and in more ways than that of any other single type of employee in an organization. Once the sale has progressed to the point at which the customer has the opportunity to experience your product or service, your credibility is being put to the acid-test. Any sign of hesitation or reluctance on your part to help the customer achieve total satisfaction will be remembered and will make a durable relationship with the customer exceptionally difficult to establish. From a positive perspective, however, if you regularly follow up after a sale to ensure customer satisfaction, the customer will come to rely on you as a valuable resource person who is worthy of future business.

Every Post-Sale Contact You Make with a Customer Should Have an Objective

Be certain that as an individual sales rep you become strongly associated with benefits. Make sure that whenever the customer thinks about you, or you are called to his or her attention via your card, your sales brochures, or other sales aids, the customer receives some reward. The ideal occurs when the customer thinks to him or herself, "When Mary Thomas contacts me there is always something of value in that contact." The benefit you provide need not be dramatic; it is more important that the contacts be regular. For instance, in July a rep may drop off a schedule of seminars the rep's company is sponsoring for customers. In August the rep might contact the buyer with information about a new preventive maintenance program. September's contact could involve an invitation to the rep's hospitality suite at a local trade show. Each of these seemingly minor encounters with the customer provides the professional salesperson with opportunities to (1) check on customer satisfaction, (2) get some referred sales leads, (3) keep tabs on any competitive efforts to wrest away the account, and (4) establish the foundation for the next product or service sale.

SUMMARY

1. A salesperson's perspective on objections is important. Guidance was provided on the general subject of objections and then specific types of objections were identified and analyzed. Suggested approaches toward handling objections were provided.

2. The reasons people give for not wanting to buy a product or service are not always the true explanation for their reluctance. Hidden objections were explained and a method of coping with them was explained.

3. Customers transmit messages not only verbally but also through their body language or nonverbal signals. Three types of nonverbal signals were identified and advice was given on how a sales rep should respond to each type of signal.

4. Gaining a customer's commitment to make a purchase is usually referred to as closing. A variety of ways exist for a rep to accomplish a close. Several of the principal types of closes were identified and the circumstances in which they would work were identified.

5. Follow-up or post-sale contacts with a buyer are crucial to the establishment of a durable relationship. A professional sales representative knows that closing a sale does not mean the end of the salesperson's responsibilities toward the customer. A number of benefits can be obtained by the sales rep as he or she ensures that the buyer is receiving the full measure of benefits expected when the purchase decision was made.

QUESTIONS FOR DISCUSSION AND REVIEW

1. Why is an objection-free sales presentation usually not desirable from a sales rep's standpoint?

2. What are "hidden objections," and why is it sometimes desirable to use the third-party technique in dealing with them?

3. Why should a salesperson immediately stop saying or doing whatever he or she has been saying or doing when the customer displays a red signal? Do green signals indicate that the salesperson should continue to the completion of a prepared sales presentation? Explain why or why not.

4. When a prospective buyer says, "Your price is too high," what might the person be telling you?

5. Review the description of the various communication styles (drivers, amiables, and so forth) contained in the Presentation Dynamics section of Chapter 8. Assuming all other factors are equal, would a sales rep be able to use a trial close as quickly on a customer who is an analytical as on one who is a driver? Why or why not?

6. What must a rep be careful to do when using a summary close?

7. What is an assumptive close? Give an example of such a close.

8. Even if you know a customer cannot purchase anything more from you in the near future, why should you continue to make contact with him or her? Give three reasons.

9. Describe the three methods successful sales reps have been found to use when dealing with price objections. Which one of the three methods would seem to be the best way to find out whether competitors have quoted the customer a lower price?

10. What is the best way to find out what is causing a customer to deliver yellow signals? Describe how the third-party technique might be used in such situations.

11. How should a salesperson interpret the phrase "closing a sale?" Why is the proper interpretation important in successful relationship management?

CASE 10-1   COLUMBO THE DUMBO

As he braked his Toyota to a halt at a stop sign, Frank Columbo thought about the sales meeting he had just conducted. He had met with Luis Mendoza, who owned a furniture store in Sierra, Arizona. Mendoza's store, La Casa, sold expensive furniture and interior design consulting services. Columbo's objective had been to sell Mendoza a series of full-page advertisements in Columbo's newspaper, *The Stephens Star*.

As Columbo drove back to his office he reviewed what had happened in the meeting. He recalled that Mendoza had seemed very interested in examining each of the three advertising layouts Columbo had brought with him. They had talked about a few minor modifications in the text of the ads and the schedule for when the ads would run in the newspaper.

The problem in their meeting seemed to arise, as Columbo recalled, when Mendoza had asked about the price of the proposed advertising plan. I know, Columbo said to himself, that I thoroughly explained why *The Stephens Star's* advertising rates have risen in the past six months. I covered the costs of our labor in producing the ads, the increased costs of newsprint, and even the increasing costs of delivering newspapers. No, he thought, there was nothing I could have said to more completely explain why our advertising prices had to be increased. Mendoza just seemed to tune me out when I started explaining our situation. From sitting on the edge of his chair when we were looking at the ads, he changed his posture to leaning back in his chair and crossing his arms.

Frank Columbo's last thought on the subject occurred as he pulled into his parking lot at the *Star's* offices. He wondered why Mendoza apparently hadn't been able to see the newspaper's position.

QUESTIONS

1. What was the most fundamental problem in this situation?

2. How could Frank Columbo have dealt with the "price problem?"

3. Is there any evidence in this case of positive or negative body language by the prospective buyer?

4. Using the communication model explained in Chapter 2, explain what has happened in this case.

CASE 10-2 A FOLLOW-UP SALES VISIT

Lori Wheeler, a sales representative for Hawkeye Landscaping Service Incorporated, punched in Frank Gold's number on her cellular telephone. "Frank, can you tell me whether the warranty policy on our privet shrubs permits a customer to transplant the shrubs and still be covered? The situation is this. I was just out at the Ames Corporation offices talking to Joe Mancuso, their physical plant manager. We sold them about $20,000 worth of trees and shrubs approximately six months ago. About two months ago Joe's work crews had to create some drainage systems and it required them to dig up some of the shrubs we had planted for them. They replanted the shrubs a few feet away from the original site. Some of the shrubs are turning brown and they'll have to be replaced. I told the customer we would cover it for him."

Earlier, Wheeler had been in the office of one of her best customers, following up with the Ames Corporation to see how satisfied they were with the landscaping they had purchased from the Hawkeye Company. The following dialogue had occurred between Wheeler and Mancuso:

Wheeler: Joe, as I drove through your gate I was really impressed with how attractive your grounds and new office building look. I'll bet you get a lot of compliments, don't you?

Mancuso: Thanks, Lori. Yeah, I've heard a lot of people comment on how much better things look compared to our old building. We've had the normal amount of adjustments to make since we moved here, but this is better.

Wheeler: Those sugar maples we planted next to the building will be beautiful in the fall in a couple of years. As I recall, you mentioned several months ago you had some plans to create a jogging and walking trail for your employee wellness program. Have any idea when that may be under construction? I have some ideas I'd like to share with you about that.

Mancuso: We're still going to do that, Lori, but before we could start on it we had to take care of some areas on our property that weren't draining very well. After a lot of rain there were some areas where we had water standing for two or three days. My people have just completed a drainage system to fix that.

Wheeler: How is it working?

Mancuso: Very well. While we're on that subject, we had to move about two dozen shrubs your company planted. We just dug them up and replanted them a few feet away from a drainage pipe we had to bury in the ground.

Wheeler: I see. How are the shrubs now? Are they taking root again and growing?

Mancuso: One of my guys was in here yesterday and he said they were looking pretty bad. I know your company offered a warranty for one year on all the plants and shrubs we purchased.

Wheeler: That's true, Joe. Of course, we didn't know about this construction work that had to be done and the replanting of the shrubs. When the workers replanted the shrubs did they prepare the new beds with fertilizer and mulch?

Mancuso: I really don't know, Lori. Would that be important?

Wheeler: (laughing) It usually spells the difference between a healthy shrub and a dead one. I'll tell you what, Joe, even though I think the warranty doesn't apply when you dig the trees or shrubs up and transplant them, I'm going to recommend that my company replace those few shrubs at no cost to your company.

Mancuso: O.K., we appreciate that. I imagine we should have called you before we moved those shrubs, but you know how my boss Mr. Powers is. He wants everything done yesterday. Lori, I guess I'll owe you one if you can get these things replaced.

Wheeler: Well, Joe, I'll remember that. When you get ready for that jogging path I want to take you out to see something we did for the Ralston Company. They have a fitness center and a running path on their corporate grounds and we helped them landscape those grounds. I think you'll be impressed. I've got to go now, but I'll recommend we replace your shrubs next week, O.K.?

Mancuso: I like to do business with you, Lori. You take care of us.

Wheeler: Thanks, Joe. Give me a call now if I can help you before I see you again in about a month.

Mancuso: O.K., will do.

QUESTIONS

1. What type of relationship seems to have been formed between the sales rep for Hawkeye Landscaping and the customer?

2. Should Lori Wheeler request that Joe Mancuso get a copy of the warranty contract and read the conditions under which the warranty would be in force? Why or why not?

3. Would it have been advisable for the salesperson to have stayed away from this customer until they were just about ready to begin the next construction project? Why?

4. If anyone at Hawkeye questions Wheeler's judgement about granting an exception to the warranty, what justification can she use?

NOTES

1. David Mercer, *High-Level Selling* (Houston, Texas: Gulf Publishing Company, 1990), 130.
2. Tom Hopkins, *How To Master The Art of Selling* (New York: Warner Books, 1982), 87.
3. Richard Kern, "The Art of Overcoming Resistance," *Sales and Marketing Management* (March 1990): 101.
4. Ibid.
5. Paul H. Schurr, Louis H. Stone, and Lee Ann Beller, "Effective Selling Approaches to Buyers' Objections," *Industrial Marketing Management* 14 (1985): 195–202.
6. Ibid.
7. Ibid.
8. Clifton J. Reichard, "Industrial Selling: Beyond Price and Persistence," *Harvard Business Review*, no. 2 (March–April 1985): 127–33.
9. Adapted from Schurr et al., "Effective Selling Approaches to Buyers' Objections," 195–202.
10. Rolph Anderson, *Professional Personal Selling* (Englewood Cliffs, New Jersey: Prentice Hall, 1991), 220.
11. Gerhard Gschwandtner, "How to Read Your Prospect's Body Language," *Industrial Marketing* 66 (July 1981): 54–59.
12. Kerry L. Johnson, *Subliminal Selling Skills* (New York: AMACOM - American Management Association, 1988), 128–29.
13. Ronald D. Balsley and E. Patricia Birsner, *Selling: Marketing Personified* (Hinsdale, Illinois: The Dryden Press, 1987), 268.
14. Anthony Allessandra, James Cathcart, and Phillip Wexler, *Selling by Objectives* (Englewood Cliffs, N.J.: Prentice Hall, 1988), 213.
15. David L. Kurtz, H. Robert Dodge, and Jay E. Klompmaker, *Professional Selling*, 4th ed. (Plano, Texas: Business Publications, Inc., 1985), 264.
16. Ibid.
17. Michael P. Wynne, *Sci-Tech Selling* (Englewood Cliffs, N.J.: Prentice-Hall, Inc., 1987) 148–53.

PART FOUR

Relationship Management Inside the Organization

CHAPTER 11

The Salesperson's Organization

LEARNING OBJECTIVES

After studying this chapter, you should be able to:

1. Describe the meaning and influence of an organization's mission and corporate culture on its operations.

2. Identify four different types of corporate culture.

3. Describe the various functional orientations an organization might have, including sales, marketing, technology, and manufacturing.

4. Identify six organizational structures and the implications of each for the role of the salesperson.

5. Explain the influence of intra- and interdepartmental, vertical and horizontal, and formal and informal relationships on the salesperson.

6. Define the key terms used in this chapter.

KEY TERMS

- company mission
- corporate culture
- manufacturing-oriented company
- technology-oriented company
- sales-oriented company
- marketing-oriented company
- functional organization
- geographic or territorial organization
- product organization
- customer or market organization
- product-market organization
- key or major account organization
- intradepartmental relationships
- interdepartmental relationships
- strategic, administrative, and operative managers
- formal organization
- informal organization

J ULIE ZIMMER, who had recently completed her undergraduate degree in marketing, was reviewing her first day as a Sales Representative with her new employer, a major pharmaceutical company. During the day, she had a meeting with her supervisor, John Collier, who was a District Sales Manager. Mr. Collier had introduced her to Tim Mason, National Sales Manager, and Mary Lou Roberts, who was the Vice President of Marketing. In talking with John Collier, Julie discovered that the company had just recently switched from a geographic to a product sales organization structure and that the role of each salesperson had changed to some degree. She also remembered that the Vice President of Marketing, Mary Lou Roberts, who had recently been hired from a competitor, stressed the importance of the company maintaining its strong technological orientation due to the nature of the pharmaceutical business. Julie also recalled the warm greeting and extensive company-related information she had received from Doris Brown, who was John Collier's secretary. In addition, Julie thought about the comments of some of her sales colleagues who at lunch had mentioned the great deal of influence that Tim Mason had on both sales and marketing activities. He had been with the company for almost twelve years. Other sales representatives had also acknowledged the extensive influence that the research and development department had on company operations. Julie had found the various people she met to be very interesting and, for the most part, congenial, although she realized there were more things to learn about the company and her new associates in the days ahead.

One of the challenges and requirements for a professional salesperson, such as Julie Zimmer, is to have a thorough understanding of the organization or company he or she represents. Although every person is surrounded by and involved with many organizations each day, one of the organizations that accounts for a majority of a person's time is his or her employer. Since organizations can be rather complex systems, the task for both new and established salespersons is to become knowledgeable about the organizational structure and people in his or her company.

One of the first things for a salesperson to assess is how the company or organization defines itself in terms of the business or businesses in which it is engaged. One input to this determination will be the company mission, a broad statement of what the company considers its overall purpose and direction. The mission will be influenced by the management philosophy that has been adopted and practiced by the company. Management's philosophy is often referred to as the corporate culture. The company's mission and corporate culture define the nature of the role and importance of sales in the organization.

An understanding of the company's basic organizational structure is also very important. In addition, a critical dimension to identify is the number of departments, units, or divisions within the company and their relationships to one another. Various levels of management in the organization will have different functions and perspectives that a salesperson should understand, even though he or she may not directly interact with each level.

Finally, the salesperson should devote some time to discovering not only the formal organization of the company, as depicted in the organizational chart, but also the informal organization that may, but frequently does not, reflect the formal structure. The informal aspect of the organization is critical to understand, since key individuals will have varying levels of responsibility and authority that may not be related to their formal position in the organization. Let's begin our discussion with a closer look at the company mission.

COMPANY MISSION

An initial step for the new salesperson in understanding his or her organization is to become aware of the company's business mission. In some organizations, the business mission may be explicitly stated in a number of documents, such as a company's strategic plan, its annual report, or other materials. In other organizations, the mission of the company may be implicit; individuals in the organization have a sense of what is expected or valued by the business. In still other organizations, the business mission may be nonexistent.

The purpose of a mission statement is to stake out broad areas in which the firm can or cannot operate.[1] Another important aspect of the mission statement is to serve as the foundation on which detailed objectives, strategies, and tactical plans can be worked out.[2] The actual development of a mission statement may be based on answering questions such as "What is our business? Who is the customer? What is value to the customer? What will our business be? What should our business be?"[3]

The **company mission** has been defined as the fundamental, unique purpose that sets a business apart from other firms of its type and identifies the scope of its operations in product and market terms.[4] Although there may be a variety of mission statements, it has been suggested that a truly effective mission statement should meet the following criteria:

1. It should define what the organization is, and further, what the organization aspires to be.

2. It should be limiting enough to exclude some ventures and broad enough to allow for creative growth.

3. It should distinguish a given organization from all others.

4. It should serve as a framework for evaluating both current and prospective activities.

5. It should be stated in terms sufficiently clear to be widely understood throughout the organization.[5]

As can be seen from this list, a company salesperson who knows the mission statement will have a better understanding of where the organization is now and where it hopes to be in the future. In addition, the sales representative will have a greater sense of what differentiates his or her firm from competitors. Finally, while specific objectives, strategies, and tactics will be assigned to the salesperson, the mission statement may provide a critical frame of reference by which to judge the appropriateness or desirability of certain activities that one might undertake in performing one's job.

The mission statement of the Wallace Company, Inc., a winner of the 1990 Malcolm Baldrige National Quality Award, highlights that its business is in quality industrial distribution. In addition, its mission pinpoints the company's commitment to quality products, fair prices, and high levels of service, honesty, and integrity in dealing with its customers. The mission statement also emphasizes the importance of building open, honest and mutually-beneficial, long-term relationships with both its customers and suppliers. In addition, the key activities of teamwork and communication are also mentioned. For a professional salesperson, the Wallace Company's mission statement would serve as the general philosophy or creed by which the company operates and expects individuals working for Wallace to function.

In addition to formal mission statements, many companies define the scope of their businesses in customer terms as opposed to product terms. For example, IBM sees itself as "a business problem-solving company" as compared to "a computer company." Similarly, Brunswick has moved over time from a "bowling" to a "recreation" company. The above distinctions may appear minor, but the key idea is that major companies define themselves in market or customer terms as contrasted to product terms.[6] Defining one's business in customer terms rather than product terms is important since customer needs will outlast particular products. Although the need will exist continuously for problem solving or recreation, the specific items to satisfy those needs will change significantly over time with either improved or to-

Figure 11-1 A mission statement may be explicitly stated in a company's strategic plan, annual report, or other materials.

tally new products and services. Exhibit 11-1 provides additional examples of differences between product and customer orientations for various companies.

The examples of the Wallace Company, Inc., and those listed in Exhibit 11-1 reveal how a company's formal mission statement or definition can further clarify what a company sees as important for the organization as a whole. Perceptive employees, including members of the sales staff, should fully understand the values of the company's top managers and the direction they are planning to take the company. In essence, the sales representative should make sure that he or she is pulling in the same direction as others in the company.

Product Orientation	Company	Customer Orientation
Telephones	AT&T	Communication
Oil and gas	Mobil	Energy
Railroads	Union Pacific	Transportation
Movies	Universal Studios	Entertainment
Bowling balls	Brunswick	Recreation
Computers	IBM	Problem solving
Banking	Chase Manhattan	Financial services

Exhibit 11-1 Product Versus Customer Orientations

Corporate Culture

The company's mission will also be affected by the culture that exists in the organization. During the 1980s, the issue of corporate culture became one of the most discussed management concepts in business periodicals. The definitions of **corporate culture** stress a group of beliefs, values, customs, and behaviors that may be unique to each company.[7] Examples of companies with well-recognized corporate cultures include Delta Air Lines (customer service and teamwork), Digital Equipment Corporation (innovation and freedom of responsibility), International Business Machines (marketing-driven service philosophy), and Atlantic Richfield Company (entrepreneurship).[8] In addition, companies often define themselves with a slogan that becomes associated with only that company, such as DuPont's "Better things for better living through chemistry," or Sears's "Quality at a good price." Although stated beliefs and values may be considered only slogans, the professional salesperson should realize that formal company statements say a lot about how top management envisions the company.

A classic example of a company that had to attempt to undergo a change of its corporate culture was American Telephone and Telegraph (AT&T).[9] Due to actions in 1981 and 1982 by the Federal Communications Commission and the Department of Justice, AT&T was faced with deregulation and forced into a competitive, nonmonopoly market. AT&T was required to form a separate subsidiary, which became AT&T Information Systems, and to divest a major part of each of its twenty-two Bell Company subsidiaries in the span of only two years. As many have noted, AT&T was faced with "culture shock." After operating as a protected monopoly for such a long period of time, the shock of being placed in a competitive arena was a major problem faced by company management and employees. A relatively quick adjustment to a radically different business environment was not only necessary, but mandatory for the company's success and survival. Since earlier attempts by AT&T to alter its operating style had not met with success, the challenge of changing the ways things were done by an organization having approximately one million employees was a monumental task.

Studies of corporate culture have resulted in a classification of organizational cultures based on the degree of risk associated with a company's activities and the speed of feedback on the success or failure of operating decisions. Companies may be considered tough guy/macho (high risk/fast feedback), work hard/play hard (low risk/fast feedback), bet your company (high risk/slow feedback), or process (low risk/slow feedback). Examples of companies listed under each of these headings or categories can provide a salesperson with further insight into what to expect in his or her company. For example, the selling field is often most associated with the work hard/play hard culture, which includes such companies as Frito-

Lay, IBM, and McDonald's.[10] In this culture, attention to customer needs and customer service dominates. Other cultures will also dictate the extent to which sales and marketing play a major or minor role in the company.

Role of Marketing and Sales in the Organization

The company mission and corporate culture will have a major effect on a company's orientation. In a given organization, marketing and sales may have a minor, equal, or major role in comparison to other business functions. The orientation a company adopts and practices may be due to a number of factors, including the competitive environment the company faces, the backgrounds of top management, and the company's strategic initiatives in the marketplace.

Exhibit 11-2 shows four possible company orientations: manufacturing, sales, technology, and marketing. Each orientation can be compared or contrasted on a number of different dimensions such as typical strategy, normal structure, key sys-

Exhibit 11-2 Company Orientations

	Manufacturing-Oriented	Sales-Oriented	Technology-Oriented	Marketing-Oriented
Typical Strategy	Lower Cost	Increase volume	Push research	Build share profitability
Normal Structure	Functional	Functional or profit centers	Profit centers	Market or product or brand; decentralized profit responsibility
Key Systems	Plant P&Ls Budgets	Sales forecasts Results versus plan	Performance tests R&D plans	Marketing plans
Traditional Skills	Engineering	Sales	Science and engineering	Analysis
Normal Focus	Internal efficiencies	Distribution channels, short-term sales results	Product performance	Consumers Market share
Typical Response to Competitive Pressure	Cut costs	Cut price Sell harder	Improve product	Consumer research, planning, testing, refining
Overall Mental Set	"What we need to do in this company is get our costs down and our quality up."	"Where can I sell what we make?"	"The best product wins the day."	"What will the consumer buy that we can profitably make?"

Source: Edward G. Michaels, "Marketing Muscle," *Business Horizons* (May–June 1982): 72. Reprinted from *Business Horizons*, May–June 1982. Copyright 1982 by the Foundation for the School of Business at Indiana University. Used with permission.

tems, traditional skills, and normal focus. In the **manufacturing-oriented company**, engineering skills tend to dominate with a resulting emphasis on a lower-cost strategy and internal efficiencies. This type of company tends to have an internal orientation with a great deal of attention devoted to budget systems and cost-cutting programs. Examples of manufacturing- or production-oriented companies are Mobil and most energy corporations, which place an above-average emphasis on the exploration for and production of various energy resources.

In comparison to the manufacturing-oriented company, the **technology-oriented company**, such as 3M Corporation or Polaroid, has a strategy emphasizing research and product performance. The purpose of such a company is to design and develop the best product and then to also be able to have product improvements that make the original product even better. New product development and state-of-the-art technology are high priorities. Both the manufacturing and technology orientations resemble to some degree the production concept that placed primary focus on the product rather than the customer and his or her needs (see Chapter 1).

The **sales-oriented company** and the **marketing-oriented company** are really more similar than different. The differences sometimes tend to be overstated. In some companies, sales and marketing are separate departments or units while in others the sales activity is a subset of marketing. As shown in Exhibit 11-2, sales orientation describes a company that has adopted the *sales* as opposed to the *marketing* concept. The sales concept suggests companies focus on the product and use selling and promotion to generate profits and sales volume. The focus is on short-term sales volume increases with aggressive selling and price cutting in dealing with dealers and distributors. In essence, the sales-oriented company is looking for a market for a product that has already been manufactured.

The marketing-oriented company is characterized by analysis, planning, and research to discover what customers want or need. These steps occur before the actual production of the product takes place. Under the marketing concept, the company strives for profits, market share, and customer satisfaction in order to gain brand or supplier loyalty and positive word-of-mouth recommendations. Examples of sales- and marketing-oriented companies include Procter and Gamble, IBM, McDonald's, and Frito-Lay.

Although a professional salesperson has a role in any of the four company orientations described above, the relative importance of the sales activity varies significantly among companies with different orientations. A professional salesperson should obtain a good understanding of how the sales function is viewed within the organization he or she represents.

SALES ORGANIZATIONAL STRUCTURES

In addition to the company's mission and corporate culture, its organizational structure is a major factor that affects the entire company in which a salesperson may work. We will discuss six organizational structures that will directly affect the salesperson's position and activities: functional, geographic, product, customer, product-market, and key account organizations. A review of the company's organizational chart should provide some valuable insight for either new or existing sales personnel. Also, the salesperson should study the specific organizational structure within the marketing and sales department.

Functional Organization

One of the most common forms of organizational structure is by function. A **functional organization** includes a number of functional marketing specialists in such areas as sales, marketing research, and marketing communications among others (see Exhibit 11-3). It does not divide the sales force into any specialized group or division or focus on any major product or customer. Although this organizational structure may be the simplest to implement, most companies use a functional organization as only the starting point in organizing their sales and marketing activities. In those companies that do use a functional approach, one is likely to see similar customers, with similar product or service needs, and little variation between or among market areas.

Geographic Organization

Another organizational alternative takes a functional sales organization and divides the sales force into geographical groups (see Exhibit 11-4). A **geographic** or **territorial organization** acknowledges customer differences due to their respective locations. For example, a company that sells recreational equipment

---

Exhibit 11-3 Functional Sales Organization

Vice President of Marketing

| Marketing Research Manager | Distribution Manager | National Sales Manager | Marketing Communications Manager |

Sales Representatives

Exhibit 11-4 Geographic or Territorial Sales Organization

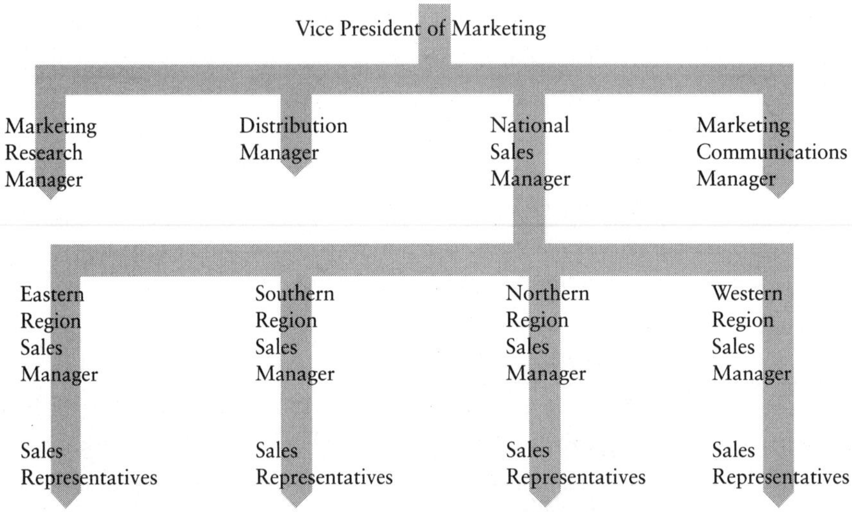

Vice President of Marketing

Marketing Research Manager

Distribution Manager

National Sales Manager

Marketing Communications Manager

Eastern Region Sales Manager

Southern Region Sales Manager

Northern Region Sales Manager

Western Region Sales Manager

Sales Representatives

Sales Representatives

Sales Representatives

Sales Representatives

may find it appropriate to divide the sales force by region since recreational interests may vary in the Eastern as opposed to the Western states due to climate and life style. A geographic or territorial organizational structure may also provide a company and its sales representatives a number of benefits. For the company, this arrangement may enable better control of the sales force since each sales representative is responsible for a given geographical area. For the salesperson, he or she may be able to provide better coverage of the territory and quicker response to local competitive conditions.

Product Organization

As the company's products or customers become more numerous and diverse, additional adaptations to the basic functional organization are likely to occur. A common organizational structure for companies with a large number of products, particularly when the products are technical or dissimilar and unrelated, is the product organization (see Exhibit 11-5). The major advantage of a **product organization** is that each product group or individual product receives a level of attention from sales and marketing personnel that may not be possible with only a functional or geographic organization. The actual product organization can take a number of forms. The sales force can be divided into groups that sell a specific product or group of products. In this situation, the salesperson becomes a product specialist who may sell to a variety of customers. The possibility also exists that two or more salespersons from the same company may be calling on the same customer since each salesperson would be handling only one product or product group. An alternative is for product managers to serve as staff specialists while the

Exhibit 11-5 **Product Sales Organization**

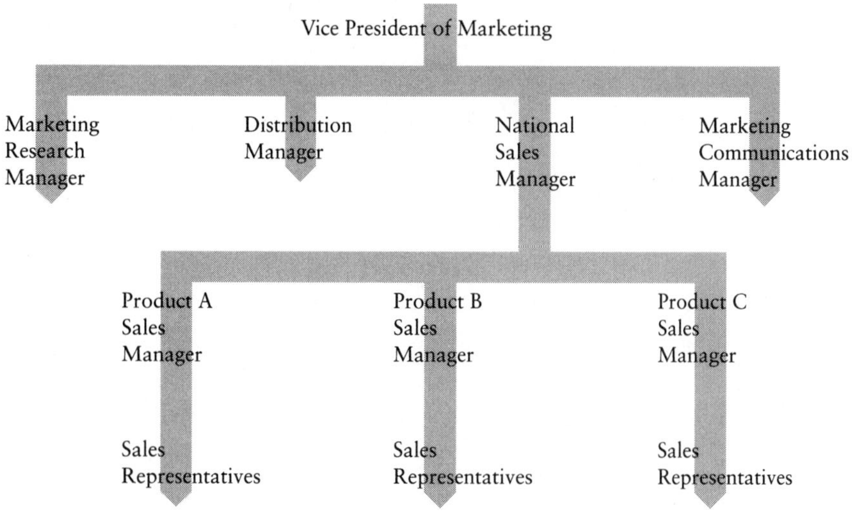

Vice President of Marketing

Marketing Research Manager — Distribution Manager — National Sales Manager — Marketing Communications Manager

Product A Sales Manager — Product B Sales Manager — Product C Sales Manager

Sales Representatives — Sales Representatives — Sales Representatives

sales force, rather than being divided by products or product categories, remains the same, as in a functional or geographic organization. Companies such as Procter and Gamble, General Foods, and Pillsbury are examples of this arrangement.[11] These product specialists must interact not only with those in sales but also individuals in advertising, market research, distribution, and customer service.

Customer Organization

Just as the number of products may be numerous, the customer base of the salesperson's company may be diverse as well. Faced with numerous market segments that do not have similar needs, a company may adopt a **customer** or **market organization** (see Exhibit 11-6). In this situation, the company may pinpoint its marketing and sales efforts to specific types of customers, such as the consumer market, the industrial market, or the government market. Differences in the product needs or the organizational buying behavior of these groups may warrant a customer or market specialization depending on the sales volume and profit that can be generated from each customer group. IBM, Xerox, and General Electric are a few companies that have adopted this type of organizational system.[12] Although both product and customer or market organization may be appropriate for a given company, the cost of either alternative may be significant.

Product-Market Organization

The **product-market organization** has an even more specialized organizational structure. It may use both product managers and market managers in the role of

---

Exhibit 11-6 Customer Sales Organization

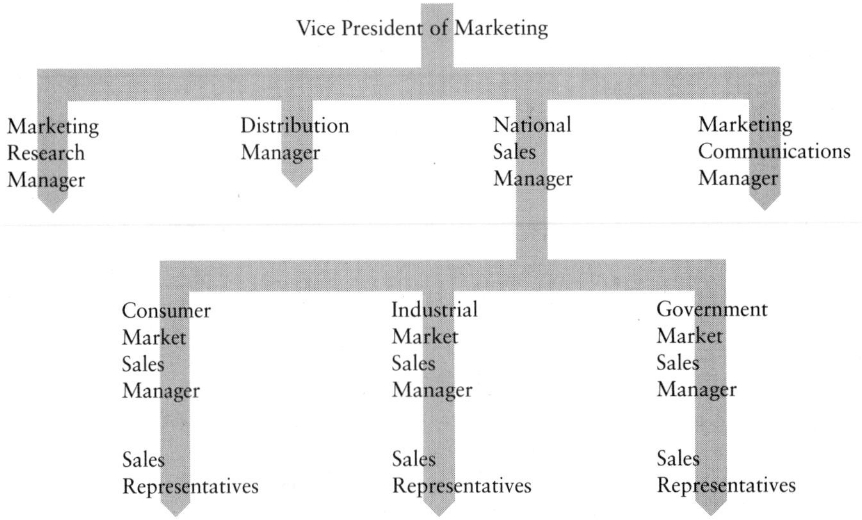

Vice President of Marketing

Marketing Research Manager

Distribution Manager

National Sales Manager

Marketing Communications Manager

Consumer Market Sales Manager

Industrial Market Sales Manager

Government Market Sales Manager

Sales Representatives

Sales Representatives

Sales Representatives

---

staff specialists (see Exhibit 11-7). When the products and customers or markets are numerous and different, the sales force may need to rely on product and market specialists to aid the marketing of each product.[13] DuPont, which has both product managers (nylon, dacron, orlon, rayon, and acetate) and market managers (women's clothing, men's clothing, household furnishings, and industrial fabrics), is an example of this structure.[14]

Key Account Organization

The most specialized sales force organization occurs when a company adopts a **key** or **major account organization** for select customers. This type of organization allows sales representatives to devote their full attention and time to one account. The rationale is that this one customer accounts for a disproportionate amount of sales and thus justifies a one-to-one relationship. Key accounts are a result of the 80-20 rule, which suggests that 80 percent of a company's revenue comes from only 20 percent of the company's customers. Some or all of the customers in that 20 percent may be key or major accounts.[15]

Which Structure Is Best?

Regardless of the type of organizational structure a company has adopted and implemented, the professional salesperson must be acutely aware of the differences between the types of sales organization structure. As shown in Exhibit 11-8, the salesperson will be engaged in full-line selling (all the company's products or services) in a functional organization, but will have no specialization, which results in

Exhibit 11-7 *Product-Market Sales Organization*

Vice President of Marketing

Marketing Research Manager

Distribution Manager

National Sales Manager

Marketing Communications Manager

Product Managers

Product A

Product B

Product C

Market Managers

Consumer Market

Industrial Market

Government Market

Sales Representatives

the salesperson being a generalist. In a geographic or territorial organization, the salesperson becomes a territory manager even though he or she still sells the entire product line. The salesperson's role becomes that of a specialist in product or customer specialization. Under a key or major account arrangement, the salesperson develops a one-to-one relationship with the customer. In all of these situations, the salesperson must fully understand his or her role in the organization and the expectations of others inside and outside the company.

Exhibit 11-8 *Sales Organizational Structures and the Role of the Salesperson*

Structure	Advantage	Disadvantage	Role of the Salesperson
Function	Full-line selling	No specialization	Generalist
Geographic or territorial	Full-line selling	No specialization	Territory manager
Product	Product specialization	Limited to a product or product group	Product specialist
Customer or market	Customer specialization	Limited to a customer or customer group	Customer or market specialist
Combination (e.g., product and customer)	Multispecialization	Very limited products or customers	Liaison with staff specialists
Key or major account	In-depth customer knowledge	Tied to one customer	Account or company specialist

INTRADEPARTMENTAL AND INTERDEPARTMENTAL RELATIONSHIPS

An important aspect of the salesperson's orientation will be the development of an understanding and appreciation of the departmental relationships that exist in his or her company. Even though the suggestion is often made that sales personnel may operate on their own with little direct supervision, the effect of various company departments on sales force performance should not be underestimated. Two departmental relationships are of extreme importance to the salesperson. **Intradepartmental relationships** refer to the salesperson's relationships with others in marketing and sales. For example, the sales force may interact with individuals from marketing research, advertising, and customer service. In **interdepartmental relationships**, the salesperson must be aware of the relationships that exist between sales or marketing personnel and other functional units in the organization, such as manufacturing or finance. The nature of intradepartmental and interdepartmental relationships will be greatly influenced by the corporate culture and the company's organizational structure.

Departmental relationships, whether intra- or interdepartmental, will have an impact on the salesperson in a number of ways. First, if the corporate culture of the salesperson's company is predominantly sales, manufacturing, or technology, it is likely that one of those departments will have more influence than the others on product strategies and markets the company pursues. For example, Procter and Gamble or Frito-Lay, often recognized as marketing-dominated companies, are likely to have a strong sales orientation, which may result in sales and marketing personnel having the major input on the directions the company takes.

The salesperson should also understand that the more complex the organizational structure of his or her company, the more numerous the intra- and interdepartmental relationships are likely to be. A simple comparison of a territorial organization with a product-market organization reveals the possibility of numerous additional relationships that the salesperson would encounter in the more complex organization. Due to the increased number of relationships that he or she will encounter, the demands on the salesperson's time will increase rapidly as the organization becomes more and more specialized.

A final factor highlighting the importance of departmental relationships is the need for organizations to develop integrated and coordinated operations at both the department and company levels. The tendency for conflict rather than cooperation between or among departments must be minimized so a timely and appropriate response can be made by the company to its customers. The ability of the company's sales personnel to develop strong intra- and interdepartmental relationships will be the major ingredient in the achievement of successful company efforts in the marketplace.

VERTICAL AND HORIZONTAL RELATIONSHIPS

With an increased understanding of departmental relationships, the salesperson will also become aware of the vertical and horizontal dimensions of organizational relationships. A salesperson's principal vertical relationship will be the interactions with his or her supervisor, whether a departmental, district, regional, or national sales manager. Although this is probably the most immediate and important relationship inside the company, the salesperson should also be aware of other vertical relationships.

Because of the number of management levels in an organization, managers have various responsibilities and different perspectives. Management levels include **strategic**, **administrative**, and **operative managers**. Each management level differs to some extent on the time spent on major functions and the time horizon for which they manage—for example, long-term (year or more) or short-term (daily or weekly). Strategic (top) managers, which would include the marketing vice president, spend a considerable amount of time on planning and organizing activities with less time spent on staffing, directing, and controlling operations (see Exhibit 11-9). In addition, the strategic manager often focuses attention on programs or activities a year or more in the future. In contrast, an operative or first-line manager, such as a district or regional sales manager, may be spending more time on staffing, directing, and controlling and less time on planning and organizing. His or her focus is on a shorter time frame such as weekly and monthly sales performance. A national sales manager falls somewhere between the strategic and operative managers into an administrative or middle-manager category in which functions and time horizons are a combination of the other two management categories. The importance to the salesperson of knowing the functions and time horizons of the various managerial levels is to ensure that, when he or she deals with different managers, each manager's perspective is considered. Failure to understand a manager's perspective may negatively influence the assessment of the salesperson by key management personnel.

Management Levels

Management Functions	Strategic	Administrative	Operative
Planning	High	Medium	Low
Organizing	High	Medium	Low
Staffing	Low	Medium	High
Directing	Low	Medium	High
Controlling	Low	Medium	High

Exhibit 11-9 Emphasis of Strategic, Administrative, and Operative Managers on Management Functions

Figure 11-2 Peers are important to a salesperson's intracompany relationships and serve as points of reference.

Although the vertical relationships within an organization may overshadow the horizontal relationships from the salesperson's point-of-view, he or she should also be aware of the horizontal relationships. In any organization, a salesperson will have a number of peers who are in the same or a similar position in the company. Two important considerations about these relationships are the use of one's peers for guidance and as a frame of reference. Particularly for new sales personnel, one's peers may be able to provide guidance and information on the organization's corporate culture and departmental relationships, the salesperson's supervisor, or simply how things are done in the company.

In addition to guidance and information, the salesperson should also realize that other salespeople may serve as a frame of reference. Comparing oneself to other salespeople may tell an individual how well he or she is doing in the company. Whether or not the salesperson uses peers as a frame of reference, he or she should expect the sales supervisor to compare each salesperson to others under his or her supervision. Just as there can be conflict or cooperation at the departmental level, the same is true for relationships at the individual level.

FORMAL AND INFORMAL RELATIONSHIPS

A salesperson's attempt to more fully understand the organization for which he or she works will also focus on what is known as the formal, as opposed to the informal, organization. A **formal organization** is created by management to specify individual responsibilities and authority, while the **informal organization** is an outgrowth of human interaction and develops with or without formal management approval.[16] The major reason for more attention on the formal organization is that this is the easier of the two to understand. The company's employee orientation will normally include an overview of key officials and their respective positions or titles. The company's organizational chart may be used to give a new salesperson the "big picture." It should be noted, however, that often the formal organizational chart is out of date due to personnel turnover or reorganization of the company's structure.

Even if the salesperson is able to obtain up-to-date information on the company's formal organization, he or she may be missing the even more important network of individuals and activities in the company's informal structure. Due to corporate culture, length of time with the company, interpersonal skills, and knowledge of critical information, a given employee in an organization may have a degree of influence on company operations that is disproportionate to his or her formal position.

The salesperson who makes the assumption that the formal organizational structure actually depicts the way things work may develop a narrow view of how the organization operates. This false assumption would be particularly troublesome if the effectiveness of the salesperson was determined to a large extent by the informal organization. For example, an administrative assistant or secretary to a district, regional, or national sales manager, due to the length of time in the position, may serve as a key information source for sales personnel as well as being the gatekeeper for the sales manager. Another example might be the extraordinary level of influence a senior salesperson may have on a sales manager based on the length of time the two have known each other. Although the formal organizational chart would not indicate the depth of these relationships and the influence of the secretary or senior salesperson, these are examples of informal relationships the salesperson should discover in order to increase his or her effectiveness.

The existence of informal relationships will occur not only in the sales department, but also throughout the organization. Informal, as well as formal, relationships between strategic, administrative, and operative managers may greatly affect what, when, and how things are done. A sales manager may have good or poor relationships with individuals in manufacturing, personnel, and accounting. The ability of the sales manager to get others to schedule more production, to process new personnel more quickly, or to approve a customer's credit faster may depend on the informal relationships one has developed over time.

For the professional salesperson like Julie Zimmer, there are a number of challenges in attempting to understand his or her organization. Knowledge of the company's mission, corporate culture, functional orientation, and intra- and interdepartmental, vertical and horizontal, and formal and informal organizational relationships may be critical factors in the salesperson's success in dealing with company personnel and the company's customers. Chapter 12 will discuss relationships within marketing and sales units and Chapter 13 focuses on relationships between sales and nonmarketing functions or departments.

SUMMARY

1. The organizational mission statement will define what a company is or aspires to be as well as what the company will not be.

2. Corporate culture is a group of beliefs, values, customs, and behaviors that are unique to a company.

3. The importance of sales in a company will depend to a large degree on the dominant functional orientation, whether sales, marketing, manufacturing, or technology.

4. Each sales organizational structure requires a different role for the professional salesperson.

5. To be effective, the salesperson should have a thorough understanding of the various relationships existing in the company including intra/interdepartmental, vertical/horizontal, and formal/informal.

QUESTIONS FOR DISCUSSION AND REVIEW

1. What criteria should be used to judge the effectiveness of a company's mission statement?

2. In terms of degree of risk and speed of feedback, what are the characteristics of a sales-oriented corporate culture?

3. What would be the typical strategy in a manufacturing-oriented company? Sales-oriented company? Technology-oriented company?

4. Compare and contrast the advantages and disadvantages of a geographic or territorial structure versus a customer or market structure? What would be the role of the salesperson under each?

5. How does the 80-20 rule relate to a sales organizational structure of key or major accounts?

6. In terms of the salesperson, what would be the difference between intradepartmental versus interdepartmental relationships? Give an example of each.

7. In dealing with a strategic versus an operative manager, what should the salesperson know about the two managers?

8. Informal relationships in an organization may be just as important or even more important than some formal relationships. Why or why not?

9. It is important for the salesperson to understand the definition of his or her company in customer terms rather than in product terms. Why or why not?

CASE 11-1 JULIE ZIMMER'S FIRST WEEK

The first week in her new job had been very exciting and interesting for Julie Zimmer. What occurred on her first day at work seemed more like a month ago than only five days. She had been very busy with a number of meetings and had received a lot of new information about company policies, procedures, products, and personnel.

Of all the things that occurred during her first week on the job, she recalled especially her conversation at the end of the week with Doris Brown, secretary for John Collier, who was Julie's sales manager. Doris Brown had been John Collier's secretary for almost six years. Julie remembered the coversation as going something like the following:

Doris: Julie, how has your first week been?

Julie: It's been very busy and exciting to learn more about such a dynamic company. I hope I can remember everything I have been told about the company, its products, and customers.

Doris: You will do fine. Mr. Collier thinks a lot of you or otherwise he would not have hired you.

Julie: I hope so. I do wonder if I made a good impression on Ms. Roberts and Mr. Mason, whom I met earlier this week.

Doris: I'm sure you did. Besides, Mr. Collier and Mr. Mason have worked side by side for the past eight years and have been instrumental in making this company a sales leader in the industry. They tend to see people in the same way. Also, Mr. Mason knew Ms. Roberts when she worked for one of our competitors.

Julie: There seems to be a lot of competition between sales and marketing with research and development in the company. Also, there even seems to be competition among the members of the sales force.

Doris: Julie, that's the nature of this company. Competition within the company is seen as critical to developing and marketing the best products. Our company's president fosters competition to get the best results. People who do not produce results in this company are replaced. Since last year, about 10% of the sales personnel reporting to Mr. Collier are no longer here, and for the company, the percentage of turnover among sales personnel was almost 20%.

Julie: Well, so far, I like what I see. I like working for a leading company.

Doris: Don't worry, Julie, this is only your first week. You can't expect to know everything you need to know in just a few days. If I can help you in any way, please do not hesitate to let me know. Have a good weekend.

Julie: Thanks, Doris. I hope you have a good weekend as well. See you on Monday.

QUESTIONS

1. What type of relationship do Julie and Doris have?

2. Based on the opening vignette in this chapter about Julie's first day on the job and the conversation cited above, what should Julie have learned about her new employer?

3. From Julie Zimmer's perspectives, what are the potential advantages and disadvantages of her relationship with Doris Brown?

CASE 11-2 COMPUTER CONCEPTS, INC.

Alisha Brooks has just been hired by Computer Concepts, Inc., as its National Sales Manager. She held a similar position with one of Computer Concepts' major competitors. Computer Concepts has been in business for almost five years. Although the company initially did well in the marketplace for personal computers, recent performance in profits, sales, and market share has not met established objectives.

Computer Concepts was created by a partnership between Jack Evans and Bob Hoover. The two partners attended college together and both majored in computer science. Due to their strengths in new product development, the company has been a technological leader in the industry.

With the rapid growth of the computer industry and increased competition, major ingredients for success were continuous new product development with a special emphasis on aggressive marketing and sales programs. Jack and Bob now realize that they may have placed too much emphasis on being a technological leader while giving inadequate attention to sales activities.

The shift from a technological orientation to a sales and marketing orientation would be a major development for Computer Concepts. Jack and Bob have decided to have a planning session with Alisha to decide what a change in operating philosophy would imply for the company's operations. The question is not really whether or not to make the change, but how to best implement it.

QUESTIONS

1. In defining the business of Computer Concepts, Inc., what would be a product-oriented definition? A customer-oriented definition?

2. What would be characteristics of a technology-oriented company?

3. What would be some of the major differences between a sales-oriented and a marketing-oriented company?

CASE 11-3 WHOLESALE FOOD COMPANY

The Wholesale Food Company, headquartered in Houston, Texas, has been in business for over forty years. The company sells a wide range of food products to grocery stores, restaurants, and institutions such as schools, hospitals, and prisons.

Ed Foster is the sales manager for Wholesale Food Supply. He has held this position for the past five years. Previously, he was a sales representative for a company in the Southwest, in a territory consisting of Texas, Oklahoma, New Mexico, and Arizona.

The company's sales force was originally a functional organization due to its relatively similar products and customers. The company first sold its products only to individual grocery stores or grocery chains. With the growth in the number and types of food products carried by the company and its expansion to the restaurant market, the Wholesale Food Company switched from a functional to a geographic organization. Each salesperson sold all of the firm's products to the grocery outlets and restaurants within his or her territory.

During the past two years, the company, due to Mr. Foster's suggestion, has added the institutional market as a major customer group. Within each of the three major customer groups (groceries, restaurants, and institutions), Mr. Foster has identified a select number of customers accounting for a disproportionate share of the company's sales and profits. He has decided it is time to reassess whether the geographic or territorial sales organization is still appropriate. Also, he is concerned how a change in the sales organizational structure might affect the role of his sales representatives.

QUESTIONS

1. Given Wholesale Food Company's present situation, what would be the limitations of a geographic sales organization?

2. What type or types of sales organization might be most appropriate for the company at this time? Why?

3. How would your answer in Question 2 affect the role of the sales representatives of the Wholesale Food Company?

NOTES

1. Robert E. Linnemann, *Shirt-Sleeve Approach to Long-Range Planning for the Smaller Growing Corporation* (Englewood Cliffs, N.J.: Prentice-Hall, 1980), 41.

2. George A. Steiner, *Strategic Planning—What Every Manager Must Know* (New York: The Free Press, 1979), 149.

3. Philip Kotler, "Strategic Planning and the Marketing Process," *Business* (May–June 1980): 4.

4. John A. Pearce and Richard B. Robinson, Jr., *Formulation and Implementation of Competitive Strategy* (Homewood, Ill.: Richard D. Irwin, 1982), 81.

5. Vern J. McGinnis, "The Mission Statement: A Key Step in Strategic Planning," *Business* (November–December 1981): 41.

6. Theodore Levitt, "Marketing Myopia," *Harvard Business Review* (July–August 1960): 45–56.

7. Terrence E. Deal and Allan A. Kennedy, *Corporate Cultures* (Reading, Mass.: Addison-Wesley, 1982), 3–36. See also John Sedgewick, "Corporate Culture: Customers First," *Business Month* (June 1989): 28.

8. "Corporate Culture: The Hard-to-Change Values That Spell Success or Failure," *Business Week* (October 27, 1980): 148.

9. W. Brooke Tunstall, "Cultural Transition at AT&T," *Sloan Management Review* (Fall 1983): 15–26.

10. Deal and Kennedy, *Corporate Cultures*, 107–27.

11. William J. Stanton and Richard H. Buskirk, *Management of the Sales Force* (Homewood, Ill.: Richard D. Irwin, 1987), 71.

12. Ibid., 74.

13. B. Charles Ames, "Dilemma of Product/Market Management," *Harvard Business Review* (March–April 1971): 66–74.

14. Philip Kotler, *Marketing Management: Analysis, Planning, and Control* (Englewood Cliffs, N.J.: Prentice-Hall, 1984), 727.

15. Richard T. Hise and Stanley H. Kratchman, "Developing and Managing a 20/80 Program," *Business Horizons* (September–October 1987): 66–73.

16. Justin G. Longenecker and Charles D. Pringle, *Management* (Columbus, Ohio: Charles E. Merrill, 1984), 289.

CHAPTER 12

The Salesperson's Relationships Within the Marketing Department

LEARNING OBJECTIVES

After studying this chapter, you should be able to:

1. Understand the components of the job description, including organizational relationships, for the professional salesperson.

2. Acknowledge the importance of the salesperson-sales manager relationship.

3. Identify the critical relationships the salesperson may have with various marketing personnel.

4. Explain why intradepartmental conflict exists as well as why cooperation within the marketing department is so critical for the salesperson's success.

5. Define and describe "integrated marketing" at the marketing departmental level.

6. Define the key terms used in this chapter.

KEY TERMS

- position or job description
- organizational relationships
- job qualifications
- network of relationships
- work styles
- integrated marketing and selling
- line versus staff
- empathy

PETE WILKERSON has been a Sales Representative for the past fourteen years with the Crandon Company, a producer of containers for the soft drink and beer industries. During those fourteen years, both the soft drink and beer industries have undergone major changes, primarily in the number and variety of competitors. Currently, there are fewer customers on which to call, but each account has grown in size and importance to the Crandon Company. Pete Wilkerson's Sales Manager, Gordon White, recently held a sales staff meeting to highlight some change in sales force strategy that the Crandon Company would be making in the next six months. Gordon White discussed the possibility of introducing two new selling approaches, key or major account selling and telemarketing, to the marketing of containers to both large and small accounts, respectively, in the soft drink and beer industries. Since he has been a field salesperson for the past fourteen years, Pete Wilkerson is somewhat concerned as to how these changes will impact his position in the company. Gordon White has stated that the 1990s will call for new selling strategies although the traditional field salesperson-customer interaction would also continue to be critical to the company's success.

Relationship management includes an external and internal dimension. Although the primary emphasis of professional selling should be placed on new or existing relationships between the seller and the prospect or customer, an effective sales representative will also need to have an awareness and understanding of the relationships he or she must develop and maintain with departments and individuals inside his or her own company. In this chapter, both interpersonal and intradepartmental relationships within the marketing department will be discussed. In Chapter 13, the relationships among sales and nonmarketing areas of the organization will be presented. The objective of these two chapters is to highlight the extent and importance of relationship management within the seller's organization. The effectiveness and productivity of a professional sales representative, such as Pete Wilkerson, will depend greatly on how well not only the external, but also the internal relationships are managed.

THE SALESPERSON'S POSITION IN THE ORGANIZATION

The first step for the professional salesperson in understanding his or her role in the organization, particularly in the marketing department, is to have a thorough knowledge of the **position or job description**. Most organizations provide a written job description that includes the job or position title, duties and responsibilities, organizational relationships, and job qualifications for the position.[1] Some of the key components of a job description are presented in Exhibit 12-1.

Due to the variety of sales positions, there are numerous job titles that are used by various companies. Different position titles may mean different types of sales positions or may simply mean the same basic type of selling position under two or more different titles. Whether the selling position is referred to as sales, marketing, or account representative, key considerations will be the types of customers and products the salesperson will handle. Responsibility for consumer versus industrial products or services or both will greatly affect the scope of the sales position. In addition, the type of customer, whether consumers, resellers (wholesalers, retailers, or industrial distributors), manufacturers, nonprofit organizations, or government (local, state, or federal), will significantly influence the nature of the selling task.

One of the major aspects of the job or position description for the salesperson to fully understand is his or her duties and responsibilities. Specific attention must be given to the different selling and nonselling activities that constitute the sales position. For example, a salesperson selling hospital, surgical, and patient care items to surgical supply distributors, hospital administrators, and physicians may be asked to do both creative selling of existing products and missionary selling, educating the various types of customers about new products. Missionary selling would be particularly relevant to calls on physicians who recommend some products for use by hospitals rather than ordering the products themselves. Besides selling, the salesperson may be called upon to do promotional and merchandising work. Examples of these nonselling duties could include training dealer or distributor personnel, conducting market surveys, setting up product or promotional displays, and supervising test marketing of new products or services. Since most companies place greater emphasis on selling activities for most sales positions, the salesperson must be careful to balance his or her activities and time between selling and nonselling tasks.

In addition to duties and responsibilities, the salesperson must also understand the implications of the job description in terms of **organizational relationships** within the company. A salesperson will normally be assigned to a district, department, or division within the company. The salesperson must know who his or her supervisor is and the form of the reporting relationship. The salesperson will most

Exhibit 12-1 Position or Job Description for Sales Personnel

Position or Job Title

Sales trainee, representative, coordinator, consultant, analyst, engineer, associate, or counselor
Marketing representative, analyst, specialist, service representative
Account representative, manager, executive, coordinator

Products or Services Sold

Consumer and/or industrial products
Consumer and/or business services

Customers

Consumers
Retailers, wholesalers, distributors
Manufacturers
Government
Nonprofit organizations

Organizational Relationships

Supervisor, superior, or sales manager
Marketing staff personnel
Nonmarketing staff and line personnel
Territory, department, or division
Reporting requirements

Duties and Responsibilities

Selling activities
Nonselling activities

Job Qualifications and Expectations

Education
Sales experience
Product/service knowledge
Personality
Physical requirements
Willingness to travel
Willingness to relocate
Promotion and advancement opportunities

likely be required to keep the supervisor or superior informed by face-to-face meetings and telephone calls as well as daily, weekly, or monthly call reports depending on the type of sales position. The salesperson will often be required to file expense reports at regular intervals. Company guidelines may be included in the job description that specify under what situations the salesperson should contact marketing staff personnel (advertising, market research, customer service, distribution, and product or market managers). And interactions with nonmarketing areas such as research and development, manufacturing, personnel, accounting, or the legal staff may be spelled out for the salesperson.

Finally, the salesperson should be aware of the **job qualifications** or hiring specifications for the position. Job qualifications give a good indication of what is expected of each sales representative in terms of education, sales experience, product or service knowledge, and personality and physical requirements of the position. This part of the job description may also indicate if the salesperson is expected to travel or relocate. Although often not part of a job description, some companies will also include possibilities for promotion, advancement, or professional development, such as support for advanced education or attendance at seminars and workshops.

The Salesperson-Sales Manager Relationship

The sales representative's understanding of his or her position is only the first step in building strong and lasting relationships within the company. A critical rela-

Figure 12-1 The salesperson will most likely keep superiors informed through face-to-face meetings, phone calls, and reports.

tionship for the salesperson to acknowledge and develop is the one with his or her superior, the sales manager. Whether one reports to a departmental, district, regional, divisional, or national sales manager, an effective relationship with one's boss will lead to better performance, greater rewards, and possibly even promotion opportunities.

Since an organization can be seen as a **network of relationships**, one might conclude that the most important relationship is the one between superior and subordinate. Many people, however, including sales representatives, often do not take the time and initiative to fully develop this relationship. It has been suggested that managing the boss requires an understanding of both the boss and his or her context as well as one's own situation and needs.[2] The key question then is How can the sales representative develop this relationship? Exhibit 12-2 presents a number of ideas for new or experienced sales representatives to consider.

The Sales Manager's Perspective

First, the sales representative should understand his or her boss's goals and the context within which the boss works or operates. What are the sales manager's

Exhibit 12-2 Managing the Relationship with Your Boss

Make Sure You Understand Your Boss and His/Her Context, Including:

His/her goals and objectives
The pressures on him/her
His/her strengths, weaknesses, blind spots
His/her preferred work style

Assess Yourself and Your Needs, Including:

Your own strengths and weaknesses
Your personal style
Your predisposition toward or dependence on authority figures

Develop and Maintain a Relationship That:

Fits both your needs and styles
Is characterized by mutual expectations
Keeps your boss informed
Is based on dependability and honesty
Selectively uses your boss's time and resources

Source: John J. Gabarro and John P. Kotter, "Managing Your Boss," *Harvard Business Review* (January–February 1980): 99.

goals or objectives for the sales organization? Is the emphasis on sales volume, market share, profitability, customer service, or overall growth? Does the sales manager have both short- and long-term goals for his or her department? Is more emphasis placed on short-term actions or long-term results? The sales representative must also have an understanding of the pressures the boss faces. For example, what type of relationship does the sales manager have with his or her superior? Is the sales manager under a mandate from his or her superior to achieve a particular objective or goal? If so, what is the time frame? Due to his or her performance, or competition, or the general condition of the economy, the sales manager may be under a great deal of pressure to meet specific monthly, quarterly, or annual goals in market share, sales, or profits. Pressure on the sales manager from upper management will have a direct effect on the sales manager's relationship with the sales representative. The salesperson must be effective so that the sales manager is viewed as successful and valuable to the organization.

Another dimension the professional salesperson must consider in assessing his or her boss is the superior's strengths and weaknesses. Just as the salesperson is better at some activities than others, the same is also true of the sales manager. The sales manager may be better at planning than implementation, better at oral than written communication, or more task- than people-oriented. The suggestion has been made that all managers tend to develop a managerial style—that is, some combination of a people and task orientation from an emphasis on one or the other to a more equal combination of the two. The sales manager will thus have a **work style** the salesperson must understand and adapt to in order to be effective in the organization. What may appear as relatively simple may be very important to getting along with the boss. Acknowledgment by the salesperson that the sales manager reacts best to written versus oral communication, or informal as opposed to formal meetings, may be a key step in developing a better and more productive relationship.

The Salesperson's Perspective

Besides understanding the boss's goals and work style, the salesperson will need to assess himself or herself in order to foster the development of a strong relationship with the superior. Just as the sales manager has strengths and weaknesses, so does the sales representative. Although the sales manager is critical to the relationship, the salesperson has more control over how he or she acts or reacts to the sales manager. The salesperson, however, should not expect the basic personality of either of them to change. The salesperson's task is to determine what he or she does well and what needs improvement to make him or her more effective in the organization. For example, the salesperson may realize that, although he or she is very good at oral communication, written memos and reports are very difficult. If the sales manager desires or demands written reports on customers and competitors, the salesperson may need to develop a plan to improve this skill. Another instance may be the situation in which a salesperson realizes he or she needs improvement managing selling versus nonselling time. For example, too much time spent on nonselling activities to the exclusion of selling activities may be due to the salesperson's lack of self-confidence in dealing with certain types of customers. Failure to correct this limitation may not only lead to missed sales opportunities, but also to a poorer relationship with the sales manager.

The salesperson's self-assessment should include not only an analysis of strengths and weaknesses, but also an understanding of the mutually dependent relationship between the salesperson and the sales manager. When mutual dependence exists, the sales representative is normally more dependent on the sales manager than vice versa, since the manager may determine to a large degree the salesperson's assignments, rewards, and advancement opportunities within the company. Since sales representatives are often characterized as independent individuals who work well on their own or with little direct supervision, the tendency is for salespeople to resent this dependence on the sales manager.

Sometimes a sales representative may react by becoming either counterdependent or overdependent. A salesperson who is counterdependent will often further resent and rebel against the boss's directions. The salesperson may see the sales manager as an obstacle that he or she must go around or at least tolerate to be successful. This behavior may cause the sales manager to lose confidence or trust in the salesperson. As a result, their relationship will worsen, or at least not improve. The response by the salesperson who becomes overdependent is the other extreme. The overdependent salesperson will often suppress anger or frustration and agree with the sales manager's decisions and actions even if he or she actually disagrees. The result is that a productive give-and-take working relationship becomes one marked by total dominance by the sales manager. Real differences of opinion between the salesperson and the sales manager are not confronted, and the relationship becomes less effective over time.

Developing and Maintaining the Relationship

An assessment by the salesperson of the sales manager and himself or herself may provide the foundation for developing and maintaining a productive working relationship. However, just assessing the strengths and weaknesses of each person is not enough. As noted in Exhibit 12-2, a good working relationship is one that accommodates the preferred work styles of both the salesperson and the sales manager. A common example of developing compatible work styles is when a sales manager is characterized as a "reader" or a "listener." According to management expert Peter Drucker, if your boss is a listener, you brief him or her in person then follow it up with a memo. If your boss is a reader, you cover important items or proposals in a memo or report, then discuss them in person.[3] This is a relatively simple example of how a sales representative would adjust to the sales manager's work style to further develop their relationship.

The salesperson should give further consideration to making sure the salesperson-sales manager relationship is characterized by mutual expectations. Does the salesperson know, or simply assume, that he or she knows what the sales manager wants or expects? Dealing with a straightforward boss may not be a problem, but working with a sales manager who is vague or gives general as opposed to specific instructions may be a quite different situation. The burden is on the salesperson to discover the sales manager's expectations and to adapt to them.

An effective relationship will also depend on the extent to which the salesperson keeps the sales manager informed of what is going on with the salesperson's territory, department, or customers. Although the salesperson may assume the sales manager already knows what he or she is doing, this may not necessarily be the case. The salesperson may also feel that there is not enough time to keep the sales manager informed of everything. The salesperson should remember that most people, including sales managers, do not like surprises, particularly when the surprise is bad news.

It probably goes without saying that the salesperson-sales manager relationship should be based on dependability and honesty between the two individuals. If the salesperson often fails to deliver on promises made to the sales manager, the sales manager will soon question the dependability of the salesperson. Even more important than dependability is honesty between the superior and the subordinate. Less than total dependability may be tolerated, but dishonesty normally will not. The credibility of the salesperson may be so severely damaged by dishonesty that the salesperson-sales manager relationship is not only harmed, but injured beyond repair. If the dishonesty is of a very serious or continuous nature, it may even lead to the dismissal of the sales representative.

A final consideration for the salesperson in developing a productive and effective working relationship with his or her sales manager is to selectively use the sales manager's time and resources. In any organization, a manager has only limited time and resources to deal with never-ending opportunities and problems. If

Exhibit 12-3 **Rate Your Relationship with Your Boss**

Instructions: Answer the following questions by writing yes or no in the blanks at the left.

_____ 1. Do you sometimes do things your boss's way even though you may disagree?

_____ 2. Have you tried to discover your boss's goals?

_____ 3. Are you aware of things that you do that upset your boss?

_____ 4. Are you able to accept a healthy dependent relationship with your boss?

_____ 5. Are you fully aware of how your boss likes to do things?

_____ 6. Do you keep your boss fully informed about what is happening?

_____ 7. Do you avoid surprising your boss?

_____ 8. Have you made honest attempts to adjust your style somewhat to please your boss?

_____ 9. Are you aware of the major pressures that affect your boss?

_____ 10. Do you have a sincere desire to improve your relationship with your boss?

Source: *Applied Management Newsletter*

the salesperson is not selective in asking for the sales manager's time for important as opposed to trivial matters, the salesperson may lose influence and even credibility. For example, a desire to discuss each customer prospect, regardless of potential sales, with the sales manager may be desirable from the salesperson's point-of-view, but not realistic or possible given the other demands placed on the sales manager. Exhibit 12-3 provides a self-checklist for a salesperson to rate his or her relationship with the boss.

THE RELATIONSHIPS BETWEEN SALES PERSONNEL

In addition to the salesperson-sales manager relationship, the professional salesperson must also be aware of the various individuals involved in his or her firm's selling activities. Just as companies have to design marketing mix and promotional mix strategies, leading sales organizations are currently planning and implementing a personal sales force mix. The personal sales force mix for a company may include traditional field sales personnel, telemarketing specialists, technical support personnel, manufacturers' representatives, and key/national/major account salespersons or sales teams. Exhibit 12-4 presents the personal sales force mix.

Exhibit 12-4 **Personal Sales Force Mix**

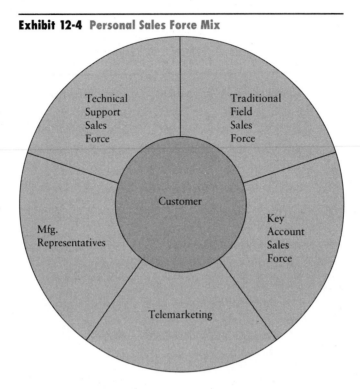

The traditional *field sales force* is defined as individuals employed by a firm to interact with customers on a face-to-face basis. The field sales representative may have several dozen or more customers and may cover a territory and may also specialize in a product or a type of customer.

The *telemarketing salesperson's* most distinguishing feature is quite obvious—the use of the telephone as the primary mode of interaction with customers. Telemarketing sales reps can be used to supplement or substitute for field sales representatives. They are being used to accept orders from customers, qualify sales leads to be turned over to field sales reps, make appointments for field people, and conduct full-scale selling operations for selected accounts.

Technical support representatives are in use by such companies as AT&T, IBM, and Hewlett-Packard. Mainly, they are employed to "back up" a field salesperson who may have cultivated the relationship with a prospective buyer. In some cases, the "tech rep" is part of a sales team that includes another salesperson who specializes in identifying and satisfying customer needs by recommending an appropriate product or service.

Manufacturers' representatives may also be used in a company's sales force mix. Nike, the athletic shoe manufacturer, uses hundreds of manufacturers' representatives. Manufacturers typically develop contractual agreements with several rep organizations. The rep organization is compensated by the manufacturer on a commission basis for products sold.

Key account, national account, major account—all of these are names used to identify a salesperson (or team of people) assigned to a particularly important customer. Firms using the key account system have recognized that a few of their customers account for a very large percentage of the firm's total sales. The firm, by assigning significant resources to the account, is endeavoring to create a relationship that competitors will find difficult to break.

Each of these sales force types, when combined appropriately with one or more of the other sales forces, can play a role in the overall enhancement of a firm's personal sales strategy. Some definite reasons can be identified for companies using a mixture of sales forces. The explanations require an examination of environmental conditions.

One of the most obvious reasons for using a mix of sales forces is the unrelenting rise of sales costs associated with face-to-face selling. The average cost of a business-to-business sales call has been increasing at an annualized rate of just over 11%.[4] This situation has been identified as the primary cause which is pushing more and more companies to use telemarketing.[5]

Another reason for diversifying sales efforts is the shift in power which comes about when buyers become fewer. In industries where the number of competing firms is shrinking, the survivors take on added significance to their vendors. Vendors to breweries, for instance, have seen their customer base shrink from several dozen to less than ten companies which account for a disproportionate share of all beer that is sold. To keep the business of an Anheuser-Busch, a Miller, or a Coors, the firms selling to these giants have rightfully labelled these customers "key accounts." Another reason for creating key accounts and developing a part of a sales organization to exclusively sell to them is the rise of "strategic partnering." Recent research revealed that the creation of long-term relationships between a buyer and a carefully chosen relatively small number of suppliers furnishes incentive to sellers to create a key account sales group. Careful nurturing of the strategic partnership requires a dedicated salesperson or team of sales personnel.[6]

Technology is changing so fast in many cases that today's salesperson sometimes needs technical specialists to support him or her. Thus the technical support sales group has added a needed ingredient to some firms' sales force mix. The presence of such a resource is also being used as a differentiating feature by some vendors who can point to their technical support personnel as standing ready to better serve customers. As purchasers take a more proactive role in evaluating and choosing long-term suppliers, they are using the presence (or absence) of technical support sales personnel as a criterion in supplier evaluations.[7]

The final reason cited here for diversifying a firm's selling forces involves the quest for new markets. One way to test a new market before making a heavy commitment of a company's human and financial resources is to use manufacturers' representatives.[8] A rep's knowledge of a market can help the marketer jump start the marketer's entry.

THE RELATIONSHIPS BETWEEN SALES AND OTHER MARKETING FUNCTIONS

The salesperson must not only develop an effective working relationship with the sales manager and other sales personnel, he or she must also be able to work well with the individuals responsible for other marketing functions. Although the salesperson represents the entire company to the customer, his or her ability to satisfy the customer's needs and problems will depend to a large degree on the abilities of other marketing personnel in the company. One of the key ingredients of the marketing concept as a business philosophy is that all of the marketing department's activities must be effectively coordinated and integrated in order to serve the customer. Stating a belief in **integrated marketing and selling** and achieving it are two different things, as new salespersons quickly learn. A key challenge for the professional salesperson in dealing with the company's customers is to understand the role and perspective of each of the major marketing functions or activities (see Exhibit 12-5).

Advertising, Sales Promotion, and Merchandising

The salesperson's relationship to advertising personnel is probably more direct than to any other marketing activity. Both sales and advertising are charged with the responsibility of stimulating demand for the company's products or services. The blending of promotional methods, such as personal selling and advertising, requires coordination of the planning and implementation of a company's efforts. If an advertising or sales promotion plan is implemented using television, radio, newspapers, magazines, coupons, or contests without effective coordination with the sales force, demand may be stimulated, but the product may not be available.

In addition, for the sale of products to wholesalers and retailers, merchandising activities such as training or displays provided by the sales representative may be a key activity. Advertising personnel may be able to design campaigns that provide sales aids, sales leads, or that presell prospects before the salesperson meets them. Or the sales representative, through day-to-day interaction with customers, may be able to furnish advertising personnel with key information that may influence the selection of advertising themes, media, and schedules, among other items.[9]

Marketing Research and Information Systems

A key marketing activity necessary for the success of a company in meeting the needs of the marketplace and making better marketing decisions is the collection and use of marketing information. Although the spotlight has been on marketing research in most companies, the adoption of computer technology has created sophisticated marketing information systems. The information systems focus on gathering information from sources inside and outside the organization to enable the company to capitalize on opportunities and minimize threats. A salesperson's success may depend to a large degree on obtaining information on prospects, customers, competitors, and economic or social trends that may have an impact on the sale of the firm's product or service. In addition to external information on customers and competitors, the sales representative can also benefit from internal in-

Exhibit 12-5 Relationships in the Marketing Department

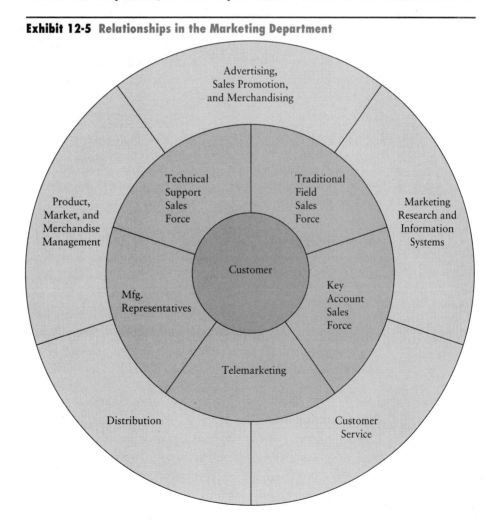

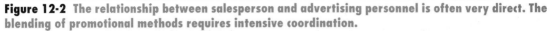

Figure 12-2 The relationship between salesperson and advertising personnel is often very direct. The blending of promotional methods requires intensive coordination.

formation from research and development, production, or accounting on new-product development, production schedules, or credit-worthiness of selected prospects and customers. Marketing data for use by the salesperson to analyze sales expenses, profitable versus unprofitable order sizes, and sales forecasts for coming months may be extremely helpful in making the salesperson more effective and efficient in his or her selling activities. The salesperson also needs to realize that in order for marketing research personnel to be effective, the salesperson may be called upon to supply or help collect data about customers or competitors that they alone would be unable to collect as rapidly, if at all. The interaction between the sales staff and marketing research personnel should be a two-way, mutually beneficial relationship.

Customer Service

Customer service is as important a marketing activity as advertising, sales promotion, merchandising, or marketing research. The use of marketing research and advertising to aid the salesperson in making the sale must be coupled with an effective customer service program to support the salesperson and the customer after the sale has been made. Effective communication between sales and service personnel is crucial in keeping the customer satisfied and building salesperson, brand, or supplier loyalty. Although customer service is important for all types of products, the salesperson who sells service-intensive products, such as automobiles or computers, must rely heavily on customer service personnel. In automobile sales, a warranty of seven years or 70,000 miles has become a critical aspect in the sale of one brand over another. In fact, with some products, such as communications or information processing systems, the service package that accompanies the product may be equally or even more important than the product itself. Part of the success of companies such as IBM, Caterpillar, and Xerox is due to strong service orientations that supplement and complement their products. The salesperson cannot lose sight of the fact that many customers and prospects are attracted to and retained by an effective product offering that includes service during and after the sale. Customer service representatives may be able to provide additional insight for the sales representative as to what product and service aspects should be stressed to prospects.

Distribution

One of the key marketing activities that is often forgotten or undervalued in marketing and sales is the physical distribution function. Although advertising, market research, and customer service may be given more emphasis in many companies, the company's success may be largely dependent on its ability to have its products or services at the right place, at the right time, and in the right amount. Physical distribution involves planning, implementing, and controlling the physical flows of materials and final goods from points of origin to points of use at a profit.[10] The major activities included in physical distribution are presented in Exhibit 12-6.

The success of the professional salesperson will depend to a large extent on effective distribution planning based on sales forecasts. The interaction of physical distribution personnel with production managers plays a key role in the overall effectiveness of inventory management. Obtaining materials for the production of the product is only the first step for the physical distribution manager. Based on sales forecasts supplied by marketing research and sales personnel, production schedules are developed. Once the product is manufactured, decisions on inventory management, packaging, warehousing, shipping, and transportation must be made and coordinated with other marketing and sales personnel.

Customer service focuses on effective order processing to ensure time, place, and form utilities. In addition, the salesperson is also concerned that the exchange or possession utility is enhanced by the physical distribution function. Failure to

Exhibit 12-6 Major Activities of Physical Distribution

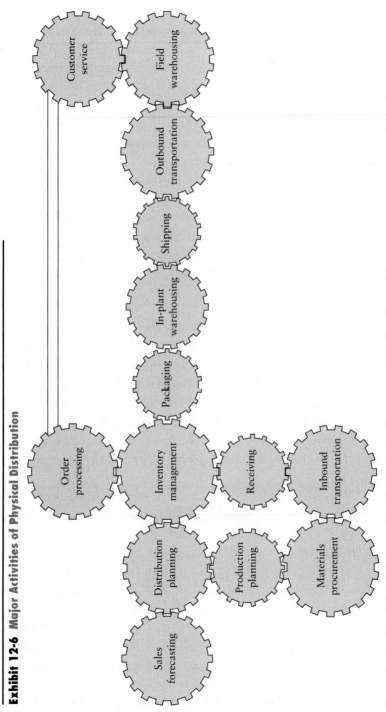

Source: Reprinted from Wendell M. Stawart, "Physicial Distribution: Key to Improved Volume and Profits," *Journal of Marketing* (January, 1965): 66, published by American Marketing Association.

have the product available at the right time or place or in the right amount will result in a lost sale, which may or may not be recoverable in the future. Effective market research, advertising, and selling activities can be voided when the physical distribution process breaks down in any activity from materials procurement to field warehousing of the finished product. The challenge is to balance the need for customer service and satisfaction of customer needs at a profit. Although it may seem that the salesperson is totally separate from the physical distribution function, lack of attention by the salesperson to developing this relationship and acknowledging its importance may greatly limit his or her effectiveness.

Product, Market, and Merchandise Managers

In larger industrial and consumer product companies, there may be product, market, or merchandise managers (see Chapter 11). Depending on the type of product or market management used by a company, the salesperson will interact with these personnel to some degree. For example, at General Foods' Post Division, product group managers are in charge of cereals, pet food, and beverages. In addition, within the cereal group, product managers are responsible for nutritional, children's presweetened, and family cereals with brand managers for each specific brand of cereal.[11] Product group, product, and brand managers interact with the sales managers and the sales force.

The major duties of product and market managers are shown in Exhibit 12-7. Specifically, a product or market manager is responsible for developing long- and short-range product or market strategies and plans, including sales forecasts. The product or market manager must also work closely with sales, distribution, and ad-

1. Develop a long-range and competitive strategy for the product or market.
2. Prepare an annual marketing plan and sales forecast.
3. Work with advertising and merchandising agencies to develop copy, programs, and campaigns.
4. Stimulate interest and support of the product or market among the sales force and distributors.
5. Gather intelligence on the product or market, customer and dealer attitudes, and new problems or opportunities.
6. Initiate product improvements to meet changing market needs.

Exhibit 12-7 Major Duties of Product and Market Managers

Source: Philip Kotler, *Marketing Management: Analysis, Planning, Implementation, and Control*, 6e, Copyright 1988, p. 709. Adapted by permission of Prentice Hall, Inc., Englewood Cliffs, New Jersey.

vertising personnel, as already discussed. In addition, the manager may be responsible for monitoring the product's performance, customer attitudes toward the product, and initiation of product changes or improvements.

In most organizations, product and market managers are staff personnel, but in a few instances, they may be in line positions with direct authority over sales personnel. When product or market managers are in line positions with sales personnel reporting to them, lines of communication and areas of responsibility and authority may be well defined. However, when the relationship between the salesperson and the product or market manager is of the **line** (sales) **versus staff** (product or market manager) type, it is not unusual for poor coordination and even conflict to arise. The expectations that the product or market manager and the salesperson have of one another's appropriate role may not coincide. For sales personnel to be effective, however, input and support from product and market managers may be critical. Poor working relationships will hinder the overall marketing effort of the company, and the end result will be a high level of frustration among the company's marketing and sales personnel or, at worst, lost customer sales.

CONFLICT AND COOPERATION BETWEEN SALES AND MARKETING

The numerous relationships sales personnel may have with individuals in advertising, market research, customer service, distribution, and product or market management must be integrated at the departmental level to enhance the likelihood of success in attracting and retaining customers. Although personnel assigned to each marketing activity, such as advertising or market research, may easily recognize the need for cooperation, conflict often arises. Marketing personnel who are responsible for various marketing functions or activities will have different perspectives about what is most important. Due to a functional bias, competition for resources, or a desire to influence the future direction of marketing activities, marketing and sales personnel may tend to look out for their own self-interest.

Exhibit 12-8 lists the major marketing functions and activities and contrasts their emphasis with that of the sales function. The advertising-sales relationship is marked by differences in time horizons (annually, monthly, weekly) or the long- as opposed to short-term effects of promotional programs. In addition, advertising personnel may be accustomed to relatively slow feedback, and sales personnel may desire fast feedback.

The marketing research-sales relationship might be characterized as an orientation difference from continuous data collection by research personnel to peri-

Exhibit 12-8 Potential Conflicts Within the Marketing Department

Function or Activity	Their Emphasis	Emphasis of Sales
Advertising, sales promotion, and merchandising	Annual focus Slow feedback Long-term	Monthly or weekly focus Fast feedback Short-term
Marketing research and information systems	Continuous data collection Scientific method Exploratory research	Periodic data collection Quick and easy analysis Cause-and-effect research
Customer service	Standard response Single-contact orientation Efficiency	Personal response Multicontact orientation Effectiveness
Distribution	Centralized Cost-effective Cost Large order size	Decentralized Demand-responsive Service Small order size
Product, market, and merchandise management	Planning Strategy Long-range	Implementation Tactics Short-range

odic collection by sales personnel. Marketing researchers might employ sophisticated scientific research techniques for exploratory research while the salesperson may prefer quick-and-easy data collection and analysis to determine cause-and-effect relationships between promotional programs and sales results.

Although the need for cooperation between sales and customer service may be readily apparent, the sales staff may expect a more personal approach to customer inquiries for assistance, refunds, exchanges, complaints, or postsale service. Differences of opinion as to whether customer service is a one-time interaction with a customer versus an ongoing relationship may also arise. In addition, sales personnel may feel that customer service should do whatever is asked by the customer in order to develop customer loyalty, while customer service personnel may want to balance the need for customer service against its cost.

The sales-distribution relationship may also result in differences of opinion with respect to the location of centralized or decentralized distribution outlets. Other potential conflicts may arise over the sales department's desire for demand-responsive distribution systems, while distribution personnel must consider the cost-effectiveness in their response to customer needs. Disagreements over the feasibility and practicality of minimum order sizes, length of delivery time, and speed of order processing may also develop between sales and distribution personnel.

In dealing with product and market managers, sales personnel may feel that the product and market specialists engage far too much in planning, with too little emphasis or appreciation for implementation. The staff specialists may view strategy and long-range performance as the key factors for success, and sales personnel may believe tactical, day-to-day decisions and activities are the foundation for short- as well as long-range success.[12]

The adoption and implementation of the marketing concept requires an effective, integrated marketing effort. The marketing department's focus on the customer with the hope of generating profits and customer satisfaction requires intradepartmental cooperation with minimal conflict. Each marketing function, including sales, will have a primary emphasis or perspective; the key will be integrating and coordinating the various activities. Sales personnel should develop **empathy**, the ability to see the points-of-view of marketing personnel as well as their own. An appreciation of the roles and responsibilities of each marketing function will enable the salesperson to develop and maintain effective working relationships with key marketing personnel. The salesperson's success in dealing with customers will be dependent mainly on how well the salesperson works with other marketing personnel in his or her company.

SUMMARY

1. To be effective, the salesperson must be able to develop and maintain strong working relationships with key individuals responsible for marketing as well as sales activities.

2. The job description for a sales position will include information about the position's title, duties and responsibilities, organizational relationships, and job qualifications, which the salesperson should fully understand.

3. To correctly manage the relationship with his or her sales manager, the salesperson must have a good understanding of the superior's goals and objectives, strengths and weaknesses, and preferred work style.

4. The salesperson must be able to understand the perspective and role of the individuals who perform other marketing functions such as advertising, sales promotion, merchandising, market research, customer service, distribution, and product or market management.

5. The task of the salesperson to develop an integrated and coordinated sales effort, based on strong intradepartmental relationships, may be affected by

conflict among marketing personnel with differing biases and perspectives and by demands against limited resources.

QUESTIONS FOR DISCUSSION AND REVIEW

1. How can the job description assist the salesperson to better understand his or her place in the organization?

2. In a salesperson-sales manager relationship, what would be some examples of a sales manager's preferred work style?

3. What would be two characteristics of a good relationship between the salesperson and sales manager?

4. Why is the sales-distribution relationship so important?

5. Why must marketing research personnel and the sales staff rely on one another?

6. What reasons might exist for potential conflict between sales personnel and product or market managers?

7. What is meant by the term *integrated marketing*?

8. A salesperson is no more effective than the marketing organization that supports him or her. Why or why not?

CASE 12-1 THE CRANDON COMPANY'S NEW SELLING STRATEGY

During the six months that followed his presentation to the sales force, including Pete Wilkerson, Gordon White has done a great deal of thinking about what a change in selling strategy would mean for the Crandon Company. (See opening vignette to this chapter.) He has mulled over in his mind such issues as what accounts of Crandon's would warrant key or major account status and what criteria should be used to make this determination. Gordon has also thought about which accounts accustomed to face-to-face selling coverage would be converted to accounts covered by telemarketing due to their decreasing buying potential in containers. In addition, either new selling approach also has to be evaluated for the likely impact on both sales and profits for the company.

Gordon White has also become aware recently that the sales force has some degree of anxiety about the addition of key or major account selling and telemarketing as new strategies. Those sales personnel who have been with the company for a number of years are especially concerned about what the change in selling strategy would mean to their daily selling activities. For example, Pete Wilkerson has been a very successful and productive field salesperson for the Crandon Company as have several of his sales colleagues who have been with the company for anywhere from seven to fifteen years.

As Gordon White prepares for his next meeting with his sales force to discuss the actual implementation of the new selling strategies during the next month, he wonders what items would be best for him to cover in this meeting. Gordon realizes that the success of the Crandon Company and his success as a sales manager are largely dependent on a productive and happy sales force.

QUESTIONS

1. In terms of the salesperson-sales manager relationship, what should Gordon White assess, given the upcoming change in selling strategies?

2. In terms of the salesperson to salesperson relationship, what should Gordon White expect or anticipate?

3. In terms of the salesperson-customer relationship, what might be some concerns?

CASE 12-2 BETH'S BOSS

Beth Thompson, a sales representative for a major cosmetics company, has begun to have second thoughts about whether or not she can develop a good working relationship with her sales manager, Thea Branch. Beth has been in her present position for just over two years; Thea was hired as the new Divisional Sales Manager only six months ago. At the same time Thea was hired, the national sales manager's slot, the position to which she reported, was filled by Adam Alexander due to the retirement of the former national sales manager.

Although Beth realizes that Thea Branch is new to the organization, she feels Thea seems to have little time to discuss her situation, particularly some problems she is having with turning prospects into established customers. Due to what Beth believes is a decreasing amount of quality selling time because of time spent filing written customer call and expense reports, she is sometimes late with her reports. In addition, she often finds it necessary to respond with telephone calls or quick face-to-face meetings when asked for information by her sales manager.

To many of the sales staff, including Beth, it appears that Thea Branch is spending an unusual amount of time with Adam Alexander in assessing the future direction of various cosmetic product lines. Mr. Alexander's reputation is one of being a very demanding person who sees nothing unusual about twelve- to fourteen-hour days. In order to stay a step ahead of Mr. Alexander, Thea Branch has asked for monthly written updates on how each salesperson is doing in existing accounts, new customers, expenses, competitive actions, and distributor attitudes, among other items. Beth thinks much of the monthly report is a waste of her valuable selling time.

QUESTIONS

1. Why do you believe Beth is so upset with her sales position at this particular time?

2. What is Beth failing to recognize or consider in her relationship with Thea Branch?

3. How might Beth attempt to improve her relationship with Thea Branch?

CASE 12-3 LINE VERSUS STAFF

John Bowman, a Sales Associate for Knight Consolidated, a manufacturer of portable swimming pools, is beginning to believe the staff of his company is having more influence on operations than line personnel. Specifically, John feels that the company's marketing research and customer service personnel are beginning to ask the sales force, including himself, to do too many nonselling activities.

Recent requests from marketing research personnel include members of the sales force providing information every two weeks on competitive activity in each salesperson's district. In addition, the customer service manager received permission from the marketing vice president to ask the sales staff to provide detailed records on customer turnover and an explanation for each occurrence.

John believes the marketing researchers and customer service representatives should do their jobs and let the sales staff do what they were hired to do—sell! John knows that many members of the sales force want marketing research to uncover the reasons why customers use one brand of product over another. Some members of the sales force also want customer service to play a more active role in sales support during the sales process, not just after the sale has been made.

Joan Sanders, the company's Sales Manager, has indicated to the sales staff that if Knight Consolidated is to reach its full potential, all the marketing units, including sales, marketing research, and customer service, must work together in an integrated and coordinated manner in order to respond to customers' needs, wants, and problems. She also has indicated that the company's marketing vice president expects teamwork within the marketing department.

QUESTIONS

1. What do you see as the principal problem between marketing research and sales? Between customer service and sales?

2. What would be the desired relationship among market research, customer service, and sales?

3. Assuming the situation is marked by a lack of cooperation or even conflict, how might the problem be resolved?

NOTES

1. William J. Stanton and Richard H. Buskirk, *Management of the Sales Force* (Homewood, Ill.: Richard D. Irwin, 1987), 114.

2. John J. Gabarro and John P. Kotter, "Managing Your Boss," *Harvard Business Review* (January–February 1980): 92–100.

3. Ibid., 98.

4. William A. O'Connell and William Keenan, Jr., "The Shape of Things to Come," *Sales & Marketing Management* (January 1990): 36–41.

5. Carlton A. Pederson, Milburn D. Wright, and Barton A. Weitz, *Selling: Principles and Methods*, 9th ed. (Homewood, Ill.: Richard D. Irwin, Inc., 1988).

6. Michiel R. Leenders and David L. Blenkhorn, *Reverse Marketing: The New Buyer-Supplier Relationship* (New York: The Free Press, 1988).

7. Larry C. Giunipero, "Supplier Evaluation Methods," *NAPM Insights* 1, no. 6 (June 1990): 21–23.

8. Thomas R. Wotruba and Edwin K. Simpson, *Sales Management: Text and Cases* (Boston: PWS Kent Publishing Co., 1992).

9. Richard R. Still, Edward W. Cundiff, and Norman A.P. Govoni, *Sales Management: Decisions, Strategies, and Cases* (Englewood Cliffs, N.J.: Prentice Hall, 1988), 208.

10. Philip Kotler, *Marketing Management: Analysis, Planning, Implementation, and Control*, 6th ed. (Englewood Cliffs, N.J.: Prentice Hall, 1988), 577.

11. Ibid., 708–9.

12. Gerald P. Michaelson, "Sales Versus Marketing Can Lead to Senseless Warfare," *Marketing News* (November 8, 1985): 3–4.

CHAPTER 13

The Salesperson's Relationships with Nonmarketing Areas

LEARNING OBJECTIVES

After studying this chapter, you should be able to:

1. Understand the different types of relationships among sales, research and development, production, finance and accounting, purchasing, personnel, legal, and public relations.

2. Identify areas of cooperation and conflict among sales and nonmarketing areas.

3. Understand the six methods that may be used to resolve conflicts among departmental units.

4. Acknowledge and understand the meaning and importance of integrated marketing at the company level.

5. Define the key terms used in this chapter.

KEY TERMS

- conflict
- goal orientation
- time orientation
- formal structure
- interpersonal orientation
- avoidance
- accommodation
- compromise
- bargaining
- authority
- problem-solving
- coordinated marketing
- internal marketing

THE RELATIONSHIP between sales, marketing, and other departments in an organization sometimes may undergo dramatic changes due to developments both inside and outside the company. An example of such a change is the Du Pont Company, which puts customers first by training the entire organization to think marketing. Until recently, Du Pont's business perspective was influenced by a scientific orientation—a business-to-business marketing outlook as opposed to a business-to-consumer approach—and technological and economic strength. Du Pont's corporate culture revolved around product innovation. Today, rather than relying primarily on technology for company success, Du Pont also emphasizes marketing by encouraging company personnel to think first of customer needs and how Du Pont can meet those needs. The overall goal for the company is to create a marketing community involving the entire corporation. The key steps taken by Du Pont to build this marketing community include seeing the company as market-driven (measuring what is done against marketplace performance, including sales, marketing, finance, personnel, and research and development, among others) and making a top-to-bottom commitment to marketing and the company's customers.[1]

The salesperson's relationships within the marketing department are only one part of the various relationships that he or she must acknowledge, develop, and maintain in order to enhance his or her effectiveness. In contrast to intradepartmental relationships, interdepartmental relationships, as shown in Exhibit 13-1, include a variety of functions, such as research and development, production, and accounting, which may be directly or indirectly related to the sales and marketing function. The achievement of an integrated marketing effort throughout the salesperson's company in line with the marketing concept philosophy is normally the company's ideal objective.

Although the marketing concept calls for an integrated, cooperative, and harmonious relationship within and between departments, a number of factors often limit the accomplishment of this objective. First, differences of opinion may exist

Exhibit 13-1 Interdepartmental Relationships

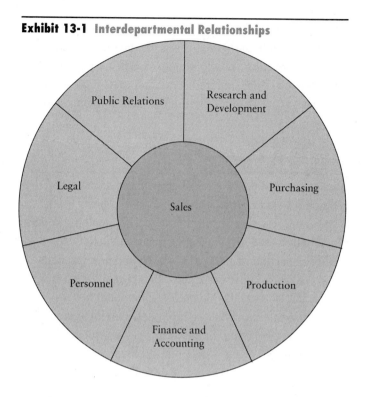

as to what constitutes the best interests of the organization. Each department may view their efforts as responsible for the success of the company. Second, there may be tradeoffs between the well-being of the department and the well-being of the company. What is good for marketing, production, or accounting may or may not contribute to the overall effectiveness of the organization. For example, the production of a few products in large quantities may be cost-effective, but may not contribute to satisfying market demand for new product introductions. Third, many individuals within a company may develop stereotypes of other departments, which may contribute to a lack of understanding or even conflict. Sales personnel may be viewed as "hucksters" by others in the company, while sales may view people in accounting as "penny-pinchers" who have no understanding or appreciation of what sales personnel do or their importance to the organization. Finally, in the competition for resources and attention from top management, each department will have a degree of self-interest that will naturally contribute to a certain level of competition or conflict.[2]

Although there are a number of reasons why conflict rather than cooperation may develop, the fact that all of the departments within a company have a direct or, at least, an indirect influence on customer satisfaction should not be forgotten. The roles of sales and marketing, research and development, and production may be readily apparent; but other functions such as personnel, accounting and finance, purchasing, legal, and public relations also have an effect on the degree to which a company is customer-oriented and focused on customer satisfaction.

DEPARTMENTAL RELATIONSHIPS

Just as the effectiveness of the salesperson in any organization depends on his or her relationships with other marketing personnel in advertising, market research, or customer service, relationships with nonmarketing departments are also critical to success. Although sales and marketing may be seen as the company's link to the customer, other departments, such as research and development or production, play a key role in the overall success of the company's marketing and sales effort. To be more productive, the salesperson must understand the perspectives of each of the company's departments, including how a department's point-of-view may differ from that of sales and marketing. Some of the key interdepartmental relationships are shown in Exhibit 13-2 along with the different emphases of each department.

Research and Development

The research and development activity for most large firms is located in a separate department; in smaller companies, however, the activity may be a part of production or marketing. This department is charged with the responsibility of developing new products and improving established products. A number of alternatives exist for the integration of new product development throughout a company, including a new product development committee, a new product project management team, new product managers, or new product departments that coordinate the efforts of research and development, production, marketing and sales, and other operating departments.

The salesperson should understand the differing views of sales and marketing versus research and development or engineering in many organizations. While sales and marketing want short design lead times to respond to market changes, research and development personnel desire longer lead times for product development. Also, sales personnel may want products with sales as opposed to functional features, many rather than few models, and custom as contrasted to standard components. With each of these issues, the different desires and emphases of sales and marketing compared to research and development tend to lead to disagreement and, in some situations, conflict. Although a certain level of disagreement

Exhibit 13-2 Departmental Emphases in an Organization

Departments	Their Emphases	Sales and Marketing's Emphases
Research and development	Long design lead time	Short design lead time
	Functional features	Sales features
	Few models	Many models
	Standard components	Custom components
Purchasing	Cost reduction	Revenue generation
	Economical stock levels	High stock levels
	Standard parts	Nonstandard parts
	Low cost	High quality
	Infrequent purchasing	Frequent purchasing
	Narrow product line	Broad product line
Production	Long lead times	Short lead times
	Long production runs	Short production runs
	Few models	Many models
	No model changes	Frequent model changes
	Standard orders	Custom orders
Finance and accounting	Strict justification for spending	Easy justification for spending
	Strict budgets	Flexible budgets
	Low credit risks	Medium credit risks
	Tough collection procedures	Easy collection procedures

Source: Philip Kotler, *Marketing Management: Analysis, Planning, Implementation, and Control,* 6e, Copyright 1988, p. 717. Adapted by permission of Prentice-Hall, Inc., Englewood Cliffs, New Jersey.

may lead to even better ideas, too much may cause a lack of integration and understanding between these two key functions.[3]

The salesperson's relationship with individuals in research and development should focus on areas where one party may help the other for mutually beneficial results (see Exhibit 13-3). For example, the research and development department may rely heavily on sales personnel to provide it with suggestions or ideas for

Exhibit 13-3 Issues Between Sales and Research and Development

1. Modifications to existing products
2. New product ideas
3. Updates on competitors' products
4. Customer reactions to test markets
5. Customer complaints
6. Product warranty problems

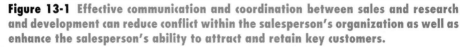

Figure 13-1 Effective communication and coordination between sales and research and development can reduce conflict within the salesperson's organization as well as enhance the salesperson's ability to attract and retain key customers.

either modifications to existing products or totally new products. In addition, updates on competitors' products may help research and development respond to changing competitive offerings. When test marketing new or improved products, sales representatives may provide a critical communication link to research and development by being the eyes and ears of the company in the marketplace. Besides reactions to new products, the relationship between sales and research and development may be improved by careful attention to customer complaints and product warranty problems. Effective communication and coordination between these two departments should enhance the salesperson's effectiveness in attracting and retaining key customers.

Purchasing

Once a product has been designed and is ready for initial product development, the materials to construct the product must be ordered. More importantly, once a

1. Sales forecasts
2. Purchasing schedules
3. Cost of materials
4. Inventory levels of materials
5. Pricing of products
6. Product warranty problems
7. Customer complaints
8. Competitor product changes
9. Shifts in marketplace demand

Exhibit 13-4 Issues Between Sales and Purchasing

decision has been made to commercialize a product for regional or national distribution, the need exists to purchase large quantities of materials or components for the new product's production.[4] The key information for this decision will be the sales forecast for the product, which may apply to existing as well as new products (see Exhibit 13-4). The sales forecast may be more questionable for new products than for existing products, but they are still critical, due to the lack of a previous track record.

Although the sales function is charged with generating revenue, the purchasing department is often expected to hold costs down. This distinction is a major underlying cause for conflict between sales and purchasing. More specifically, sales may desire high levels of stock and large lot sizes to avoid stock shortages or outages, while purchasing is expected to have only economical levels of stock. In addition, purchasing may focus on standard parts, low prices, and purchasing at infrequent intervals, while sales expects nonstandard items, high quality, and frequent purchasing to meet customer needs. The broad product line desired by sales as compared with the narrow product line that would be best for purchasing personnel is another example of differing viewpoints on how the purchasing function should operate.

Production

One of the most critical interdepartmental relationships is the one between sales and production. As noted in Exhibit 13-2, production personnel often prefer long production lead times and production runs of a few relatively standardized models. The production department desires to maintain stable levels of production with few interruptions, which it hopes will lead to cost minimization.

Sales personnel, on the other hand, want to be able to have custom orders and frequent model changes that result in short production lead times and production

1. Products to manufacture
2. Quantities to produce
3. Production schedules
4. Sales forecasts
5. Expected price and quality levels
6. Packaging
7. Inventory levels
8. Salesperson training on product knowledge
9. Technical information updates
10. Marketplace changes in demand

Exhibit 13-5 Issues Between Sales and Production

runs. Having new products available to contribute to the achievement of high sales volume and market share goals is given high priority by sales personnel.

The foregoing differing emphases of production and sales would suggest two departments that are exact opposites in viewpoint. There are, however, a number of decisions that demand sales-production cooperation.[5] As shown in Exhibit 13-5, the sales-production relationship is critical in deciding which products to manufacture and in what quantities. For a company with numerous products, priorities must be set as to which product's production schedule may take precedence over another. The production schedules will rely heavily on sales forecast data provided in part by the sales force. Key information regarding customer expectations of product price and quality will have a direct effect on the type of materials and components in the product produced.

After the product is produced, production and sales personnel must also make key decisions involving product packaging and inventory levels, among other items. Production personnel may provide product-related training for the sales staff as well as technical information updates once the product is on the market. During the same time period, sales personnel will provide the production department with key information on changes in demand occurring in the marketplace. These changes may include minor concerns or problems with the product that could lead to the eventual decline of customer interest in the product altogether. Without cooperation between sales and production personnel, the effectiveness of the salesperson in dealing with his or her customers will be adversely affected.

Finance and Accounting

Once the product has been developed, parts and materials purchased, and production completed, the salesperson's attention may increasingly focus on his or

1. Budgets
2. Cost information for pricing decisions
3. Discounts
4. Credit checks
5. Customer billing
6. Collection of accounts
7. Sales and marketing cost analysis

Exhibit 13-6 **Issues Between Sales and Finance and Accounting**

her interaction with prospects and customers. Although often overlooked, a key support area for the salesperson is finance and accounting. Although disagreements may arise between sales and finance and accounting over various issues, such as justifications for spending, acceptable levels of credit risk for customers, or collection procedures for past due accounts, the finance and accounting department can aid the selling staff in a number of areas (see Exhibit 13-6).

The salesperson may rely heavily on finance and accounting personnel to develop budgets that will guide the level of sales effort for the salesperson's territory, product, or customer group. In addition, the salesperson may need assistance with cost information for making pricing decisions, including discounts and better ways to control selling expenses. In dealing with his or her customers, the salesperson may also want finance and accounting personnel to provide information on the credit worthiness of a customer, accurate and timely customer billing, and collection procedures that will strengthen rather than weaken future salesperson-customer relationships. Periodically, the sales staff may desire sales and marketing cost analyses from finance and accounting to help identify areas for increased or decreased effort such as territories, products, customer groups, order sizes, or other items.

Many salespeople tend to stereotype personnel in finance and accounting as people interested only in controlling operations rather than aiding customer development and maintenance. Cooperative efforts by sales and finance and accounting may be a critical aspect of building long-term customer relationships by the salesperson.

Personnel, Legal, and Public Relations

The salesperson's relationships with research and development, purchasing, production, and finance and accounting may be very apparent as inputs to his or her success, but other departments may also have an effect. One of these departments, personnel, may be seen as affecting the salesperson only when he or she joins the organization. In many companies, however, the personnel department is also responsible for the coordination and delivery of training on company policies, products, customers, competitors, and selling techniques. Information and instruction on these issues may go a long way toward helping the salesperson develop his or her abilities and achieve personal and professional goals.

The interdepartmental relationship between sales and legal may be forgotten until the need arises or, as is often the case, a legal problem presents itself. The salesperson may need the help of the legal department regarding contracts with customers as well as legal issues involved in pricing decisions, including customer discounts. In addition, questions about product warranties, distributor or dealer relations, or acceptable promotional practices may arise; and issues regarding the salesperson's relationships with competitors' personnel or industry trade associations may have an impact on what the salesperson can or cannot do.

In many organizations, the departmental relationship between sales and public relations may be one of the least developed relationships. Sales personnel may readily see the importance of a good working relationship with the advertising and sales promotion staff, but often overlook individuals in public relations. However, because of its responsibility for company publications such as newsletters, catalogs, product announcements, and trade shows, the public relations department may be able to assist the salesperson in doing his or her job by providing items that serve as selling supplements. The total marketing effort of the company may receive a big assist from the organization's public relations efforts.

Each of these departments may help the salesperson be more successful in representing the company to the customer. Converting a prospect to a customer and retaining that customer over the long haul may hinge not only on the salesperson's abilities, but on how well the salesperson understands, develops, and maintains relationships with key nonmarketing areas in the company.

INTERDEPARTMENTAL CONFLICT

The salesperson's relationships with individuals in other departments may involve a level of conflict or competitiveness that may interfere with achieving an integrated marketing effort. As a first step, the salesperson should understand what conflict is and why conflict arises in any organization. **Conflict** can be defined as any kind of opposition or antagonistic interaction between two or more parties.[6] Thus, conflict may range from minor disagreements to situations marked by a desire by one party to dominate another party.

A key consideration in understanding and adapting to interdepartmental conflict is for the salesperson to understand why conflict arises. As one might expect, conflict may be due to a number of factors. One suggestion is that conflict is due to circumstances related to communication (for example, misunderstanding due to ambiguous or incomplete information), structure (interdependence of two or more groups to achieve their goals), or personal factors (incompatibility of personal goals with the behavior required by one's job or position).[7]

Exhibit 13-7 lists several more specific sources or causes of conflict between groups, departments, or individuals. It is not uncommon for a department or an individual to be in competition for limited resources. Even very successful organizations do not normally have sufficient money, personnel, equipment, or facilities to satisfy each department. Desires for increased budgets, new personnel, and improved facilities may all be part of a department's or individual's desire to gain more power and influence in the organization. When this occurs between areas such as sales and production, or sales and research and development, conflict is often the end result.

Conflict may also arise due to role-based conflicts. While sales is charged with generating revenue and fostering customer relations, production is often focused on cost-effectiveness. Different roles or expectations for different departments frequently result in disagreement over what is the most important emphasis for the organization. In worse situations, poorly defined responsibilities may mean a misunderstanding of which department is responsible or has authority for a given activity, such as sales force hiring decisions (sales versus personnel), new product plans (sales versus research and development), or customer relations (sales versus public relations). Poorly defined or overlapping responsibilities or lack of authority will undoubtedly lead to some form of conflict between or among departments.

Some sources of conflict related to different roles in the organization include clashes of values, interests, and organizational climates. As discussed in Chapter 11, each and every organization will have a dominant value system, set of beliefs,

Exhibit 13-7 Sources of Conflict

Competition for limited resources
Drives for power acquisition
Role-based conflicts
Poorly defined responsibilities
Clashes of values and interests
Organizational climate
Introduction of change

Source: Andrew J. Dubrin, *Fundamentals of Organizational Behavior* (New York: Pergamon Press, 1974), p. 303.

climate, or culture. It is not unusual to find that a particular company has a greater emphasis or interest in research and development, production, sales and marketing, or technology, among other possibilities. When this occurs, a given department will have a much greater influence on the company's present and future direction. In addition, the dominant department's influence is likely to have an effect on the allocation of resources and the power relationships inside the company.

A final major source of conflict is the introduction of change to the organization. An example would be the effect that deregulation had on the airline and telecommunication industries. Companies in each of these fields had to adjust quickly from a stable environment with relatively little competition to unstable environments marked by intense competition for customers, which affected each company's operations (as well as company survival, in a few cases). Companies such as IBM and AT&T are just two examples of corporations that were forced to respond to a changing competitive environment. Internal battles between individuals and departments frequently arise over how to adapt or respond to such dramatic changes. A salesperson should not be surprised that a company in a very competitive industry or turbulent environment is likely to have a certain level of conflict that must be controlled or managed if the company is to be effective in the marketplace.

The preceding discussion highlighted various relationships between sales and nonmarketing areas in an organization. Departmental differences are due partially to the extent to which various departments perform different tasks and deal with different parts of the organization's environment. Because of those differences, departments vary in their goal orientation, time orientation, formal structure, and interpersonal orientation. Examples of each of these differences are presented in Exhibit 13-8 in terms of research, production, and sales departments.

In terms of **goal orientation**—which is the primary emphasis or focus of a department—sales often has an orientation centered on customer problems and market opportunities. This sales orientation is less exact than production's goal for

Exhibit 13-8 Departmental Differences

	Research	Production	Sales
Goal orientation	Scientific knowledge	Unit costs	Customer problems and market opportunities
Time orientation	One year or more	One day to one month	One month to six months
Formal structure	Low	High	Medium
Interpersonal orientation	Medium	Low	High

unit costs, but more exact than research's goal of scientific knowledge. In contrast, **time orientation**—how long it takes a department to know the results of its actions—is very short for production, moderate for sales, and long for research. In terms of **formal structure**—the relative strictness of rules, span of control, and frequency and specificity of supervisory control—the research department is normally the lowest, with production the highest, and sales somewhere in the middle. The **interpersonal orientation** dimension—which focuses on the relative openness, sociability, and permissiveness of relationships within a department—tends to be highest in sales, followed by research and then production. One can see how different each of the three departments is on these four dimensions. Studies show that the greater the differences between departments, the greater the difficulty of coordinating interdepartmental activities and the more likely that interdepartmental conflicts will arise.[8]

RESOLVING DEPARTMENTAL CONFLICT

Due to the number of different activities, functions, and departments involved in selling a product or service to a customer, a sales representative should expect that conflict will arise periodically. Although conflict cannot always be avoided, once it does arise, steps must be taken to deal with the conflict and try to alleviate it. A decision must be made as to how a given conflict will be handled. Exhibit 13-9 presents an overview of methods to resolve conflict within departments (sales and advertising) or between departments (sales and production).

The least effective method of handling conflict is the use of **avoidance**. When a conflict arises between sales and advertising on the amount of budget each

Method	Implications
Avoidance	Conflict is recognized, but nothing is done to resolve it.
Accommodation	One party gives in to another.
Compromise	Each party is willing to give a little.
Bargaining	Two parties use their power and persuasion to maximize their gain or minimize their loss vis-à-vis each other.
Authority	The issue of the conflict is taken to a higher authority.
Problem-solving	Parties to the conflict seek a solution that will satisfy the goals of each.

Exhibit 13-9 Methods to Resolve Conflict

Sources: Leon C. Megginson, Donald C. Mosley, and Paul H. Pietri, Jr., *Management: Concepts and Applications* (New York: Harper and Row, 1983), p. 439. Philip Kotler, *Marketing Management: Analysis, Planning, Implementation, and Control*, 2e, Copyright 1972, pp. 277–78. Adapted by permission of Prentice-Hall, Inc., Englewood Cliffs, New Jersey.

should be given, little or no action may be taken to resolve the conflict. The end result is that the conflict, disagreement, or competition for resources continues. In addition, the conflict may worsen over time to the point that sales and advertising personnel find it difficult to work with one another.

Depending on the issue, one of the two parties in a conflict may decide it is better to use **accommodation**, in which one party gives in to the other's demands. Although they may not want to be held to strict spending guidelines, the sales force, particularly the sales manager, may decide to yield to the desires of finance and accounting on this issue in order to continue selling activities without interruption. Using accommodation is not appropriate for all conflicts and disagreements, but it may be advisable for some issues that may not be worth the time and effort required to "do battle" when compared to the likely end result. Also, if the sales staff uses accommodation on a particular issue, it may increase the chances that the other party—in this case finance and accounting—may be willing to accommodate sales on a future disagreement.

Closely related to accommodation is the **compromise** method, which refers to each party's being willing to give a little to resolve a conflict. If the sales department wants the production department to increase the inventory of a particular product, sales personnel might be willing to specify which other product or products can be cut back, even though, ideally, sales personnel want the same production levels of all products. Although production personnel do not want to alter production schedules, they may be more willing to do so if sales personnel are willing to change their expectations of production levels in order to solve this problem.

Although accommodation and compromise may quickly lead to resolving conflicts between sales and other departments in the company, it would not be unusual to find conflicting departments using bargaining to handle conflicts. **Bargaining** occurs when two parties use their power and persuasion to maximize their gain or minimize their loss vis-à-vis the other party. A conflict between sales and distribution personnel may occur because the sales staff wants quicker order processing and delivery. Distribution personnel may counter with the demand that sales representatives will need to do a better job at sales forecasting and negotiation with customers if distribution is to set reasonable delivery schedules. This may sound very much like compromise, depending on the overall influence of sales or distribution in the company, but one party may end up on the better end of the deal. In some cases, this type of disagreement is not resolved, and the problem either continues or another method to resolve the conflict must be sought.

In conflict situations marked by avoidance or bargaining, the eventual use of authority as a method to resolve the conflict is often necessary. **Authority** simply refers to taking the conflict issue to a higher level, which normally is the conflicting parties' superior. A disagreement between sales and marketing research over who should collect data about buying practices of customers may be an issue that is not easily resolved. Sales personnel may expect the marketing research staff to be responsible for this activity, while marketing research personnel may believe the sales staff can best interact with the company's customers. Due to time and budget limitations, each unit may be unwilling to budge from its position that the other unit should perform this activity. In such a situation, the issue may have to be resolved by the vice president of marketing or whatever executive is in charge of sales and marketing research. Intradepartmental conflicts may easily resort to a higher authority, but interdepartmental conflicts between sales and research and development or production, for example, may mean taking the issue to the firm's top management if it cannot be worked out by the department supervisors.

Although a higher authority may be needed in some situations, problem-solving is the best method of resolving intra- and interdepartmental conflicts. With **problem-solving**, parties to the conflict seek a solution that will satisfy the goals of each of them. In this way, both parties may in fact gain or benefit, and at least neither party would lose. The earlier conflict cited between sales and production, which used compromise, could also be approached from a problem-solving stance. In using problem-solving, sales personnel may get production to increase the production levels of a given product to satisfy the sales staff's desires. In addition, the longer production run on one product may be offset by the reduced production runs on one or more other products that the sales staff is willing to cut back. In this case, overall production costs may not increase. The sales staff may be better off, and production may at least be no worse off.

The problem-solving method is particularly useful to sales personnel in resolving conflict since this technique sets the stage for future cooperative efforts with other marketing functions or nonmarketing departments. Since neither party has lost, a good working relationship has been established, and the likelihood is greater that future disagreements may be handled successfully. The use of problem-solving, as opposed to the authority method, may also elevate higher management's opinion of sales personnel because they are able to work out problems and disagreements without always involving their superiors.

Although conflict is inevitable in any organization, how the sales staff deals with conflict ultimately determines how good the working relationships are with other personnel throughout the organization. Strong intra- and interdepartmental relationships built on respect and trust should enable sales personnel to better respond to customer needs. The salesperson's customers may also come to see the sales representative as an individual who has considerable influence representing the customer's interests in his or her company.

Figure 13-2 Serving customers well, a critical task of market-oriented companies, should not be the focus only of customer service personnel.

INTERDEPARTMENTAL COOPERATION AND THE MARKETING CONCEPT

A key element of a company's practice of the marketing concept is its ability to generate profits and customer satisfaction. To do so, a coordinated or integrated marketing effort must be established. **Coordinated marketing** means the various marketing functions (for example, sales, market research, advertising) must be integrated with each other, and marketing must be integrated with other departments in the company.[9] It has been suggested that in addition to marketing to customers—that is, external marketing—successful companies first must engage in internal marketing. **Internal marketing** is the task of successfully hiring, training, and motivating company employees to serve customers well.[10] In marketing-oriented companies, customers are the principal focus, with particular attention given to the relationships between customers and the company's front-line personnel, the sales force.

Stating a belief in the marketing concept and actually practicing it are two very different things. A company's departments tend to view each other as adversaries competing for limited resources or increased influence. If each function or department in a company were reoriented to consider the next organizational level as its "customer," the adversarial nature of departmental relationships may decrease or end.[11] As an example, research and development would serve produc-

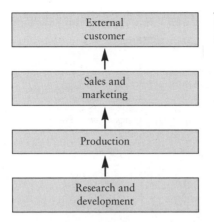

Exhibit 13-10 A Company's Internal Customers

tion, which in turn would serve sales and marketing (see Exhibit 13-10). While the company's customers would be the overall focus, departments in the company would be both marketers to and customers of other departments.

In order to build and develop this operating philosophy within the company, key changes would be needed. First, a company may want to develop multifunctional teams (purchasing, research and development, production, marketing) that would examine the needs of both internal and external customers. Rather than considering these needs in isolation from one another, departmental representatives would work as a team. Second, they would place an increased emphasis on the problem-solving method to resolve differences as opposed to the avoidance, bargaining, or authority methods. The objective would not be for one department to win over another, but for the company as a whole to be in a better position to effectively and efficiently meet customer needs. A third step, and possibly the most crucial, would be to modify or reorient the company's reward system.[12] Instead of rewarding various departments for meeting their own objectives, rewards would be given to departments that fill internal customer needs (for example, research and development satisfying production or production satisfying marketing and sales) and contribute to the overall satisfaction of the company's customers as measured by profits, market share, or return-on-investment, among other measures. Intra- and interdepartmental cooperation, coupled with a focus on the company's external customers, would be the keys to attracting and retaining customers and providing a competitive edge for the company's sales force. (See Exhibit 13-11.)

Exhibit 13-11 Intradepartmental and Interdepartmental Relationships

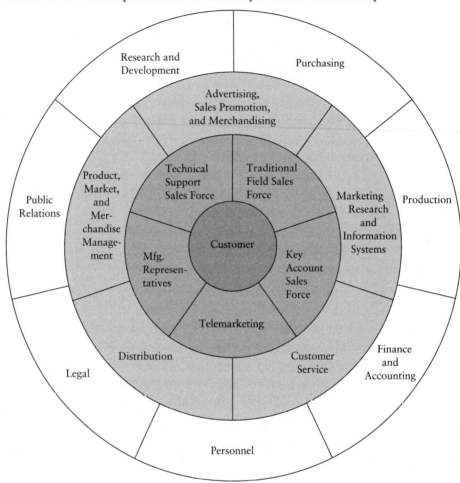

1. Sales personnel must understand the perspectives of other company personnel in research and development, purchasing, production, finance and accounting, personnel, legal, and public relations.

2. The relationships with other departments in the organization are likely to be marked by periods of both cooperation and conflict. A sales representative

needs to be aware of the various causes or sources of conflict between or among departments.

3. To be more effective in one's position, a salesperson should be knowledgeable of the various methods by which conflict can be resolved including avoidance, accommodation, compromise, bargaining, authority, and problem-solving.

4. A coordinated marketing effort by a company requires intradepartmental and interdepartmental cooperation.

5. The practice of the marketing concept means that all the employees of a company in the various departments are focused on how their duties and responsibilities have an impact on the company's customers.

QUESTIONS FOR DISCUSSION AND REVIEW

1. Compare and contrast the different emphases between sales and production and between sales and finance and accounting.

2. What is meant by the term *conflict*?

3. Conflict arises for a variety of reasons. What are three sources or causes of conflict?

4. Departments may differ in goal, time, and interpersonal orientation as well as formal structure. Discuss the differences between sales and production on these dimensions.

5. In resolving conflict, what are the differences among compromise, bargaining, and problem-solving?

6. Describe the concept of coordinated marketing. How does internal marketing affect coordinated marketing?

7. How do departments within a company serve as customers of other departments in the company?

8. Discuss three ways in which coordinated marketing could be implemented in a company.

9. Discuss the pros and cons of the following statement: In terms of a company's overall operations, the sales function is much more critical to the firm's success than the production function.

10. In dealing with interdepartmental relationships, sales personnel should strive to increase their level of influence in the company to maximize their gain, or at least to minimize their loss. Agree or disagree? Why?

CASE 13-1 INTERDEPARTMENTAL COOPERATION OR CONFLICT?

Jim Sanders was eagerly awaiting the weekly golf outing with Wendy Adair and Jack Madden. Jim, Wendy, and Jack were all employed by Information Management, Inc., a manufacturer and marketer of computer hardware systems. Jim, who was in sales, had been with Information Management, Inc. for the past four years. During that time, he had developed a good working relationship with Wendy, who worked in research and development, and Jack, who was in the production department. While they tried not to discuss work projects during their weekly golf match, they often ended up talking about either new products on the market or products in the development stage.

As they began their round of golf, both Wendy and Jack were commenting about the latest product that Information Management, Inc., had introduced to the market. The new product, the XL24 computer, was the latest technology in portable computers. Wendy commented that she thought this new product had a real chance of making Information Management the market leader in portable computers. Jack said the production department had anticipated large orders for the new product, although to date, the anticipated demand had not developed. Both Wendy and Jack felt that the working relationships among research and development, production, and sales had to be more coordinated and cooperative for market success, even if the new product was leading-edge technology.

After they concluded their round of golf, Jim Sanders started his fifteen minute drive from the golf course to his home. While he had enjoyed the round of golf with Wendy and Jack, he was troubled by the apparent lack of cooperation between the three key areas of Information Management, Inc. After finishing dinner that evening with his family, he retired to the den to contemplate how the interdepartmental working relationships at Information Management, Inc., could be improved.

QUESTIONS

1. In terms of the sales-research and development working relationship, what could be possible areas for conflict and cooperation?

2. With respect to the sales-production relationship, what could be possible areas for conflict and cooperation?

3. How does this case situation relate to a company's internal and external customers?

CASE 13-2 DIAGNOSING THE CAUSES OF CONFLICT

The Nelson Company, a manufacturer of industrial valves and meters, has been in business for forty years. John Jenkins, Sales Manager, and Jill Brown, Production Superintendent, have both been with the company for the past twelve years. The Nelson Company is well respected by its competitors, but the company has seen its market share slip during the past two years, which has had a negative impact on the firm's financial resources.

John Jenkins and Jill Brown report directly to the President of the Nelson Company, Sam Taylor. Mr. Taylor, who has been with the company since its beginning, is scheduled to retire in two years, when he will be sixty-five years old. Given their time with the company, the likely successor will be either Jenkins or Brown, although it is not clear if outside candidates will also be considered.

To try to reverse the company's declining market share, Sam Taylor decided to concentrate on becoming more competitive by exercising greater control over production costs and transferring dollars from the advertising to the sales budget, since in selling industrial products the promotional program relies more heavily on personal selling than advertising. Sam Taylor also appointed Jenkins and Brown to co-chair a company task force to determine what else the company can do to turn the current situation around quickly.

QUESTIONS

1. Even before considering the specifics of the case, what differences of opinion would you expect between Jenkins and Brown given their positions in the company?

2. Given the material presented in the case, what are likely to be three sources or causes of potential conflict?

3. How does Sam Taylor affect the potential conflict between John Jenkins and Jill Brown?

CASE 13-3 DEVELOPING A COORDINATED SALES AND MARKETING EFFORT

Sandy Evans, sales manager for Toys for Kids, is very concerned about the lack of cooperation between her sales representatives and the company's product development and production departments. With a declining birth rate and the resulting smaller families, competition in the toy market geared to children age twelve and under has become particularly intense.

Ms. Evans believes only a coordinated and integrated sales and marketing approach by the company will enable it to be effective in the toy market. In essence, all of the company's departments will need to pull in the same direction, with the ultimate focus on satisfying customers' needs and wants. This is very challenging, since the market for toys includes children and their parents who often make a joint child-parent decision to buy a toy.

Ms. Evans has called a meeting of her sales force for one week from today. She knows the present situation is marked by a lack of cooperation and some conflict and must change as soon as possible. She is not sure why the working relationships between sales and the other departments have not developed into a coordinated and integrated effort. The success of Toys for Kids is the issue at hand, and Sandy Evans knows her future with the company is also at stake.

QUESTIONS

1. If you were Sandy Evans, what would be your major objective at the meeting with the company's sales representatives?

2. What issues could Sandy Evans stress with respect to the product development/production/sales relationship?

3. How could Sandy Evans use the internal marketing concept in this situation?

NOTES

1. Edward E. Messikomer, "Du Pont's 'Marketing Community,'" *Business Marketing* (October 1987): 90, 92.

2. Philip Kotler, *Marketing Management: Analysis, Planning, Implementation, and Control* (Englewood Cliffs, N.J.: Prentice-Hall, 1972), 277.

3. Paul D. Klimstra and Ann T. Raphael, "Integrating R&D and Business Strategy," *Research Technology Management* (January–February 1992): 22–28. See also Massoud M. Saghafi, Ashok Gupta, and Jagdish Sheth, "R&D/Marketing Interfaces in the Telecommunications Industry," *Industrial Marketing Management* (1990): 87–94.

4. Joseph G. Ormsby and Dillard B. Tinsley, "The Role of Marketing in Material Requirements Planning Systems," *Industrial Marketing Management* (1991): 67–72. See also Alvin J. Williams and William C. Smith, "Involving Purchasing in Product Development," *Industrial Marketing Management* (1990): 315–19.

5. Caron H. St. John and Ernest H. Hall, Jr., "The Interdependency Between Marketing and Manufacturing," *Industrial Marketing Management* (1991): 223–29.

6. Leon C. Megginson, Donald C. Mosley, and Paul H. Pietri, Jr., *Management: Concepts and Applications* (New York: Harper and Row, 1983), 437.

7. Ibid.

8. Don Hellriegel and John W. Slocum, Jr., *Management* (Reading, Mass.: Addison-Wesley, 1982), 666.

9. Philip Kotler, *Marketing Management: Analysis, Planning, Implementation, and Control*, 6th ed. (Englewood Cliffs, N.J.: Prentice-Hall, 1988), 20.

10. Ibid., 21.

11. Charles O'Neal, "Applying the Marketing Concept to Satisfy Internal 'Customers,'" *Marketing News* (March 14, 1988): 18.

12. Ibid.

PART FIVE

Strategic Alternatives and Tactical Actions

CHAPTER 14

The Salesperson's Self-Management Process

LEARNING OBJECTIVES

After studying this chapter, you should be able to:

1. Identify the steps in the personal planning process.
2. Describe customer analysis vis-à-vis customer classification.
3. Describe the expected value analysis of prospects.
4. Describe the calculations necessary to determine a salesperson's effective selling time.
5. Identify the major time wasters for sales representatives and ways to minimize them.
6. Explain the meaning and causes of stress and the methods for reducing stress.
7. Define the key terms used in this chapter.

KEY TERMS

- diagnosis
- prognosis
- objectives
- strategy
- tactics
- controls
- customer maintenance
- customer development
- 80-20 rule
- effective selling time
- stress
- stressors
- strain

CHARLIE BATES was a Sales Representative for a major company in the life insurance field. He thoroughly enjoyed selling life insurance and consistently was a top producer in his district. While other salespeople were playing golf and tennis with their customers, Charlie put all of his energy into selling. He felt playing golf was a waste of time and he did not enjoy playing tennis. To his co-workers, Charlie was friendly but highly competitive. He liked to win—not just once in a while, but all the time. Charlie always seemed like he was in a hurry. He hated sales meetings and rarely took time to interact with his customers on anything but a business basis. Charlie's sales manager thought Charlie was a great time manager. Charlie's colleagues were not so sure. From your perspective, what are the pros and cons of Charlie's behavior?

Effectively managing his or her time in dealing with a wide variety of individuals and organizations is one of the major challenges for the professional salesperson. Relationship management, both inside and outside the salesperson's company, is time-consuming but critical to the salesperson's success. Outside the company, the salesperson must devote adequate time and attention to existing customers and potential prospects for the company's products or services. Inside the organization, the relationships with other marketing personnel in areas such as advertising and marketing research, as well as nonmarketing personnel in production and finance, must be developed and maintained in order for the salesperson to be more effective in fostering strong customer relationships. In addition, time commitments for family and friends often present the salesperson with conflicting choices or situations that may be difficult to resolve.

A professional sales representative's productivity and effectiveness will depend to a large extent on how well he or she can balance competing demands for a limited amount of time. The salesperson must first and foremost be good at self-management since successful people rely mainly on managing themselves as opposed to being managed by others. This is particularly true in most selling situations, since the salesperson often is not in direct and frequent face-to-face contact with her or his superior. The challenge then is to understand how a salesperson can best respond to the various demands that are placed on his or her limited amount of time.

A PERSONAL PLANNING PROCESS

A starting point in the salesperson's self-management process may simply be developing an understanding of where he or she is at the present time and what needs to be done for the future. Frequent attention is given to planning sales presentations, product demonstrations, or calls on prospects. The salesperson, however, may view each activity separately rather than stepping back and looking at the big picture of his or her professional development and productivity.

A technique for beginning the task of self-management is the use of a personal planning process (see Exhibit 14-1), which includes six steps with an accompanying question for the salesperson to consider at each step.[1]

Step 1: Make a Diagnosis

In the first step, **diagnosis**, the salesperson attempts to define where he or she is and why this situation has occurred. The purpose of step 1 is to provide a benchmark or status report on what the salesperson has achieved to date. For example, the salesperson may define the present situation in terms of the amount of sales made to different customers, the likelihood of converting certain prospects into customers, new accounts that have been gained, or old accounts that have been lost. This assessment may give the salesperson a key reference point for future comparisons.

Step 2: Make a Prognosis

The second step of the personal planning process, **prognosis**, focuses on assessing where the salesperson is heading in the near future. The assumption is made that the salesperson will continue to conduct his or her activities in much the same manner as in the past. Step 2 allows the salesperson to forecast whether things are

Steps	Questions
1. Diagnosis	Where am I now and why?
2. Prognosis	Where am I headed?
3. Objectives	Where should I be headed?
4. Strategy	What is the best way for me to get where I'm going?
5. Tactics	Who? What? When? Where? Why? How?
6. Controls	Have I accomplished my objectives?

Exhibit 14-1 Personal Planning Process

likely to stay the same, deteriorate, or improve. Depending on upcoming changes in a company's new product development program, changing economic conditions, or the entry or exit of a competitor, the future may look better, worse, or about the same from the salesperson's perspective. Just as a company looks at the past, present, and future, the salesperson needs to evaluate the present situation, anticipated changes, and the effect of these on his or her chances for success.

Step 3: Establish Objectives

The third step, **objectives**, focuses on answering the question of where the salesperson would like to be at a certain time in the future. This is different than step 2, which centers on where the salesperson will be, not necessarily where he or she would like to be with respect to sales, customer relations, or new accounts, among other issues. Just as one would set objectives for a new product or a new market, the salesperson would plan for what he or she wants to accomplish in the next month, quarter, or year. The salesperson's answers to the questions for the prognosis and objectives steps may or may not be the same. If the answer is the same, the salesperson may consider himself or herself on track. If, however, the answers differ, the difference between where things are versus where they should be headed may highlight the actions or decisions the salesperson must make to reach the desired situation. This step is critical for the salesperson, since working without a strong sense of direction or well-stated goals may lead to a great deal of activity, but not necessarily in the desired direction or with the desired result.

Step 4: Determine a Strategy

Strategy, step 4 of the personal planning process, is centered on defining the best way(s) for the salesperson to achieve his or her objectives (step 3). Although a great many activities may be available, the salesperson should undertake the ones most appropriate for meeting his or her objectives. For example, a salesperson who wants to increase overall sales in dollars and units could spend more time with prospects, major or key accounts, small accounts that might become larger ones, or any combination of these. The key question is which specific action or actions would be the most effective; rarely will there be a simple and direct answer. The salesperson will need to balance and weigh various alternative actions that may be taken to accomplish each objective. Failure to address the strategy question may cause the salesperson to go off in all directions, with little order or priority.

Step 5: Identify Tactics

Once the salesperson has specified the objectives and strategies, his or her attention must shift to tactics. **Tactics** represent the specific detailed actions that will be taken to implement a strategy and accomplish an objective. More specifically, tactics will state the who, what, when, where, why, and how of an action to be taken. The best objectives and strategies a salesperson has may have little if any effect if the tactics are not addressed. For example, a sales representative may be very concerned about staying competitive with a competitor's new product development efforts. The salesperson must design a strategy with accompanying tactics to deal with the problem, which may call for careful coordination among the salesperson and personnel in research and development and in production. In addition, the salesperson may want to test reactions of customers, such as dealers and distributors of the company's products, with periodic marketing research surveys and occasional test markets of new product improvements or modifications. Without coordination among individuals and groups inside and outside the salesperson's company, the salesperson's company may not act or react in a timely manner to major changes in the marketplace.

Step 6: Establish Controls

The final step in the personal planning process, **controls**, refers to the salesperson's measures or assessments of progress to determine whether or not the objectives have been accomplished. Step 6 may also provide feedback not only on objective accomplishment, but also on the effectiveness of particular strategies or tactics. Without periodic assessment of the progress that has been made, the salesperson will not have an indication of whether things should continue as is or undergo a major revision. If the strategy the salesperson laid out to achieve greater dollar and unit sales, such as focusing more attention on major accounts, is not working then steps must be taken to either make the strategy work or select a different strategy. Likewise, the controls or evaluation step may pinpoint problems in tactics. The failure of a company to be competitive in the marketplace may be due to an inadequate marketing information system, which fails to anticipate customer reactions as well as those of competitors. Isolating the problems related to who, what, when, where, why, or how may then allow the salesperson to make an appropriate decision to correct the problem or shortcoming.

Using the six steps and questions of the personal planning process allows a salesperson to quickly assess where things are, where things are headed, the best way or ways to get there, and the steps necessary to do so. This relatively simple approach can aid the salesperson's efforts at self-management. Specific questions, however, will remain as how to best handle key constituencies outside and inside the salesperson's company.

CUSTOMER AND PROSPECT ANALYSIS

Once the sales representative has a good idea of the amount of time he or she will need for various selling and nonselling activities, an in-depth analysis of customers and prospects is needed. In very general terms, a salesperson must spend time on both customer maintenance and customer development. **Customer maintenance** refers to those activities undertaken to ensure that existing customers remain loyal to the salesperson's company.[2] This may include devoting the necessary time and effort to assure that a customer's existing needs or problems are satisfied, as well as staying on top of new developments in the customer's operations. In contrast, **customer development** includes those activities that identify and attract potential customers or prospects to do business with the salesperson.[3] Since a certain amount of turnover of existing customers is bound to occur over time, customer development is critical for the salesperson's and the company's long-run success. The task is to effectively balance the time allotted to customer maintenance and customer development. Failure to devote adequate time to each of these major activities will mean that the overall productivity of the salesperson will decline in either the short- or long-run.

Customer Analysis

In order to best utilize the time available, a sales representative must have a very clear picture of the range of customers she or he currently serves. Although every customer is important, it is also true that some customers are more important than others. A common rule-of-thumb is that a very small percentage of a salesperson's customers may account for a very large percentage of total sales. This situation is often referred to as the **80-20 rule**—meaning that 80 percent of sales come from 20 percent of customers or products. The implication of the 80-20 rule is that a salesperson must be sure to spend the right amount of time on the right customers. Conversely, spending too much time on average or marginal customers may lead to less productivity or effectiveness by the salesperson in meeting sales objectives. It is important for a salesperson to recognize that another implication of the 80-20 rule is that 20 percent of sales may come from 80 percent of the total number of customers. A salesperson can quickly realize that not all customers are to be treated equally with respect to the time allotted to each.

In order to spend the appropriate amount of time on various customers, the salesperson needs to develop some customer classification system based on a thorough analysis of existing customers. Exhibit 14-2 presents a customer classification system based on annual sales to each customer. Other methods of classifying customers could be by annual profits generated from sales to a customer and average order size. Exhibit 14-2 shows that Caron Smith, a Sales Representative for the XYZ Company, has seventy-five customers, with sales of over $50,000 per year to ten customers, $30,000 to $50,000 to twenty-five customers, and below $30,000 to forty customers. In this example, Smith has decided, based on annual sales to each customer category, that those customers in category A will be called on once per month or twelve times a year. In contrast, customers in categories B and C will be called on six and four times per year, respectively. The key point is that the number of sales calls or the amount of time spent with each customer will depend on the amount of sales each has generated, or is likely to generate, for the sales representative.[4]

Although the customer classification system presented in Exhibit 14-2 appears relatively straightforward, there are some other customer analysis issues that are not easy to resolve. First, whether a customer is placed in category A, B, or C, the customer is likely to want more attention and time than the salesperson has allocated to that account. Customers in category A may desire to see the sales representative twice rather than once a month. Second, difficult decisions will face the salesperson when customers in any category are very close to the upper or lower limits of the category. For example, a customer that generates annual sales of $45,000 may deserve more than bimonthly sales calls, but not necessarily every month. Similarly, an account that has declined from $80,000 annual sales to $52,000 may not justify a monthly sales call, particularly if future sales to this customer are likely to decrease even further. A third consideration for the salesperson to address is what to do with accounts that appear at the bottom of category C. The call frequency may be reduced to once every six months, or the salesperson may de-

---

Exhibit 14-2 Customer Classification System

Salesperson: Caron Smith
Company: XYZ Company

Category	Number of Customers	Annual Sales	Call Frequency	Total Number of Calls
A	10	$50,000 and above	Monthly	120
B	25	$30,000 to $50,000	Bimonthly	150
C	40	$30,000 and below	Every three months	160

cide the account does not justify a face-to-face sales call and can be handled by telephone. Finally, a sales representative will need to continually analyze customers to determine whether they should be reclassified to a higher or lower category in terms of sales call frequency. Due to "opportunity costs," there may come a time when a customer may be dropped completely if other accounts have more actual or potential sales for the salesperson to develop. The bottom line for customer analysis and classification will be the value of the customer in relation to the limited amount of selling time the salesperson has available.

Prospect Analysis

Just as customer maintenance is a very important activity for the salesperson, adequate time and effort must also be devoted to the task of customer development. Although there may be numerous prospects for the salesperson to call on, a key consideration is to determine which potential prospects should or should not receive attention. One method of making this decision is for the salesperson to use an expected value analysis of prospects (see Exhibit 14-3).[5]

The salesperson will need to have an estimate of each prospect's dollar purchases for the salesperson's product or service to perform an expected value analysis. This information may be gained by simply asking a customer about how much he or she spends each year on a certain product category. If direct questioning is not appropriate or feasible, the estimate might be gained from a marketing research study, such as a questionnaire sent to various prospects. Another option is to determine the purchases of a product or service made in a particular geographic area and then estimate the percentage of those purchases that each prospect in the area is likely to have made during the past year. At best, this estimate of dollar purchases for each prospect is inexact. A rough estimate, however,

Exhibit 14-3 Expected Value Analysis of Prospects

Prospect	Prospect's Purchases	Probability of Converting a Prospect to a Customer (Percentage)	Expected Value	Customer Category
#1	$ 80,000	40	$32,000	B
#2	$ 40,000	20	$ 8,000	C
#3	$ 60,000	75	$45,000	B
#4	$120,000	50	$60,000	A

is better than no estimate at all. Without some procedure or technique of analyzing prospects, the salesperson will be unable to identify the best prospects to pursue.

Once the salesperson has an estimate of each prospect's dollar purchases of the product or service for a particular time period, he or she must also estimate the probability of converting the prospect to a customer, as shown in Exhibit 14-3. If probabilities were not considered, prospects 1, 3, and 4 would be placed in category A of the customer classification system (Exhibit 14-2), since the annual sales to each would be over $50,000, and prospect 2 would be a category B customer. In almost all cases, however, a salesperson will not rate a prospect as being 100 percent likely—an absolute certainty—to become a customer. A salesperson thus must make a professional judgment as to the probability that a prospect will become a customer for his or her company. Although this estimate is subjective, it still may be appropriate, provided a degree of realism is used in making the estimates.

In Exhibit 14-3, the probability of converting a prospect to a customer ranges from a high of 75 percent for prospect 3 to a low of 20 percent for prospect 2. In order to calculate the expected value of each prospect in terms of sales to that account, the probability is multiplied by the prospect's estimated dollar purchases— for example, for each prospect in Exhibit 14-3: $80,000 \times .40 = $32,000$; $40,000 \times .20 = $8,000$; $60,000 \times .75 = $45,000$; and $120,000 \times .50 = $60,000$. Once he or she has made these calculations, the salesperson has a much better assessment of each prospect's dollar potential as a customer. For each of the four prospects in this example, prospect 4 would be a category A customer, prospects 1 and 3 would be category B customers, and prospect 2 would be a category C customer. It is interesting to note that even though prospect 1 has larger dollar purchases of the product or service than prospect 3, the higher probability of converting prospect 3 to a customer, as compared to prospect 1, results in prospect 3 being a better prospect in terms of expected value.

The purpose of prospect analysis using the expected value technique is to make sure the appropriate attention and effort are given to the right prospect. At the same time, the salesperson does not want to pay too much attention to the wrong prospects. Given the expected value of each of the prospects in Exhibit 14-3, prospect 4 would be called on monthly, prospects 1 and 3 bimonthly, and prospect 2 once every three months. In this way, prospects and customers of similar value in either actual or potential dollar purchases would receive the same number of sales calls. The salesperson should not forget that prospecting and effective prospect analysis is a continuing activity since existing customers may change over time due to competitive sales efforts, moves or relocations, and possible dissatisfaction with the salesperson and his or her company or product. The salesperson thus has to balance keeping customers or customer maintenance with attracting new customers or customer development in order to be successful in both the short- and long-term.

Customer and prospect analysis is only half of the analysis that the salesperson must conduct in order to effectively plan how to further customer maintenance and development. The other key factor is the amount of effective selling time that the salesperson has to conduct these activities. **Effective selling time** refers to the actual time spent selling to customers or prospecting for new business. Factors that limit selling time include traveling and waiting time, reports, paperwork, and meetings.

The first step in determining a salesperson's effective selling time should be an analysis of the total selling days available. As shown in Exhibit 14-4, the 365 days in a calendar year would be reduced by days devoted to vacations, holidays, and weekends. The remaining time available for selling would be further reduced by time spent doing paperwork; attendance at conventions and conferences; and absences due to illness, jury duty, or some other reason. Exhibit 14-4 shows that effective selling time amounts to only 236 days or approximately 65 percent of the year.[6]

The 236 days of effective selling time would also be further reduced for those sales representatives whose position requires extensive travel. Exhibit 14-5 shows the various numbers of effective selling days that would result depending on the amount of travel a salesperson was required to do. Assuming the salesperson works an eight-hour day and travels an estimated 50 miles per hour by automobile, the salesperson who travels 5,000 miles per year would lose an additional 12.5 travel days, further reducing effective selling time from 236 to 223.5 days. By com-

Calendar year (days)		365
Minus	Vacations	10	
	Holidays	5	
	Weekends	104	
Total		119	**246**
Minus	Nonselling time due to paperwork, meetings, conventions, illness, jury duty, etc.	10	
Effective selling time (days)		**236**

Exhibit 14-4 Effective Selling Time

Exhibit 14-5 Effective Selling Time Minus Travel Time

Travel (miles per year)	Effective Selling Time**	Travel Time**	Net Effective Selling Time**
5,000	236	12.5	223.5
10,000	236	25	211
15,000	236	37.5	198.5
20,000	236	50	186

*Assumes travel at an average of 50 miles per hour.
**Computed in days.

parison, a salesperson traveling 20,000 miles per year would lose a total of 50 selling days from 236, leaving only 186 days. One can quickly see how extensive travel will drastically reduce a salesperson's amount of effective selling time.[7]

To effectively assess the impact of the salesperson's work-load potential on customer maintenance and development, an additional factor must be considered. The number of effective selling days after travel as shown in Exhibit 14-5 must be analyzed with respect to the number of sales calls per year that a sales representative can make. This calculation will depend on the average length of each sales call. By taking the number of effective selling days times eight hours per day and then dividing by the average length of a sales call, the total number of sales calls per year can be determined. For example, in Exhibit 14-6 the salesperson who travels 10,000 miles per year would have 211 effective selling days and would be able to make 1,688 one-hour sales calls per year ($8 \times 211 = 1,688$). By comparison, if the same salesperson's sales calls averaged two hours each, only half of the 1,688 calls or 844 calls on customers and prospects would be possible.[8]

The calculation of total effective selling days is a key factor in assessing the work load that a salesperson can undertake. Modifications to the number of effective selling days due to travel time and the average length of each sales call are

Exhibit 14-6 Annual Sales Calls

Travel (miles per year)	Effective Selling Time (days)	Average Length of Sales Calls (Hours)			
		1	2	3	4
5,000	223.5	1,788	894	596	447
10,000	211	1,688	844	563	422
15,000	198.5	1,588	794	529	397
20,000	186	1,488	744	496	372

Figure 14-1 The take-anywhere convenience of laptop computers allows salespeople to manage their time more efficiently.

required to determine the total number of calls a salesperson can make annually. The total annual sales calls can then be compared to the total calls required to be made on the salesperson's various customers and prospects.

TIME MANAGEMENT

One of the major problems confronting salespeople is the need to perform a wide variety of duties in a limited amount of time.[9] The salesperson must be constantly servicing existing customers as well as seeking potential new customers. In addition, he or she must maintain effective working relationships with company marketing and nonmarketing personnel. To become a more effective salesperson, the salesperson must also find time to keep abreast of new product information, changes in company policies and procedures, and professional development activities. In essence, the sales representative must become an excellent time manager.

In looking at the issue of time management, an appropriate starting point may be to analyze how salespeople actually spend their time. A survey of industrial salespeople (see Exhibit 14-7) indicates that salespeople spend only 25 percent of their time in face-to-face selling. In contrast, 47 percent of a salesperson's daily activities is spent traveling, waiting for interviews, doing paperwork, and attending sales meetings. The actual time spent selling, including service calls, totals only 50 percent of the salesperson's time. Thus, only half of the salesperson's time is spent on revenue-generating activities. Although each of the activities in Exhibit 14-7 may be important to the salesperson, efforts must be taken to improve the salesperson's time management.

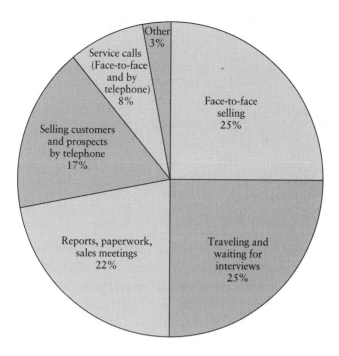

14-7 How an Average Salesperson Spends a Working Day

Source: McGraw-Hill Research 1986 "How Salespeople Spend Their Time" survey.

Time Wasters

Although everyone would acknowledge the importance of managing time effectively, a key aspect of doing so is the recognition and control of things that waste the salesperson's time. Exhibit 14-8 lists some of the most common time wasters as ranked by sales representatives. It is interesting to note that the top two time wasters are telephone interruptions or drop-in visitors. Another frequently mentioned time waster is meetings, which also appeared as a major time commitment for the salesperson in Exhibit 14-7. The rest of the time wasters listed in the exhibit, such as lack of self-discipline, lack of objectives, and procrastination, indicate poor self-management by the salesperson. Just as customer relationships must be managed, the salesperson must also be able to effectively manage the most scarce resource of all, his or her time.

A common problem for many salespeople is misallocating the amount of time and effort that is placed on various customers and prospects. The salesperson tends to give equal time to all accounts even though the accounts or customers may vary significantly in their sales and profit potential. To be effective, the salesperson must set objectives and priorities that will enable him or her to be the most productive. Exhibit 14-9 compares recommended selling times with actual selling times for various customer groups according to customer profitability. Dividing the salesperson's sixty accounts into three categories (A, B, or C) depending on

1. Telephone interruptions
2. Drop-in visitors
3. Lack of self-discipline
4. Crises
5. Meetings
6. Lack of objectives, priorities, and deadlines
7. Indecision and procrastination
8. Attempting too much at once
9. Leaving tasks unfinished
10. Unclear communication

Exhibit 14-8 Time Wasters for Sales Representatives

Source: Michael LeBoeuf, "Managing Your Time, Managing Yourself," *Business Horizons* (February 1980): 42. Reprinted from *Business Horizons*, February 1980. Copyright 1980 by the Foundation for the School of Business at Indiana University. Used with permission.

their relative profitability and assessing each group's total net profit and percentage of total net profit yields a rough estimate of the appropriate percentage of selling time for each account category.[10] The most interesting discovery will be a calculation of the actual percentage of selling time spent on each category of accounts. In the example in Exhibit 14-9 one can see that the amount of time spent on customer categories A and B is less than what is considered appropriate, while the amount of time spent on category C is two-and-one-half times what it should be. The salesperson in this example has a serious misallocation of time since the least profitable accounts are being overemphasized, and the most profitable accounts, particularly category A, are being underemphasized. This same type of analysis could also be conducted using sales and size of orders as well as the profitability measure shown in this example.

Exhibit 14-9 Selling Time and Customer Profitability

Customer Group*	Total Net Profit	Percent of Total Net Profit	Appropriate Percent of Selling Time	Actual Percent of Selling Time
A accounts	$6 million	60	60	50
B accounts	$3 million	30	30	25
C accounts	$1 million	10	10	25

*Assumes 20 accounts in each group.

Time Savers

The acknowledgment that one wastes time is only part of the task of striving for better time management.[11] The salesperson must also become more skilled and conscious of the need to employ time-saving strategies. A starting point in this process is to become aware of the dollars-and-cents value of the salesperson's time.

For example, assuming a salesperson works forty hours per week for a total of fifty weeks per year, the value of one hour of his or her time is shown below according to different levels of yearly earnings:

Yearly Earnings	Value of One Hour
$30,000	$15
$40,000	$20
$50,000	$25
$60,000	$30

One can quickly see from the above examples the value of one hour of a salesperson's time. The salesperson must be sure, therefore, to carefully use the limited time available on the most important selling activities. A quick calculation shows that if a salesperson is only selling 50 percent of the available time, then the hourly value of actual selling time would double—$30 per hour for those making $30,000 per year and $60 per hour for those making $60,000 per year.

Knowing the value of one's time should cause the salesperson to look for ways to better manage his or her time in order to increase productivity. An informative exercise for the salesperson would be to compare how he or she plans to spend time for a coming week to how the time is actually spent as the week progresses. For most individuals, chances are that the planned versus the actual time spent on different selling and nonselling activities would not be the same, with more time most likely spent on nonselling as opposed to selling.

Exhibit 14-10 lists some major steps a salesperson might take to further enhance effective time management. A key starting point might be to plan for the next day or the next week before that day or week actually begins. For many people, planning their time does not often begin until that particular day or week has already begun. In planning the next day or next week, the salesperson should make certain he or she does not overplan. Planning too many activities with little or no leeway for delays or interruptions may cause the salesperson more frustration as he or she is always trying to catch up. As each day passes, the items not completed the previous day are then added to the following day; sooner or later, they either overwhelm the salesperson or cause him or her to feel overwhelmed, which will adversely affect performance.

In scheduling various activities, the salesperson should prioritize the things that must or should be done from the very important to the least important. Using something as simple as the form shown in Exhibit 14-11 may help the salesperson schedule time. Priority A items would be tasks that have the highest priority and must be done first; B items would be things to do when most, if not all, A items had been handled; while C items would be those to take care of if possible, but they could be deferred to a later time if necessary. In essence, the salesperson would

1. Planning the day's work
2. Planning the week's work
3. Prioritizing activities
4. Scheduling recurring versus nonrecurring activities
5. Grouping similar work
6. Scheduling waiting versus working time
7. Knowing the best time of the day or week
8. Planning interruption-free time

Exhibit 14-10 Effective Time Management Steps

end up with things that must be done, things that should be done, and things that would be nice to do if time permits. The important point is that the salesperson must effectively prioritize the numerous activities that must be addressed.

The salesperson should also consider classifying the various activities to be completed into recurring versus nonrecurring activities. The salesperson may know that a certain activity, such as completing monthly call reports on customers and prospects, must be scheduled each and every month. On the other hand, going to a seminar on new product developments may occur randomly as the need arises or only once a year at a time that cannot be determined in advance. To avoid the problems of starting, stopping, and restarting each of these activities, the salesperson may also want to group similar work, such as telephone calls to customers and prospects or monthly paperwork. Avoiding the start-stop-start pattern can be a major time saver.

Another consideration for the salesperson in order to save time is to plan what he or she will do when confronted with waiting versus working time. Since a salesperson frequently has to wait to meet customers and prospects, he or she should decide what to do during this period to maximize the use of the waiting time. Making notes about a customer or prospect or planning the next day or week might be appropriate activities.

A final consideration for the salesperson—possibly the most important in terms of saving time—is deciding what is the best time of the day or week for the salesperson to tackle the most difficult activities. Since most individuals are known to be "morning" persons or "night" persons, a salesperson should be sure to use his or her best and most productive time whether it be morning, afternoon, or night to deal with critical activities, if at all possible. The salesperson should also do everything possible to ensure that this most productive time period is guarded from interruptions so time is not lost to less important activities that could be handled at other times.

Exhibit 14-11 Daily Priority Planning

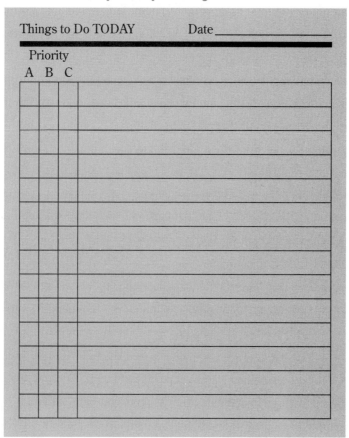

Things to Do TODAY   Date_____

Priority
A   B   C

Effective time management in dealing with customers, prospects, and the salesperson's company personnel should result in a number of benefits. First, the optimum amount of time will be spent with customers and prospects in accordance with their present or future value to the salesperson's company. Second, sales costs should be reduced since the salesperson will be more productive, particularly with respect to customer maintenance and customer development. Third, the salesperson's morale level and self-confidence should increase as he or she becomes more effective and efficient in dealing with the various demands placed on his or her limited amount of time.

STRESS MANAGEMENT AND THE SALESPERSON

The tasks of customer maintenance, customer development, and personal time management often will place large demands on the salesperson's ability to handle a wide range of activities with competing priorities. A salesperson has responsibilities to customers, prospects, and company personnel, as well as to family and friends, all of whom desire part of the salesperson's time. The end result of attempting to satisfy competing demands is that the salesperson often experiences a certain degree of stress. **Stress** refers to feelings of frustration, fear, conflict, pressure, anger, inadequacy, guilt, loneliness, or confusion. Because a salesperson's job requires dealing with a variety of people with varying needs and expectations, stress is extremely likely to occur.[12]

The causes of stress are **stressors**, which may be either external events such as not converting a prospect into a customer, or internal events such as thinking or believing you will not be able to convert a prospect into a customer. If stress is left unchecked or uncorrected, it may reach the point of **strain**, in which the salesperson may experience actual damage to his or her ability to deal with everyday situations[13]—avoiding prospecting activities for fear of failure, interacting less with customers or company personnel, or isolating oneself from family or friends.

A salesperson should recognize that everyone suffers from a certain degree of stress from daily activities. He or she should also be aware that there are many different classifications of stressors, such as positive-negative, daily-traumatic, and conscious-unconscious. For example, a negative stressor may be the loss of an account, and a positive stressor might be the assignment of the salesperson to a new and larger territory. Although the first would be a negative experience and the second a positive one, both could cause increasing stress. Similarly, stress can be traumatic, as in the case of the death of a spouse or child, although most stressors are daily occurrences such as difficulty getting along with one's boss or co-workers. Although both can be equally harmful, daily stressors are particularly so since they accumulate over time. Other stressors include conscious versus unconscious. A salesperson may fail to recognize or choose not to recognize that he or she is experiencing stress, and may attempt to ignore the situation.[14] If the salesperson's relationship with a customer or prospect is less than desired, the sales representative may choose to downplay or ignore the situation even though it exists and needs attention.

Indications that a salesperson is suffering from stress can be noted in a variety of behaviors such as the following:[15]

Renewal: requiring longer periods of time to renew or recharge oneself
Concentration: losing concentration or being easily distracted
Memory: forgetting key information easily remembered in the past
Sleep: getting too much or too little sleep
Appetite: overeating or loss of appetite
Patience: becoming impatient, often to the point of outright anger
Motivation: lacking drive, energy, or desire to perform the job

Mood: feeling depressed, sad, hopeless, or in some cases hyperactive
Relating: being unable to relate to others as indicated by withdrawal, hostility, or
                    rudeness

A classification system for individual behaviors, which has frequently been noted in different studies, is the comparison of Type A and Type B behaviors. Excessive competitive drive, hyperaggressiveness, impatience, and a compelling sense of time urgency are characteristic of Type A behavior. In addition, Type A behavior is seen as an attempt to accomplish more tasks, achieve more recognition, or participate in more events in less time, often in the face of real or imagined opposition from other persons. Indications that a person is Type A are found in descriptions such as the following:

Is highly competitive about everything

Always hurries even when not pressured

Becomes uneasy when waiting

Holds feelings in

Has few interests outside of work

Takes work very seriously

Always feels responsible

Is hard driving

Figure 14-2 Reserving time to relax with one's family—a stress-reducing activity—is an important component of the sales rep's time management program.

Type A behavior is very likely to lead to high stress levels if left unchecked. However, there are ways to reduce Type A behavior. The salesperson, as part of his or her time management program, should ensure that time is reserved for activities that will reduce stress from either the job, family, or some other source. Stress-reducing activities include physical exercise, reserving time to be alone, not working through the lunch hour, and sharing stress with a close friend or colleague in order to talk it out. Besides these behavioral steps, the salesperson should also attempt to make attitudinal changes that may decrease the level of stress. A certain amount of stress may be self-induced, due to the salesperson's attitudes. For example, people who feel they must always do a good job, want to change people or situations, dislike it when anything goes wrong, always want to be helpful to others, feel compelled to always be improving themselves, or place their work as the most important thing in their life may be holding attitudes that lead to increased stress. Although many of the above attitudes are appropriate, the problem arises when they are taken to the extreme.

A certain amount of stress is normal for all people and may, at certain levels, lead to increased and improved performance, but too much stress may be a limiting or damaging factor for a salesperson's performance and effectiveness. The salesperson must realize stress is very likely due to the demands of his or her position to serve customers, company personnel, family, and friends.

Recognizing the likelihood of stress and taking steps to reduce it can help the salesperson become more successful in developing work and social relationships that lead to greater personal satisfaction and higher productivity.

SUMMARY

1. To engage more effectively in self-management, a salesperson may use the personal planning process, which includes diagnosis, prognosis, objectives, strategy, tactics, and controls.

2. The salesperson should strive to balance customer maintenance and customer development activities by using a customer classification system and an expected value analysis of prospects.

3. A salesperson's effective selling time will depend on the number of hours or days available for selling activities, travel time, and the average length of each sales call.

4. The salesperson must take steps to maximize the time available for selling and minimize or control activities that are time wasters.

5. The salesperson should recognize that he or she may experience some degree of stress and should learn to deal with it in order to enhance his or her productivity.

QUESTIONS FOR DISCUSSION AND REVIEW

1. What is the difference between the diagnosis and prognosis steps of the personal planning process?

2. What would be the basis for classifying a customer as an A, B, or C account?

3. In prospect analysis, the key factor is the probability of converting a prospect to a customer. Yes or no?

4. What is the meaning of the term *effective selling time*?

5. What are three major time wasters for the salesperson? What methods can be used to deal with time wasters?

6. What are the differences among stress, strain, and stressors?

7. What are the indications that a salesperson may be experiencing stress?

8. The most effective sales representatives are very good at self-management. Yes or no? If yes, what are the indications of good self-management techniques?

9. Stress is normal for all individuals. Although a salesperson may experience more stress than some people in other occupations, stress may work to the salesperson's advantage. Agree or disagree?

10. Customer maintenance and customer development are both important activities, but in the final analysis customer maintenance is the key. Agree or disagree? Why?

CASE 14-1 A DAY IN THE LIFE OF A PROFESSIONAL SALESPERSON

Elyssa Kirchner has been a Sales Representative for a major pharmaceutical company for the past sixteen months. While she has done reasonably well in terms of servicing existing customers and attracting new ones, she feels pressure to perform even better as she progresses through her second year with the company. Elyssa knows that the more experienced sales representatives with the company have often told her about the competing demands on their time from individuals both inside and outside the company. Even though Elyssa is not married, she realizes that she needs time for activities away from her work that will help her maintain a healthy professional and personal balance in her life. She admitted to one of her close friends in the company that she does feel more stress even though she believes she is effectively planning her work days.

As Elyssa prepares for her next week on the job, she looks over her appointment schedule for the next day, which is Monday. Her schedule is as follows:

7:30 to 8:30 a.m.	Breakfast with Tom Jenkins (current customer)
8:45 to 9:30 a.m.	Paperwork and telephone calls in the office
9:30 to 11:00 a.m.	Meeting with advertising and sales promotion personnel on a promotional campaign for a new product
11:00 to 11:45 a.m.	Telephone calls to customers and prospects to set up appointments for the following week
Noon to 1:00 p.m.	Lunch with Jerry Jones (Elyssa's sales manager)
1:30 to 2:15 p.m.	Meeting with Gayle Finley (current customer)
2:30 to 3:45 p.m.	Meeting with Sandy Day (prospect)
4:00 to 5:00 p.m.	Paperwork and telephone calls in the office
6:30 to 8:30 p.m.	Dinner with Jim Brock (prospect)

QUESTIONS

1. In terms of hours spent on various activities, what percentage of her time for Monday will be spent on selling activities versus nonselling activities?

2. With respect to customer maintenance and customer development, what is your assessment of Elyssa Kirchner's time management?

3. If the above schedule is a typical day for Elyssa Kirchner, what advice would you give her in terms of time management?

CASE 14-2 CUSTOMER MAINTENANCE AND DEVELOPMENT

Emilynn Shaw, Sales Manager for Canyon Coatings, Inc., was in the process of reviewing the customer maintenance and development activities of one of her sales staff. She had the following information available to her:

Michael Reed

His territory required approximately 10,000 miles per year in travel and he currently had the following number and type of customers and prospects:

10 A customers and 4 A prospects

20 B customers and 10 B prospects

40 C customers and 25 C prospects

His call rate for each customer or prospect was monthly for type A, every two months for type B, and every three months for type C. His sales calls on both customers and prospects averaged three hours. If you were Ms. Shaw, what would be the answers to the following questions:

QUESTIONS

1. How many total sales calls per year are made on customers?

2. How many total sales calls per year are made on prospects?

3. Using information from Exhibits 14-5 and 14-6 and assuming that Michael Reed has 236 days of effective selling time per year and averages 50 miles per hour while traveling, what is your assessment of the situation?

CASE 14-3 PROSPECT ANALYSIS

Sally Evans, a Sales Representative for a major consumer goods organization, has identified five promising prospects. She is interested in spending the appropriate amount of time with each prospect.

QUESTIONS

Given the information in Exhibit 1 below,

1. What is the expected value of each prospect?

2. What is the number of annual sales calls for each prospect?

3. In conducting prospect analysis, such as in this example, what would concern you the most?

Exhibit 1 Prospect Analysis for Sally Evans

Prospect	Purchases	Probability of Converting the Prospect to a Customer	Expected Value	Number of Calls Per year
#1	$40,000	20%		
#2	$20,000	60%		
#3	$50,000	10%		
#4	$80,000	5%		
#5	$60,000	10%		

Call rates: $10,000 and over (monthly)
$5,000 to $10,000 (bimonthly)
Less than $5,000 (every three months)

NOTES

1. Philip Kotler, *Marketing Management: Analysis, Planning, and Control* (Englewood Cliffs, N.J.: Prentice-Hall, 1972), 366–71.

2. Thomas R. Wotruba, *Sales Management: Concepts, Practice, and Cases* (Santa Monica, Ca.: Goodyear Publishing, 1981), 143.

3. Ibid.

4. For further information on customer classification, see Porter Henry, "The Important Few—The Unimportant Many," *1980 Portfolio of Sales and Marketing Plans* (New York: Sales and Marketing Management, 1980), 42–45. See also Raymond W. LaForge, Clifford E. Young, and B. Curtis Hamm, "Increasing Sales Productivity Through Improved Sales Call Allocation Strategies," *Journal of Personal Selling and Sales Management* (November 1983): 52–59.

5. C. Robert Patty and Robert E. Hite, *Managing Salespeople* (Englewood Cliffs, N.J.: Prentice-Hall, 1988), 147.

6. Ibid., 148.

7. Ibid.

8. Ibid., 149.

9. William A. Weeks and Lynn R. Kahle, "Salespeople's Time Use and Performance," *Journal of Personal Selling and Sales Management* (Winter 1990): 29–37. See also Harish Sujan, Barton A. Weitz, and Mita Sujan, "Increasing Sales Productivity by Getting Salespeople to Work Smarter," *Journal of Personal Selling and Sales Management* (August 1988): 9–19.

10. Richard T. Hise, *Effective Salesmanship* (Hinsdale, Ill.: The Dryden Press, 1980), 345–47.

11. Carl K. Clayton, "How to Manage Your Time and Territory for Better Sales Results," *Personal Selling Power* (March 1990): 46. See also "Seven Thieves of Time That Can Steal Your Sales Away," *Personal Selling Power* (January–February 1990): 48–49.

12. Michael E. Cavanagh, "What You Don't Know About Stress," *Personnel Journal* (July 1988): 53. See also W. E. Patton, III, and Michael Questell, "Alcohol Abuse in the Sales Force," *Journal of Personal Selling and Sales Management* (November 1986): 39–51; W. E. Patten, III, "Drug Abuse in the Sales Force," *Journal of Personal Selling and Sales Management* (August 1988): 21–33.

13. Cavanagh, "What You Don't Know About Stress," 53.

14. Cavanagh, "What You Don't Know About Stress," 54–55.

15. Cavanagh, "What You Don't Know About Stress," 55.

CHAPTER 15

Emerging Trends and Technologies in Selling

LEARNING OBJECTIVES

After studying this chapter, you should be able to:

1. Recognize when it is appropriate to use face-to-face selling, national account management, and telemarketing.
2. Explain the rationale for national account management.
3. Describe how telemarketing can have an impact on various aspects of professional selling.
4. Explain the relationship of telemarketing to order processing, sales support, account management, and customer service.
5. Describe how customer service is a major factor for success in selling.
6. Explain the value of customer service in terms of communication, objectives, economics, and credibility.
7. Define the key terms used in this chapter.

KEY TERMS

- national account management
- selling center
- telemarketing
- customer service

N TODAY'S HIGHLY saturated marketing environment, customer service is one of the only ways left to grow market share. Every company serious about customer service should have a plan in place for getting feedback from its customers. Xerox, for example, surveys roughly 40,000 customers a month, getting back about 10,000 responses. Similarly, General Electric's GE Answer Center, which receives over three million calls per year, logs about 30% of its inquiries from customers who phone in before making a purchase, another third from those with questions on how to operate GE products, and the rest from people with service problems or other questions.[1]

NEW SELLING STRATEGIES

The role and activities of the professional salesperson are undergoing major changes due to the costs and potential revenues from serving various types of customers. As the cost of each industrial sales call has risen to over $200, along with the need for four to five sales calls to close a sale, closer attention is being paid to how best to serve diverse customer types and sizes.[2] Although past buyer-seller relationships have focused almost exclusively on face-to-face selling techniques, the 1990s will see greater use of national account management and telemarketing.

Exhibit 15-1 shows that the traditional use of face-to-face selling included small, medium, and large accounts, and ranged from prospecting for customers to closing, after-sale service, and reordering. In contrast, Exhibit 15-2 reveals how national account management and telemarketing have entered the picture. Specifically, national account management will be used primarily to serve large accounts because of their revenue potential, and telemarketing will be used for small accounts due to the costs of serving these accounts. It is important for the professional salesperson to understand the meaning and use of both national account management and telemarketing with respect to the development and maintenance of customer relationships.

NATIONAL ACCOUNT MANAGEMENT

A truism of selling is that a relatively small number of customers account for a disproportionately large share of sales. This is known as the 80-20 rule—80 percent

Traditional Stage in Selling Process

Account Size	Prospect/ Qualify	Present/ Close	Service/ Reorder
Large	Face-to-Face Selling (FTF)	FTF	FTF
Medium	FTF	FTF	FTF
Small	FTF	FTF	FTF

Exhibit 15-1
Traditional Selling

Source: Richard Cardozo and Shannon Shipp, "New Selling Methods Are Changing Industrial Sales Management," *Business Horizons* (September–October 1987): 26. Reprinted from *Business Horizons*, September–October 1987. Copyright 1987 by the Foundation for the School of Business at Indiana University. Used with permission.

of the customers contribute 20 percent of the sales or profits, or 20 percent of the customers account for 80 percent of the sales.

In recent years some companies have recognized the importance of the high-volume/high-profit customer by deciding to identify these customers and then assign special sales attention to them. To do this, these companies have restructured their marketing operations to include **national account management**, thereby dedicating a portion of their staff, either an individual or sales team, to serving those major or key accounts.[3]

New Stage in Selling Process

Account Size	Prospect/ Qualify	Present/ Close	Service/ Reorder
Large	National account management (NAM)	NAM	NAM
Medium	Telemarketing (TM)	FTF	FTF and TM
Small	TM	TM	TM

Exhibit 15-2 New Selling Strategies

Source: Richard Cardozo and Shannon Shipp, "New Selling Methods," p. 26. Reprinted from *Business Horizons*, September–October 1987. Copyright 1987 by the Foundation for the School of Business at Indiana University. Used with permission.

National Account Rationale

From the seller's standpoint, the most obvious reason to give national account status to a key customer is to protect the business revenues generated by that account. Another reason is to help develop solutions to complex problems that may affect many areas of a customer's company. The "product" then becomes an augmented product—the basic product plus planning, installation, and maintenance assistance that can help facilitate the client's overall operations.

Each special customer is assigned a national account team composed of specialists trained to help solve that customer's particular problems. In contrast to the traditional marketing approach, which focuses attention on the product and has little or no concern for related or needed services, the national account team provides expertise, resource personnel (technical consultants), and postsale service personnel. The team creates a differentiated or customized product or service to fit the customer's particular needs. This is known as the holistic approach to marketing.

An example of how a national account sales team can add value to a product is the sale of telemarketing by American Telephone and Telegraph's (AT&T) Long Lines Division. Instead of merely selling the product—WATS (wide area telephone service) lines (800 service) or equipment—a national account sales team is assigned to a key customer to analyze the customer's total marketing communications program; to recommend the appropriate telemarketing application; and to render assistance in staffing, training, and administering a telemarketing center.

In a competitive situation, a coordinated team of personnel dedicated to solving customer problems is a very formidable opponent. It must be pointed out, however, that while marketing a product using the holistic approach may solve many

Figure 15-1 A well-coordinated team permits the buying decision to be "pulled" through a customer's organization rather than laboriously "pushed" through it.

complex problems, this does not mean that only companies providing national account sales teams can or will extend such complete solutions to their customers. But a customer who receives national account service is more likely to recognize the value of the augmented products and services.

An additional reason for the upsurge in national account management is its obvious compatibility with the marketing concept and the business rewards that accompany such compatibility. Comparing the expense of marketing in the national account mode vis-a-vis the costs associated with geographic or product-line bases might indicate that the national account sales team approach is too costly. But by allowing each sales team to devote full attention to the penetration of one customer organization and the cultivation of the decision-maker's respect, the team recommendations are more likely to be considered credible. Thus, sales revenues will probably far outweigh the costs of a high-overhead sales operation.

Exhibit 15-3 shows how specialists on a national sales team interact with their counterparts in a customer's company to achieve solutions. The salesperson first plans the sales project so that the various participants know at what point in the sales cycle their contributions will be required. In addition, the specialists are told what person or department to interact with to convey their specialized knowledge. Because the specialists "sell" the product to their counterparts in the customer's firm, the sales representative eventually benefits from the influence that the customer's specifications engineer and production manager exert on the ultimate decision maker. When a team is well-coordinated, the buying decision is "pulled" through the customer's organization (from higher to lower levels) rather than laboriously "pushed" (from lower levels to higher) as is done in a more traditional sales atmosphere.

Importance of Environment

Professional salespersons are familiar with the role the business environment plays in determining a corporation's success. A firm that uses the national account

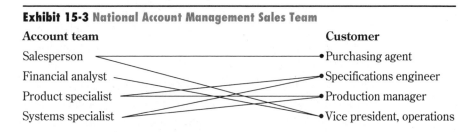

Exhibit 15-3 National Account Management Sales Team

Account team	Customer
Salesperson	Purchasing agent
Financial analyst	Specifications engineer
Product specialist	Production manager
Systems specialist	Vice president, operations

Source: Reprinted by permission of the Georgia State University Business Press from *Business* magazine. "Managing a National Account Sales Team," by John I. Coppett and William A. Staples (April–June 1983): 42.

organization structure in its marketing and sales operations is confronted with a specialized business environment for each of the national accounts the firm serves. For example, if the customer's industry has been severely affected by an economic downturn, then the account team may find that its own sales objectives are hard to achieve.

In focusing on the customer's environment, the account team must understand two facets of the total business environment: the external and internal environments. The external environment of a firm yields more readily to analysis and prediction. It includes such issues as social customs, political and legal practices, technological conditions, and economic influences.

A less obvious (but no less significant) environment affecting a national account team's operation is the customer's internal environment.[4] Every national account salesperson would be well advised to devote effort to an analysis of the customer's internal environment. Although not an exhaustive checklist for a complete audit of this area, Exhibit 15-4 includes some questions that should be useful in beginning this analysis. Answers to these questions can provide insight into the internal environment of the customer's organization, improve the understanding of the customer's firm, and provide information for better proposals and presentations.

The national account approach to selling is an extreme example of micromarketing. When one customer is so large and potentially profitable to a company that a sales team is devoted exclusively to that customer, then great efforts should be made to staff the national account team with properly trained people. If the team uses strategic approaches that incorporate sound marketing principles, the "product" sold by the account team will be an extremely formidable competitor in the marketplace. Under such circumstances, the attacks of rivals, relying on lower prices or superficial advertising claims, will have great difficulty in penetrating the national account.

SELLING CENTERS

The use of national account management has often focused on the relationships between or among one or more individuals in both the seller's organization and the buyer's organization. A new development that relates to national account management is the selling center concept. Similar to the buying center concept which was discussed in Chapter 2, the **selling center** includes representatives from various functional areas in the sales organization who are grouped together to form a selling team in order to better respond to the special requirements of key buyers. As shown in Exhibit 15-5, the selling firm's organizational selling center involves interdepartmental cooperation among not only marketing and sales personnel, but

Exhibit 15-4 **Analysis of the Customer's Internal Environment**

1. **What are the company's objectives, and how does it measure objective attainment?**

   Example: Share of market attainments may be viewed as vitally necessary. If so, any sales presentations made to executives should recognize this fact. Proposals should clearly describe how and why a purchase will contribute to a customer's gains in share of market.

2. **What is the reward system that encourages objective attainment and punishes failure?**

   Example: Firms that severely punish nonperformance in their managerial ranks may produce an extremely conservative atmosphere. When such a situation confronts a sales team, care must be taken to gather an abundance of success stories showing how other adopters of a product or service have minimized their risks.

3. **What are the methods utilized to groom future managerial talent?**

   Example: Knowledge of how a customer's "fast track" operates is important. If the normal tenure in one position is two years or less for a rapid corporate climber, a sales team must be prepared for questions that probe the short-term benefits and how quickly those benefits will become apparent.

4. **What seems to be the decision-making style of most of the firm's major decision makers?**

   Example: A sales team dedicated to serving a major customer became aware of the customer's acceptance and use of the Japanese management approach that emphasizes consensus development. As a result, the sales team was careful to gather endorsements for their proposed system from the customer's department heads who would be affected by the system. The customer's decision maker, assured that a consensus had been developed, quickly gave approval to the sales team.

5. **What is the apparent basic business philosophy inculcated in the client's organization (e.g., technical superiority, marketing aggressiveness)?**

   Example: Business executives who take pride in projecting an image of marketing aggressiveness appreciate sales teams that also exhibit these tendencies. Knowing that this situation prevailed in a customer's firm allowed a national account team to prepare a proposal emphasizing the competitive advantage that would be attainable through the adoption of the proposed product.

Sources: Mack Hanan, James Cribbin and Herman Heiser, *Consultative Selling* (NY: American Management Association, 1970), Mack Hanan, James Cribbin, and Jack Donis, *Systems Selling Strategies* (NY: American Management Association, 1978).

also manufacturing, research and development, engineering, and physical distribution among others. The composition of a selling center will vary from company to company as well as from one selling situation to another. However, the various participants in the selling center may assume a variety of roles in the selling activity

Exhibit 15-5 Exchange between Selling Centers and Buying Centers

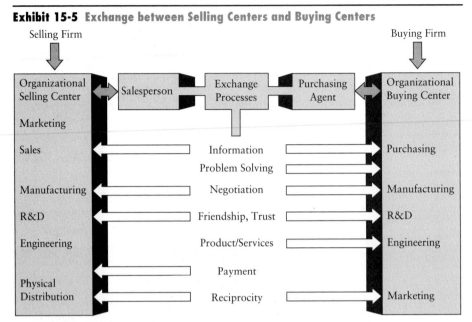

Source: Michael D. Hutt, Wesley J. Johnston, and John R. Rouchelto, "Selling Centers and Buying Centers: Formulating Strategic Exchange Patterns." *Journal of Personal Selling and Sales Management,* (May 1985): 34. Used with permission.

including not only being responsible for initiating the buyer-seller interaction, but also approving, consulting, informing, and implementing activities throughout the initiation, development, and maintenance of the buyer-seller relationship.[5]

In comparison, the buying firm's organizational buying center also may include a variety of departments which interact with one or more departments from the selling center. Typical departments involved in a buying center, as shown in Exhibit 15-5, include purchasing, manufacturing, research and development, engineering, and marketing. The degree of involvement between or among departments in the selling and buying centers will depend to a large extent on the nature of the organizational selling situation. Similar to the types of organizational buying situations or decisions discussed in Chapter 5, Exhibit 15-6 presents the various organizational selling situations including new, modified, and routine selling tasks. As shown in Exhibit 15-6, as one moves from a routine selling task to a modified and then to a new selling task, the emphasis shifts from more individual or salesperson involvement to more team or functional department involvement in the selling activity.

It is important to note also in Exhibit 15-5 that the exchange process between the selling and the buying centers may involve a number of things in addition to the traditional transaction of selling a product or service for the payment of money.

Exhibit 15-6 Organizational Selling Situations

	New Selling Task	Modified Selling Task	Routine Selling Task
Functional Representation	Diverse functional areas participate in selling center.	Limited functional representation in selling center.	Salesperson executes selling strategy.
Transactional Interdependence	High	Moderate	Low
Level of Task Uncertainty	High	Moderate	Low
Degree of Coordination Required	Extensive negotiation and a high degree of coordination among selling center participants.	Negotiation and coordination among the relevant functional areas comprising selling center.	Salesperson seeks assistance from other functional areas by exception.
Decision-Making Roles	Several functional areas may assume implementation roles.	Salesperson and Sales Manager involved in consultation/negotiation with other departments.	Salesperson responsible for implementation.
Coordination/ Control Strategy	Selling team.	Meetings, frequent contact among managers.	Written plans and established procedures.
Example:	New product line introduction; entry into new market segment with different service requirements.	Product modification in response to changing customer requirements.	Implementing strategy for established product line.

Source: Michael D. Hutt, Wesley J. Johnston, and John R. Rouchelto, "Selling Centers and Buying Centers: Formulating Strategic Exchange Patterns." *Journal of Personal Selling and Sales Management* (May 1985): 36. Used with permission.

As noted in Exhibit 15-5, the exchange process also includes information, problem-solving, negotiation, friendship, trust, and in some cases, the possibility of reciprocity in which both the selling and buying firms sell products or services to each other.[6] A challenge for the professional salesperson with the increased use of the selling center concept is to effectively handle intradepartmental and interdepartmental relationships in his or her company in order to be better able to respond to the needs of the buyer or purchasing agent and the other individuals and departments in the buyer's organization.

TELEMARKETING

The field of selling regularly experiences innovations that are rooted in some form of information technology. Usually, the driving force behind these innovations is a quest for improved productivity and competitive advantage. One form of information technology, telemarketing, is being adopted by more and more firms. **Telemarketing** refers to a system staffed by trained specialists who use telecommunications and information technologies to implement marketing strategies cost-effectively.[7] Exhibit 15-7 identifies the major components of the processing system within a telemarketing center. In essence, various forms of media (radio, television, magazines, newspapers, and direct mail) directed at customers result in telephone or mail inquiries. Members of the telemarketing center process the various requests or collect information that will aid in serving the customer's product or service needs or solving a customer's problem or request for information or assistance. The telemarketing center is then able to provide various information and reports to other departments within the organization (see Exhibit 15-8).

In order to highlight the growing importance of telemarketing and its impact on selling in various companies, four areas of application are presented: order processing, sales support, account management, and customer service. Each of these areas plays a key role in the salesperson-customer relationship. In addition, the salesperson's relationship to departments within his or her organization are also affected by telemarketing operations.

Exhibit 15-7 Telemarketing Center Processing System

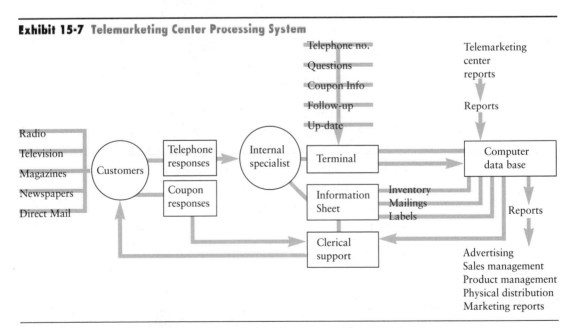

Source: John I. Coppett and Roy Dale Voorhees, "Telemarketing: A New Weapon In the Arsenal," *Journal of Business Strategy* (Summer 1983): 81.

Exhibit 15-8 Telemarketing Center Information to Other Departments

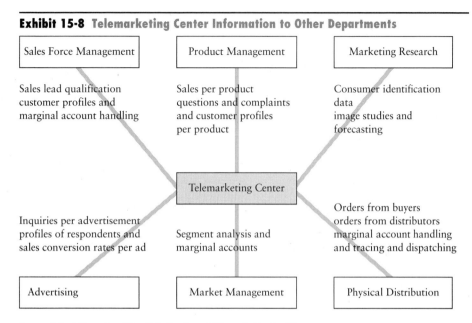

| Sales Force Management | Product Management | Marketing Research |

Sales lead qualification
customer profiles and
marginal account handling

Sales per product
questions and complaints
and customer profiles
per product

Consumer identification
data
image studies and
forecasting

Telemarketing Center

Inquiries per advertisement
profiles of respondents and
sales conversion rates per ad

Segment analysis and
marginal accounts

Orders from buyers
orders from distributors
marginal account handling
and tracing and dispatching

| Advertising | Market Management | Physical Distribution |

Source: John I. Coppett and Roy Dale Voorhees, "Telemarketing," p. 81.

Order Processing

On the most basic level, order processing consists of handling orders that customers initiate over the telephone (see Exhibit 15-9). The caller has probably used an 800 service number that was listed in an advertisement, direct mail piece, or catalog. A recent study of 700 U.S. industrial firms and other kinds of businesses revealed that 65 percent used the phone for sales and/or lead generation.[8] By delving into a data base that reveals the inventory status of a product, the telemarketing specialist can inform customers about the availability of the product, its probable shipping date, and other information pertaining to the transaction. The opportunities to collect useful information for improving the marketing program are too numerous to cite more than one or two brief examples.

Digital Equipment Corporation (DEC) maintains an order processing operation for a product line of approximately 30,000 items sold at prices ranging from $20 to over $15,000. The products are listed in DEC's catalog. The telemarketing program started in the late 1970s to allow sales personnel to perform their expected role as sales engineers rather than order takers. About fifteen telemarketing specialists handle 14,000 calls per month coming from a customer data base of approximately 9,000 accounts. Orders have increased steadily through the telemarketing center, thus permitting the field sales force to increase its productivity.[9]

Another well-known adopter of telemarketing, Fingerhut, began telemarketing in 1979 to solve the problems associated with missing information on incoming

Exhibit 15-9 **Telemarketing and Order Processing**

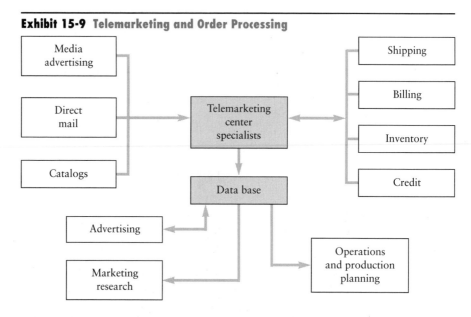

mail orders. When such errors occurred, they drove up the costs of filling orders, thus reducing profits. After turning to telemarketing to expedite orders and to ensure that they were correct, Fingerhut realized that the telephone contact with a customer also allowed an opportunity to sell additional merchandise. The potential for increased sales and profits is indeed impressive when one realizes that Fingerhut representatives make between 18,000 and 25,000 contacts daily.[10]

Sales Support

Some Fortune 500 companies have determined that more than half of their business comes from the direct initiative of prospects and customers and that only about 25 percent of the salesperson's time is required to close that business.[11] The evidence is overwhelming that sales personnel can and should be more productive if given the opportunity to "work smarter." One avenue for improvement is telemarketing. Some of the more prominent means of support are qualifying leads (see Exhibit 15-10) and making appointments for outside salespeople. A telemarketing sales support person can call and qualify 1,000 leads in twenty workdays; whereas if the leads had been qualified by a face-to-face sales visit, the time period would have been much longer, interest would have waned, and the chances of success would have been diminished.

American Airlines supports their field sales teams with telemarketing. When they began marketing Air-Pass, a long-term transportation agreement costing $20,000, the telemarketing group was created to qualify the leads American Airlines had acquired through direct mail and advertising. In some cases, the tele-

Exhibit 15-10 Telemarketing and Sales Support

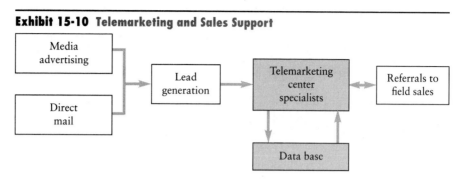

marketing reps even closed sales on this big-ticket item thereby enhancing the profit margin on the new program even more than would have been the case using expensive face-to-face sales calls.

By identifying the advertising medium that generated the lead, the quality of the lead, and the eventual disposition of the lead (that is, sales versus no sales), the telemarketing center can provide vital information for use in allocating advertising expenditures. The center can also determine if significant differences exist among sales personnel in closing sales when high-quality sales leads are being furnished. The implications for supervision and training are obvious. These are only a few of the more obvious uses of the telemarketing "nerve center."

Account Management

Account management involves maintaining a relationship with a customer entirely through the telemarketing center. An inside telemarketing sales specialist may either supplement or replace the outside salesperson's efforts in dealing with particular customers. Usually companies assign marginal accounts to be handled this way. In cases where the sales volume of an account is not large enough to justify sending a field representative to call on the account, the business will be turned over to an inside sales representative who will maintain the relationship. The entire cycle for all customer contacts is, in many cases, handled by the telemarketing specialists. This can include ordering, billing, credit, complaints, and product information (see Exhibit 15-11).

Most frequently, account management is used to conduct business with accounts that have proven to be marginally profitable under traditional face-to-face sales conditions. Some examples of well-known firms that practice full-account management in their telemarketing centers are:

Kelly-Springfield: employs more than thirty people to serve 3,000 accounts per week.

Valvoline, a division of Ashland Oil: receives over 90 percent of its orders over the phone; each order averages $10,000.

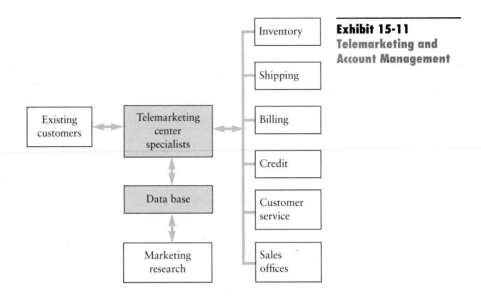

Exhibit 15-11
Telemarketing and
Account Management

Montgomery Ward Insurance Group: sells about $150 million worth of life insurance a year by phone.

Great North American Stationers: uses a telemarketing sales force to sell desk-top supplies; garners approximately $14 million of sales rather than the $25,000 it made only ten years ago.[12]

Customer Service

Rather than regarding customer service as a cost that needs to be kept as low as possible (or as low as customer demands will permit), there is a growing recognition that service is a potent marketing tool.[13] Telemarketing is a very popular, cost-effective way to deliver a program of customer service that is characterized by high-quality response to buyers' needs. Customer calls range from product information (in the case of a customer considering a purchase or needing assistance in using something already purchased) to service-related information (in the case of customers trying to locate a dealer, determine the status of an account, or resolve questions about shipping or billing).

Customer service specialists usually take calls over a toll-free 800 service number (see Exhibit 15-12). Depending on the kind of service they render, the specialists may need intensive product training so they can respond to the callers. Access to customer files, inventory data, and shipping and billing records is also frequently necessary. Automated data bases become almost a necessity as the service representative interacts with callers. Although the need for information is great in such centers, possibilities to collect enormous amounts of useful infor-

Exhibit 15-12 Telemarketing and Customer Service

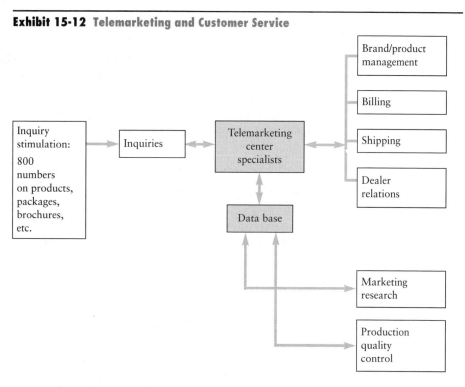

mation abound. Among the things that can be learned through the collection of information in a service center are:

Demographic information

Identification of product problems by model, type of defect, and area of distribution

Life-expectancy of products

Ideas for potential new products[14]

The General Electric (GE) Answer Center is a good example of how telemarketing is functioning to permit a faster response to customer inquiries. The 200-person staff handles approximately 2.4 million calls annually. The calls include questions about GE dealer location, product information, and customer assistance on how to make minor repairs on GE appliances.[15]

CUSTOMER SERVICE

Selling products or services to customers using face-to-face selling, national account management, or telemarketing are key strategic decisions that the sales representative must make to be more productive and to efficiently use his or her time. Customer service is associated with each of these selling techniques and is very critical in retaining the customer once the initial purchase has taken place. **Customer service** may be defined as responding to the needs and problems of the customer. In situations where products are similar, the level of customer service provided by a company and its sales force may be the deciding issue. In addition, customer service is likely to be the key in developing long-term customer relationships.

At a time when customer service has become a strategic competitive tool for companies, there appears to be a feeling by many in the United States that the overall quality of customer service has declined. A key question then is why customer service is judged to have declined in quality. One reason is that customer expectations about the appropriate response of a seller have increased.[16] For instance, electronic order exchange (EOE) systems provide buyers who are linked to suppliers through EOE systems with opportunities to electronically enter purchase orders, make inquiries about inventory availability, and check on ordering and shipment status.[17] Such levels of automation create images among customers of speed, accuracy, and overall responsiveness to customer requirements. Notwithstanding these images, if the customer comes in contact with individuals who are inept or uncaring, that seller's service is likely to be judged to be poor. Another reason for exerting efforts to improve is that customer service is often considered by companies to be a necessary evil.[18]

Thus, there is the scenario where buyers' concepts of service are broadening so much that they expect vendors to provide services that will prevent the emergence of problems (for example, EOE permitting just-in-time inventory management). With the improvement in the technology that provides the infrastructure of good customer service comes the responsibility of sellers to make sure that technologically based "promises" can and will be fulfilled by the sales personnel interacting with the buyer.

To develop a competitive advantage and capitalize on the importance of customer service, the professional salesperson should consider communication channels, objectives, economics, and credibility. Each of these areas is crucial to an effective customer service program.

Communication Channels

Providing customers and potential customers with opportunities to ask questions, voice complaints, submit orders, and trace shipments is absolutely indispensable to excellent customer service. Most firms have several channels or methods available to buyers and potential buyers. The salesperson would be well advised to analyze each communication channel to the target market(s) and ask the question,

"How could these communication methods be changed to provide our company with a differential advantage?"

Two companies that have established easy-to-access communications channels for customers are Whirlpool and GE. Whirlpool's "cool line" provides customers with a means of accessing (at no cost to the caller) product technicians who can coach do-it-yourselfers through minor repairs on Whirlpool products. GE has a huge telemarketing facility in Louisville, Kentucky, which annually handles over 2 million calls per year. One of the reasons that some forms of telemarketing are growing so fast is that people prefer to call in orders or receive assistance by communicating with a representative of a firm rather than writing a letter or going to a distribution outlet.

A note of caution must be inserted, however, lest the impression be given that providing telemarketing or other high-tech forms of communication will solve customer service problems. Indeed, the provision of these easy-to-access communication methods may result in a marked increase in voiced complaints and requests. The interpretation of this could be that customer service quality is deteriorating instead of improving. Such a gloomy assessment may be inaccurate. The perceived decline in customer service quality may be due to the easy-to-use communication methods.

Excellent customer service is not attained entirely by having communication channels to handle postpurchase problems. American Hospital Supply's ASAP ordering system, American Airlines' SABRE, and United Airlines' APPOLO reservation systems are some of the better-known ways companies link themselves to customers to facilitate order processing. In such cases, customer service is being rendered to stimulate sales, not to solve postpurchase problems. Instead of viewing customer service from a reactionary perspective, these firms are proactively employing effective customer service to garner more sales.

Objectives

The nature of customer service objectives is very important. One of the problems is that customer service has often been regarded as complaint handling. Without dismissing that activity as unimportant, it is also necessary to realize that most customer service departments should be managed so as to attain more than the resolution of complaints. Objectives should reflect the expanded possibilities available to customer service. Some customer service groups have become proficient at selling related products or services, as well as answering questions and/or resolving complaints.

The test that can be applied to customer service situations is the percentage of customers who are repeat buyers after having been in contact with a firm's customer service group. As a benchmark statistic, the research findings of the Technical Assistance Research Program (TARP) can be used.[19] TARP's research revealed that when the customer's complaint was resolved and the purchase involved $5 or less there was a 70 percent probability the consumer would make another purchase from the company that had resolved the difficulty. When the situation involved $100 or more and the problem was resolved to the customer's satisfaction, the probability of continued transactions was 54 percent. These statistics, generated from negative circumstances, can be used as broad guidelines. Sales personnel should expect customer retention rates to be equal to or exceed these statistics when their company's customer service activities are effectively responding to customer needs.

Economics

The American Management Association estimates that it now costs six times as much to win a new customer as it does to keep an existing one.[20] To emphasize the value of customer retention, a Technical Assistance Research Program study determined that car owners loyal to a car manufacturer can return as much as $142,000 in profit to the manufacturer over the life of the typical car buyer.[21] Even in an age where families move frequently, a supermarket that can keep a customer purchasing most of his or her groceries for three years from the same supermarket stands to make a profit of $22,000.[22]

Analyzing the frequency of use of the customer service offerings is akin to a product line review to determine what products should be deleted. This can be a

Figure 15-2 A responsive customer service organization constitutes a formidable competitve advantage.

valuable exercise, particularly if new market segments have been added since the customer service program began.

An example of the benefits to be achieved from assessing new modes of customer service delivery involves the 3M Company. 3M provides an 800 number for customers to call and talk to a technician when they experience difficulties with a 3M product.[23] Through this mode of delivery of responsive customer service, the 3M Company has avoided the cost of a premature visit by a technician. This is in addition to having provided a more timely and convenient solution to the customer.

Credibility

Perhaps no other single attribute of customer service has as great a potential to bolster or damage a company's image than the personal credibility of the salesperson. Employees who tell customers what they think the customers want to hear concerning installation or delivery dates and prices and then, subsequently, have to make excuses or render apologies will quickly ruin a company's reputation. Unfortunately, this has occurred so much that consumers are, in many cases, becoming hardened cynics.[24]

In analyzing customer service performance in terms of accuracy of information, a salesperson may find it useful to consider several questions.

1. When dates or times are quoted in response to shipping, delivery, and/or installation questions, in what percentage of cases is the quoted time or date met?

2. How current is the information that is available to customer service personnel who are fielding various customer questions?

3. To satisfactorily handle the most frequently encountered requests, what is the necessary level of precision and accuracy? Will ranges (for example, three to five days) be satisfactory or is an exact date, time, or amount required? (The greater the precision required, the more need for real-time, on-line information.)

Effective customer service may well be the key ingredient to retaining customers. Whether the salesperson is dealing with major accounts, marginal customers, or those in between, customers' feelings, perceptions, and beliefs about how well they are taken care of by the salesperson and his or her company are critical. The salesperson should remember that while customers may remain loyal to a company or business due to its reputation, its product or service, or the salesperson, an important factor to add to this list is customer service. Although attracting new customers is extremely important, retaining existing customers is equally, if not more, important.

SUMMARY

1. Traditional face-to-face selling is being supplemented by national account management and telemarketing.

2. National account management is particularly appropriate for that small percentage of customers who account for a high percentage of a company's sales.

3. National account management may be one salesperson or a sales team for each major or key account.

4. Telemarketing is a new form of information technology that can be used to service various customers, particularly small or marginal accounts.

5. Telemarketing's applications for building customer relationships include order processing, sales support, account management, and customer service, among others.

6. Customer service, which is responding to the needs and problems of customers, has become a strategic competitive tool for companies.

7. Key issues relating to customer service that the salesperson should consider include communication channels, objectives, economics, and credibility.

8. The integration of effective customer service with face-to-face selling, national account management, or telemarketing is likely to be the key activity in developing and maintaining long-term customer relationships.

QUESTIONS FOR DISCUSSION AND REVIEW

1. In terms of account size and stage of the selling process, compare the situations in which face-to-face selling, national account management, and telemarketing would be used.

2. What is the primary rationale for national account management?

3. Although national account management may be expensive to implement, why may it be worthwhile to do so?

4. Telemarketing is simply selling over the telephone. Why is this statement not true?

5. How would the use of telemarketing differ in its application to sales support versus customer service?

6. Why might telemarketing be seen as a threat to the sales force? Why should telemarketing be seen as an effective supplement to the salesperson?

7. Why is the area of customer service becoming even more important?

8. Will the salesperson in the future need to be more adaptable and flexible than in the past? Why?

CASE 15-1 COMPETITECH A

Brenda Johnson, Vice President of Marketing, is confronted with a major problem. Her company, Competitech, which is a retailer of computer supplies, has recently started to feature a toll-free 800 number in all its advertisements, direct mail pieces, and catalogs. The public is responding very well to this easy-to-use, economical method of ordering products. Response rate reports indicate that sales should be up by 12 to 15 percent. Actual sales, however, are just about the same as before Competitech started using telemarketing. As Ms. Johnson studied the reports, she saw that her three telemarketing service representatives had received approximately 4,000 calls during the past twenty working days. Brenda Johnson was pleased to note that about 50 percent of the callers had never previously purchased anything from Competitech. The fact that the telephone is ringing but the cash register isn't is cause for deep concern.

Brenda Johnson decides to call a meeting of the managers of the telemarketing operation, the shipping and inventory management group, the mail order department, and customer service. The meeting focuses on determining where and how business is being lost. The groups of managers are devoting most of their attention to the steps of order processing as depicted in Exhibit 1.

When the telemarketing personnel receive a call for a computer part or a software package, they record the customer's name, address, product identification information, and credit card information; then they ask the caller where he/she had seen the Competitech advertisement or other promotional information. Ms. Johnson considers this

Case Exhibit 1 Order-Processing Operations

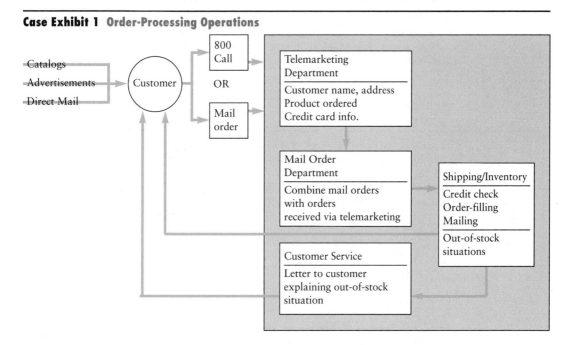

last bit of information vital to learn which media are stimulating the most responses. At the end of the workday, the telemarketers send all their orders to the mail order department where that day's orders are combined. The orders are then passed on to the shipping and inventory management department. Shipping and inventory verify creditworthiness if the order needs it, and order pickers fill each request and prepare the products for shipment.

If the requested merchandise is out of stock, a written notice of the shortage and the customer's name and address is given to the customer service group. Customer service sends a letter apologizing for the temporary delay in completing the order and indicates when Competitech expects to ship the back-ordered product.

The telemarketing group is beginning to receive calls from customers stating that they do not want to wait for back orders and therefore wish to cancel their request. In some situations, customers angrily say they would never have done business with Competitech if they had known about this delay.

Ms. Johnson realizes that Competitech is not only losing an opportunity to capitalize on the new business but, even worse, is alienating some customers. She wonders if telemarketing might hold the solution to some of the problems.

QUESTIONS

1. What could the telemarketers do if they had on-line computer access to inventory status information?

2. How could telemarketing be used to more efficiently support the customer service function?

3. What information does Ms. Johnson need to determine where the problem(s) are in Competitech?

4. Assuming the telemarketing representatives knew what the inventory status was of every product Competitech sold, how could Ms. Johnson motivate the telemarketing personnel to sell more?

CASE 15-2 COMPETITECH B

Background material for this case is provided in the Competitech A case. Students should read the Competitech A case before analyzing Competitech B.

This discussion is occurring one year after the difficulties described in the original Competitech A case were resolved. Brenda Johnson, Vice President of Marketing, is meeting with Frank Thomas who is the Telemarketing Center Manager.

Johnson: Frank, after we solved the problem of how to coordinate our telemarketing order processing activity with the inventory control people, our sales and profits have really increased. Our sales are up almost thirty percent over last year and customer problems are greatly reduced in numbers. Top management is very pleased with your department.

Thomas: Thanks, Brenda, I'll pass that on to the people on the phones. You know I've been in this telemarketing business for almost ten years and this is the best group of people I have ever worked with. They're really customer-oriented.

Johnson: I know. Last week I was at an AT&T seminar. One of the things they mentioned got me to thinking about our center and how we could do an even better job with telemarketing.

Thomas: What do you have in mind?

Johnson: Well, right now all of our business is generated by in-coming calls. Customers call us after they see one of our ads or get one of our catalogs. The customer, however, is taking the initiative in these situations. What the AT&T people were recommending was an "out-call" sales program. Rather than just wait for in-coming calls to be placed, they recommended that we also make calls from our center to prospective customers. In that way we can use our center more efficiently and increase sales even more. We would still be selling the same products. What do you think?

Thomas: There is a big difference between being an order taker and an order getter. Let me get back with you next week with a plan that will test the feasibility of this.

Johnson: Good!

QUESTIONS:

1. What are the major factors that Frank Thomas needs to consider as he designs a plan?

2. Describe some of the major "people problems" that will need to be anticipated by Thomas if this expansion occurs?

3. Assuming that it is technically feasible for Competitech to proceed with this expanded use of telemarketing, with what target market would you suggest they start?

4. How would you suggest that the telemarketing operators obtain new leads from which additional business might be secured?

CASE 15-3 NATIONAL TIRE SUPPLY

Bob Finley, Sales Manager of National Tire Supply, is facing a situation all sales managers would like to confront. His company has become very successful in supplying tires to businesses who have truck fleets between 5 and 300 vehicles. Through superior customer service from his twenty-five sales representatives, National Tire Supply has become one of the three leading firms in supplying replacement tires for industrial customers in the business of long-haul trucking.

Mr. Finley has divided his customers into three primary groups based on annual sales volume to each customer. Category 1 purchases about 60 percent of all the tires sold by National Tire Supply during a given year. Categories 2 and 3 account for 30 percent and 10 percent, respectively, of annual sales. He has also noted that the number of customers totals 100 in category 1, 300 in category 2, and slightly more than 500 in category 3.

Although the sales representatives of National Tire Supply are servicing the company's over 900 customers, Mr. Finley believes that sales force productivity might be increased with the adoption of different selling strategies. He is aware that high levels of customer service must be maintained to keep the business the firm already has. He also has instructed the sales force on the importance of retaining existing customers, although gaining new customers is also necessary.

QUESTIONS

1. What rule is exhibited by National Tire Supply's current situation?
2. Based on the current situation of National Tire Supply, what new selling strategies would you recommend to Mr. Finley?
3. How might telemarketing affect the company's activities in order processing?
4. What advice or suggestions would you make to Mr. Finley for maintaining high levels of customer service?

NOTES

1. Barry Farber and Joyce Wycoff, "Customer Service: Evolution and Revolution," *Sales and Marketing Management* (May 1991): 44 and 48.
2. *LAP Report* (New York: Laboratory of Advertising Performance, McGraw-Hill Research, 1984).
3. John I. Coppett and William A. Staples, "Managing a National Account Sales Team," *Business* (April–June 1983): 41–44.
4. "Corporate Culture," *Business Week* (October 27, 1980): 148–60; Tom Peters, "The Planning Fetish," *Wall Street Journal* (July 7, 1980): 10.
5. Michael D. Hutt, Wesley J. Johnston, and John R. Rouchelto, "Selling Centers and Buying Centers: Formulating Strategic Exchange Patterns," *Journal of Personal Selling and Sales Management* (May 1985): 33–40.
6. Ibid.
7. John I. Coppett and Roy Dale Voorhees, "Telemarketing in Distribution Channels," *Industrial Marketing Management* (April 1983): 105–12.
8. Murray Roman and Bob Donath, "What's Really Happening in Business/Industrial Telemarketing," *Business Marketing* (April 1983): 82–90.
9. Ibid.
10. Ibid.
11. Richard L. Bencin, "Electronic Marketing 1990," *Telephone Engineeer and Management* (February 15, 1983): 81–83.
12. Ray Smith, "Telemarketing Works," *Telephone Engineer and Management* (February 5, 1984): 10.
13. "Making Service a Potent Marketing Tool," *Business Week* (June 11, 1984): 164–70.
14. Ibid.
15. Ibid.
16. "In the Service Sector, Nothing Is Free Anymore," *Business Week* (June 8, 1987): 144.
17. Martin A. Weiss, "Implications of Electronic Order Exchange Systems for Logistics Planning and Strategy," *Journal of Business Logistics* 5 (1984): 17–39.
18. Diane Lynn Kastiel, "Service and Support: High Tech's New Battleground," *Business Marketing* (June 1987): 54–66.
19. "Making Service a Potent Marketing Tool," 164–70.
20. "Telemarketing Turns Customer Service into a Profit Center," *Telemarketing* (September 1983): 13.
21. "Making Service a Potent Marketing Tool," 164–70.
22. Ibid.
23. "Telemarketing and Technology: Special Section," *Forbes* (September 1, 1985): 1.
24. "Gluttons for Punishment? Fliers Continue Using Airlines They Hate," *Wall Street Journal* (November 19, 1987): 29.

PART SIX

Professional Selling as a Career

CHAPTER 16

Ethical and Legal Issues in Professional Selling

LEARNING OBJECTIVES

After studying this chapter, you should be able to:

1. Explain the meaning of ethics.
2. Describe three methods or guidelines for ethical behavior.
3. Identify ethical issues from both the seller's and buyer's points-of-view.
4. Describe major ethical issues confronting the salesperson in terms of his or her company, customers, prospects, and competitors.
5. Describe the major federal laws that have an impact on the field of selling.
6. Explain the seller's and buyer's obligations under the Uniform Commercial Code.
7. Define the key terms used in this chapter.

KEY TERMS

- ethics
- ethical behavior
- golden rule
- model of utility
- enlightened self-interest
- sharp practices
- reciprocity
- credibility
- tying contract
- price discrimination
- express warranty
- implied warranty

BECKY DORRIS is a Sales Representative for a major supplier of maintenance supplies for firms in the pulp and paper industry. She has been with this company for almost two years. One of her key prospects is Ian Christison, the purchasing manager for Allied Industries. In talking with Ian Christison, Becky Dorris realizes the maintenance supply contract with this company would total approximately $40,000 annually. For Becky Dorris, Allied Industries would be a major account that would reflect extremely well on her sales productivity. In addition, by gaining this account, Becky Dorris would more than meet her quota for the year, which would result in a substantial year-end bonus. After meeting with Ian Christison on a number of occasions, the time has arrived for the sale to be closed. Although all of their meetings have been going well, there is a sudden turn of events when Ian Christison tells Becky Dorris that, given the size of the order, he would expect some type of gift in return. Mr. Christison mentions he is very interested in a new outboard motor for his boat since he is an avid fisherman. The cost of the motor, according to Christison, is $500 to $600.

Becky Dorris realizes the importance of this order. She is also aware the company she represents does not encourage anything other than small gifts, such as pens, calendars, or taking prospective customers out for meals or entertainment, such as golfing or fishing. Becky Dorris is very perplexed as to what her next move should be.

The above example is just one type of situation a sales representative may be placed in when dealing with various customers or prospects. Becky Dorris's uneasiness may be due to a variety of factors. First, she may be fearful of losing a major account to her competitors, which her sales manager may see as poor performance on Dorris's part. Second, she may be concerned that as a relatively new salesperson for this company, she is under the gun to produce if she is to be retained by her employer. Third, for purely financial reasons, she may feel pressure to agree to Christison's request in order to qualify for the year-end bonus. Fourth,

Becky Dorris may be uneasy about what to do in this situation since it appears that her company does not exclude these activities, but merely discourages them. Finally, Dorris may believe that if she does it for this sale then Christison will expect it each year the contract comes up for renewal. In particular, Christison might even request a more expensive gift in the following years. Also, other customers that Dorris calls on may find out about the gift and may request or expect her to do the same for them.

In the daily activities of a professional salesperson like Becky Dorris, similar events are likely to occur. Sales representatives must deal with relationships with various individuals, including prospects, customers, competitors, and fellow employees within their own organizations. The challenge is to determine what guidelines or procedures should be followed to minimize situations like the one faced by Becky Dorris. A professional salesperson may be confronted by issues relating to ethics, the law, or both. The following sections are devoted to coverage of relevant guidelines for dealing with a wide variety of ethical and legal questions.

ETHICS AND ETHICAL GUIDELINES

A starting point for dealing with ethical issues is to define what is meant by the term *ethics*. **Ethics** is a system or code of morals of a particular profession, group, or person.[1] Ethical behavior refers to just or right standards of interaction between parties in a situation. A more precise definition of **ethical behavior** is the use of recognized social principles involving justice and fairness in business relationships. These relationships may involve areas of trust between parties in gray areas outside the law.[2] It is important to note that even those issues that might be considered unethical may not be illegal, although a salesperson is advised not to engage in either unethical or illegal activities.

Although there may be agreement on the meaning of ethics, problems often arise, since most ethical dilemmas in professional selling don't always have simple answers. Also, individuals will often judge issues differently—from ethical to unethical. In essence, rather than being straightforward, black or white issues, many fall in a gray zone. For example, presented with Becky Dorris's case, others may suggest she should give the gift, give the gift with the stipulation that it is a one-time occurrence, or not give the gift, among various possible alternatives.

In analyzing one's own ethics, it may be important to review some of the major operational models that have been suggested for dealing with ethical dilemmas. One such approach or model is the **golden rule**. This model suggests that professional salespersons should treat others as they would want to be treated.[3] For example, if a salesperson expected a customer to guard the confidentiality of information about his or her company's bid on a contract from other competitors, the salesperson should also be sure to retain in confidence information provided by the customer. One can see that the golden rule approach to ethical decisions makes a great deal of sense, but there may still be differences of opinion about its application or appropriateness among salespersons and customers.

A second method or guideline for dealing with ethical situations is a **model of utility**, which is based on the principle of maximizing happiness for the greatest number of people.[4] In buyer-seller relationships, the salesperson could weigh the benefit for the salesperson's company against the benefit for the customer's company. This perspective may focus more on a win-lose point-of-view than on a win-win perspective. Salespersons who view selling as a transaction may see everything as win-lose; more enlightened sales representatives who practice relationship selling would be looking for long-run, win-win situations.

A third method of looking at ethical problems is the **enlightened self-interest** model, which suggests that an individual should pursue personal gain in a way that minimizes harmful consequences for others.[5] This approach would seem to indicate an even greater move toward a win-lose situation. The professional salesperson, however, should desire to benefit from dealing with a customer at the same time that the customer benefits. One can easily see that if the interaction between the salesperson and the prospect or customer is in any significant way harmful to the buyer, the relationship is not likely to develop into a long-term—and maybe not even into a short-term—situation.

Exhibit 16-1 presents these three methods or guidelines for dealing with ethical situations or dilemmas. As noted in the exhibit, it would appear that the golden rule method is the most compatible with the practice of relationship selling. A challenge is for a professional sales representative to determine what method or guideline he or she will use in handling ethical situations. The salesperson may also be able to gain guidance in this area by reference to professional association and company codes or policies on ethical behavior.

Exhibit 16-1 Ethical Guidelines

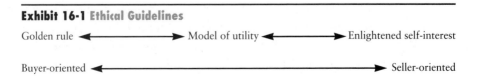

PROFESSIONAL ASSOCIATIONS AND CODES OF ETHICS

A professional salesperson may gain some insight on ethical behavior by referring to the code of ethics formulated by his or her professional association. One such association, the American Marketing Association, has drafted a code of ethics, which is shown in Exhibit 16-2. It is interesting to note several of the key points presented in the AMA Code of Ethics. First, under Responsibilities of the Marketer, the idea is advanced that the marketer, in this case the salesperson, should seek to serve consumers, organizations, and society by accepting responsibility for his or her actions. This code of ethics also refers to the practice of honest and fair marketing and selling activities, which do not involve conflicts of interest.

It is also interesting to note that under Rights and Duties of Parties reference is made to participants in the exchange process, the seller and buyer. Key issues raised relate to good faith discharge of obligations between the parties: that the products or services offered for sale are safe and fit for their intended use; that there are no deceptive communications; and that there is a procedure for handling problems, disputes, or grievances between the buyer and seller. These guidelines suggest appropriate behavior for the salesperson, the marketing function, and the company as a whole in dealing with the buyer-seller relationship.

The final section, Organizational Relationships, highlights the importance of ethical behavior in dealing with employees, suppliers, or customers; and offers a professional salesperson guidance on issues relating to maintaining confidentiality on privileged information, meeting the obligations of contracts or other agreements, and avoiding situations that would benefit the salesperson at the expense of his or her own company or the company's customers.

Although the professional salesperson may use the AMA's Code of Ethics as a starting point, he or she may also find it helpful to look at the ethical dimensions of the buyer-seller relationship from the buyer's point-of-view. One method of doing this would be to have knowledge of the code of ethics or standards of practice of professional buyers.

PRINCIPLES AND STANDARDS OF PURCHASING PRACTICE

A major professional organization for buyers is the National Association of Purchasing Management. Similar to the AMA, this association also has a code of ethics or principles and standards of purchasing practice (see Exhibit 16-3). The three major principles that should guide the purchaser or buyer include loyalty to your company, justice to those with whom you deal, and faith in your profession.

The National Association of Purchasing Management has derived a set of standards of purchasing practice based on these three principles. As shown in Exhibit

Exhibit 16-2 American Marketing Association's Code of Ethics

Members of the American Marketing Association (AMA) are committed to ethical professional conduct. They have joined together in subscribing to this Code of Ethics embracing the following topics:

Responsibilities of the Marketer

Marketers must accept responsibility for the consequences of their activities and make every effort to ensure that their decisions, recommendations, and actions function to identify, serve, and satisfy all relevant publics: consumers, organizations and society. Marketers' professional conduct must be guided by:

1. The basic rule of professional ethics: not knowingly to do harm;
2. The adherence to all applicable laws and regulations;
3. The accurate representation of their education, training and experience; and
4. The active support, practice and promotion of this Code of Ethics.

Honesty and Fairness

Marketers shall uphold and advance the integrity, honor, and dignity of the marketing profession by:

1. Being honest in serving consumers, clients, employees, suppliers, distributors and the public;
2. Not knowingly participating in conflict of interest without prior notice to all parties involved; and
3. Establishing equitable fee schedules including the payment or receipt of usual, customary and/or legal compensation for marketing exchanges.

Rights and Duties of Parties

Participants in the marketing exchange process should be able to expect that:

1. Products and services offered are safe and fit for their intended uses;
2. Communications about offered products and services are not deceptive;
3. All parties intend to discharge their obligations, financial and otherwise, in good faith; and
4. Appropriate internal methods exist for equitable adjustment and/or redress of grievances concerning purchases.

It is understood that the above would include, but is not limited to, the following responsibilities of the marketer:

In the area of product development and management:

Disclosure of all substantial risks associated with product or service usage
Identification of any product component substitution that might materially change the product or im-

pact on the buyer's purchase decision

Identification of extra-cost added features

In the area of promotions:

Avoidance of false and misleading advertising

Rejection of high pressure manipulations, or misleading sales tactics

Avoidance of sales promotions that use deception or manipulation

In the area of distribution:

Not manipulating the availability of a product for purpose of exploitation

Not using coercion in the marketing channel

Not exerting undue influence over the resellers' choice to handle a product

In the area of pricing:

Not engaging in price fixing

Not practicing predatory pricing

Disclosing the full price associated with any purchase

In the area of marketing research:

Prohibiting selling or fund raising under the guise of conducting research

Maintaining research integrity by avoiding misrepresentation and omission of pertinent research data

Treating outside clients and suppliers fairly

Organizational Relationships

Marketers should be aware of how their behavior may influence or impact on the behavior of others in organizational relationships. They should not encourage or apply coercion to obtain unethical behavior in their relationships with others, such as employees, suppliers or customers.

1. Apply confidentiality and anonymity in professional relationships with regard to privileged information.
2. Meet their obligations and responsibilities in contracts and mutual agreements in a timely manner.
3. Avoid taking the work of others, in whole, or in part, and representing this work as their own or directly benefiting from it without compensation or consent of the originator or owner.
4. Avoid manipulation to take advantage of situations to maximize personal welfare in a way that unfairly deprives or damages the organization or others.

Any AMA member found to be in violation of any provision of the Code of Ethics may have his or her Association membership suspended or revoked.

Source: American Marketing Association. Reprinted with permission.

Exhibit 16-3 **National Association of Purchasing Management's Principles and Standards of Purchasing Practice**

LOYALTY TO YOUR COMPANY
JUSTICE TO THOSE WITH WHOM YOU DEAL
FAITH IN YOUR PROFESSION

From these principles are derived the NAPM standards of purchasing practice. (Domestic and International.

1. Avoid the intent and appearance of unethical or compromising practice in relationships, actions, and communications.

2. Demonstrate loyalty to the employer by diligently following the lawful instructions of the employer, using reasonable care and only authority granted.

3. Refrain from any private business or professional activity that would create a conflict between personal interests and the interests of the employer.

4. Refrain from soliciting or accepting money, loans, credits, or prejudicial discounts, and the acceptance of gifts, entertainment, favors, or services from present or potential suppliers that might influence, or appear to influence, purchasing decisions.

5. Handle confidential or proprietary information belonging to employers or suppliers with due care and proper consideration of ethical and legal ramifications and governmental regulations.

6. Promote positive supplier relationships through courtesy and impartiality in all phases of the purchasing cycle.

7. Refrain from reciprocal agreements that restrain competition.

8. Know and obey the letter and spirit of laws governing the purchasing function and remain alert to the legal ramifications of purchasing decisions.

9. Encourage all segments of society to participate by demonstrating support for small, disadvantaged, and minority-owned businesses.

10. Discourage purchasing's involvement in employer-sponsored programs of personal purchases that are not business related.

11. Enhance the proficiency and stature of the purchasing profession by acquiring and maintaining current technical knowledge and the highest standards of ethical behavior.

12. Conduct international purchasing in accordance with the laws, customs, and practices of foreign countries, consistent with United States laws, your organization policies, and these Ethical Standards and Guidelines.

Source: Reprinted with permission from the publisher, the National Association of Purchasing Management, *Principles & Standards of Purchasing Practice*, adopted January, 1992.

16-3, some of the same guidelines given in the American Marketing Association's Code of Ethics are also expressed here. The salesperson should understand that just as there are professional salespersons who abide by ethical guidelines, there are many professional buyers or purchasing managers who do likewise. Exhibit 16-4 shows some of the similarities between the American Marketing Association's and National Association of Purchasing Management's codes of ethics.

To give the salesperson some additional information on the ethical improprieties that are likely to confront a professional buyer, we discuss the issues of gifts, sharp practices, reciprocity, competitive bidding, and negotiation.

Gifts

A general statement of conduct for buyers would be that gifts from sellers, suppliers, or vendors should not be accepted. In many industries, however, it is a common practice for sales personnel to provide different types of gifts or favors for purchasing personnel. Exhibit 16-5 presents the results of a study sponsored by the National Association of Purchasing Management. The exhibit lists various gifts or favors that are acceptable to buyers, offered to buyers, and actually accepted by

Exhibit 16-4 Similarities Between the American Marketing Association's and National Association of Purchasing Management's Codes of Ethics

	American Marketing Association	National Association of Purchasing Management
Integrity	Marketers shall uphold and advance the integrity, honor, and dignity of the marketing profession by: 1) being honest in serving consumers, clients, employees, suppliers, distributors, and the public.	Avoid the intent and appearance of unethical or compromising practice in relationships, actions, and communications.
Gifts	In the area of promotion, avoidance of false and misleading advertising; rejection of high-pressure manipulations or misleading sales tactics; and avoidance of sales promotions that use deception or manipulation.	Refrain from soliciting or accepting money, loans, credit, or prejudicial discounts, and the acceptance of gifts, entertainment, favors, or services from present or potential suppliers which might influence, or appear to influence, purchasing decisions.
Relationships	Marketers should be aware of how their behavior may influence or impact on the behavior of others in organizational relationships. They should not demand, encourage, or apply coercion to obtain unethical behavior in their relationships with others, such as employees, suppliers, or customers.	Promote positive supplier relationships through courtesy and impartiality in all phases of the purchasing cycle. Handle information of a confidential or proprietary nature to employers and/or suppliers with due care and proper consideration of ethical and legal ramifications and governmental regulations.

Source: Marilyn Lester, "Sales Ethics: Comments from the Other Side," *NAPM Insights* (September 1990): 26.

buyers. As one might expect, the items most likely to be accepted by buyers are meals, holiday gifts, and tickets to events. In contrast, the items least likely to be accepted or offered are major dollar items such as vacation trips and automobiles. Whether or not any of these gifts are accepted may depend on whether or not the buyer's company has policies on receiving gifts and the ethics of the buyer.

Sharp Practices

Although accepting gifts may be seen from a variety of viewpoints from positive to negative, sharp practices are usually viewed very negatively. **Sharp practices** include evasion and indirect misrepresentation that may be just short of fraud, which is illegal. Examples of sharp practices by a buyer would include the following:

EXHIBIT 16-5 Gifts Acceptable to, Offered to, and Accepted by Buyers

Favor Description	A. Acceptable to Buyers "Yes"	B. Offered to Buyers "Yes"	C. Actually Accepted "Yes"
Advertising souvenirs	72%	26%	25%
Lunches	68	83	75
Tickets (sports, theater, etc.)	37	57	38
Dinners	48	67	51
Golf outings	28	43	25
Food and liquor	28	46	30
Holiday gifts	43	67	47
Trips to vendors' plants	31	51	30
Small value appliances	6	19	7
Discounts on personal purchases	11	24	9
Clothing	7	11	6
Loans of money	1	3	0
Vacation trips	2	10	2
Large appliances	1	4	0.4
Automobiles	1	2	0.4
Other ("contest")	0.4	2	0.4

Source: Robert L. Janson, *Purchasing Ethical Practices* (Tempe, Ariz.: Center for Advanced Purchasing Studies/National Association of Purchasing Management, Inc., 1988), 32 pages. It is available in most major libraries (Library of Congress Call Number 88-071748). Single copies are available gratis by written request to the Center for Advanced Purchasing Studies, Arizona State University Research Park, P.O. Box 22160, Tempe, Arizona 85285-2160. CAPS is a national research organization resulting from an affiliation agreement between the College of Business at Arizona State University and the National Association of Purchasing Management. Research reports on a variety of purchasing-related subjects of national importance are released periodically.

Figure 16-1 Among gifts most likely to be accepted to buyers are tickets to entertainment events.

1. A buyer talks in terms of large quantities to encourage a price quote on that basis, but then places a smaller order with the intent of getting the lower price, which may not be deserved.

2. Bids are obtained from unqualified suppliers whom the buyer would not patronize. These bids are then played against the bids of other suppliers in order to gain a price or other advantage.

3. Obscure terms in the contract, which are benefits to the buyer, are buried in small print in the contract.[6]

Reciprocity

Reciprocity is the practice by a buyer of giving preference to a supplier who is also a customer of his or her company. Although many companies have a policy stating that when factors such as price and service are equal, the company prefers to buy from its customers, this practice could be illegal. The illegality would be due to the practice of reciprocity causing a restraint of trade between the buyers and other suppliers or sellers. Even if the practice is not illegal, blind use of reciprocity may result in less than competitive products or services being used when other, better alternatives exist.[7]

Competitive Bidding

In purchasing, the assumption is often made that the low bidder will be awarded the contract or order. A professional buyer could engage in some of the following improprieties with respect to competitive bidding:

1. Failure to keep competitive price information confidential such as letting a vendor know the bids of other vendors.
2. Failure to notify unsuccessful bidders promptly in order that a vendor may use resources on other bids.
3. Allowing a given supplier to make more than one bid when other suppliers are not given this opportunity.
4. Accepting a late bid after an announced closing date, which would favor the late bidder who had more time to prepare the bid.[8]

Negotiation

In comparison to competitive bidding, which often focuses primarily on bids based on price, negotiation centers on proposals. A vendor's proposal may include many key factors other than price that are subject to negotiation or modification between the buyer and seller. During negotiation, a buyer engaging in unethical behavior could be involved in one or more of the following situations:

1. The buyer does not inform all vendors of all of the factors or criteria that will be used to select the successful proposal.
2. The buyer gives one vendor either more or different information than another vendor.
3. Due to an easily recognized error on the part of a vendor or supplier, a buyer unfairly takes advantage of a proposal rather than allowing the vendor to make a recalculation.[9]

Although there are numerous areas of ethical improprieties that could develop between buyers and sellers, it is important for the professional salesperson to be aware of possible unethical behavior by buyers. Exhibit 16-6 reveals purchasing managers' attitudes toward whether a given purchasing practice poses an ethical problem.

Exhibit 16-6 Purchasing Managers and Ethical Problems

	Percent Replying "Definitely Yes" or "Probably Yes"		
Practices	*An Ethical Problem?*	*Have Stated Policy Now?*	*Want a Stated Policy?*
1. Acceptance from a supplier of gifts like sales promotion prizes and "purchase volume incentive bonuses."	83%	71%	89%
2. Giving a vendor information on competitors' quotations, then allowing him to requote.	77	55	86
3. Acceptance of trips, meals, or other free entertainment.	58	70	83
4. Preferential treatment of a supplier who is also a good customer.	65	45	68
5. Discrimination against a vendor whose salespeople try to deal with other company departments directly rather than go through purchasing.	35	38	62
6. Solicitation of quotations from new sources, when a market preference for existing suppliers is the norm, merely to fill a quota for bids.	23	37	59
7. To a supplier, exaggerating the seriousness of a problem in order to get a better price or some other concession.	68	28	57
8. According special treatment to a vendor who is preferred or recommended by higher management.	65	28	56
9. Attempting to avoid a cancellation charge when the cancellation involves an order already being processed by the source.	40	22	52
10. Allowing personalities—like of one sales representative or dislike of another—to enter into supplier selection.	63	24	46
11. Use of the company's buying power to obtain price or other concessions from a vendor.	22	29	46
12. To obtain a lower price or other concession, informing an existing supplier that the company may use a second source.	34	26	42
13. Seeking information about competitors by questioning suppliers.	42	19	34

Source: William Rudelius and Rogene A. Buchholz, "Ethical Problems of Purchasing Managers," *Harvard Business Review* (March–April 1979): 8–9.

CODES OF ETHICS: THE COMPANY PERSPECTIVE

A salesperson's behavior may be influenced by policies on ethics of professional associations such as the American Marketing Association. In addition, the policies and practices adhered to by buyers that the salesperson calls on may also have an impact on a salesperson's ethical behavior. Another major effect on the degree to which a salesperson engages in ethical or unethical behavior may be the existence and enforcement of an ethics policy in his or her own company.

The suggestion has been made that for a company's ethical policies to be effective they should be in writing. Although there may be problems in developing written ethics for a company in terms of time, cost, and operationalizing the policy from general to specific situations, the benefits are likely to outweigh these problems. Major advantages of a written policy could include a focus of management and employee attention on key ethical issues, effective communication of the importance of the policy to all employees covered, the provision of a justification for an employee to act in a certain manner (for example, a policy that does not allow gift giving), and the identification of the penalty for employees who do not follow the policy.[10]

Although there may be agreement that a written ethics policy would be most effective, there are often relatively brief statements by companies of what is expected of their employees in terms of ethical behavior. The following are two examples of relatively brief statements of an ethics policy.

EDS, a major software systems company in Dallas, Texas, poses the following questions for its employees to ask:

1. Would we want to do business with ourselves?
2. Are we exercising the level of professional standards and ethics that would permit our customers to have complete trust in us?[11]

Eli Lilly, a manufacturer and marketer of pharmaceuticals, agricultural chemicals, medical instruments, and diagnostic products in Indianapolis, Indiana, states: "No Lilly employees should do anything or be expected to take any action that they would be ashamed to explain to their family or friends."[12]

General Dynamics' ethics program represents one of the most ambitious. The company has nine full-time ethics directors with one for each of its major divisions. The company also has almost thirty hot lines for employees to use to get answers to ethics-related questions. General Dynamics started the program in 1985. Employees are asked to sign a statement that they have received a copy of the company's standards of business ethics and conduct. The definition of ethics used includes telling the truth, being fair, and doing no voluntary harm.[13]

General Dynamics has established the following rules for its sales representatives:

1. If it becomes clear that the company must engage in unethical or illegal activity to win a contract, it will not pursue that business further.

2. To prevent hidden interpretations or understandings, all information provided relative to products and services should be clear and concise.

3. Receiving or soliciting gifts, entertainment, or anything else of value is prohibited.

4. In countries where common practices indicate acceptance of conduct lower than that to which General Dynamics aspires, salespeople will follow the company's standards.

5. Under no circumstances may an employee offer or give anything to customers or their representatives in an effort to influence them.[14]

Although the statements and policies on ethics by EDS, Eli Lilly, and General Dynamics give members of their sales forces guidance on appropriate behavior, the key is often top management commitment and company enforcement of the policy. For an ethics policy to be effective at the company level, it has been suggested that top management must create a corporate culture that values ethics and social responsibility as well as profits and efficiency.[15]

The guidance for the professional salesperson offered by professional association and company codes of ethics is extremely important. These guidelines may enable the salesperson to more fully develop his or her own personal code of ethics by which to work in today's business environment.

THE SALESPERSON'S CODE OF ETHICS

The professional salesperson will probably develop his or her own code of ethics over time due to increasing levels of knowledge and experience in selling activities. As shown in Exhibit 16-7, the codes of ethics of the salesperson's professional association and company may serve as key ingredients in formulating his or her own code of ethics. In addition, the salesperson will be affected by his or her interaction with customers and competitors. The result will be a set of values and attitudes that influence the type of behavior exhibited by the salesperson. For example, a belief in the value of honesty and integrity may lead the salesperson to have a strong attitude that all dealings with customers should be not only legal, but ethical as well. The salesperson's behavior such as not divulging confidential information or not using high-pressure selling tactics would be the result of basic values and attitudes developed over time. In dealing with his or her employer, cus-

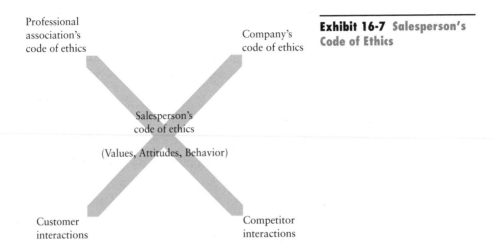

Exhibit 16-7 Salesperson's
Code of Ethics

tomers, and competitors, the salesperson should be aware of potential ethical issues that may arise. Exhibit 16-8 provides a list of some of these major issues.

Company Issues

Major ethical issues that may arise with respect to the company include misrepresentation of information, such as overstating customer call reports or padding
expense accounts by the salesperson. Certain forms of misrepresentation by an individual may not only be unethical, but also illegal. The salesperson should be on
guard to avoid not only the misrepresentation of information, but also the use of
company assets for personal benefit (for example, use of expense money for personal, nonbusiness reasons) or a conflict-of-interest such as investment or involvement in a company to which one sells. Other areas to guard against are the
disclosure of proprietary information about the company that should not be known
to noncompany personnel, such as a trade secret involving a new product. In addition, if a salesperson were to leave his or her employer, it would be inappropriate and unwise to disparage the company. Bad-mouthing one's employer will not
only affect any future relationships with that company, but also may become
known to other companies who would not look favorably on the practice.

Customer and Prospect Issues

Ethical dilemmas may be even more likely to develop when the salesperson is dealing with customers and prospects. Just as misrepresentation of one's company is
an issue, misrepresentation of the salesperson, his or her company, or his or her
products or services is also to be avoided at all times. The professional salesperson should also avoid high-pressure selling tactics with prospects and customers,

Exhibit 16-8 Ethical Issues of the Salesperson

THE SALESPERSON'S COMPANY

Misrepresentation of call reports

Misrepresentation of expense accounts

Use of company assets for personal benefit

Conflict-of-interest situations

Disclosure of proprietary company information

Disparagement of the company

THE SALESPERSON'S CUSTOMERS AND PROSPECTS

Misrepresentation of yourself

Misrepresentation of your company

Misrepresentation of your products or services

Use of high-pressure selling tactics

Inappropriate gift-giving

Disclosure of proprietary customer information

Overstocking or understocking a customer's supply of your product

THE SALESPERSON'S COMPETITORS

Disparagement of a competitor's company

Disparagement of a competitor's product or service

Disparagement of a competitor's sales representative

since this type of behavior is likely to lead, at best, to transaction– as opposed to relationship–selling. At worst, it will lead to alienation of the prospect or customer and a lost sales opportunity. Another practice to be avoided by the salesperson is the offering of gifts or favors that might be considered inappropriate by either the customer or the salesperson's company. In dealing with each customer, the salesperson should also ensure that he or she does not disclose proprietary customer information, such as proposed new product introductions. Finally, in looking out for the customer's interests, the salesperson should also not engage in selling practices that cause the customer to be over- or understocked with products for the benefit of the salesperson. This type of behavior will also not lead to a long-term beneficial buyer-seller relationship.

Competitor Issues

A final area for the professional salesperson to consider in developing his or her own code of ethics is relationships with competitors. Although an adversarial view of selling would see each competitor as an enemy to be defeated, care must be taken to treat competitors professionally. A common practice for inexperienced sales personnel is to sell to prospects and customers by including disparagement of a competitor's company, its products or services, or even the competitor's sales representative. Not only is this inappropriate and unprofessional behavior, it is unethical. Knowledgeable customers or prospects may also view the salesperson who engages in this practice as grasping for ways to cut down the competition rather than showing how the salesperson's products or services meet or exceed the capabilities of each competitor's offerings. This behavior will not add to the perception by others of the salesperson as a sales professional.

In interactions with one's company, customers and prospects, and competitors, the salesperson must realize that his or her credibility is on the line. **Credibility** refers to the ability to be believed and trusted as well as being reliable. Engaging in any unethical behavior is likely to diminish or even destroy a salesperson's credibility. Although it may take years to develop one's credibility with peers, customers, and competitors, engaging in unethical behavior (see Exhibit 16-8) can destroy one's credibility in a very brief time. Every professional salesperson should carefully guard his or her personal and professional credibility, based on ethical behavior.

LEGAL ISSUES IN PROFESSIONAL SELLING

Besides the number of issues dealing with ethics in professional selling, the professional salesperson should also understand a number of legal issues that affect selling. Although a salesperson may be able to consult his or her company's legal counsel on specific issues, a general knowledge of major legal statutes affecting selling practices is important, since ignorance of the law is not an appropriate defense for illegal behavior. Major areas of law are presented, including federal and state laws as well as the Uniform Commercial Code.

The laws regulating business practices focus on three issues: (1) legislation to protect one business firm from another in order to prevent unfair competition; (2) legislation to protect consumers or customers from unfair or deceptive business practices; and (3) a more general purpose, to protect the greater interest of society against inappropriate business practices.[16] Although laws affecting the buyer-seller relationship may be of most concern or interest, other legislation and statutes may also have an impact on selling activities.

Federal Laws

Some of the major federal legislation pertaining to marketing and selling activities include the following:

Sherman Antitrust Act of 1890: Prohibits monopolies or attempts to monopolize, contracts, combinations, or conspiracies in restraint of trade in interstate and foreign commerce.

Clayton Act of 1914: Supplements the Sherman Antitrust Act and prohibits certain practices such as price discrimination, tying contracts, and exclusive dealing where the effect may be to substantially lessen competition or create a monopoly.

Federal Trade Commission Act of 1914: Declares that unfair methods of competition in commerce are unlawful.

Robinson-Patman Act of 1936: An amendment to the Clayton Act of 1914. Defines as unlawful price discrimination which may serve to injure, destroy, or prevent competition. Grants the Federal Trade Commission the right to establish limits on quantity discounts and to prohibit promotional allowances or the provision of services except where made available to all on proportionately equal terms.

Wheeler-Lea Act of 1938: Prohibits unfair and deceptive acts and practices regardless of whether competition is injured.

Figure 16-2 Major legislative acts and statutes affect selling practices.

Magnuson-Moss Warranty/FTC Improvement Act of 1975: Authorizes the Federal Trade Commission to determine rules and regulations concerning consumer warranties and provides for consumer access to means of redress, including class action suits. Expands the Federal Trade Commission's powers over unfair or deceptive acts or practices.

Many of the laws described above have a major impact on business-to-business dealings between companies as compared to those between a company and the ultimate consumer. A key consideration in complying with these laws is to avoid unfair methods of competition that may injure, destroy, or prevent competition. Such practices might include attempting to force a buyer to buy one product in order to obtain another product (**tying contract**) or offering a given customer a price reduction or additional promotional allowances while not offering the same to other customers on a proportionately equal basis (**price discrimination**). These practices fall under the antitrust laws, such as the Sherman Antitrust and Clayton Acts presented above. Exhibit 16-9 offers ten guidelines for sales personnel to follow to comply with antitrust legislation.

Exhibit 16-9 Guidelines for Antitrust Compliance

1. Don't discuss with customers the price your company will charge others.
2. Don't attend meetings with competitors (including trade association gatherings) at which pricing is discussed. If you find yourself in such a session, walk out.
3. Don't give favored treatment to your own subsidiaries and affiliates.
4. Don't enter into agreements or gentlemen's understandings on discounts, terms or conditions of sale, profits or profit margins, shares of the market, bids or the intent to bid, rejection or termination of customers, sales territories or markets.
5. Don't use one product as bait for selling another.
6. Don't require a customer to buy a product only from you.
7. Don't forget to consider state antitrust laws as well as the federal statutes.
8. Don't disparage a competitor's product unless you have specific proof that your statements are true. This is an unfair method of competition.
9. Don't make either sales or purchases conditional on the other party's making reciprocal purchases from or sales to your company.
10. Don't hesitate to consult with a company lawyer if you have any doubt about the legality of a practice. Antitrust laws are wide-ranging, complex, and subject to changing interpretations.

Source: Reprinted from January 27, 1975 issue of *Business Week* by special permission, copyright 1975 by McGraw-Hill, Inc.

Cooling-off Rule

Most of the legislation cited above deals with antitrust legislation, but one specific area of the buyer-seller relationship—door-to-door or direct selling—is very noteworthy. In response to high-pressure selling tactics in sales made to individuals in their homes, the Federal Trade Commission in 1974 adopted a Trade Regulation Rule focusing on door-to-door transactions of $25 or more. The essence of this rule is that it allows a buyer to cancel the sale during the three working days immediately following the day on which the sale was originally made. The seller must furnish the buyer a Notice of Cancellation (see Exhibit 16-10) and must inform the buyer in writing, as part of the sales contract, that the buyer has the option to cancel the contract at any time prior to midnight of the third business day after the date of the contract. If the seller fails to comply with the requirements of the cooling-off rule, the noncompliance would constitute an unfair or deceptive trade practice.

State Laws

Although it is impossible to discuss the various laws across all fifty states that would have an impact on the salesperson, one occurrence is important to note. In many states, there now exists what are known as "little FTC laws," which focus on consumer protection issues at the state and local levels. The major purpose of these laws is to prevent deceptive acts or practices in buyer-seller interactions. A good example of the issues addressed by these acts is provided in Exhibit 16-11, which is taken from the Texas Deceptive Trade Practices and Consumer Protection Act, which is enforced by the Office of the Texas Attorney General. The local county and district attorneys also have legal authority in consumer protection and consumer fraud.

UNIFORM COMMERCIAL CODE

The Uniform Commercial Code (UCC) is the primary legal guide for business or commercial practice in the United States. The code was drafted in 1952 and the final version was enacted in 1958. The code provides some very specific definitions of concepts and terms related to the buyer-seller relationship. Some of the key terms include:

Buyer: a person who buys or contracts to buy goods

Seller: a person who sells or contracts to sell goods

Sale: the passing of title from the seller to the buyer for a price

Exhibit 16-10 Notice of Cancellation Required by the Cooling-off Rule

Notice of Cancellation

(enter date of transaction)

You may cancel this transaction, without any penalty or obligation, within three business days from the above date.

If you cancel, any property traded in, any payments made by you under the contract or sale, and any negotiable instrument executed by you will be returned within 10 business days following receipt by the seller of your cancellation notice, and any security interest arising out of the transaction will be canceled.

If you cancel, you must make available to the seller at your residence, in substantially as good condition as when received, any goods delivered to you under this contract or sale; or you may if you wish, comply with the instructions of the seller regarding the return shipment of the goods at the seller's expense and risk. If you do make the goods available to the seller and the seller does not pick them up within 20 days of the date of your notice of cancellation, you may retain or dispose of the goods without any further obligation. If you fail to make the goods available to the seller, or if you agree to return the goods to the seller and fail to do so, then you remain liable for performance of all obligations under the contract.

To cancel this transaction, mail or deliver a signed and dated copy of this cancellation notice or any other written notice, or send a telegram, to

_____, at _____
(name of seller)   (address of seller's place of business)

no later than midnight of _____.
                                        (date)

I hereby cancel this transaction.

_____
(date)

_____
(buyer's signature)

Source: Donald W. Jackson, Jr., William H. Cunningham, and Isabella C.M. Cunningham, *Selling: The Personal Force in Marketing* (New York: John Wiley and Sons, 1988), p. 448. Copyright 1988 by John Wiley and Sons, Inc. Reprinted with permission.

Good faith: honesty in fact and the observance of reasonable commercial standards of fair dealing in the trade

Receipt: taking physical possession of the goods[17]

In essence, a sale is a contract that by its terms transfers the merchandise from the salesperson to the customer for a price, which may be either money or a promise

Exhibit 16-11 Deceptive Acts or Practices of the Texas Deceptive Trade Practices and Consumer Protection Act

1. Passing off goods or services as those of another.
2. Causing confusion or misunderstandings about the source, sponsorship, approval, or certification of goods or services.
3. Using deceptive representations or designations of geographical origin in connection with goods or services.
4. Representing goods or services as having sponsorship, approval, characteristics, uses, or benefits that they do not have.
5. Representing goods as being original or new when they are deteriorated, reconditioned, reclaimed, used, or secondhand.
6. Representing goods as being of a particular standard, quality, or style when they are not.
7. Disparaging the goods, services, or business of another by a false or misleading representation of facts.
8. Making false or misleading statements concerning the reasons for the existence of, or the amount of, price reductions.

Source: Donald W. Jackson, Jr., William H. Cunningham, and Isabella C.M. Cunningham, *Selling: The Personal Force in Marketing* (New York: John Wiley and Sons, 1988), p. 448. Copyright 1988 by John Wiley and Sons, Inc. Reprinted with permission.

to pay.[18] The salesperson should have a good understanding of the obligations of the seller and buyer under Article 2 (Sales) of the Uniform Commercial Code.

Seller's Obligations

The seller's major obligations are to transfer title of the merchandise, deliver possession of the goods, and fulfill warranty obligations. With respect to transfer of the title, the seller must provide clear title to the product or products; failing to do so would be a breach of warranty of title. In the delivery of the goods, it is expected that the goods will be delivered in a single delivery unless specified otherwise in the contract. The seller is also expected to make the goods available to the buyer during reasonable hours and for a reasonable period of time in order that the buyer can take possession. In addition, the seller retains the risk of loss of the merchandise until the delivery obligation has been completed.[19]

Regarding fulfillment of warranty obligations, a sales contract carries an assumption of responsibility by the seller for the quality, character, or suitability of the merchandise. Two types of warranty—express and implied—are critical at this point. An **express warranty** is based upon the contract and is the result of negotiation of the terms of the sales contract. An **implied warranty** represents obligations assumed by the seller by operation of the law. The seller has two implied warranties—one of merchantability (merchandise is fit for the ordinary purpose for which it was intended) and one of fitness for a particular purpose (merchandise will fit the particular purpose of the buyer).[20]

The seller must be aware of each of these three warranty obligations and the implications of each for the merchandise that he or she is selling. It is also important for the salesperson to know the buyer's obligations.

Buyer's Obligations

The buyer's two major obligations are to pay the contract price and to accept ownership of the goods. Ordinarily, paying the contract price is not a problem since the price is stated in the contract. When it is not stated in the contract, the expectation is that a reasonable price will be paid by the buyer.[21]

A buyer may accept ownership of the goods in three different ways. First, the buyer may positively accept ownership of the merchandise without reservation. Second, the buyer will use the product in a manner that is inconsistent with the rights of the seller, such as before title to the product has actually been transferred from the seller to the buyer. Third, the buyer can accept the product by failing to reject the merchandise by informing the seller of a desire not to accept. If the buyer does choose to reject the seller's merchandise, the buyer must react within a reasonable period of time, must give notice of rejection to the seller, and must protect the seller's merchandise in the meantime.[22]

Breach of Contract by the Seller or Buyer

The salesperson should also be aware of actions that would breach a contract with a customer. The salesperson could breach a contract by disclaiming the contract, failing to make an agreed delivery, or sending goods that don't conform to the contract specifications.[23]

On the other hand, a buyer would breach a contract with a wrongful refusal to accept merchandise, a wrongful returning of merchandise, a failure to make a payment when it is due, an inability or unwillingness to proceed with a contract, or insolvency.[24]

If the buyer or customer wrongfully rejects the goods or becomes insolvent, the seller can take a number of possible actions including withholding delivery of any undelivered goods, recovering the merchandise from the insolvent customer, stopping delivery of any products in transition from the seller to the buyer, reselling the goods and recovering damages or recovering damages if the goods cannot be resold, or simply canceling the contract.[25]

The pervasive issues of ethics and law that surround the professional salesperson are numerous and important. Ethical and legal behavior by the sales representative go hand in hand. Failure to abide by recognized ethical and legal standards will endanger the salesperson's career and his or her company. To be recognized as a professional, the salesperson must possess attitudes and exhibit behavior that coincide ethically and legally with the image of a professional.

SUMMARY

1. Ethics refers to a system or code of morals of a particular profession, group, or person.

2. Three major methods or approaches to deal with ethical dilemmas include the golden rule, the model of utility, and enlightened self-interest.

3. Professional associations, such as the American Marketing Association and the National Association of Purchasing Management, can offer guidance to professional sales personnel with respect to ethical behavior.

4. A salesperson's code of ethics includes issues relating to his or her company, customers, prospects, and competitors.

5. Major pieces of federal legislation such as the Sherman Antitrust Act and the Federal Trade Commission Act focus on business-to-business relationships and buyer-seller relationships.

6. An important legal statute regulating door-to-door direct selling is the cooling-off rule.

7. Key aspects of Article 2 (Sales) of the Uniform Commercial Code cover the obligations of the seller and the buyer with respect to contractual relationships.

8. A salesperson's credibility is based on ethical and legal behavior.

QUESTIONS FOR DISCUSSION AND REVIEW

1. A person is either ethical or not ethical. Agree or disagree?

2. How would you define the term *ethical behavior*?

3. If you had been Becky Dorris in the opening vignette, what would you have done? Why?

4. Why is it important for a salesperson to know potential ethical dilemmas the buyer might face?

5. What do the terms *sharp practices* and *reciprocity* mean?

6. When would reciprocity be inappropriate in the buyer-seller relationship?

7. Why is it important for a company's code of ethics to be in writing?

8. What are some of the major ethical situations faced by the salesperson with respect to his or her company? customers and prospects? competitors?

9. What are the provisions of the cooling-off rule?

10. What are the major obligations of the buyer and the seller under the terms of Article 2 of the Uniform Commercial Code?

CASE 16-1   AN ETHICAL DILEMMA

Sue Jacobs and John Neece were two sales representatives for the Empire Company which sold lawn care products to wholesalers and retailers for ultimate sale to homeowners and commercial property managers. Sue and John had become friends as a result of being members of a sales training class conducted for employees by the Empire Company. Sue was assigned the western Tennessee territory and was based in Memphis while John's territory was in eastern Tennessee and he lived in Knoxville.

The sales force of the Empire company was paid a salary and a bonus based on the amount of product sold during each quarter of the year. It would be possible to earn a total yearly bonus equal to your salary. The company used this system to stimulate sales and level out production of lawn care products over the entire year as opposed to heavy concentration in only the spring and summer months.

In her most recent telephone conversation with John Neece, Sue Jacobs had discovered that John had overstocked his customers in some quarterly periods in order to receive an especially high bonus for that time period. In order to achieve this level of sales in a particular quarter, John told Sue that he engaged in some very aggressive selling, since some customers were reluctant to place such large orders initially.

John went on to tell Sue that in order to consistently gain a bonus he had decided to overstock various customers each quarter with product. While some customers went along with the idea, some others did not. In order to handle those who did not want to buy such large amounts, John Neece decided that if a customer did buy in large amounts, he would use part of his quarterly bonus to purchase a very nice gift for that customer.

While Sue considered John a friend, she was very concerned about what John had told her, since she questioned the ethics of the situation. She knew that the Empire Company did not approve of costly gifts for customers. However, Sue also realized that John had caught the attention of the regional sales manager who had noticed his impressive sales volume during the past year. Sue Jacobs was pondering what actions she should take.

QUESTIONS

1. What do you think of the selling practices of John Neece?

2. What risk is John Neece taking given his present sales practices?

3. What would be your advice to Sue Jacobs?

CASE 16-2 MEETING THE COMPETITION

Sue Adams is a Sales Representative for a wholesaler who sells electrical and plumbing supplies to various commercial building and residential contractors. She has consistently been one of the top ten salespeople for the company in annual dollar volume of electrical and plumbing supplies sold. She has been with the company for the past five years.

During the past few years, a number of mergers and acquisitions have dramatically reduced the number of wholesalers in this industry. There has also been a significant increase in the level of competition for customers, particularly for commercial, as opposed to residential, contractors.

A practice has developed in the selling of supplies that Sue feels she must deal with in order to stay competitive with her competitors. More and more of Sue's competitors are offering substantial gifts to customers based on the size of the purchase order. For example, Sue knows of competitors' sales representatives giving gifts, such as a set of golf clubs, a personal computer, and season tickets for sporting events. Sue's company has a policy of not giving gifts other than their advertising-related items such as calendars, pencil and pen sets, and coffee mugs.

One of Sue's key prospects, D&B Builders, Inc., is represented by its purchasing agent, Arnold Fawks. Mr. Fawks has told Sue his company is about to place an order for almost $35,000 of electrical and plumbing supplies for installation in a new commercial building. Sue knows, from previous meetings, that Mr. Fawks is an avid golfer who plays golf regularly. She realizes he would be very pleased to receive golf-related gifts. Sue also knows that competitors are likely to offer him these types of gifts in order to gain the large dollar order. Sue Adams is contemplating how she should respond in this situation.

QUESTIONS

1. What alternatives are open to Sue Adams?

2. If Sue Adams believes giving gifts to customers and prospects is a competitive advantage for those doing so, what should she do?

3. What would be important for Sue Adams to know about Arnold Fawks and his company?

4. What would you do if you were in Sue Adams's place?

CASE 16-3 WALT WILLIAMS'S EXPENSE ACCOUNT

Walt Williams has been a Sales Representative for Diamond Products for the past twelve years. Diamond Products is a manufacturer and marketer of jewelry items to retail stores throughout the United States. Walt Williams works out of his district office in Des Moines, Iowa. His territory includes all of Iowa, eastern Nebraska, Minnesota, and Missouri.

To stay in close contact with his customers, Walt Williams travels throughout his territory approximately three weeks of every month. He has noticed the costs for lodging and meals have increased over the past year. He has a company car and a company credit card for all automobile-related expenses. Lodging and meal expenses are to be itemized, documented by a receipt, and turned in to his company for reimbursement. Only legitimate business-related expenses are reimbursed by the company, although Diamond Products does not list specific expenses that will not be reimbursed.

Due to the hiring of a number of new sales representatives in the past few years, Walt Williams feels his salary is not appropriate given the salary levels of the new sales personnel. Although all sales representatives for Diamond Products are on straight salary, Walt believes his salary should be about $3,000 more than it presently is because of his length of service to Diamond Products. His annual salary review is not for ten more months, but Walt is thinking of ways to boost his salary or, at least, lower his personal, as opposed to business-related, expenses.

QUESTIONS

1. What measures might Walt Williams take to boost his salary or lower his personal expenses that could pose major ethical dilemmas?

2. What do you think should be the first course of action for Walt Williams to take?

3. If Walt Williams were to pad his expense account, do you think that would be unethical? Illegal? Why or why not?

NOTES

1. *Webster's New World Dictionary* (New York: William Collins/World Publishing Company, 1978), 481.

2. John Browning and Noel B. Zabriskie, "How Ethical Are Industrial Buyers?" *Industrial Marketing Management* 12 (1983): 219. See also Marilyn Lester, "Sales Ethics: Comments from the Other Side," *NAPM Insights* (September 1990): 25–27; and Cornelia H. Tuite, "It May Be Legal, But Is It Ethical," *NAPM Insights* (September 1990): 8.

3. Duane R. Kullberg, "Right and Wrong: How Easy to Decide?" *New Accountant* (September 1988): 19.

4. Ibid.

5. Ibid., 20.

6. Robert I. Felch, *Proprieties and Ethics in Purchasing Management* (Oradell, N.J.: National Association of Purchasing Management, 1986), 3–4.

7. Ibid., 4.

8. Ibid., 4–5.

9. Ibid., 5.

10. William Rudelius and Rogene A. Buchholz, "What Industrial Purchasers See as Key Ethical Dilemmas," *Journal of Purchasing and Material Management* (Winter 1979): 9–10. See also William C. Pursch and Robert A. Holmes, "Making Ethics Work in Business," *NAPM Insights* (September 1990): 10–11.

11. Jules Abend, "Corporate Ethics: An Overview," *New Accountant* (September 1988): 4.

12. Ibid.

13. Ibid., 5–6.

14. "This Industry Leader Means Business," *Sales and Marketing Management* (May 1987): 44.

15. Philip Kotler and Gary Armstrong, *Principles of Marketing* (Englewood Cliffs, N.J.: Prentice-Hall, 1989), 612.

16. Philip Kotler, *Marketing Management: Analysis, Planning, Implementation, and Control*, 6th edition (Englewood Cliffs, N.J.: Prentice-Hall, 1988), 156–57.

17. Robert N. Corley, Eric M. Holmes, and William J. Robert, *Principles of Business Law* (Englewood Cliffs, N.J.: Prentice-Hall, 1983), 797–98.

18. Joseph P. Vaccaro, "The Law and Selling," *Journal of Business and Industrial Marketing* (Winter 1987): 45–46.

19. Ibid., 46.

20. Ibid., 47. See also Karl A. Boedecker, Fred W. Morgan, and Jeffrey J. Stoltman, "Legal Dimensions of Salespersons' Statements: A Review and Managerial Suggestions," *Journal of Marketing* (January 1991): 70–80.

21. Ibid., 47–48.

22. Ibid., 48.

23. Ibid., 50.

24. Ibid.

25. Ibid.

CHAPTER 17

The International Scene

LEARNING OBJECTIVES

After studying this chapter, you should be able to:

1. Understand the factors affecting buyers and sellers from different cultures.

2. Explain how cultural barriers can complicate suppliers' efforts to meet demand for their product or service in a foreign culture.

3. Describe a situation in which a salesperson might jeopardize a relationship with a customer from another culture by using a stereotype.

4. Describe how the social status of salespeople in various cultures affects their credibility when communicating with prospective buyers.

5. Explain how body language differs in various cultures and why sales reps should be aware of the differences.

6. Demonstrate some guidelines for "internationalizing" English.

7. Describe how an interpreter should be used.

8. Identify at least two do's and don'ts that should govern behavior when interacting with people in China, Japan, Russia, France, and the Arab countries.

9. Explain what the Foreign Corrupt Practices Act is and what it allows.

10. Define the key terms used in this chapter.

KEY TERMS

- cultural barriers
- proxemics
- language of time
- language of space
- language of things
- language of friendship
- language of agreements
- ethnocentrism
- high-context language
- the inner circle
- future favor
- inner debt

T'S 2 P.M. and you have been waiting three hours for what was supposed to be an 11 a.m. meeting with a high official in a Latin American country. This is the second time he has kept you waiting. Is he sending you a message?

You have a meeting with a trader in Cairo whom you have heard is one of the best. You walk down a dirty side street into his office and note that it's no more than eight feet by eight feet with the dingiest furniture you have ever seen. Is he the wrong person with whom to do business?

You have just completed lengthy negotiations with the Chinese. Only yesterday you signed the contract, and today they are claiming that the contracted price is too high and they want to change it. Are they being dishonest in trying to change the terms of the contract?

The leader of the Japanese negotiation team has been introduced to you as the most senior official at the table. Do you address all your comments and concerns to him, and do you try to develop a more personal relationship with him?

In Mexico you meet a very senior executive whom you vaguely remember from your last sales trip. He greets you as a long-lost friend and invites you to tour the city sights with him. You have one day left in the city and desperately want to finalize the business deal. Do you make it clear that you don't have the time and would like to discuss business immediately?[1]

These situations are not unusual in international sales; each reflects a variance with our North American values. To be successful in establishing and maintaining strong relationships with people in other cultures, the professional salesperson must quickly adjust to different values. In the first situation, the value of time is involved. United States businesspeople consider it a serious breach of etiquette to ignore or be late for appointments. But the way time is regarded and managed differs from one culture to another.

The second scene reveals how you must adjust to another culture's use of symbols. We often draw conclusions about a person's organizational status by looking at the office furniture, the internal decor, and the location of the office. In some cultures, physical surroundings are not so important.

Agreements (particularly written contracts) carry a great deal of importance among North American business people. As a result, the average sales rep would no doubt be upset with people who sign a contract and then start to renegotiate. The third situation above reveals that not all cultures regard contracts the way we do.

The fourth scene points out a difference in leadership styles. We are used to "the boss" speaking for a group when negotiations are being conducted. The Japanese, however, approach problems as a team, and therefore sales reps should not ignore the other team members.

The fifth situation presents a variance between North American and Latin American interpersonal relationships. The tendency in the United States is to do business in an impersonal way and think of friendship as a by-product that may, eventually, be enjoyed between the buyer and seller. In Latin American countries the personal relationship has to come first. Out of the personal relationship may come business.[2]

As your sales career matures, you may be assigned foreign accounts. Sometimes, you will live in another country and find it necessary to adjust to the new country's values. At other times, your responsibilities may require your calling on accounts in various countries, thereby necessitating a rapid adjustment of your sensitivity to cultural differences.

This chapter contains four major sections. First, we introduce a model that identifies some key factors influencing the interactions of customers and salespeople when they come from different cultures. Second, we examine the way cultural differences can affect interpersonal communications. Third, some do's and don'ts for salespeople conducting business in Japan, Germany, and elsewhere are provided. Finally, the chapter concludes with a section on legal and ethical business practices as interpreted by the Foreign Corrupt Practices Act.

A MODEL IDENTIFYING FACTORS AFFECTING BUYER-SELLER RELATIONS WHEN CULTURAL DIFFERENCES EXIST

Exhibit 17-1 is a descriptive model. Although it cannot be used to predict the outcome of a specific meeting between a salesperson and a potential buyer, it will help you understand the complexities encountered when a salesperson (or a team of salespeople) interacts with a potential buyer who comes from a different cultural background. Specifically, the model serves several important purposes. First, as we look at its component parts (represented by the various levels in the pyramid), we can easily detect that there are a number of factors *other than cultural differ-*

Exhibit 17-1 **Factors Affecting Buyer-Seller Interaction When Participants are from Different Cultural Backgrounds**

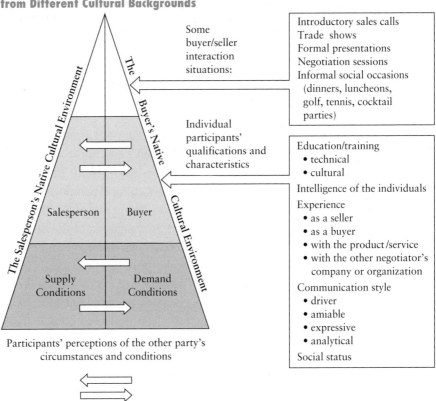

Some buyer/seller interaction situations:

Introductory sales calls
Trade shows
Formal presentations
Negotiation sessions
Informal social occasions
   (dinners, luncheons,
   golf, tennis, cocktail
   parties)

Individual participants' qualifications and characteristics

Education/training
 • technical
 • cultural
Intelligence of the individuals
Experience
 • as a seller
 • as a buyer
 • with the product/service
 • with the other negotiator's
   company or organization
Communication style
 • driver
 • amiable
 • expressive
 • analytical
Social status

The Buyer's Native Cultural Environment

The Salesperson's Native Cultural Environment

Salesperson   Buyer

Supply
Conditions   Demand
Conditions

Participants' perceptions of the other party's
circumstances and conditions

ences that influence a salesperson's and a potential buyer's behavior when they are in each other's presence. Too often, we ascribe any difficulty arising between a salesperson and a prospect from different cultures to the differences between their cultures. But in addition, the sales rep and the buyer may each have different levels of experience and expertise in their respective roles. In many cases, there will be a difference in their intelligence levels. Furthermore, one may be a "driver" and the other may be an "amiable" (see Chapter 8 for review). These highly personal factors will have an impact on the successful formation of a relationship and the sales from it. When these factors are mixed with a difference in cultural backgrounds, circumstances become even more challenging.

The model also accounts for a variety of social circumstances in which salespeople communicate with customers and/or potential customers. Understanding what constitutes appropriate behavior is important when the focus is on buyer-seller interactions conducted between people from the same culture. It is even more challenging when the people involved are from different cultures. The cultural background of the participants serves as an important influence on the outcome whether the relationship is being formed or maintained on a golf course in Tokyo or a boardroom in Berlin.

Finally, the model's design reminds us that *both* the buyer and the seller have been thoroughly conditioned by their respective cultural backgrounds. Cultural conditioning occurs over many years and so permeates an individual's views on life in general and business in particular that it requires a conscious effort to recognize other cultural perspectives. For instance, it is difficult for a salesperson to adjust to being kept waiting an hour or more by someone in whose culture time is not considered important. If the salesperson has the intellectual and emotional capacity to understand and accept other cultural perspectives, communication with a prospective buyer can be conducted much more effectively.

We now turn our attention to a brief analysis of the major components of the model. The first and most basic component is supply and demand.

Supply and Demand Conditions

Regardless of the cultures involved, any seller at any time will have a supply "condition." If the sales rep's firm has excess product on hand, the rep may offer generous terms to potential buyers. Conversely, in times of scarcity, a sales rep may only be able to partially satisfy a buyer. The buyer, likewise, has a demand level for a particular product that may be strong or weak. When it is weak (or even nonexistent), a salesperson may try with varying amounts of success to increase the potential buyer's *awareness* of a need, thus leading to the eventual purchase of the seller's product (see "Problem or Need Recognition" in Chapter 4).

How do cultural environments of the seller and buyer affect supply and demand satisfaction? If a seller has a sufficient amount of a product to fulfill the demands of a potential buyer, why isn't the transaction simply conducted? Because, in many cases, *cultural barriers* hamper the transaction. Culture was defined in Chapter 4 as that set of values, ideas, attitudes, and other symbols and objects created by people, that shapes human behavior.[3] A **cultural barrier** is, therefore, a value, idea, attitude, or way of thinking or behaving that hinders or prohibits someone from a particular culture from accomplishing something in another culture. Language differences, laws, and religious customs are some of the things that can result in cultural barriers and make the conduct of business difficult.

For example, a U.S. company wanting to establish a chain of stores in Japan may be informed that it must first become partners with a Japanese company before the Japanese government will permit operations in Japan. A legal requirement to engage in a joint venture is one example of a cultural barrier.

Cultural barriers are not erected exclusively by other countries to make life more difficult for U.S. firms. A German sales representative trying to become a supplier to Wal-Mart may encounter a cultural barrier in the form of Wal-Mart's "Buy American" policy. Wal-Mart's decision to purchase from companies whenever comparable quality products made in America can be found is a cultural barrier to the German salesperson.

Just as an alert, well-prepared salesperson strives to learn about a customer's demand conditions when both the buyer and seller are Americans, so also must a sales rep seek to understand a buyer's demand conditions when the buyer is from another culture. Difficulties may be introduced to the selling situation by cultural barriers. Although the sales rep for the German manufacturer may not be able to get Wal-Mart to change its policy and thereby remove the barrier, he or she can attempt to overcome it by convincing the Wal-Mart buyer that the German product is a better value for Wal-Mart and its customers than other products that may be in competition. Situations such as this eventually come down to interactions between individuals—salespeople and purchasing agents or buyers—who possess varying degrees of skill and knowledge. A brief analysis of this component of the model consitutes the next step in our examination of factors affecting interactions between buyers and sellers who come from different cultures.

Individual Skills, Knowledge, Communication Styles, and Status

Regardless of a supplier's capacity and a buyer's present or potential demand conditions, the supplier and the buyer will be represented by individuals. The supplier will be represented by a salesperson or, in some complex situations, by a sales team. The potential buyer may be a purchasing agent, a buying committee, or a private citizen. Whatever the circumstances, the people involved will have varying amounts of information about their situation and about each other. They will possess different skills and, of course, in most cases their personal needs will not be the same at any moment in time. All too frequently, these individual differences are ignored when we analyze business dealings with people from other cultures. We tend to stereotype people from other cultures by ascribing some universal characteristic(s) to all the people who come from that culture. For instance, not all Scots are thrifty people; not all British people like fish and chips; nor do all Americans like hot dogs. Articles and books abound on "how to do business" with the Japanese, Germans, Russians, Chinese, and others. The uncritical reader may forget that in a sales situation we are ultimately dealing not with a nationality but with an individual. In the same way, a foreign salesperson who stereotypes all U.S. busi-

Figure 17-1 Business dealings with people from other cultures should be predicated on basic respect for other human beings.

ness people as impatient, aggressive "deal-makers" will be unprepared for the American who knows how to conduct business on an international level.

Just as we have inserted a word of caution to you about simplistic articles and books, we now caution you as you read this chapter to not forget that in sales calls, presentations, trade shows, and other settings there are individuals involved. Although the person's mannerisms, terms of speech, and physical surroundings will be influenced by their native culture, these people bring varying amounts of intelligence, skill, and experience to a particular purchasing situation.

The most important point to remember and put into practice when dealing with people from other cultures is to *be sensitive to general tendencies they may exhibit but never forget that you are interacting with another human being.* Basic respect for another person travels very easily from culture to culture. What specific actions signal respect (or disrespect) will, however, vary from one culture to the next. We provide some guidance on this later in the chapter.

Settings in Which Buyer-Seller Interactions Occur

At the top of the model in Exhibit 17-1 is the "buyer seller interaction." A wide variety of situations bring salespeople into contact with potential buyers and established customers. People's behavior toward each other is influenced by factors such as their perceptions of the other's intentions and behavior toward them. For example, in the United States when a salesperson calls a prospective buyer and asks for an appointment, the prospect knows the general purpose of the proposed visit. Even though a sale may not occur on the first visit, there is usually little or no ambiguity about the situation. Business is what both parties expect to discuss and, in some cases, the quicker the better. In other cultures, however, the interaction usually proceeds in a different way. First, the salesperson needs to find someone to introduce him or her to the prospective buyer. Then one or more appointments will be necessary to permit the buyer and the seller to "get to know each other." After that stage has been accomplished, then business will be discussed.

Not all business abroad is conducted in the traditional office environment. Deals are made in restaurants, in clubs, on tennis courts and, of course, on golf courses. In some cases, it is more important to know *when* to do business than to know what to say. Should you assume, for instance, that after toasting your Japanese dinner guest whom you have just met, you may begin discussions about the arrangements for a purchase?

Effective communication, particularly between people from different cultures, requires sensitivity not only to what is said but also to who in a group makes a statement, body language signals, and even, in some situations, what is *not* said. The next section analyzes the important subject of communication between persons from different cultures.

COMMUNICATION

The Communication Process Model (Exhibit 17-2) depicts the essential components of communication between a sales rep and any customer, whether foreign or not. In the model, the salesperson is considered the source, and the customer/client is the receiver. We should not forget, however, that these roles rapidly change back and forth in a face-to-face sales situation.

In Chapter 2 we learned that it is crucial to successful communication for the sales message to be encoded in such a way that it can be accurately decoded. This is, of course, the essence of effective communication *in any culture*. Later in this section we will present some guidance on how to use English in foreign countries to minimize misunderstandings. First, however, we will examine how salespeople are perceived in various parts of the world.

Exhibit 17-2 The Communication Process

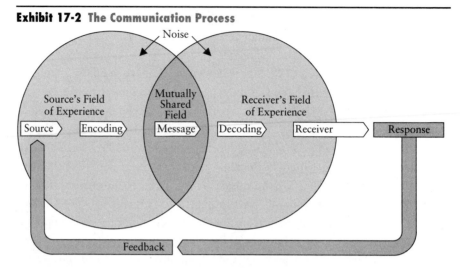

Source: From *Principles of Marketing* by Thomas C. Kinnear and Kenneth L. Bernhardt. Copyright © 1990, 1986 by Scott, Foresman and Company. Reprinted by permission of HarperCollins Publishers.

Perceived Status of the Source and the Receiver

How does the receiver (that is, the prospective customer) perceive the salesperson who, in the communication model, is the source of the communications? Much of our success in communicating with someone depends on how we are perceived. If you are regarded as a skilled professional who can provide solutions to a customer's problems, communications between you and a customer are much more likely to be mutually satisfying. If you are functioning in a culture where salespeople are perceived as unacceptable in some social circles, communication will be much less likely to succeed. In some European countries, salespeople do not enjoy professional status. For example, salespeople in France, in an effort to avoid the social stigma attached to selling, refer to themselves as "commercial attachés."[4]

In China merchants and salespeople have low social status.[5] Japanese, although less prone to automatically assign salespeople to a low status, are concerned about where an individual is located in the organizational structure. Do you have managerial status in your company? Do you have people reporting to you? How much authority and responsibility do you have? These questions help the Japanese customer locate the salesperson in a company's hierarchy. After determining what the salesperson's status is, the Japanese businessperson reacts appropriately to the sales rep's communication efforts. Knowing this is important, consultants to U.S. firms advise American salespeople to have business cards printed in Japanese with the rep's title indicated on the card. Also, to get the communication process started as successfully as possible, consultants recommend that the business cards be tastefully engraved and printed on the best possible paper.[6] The extra expense will pay dividends in enhancing the sales rep's status.

What does one's social status have to do with communication? Shouldn't a person's proposals be judged entirely on their merits? Ideally, the answer to the second question is, "Yes." One of the most important points a person must accept when selling abroad, however, is that U.S. ideals cannot be imposed on foreign buyers. Therefore, the smart sales professional will analyze his or her status as it will be perceived by a customer. You will need to present yourself in ways that will not put you on the defensive when meeting a prospective customer for the first time.

The status of the receiver or customer is also an important factor in successful communication. Americans react to other people's status in a way that may be inappropriate in some cultures. In the opening vignette involving a Japanese negotiation team, a U.S. salesperson could jeopardize communications with the negotiating team by adhering to the typical U.S. practice of directing communications toward the highest-level manager in the customer's group. Such an approach in a meeting with members of a Japanese company would be ill-advised. Because the Japanese apply a team approach to decision making, it would be risky to ignore the other team members even if they do not have the same status as the team leader. In addition to status, we must also consider the way various messages are encoded and decoded.

Encoding

Encoding is the use not only of words but also of physical movements (body language) as well as of symbols, such as gifts and even colors. Green, for example, signifies disease in countries such as Brazil; therefore, marketers must be careful about packaging their products. Since so much communication occurs nonverbally, let us look first at body language signals used in some foreign cultures.

Body Language

One interesting difference to which American businesspeople abroad have to adjust is the physical space in which business conversations occur. The study of personal space and the movement of people within it is called **proxemics**.[7] The distance in a room at which we feel comfortable while engaging in certain types of discussions is a form of nonverbal communication determined partly by our culture.

Sales relationships in North America usually are conducted at distances of four to twelve feet. This, of course, does not include shaking hands. In Latin America, according to noted anthropologist Edward T. Hall, the sales or business conversation occurs at a much shorter distance than in the United States. Latin Americans cannot talk comfortably with each other unless they are very close to the distance that evokes either sexual or hostile feelings in North Americans.[8]

Arab businesspeople use a lot of bodily contact in their conversations; therefore, they also tend to conduct business at close range. Interestingly, the Western "backslap" is considered rude and vulgar by most Arabs.[9] The penchant for close physical contact among Middle Easterners and Latin Americans is not shared by some other cultures. Koreans, for example, avoid physically touching another person. They consider it an affront to the person unless there is a well-established bond of close friendship or childhood ties.[10] Likewise, the Chinese do not like to engage in greetings that involve more than a slight bow.

Another important facet of body language is the use of one's hands and (in some cultures) the display of feet. For instance, a thumbs-up signal might mean "okay" to you, but it is an obscene gesture in the Middle East.[11] The "A-OK" sign of forefinger and thumb in a circle used in the United States means a variety of things abroad. In Japan, it symbolizes money. In France, it means you think someone is worthless (a "zero"). In Malta, it is interpreted as a signal that the communicator wishes to engage in homosexual activity.

When dealing with Arabs you should be careful about how you use your hands *and* feet. Putting your hands on your hips may appear to be a challenging gesture to your Arab business contact. A more serious *faux pas* is exposing the soles of your feet. Arabs consider this very rude.

Figure 17-2 Proxemics, one facet of body language, differs among cultures.

Eye contact is another important aspect of body language. Salespeople in the United States are usually advised to maintain good eye contact. This does not mean staring at the prospect; it means making frequent direct eye contact while avoiding the "shifty" look. Our approach to eye contact and what it means is not universal, however.

Because of their belief that a person's eyes are a window to the soul, Arabs tend to look initially at another person's eyes. This permits them to know more about a person's character. Contrasted sharply with the Arab approach is the Japanese gaze. The Japanese lower their eyes or look downward when showing respect to another party. In Latin American and some African cultures, how long one maintains eye contact with another person is determined by the other person's relative social rank. Prolonged eye contact from an individual of lower status is considered disrespectful.[13]

Usually when we think of encoding messages to be interpreted by someone else, we also think of what we will actually say. This leads us to examine some guidelines for the use of English when transacting business with people whose native language is not English.

GUIDELINES FOR INTERNATIONALIZING ENGLISH

English is considered the world's business language for two reasons. First, most Americans involved in world trade speak only English. Second, even when Americans are not involved, English is likely to be the participants' language in common. Below are several propositions for dealing with non-English-speaking people.

1. Practice using the most common 3,000 words in English, that is, those words typically learned in the first two years of language study. Be particularly careful to avoid uncommon or esoteric words; for example, use "witty" rather than "jocose," or "effective" rather than "efficacious."

2. Restrict your use of English words to their most common meaning. Many words have multiple meanings, and nonnative speakers are most likely to know the first or second most common meanings.

3. Whenever possible, select an action-specific verb ("ride the bus") rather than a general action verb ("take the bus"). Verbs to avoid include "do," "make," "get," "have," "be," and "go." For example, the verb "get" can have at least five meanings (buy, borrow, steal, rent, retrieve), as in "I'll get a car and meet you in an hour."

4. In general, select a word with few alternate meanings ("accurate" has only one meaning) rather than a word with many alternate meanings ("right" has twenty-seven meanings).

5. Conform to basic grammar rules more strictly than is common in everyday conversation. Make sure that sentences express a complete thought, that pronouns and antecedents are used correctly, and that subordination is accurately expressed.

6. Avoid "word pictures," constructions that depend for their meaning on invoking a particular mental image ("run that by me," "wade through these figures," "slice of the pie").

7. Avoid terms borrowed from sports ("struck out," "field that question," "tackle that problem"), the military ("win the marketing war," "outflank the competition"), or literature ("Catch-22").[14]

In some cases, you will find it necessary to use an interpreter. This adds another participant to the encoding-decoding process depicted in Exhibit 17-2.

Guidelines for Using an Interpreter

Harris and Moran, consultants to people doing business overseas, provide anyone thinking of using an interpreter with some helpful guidance. Several of their guidelines are listed below.

1. Brief the interpreter in advance about the subject. (Select an interpreter knowledgeable about the product or service if possible.)

2. Speak clearly and slowly.

3. Do not talk for more than a minute or two without giving the interpreter a chance to speak.

4. While talking, allow the interpreter time to make notes of what is being said.

5. Permit the interpreter to spend as much time as needed in clarifying points whose meanings are obscure.

6. During meetings, write out the main points discussed. In this way, both parties can check their understanding.

7. Don't be concerned if a speaker talks for five minutes and the interpreter covers the speech in half a minute.[15]

Although interpreters are sometimes necessary to facilitate encoding-decoding, you will still need to understand (decode) the various business practices you will encounter overseas.

Decoding

Edward T. Hall, a renowned anthropologist, has alerted American businesspeople to a variety of unspoken yet powerful "languages" they will confront overseas. Hall divided "silent" languages into five categories—the languages of time, space, things, friendship, and agreements.[16]

The Language of Time

Everywhere in the world people use the **language of time** to communicate with each other. For instance, in America if someone does not respond within a few hours or a day to a telephone message we have left for them, we tend to interpret that as a signal that the person is not interested in talking to us. In many foreign countries, this would be a very incorrect interpretation.

Time in the United States is treated very differently than in Ethiopia, where the time required for a decision is directly proportional to its perceived importance. Minor bureaucrats try to elevate their status by taking a long time to make a decision. Doing so makes their work appear more important. Imagine the problems the typical hard-charging American salesperson will encounter when he or she tries to prod the Ethiopian business contact.

Arabs also regard time differently than Americans. The time required in the Arab East depends on the relationship. Close relatives get first priority while others are kept waiting. Also, Arabs seem to be evasive when someone tries to pin them down on when an event or action will occur. Hall interprets the Arabs' reluctance to make a time commitment as indicating that Arab businesspeople tend to take their commitments more seriously than we do. This will be discussed more thoroughly under the language of agreements.

The Japanese have detected a weakness in Americans' perception of time. They have learned that our impatience makes us vulnerable in negotiations. One of them expressed it: "You Americans have one terrible weakness. If we make you wait long enough, you will agree to anything."

The Language of Space

The **language of space** varies considerably around the world. Americans not only analyze the amount of space a customer has in his or her office; we also check to see *where* the office is located. Does the person have an office at the "right address"? Is the office located in an area of the building in which one would expect to find a powerful executive? For instance, a corner office is usually considered to be a signal of a more powerful manager. Another signal is that the higher the office is located in a building relative to other offices in the firm, the more powerful its occupant. Thus, someone whose office is on the top floor of a company's building and in a corner location is perceived by most American businesspeople to be a relatively powerful manager.

A French executive, however, may have an office in the middle of his or her business domain. If the French firm occupies a ten-story building, the top French executive will likely be on the fifth floor and have an office in the center of the floor space.

The Language of Things

Lacking a fixed class system and having an extremely mobile population, Americans have become highly sensitive to how others use material possessions—the **language of things**. Americans view each other's possessions as signaling their status in society. Decoding a person's status in other cultures, however, cannot be accurately accomplished using our value system. Even the British, as closely attuned as they are to our culture, view possessions differently from the way Americans do. Their values of tradition and dependability make them less attracted to fashion-oriented products.

In the opening vignette that takes place in Cairo, the knowledgeable salesperson would ignore the physical surroundings of the trader's office, rather than decoding it by U.S. standards. He or she would realize that the trader's friends and associates in important positions are of much more value to him than are thick carpet, mahogany desks, and other office fixtures.

The Language of Friendship

How long will the friendships continue that you now value so highly? In the **language of friendship**, Americans sometimes pay a high price in interpersonal relationships because of our mobility. Frequently, as we strive to get ahead, we move from one city to another. Usually we make new friends and often tend to lose touch with people we worked and socialized with in our former locations. As a general rule in other countries, friendships are not formed as quickly as in the United States, but they tend to go much deeper, last longer, and involve real obligations.

In our society we usually expect reciprocity from our friends. If we do them a favor, at some point we expect them to return the favor. In India, however, one who does a friend a favor is assumed to be rewarded by having a more positive feeling. In effect, a good deed, according to the Indian perspective, is its own reward.

Africans, as a general rule, place such a high value on friendship that normally before a meeting begins, there is a general talk about events that have nothing to do with business issues.[17] Latin Americans view their friends as a form of disaster protection. Even if the Latin American businesspersons' friends are not faring so well themselves, he or she knows that the friends can still be depended on for help.

When selling in other cultures, U.S. sales reps should be sensitive to the powerful influence friendships have on business affairs. Friendship before business requires that Americans spend more time than they normally would in making a sale. To do otherwise is to risk being considered rude and abrasive.

The Language of Agreements

In the **language of agreements**, Americans tend to think in formal terms. In reality, however, agreements don't necessarily have to be spelled out technically in written contracts. In some cultures, moral practices are understood and adhered to by the vast majority of the populace. Written contracts in such cultures tend to be regarded as signals that one party does not trust the other party in a transaction. Moslems, for instance, view a written contract as a poor reflection on their honor. Unless the contract matter is handled very delicately, a business deal can fail because of their perceptions of the meaning of written agreements.

Greek businesspeople view a contractual agreement as just the opening round of negotiations. After a U.S. sales rep gets a signed agreement with a customer in Greece, the sales rep should not be surprised if the customer continues to negotiate. Negotiation efforts will continue until the goods or services are delivered to the buyer.

Americans assume that prices, delivery time, and quality of goods are constants as spelled out in the contract. To the Korean, however, a change in the economy, the political situation, or even personal circumstances may be reason enough to invalidate a contract.

To gain a better understanding of what it is like to sell to some of America's leading trading partners, we now focus on China, France, the Arab countries, Russia, and Japan.

SALES PRACTICES: SOME DO'S AND DON'TS

Obviously cultures are much more complex in each of the above-mentioned countries than can be described here. Try, however, to project yourself into the role of a salesperson attempting to establish a relationship in one of these countries. You will quickly realize that just because a sales practice or technique has been successful for you in the United States doesn't mean it will be effective (or even polite) in another country. The tendency to think, "If it's good enough for us, it's good enough for them," is called **ethnocentrism**. Falling prey to ethnocentrism is usually disastrous to salespeople who function in markets outside the United States.

Keep in mind, therefore, that some of the advice you have been given on how to deal with sales openings, negotiations, handling objections, and closing will not work in many foreign cultures the way it does in the United States. For instance, an appeal to greater individual productivity that might be very effective in selling PCs in an American office would be ill-advised when selling the same product in China.

Sales Relationships with the Chinese

The Great Wall of China was erected more than 2,300 years ago to keep invading armies from penetrating China's boundaries. As out-of-date as the Great Wall is militarily, there has been no appreciable trade with China until recently. Consequently, most of us have little practical knowledge about the country and its people.

Perhaps most of our information concerning China revolves around its ties to the Communist Party. Even that information is not complete enough for most Americans to talk intelligently about Chinese politics. Therefore, when in the company of Chinese businesspeople, one should not make any comments (especially jokes) about political events in China.

One thing the Chinese have in common with the Japanese is their patience in conducting negotiations. Do not expect to complete a sale quickly. Not only are the Chinese very slow and thoughtful in their transactions, but they prize sincerity and a serious manner in the people with whom they are dealing. The sales rep who is normally an aggressive, assertive sort in the United States should learn to slow down and avoid seeming to "push" a sale. Above all, keep your feelings in check and do not show emotion. To do otherwise is, in the opinion of the Chinese, a form of weakness.

Sales appeals must focus on how a product or service could benefit a *group* of people. Appeals based on how well a product or service would help the individual will not be successful. In addition, a Chinese buyer will not respect a sales rep who attempts to make himself or herself the center of attention. The rep should position his or her *company* as a team of people working together to solve the Chinese customer's problem.

Many times the Chinese customer will use the services of an interpreter even if he or she understands English. The reason is that the extra time needed for translation gives the Chinese buyer added time to think about the negotiations.

Whereas the Chinese seldom reveal outward signs of emotion, this is certainly not true of the French, who seem to enjoy displays of emotion even more than Americans.

Sales Relationships with the French

French society is very stratified, encompassing distinct, well-defined social classes. Upward movement of more than one level in a generation is very rare. Social interaction between people in different classes is affected by class differences. Earlier in this chapter we mentioned the relatively low status of salespeople in France. It is necessary instead to act as a "consultant" who, incidentally, has "solutions" (that is, products and/or services) that are for sale to clients or customers.

Be prepared for confrontations when selling in France. Whereas most Americans want to be personally liked, the French do not seem to possess this trait. The French are hard to impress and do not seem to be particularly interested in people who try to impress them.[18] You should not be discouraged by what Americans would judge to be arguments when meeting with a French sales prospect. A conversation in which disagreements are exchanged can be considered stimulating by the French, while Americans will likely be embarrassed. Recognize an "argument" for what it is and maintain your poise.

Sales appeals to the French buyer based on competitiveness are not usually as effective as such appeals are in the U.S. The social ideals of "liberty, equality, and fraternity" seem to permeate the French approach to competition. The idea of equality and all its implications diminishes a French business executive's zeal to "get ahead" of his or her competitors. Appeals to craftsmanship are, however, likely to be successful. The French take great individual pride in a job or assignment well done. This is difficult for many Americans to understand, because most of the time our pride in excellent performance is based on being superior to our competitors.

Sales Relationships with the Russians

Business deals with the Russians require much time and patience, but not because of their desire to get to know the salesperson better. Most of the time consumed in a business deal results from the time it takes to find the Russian trade official authorized to make a purchase.

The successful U.S. sales rep must have perseverance and flexibility during negotiations with the Russians. It is not uncommon for negotiations for large purchases such as manufacturing plants to drag out over a year. During such periods, it is usually a mistake to give the decision makers the impression that you are trying to rush them. Russians do not like to be rushed by aggressive American sales reps.

Salespeople accustomed to negotiating in the U.S. business environment will be shocked at how Russian purchasing agents handle competitive bids. It is considered unethical in the United States for purchasing agents to reveal other sales-people's bids to competing sales reps.[19] In Russia where bids are employed to play competing vendors against each other, it is not so judged. The rationale is that, ultimately, the buyer will "win" as competitors struggle to lower their asking prices. Another related negotiation tactic is to start with what may be the weakest competitor who is seeking the business. They will wring concessions out of that vendor and then try to impose those concessions on the other contenders.

Russian negotiators do not respect vendors who make large concessions to them. Understandably, they perceive that large drops in prices or the additions of significant services mean that the seller was initially trying to make an exorbitant profit.

Before you quote a final price, make sure all the services and other details (that is, delivery dates, locations, warranty conditions, and so on) are explicitly agreed to. Otherwise, you may find the Russian buyer trying to get extra concessions, such as more service after the sale, after a price is set.

When establishing contact with buyers in Russia, you would be well advised to seek expert guidance from U.S. government officials who are familiar with the Russian system. The Russians are very protocol-conscious. Because of the complexity of their society, you could overlook or unknowingly slight an important Russian trade official.

Sales Relationships with the Arabs

Salespeople and other "people of commerce" are highly respected by the Arabs. (Mohammed the Prophet was considered a man of commerce and married a woman of commerce.)[20] Relationship management among traders has been skillfully practiced by Arabian businesspeople for many centuries.

Be prepared to wait when you are selling to the Arabs, because they have a fatalistic view of time. If you cannot control your destiny, then why should you plan and set schedules? This, in the eyes of many Americans, leads to chaotic situations in which appointments to meet seem to be ignored.

Even when you do meet with your prospective customer, you should plan to spend at least the first meeting (or perhaps the first several meetings) getting to know the other party. Arabs tend to do business because they like the salesperson rather than because they are impressed with the rep's company.

The Arab buyer is not an impassive, unemotional person. The Arabs have what is known as a **high-context language**: what one does with his or her hands, facial expressions, and even noises all mean something in addition to what is actually being said. For instance, the Arab buyer who arches his eyebrows and clucks his tongue is signaling disapproval.

There are several things a U.S. sales rep should keep in mind as he or she builds a relationship with an Arab customer. First, you will be functioning in a male-dominated society. Second, your business cards should be printed in English and Arabic, and your card should be offered to your contact with the Arabic side showing. Third, you should be careful of what you say about a picture, vase, or other item in your host's office. Tradition requires the Arab to offer the possession to the guest when the guest expresses strong admiration. Although it is acceptable to politely decline the offer, it is safer not to have this awkwardness occur. Fourth, although the Arabs are extremely hospitable (for example, a visitor may stay in an Arab's home three days), they do expect you to return their hospitality. Gifts of equal value must be exchanged, and if you are invited into your customer's home, you are expected to return the hospitality in as nearly equal a manner as possible. Finally, you should avoid asking any questions about your Arab customer's wife or any female child above the age of twelve. This situation, once again, reflects the male dominance in that culture. The origins of this practice are ancient.

Sales Relationships with the Japanese

Perhaps the single most important thing for Americans to realize about business dealings with the Japanese is the value the Japanese place on "saving face."[21] If you use this as a guiding principle, other advice about how to deal in Japan becomes very logical. Another important point to guide your behavior is that a Japanese prospective customer is, initially, more interested in knowing about the person with whom he or she is dealing than about the products or services involved. This is in contrast to many American buyers who seem to be largely indifferent to the sales rep as an individual.

Edward and Mildred Hall, noted anthropologists, offer an abundance of useful guidelines in sales negotiations with the Japanese.[22] First, they advise never asking questions unless you are sure your Japanese prospect can answer them. If you have a series of questions to pose in a sales meeting, it would be advisable to submit them in advance so that your Japanese customer can formulate answers. Also, try to avoid asking direct questions ("Will this product be useful to you?"). The Japanese manner can be summarized as one of indirection. The Japanese will avoid asking direct questions and will tend to evade direct questions that are asked of them. The reason for this is their fear that refusal or rejection will upset the much-valued harmony between the buyer and the seller. Try to avoid having to directly refuse a Japanese proposal. If you must do so, remember to state your reasons as fully and politely as possible.

When a Japanese businessperson extends an invitation to you to come to dinner or engage in some other social event, be sure to accept. This is a very important part of relationship building even though you may not discuss any business during the social event. Look to your Japanese host to alert you to the appropriate time to discuss business.

Once negotiations have started, do not make the mistake of revealing your time deadline. Remember that the Japanese believe most Americans are too impatient. If the Japanese negotiator knows you must meet a tight deadline, he or she may stall for time in hopes that you will make concessions to speed up negotiations. Be patient and let your Japanese counterpart know you will be patient. Watch for body language signals you might unconsciously give that would undermine your patient image.

Be prepared for what may seem to you to be long periods of silence during the negotiations. The Japanese say, "Eloquence is silver. Silence is golden."[23] As they use the period of silence to reflect on the negotiations, you too can benefit from the pause by reflecting on what is occurring.

Hall and Hall also recommend what seems to be in the realm of common sense: be prepared. Japanese businesspeople respect technical and business competence. Be sure you not only know your product or service but also thoroughly understand how your company will support the product's delivery, installation, and postsale service. Any financial arrangements, training programs, and production schedules that will have an impact on the transaction should be known by the salesperson who hopes to impress the Japanese buyer.

GIFT-GIVING AND BRIBES

Chapter 16 described some of the principal legal statutes and ethical policies that govern salespeople's behavior in the United States. Sales reps functioning outside the United States sometimes encounter legal and ethical situations that are not as clearly defined as they are in domestic markets. We will analyze some reasons why Americans become puzzled and sometimes respond angrily or awkwardly when confronted abroad by what they consider extortion.

In addition, we will examine how some companies can legally and ethically respond to buyers' requests for gifts when the requests come during overseas operations. As a point of departure in exploring this aspect of international sales, we turn first to a brief examination of the Foreign Corrupt Practices Act.

Foreign Corrupt Practices Act

In 1977 Congress passed the Foreign Corrupt Practices Act (FCPA), which prohibits U.S. companies, their subsidiaries, and their representatives from making payments to high-ranking foreign government officials or political parties.[24] Pay-offs continue in overseas sales, however, because sales reps from other countries who compete against U.S. sales reps aren't as restricted in their use of payoffs. For example, European and Japanese governments view such payments as merely a cost of doing business.

Realizing the seriousness of the situation, many U.S. corporations—notably DuPont, General Motors, IBM, and Lockheed—have spelled out in detail what employees can and cannot do.[25] When a company has explicitly stated what actions are or are not permitted, your decisions about gifts or payments are considerably easier. But not all reps work for such multinational giants. They must occasionally wrestle with such questions as: When can gifts be given to facilitate a sale? Are buyers' requests for gifts to be considered illegal? Part of the answer to such questions lies in examining the cultural context in which the sale is occurring. For instance, a request from a British government purchasing agent that you provide him with $5,000 for buying your pneumatic drill would be different from a similar request from a minor government official in Kenya. Why? Primarily because of cultural tradition; in Britain the tradition of business ethics prohibits such behavior, whereas in Kenya it would be a common practice.

Even the FCPA recognizes such situations. The FCPA does not forbid payments to all parties who may request a payoff. On the contrary, it explicitly allows "facilitating payments" (or "grease payments") to persuade foreign officials to perform their normal duties, at both the clerical and ministerial levels. The law establishes no monetary guidelines but requires companies to keep reasonably detailed records that accurately and fairly reflect the transactions.[26]

Professor Jeffrey A. Fadiman analyzes a variety of situations occurring in Third World countries that we would dub criminal behavior in the United States. Fadiman states, "What may initially appear as begging, bribery, or blackmail may be revealed as local tradition, cross-cultural courtesy, or *attempts to make friends.*" He cites three traditions that form the background for payoffs in Third World countries: the inner circle, the future favor, and the gift exchange.[27]

The Inner Circle

Societies that are not yet industrialized may exhibit some characteristics of tribal and communal organizations. Communal societies tend to view people as either "brothers and sisters" or "strangers," a practice that can be traced back to the very fundamental need to ensure the protection and survival of the group. If you are accepted into the **inner circle** of "brothers and sisters," this opens up an amazing network of contacts that, from a business standpoint, can be quite lucrative. One way of gaining access to a society's inner circle is to incur from one of the group members an obligation to repay you because he or she "owes you a favor."

The Future Favor

Every time a favor (such as giving a gift) is performed, a **future favor** is expected to pay off the obligation. Relationships among people within the inner circles of non-Western nations function through such favors. The Western businessperson unaccustomed to this situation is interested in generating sales to improve his or her company's profits. The Third World businessperson is more interested in creating obligations that will, in turn, lead to stronger, more durable interpersonal relationships between the buyer and the seller.

The Gift Exchange

If the U.S. sales rep does not realize that the Third World buyer holds to a different value system, he or she is unlikely to take the initiative in doing the buyer a favor by giving him or her a gift when a deal is finalized. Knowing this, the buyer may ask for a gift (money or some product or service). If it is forthcoming, the buyer now has, at least in his mind, established within the seller's mind an **inner debt** (*giri* in Japanese). The debt may be paid by the buyer's future purchase of another product from the seller who, in turn, is expected to repay the debt with another gift. Thus, the cycle becomes unending and the relationship is cemented. Is it unlawful or unethical? Those in the United States and in most Western industrialized countries would think so. Thus, it is very difficult when sales reps are sent abroad to keep from moralizing about these practices.

If you are going to give a gift to someone from another country, what should you choose? Are there some items you should avoid? Fortunately, there are a number of excellent sources to consult before you go shopping. *Business Week* magazine usually has a comprehensive supplement to one of its weekly issues in October that gives many useful suggestions to the person shopping for a gift for someone from another country. Also, the Parker Pen Company has compiled an extremely useful book, *Do's and Taboos Around The World* (available through John Wiley & Sons Publishing Company). *Sales & Marketing Management* magazine also sometimes features useful articles and information (see Exhibit 17-3).

A Potential Solution

Fadiman proposes that managers (and salespersons) consider two options. The first option is to regard every request for a gift or payoff as extortion and every petitioner as a potential thief. The second option is to create a "donation strategy." This would entail the selling company's making a donation to medical, educational,

Exhibit 17-3 International Gift Gaffes

Here are some recommendations on what to avoid when giving gifts to business associates who may have different cultural or religious backgrounds. Although some of these points may seem inconsequential, to others they're extremely important and should be strictly heeded.

The Arab World

1. Never give any alcoholic beverage as a gift, in spite of the fact that you may have seen an Arab business associate drink while in another country.
2. Don't send a card with a picture of your family; Moslems regard the family as a private matter.
3. Don't bring or send a gift for your host's wife (or wives).
4. Don't give food, which may offend an Arab's sense of hospitality.
5. Don't give a sculpture depicting an animal or human form; in Islamic cultures these are considered graven images and may offend.
6. Never offer anything with your left hand.

Australia

Australia, although fundamentally a British-based culture, has extremely strict quarantine laws that business gift givers should be aware of. All meats (even canned), straw articles like baskets and hats, certain "origin-related" wood products, feathers, and dairy products, including cheeses, are banned.

China

1. It's not wise to give commemorative medals or tokens, since they may be mistaken for foreign currency, which the Chinese aren't allowed to accept as gifts.
2. Avoid giving clocks to older, more traditional Chinese; the English word "clock" is a homonym for the Chinese word for "funeral."
3. Avoid writing in red ink, unless a card is preprinted, since it means you're cutting off a friendship.

Italy

1. Don't give chrysanthemums—they're symbols of mourning.
2. The number 17 is considered an unlucky number (13 is the luckiest) for flowers as well as overall good fortune.
3. Avoid giving anything purple, the color of death in Italy.

Japan

1. Avoid the number 4 and 9 anywhere on gifts, since they have homonyms that connote death and suffering.
2. Gifts that consist of less than 10 items should be given in odd numbers. Place settings and tea cups, for example, are sold in Japan in sets of five.

Korea

1. Again, the number 4 is considered unlucky, so never give anything in a set of four or four separate items.
2. Don't give shoes as a gift—it implies that the giver wishes to kick the person receiving the gift.

Source: "Beware the Purple Pigskin Clock!" *Sales & Marketing Management* (August 1990): 76.

or agricultural projects at the provincial, district, or even village level, focusing consistently on the geographic areas from which the buyer comes. Many U.S. companies now simply donate funds. For example, those in Bali contribute large sums to local temples; those in Senegal donate to irrigation projects.[28] In such cases, U.S. businesses and their personnel can remain competitive on the international stage while also enhancing the social welfare of Third World countries.

Of course, the decision to treat requests for gifts as though they were opportunities for donations is a matter requiring consideration by top management. No first-line salesperson or even sales manager would realistically expect to decide on how such delicate matters should be handled. As a sales rep operating in a "global village," you may very well be confronted with situations similar to those described in this chapter. When you are, and if your company has no established policy, you should refer the matter to your senior managers and legal counsel for guidance.

SUMMARY

1. The basis for any interaction between a salesperson and a customer or potential customer is supply and demand. In a relationship management-oriented selling approach, the sales rep attempts to ensure that a customer, even if he or she has no immediate need, continues to regard the sales rep's company as the optimal source of supply when the product or service is needed.

2. Cultural barriers sometimes hamper smooth supply-demand relationships.

3. It is crucial for salespeople to remember that they are dealing with individuals and to recognize their customers as individuals. Stereotyping people from other cultures leads to false and damaging assumptions.

4. The particular setting in which a salesperson and a customer meet must be factored in to realistically analyze a cross-cultural sales situation. For instance, playing a round of golf with Japanese executives is not the same as playing with Americans.

5. The ability to properly decode the spoken and unspoken communication signals transmitted by a customer or group of customers is one of the keys to successful selling. The other key is the proper encoding of information you wish to impart to your customer.

6. The salesperson and the customer possess status that will affect how each party perceives and interprets the other party's statements. A U.S. sales rep needs to understand how salespeople are perceived in the customer's country.

7. A U.S. sales rep should examine his or her notions about what signals accurately identify another person's social standing. For example, not all people who occupy dingy or unassuming offices abroad are poor or lack power.

8. The body language and especially hand gestures salespeople sometimes use must be analyzed to avoid embarrassment on the international scene.

9. Communications between U.S. salespeople and foreign customers can be improved if the salesperson will employ the guidelines to internationalize English and, when an interpreter is necessary, use the individual wisely.

10. Understanding the various silent languages in overseas trade requires that the salesperson analyze cultural differences in the way his or her customers view time, space, things, friendship, and agreements.

11. Patience and the suppression of emotions will pay dividends when dealing with Chinese buyers.

12. French customers are prone to express their emotions and even enjoy conversations that may appear to Americans to be arguments. Sales appeals to a French buyer based on winning competitive battles are less effective than appeals to the buyer's respect for craftsmanship.

13. A Russian negotiator, when several companies are bidding for business, may attempt to play one company against the others. Patience and firmness are traits the Russian negotiator respects.

14. A salesperson should not be alarmed at the Arab customer's habit of not keeping appointments on time and should be prepared to spend the first part of the initial meeting (or even several meetings) in establishing personal rapport. Arab buyers seem to be more concerned with the individual with whom they are doing business than with the person's company.

15. U.S. sales reps should take great care to help the Japanese customer "save face" and never embarrass or put the Japanese buyer in an obvious position of weakness, such as by asking direct questions the customer cannot answer. Sales reps should also maintain their poise at all times and prepare carefully prior to meeting with Japanese customers.

16. The Foreign Corrupt Practices Act makes it illegal to give payments to high-ranking officials or their political parties for the purpose of making a sale or increasing the profits from a sale. Donations to hospitals, agricultural projects, schools, or other institutions, however, can legally benefit a buyer's country, region, or village.

QUESTIONS FOR DISCUSSION AND REVIEW

1. What are cultural barriers? Identify three and explain how they hamper a free flow of goods and services between two countries.

2. What are stereotypes, and why are they dangerous insofar as salespeople are concerned?

3. Examine Exhibit 17-2 and explain how a stereotype could be a form of "noise." Give an example showing how it will affect the encoding-decoding process.

4. Why does "cultural environment" run up and down both sides of the pyramid in Exhibit 17-1?

5. Describe the various silent languages that were explained in this chapter.

6. After analyzing a sales training program designed to prepare sales reps for overseas assignments, a consultant says, "I think this program suffers from ethnocentrism." What does the consultant mean?

7. Are all payments to purchasing agents or government officials at any level considered illegal under the Foreign Corrupt Practices Act? Explain.

8. What advice would you give to a salesperson who, after meeting with a Japanese customer, reported, "The sale is sewn up. I got the customer to agree with everything I said"?

9. If you are selling to a Russian purchasing agent who you know is soliciting bids from your competitors, what can you expect to encounter in your negotiations?

10. What are the inner-debt and future dept concepts and how do they, presumably, foster long-lasting relationships among buyers and sellers in some foreign countries?

CASE 17-1 THE ART OF GIFT GIVING

John Malloch listened to Sue Foster wrap up the training program sponsored by Universal Communications Company. Sue was explaining to John and several other people Universal's approach to giving gifts to people in buying positions overseas.

Sue: "What I am about to tell you will shock you if you know anything about our purchasing department's code of ethics. What I am going to advise you to do would never be acceptable here. I can assure you, however, that our company's top management and our legal staff have considered this and they have approved it.

"Our policy is basically this. You have in front of you our company catalog with products you can give as gifts to people abroad who you believe have helped you in getting a sale made. You'll see there are many items, such as gold and silver pen and pencil sets, golf putters, tennis racket carrying cases, articles of clothing, and so forth. You'll also note that each item has our corporate logo stamped or engraved on it. Each item is absolutely top-quality merchandise. You should order large quantities of these goods so you can avoid ever being out of any item you might need as a gift. Now here is the important thing to keep in mind. Some of the purchasing agents you will do business with believe they will be doing you a favor if they ask you for a gift for themselves after they have given you an order from their company. Don't wait for them to ask. Take the initiative and give them a gift *before* they feel compelled to ask. In other words, beat them to the punch. As long as you give them items from this catalog, there is absolutely no problem. Technically or legally, these gifts with our logo on them are promotional items. In our legal system, these are not in violation of our laws. Are there any questions?"

John Malloch raised his hand and said, "What about cases in which we have very large accounts of, say, over $50 million per year and there is a constant stream of purchases going on? I can't be running out to the customer's plant every day or so with a coffee cup or a pen set."

"Glad you asked, John. In those cases, our top management has met with the managements of those accounts. I don't know the details, but in the case of our key accounts, the super-large customers, you won't be approached by lower-level people. If you are, they are out of line."

As John and the other people left the session Sue caught up with John and said, "I know it goes against the grain to do something overseas you have been told not to do here in the States."

"It sure does, Sue. My brother works in purchasing right here in this building. Once a year for ten years he has signed a statement indicating he has read and understands Universal's policy on accepting gifts. Now here I am with a catalog ordering probably several thousand dollars worth of stuff to give away in my new job overseas."

"Well," Sue said, "What do they say—to get along, go along?"

Questions

1. What cultural practice described in Chapter 17 is illustrated in this case?

2. How might Sue Foster diminish the discomfort John Malloch and other salespeople may be feeling by describing the practice referred to in the preceding question?

3. Are there any ethical problems in this case? Explain.

4. In the case, mention is made of Universal's very large accounts. How might Universal's top management legally give a "gift" to its major accounts?

Case 17-2 A Lesson in the Art of Japanese Deal-Making

Franklin Stubbs ran a polishing cloth over his shoes as he listened to Shin Yamota. Yamota was briefing Stubbs on what to expect at a dinner party they were hosting later that evening for a very important customer. The conversation had been going on for about fifteen minutes.

Yamota said, "There will be six of us—three people from SFC and three of us. Their senior manager's name is Toyoo Ohkawara. That's pronounced *Oh-ka-wara* with the accent on the wara. He will be your dinner partner and he will sit across from you. I will be seated next to you on your left, and my assistant will be to my left."

"Okay," said Stubbs, "and am I correct? Do I bow to Toyoo and give him my card first and then present my card to each of his guys?"

"That's correct. Be sure you give them the cards with the side up that is printed in Japanese."

This crash course in Japanese business etiquette was necessary because Franklin Stubbs had never made a business trip to Japan. Stubbs was Vice President of Sales for Rolemore Paper Company in Spokane, Washington which has recently become a partner with Sanbo Trading Company in Kobe, Japan.

Shin Yamota was a senior partner in the Sanbo Company who had been calling on different purchasing agents in the SFC Corporation for several months. SFC-Japan is a leading fast-food chain of 400 stores in Japan. Sanbo Company, in the person of Shin Yamota, was attempting to sell paper supplies (cups, napkins, food wrappers, and straws) to SFC. Yamota had made progress in his talks with SFC personnel, but now SFC's management wanted to meet a representative of the U.S. company that would be making the products. Rolemore would manufacture the cups, napkins, and other supplies and ship them to Japan where Sanbo would act as the distributor. The dinner meeting was, therefore, a major opportunity for both Sanbo and Rolemore. If Stubbs and Yamota could cement relations with important people from SFC, the Japanese trading company and the U.S. manufacturer would both benefit.

Yamota: We will start the meal with saki. You will be expected to offer a toast to Mr. Ohkawara. I have written a very short sentence or two and will give you some help in pronouncing the words in Japanese. Our guests will appreciate your trying to speak our language even though they know it is somewhat difficult for you.

Stubbs: Okay. That's fine. About all I know now is *arigato* (thank you).

Yamota: Don't worry. Ohkawara and his people all speak English and are quite willing to do so, but some evidence on your part that you are willing to speak Japanese will do us a lot of good.

Stubbs: I'll try. Now tell me, when should we get down to business?

Yamota: That opportunity may not present itself at all tonight. We shouldn't be disappointed if we don't talk business. The best thing for you to do is to let me tell our guests about your position at Rolemore. They will want to know how much authority you have. I can tell them that more tactfully than you can.

Stubbs: (somewhat impatiently) Okay, okay, but here it is Monday evening, and I need to be back in Seattle by Wednesday night.

Yamota: Don't mention that or even suggest you have a deadline. Ohkawara and his people will stall us if you indicate your impatience.

QUESTIONS

1. What advice is Yamota giving Stubbs that is supported by information in the chapter?

2. What is the biggest error Stubbs could make if he ignores Yamota's advice?

3. What Japanese cultural value would cause the SFC executives to choose not to talk business at the dinner party?

CASE 17-3 JOAN TURNER'S CONVERSATION WITH A FRENCH CUSTOMER

Joan Turner has been selling automotive parts and installation equipment to automobile manufacturers for twenty years. Recently, her company exhibited its products at a trade show in London. One of the many visitors who viewed the Safety Webbing Company's exhibit was a purchasing agent from Franc Automotive Manufacturing Company. Franc has several manufacturing plants located throughout France, but its headquarters and safety-testing facilities are on the outskirts of Paris.

Ms. Turner contacted the purchasing agent who saw the exhibit and he, in turn, suggested that she set up an appointment with Dr. Jean Laval, a safety design engineer. Dr. Laval is in charge of testing a new automobile Franc will be selling in Europe and Canada in two or three years. Turner and Laval are seated in his office discussing Safety Webbing's passenger restraint system.

Laval: Ms. Turner, what is it about your restraint system that makes it better than your competitors'?

Turner: I'm very glad you asked that question, Dr. Laval. For one thing, we have over twenty years' experience in making seat belts and harnesses for racing cars and automobile manufacturers in the United States. We have the largest market share of any manufacturer of seat belts in the United States. . . .

Laval: (interrupting her in midsentence) That's of no consequence as far as I'm concerned. Tell me why your products are better. My colleagues tell me there are three or four other manufacturers who have a superior product.

Turner: I don't know what criteria your sources are using, but I can assure you that we will let you choose any tests you want to conduct, and our products will be evaluated as superior in overall quality.

Laval: Aha, now there is a suitably ambiguous phrase—"overall quality."

Turner: Dr. Laval, what specific qualities or features are most important to you, an expert, in auto safety engineering?

QUESTIONS

1. Dr. Laval seems to be trying to provoke an argument with Ms. Turner. Should Ms. Turner believe that Laval has a prejudice against her company and its products?

2. How can Ms. Turner use the art of asking good questions to her advantage?

3. Was it a mistake for Ms. Turner to mention that her firm has the largest share of the United States market? Why?

4. From what we know about French respect for craftsmanship, what would you advise Ms. Turner to do in her conversation with Dr. Laval?

NOTES

1. Jonathan L. Calof and Henry W. Lane, "So You Want to Do Business Overseas? Or Ready, Fire, Aim," *Business Quarterly* 52 (Winter 1987): 52–57.

2. Brian H. Flynn, "Homing in on Foreign Sales Customs," *Business Marketing* (June 1987): 90–92. See also John S. Hill, Richard R. Still, and Unal O. Boya "Managing the Multinational Sales Force" in *International Marketing Review*, Vol. 8, No. 1 (1991): 19–31.

3. William H. Cunningham, Isabella C. M. Cunningham, and Christopher M. Swift, *Marketing: A Managerial Approach* (Cincinnati, Ohio: South-Western Publishing, 1987), 154.

4. Ibid. See also Hill, Still, and Boya "Managing the Multinational Sales Force," 19–31.

5. Esther Lee Yao, "Venturing Through China's 'Open Door,'" *Business Marketing* (February 1988): 63–66.

6. Edward T. Hall and Mildred Reed Hall, "Selling to a Japanese," *Sales and Marketing Management* (July 1987): 58–61. See also Perry W. Buffington, "Practical Protocol" *Sky* (November 1991): 79–81; and Roger E. Axtell, *Do's and Taboos Around the World*, 2nd ed. (New York: John Wiley & Sons, Inc., 1991), 8.

7. Anthony Alessandra, James Cathcart, and Phillip Wexler, *Selling by Objectives* (Englewood Cliffs, N.J.: Prentice-Hall, 1988), 288. See Also James C. McElroy, Paula C. Morrow, and Sevo Eroglu, "The Atmospherics of Personal Selling," *Journal of Personal Selling & Sales Management*, Vol. X (Fall 1990): 31–41.

8. Edward T. Hall, *The Silent Language* (Garden City, N.Y.: Doubleday, 1959), 209.

9. Philip R. Harris and Robert T. Moran, *Managing Cultural Differences*, 2nd ed. (Houston, Tex.: Gulf Publishing Company, 1987), 476.

10. Ibid., 411.

11. "Some Gestures Not Necessarily A-OK Abroad," *Houston Post* (February 12, 1989): A34. See also Axtell, *Do's and Taboos*, 41–49.

12. Harris and Moran, *Managing Cultural Differences*, 476.

13. Ibid., 44. See also "Look'em In The Foot," *Houston Post* (March 7, 1991): B1.

14. D. I. Riddle and Z. D. Lonham, "Internationalizing Written Business English: Twenty Propositions for Native English Speakers," *The Journal of Language for International Business* (Spring 1985).

15. Harris and Moran, *Managing Cultural Differences*, 87–96. See also Masumi Muramatsu, "The Perils of an Interpreter," *Speaking of Japan*, Vol. 10, No. 110 (February 1990): 4–11.

16. Edward T. Hall, "The Silent Language in Overseas Business," *Harvard Business Review* (May–June 1960): 87–96. See also Vern Terpstra and Kenneth David, *The Cultural Environment of International Business,* Third Edition, (Cincinnati, Ohio: South-Western Publishing Company, 1991), 112–16; Buffington, "Practical Protocol,": 79–81.

17. Harris and Moran, *Managing Cultural Differences*, 484.

18. Ibid., 448. See also Pat Rosen, "French Influence Found in Varied City Businesses," *Houston Business Journal* (July 2, 1990): 14B.

19. Michael R. Leenders, Harold E. Fearon, and Wilbur B. England, *Purchasing and Materials Management*, 9th ed. (Homewood, Ill.: Irwin, 1989), 297–98.

20. Harris and Moran, *Managing Cultural Differences*, 473. See also Axtell, *Do's and Taboos*, 27.

21. Harris and Moran, *Managing Cultural Differences*, 391.

22. Edward T. Hall and Mildred Reed Hall, *Hidden Differences: Doing Business with the Japanese* (New York: Doubleday, 1987). See also Ted Holden and Suzanne Woolley, "The Delicate Art of Doing Business in Japan," *Business Week* (October 2, 1989): 120; and David N. Burt, "The Nuances of Negotiating Overseas," *Journal of Purchasing and Materials Management* 25, no. 1 (Spring 1989): 52–56.

23. Hall and Hall, "Selling to a Japanese," 61. See also Dean C. Barnlund, "Public and Private Self in Communicating With Japan," *Business Horizons* (March–April 1989): 32–40.

24. Jean-Pierre Jeannet and Hubert D. Hennessey, *International Marketing Management: Strategies and Cases* (Boston, Mass.: Houghton Mifflin, 1988), 125–26. See also "Doing Business Abroad With Fewer Restraints," *Wall Street Journal* (June 5, 1990): B1.

25. Ibid., 126.

26. Jeffrey A. Fadiman, "A Traveler's Guide to Gifts and Bribes," *Harvard Business Review* (July–August 1986): 122–36.

27. Ibid. See also Axtell, *Do's and Taboos*, 141–145; Sondra Snowdon, "Wordly Gifts and Protocol Tips," *Business Week* (October 20, 1989): 56–58; and Dawn Bryan, "Beware the Purple Pigskin Clock!" *Sales & Marketing Management* (August 1990): 74–80.

28. Ibid.

CHAPTER 18

Sales Career Management

LEARNING OBJECTIVES

After studying this chapter, you should be able to:

1. Describe how the marketing concept can be applied to career management in the personal sales field.

2. Explain the significance of environmental influences on the career opportunities confronting salespeople in the 1990s.

3. Describe each of the personal marketing mix variables you have to work with to make yourself a valuable sales resource to an employer.

4. Illustrate the four stages of a career life cycle and describe what happens to salespeople in each stage.

5. Define the key terms used in this chapter.

KEY TERMS

- macroenvironmental factors
- globalization
- intra-industry concentration
- national account or key account sales team
- stress interview
- geographic mobility
- functional mobility
- career pathing

- staff positions
- line personnel
- career life cycle
- achievement level
- preparation phase
- development phase
- maturity phase
- decline phase

FRANK BROWER AND JOAN FULLER were recently hired by the Apex Corporation. During their first month at Apex, they attended a company social function honoring a sales rep who was retiring after thirty years of service. They listened to various people tell about the retiree's accomplishments. One of the speakers, Apex's vice president of sales, climaxed the session by presenting the new retiree with a gift and reflecting on his contributions. The vice president remarked that it had become a growing rarity to see sales personnel who stay with a company for thirty years. "Now," he said, "everyone seems to 'try on' a company like an article of clothing. If it doesn't instantly satisfy them, they shed it and move on to another situation—to another company."

After the retirement party, Frank and Joan reflected on the comments over cups of coffee. "Would you have stayed with Apex for thirty years?" asked Joan. "I don't know," Frank responded, "Joe was making over $100,000 a year when you consider his salary plus commissions. He's been a top producer here for the past ten years. One guy told me his income is more than some managers who are two levels above him, because they aren't on salary plus commission."

"Now that we're out here in the 'real world,' do you ever feel that Apex bought us in much the same way they buy raw material for their manufacturing operations?" Joan asked.

"That may be," Frank said. "After all, why do you think they call the personnel department Human Resources? One of their major responsibilities is to keep a steady supply of human resources coming into the company and keep tabs on what departments need more resources such as engineers or salespeople. The screening tests we took, I think, helped the company ensure that we met their specifications in the same way that a purchasing agent uses buying specs to determine whether a brand of product should be purchased."

Joan smiled and asked, "So what's the moral of your story, Frank?"

"Don't become an obsolete product," Frank said.

In Chapter 1 we asked the question, "What is a professional?" In numerous ways we have examined what professional salespeople do and what skills they must have. Now that we have reached the conclusion of this book, it is appropriate to take a long-range perspective and ask another question: "How will you manage your sales career?" The purpose of this chapter is to provide a perspective that will help you analyze your future career decisions. As you proceed through this chapter, you will not find descriptions of selling in retailing environments, selling in manufacturing, and so forth. We have chosen to avoid compartmentalizing selling in this fashion. Instead, we have concentrated on decisions you must and will make at different stages in your career.

Initially, you are asked to consider the implications for career management if you agree with Frank Brower's opinion. He stated that human resources departments acquire people for their respective companies in much the same way purchasing agents buy materials and supplies to keep a company running. One of the most important implications of this view is that *you must be a skillful marketer of your most valuable product—yourself.*

The second major section in this chapter analyzes individuals' career life cycles in sales. At this point, you should be familiar with the concept of a career life cycle. It will prove beneficial to consider how you can use life cycle analysis to give you some insights about different career stages.

For readers interested in immediate assistance in launching a sales career, Appendix B gives pointers and guidance on writing resumés and engaging in interviews.

THE HUMAN RESOURCES PERSPECTIVE

The statement, "People are our most important resource," has become a cliché. Executives' speeches to audiences, annual reports, and company newsletters and magazines frequently contain the proclamation that the people who work for a company are that company's most vital resource. Although the statement may be reassuring to employees, it should cause all of us to reexamine how we as individuals are regarded by the firms and organizations that employ us. Analyzing this perspective will provide useful insights.

Initially, let us ask what *other* resources the users of this cliché have in mind. Economists have long used people, money, material, land, labor, and capital to describe the resources needed by an organization. How are these resources acquired? They are purchased. People are paid for their services to a company, and any firm must have a sufficient supply of suitably skilled people to stay in business.

Furthermore, as business conditions change, the firm's needs for different skills in its work force also change.

The acquisition and maintenance of an effective sales force staffed by intelligent, motivated individuals are the keys to marketing victory. Knowing this, corporate human resources specialists conduct vigorous, expensive search and screening efforts to acquire talent. For those individuals who have the appropriate skills or who appear to possess the potential for acquiring the skills, this situation is very beneficial. The graduating senior or MBA whose qualifications match the needs of corporate recruiters finds himself or herself in an enviable position. Apparently Frank Brower and Joan Fuller had the "right stuff" to be hired by Apex. In a very real sense, they sold their talents to Apex. Those two people met the hiring specifications used to select sales trainees.

Although Frank and Joan probably didn't consciously view themselves as products or resources that were being purchased, they apparently had packaged themselves in a number of ways that made the Apex purchasing agents (that is, the campus interviewer and other Apex human resources personnel) believe that Joan and Frank would be desirable assets to Apex. Now that Joan and Frank are employed by Apex, both of them must retain their value as human resources if they desire to remain and be promoted. The alternative, if they fail to live up to the potential expected of them, will be dismissal or stagnation at an entry-level job.

Joan and Frank would be well advised, therefore, to think of themselves, individually, as products that are salable to buyers (employers). By adopting this perspective, these two newcomers to the corporate world will realize the need to market themselves for the duration of their careers. They can most effectively market themselves by using the marketing concept and regarding themselves as marketing managers responsible for marketing a product (themselves). One helpful framework to guide them is found in Exhibit 18-1.

The Marketing Management Framework

As you examine Exhibit 18-1, three characteristics are important. First is the "big C" (the customer) in the center of the exhibit. A product or service's design and its price, promotion, and distribution revolve around the all-important entity—the customer. Second, each of the variables—product, price, place, and promotion—are symbolically equal in the model. A marketing manager must carefully consider each of them to provide an offering the customer will find attractive. Third, the outer ring contains variables that are relatively uncontrollable by the marketing manager. These environmental factors or conditions have an impact on customers and the marketers who serve those customers. For example, the increasing medical evidence revealing the dangers of cigarette smoking is an output coming from

Exhibit 18-1 Marketing Management Framework

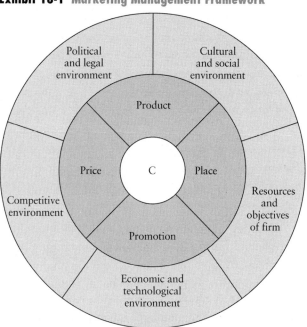

Source: Jerome McCarthy and William D. Perreault, Jr., *Basic Marketing: A Managerial Approach*, 9th ed. (Homewood, Ill.: Irwin, 1987), p. 47. Copyright © 1987 by Richard D. Irwin, Inc. Reprinted with permission.

the medical technology environment. As this is communicated via the media, it eventually influences our cultural and social environment and even has an impact on the legal environment (laws requiring cigarette manufacturers to put warning labels on packages and in advertisements). Clearly such reverberations influence consumers who in great numbers have decided to quit smoking. Therefore, a marketing manager is well advised to stay attuned to environmental changes to keep from being unpleasantly surprised and to gain a better understanding of what the future holds for his or her product/service.

How could a framework like this be useful to Frank and Joan and to you? By modifying the variables but using the same physical form of the model in Exhibit 18-1, we can analyze what you as a career manager can do to market yourself more effectively.

A Career Management Framework

Exhibit 18-2 contains the modifications mentioned above. The employer replaces the customer at the center of the model. The employer, according to our analogy, is purchasing your services as a salesperson. As we mentioned earlier, employers such as Ford, Monsanto, Boeing, and others send out purchasing agents (college recruiters) to search for talent. Years of experience and careful study by human resources specialists coupled with input from the departments that need employees make these recruiters some of the most careful "shoppers" in the world. What are some of the major forces and circumstances that influence these talent scouts in their search for human resources? This can best be answered by looking at the factors identified in the outer circle of Exhibit 18-2. Some analysts refer to these as **macroenvironmental factors**.[1] They are such broad and powerful conditions or trends that they affect, in some cases, entire industries and tens of thousands of companies. This will become apparent as we describe each trend and its impact on the acquisition of human resources. In addition, we will indicate what each condition or trend portends for salespeople trying to manage their careers in sales in the 1990s and beyond.

Reorganization

In an effort to improve productivity and reduce overhead costs, many firms have analyzed and then reduced the number of their managerial levels.[2] The result has been "flatter" organizational structures with fewer reporting levels between sales

Exhibit 18-2 **A Framework for Marketing Yourself**

representatives and executive-level management. Rather than having a multilevel structure such as depicted in part A of Exhibit 18-3, the newer structure now emerging looks more like B in the exhibit.

One of the results of this streamlining has been to push decision making and responsibility into lower levels of the organization. In the past several years, firms such as IBM, DuPont, Ciba Geigy, John Hancock Mutual Life, Coca Cola U.S.A., GTE, and V.F. Corp.'s Wrangler Division have restructured parts of their marketing and sales organizations to permit them to reduce costs and make decisions faster.[3]

What does this mean to you, a possible future employee, in companies that are being streamlined? First, as we can see in the before and after examples in Exhibit 18-3, there are fewer management positions. As one writer aptly phrased it, "There

Exhibit 18-3 **Reorganization: A Before and After Comparison**

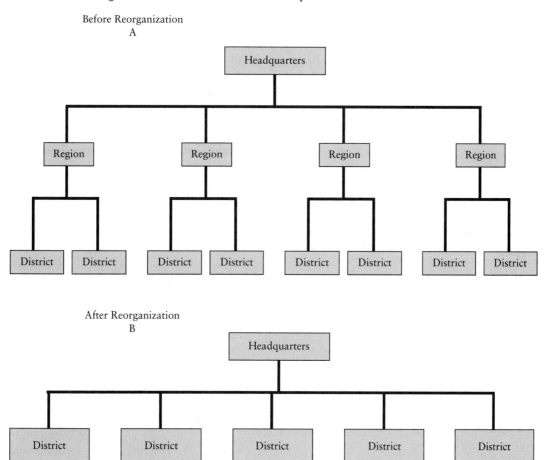

aren't as many rungs in the corporate ladder as there used to be." This can be disappointing to some people who aspire to relatively rapid promotion.[4]

The second implication is perhaps, in the long run, more challenging to firms as they analyze potential employment candidates. People who are expected to make more decisions and shoulder more responsibility must be more intellectually capable and, in general, better managers at an earlier age than their counterparts of the 1960s and 1970s.

The sales rep who must manage himself or herself in some matters previously reserved to upper management has greater autonomy. With this greater self-governance comes increased responsibility to produce results. Thus, recruiters are looking even more vigorously for the Frank Browers and the Joan Fullers who are self-starters. Individuals who can thrive on managing relationships both on an intra- as well as an intercompany basis are going to be needed in the 1990s and beyond.

Globalization

In 1992, trade barriers fell in Europe, making it easier to do business.[5] The Pacific Rim countries are rapidly emerging as contenders (in some industries as leaders) in manufacturing.[6] The effect is obvious. Competition is no longer confined to companies in an industry in the United States. The U.S. automotive industry, for example, no longer regards competition as comprising only Ford, General Motors, and Chrysler.

Although, according to some business authorities, the United States is still considered the richest market in the world, we cannot and are not ignoring opportunities to sell abroad. Companies that are household names in the United States garner very significant amounts of revenue from their global operations (see Exhibit 18-4).

Increasing **globalization**—the entire world as a possible market for goods and services—has considerable potential significance for your career. One outgrowth is an increase in internal competition among employees in firms with global operations. Human resources are becoming more interchangeable from one country to another. A manager who has caught the eye of upper-level executives as a result of solving a sales problem in the United Kingdom may be transferred to America to solve a similar problem. You may, therefore, someday find yourself competing for a promotion not just with other people in domestic divisions but with someone in another country who is also an employee of your company.

Another factor closely related to relationship management involves the management of a relationship with a customer who has divisions or operating units scattered all over the world. If your responsibility is to maintain and strengthen the relationship with Federal Express, for instance, you must know how to serve their

Exhibit 18-4 **A Dozen Top Global Players**

Company	Foreign Sales as % of Sales	Best-Selling Product Abroad	Biggest Market Abroad
Boeing	46%	Commercial airliners	Western Europe
Caterpillar	50%	Earthmoving equipment	Western Europe
Dow	55%	Industrial chemicals	Canada
Eastman Kodak	45%	Amateur film	Britain
Ford Motor	25%	Escort subcompact	Britain
General Electric	22%	Aircraft engines	West Germany
Hewlett-Packard	52%	Computer workstations	West Germany
Merck	50%	Vasotec (blood pressure medicine)	n.a.
Outboard Marine	20%	Outboard motors	Canada
Scott Paper	38%	Bathroom tissue	Western Europe
Sun Microsystems	42%	Computer workstations	Japan
3M	46%	Pressure-sensitive tape	West Germany

Source: Charles W. Lamb; Joseph F. Hair, Jr.; Carl McDaniel, *Principles of Marketing*, 1992, p. 729. South-Western Publishing Company.

operations in Tokyo, London, and Brussels.[7] The salespeople who win and retain the most lucrative accounts in the 1990s must be capable of providing service to customers wherever they need it.

Intra-industry Concentration

Every five years the U.S. Department of Commerce conducts a census within U.S. business. Part of the census involves an analysis of the extent to which the largest firms in an industry account for the sales activities in that industry—called **intra-industry concentration**. One can, therefore, use the data to determine such things as the percentage of a specific industry's (e.g., glass containers) sales which were accounted for by the eight largest firms in that industry. In the case of the glass containers industry, for example, the eight largest firms accounted for 73% of the total sales made by glass container manufacturers.

It is not uncommon for a relatively small number of companies in an industry to dominate the sales and share of market in the industry. In the U.S. toothpaste market Procter & Gamble, Colgate-Palmolive, and Smith Kline Beecham sell approximately 80% of all the toothpaste sold in the U.S. each year.[8] The ready-to-eat cereal industry is dominated by Kellogg, General Mills, and Post who collectively account for about two-thirds of the total sales in that industry.[9]

If your firm were a supplier to the cereal industry, you would probably find it important to seek business from one or more of the major competitors. The responsibility to foster and maintain relationships with these valuable accounts falls to a salesperson or, increasingly, a team of sales representatives.[10]

Managing relationships with huge accounts such as Procter & Gamble, Kellogg, and other companies of enormous size, requires salespeople to be capable of penetrating divisions of these companies that are as large as many medium-sized companies. As a result of the value of maintaining relationships with these blue-chip accounts, some companies are tailoring their sales organizations to better serve the accounts.[11] The sales teams are called **national account or key account sales teams**.[12] The sales personnel recruited and trained to staff national or key account sales teams are usually the most talented people that recruiters can find. If you can successfully manage relationships with one of these major accounts your career will prosper.

Technology

In 1973, an article titled "The New Supersalesman: Wired for Success" appeared in *Business Week*. Although the article identified several areas where great progress had been achieved, a reading of it today reveals how different conditions are now than they were in the 1970s. Conspicuous in its absence, for instance, is any mention of two forms of information technology that are causing great changes in personal selling—lap-top computers and telemarketing—both of which have career-shaping consequences.

Lap-top computers, on the one hand, permit salespeople to interface with numerous departments and data bases in the rep's sales branch, home office, and physical distribution center. With this information management tool at the rep's disposal, customers who are used to similar tools expect the rep to answer questions for them without delay. Thus, the salesperson who is technologically better prepared to represent his or her company is also expected to be more responsive and knowledgeable.

Telemarketing, on the other hand, is permitting companies to do away with hiring and retaining field reps who are "order takers."[13] Textbook descriptions of salespeople have previously categorized reps into order getters and order takers.[14] Order getters were considered to be the creative types who engaged in stimulating demand for the product. Order takers merely noted what the customer said he or she wanted and then forwarded the order to the appropriate department. Telemarketing now permits customers to transmit their own orders, thereby negating the reason for costly face-to-face contacts with sales reps who don't add any value to a buying situation.[15] As the telemarketing trend accelerates, job opportunities

Figure 18-1 Lap-top computers allow salespeople to access data in their home offices, branches, or distribution centers.

for order getters will be all that is left. Bernard LaLonde documented this trend. He found that the proportion of orders transmitted via electronic data interchange is projected to increase from 22 percent in 1987 to 55 percent in 1995. The consequences of this are that the people with talent to creatively solve customers' problems will be in demand but "traveling clerks" will find their careers on the wane.[16]

Legal and Ethical Concerns

Men and women pursuing careers in sales find themselves confronted with situations that arouse questions about legal and ethical conduct. Chapter 16 contained specific explanations of some of these problems. Without lapsing into a rehash of these specifics, suffice it to say that employers are concerned over these departures from approved conduct.[17]

Two factors contribute to increased pressure on salespeople. One involves the economic necessity for a firm to maintain its prize customers and cultivate its relationships with them. Faced with the loss of a major account's business, some sales reps are tempted to resort to illegal or unethical means of keeping the business. A second factor is globalization. Salespeople functioning in foreign markets where "graft and corruption" are taken for granted may try to excuse their "ethical laxity" with the defense, "Everyone does it in that country."

How a professional salesperson will stand up under these pressures cannot be tested during preemployment interviews. Nevertheless, recruiters and other human resources personnel definitely are interested in trying to detect early-warning signals of potential problems before a person is hired. One very controversial tactic used by some firms is a polygraph (lie detector) test.

Each of these broad-scaled environmental trends is influencing companies' searches for sales talent. In the same manner that a marketing manager must adjust to broad environmental circumstances, so must you adjust your personal marketing strategy. What actions and decisions do you have to work with as you make the necessary adjustments in your career? The next section examines your own individual marketing mix variables.

YOUR PERSONAL MARKETING MIX

The marketing manager works with his or her product or service, the prices charged for the product/service, promotion, and placement (the four P's). You too have a mix that requires that you make some decisions. The most fundamental question confronting you is how you will manage your personal mix throughout your business career. As Exhibit 18-2 revealed, your personal marketing mix variables are your skills, your image, your mobility, and your price.

Your Skills

The recruiters you meet will have many ways of measuring the skills they deem important for success as a sales rep in their companies. Their efforts to assess your skills will range from interviews and role playing to standardized tests. One of the hiring specifications may be computer-language proficiency. Generally, when people are being hired out of college they are being "bought" on the assumption that they can be trained to conduct business as their respective employers want it conducted.

Later, however, as you progress through the initial training program and are absorbed into the work force, detecting the need to acquire new skills will largely be up to you. Your readiness to explore new approaches to selling and new communication methods will be important to your continued success. Just as products are given a face-lift and remarketed as "new and improved," so also must salespeople be provided with new tools and perspectives toward their jobs.

An example of this is the Merck Company, a well-known pharmaceutical firm. Not only is each new sales rep given intensive initial training, but every year or two each of their 1,500 salespeople is sent to a medical school to learn about the latest developments in their field.[18]

The Merck example is an institutionalized means of keeping a sales force at its peak of professional proficiency. Relying entirely on your employer to provide formal training programs is not enough, however, if you view yourself as competing with your peers for top evaluations and the increasingly scarce promotions referred to earlier. As sophisticated as many corporate training programs are, they are not sufficient. Such programs as Merck's will keep you relatively equal with your peers; but if you want to truly excel, something more is necessary. What do you need to do to develop your own self-improvement program? First, you must have an orientation point—a position in your firm to which you aspire for your next move. This position need not be one in which a promotion would be involved.

Find Your Orientation Point

Do you want to be a sales manager, a brand manager, or a marketing researcher? All of these and many others are career "next-step" possibilities from the ranks of professional sales. Each of the three positions requires a different set of skills. Our purpose here is not to describe the separate skills but rather to call your attention to the need to have an orientation point toward which you can direct some specific attention and effort. If a salesperson does not identify some reference point he or she is likely to become aware of the truth in the adage, "If you don't know where you are going, any road will get you there."

Read the Literature

Find out what publications are read by the people who occupy the position to which you aspire. If, for instance, your next goal is to be branch sales manager, you will find as you read *Sales and Marketing Management* that some articles give helpful insights on emerging trends that require new skills. After you graduate from college, you must assume the dual responsibilities of deciding what subjects you need or want to master and then, to a large extent, teach yourself.

Set a Time-Bounded Deadline

After you develop an agenda of skills you think you need to acquire, set a time target for acquiring the skill(s). As you contemplate what that date should be, take into account the need to perform your present responsibilities while pursuing a future position.

Our society and particularly the world of professional selling are changing so rapidly that there is no such condition as the status quo. We are either making strides to improve our professional skills or we are deteriorating. As your professional skills grow, it is vital to your career success that you communicate your growth to people in your company who have the power to move and promote you. An important aspect of your self-marketing management efforts is the image you project (how you "promote" yourself).

Your Image

Throughout your career in sales or other fields you will project images to your peers, subordinates, and superiors. In Chapter 8 we discussed the importance of selling yourself to new customers. It is vitally important for career management to project a desirable image to people in your company and to people in your profession who work for other firms.

The obvious part of image projection involves physical appearance. Books are written about dressing for success and how to project your thoughts orally and in writing. These are helpful but, in the end, rather superficial. More fundamental and durable than your choice of clothing is what traits you exhibit in your interpersonal contacts.

Ideally, we would like to believe that people who advance in a firm are rewarded because of outstanding performance. Many people are high performers and yet are not promoted (and the trend seems to be escalating). The frequently heard explanation is "corporate politics." Sometimes the person who was promoted has not done any better in sales than someone who was passed over. What could be the reason? In many cases, the superior was influenced by the images he or she harbored of the job candidates and how he or she believed they would respond to circumstances in a more responsible position.

Although this chapter is far too brief to thoroughly explore each of the following four questions, they are posed here to provoke self-examination. How you respond in your work life to these questions plays a major role in the image people have of you.

How Do You Respond to Challenges?

No other function in a firm is so constantly laden with challenges and the attendant stress as the sales function. If that is not abundantly clear, then we have failed to convey the true picture of the professional sales profession.

The sales quota is an example of one of the challenges most salespeople must successfully meet to retain their jobs and to advance. People respond in several ways to a challenging sales quota. Some (the creme de la creme) roll up their sleeves and start making strides toward meeting and eventually exceeding the quota. Some of these salespeople address their tasks in a quiet yet determined manner, while others seem to attack the tasks with obvious enthusiasm. Both of these groups contain people whom sales managers prize greatly and on whom the entire company depends to keep it going. It does not take long to identify these people.

Other sales reps will search for ways to "beat the system." Although they realize the need to comply with the quota demands, their approach is characterized by actions that may cause their managers to require safeguards to minimize their efforts to take shortcuts. One example is the practice of "sandbagging." A rep knows that at the beginning of the new year another quota will be introduced. If the rep is at or over quota as the current year comes to a close, the rep may delay closing some sales so that they can be applied toward next year's quota. The reaction of managers who believe a rep is sandbagging is to wonder what else the salesperson is doing to make his or her work easier. Obviously, this is not the kind of image that is beneficial to a person's career.

Another approach, unfortunately, that some people take is to whine and complain. Their first reaction to challenging requirements is negative. Some exert more energy trying to find out whether they are being treated fairly than they exert in addressing the challenge. Obviously, this image is not conducive to career enhancement.

Finally, some will simply procrastinate or attempt to deny that the challenge in the form of the quota exists. If they eventually meet the quota, it is a harrowing, last-minute, crisis performance. These people's managers who are themselves under pressure to produce results will not find their lives made any easier by such subordinates. The supervisory effort required to move the procrastinators is remembered and becomes a negative factor in the image a manager has of the procrastinator.

Are Your Good and Bad Moods Too Obvious?

If we analyze the variety of people we work and associate with, all of us can identify people whose moods are easy to detect. These individuals seem to be euphoric at times and despondent on other occasions. Some professions seem to be characterized by events that offer spectacular "highs" and deep "lows." One such profession is athletic coaching. Another involves some areas of professional sales. When one sale can net a rep a commission of $20,000 to $30,000, the emotional impact of a "win" or "loss" is significant for most people.

How people manage their emotions in times of stress is a factor in how they are perceived by others. Some companies try to evaluate how applicants for sales jobs will handle stressful situations and whether or not the applicant can maintain his or her poise. The method employed is generally referred to as a **stress interview**, in which the interviewer may pose a difficult question or ask the interviewee to do something unexpected.

One tactic used by some interviewers is to say, "Sell me this pen," as he or she hands a pen to the interviewee. A well-known telecommunications firm uses a sales assessment test. The applicant is given a brief time to read information about a fictitious company. Then a series of interviews occurs with "executives" from the company. And at least one of the interviewers plays the role of a hostile customer. The purpose is to see whether the applicant can maintain poise and confidence during stressful moments.

Mood swings are inevitable. As a salesperson, however, you must attempt to minimize the carryover of feeling or emotion from one customer contact to the next and from your interactions among management and co-workers.

How Do You Handle Authority and Responsibility?

Part of your image in a company is based on how you handle assignments in which you have authority and responsibility to manage other people. You may have been an excellent sales rep for several years, and then after being promoted to management, find yourself enjoying work less and less.[19] Hall of Fame baseball players don't always make great managers.

One of the reasons corporate recruiters frequently ask about leadership positions you have had in college or at other times is to see how you may handle authority and responsibility. Early evidence of being willing and successful in shouldering responsibility will shape your image positively.

What Do Your Physical Appearance and Mannerisms Say to Others?

Notwithstanding the warnings against stereotyping people, most of us occasionally do so. We may, for example, conclude that a person who talks slower than we do also thinks and acts slower. We may tend to ascribe, at least initially, more positive features to a person who is verbally aggressive—that is, until he or she seems to be trying to overpower us.

In Chapter 10 we described body language signals that alert salespeople learn to read. All of us should have a close friend help us analyze our body language signals. There may be some mannerisms we would like to change.

These four questions have been offered not to make you a corporate chameleon, but to make you more self-aware. Your decisions about what, if anything, you wish to change about yourself, are very personal. To refuse to think about the possibilities for a need to change can damage one's efforts to project a successful image.

Figure 18-2 How a salesperson handles assignments involving responsibilities for managing others is an important consideration when assessing career options.

Your Mobility

As you contemplate your career strategy and how you will market yourself, the mobility question inevitably surfaces. There are two mobility dimensions that will play a role in your career: **geographic mobility** and **functional mobility**.

Geographic Mobility

If we remember that employees are resources, it is reasonable to expect that a company will occasionally move its resources to operational areas where the resources will be the most useful. When J. C. Penney moved its corporate headquarters from New York City to a suburb of Dallas, Texas, many of Penney's employees were transferred. A resource, whether it is an employee or a computer system, becomes more valuable to a company when it can be transferred from one location to another.[20] To what extent are you willing to be mobile to enhance your value to an employer?

Functional Mobility

This form of mobility involves the movement of a person from one type of job to another. For example, a sales rep selling paper products for Procter & Gamble is transferred to the division that sells coffee. Other cases may involve a movement from sales to marketing research. Some large companies practice **career pathing** to groom promising young people for successively larger amounts of responsibility and give them experience in different parts of the company. This assures that, eventually, the company will have in its work force the appropriate number of people to furnish the management expertise needed in the future.

An example of a company that uses career pathing is Metropolitan Life Insurance Company. As shown in Exhibit 18-5, the path starts with a two-year stint in field sales. This permits new employees to gain an appreciation and understanding of the company and its sales practices. The next stage involves jobs as either a field training consultant, a recruiting director, or a marketing specialist at one of the company's regional offices. These assignments are considered staff positions. **Staff positions** serve as support to line positions. **Line personnel** are directly responsible for sales and operations results.

At the third stage in Metropolitan's career path a person who has performed well in previous jobs will be promoted and transferred to the line organization as a branch manager. He or she has full responsibility for a Metropolitan sales office.

Assuming this large responsibility is performed well, the next point in the career path is to a staff job as director of marketing services at Metropolitan's home

Exhibit 18-5 A Career Path for Salespeople at Metropolitan Life Insurance Company

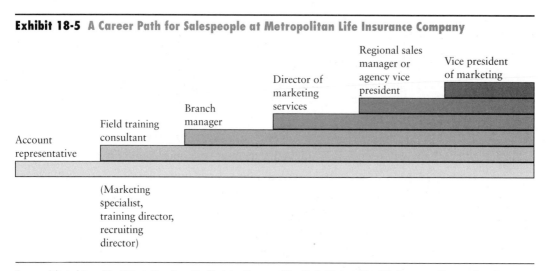

Source: Adapted from *The Metropolitan Executive Training Program* (New York: Metropolitan Life Insurance Company), p. 6. Reprinted with permission.

office in New York. This position will give the employee an additional perspective of the company and prepare him or her for even greater responsibilities.

The fifth major transition in this career path is, once again, to a line job. This is an extremely big promotion. As a regional sales manager or agency vice president, the newly minted executive is responsible for the operations of 1,100 sales office branches in a particular region.

At this point, you should be aware of the transitions a successful employee has had to make as he or she climbed the corporate ladder. A twenty-year career could easily have been consumed in the five major promotions previously described. Each promotion probably required geographic mobility and, of course, functional mobility as the employee assumed new duties and responsibilities. One of the incentives to make these transitions is financial reward.

Your Price

The pricing decisions a marketing manager makes are related to the nature of the product or service and its promotion, distribution, and competitive offerings. Your salary and other benefits paid by an employer constitute the "price" an employer pays for you—a human resource.

What price should you charge for your services? If we refer to Exhibit 18-5 and analyze that typical career path, we can obtain a more realistic answer. At the account representative stage (the first employment stage), Metropolitan, like most firms, will annually hire dozens of people to fill the beginning sales positions. The new trainees will, for the most part, be recent college graduates. They will come from an employment pool of 200,000 graduating seniors who constitute the national job market. Each year these people are the source of the supply of human resources available to Metropolitan and other employers. Metropolitan's human resources managers analyze their company's needs and the salaries other companies have been offering to similarly qualified people. Starting salaries are established under these supply and demand conditions. Metropolitan is competing not only with Travelers, Prudential, and other insurance companies, but also with Procter & Gamble, Xerox, and other companies vying for achievement-oriented people.

At this stage in the career path, the impersonal marketplace largely influences the salary and benefits package. The reason you or any other individual has little negotiating power is that the pool of job applicants is quite large. Metropolitan, for instance, may extend an employment offer to one person from among two dozen people who have applied. Thus, the negotiating power is heavily weighted in favor of the "buyer" of human resources at this stage. You, as an individual, are therefore not very powerful when it comes to setting your price in the early stages of your career.

Now let us consider the negotiating leverage an executive has who has been very successful for Metropolitan and is being offered a vice presidency. He or she will have an impressive record of accomplishments and will be a proven resource. Very few, if any, other people in the company may be capable of filling the position. Salary offers plus perks (perquisites) such as stock options, club memberships, chauffeured automobiles, and other amenities are part of the financial package successful executives can expect. Admittedly, very few people will reach such a lofty pinnacle in their career; but to the fortunate few who are able to manage their careers so they achieve this degree of success, the rewards are handsome.

Thus, in a career path's progress (whether it remains in the same company or zigzags through several companies), the freedom an individual has in establishing his or her own price depends on supply and demand. The fewer the people who can accomplish a needed task for a company, the more the bargaining power shifts from the firm toward the individual employee.

Career paths such as the one illustrated in Exhibit 18-5 can stretch over decades. If we analyze the number of people who begin their career as account representatives (sales representatives) and then look at the number of persons who become vice presidents, there is a marked disparity. What happens between these points in time to the vast majority of people? One way to determine the answer is to look at the career life cycle.

CAREER LIFE CYCLE

Exhibit 3-1 described the product life cycle. The model depicted a product's sales history in terms of sales revenues over four stages—introduction, growth, maturity, and decline. In 1974, Professor Marvin Jolson's article on a salesman's career cycle used a modified version of the product life cycle (see Exhibit 18-6). Jolson suggests that a salesperson's career moves through the stages of preparation, development, maturity, and decline.[21] Before we analyze each of these career phases, it is necessary to point out some characteristics of this model.

First, a person does not need to spend his or her entire career with one company for this model to be applicable. For instance, one approach is to be hired by a company renowned for its excellent sales training programs (for example, Corning Glass, Alcoa, American Airlines, Colgate-Palmolive).[22] After having been prepared in one of these sales training environments, a sales rep might be attracted to a smaller company, another geographic location, or a higher-paying job. Obviously the firms mentioned above do not want to become trainers for other compa-

Exhibit 18-6 **A Salesperson's Career Cycle**

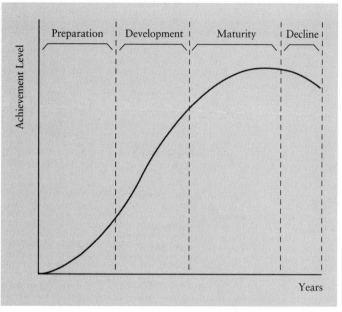

Source: Adapted from Marvin A. Jolson, "The Salesman's Career Cycle," *Journal of Marketing* (July 1974): 39. Reprinted with permission of the American Marketing Association.

nies' sales personnel. Companies such as Colgate-Palmolive and American Airlines spend sizable sums each year in preparing their salespeople and, therefore, they make strong efforts to retain them.

What about the stigma of job-hopping? And whatever happened to company loyalty? According to a *Wall Street Journal* article, a new breed of fast-track executives do more than move between specialties or companies. They zigzag their way to the top by jumping from industry to industry. And in the same article, the *WSJ* quoted a displaced executive who stated:

> *"If I made one big mistake it was getting wedded to the company," says a 15-year veteran of Westinghouse Electric Corporation who lost his controller's job when his division was sold five months ago. Less loyal co-workers who earlier jumped to jobs at different companies have already moved ahead of him.*[23]

In short, the **career life cycle** of most of us will include jobs with several companies.[24] The art of career management is knowing where you are in your career cycle and how to keep yourself in an ever-developing mode, and thus to keep from becoming an obsolete product.

Exhibit 18-7 **A Tracking Chart to Measure One Salesperson's Career Progress**

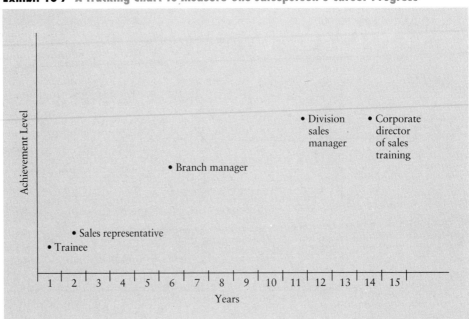

The second feature of the career life cycle model that is particularly noteworthy involves the vertical axis label (achievement level). The **achievement level** of an individual in the personal sales career field can be measured in at least two ways: the number of job assignments and the organizational levels of the jobs. For example, if over a fifteen-year span, a person had five different assignments, a chart (see Exhibit 18-7) could be developed to track his or her achievement-level progress.

The model could also measure achievement levels based on dollar sales volume. This method of analysis assumes that as a sales rep becomes more experienced and proficient in his or her job(s), the rep's sales figures will reflect the person's rate of growth and progress through the four phases of the cycle.

The Preparation Phase

Training is the essential ingredient in the **preparation phase**.[25] The rep, depending on the training policy of the company, may spend as much as six months during the first year in training programs. When training extends over a prolonged period, it is usually conducted on a stop-and-start basis. The rep goes to school for a month or six weeks, returns to the field to "practice" what he or she has learned, and then returns for additional training.

Many of the topics we have covered in previous chapters are covered in company-sponsored programs. Skills in interpersonal communications (how to listen, ask questions, negotiate, and so on), time and territory management, stress management, and product knowledge are some of the most commonly covered topics.

The Development Phase

Progress is the most apparent during the **development phase** in the career life cycle. As you examine the slope of the curve in Exhibit 18-6, you will see that the slope rises at an increasing rate. The ideal situation occurs when the rep is producing a steadily increasing growth of sales year after year or is being promoted relatively rapidly to greater responsibilities. Most people want to spend as long a period as possible in the development stage, because they enjoy the feeling of accomplishment that comes to people whose careers are developing.

How long does this phase last? It depends on the individual and the circumstances in which he or she is working. Earlier in the chapter, we described some of the reasons promotion possibilities diminish. These circumstances have nothing to do with the effort of the individual or his or her sales skills. The suggestion made earlier in this chapter about marketing yourself can be used to help you keep your career in this stage as long as possible.

The Maturity Phase

In the **maturity phase**, an individual's career slows down in its progress. This is the point where people "peak out" and attain the highest level of achievement in their profession. If sales volume is the measure of achievement level, the sales rep sells the most volume at this phase that he or she will ever sell during his or her career.

At what level does maturity occur? Since each sales rep is different, the answer to this important question must be prefaced with the phrase, "It all depends." As it was in the development phase, the ultimate point where a person peaks out in a career depends only partially on his or her talents. Other forces and factors at work in the individual's work environment, such as the economic climate and technology, cause some jobs to become more important or, unfortunately, to become expendable.

In the Metropolitan Life Insurance Company career path described earlier, some people peak out after one or two promotions. As careful as Metropolitan is in choosing each year's group of trainees, only a few eventually reach maturity at the level of vice president. Some others may reach maturity at that level as employees of other insurance companies, and a few will become vice presidents of companies outside the insurance industry.[26]

If analysts of the future business scene are correct, more of us will be hitting our peaks and maturing earlier in our working lives because there are simply fewer levels of management positions in corporate structures.[27] This poses the problem of how to be satisfied with lower levels of achievement if achievement is measured by climbing the corporate ladder. Each of us has to resolve that problem for ourselves. If you are a manager, however, you *also* will have to help some of your subordinates struggle to come to terms with their career limitations. In some cases, you may have the extremely taxing challenge of managing people who are in the next stage—the decline phase.

The Decline Phase

Ideally a person's career would end at the peak of the maturity phase. No one likes to contemplate the circumstances that cause the sales volumes of some previously productive sales reps to decline, or some reps to be demoted.[28] The **decline phase** can occur for a number of reasons—some of which extend into a person's family life and personal health. Rather than detailing the more common problems that can cause decline, we refer you to those guidelines provided earlier in the chapter. By adopting the perspective of a marketing manager and accepting the need to market yourself, we hope you will never feel the anxieties attendant with this phase of the career life cycle.

SUMMARY

1. Companies' long-term success requires that they acquire suitably qualified salespeople and train them to perform as professional sales representatives.

2. Individual employees are more likely to have a realistic perception of their role(s) in a company if they view themselves as resources needed by their employers.

3. The employee can retain and enhance his or her value to an employer by becoming a skilled marketer of himself or herself, and thus a more proficient career manager.

4. The career manager, like a traditional marketing manager, has a mix of variables that, when manipulated correctly, increases a person's value. These variables are skills, image, mobility, and price.

5. Over a salesperson's career, he or she will pass through four phases in the sales career life cycle: preparation, development, maturity, and decline. Each phase is characterized by a different rate of growth in achievement.

QUESTIONS FOR DISCUSSION AND REVIEW

1. Why is the marketing concept useful to individuals as they prepare for a career in sales?

2. What are the macroenvironmental variables influencing organizations' hiring and career path plans?

3. What are the personal marketing mix variables you can use to market yourself to an employer? At the beginning of your career, over which variable will you probably have the least control? Why?

4. Why do you suppose a typical corporate career path will have staff assignments between line assignments?

5. If the trends that were described under Reorganization continue, what do you think the major differences will be in future career life cycles compared to life cycles in the 1960s and 1970s?

6. How does this chapter reinforce the importance of a professional salesperson's ability to manage relationships?

CASE 18-1 THE MBA DECISION

Betsy Covington gazed out the window of the American Airlines plane as it landed in Cincinnati. Betsy was arriving for her second interview with Oakmont Chemical Company. Six weeks ago, Betsy talked with Oakmont's campus recruiter at State University. The recruiter asked Betsy questions about her background and her desires for a career in industry. Because Betsy's grade point average was a 3.75 out of a possible 4.0 and because she had a record of leadership in campus activities, she was an impressive job candidate. Oakmont was the fourth company that had expressed an interest in further negotiations with her.

The interviews had started in mid-October and now in early February Betsy was making her last company visit. Two of her visits prior to this one had resulted in job offers. Each of the offers was attractive. One company had offered her $26,000 to start and an opportunity to supplement her income with commissions after one year. Conceivably, Betsy could make as much as $39,000 during her second year. The other offer was for $25,000 plus a company car. Both jobs were in sales with companies that were highly respected Fortune 500 firms.

The day before Betsy left to visit Oakmont Chemical, she received a call from the director of State University's Master of Business Administration program and was asked to come by her office. When she arrived, she was told that a graduate assistantship could be arranged if she enrolled in State University's MBA program.

According to the director, Betsy could complete the MBA program in a year and a half. She also informed Betsy that the assistantship would pay all of her tuition throughout her graduate studies at State. Now Betsy not only had the job offers to weigh but also the decision about whether she should pursue an MBA under these highly advantageous conditions.

1. What should Betsy analyze as she tries to reach a decision?
2. Should she describe this latest turn of events to her would-be employers?

CASE 18-2 IS IT TIME TO CHANGE?

Incentive Marketing

For over 50 years, we have achieved market leadership in designing and implementing incentive programs for Fortune 500-sized companies, applying merchandise and travel award systems to meet clients' performance requirements.

We are known for our excellence in creative problem-solving and the overall professionalism of our Account Executives. Our expansion plans require the placement of additional Account Executives in Connecticut, Florida, Texas, Arizona, and California.

To qualify for these uniquely rewarding positions:

1. Your experience must include documented success in applying incentives to get other people to achieve goals.
2. Your skills must include creativity, client sensitivity, and team leadership.
3. Your goals must include major-league income, rapidly achieved.

If you meet this profile, you will be supported by a skilled staff of one of the largest full-service incentive agencies in the United States. You'll earn a high-level base salary and perks of equal dimension. Your income goals will be met through an open-ended commission guarantee. You'll experience more personal rewards than you probably thought possible.

Time to Change Your Professional Path?

Write to me and send your resume, in complete confidence
Joseph M. Gottschalk, President and CEO
EDGE+
2500 Bay Area Blvd.
Chicago, Illinois 50010-1058

Frank Faulkner, age twenty-nine, reread the ad he had torn out of yesterday's *Wall Street Journal*. Frank is a sales rep for Jamestown Sporting Goods Company, a leading manufacturer of a wide array of sporting goods. Faulkner went with Jamestown after he graduated from college where he majored in marketing. He has seven years of experience with the company and has been a senior sales representative for three years. Last year, Frank's total income was $55,000, which included a base salary of $30,000 and commissions of $25,000.

Although there is nothing wrong with Frank's relationship with Jamestown, he is starting to have some misgivings about his career pace. Frank's perception of promotion opportunities with Jamestown is that the company's middle-management level is slowly shrinking. In the past three years, three branch offices had been consolidated into one large regional office. Rumors persist that in the next six months two more offices will be consolidated. None of Frank's peers have been promoted during the past year.

Frank has never made any efforts to inquire about other jobs since he joined Jamestown. He was initially attracted to the company because he genuinely enjoyed the prospects of being associated with high-quality sporting goods (golf and tennis equipment, athletic shoes, and so on). As he became better acquainted with retailers and distributors in his assigned territory, he also enjoyed working with these business people. One of Frank's major responsibilities is to motivate retailers to feature Jamestown sporting goods in their advertisements and to stock a complete line of Jamestown goods. To encourage this, Frank runs contests in which the retail sporting goods store owners participate and explains special promotion programs which Jamestown sponsors.

After four years in the Houston territory, which is one of the company's largest, Frank is totally familiar with his job and all of its responsibilities. He is so comfortable, in fact, that it has started to concern him. No one from corporate headquarters has ever approached Faulkner about any positions in the Chicago office. Occasionally, Frank wonders about what his reaction would be if that happened. Sometimes at sales meetings, someone from headquarters comes out and makes a presentation. These occasions frequently result in Frank and his peers expressing mild sarcasm about the outlook on business of headquarters' staff personnel. Also, Frank senses that some of the lower-level staff people feel insecure, and this impression has grown stronger in the past two years.

Frank has started skimming "The Mart," a section in the *Wall Street Journal* where job advertisements appear. As he analyzes the various ads, he is becoming increasingly curious about how his background would be regarded by other companies. The more he looks at the ad from EDGE, the more convinced he is that he wants to test the market.

QUESTIONS

1. What environmental factor seems to be most relevant in influencing Frank's opportunities for advancement in Jamestown Sporting Goods?

2. What seems to be the career path at Jamestown? What problems does this pose?

3. What would you advise Frank to do in his efforts to manage his career?

CASE 18-3 A DISCUSSION BETWEEN TWO FORMER COLLEGE ROOMMATES

"I never dreamed there were so many questions people could ask about carpeting," said Frank Morgan to his ex-roommate Paul Cook. Frank and Paul were sitting in the State University Student Union during a break in homecoming activities. It was the first time they had visited with each other since they had graduated three years ago. Both men had started their careers in sales: Frank with LongWear Floors and Paul with Apex Glass.

"Yeah, I know what you mean," Paul responded. "We went through what seemed like a great training program at Apex, but I still felt dumb as dirt during the first six months I was in the field."

"I was 'shell shocked' at first! I knew I didn't set any academic records here at school, but still I didn't believe I was stupid, either. Best of all, the LongWear recruiters and other people in the company I talked to during pre-employment interviews seemed to think I had potential," Frank Morgan reflected. "I had to remind myself of that on several occasions when I wondered if I would ever make it."

"Last month I had my semi-annual performance evaluation review," Paul said. "I felt pretty good about what the boss had to say. I've got a dynamite boss, by the way. She really knows the business and is a great people person. She's been in the business for about ten years, but she hasn't forgotten what it's like to be starting out. During our conference she asked me to give some thought to a new follow-up training program Apex Glass is considering. She said our management realizes that new sales reps can't just go through three weeks of orientation and training and then be expected to be productive in the field. She as much as told me that if I could offer a good proposal for the contents of the follow-up program I would be in charge of it," Paul stated.

"That sounds great, Paul. What ideas do you have?" Frank asked.

"Well, one thing I would like to see is some emphasis on handling stress. You know, how to cope with the 'ups and downs' in our business. One day you think a big sale is just about to close, and the next day you discover a competitor has undercut your price and bought the business. In some cases, that's happened to me and I know I had a better product and better service. When that happens you can't let that disappointment affect your other customer contacts and your prospecting efforts."

"What else?" Frank asked.

"I'd like to see some attention devoted to knowing what our other departments do; areas like inventory control, credit, advertising and so forth. Sometimes when I have talked to people in these departments it was almost like they were working for a different company," Paul replied.

"Another thing," Paul added, "I want the new people to really share their concerns and views. I don't know how it was in your initial training program but we really didn't know enough to get involved. Mostly we just sat and listened. Many times after I was in the field, I thought of some of those training sessions and wished I could have asked the instructor for some guidance."

"Paul, you sound like you've really given this some thought," Frank said, "I hope you get a chance to implement your ideas. They sound good to me!"

"Yeah, we'll see. I get pretty excited about something like this. By this time next year, if we're both back here at homecoming, I can tell you how things are going," Paul stated.

QUESTIONS

1. In what stage in their career cycles would you say these two people are now? In what stage will Paul's trainees be in when they take his proposed program?

2. Aside from the compliments Paul has paid to his boss, what is she doing that indicates she is, in fact, a good manager?

3. What have we covered in this chapter (and in earlier chapters) that is related to Paul's proposed training course?

4. Of the two major ideas Paul has about the proposed training program which one seems to cover a topic that could only be meaningful to people who had "real world" field sales experience? Why?

NOTES

1. Philip Kotler and Gary Armstrong, *Marketing: An Introduction* (Englewood Cliffs, N.J.: Prentice-Hall, 1987), 121.
2. A.J. Magrath, "Are You Overdoing 'Lean and Mean'?" *Sales and Marketing Management* (January 1988): 46–50.
3. Ibid., 46–54.
4. "More Executives Finding Changes in Traditional Corporate Ladder as Firms Try to Refocus Workers' Career Prospects," *Wall Street Journal* (November 14, 1986): B25.
5. "Europe's Global Clout Is Limited by Divisions 1992 Can't Paper Over," *Wall Street Journal* (February 13, 1989): A1.
6. Philip R. Harris and Robert T. Moran, *Managing Cultural Differences*, 2nd ed. (Houston, Tex.: Gulf Publishing Company, 1987), 519.
7. "Mr. Smith Goes Global," *Business Week* (February 13, 1989): 66–72.
8. "Tooth-Brushers Take A Shine To Baking Soda," *Wall Street Journal* (March 2, 1992): B1.
9. "Cereal Giants Battle Over Market Share," *Wall Street Journal* (December 16, 1991): B1.
10. "Consultative Selling in the '90s," *Sales Manager's Bulletin* (1991): 5–6. See also Frank V. Cespedes, Stephen X. Doyle, and Robert J. Freedman, "Teamwork for Today's Selling," *Harvard Business Review* (March–April 1989): 44–55.
11. "National Account Marketing Swings Into The Nineties," *Business Marketing* (November 1987): 43–52.
12. John I. Coppett and William A. Staples, "Managing a National Account Sales Team," *Business* (April–June 1983): 41–44.
13. John I. Coppett and Roy D. Voorhees, "Telemarketing: A Supplement to Field Sales," *Industrial Marketing Management* (August 1985): 213–16.
14. E. Jerome McCarthy and William D. Perreault, Jr., *Basic Marketing*, 9th ed. (Homewood, Ill.: Irwin, 1987), 399.
15. Coppett and Voorhees, "Telemarketing," 213–16.
16. Bernard LaLonde, *Customer Service: A Management Perspective* (Oakbrook, Ill.: Council of Logistics Management, 1988).
17. "What's Wrong," *Time* (May 25, 1987): 14–17.
18. "Merck's Grand Obsession," *Sales and Marketing Management* (June 1987): 65.
19. "From Salesperson to Manager: Transition and Travail," *Sales and Marketing Management* (February 1992): 32–36.
20. "Unwillingness to Relocate Stifles Careers," *Wall Street Journal* (February 4, 1991): A12.
21. Marvin A. Jolson, "The Salesman's Career Cycle," *Journal of Marketing* 38 (July 1974): 39–46.
22. "America's Best Sales Forces," *Sales and Marketing Management* (June 1988): 25–31.
23. "More Executives Finding Changes in Traditional Corporate Ladder as Firms Try to Refocus Workers' Career Prospects," *Wall Street Journal* (November 14, 1986): B25.
24. Elizabeth M. Fowler, "Big Growth In Helping The Jobless," *The New York Times* (April 17, 1990): C14.
25. Jolson, "The Salesman's Career Cycle," 39–46.
26. "Would It Pay You to Switch Industries?" *Sales and Marketing Management* (January 1988): 32–36.
27. "More Executives Finding Changes. . ." *Wall Street Journal*, B25.
28. "When A Senior Salesperson Stalls," *Sales and Marketing Management* (December 1991): 111–13.

Appendix A: Telemarketing

The growth of telemarketing in the United States during the second half of the 1980s was phenomenal. From approximately 80,000 firms that were using some form of telemarketing in 1985, the number mushroomed to approximately 265,000 firms in 1990.[1] Telemarketing has been proclaimed to be the fastest growing element in the marketing communication mix.[2]

How is telemarketing being used to more cost-effectively reach customers? How do telemarketers get the names and telephone numbers of the people they call? To enhance the possibilities that the person receiving a call will make a purchase or consent to a visit by a field sales rep, what should the caller say in the first thirty seconds of the call? Answers to these questions will be provided in the following sections.

WHAT IS TELEMARKETING?

Some people say that telemarketing is a shorthand term for selling over the telephone. It is true that billions of dollars of products and services are sold over the telephone each year. Selling over the telephone, however, is *only one* application of telemarketing. Qualifying sales leads before turning them over to a field sales rep is another use of telemarketing (see Chapter 14). Providing answers to prospective customers' questions or fielding customers' complaints are also important ways of rendering better customer service. Another frequently employed telemarketing ap-

Exhibit A1 A Telemarketing Sales System

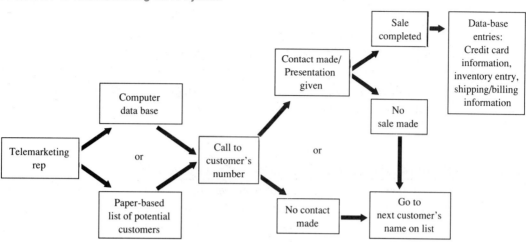

plication is account management. In this approach, all contacts with selected customers are conducted via telemarketing. After identifying the customers to whom a business can no longer justify making face-to-face field visits, the entire relationship with such customers is maintained via telemarketing. This can include ordering, billing, granting credit, transmission of product information, alerting the customers to new promotions, and other matters related to maintaining the accounts.

Telemarketing is a marketing communication system using telecommunication technology and trained personnel to conduct planned, measurable marketing activities directed at targeted audiences.[3] To provide readers with a better understanding of the true nature of telemarketing, several words and phrases in this definition are significant enough to merit closer examination: *system; trained personnel; planned, measurable marketing activities;* and *targeted audiences.*

System

A system for conducting telemarketing sales operations is depicted in Exhibit A1. One telemarketing sales rep can make approximately 120 calls on prospective buyers per day. This rate of contact far overshadows the six to ten contacts a field salesperson may be capable of achieving.

Trained Personnel

The aphorism "time is money" was never more apt than in a telemarketing operation. The telemarketing rep who is either making or receiving a call must balance the need to complete the transaction expeditiously with projecting an image of courtesy and helpfulness to the customer. This can be especially important in customer service. Managers in most successful centers conduct extensive training before permitting a new employee to field or initiate calls.[4]

The well-trained and motivated telemarketing representative can ask interest-stimulating and probing questions just as the face-to-face salesperson is trained to do. Some observers of the sales atmospheres in telemarketing and face-to-face selling contend that the telemarketing rep has a greater challenge because of the absence of body language cues from customers and the unavailability of sales aids such as product samples.

Planned, Measurable Marketing/Sales Activities

Calls to new customers are made from various lists purchased by the firm. Each call will result in either a sale or a rejection. The astute telemarketer will analyze the ratio of the number of sales to the telephone calls made to determine whether a particular list of names is yielding the expected level of success. Future purchases of additional potential customers' names from a list broker will depend on the results the telemarketer achieves with a list that was purchased or rented from the broker.

In addition to keeping tabs on the success ratios of various lists, the telemarketer will test various sales appeals the reps are using. For instance, the telemarketing reps might be told to emphasize low prices in all of their sales calls in the morning, and in the afternoon the sales approach to be emphasized might be changed to high quality. After determining which appeal had resulted in the most sales, the telemarketing manager could quickly instruct the reps to use the most successful appeal in their subsequent customer contacts.

Targeted Audiences

One of the cornerstones of marketing is the concept of targeting a market. Much of the success of such an activity depends on access to accurate information about the market. Telemarketing, when conducted effectively, permits the constant refinement of information about who is buying the product, what particular models or sizes are being purchased, and other useful marketing information. As a result of the on-line, real-time data collection and analysis capabilities, a telemarketer can quickly determine whether the initial assumptions about a target market were correct, or whether an old target market has changed.

One of the keys to success in targeting a market that will be contacted via telemarketing is in the selection of the list(s) of potential customers. The lists provide the names and telephone numbers that can be used by the telemarketer. With over 40,000 lists available, it is imperative that the telemarketing manager give considerable thought to how he or she will determine which lists to rent or purchase.[5]

TELEMARKETING LISTS

Your list of prospects *is* your market in the world of telemarketing. Before you have a list, your market is a group of people, with common demographic traits, presumed to be "out there somewhere." Once you have obtained the prospect list, your market is no longer "out there." It's in your hand.[6]

Where do you find these lists? Some telemarketers contend that the best list is obtainable from your own company records. Shipping, billing, and credit records as well as warranty applications will yield the names and other information about people and businesses that have bought other products from your company. There are several advantages to constructing a telemarketing contact list by using your own company's records. First, such lists are inexpensive. You already own the information. Second, these sources will usually yield considerable data about a customer. And third, you will have no question about how the information was obtained and whether it really applies to your business.

Other sources of names are available, of course. One common source is yellow page directories or business-to-business yellow pages. Also, there are business and city directories. Business directories are available for most major industries. They list all businesses in that industry alphabetically, geographically, by market segment, or by all three.[7] City directories list all consumers and businesses in a given city, usually by street name and number.

Magazines and other periodicals will rent their subscriber lists. These lists can be quite useful if the magazine, newsletter, or other form of periodical is oriented to a special interest group (for example, stereo hobbyists, running enthusiasts, pet owners, baseball fans). If the subscribers would also be people who are likely to be interested in your product or service, a subscription list will be useful to your telemarketing efforts.

Perhaps the best reference source to consult to facilitate your list shopping is the *Standard Rate and Data Service List Catalog*. The catalog is a compilation of almost all lists available for rent in the United States.[8] Each available list is described by title, market classification, who owns the list, the number of names on the list, the rental cost, and other conditions and restrictions. Other excellent sources of names of list owners can be found in *Telemarketing* magazine and *Direct Marketing* magazine.

A logical question to pose after securing the names and telephone numbers of prospective customers is, "How should we begin our contact with these customers?" Many successful telemarketers believe in using scripts to guide the conversation between the sales representative and the prospective customer.

SCRIPTS

Opinions vary about the value of telemarketing reps having a script to follow in conversing with customers. Some people believe a telemarketing presentation should be entirely scripted while others believe using a script stifles the natural flow of communication. Mary Ann Jones, Vice President of TELER$_x$ Marketing, Inc., advises that "the major problem with a scripted presentation isn't caused by the script itself." The problem is in how the script is delivered. If the telemarketer pauses in the wrong places, stumbles over words, or has no inflection in his or her voice, the listener can readily determine the amateurish performance. Ms. Jones recommends that telemarketing managers, rather than just handing reps a script, should first dissect the script into major components and then review each component and its purpose with the representatives. Jones contends that when reps understand *why* they are being told to use a script and what the purposes of each part of the script are, they will be more likely to deliver a presentation in a conversational tone.

There are distinctive differences in the components of a well-designed script—the introduction, attention-grabbing statement, interest-creating statements, review of benefits statement, and validation of intentions.

The Introduction

Tell the listener who is calling and the company that you represent. No one appreciates someone trying to be cute or overly aggressive in the opening seconds. The caller should also not ask "How are you today?" This is obviously an insincere gesture when neither party knows each other. A better statement immediately after identifying yourself is, "You're probably very busy so I promise I won't take much of your time." This shows empathy and sensitivity on the part of the telemarketing representative.

Attention-Grabbing Statement

A caller has only about fifteen or twenty seconds in which to establish the purpose of the call. This is definitely not the time to start talking about how well made the product is or how long the company has been in business. The listener is making up his or her mind about whether to continue to listen to you or not. Therefore, the statement you use must be customer-oriented. Knowledge of your customers and their interests is indispensable here. For instance, if you are selling subscriptions to a sports magazine and the lists contain names of people believed to be ardent baseball fans, the attention grabber could be, "Wouldn't it be great to have a box seat at the opening game of the World Series?" Another example of an interest-grabbing statement to people believed to be interested in collecting and refinishing antique furniture would be, "Wouldn't it be valuable to know how much a professional appraiser says a trundle bed or other Early American furniture is worth on today's market?"

Interest-Creating Statements

Once you have made an attention-grabbing statement or posed a question, the next stage is to follow with a statement to create interest. If a special promotional offer of a free videotape is being given to new subscribers or a booklet of reprints of the best articles from the publication is being offered, this is the place to insert this information. A statement such as "We will send a free videotape of last season's NFL highlights to everyone subscribing to *Sports Unlimited* during the next thirty days" would be appropriate. A statement designed to arouse interest is then usually followed by a question to determine if the prospective customer is interested: "Would you like to enjoy this free videotape before any of your friends get one?"

Review of Benefits Statement

"Let me tell you how easy it is to start your subscription to *Sports Unlimited*. All I need is your approval to start your subscription. Your first copy will arrive within fifteen days. If you put your subscription payment on an approved credit card, we can mail your videotape within two working days." These are all designed to show how easy it is to complete the transaction. The caller is providing specific information about how soon the potential subscriber can start enjoying the benefits of this subscription.

The script designer should anticipate the possibility of an objection or an expression of doubt being raised at this point. A good script does not assume there will be no objections or barriers to the sale. It would be inadvisable to try to build in statements such as "You may be concerned about . . . " or "In case . . . would be a problem." This might trigger doubts that the prospective buyer had not had before some potential problems were mentioned. A good script will identify several of the most commonly voiced questions or objections and have ready-made answers to which the telemarketing rep can refer. In training sessions prior to commencing actual calls, the trainer can give reps practice in using the scripted responses to some common objections.

Validation of Intentions

Assuming that the caller has aroused the interest of the prospective customer and answered all of the concerns, the next stage of the script should be to close the agreement to purchase and validate the pertinent facts.

A script can use a straightforward direct appeal close just as appropriately as a face-to-face sales rep can employ such a close. Statements such as "Mr. Smith, may we start your benefits next month?" or "Mr. Smith, would you be interested in this offer?" put the issue squarely in front of the other person.

The assumptive close can also be used in a script. Questions such as "Ms. Jones, would you prefer a six-month or the more economical one-year subscription?" or "Ms. Jones, would Tuesday of next week be convenient for us to deliver your order?" assume that the customer will buy. These questions are not focused on whether the purchase issue is in doubt. They *assume* that a sale will occur. What is left to resolve are the details—color, size, delivery date, etc.

The final stage of the script contains the questions and statements to ensure all the information is correct and to permit an order to be processed. "Okay, Mr. Howard, is your mailing address 15707 North State Street, Chicago, Illinois, 50576?" "How would you like to pay for this—by check or credit card?" "May I have the name and number of your credit card, please?" The final statements should quickly review what will be sent to the buyer. "Ms. Franklin, we will be mailing your merchandise using overnight express. Your order contains one utility bag, color red, at $10.95; one pair of pajamas, size 10, color blue, priced at $23.00; and one gray wool skirt, size 8, priced at $30.00. We certainly appreciate your business and look forward to serving you in the future."

By using the components of a script to skillfully create a guide for the telemarketing rep, a manager can get the benefits from knowing that reps will cover the essentials in a courteous yet time-efficient manner. The ultimate goal of the rep should be to deliver the script in a conversational tone.

NOTES

1. Rheva Katz, "Telemarketing and Technology," *Forbes* (September 1, 1985): 50.
2. Kenneth C. Schneider, "Telemarketing as a Promotional Tool—Its Effects and Side Effects," *Journal of Consumer Marketing* 2 (Winter): 29–39.
3. Roy Dale Voorhees and John Coppett, "Telemarketing in Distribution Channels," *Industrial Marketing Management* 12 (April): 105–12.
4. Bob Stone and John Wyman, *Successful Telemarketing: Opportunities and Techniques for Increasing Sales and Profits* (Englewood Cliffs, N.J.: Prentice-Hall, 1985), 201.
5. Rich Feldman, "Reference Guide to Merge/Purge Services," *Telemarketing* (May 1988): 61.
6. H. J. Davis, "Treatise of Telemarketing List Selection and Use," *Telemarketing* (February 1986): 36.
7. Ibid., 38.
8. Ibid., 39.

Appendix B:
Resumé Preparation and Interviewing

Welcome to the "real world" of career management! The information provided in Appendix B is meant to help you create opportunities with prospective employers. Once you have been employed as a salesperson, you will be selling products and services that will generate profits for your company. Before you become employed, however, you will be selling yourself. Your resumé is your version of a product brochure. It tells the prospective buyer (employer) what kind of "product" you are or have the potential to be. The interviews in which you participate are opportunities for you to explain and expand on your achievements and otherwise persuade the recruiter to hire you. These sessions permit you to start building a relationship with your future employer. The next several pages provide some guidance on the preparation of the resumé and some advice on interviewing.

RESUMÉ PREPARATION

There are two basic types of resumés. One type is the chronological resumé, which provides a concise description of your life during a particular period. For example, the Education section of your resumé will show the year you graduated from college and the name of the school. The next date listed would be the year you graduated from high school. The inclusion of high-school graduation information is not always appropriate. We will explain later when to mention your high-school career. In short, a resumé based on your progress over time can inform a reader about what you did during the years covered by the resumé.

The second basic type is the functional resumé. It categorizes a person's skills and provides brief descriptions of the development of those skills. An entry in a functional resumé, for example, might state under Leadership: Elected to presidency of the student chapter of the American Marketing Association in 1989, and led the local chapter to win the Southwest Chapter of the Year award.

Which is the best resumé for you? It depends on the variety of your accomplishments. This does not mean that you must have been a high academic achiever; it means that you have experienced a broad range of responsibilities, such as earning a significant amount of your college expenses, holding a job in which you were responsible for other people's safety (for example, driving a school bus), handling large sums of money, or other similar jobs. The challenge that confronts most college students when they think about developing a functional resumé is their tendency to forget or minimize the significance of what they have done.

To ensure that you don't dismiss too quickly your qualifications to use the functional resumé, you should first make a list of every organization to which you have belonged. Next, list all the jobs you have held—part-time and full-time positions. Then list any awards, honors, or scholarships you have received. Hopefully, you will have a list of at least six to eight activities, jobs, or awards. Now you should ask yourself the following questions: What kinds of responsibilities did I have in each of the situations on the list? Was I responsible for raising money, for instance, to help my group go on a trip? Was I responsible for providing excellent customer service as, perhaps, a waiter or waitress? Did I do anything during my high-school or college years that illustrates my ability to be self-reliant, such as selling on a straight commission?

If, after your self-analysis, you have determined you can credibly state that your past shows that you are self-motivated, decisive, trustworthy, or persuasive, you are ready to create your functional resumé. List the adjectives you have selected in the left margin (see Exhibit B1), then briefly describe the activities you have performed.

Once you have started analyzing your past and discovering how many things you have accomplished, you may be tempted to stretch the truth a bit. Be alert to such a temptation. Don't make a claim you can't support. Recruiters are usually adept at spotting "snow jobs." An apparently unrealistic or insupportable situation listed on a resumé will cause a recruiter to doubt all of the other information. The best advice, therefore, is to be creative but honest.

Exhibit B1 Functional Resumé

Trustworthy:	Five nights a week during 1988 and 1989, while attending SW Louisiana University, I was responsible for closing a restaurant, The Crazy Cajun; for adding the evening's receipts; and for locking the money in the safe.
Creative:	I designed, without any assistance, a brochure used in my university's College Orientation Program. I took pictures, wrote copy, and provided the artwork for the brochure, which was published in 1988.
Skillful:	I represented students majoring in business by serving on the 1989 Student Life Planning Committee. I negotiated with university administrators for a 20% increase in the amount of money the university provides to various student organizations.
Dependable:	I drove a school bus every day during my sophomore and junior years (1988 and 1989). I was responsible for the welfare and safety of 50 children ages 6 through 16. I did not miss a day, and the bus was never late.

If you decide to use a chronological resumé, you should list your educational attainments starting with your college graduation date (or anticipated date) under the major heading Education. Exhibit B2 shows how education and work experiences should be listed. Dates should be shown in descending or reverse order (for example, 1990, 1986, 1980). Your highest educational attainment should be listed first because that is the most important achievement to the recruiter.

The reader of a chronological resumé should be able to tell what a person was doing in any given year throughout the period covered by the resumé. People who are under twenty-five years old and have obtained (or will obtain) a bachelor's degree can include activities and accomplishments from their high-school and college years. Individuals older than twenty-five and those with a master's degree would be well advised to start their resumé with accomplishments, jobs, and awards attained during their undergraduate college years. The more experience you have in an industry, the more your resumé should reflect that job experience. For example, a thirty-seven-year-old should not emphasize what he or she did during college. An interviewer wants to know, in that case, what the person did during the past eight to ten years.

Regardless of what kind of resumé you decide to use, there are several guidelines you should keep in mind. First, ask yourself what traits or qualities you would look for in a job candidate if you were recruiting. Probably the stock answers come to mind—intelligence, high energy level, ability to communicate, pleasant person-

Exhibit B2 *Chronological Resumé*

Education

| 1990 | Graduated from Illinois State University. Earned B.S. in Business Administration with a Marketing major in four years. |
| 1986 | Graduated from Pleasantdale High School, Pinetree, Iowa. |

Experience

1988–1990 (September–May)	Head waitress/maitre d', Penultimate Restaurant
1988 (May–August)	Waitress, Yellowstone Lodge, Yellowstone National Park
1986–1988 (September–May)	Retail clerk, Student Union Shop, Illinois State University
1986 (May–August)	Lifeguard, Municipal Swimming Center, Pinetree, Iowa

ality, attention to detail. Some of these characteristics can be detected in personal interviews and/or aptitude tests while other characteristics can be detected by analyzing the job applicant's resumé. If the resumé is printed on good quality paper, the type is clear, and there are no typographical errors, then at least you can be sure your chances will not be diminished by the resumé itself. Unfortunately, some people's job opportunities are severely jeopardized just by the appearance of their resumé.

Second, keep your resumé short. In a survey of people who make hiring decisions, 75 percent said they frowned upon or found unacceptable a resumé longer than two pages.[1] For the majority of new college graduates, a one-page resumé should suffice.

Third, don't bother trying to state a universally acceptable job objective that will permit you to use the same resumé in applying for different jobs. Your cover letter can convey your goals, and the letter can be changed easier than the resumé.[2]

Fourth, list some of your interests and activities outside of work or school at the bottom of your resumé. If you are applying for a job that calls for high energy levels and a competitive spirit, be sure to list the activities and interests that reinforce your claims that you can do the job successfully. For example, most people would probably conclude that an avid tennis player would have a higher energy level than a bird-watcher.

Fifth, be sure to obtain the permission of each person whom you plan to list as a reference. Let him or her know when you plan to start interviewing, the type of job you are interested in, and, if possible, the names of the companies where you expect to interview. Make certain to give all your references a copy of your resumé. They will appreciate having the information, and it will help them to better answer inquiries.

Finally, and most important of all, be honest. Even if a lie or exaggeration is not spotted by the recruiter, you will be jeopardizing your future in a company if you start the relationship less than honestly with an employer.

INTERVIEWING

A good interview is one in which *both* parties contribute. Some people have the mistaken impression that a job interview is a situation in which the interviewer asks questions and the interviewee responds. You should view the meeting as an opportunity for you, the interviewee, to find out more about the job and the company as well as respond to a recruiter's questions.

Candidates for sales jobs should remember that they are being analyzed to determine their potential to successfully sell a company's products or services. Since salespeople are expected to ask good questions, an impressive job candidate should pose some questions that will not only yield some information but will reinforce his or her image as a potential employee. Questions such as, "What are the steps in your training program?" and "How will I be evaluated?" alert the interviewer to the fact that you can ask questions of fundamental importance.

As you prepare for an interview, take an extra copy of your resumé with you. Most interviewers will already have the copy you sent to them, or if the interview is occurring in a college placement center, the center's personnel will have provided the recruiter with a copy of your resumé. Occasionally, however, your resumé is misplaced or is not readily accessible. If you can quickly provide another copy, the interview can proceed smoothly and you will have given a signal that you are organized and prepared.

Be on time! In fact, plan to arrive five to ten minutes early for the appointment. If you are one of a dozen or more people the interviewer will talk to that day, any delay can irritate the interviewer and certainly does not inspire confidence in your being punctual in meeting customer appointments.

If possible, arrive in sufficient time to visit the restroom and check your appearance. You don't want to look rushed, out-of-breath, or disheveled when you meet the interviewer. A minute or two to calm yourself from the experiences of heavy traffic or other disconcerting activities will pay dividends in the way you present yourself in the first thirty seconds.

Your attire should be selected carefully. If in doubt, be conservative. There are enough guides to proper business dress so that no person should be ignorant about what is acceptable clothing for such occasions. John Molloy's *Dress for Success* can be used to help any man or woman needing guidance.[3]

Remember that the interview begins as soon as you are greeted by the interviewer. It doesn't start after the usual amenities have been concluded. Those important first few seconds set an impression about your social poise and confidence. Look directly at the person when he or she greets you and respond with a firm (but not bone-crushing) handshake if he or she extends his or her hand.

Be prepared during the interview to answer one or more of the following questions:

1. Why do you think you would be successful in sales? Warning: *do not* answer, "Because I like people." This is one of the most shopworn responses interviewers hear from inexperienced interviewees. Responses that reveal your interest in solving problems, beating competitors, or just making a lot of money are more acceptable.

2. Why are you interested in the ABC Company? Your response should reveal that you know something about the company's products and services. You should view this question as an opportunity to use the information you have collected in preparing for the interview.

3. What do you think are your major strengths and weaknesses? Be honest, but don't go overboard in praising or criticizing yourself. State two or three of your strong points and a couple of areas you hope to improve and leave it at that. Remember, this is a job interview, not a counseling session.

4. What have you done that required you to convince or persuade people to do something? This question is very relevant in a sales interview. Think back over your experiences and have a couple of examples ready to cite.

5. If you could create your perfect "dream" job, what would it be like? An interviewer is looking for an answer that reveals how you view shouldering responsibility, your attitude toward challenge, and whether you are seeking a safe, secure haven. Since most young people are expected to be building a career with some goal in mind, the interviewer will be comparing your answer with the action steps you have taken to prepare for eventually getting your dream job. If you say you want to be a vice president of marketing for a Fortune 500 company but you majored in music, the facts don't support the dream. It would be hard

to convince a recruiter that an applicant with this inconsistency should be favorably considered.

In addition to being prepared to answer these questions, you should also think about how you will respond if you are asked to engage in an impromptu role-playing exercise. Some recruiters will ask a job candidate to "sell" a pen, a necktie, or some other readily available object to them. The recruiter's purpose is not to see how polished a presentation you will make, but to see if you are willing to try and if such unusual requests will unsettle you and cause you to lose your poise. A good salesperson must have sufficient poise and self-confidence that such requests will not rattle him or her. Sales techniques and presentation skills can be improved, but it is much more difficult to improve an employee's self-confidence. The recruiter wants to know whether you have the requisite self-confidence to eventually become a winning sales rep.

Earlier, we suggested that the interview should be considered an opportunity for you to ask questions that will help you decide if you want to work for that particular firm. In addition to helping you make a better choice, the questions you ask can also be an aid in selling yourself. Many times, a person's image is influenced by the quality of the questions he or she asks.

The following are several questions you will want to ask (if the recruiter has not already provided the information):

1. How do you prepare a new salesperson to sell for your company?

2. How will I be evaluated and how often will the evaluations occur?

3. What is the typical career path for people who successfully perform in this initial job we have been discussing?

4. May I have an opportunity to visit with one of your reps, or better still, accompany a rep for a day in his or her territory?

5. What compensation method does your company use—straight salary, straight commission, or a combination of both?

The last question does not ask how much you would be paid but it does give you important information about the *method* of compensation.

When should you ask about the *level* of compensation? It is usually not advisable to ask that question during the first interview. If the interviewer asks you what amount of money you are expecting, don't evade the question. You should prepare for the question by checking with your school's placement center to find out what the salary ranges have been for jobs comparable to the one in which you are interested. Your response to such a question could be "I recently checked with the Placement Center here and they said that the salary offers ranged from $25,000 to $30,000. I'm sure your company is competitive." Make sure, however, that you are quoting figures related to comparable sales positions. A retailing position is not the same as a pharmaceutical sales position.

As the interview comes to an end, be sure you understand what the next step will be. Usually, the recruiter will make this clear but if you have not heard the recruiter explicitly state what the next contact will be, you should ask. It is a good practice, as you leave, to thank the interviewer. A statement such as, "Thank you for the opportunity to talk about the ABC Company and I will be expecting to hear from you in the next two weeks" (if that was the time period you thought the inerviewer mentioned) would be appropriate.

A short, post-interview thank-you note is appropriate if you have interviewed with someone who is not a professional recruiter. A recruiter who sees hundreds of people each month is less likely to be impressed with a note. If you decide, however, to write to thank an interviewer, be sure to keep your letter simple and brief.

If you lack experience in job interviewing, you can gain beneficial experience in a way that will not jeopardize your chances with firms in which you are most interested. Seek interviews with two or three companies in which you have little interest. Prepare for these interviews, however, with the same care you would exert if you were preparing for your first or second choices. For most people, the experience gained in the first few interviews will increase their skills significantly. It is one thing to read and think about interviewing and how you will react but it is much more valuable to get actual experience. As soon as you leave these "trial" interviews, jot down the questions you were asked and your responses. Now think about why the interviewer asked these questions and how your responses could have been interpreted. The insights you gain from such analyses will prove to be valuable.

Finally, it is vital to keep yourself in a positive frame of mind. No one likes to be rejected, and yet rejection is inevitable. Don't start immediately questioning your value and entering subsequent interviews with a defeated attitude. Successful salespeople, regardless of when they pursued their careers (the Production Era, the Sales Era, the Marketing Era), have always been resilient people. You must learn to rebound quickly and strongly so that previous setbacks don't diminsh your future chances.

If you are now an undergraduate student preparing to interview for your first full-time job after graduation, you are about the embark upon the most exciting period in your college career. Good luck and good hunting!

NOTES

1. "USA SNAPSHOTS: Keep Your Resumé Short," *USA Today* (July 28, 1989): B1.
2. John H. Noble, "Building the Perfect Resumé," *Managing Your Career* (New York: *Wall Street Journal*, 1989): 27.
3. John T. Molloy, *Dress for Success* (New York: Warner Books, 1975).

Glossary

A

Accommodation: a method of conflict resolution in which one party gives in to another.

Achievement Level: a dimension of the career life cycle that can be measured by the number of job assignments, the organizational levels of the jobs, and the dollar sales volume achieved.

Active Listening: paying attention to what the other person is saying, decoding the message, and then stating the interpretation of his or her feelings.

Administrative Managers: mid-level or middle managers who spend an average amount of time on planning, organizing, staffing, directing, and controlling activities.

Aggressive Bargaining Negotiation Strategy: a negotiating tactic whereby negotiators see themselves as adversaries who should not reveal any more information than necessary.

AIDA: an acronym comprising the first letters of the words *attention, interest, desire,* and *action.*

Alternative Evaluation: third step in the consumer's decision-making process in which the consumer compares and contrasts various potential products or services under consideration to satisfy the problem or need.

Amiables: individuals who want sales presentations that are lengthy enough to contain information on how the proposed product or service will affect people.

Analyticals: individuals who want detailed sales presentations that provide the opportunity to digest the facts and to request more information.

Assumptive Close: a closing method in which the buyer wants or needs the product or service because a sale is going to be made. The salesperson will ask a question, make a statement, or behave as though the sale is a foregone conclusion.

Attitudes or Opinions: a person's positive, neutral, or negative feelings about products, services, companies, or salespersons.

Authority: a method to resolve conflict in which the issue is taken to a higher authority.

Avoidance: a method to resolve conflict in which the conflict is recognized, but nothing is done to resolve it.

B

Bargaining: a method to resolve conflict in which two parties use their power and persuasion to maximize their gain or minimize their loss vis-à-vis each other.

Barrier Theory: when a person has agreed to a proposition in a presentation, the proposition appears to form a mental barrier for the individual.

Benefit Approach: a benefit of a product or service cited by the salesperson that is expected to appeal to a broad range of people.

Benefitizing: translating a product's or service's features into benefits believed to be of value to the customer.

Bingo Cards: advertisements in which the reader is asked to circle a number on a card that has been assigned to a particular advertiser. By circling the number, the reader can obtain information about the product, service, or company.

Body Language: any movement of our bodies that communicates something to other people.

Bogey Tactic: an aggressive bargaining tactic in which a buyer makes both a promise to buy and a threat not to buy unless some condition is met by the seller.

Boundary Spanning: the dual role of representing the company to customers and representing customers to the company, which requires the salesperson to be adept at satisfying the needs of multiple parties.

Brand-Switching Contact: a customer contact in which the contact has extensive experience with the product, but little or no experience with the sales representative.

Business Case: a report containing revenue and/or cost information justifying a sales proposal by the salesperson to a potential buyer.

Buying Center: a group of individuals who may have an impact on the decision whether or not a product or service is purchased, and who may play one or more roles including users, influencers, buyers, decision makers, and gatekeepers.

C

Canned Presentation: a standardized sales presentation in which the same phrases or statements are used in each and every sales presentation.

Career Life Cycle: the stages of a salesperson's career including preparation, development, maturity, and decline.

Career Pathing: the grooming of individuals for successively larger amounts of responsibility by giving them experience in different parts of the company.

Center of Influence Method: a prospecting method in which the salesperson attempts to cultivate an apparent expert since this expert often influences others.

Chain of Logic Presentation: a sales presentation that assumes the agreement to purchase a product or service is a logical solution to a customer's problem or potential problem and that he or she recognizes it is the logical answer.

Channeling Question: a question used to direct or redirect the conversation to subjects pertinent to the sales call, the customer's circumstances, or the products or services.

Clarifying Question: a question asked to gain more specific information and thus a better understanding of the buyer's situation.

Clean Slate Contact: a customer contact in which the contact has no previous experience with the product or the sales representative.

Closing: the culmination of the salesperson's efforts to acquire an order or the asking for the order by the salesperson.

Closing on a Minor Point: a closing method in which the salesperson focuses on a postpurchase detail in order to determine if the prospect has already decided to purchase the product or service.

Cognitive Dissonance: an assessment by the customer in which the negative aspects of the product or service bought and the positive features of the items considered, but not purchased, are reviewed.

Company Mission: the fundamental, unique purpose that sets a business apart from other similar firms and identifies the scope of its operations in product and market terms.

Compromise: a method to resolve conflict in which each party is willing to give a little.

Conflict: any opposition or antagonistic interaction between two or more parties.

Constant Affirmation: a sales presentation in which the salesperson wants the customer to agree with each point in the presentation in order to build a series of logical agreements with the customer so that the purchase decision seems the logical step to take.

Consultative Selling: a sales method that focuses on identifying the prospect's problems.

Consumer Goods: those goods and services destined for the final consumer for personal, family, or household use.

Contact Matrix: a two-dimensional model that illustrates some basic types of customer contacts.

Controls: the measures or assessments made by the salesperson to determine whether or not his or her objectives have been accomplished.

Coordinated Marketing: integration of the various marketing functions with one another and integration of marketing with other departments in the company.

Corporate Culture: the beliefs, values, customs, and behaviors that are unique to each company.

Counselor Relationship: a relationship in which the customer knows the general objective or desired condition but does not know how to implement a solution, and therefore values personalized attention and easy access to the salesperson.

Credibility: the ability to inspire belief, trust, and reliability.

Crunch Tactic: an aggressive bargaining tactic in which a buyer asks for extra features or concessions not agreed to in the original set of specifications.

Cultural Barriers: values, ideas, attitudes, or ways of thinking or behaving that hinder or prohibit someone from one culture from accomplishing something in another culture.

Culture: the values, ideas, attitudes, and other symbols and objects created by society that shape human behavior.

Curiosity Approach: an approach in which an action is

taken by the salesperson to arouse the prospect's or customer's interest in learning more about the product or service.

Customer Development: those activities that identify and attract potential customers or prospects to do business with the salesperson.

Customer Maintenance: those activities undertaken to ensure that existing customers remain loyal to the salesperson's company.

Customer or Market Organization: the organizational sales structure a company uses when it has different market segments with dissimilar needs. Specific types of customers such as the consumer, industrial, and governmental markets are the basis for this structure.

Customer Service: the process of responding to the needs and problems of the customer.

D

Decline Phase: the final stage of a salesperson's career life cycle.

Decode: a communication process in which the listener or receiver interprets the message or behavior of the source or sender.

Depth of Inquiry: a variable in the personal sales mix model that describes the extent of effort put forth by the salesperson to learn the details of the buyer's decision process.

Detail Salespeople: salespersons calling on well-educated professionals and describing highly technical or specialized products.

Development Phase: the second stage of the salesperson's career life cycle in which the salesperson's progress is the most apparent.

Diagnosis: the first step in the personal planning process in which the salesperson attempts to define his or her status and why this situation has occurred.

Differentiation Strategy: the creation of something buyers perceive as unique and of sufficient value so that the seller can receive a higher price for the product.

Direct Appeal Close: a closing method in which the salesperson simply asks in a straightforward manner whether or not the customer is interested in making the purchase.

Direct Mail: advertising such as letters, cards, and other literature sent by mail to potential customers.

Drivers: individuals who want sales presentations that provide information that will permit them to make rapid but accurate decisions.

E

Effective Selling Time: the actual time spent selling to customers or prospecting for new business.

Eighty-Twenty (80-20) Rule: 80 percent of sales are accounted for by 20 percent of the customers. The same rule or principle may also apply to some degree to the relationship between sales and products, sales and salespersons, and sales and territories.

Empathy: the ability to see another person's point-of-view and to understand the roles and responsibilities of others.

Encode: a communication process in which the source or sender of a message constructs or develops the message.

Endless Chain: a prospecting method in which persons using the product or service can identify several other people who, in their opinion, could use the same product or service.

Enlightened Self-Interest: a method of looking at ethical situations in which an individual pursues personal gain in a way that minimizes harmful consequences for others.

Ethical Behavior: the use of recognized social principles involving justice and fairness in business relationships.

Ethics: the code of morals of a particular profession, group, or person.

Ethnocentrism: the tendency to think that one's own group is the best.

Evoked Set: the range of product brands or service groups assembled by a consumer that can be considered

his or her real alternatives for consideration to purchase.

Exit Barrier: any impediment that prevents or minimizes a customer's being enticed to switch brands (e.g., good customer service often creates an exit barrier).

Expressives: individuals who use products and symbols to communicate their status and who want sales presentations that explain how the product or service is a symbol or indicator of status.

Express Warranty: a warranty based on the contract and the result of negotiation of the terms of the sales contract.

F

Family Life Cycle: the stages involved in the formation, growth, change, and dissolution of a typical two-parent family.

Flash-in-the-Pan Model: a buyer-seller relationship with an extremely short life span because the customer doesn't see any value in continuing the relationship.

Focus or Niche Strategy: the idea that a firm can serve a narrow strategic target more effectively or efficiently than competitors who are competing more broadly.

Follow-Up Contacts: responsibilities of the sales rep after a buyer has committed to make a purchase.

Formal Organization: an organization created by management to specify individual responsibilities and authority.

Formal Structure: the relative strictness of rules, span of control, and frequency and specificity of supervisory control.

Functional Mobility: the movement of a person from one type of job to another.

Functional Organization: an organizational sales structure that includes a number of functional marketing specialists in such areas as sales and marketing research. This structure does not divide the sales force into groups based on products or customers.

Future Favor: a business practice in which every time a favor is performed or a gift is given, a future favor or gift is expected to repay the obligation.

G

General Industrial Directory: a directory of all businesses in an industry listed alphabetically, geographically, by market segment, or by all three methods.

Geographic Mobility: the movement of a person from one location to another.

Geographic or Territorial Organization: an organizational structure that divides the sales force into different geographic locations, such as the northwest and southeast regions of the United States.

Globalization: competition that is no longer confined to

companies in an industry in the United States, but occurs between or among companies worldwide.

Goal Orientation: the primary emphasis or focus of a department.

Golden Rule: a belief that a person should treat others as he or she would want to be treated.

H

Hierarchy of Effects: the movement through a series of stages from unawareness to awareness to knowledge to liking to preference to conviction and finally to the act of purchase.

High-Context Language: what one does with his or her hands, facial expressions, and even noises conveys meanings in addition to what is actually being said—an especially important concept when considering interactions with international customers from different cultures.

I

Implied Warranty: a warranty that represents obligations assumed by the seller by operation of the law.

Informal Organization: an organization that is an outgrowth of human interaction and develops with or without formal management approval.

Information Search: the second step of the consumer's decision-making process in which the consumer obtains

information from both personal and impersonal sources.

Inner Circle: the concept in some cultures in which a person is considered a member of the group, and thus is likely to have access to a network of contacts that would not otherwise be available.

Inner Debt: a situation in which the buyer, at least in his or her mind, has established within the seller's mind an obligation to be paid by the buyer when he or she makes a future purchase. It occurs after an initial purchase by the buyer has been made, and the seller has given the buyer a gift for making a purchase.

Inside Selling: a selling situation where the customer comes to the salesperson, as in stores, telephone inquiries, and "800" calls initiated by advertising.

In Supplier: the seller is the customer's current supplier.

Integrated Marketing and Selling: the coordination of a salesperson's activities with other marketing personnel responsible for other marketing functions including advertising, marketing research, and customer service.

Interdepartmental Relationships: specifically, relationships between sales or marketing personnel and other functional units in the organization, such as manufacturing and finance; in general, relationships between or among departments.

Internal Marketing: the successful hiring, training, and motivation of company employees to serve customers well.

Interpersonal Orientation: the relative openness, sociability, and permissiveness in relationships within a department.

Intradepartmental Relationships: specifically, relationships between sales and other marketing functions; in general, relationships within a department.

Intra-industry Concentration: a situation in which a few of the largest producers account for a high percentage of an entire industry's production.

Introductory Approach: the most straightforward and frequently used approach in which the salesperson simply introduces himself or herself to the prospect or customer.

J

Job Qualifications: the hiring specifications for a sales position, including such items as education, sales experience, product or service knowledge, and personality.

K

Key or Major Account Organization: an organizational sales structure in which a salesperson devotes his or her full attention and time to one account.

L

Language of Agreements: how various individuals in different cultures view agreements or contracts, from a preference for written to oral contracts and the degree to which contracts or agreements are specific or general in content.

Language of Friendship: how various individuals in different cultures view relationships with others and the degree to which these relationships are valued.

Language of Space: how various individuals in different cultures view the importance of space, such as the location of one's office or business.

Language of Things: how various individuals in different cultures view the importance of various possessions or things that a person may have.

Language of Time: how various individuals in different cultures view the importance of time and the speed with which they perform various tasks or conduct business.

Learning: a change in behavior that is the result of past experience.

Life Style: how people live and how they spend their time and money.

Limited Choice Close: a closing technique in which the salesperson reduces the number of options for the customer to consider to only a few in which the customer has

shown interest even though a large number of options were originally available.

Line Personnel: individuals in decision-making roles with authority over other individuals as in the relationship between the sales manager and a salesperson. Those directly responsible for sales and operations results.

Line Versus Staff: the distinction between those individuals in decision-making roles with authority over other individuals (line personnel) as compared to those individuals in advisory roles (staff personnel).

Loose Lead: a person or an organization that does not intend to buy within a short period of time and thus is less likely to buy at all.

Low-Cost Producer Strategy: a way to create products or render services more economically than any of the other competitors in the industry.

M

Macroenvironmental Factors: broad and powerful forces and factors that can affect industries, companies, and individuals, including technology, globalization, legal and ethical concerns, reorganization, and intra-industry concentration.

Manufacturing-Oriented Company: a company whose orientation focuses on internal efficiencies and an emphasis on a lower-cost strategy.

Marketing Concept: a business philosophy based on the idea that, for long-range success, a firm should orient its products, prices, promotions, and distribution efforts to the needs and wants of an identified target group of customers.

Marketing Era: a stage in the evolution of American business from approximately 1950 to 1980, which was characterized by attention to what customers seemed to need or want before production produced the goods.

Marketing Mix: the combination of product, price, place, and promotion elements.

Marketing-Oriented Company: a company focusing on analysis, planning, and research to discover what customers want or need.

Maturity Phase: the third stage of a salesperson's career life cycle in which his or her career progress slows, but may reach its peak in attaining the highest level of achievement.

Missionary Selling: selling to individuals who decide what product someone else should buy.

Model of Utility: making ethical decisions based on the principle of maximizing happiness for the greatest number of people.

Modified Rebuy: an organizational buying situation in which the buyer has made the purchase previously and has already undergone a certain amount of information search about suppliers and their products or services and is willing to consider alternative suppliers for further analysis.

Motivation: the major force underlying a consumer's behavior that leads the consumer to act in a certain way in response to a need.

Motive: a force that leads a person to act in a certain way in response to a need.

N

National Account Management: the dedication of a portion of the sales staff, either an individual or a sales team, to service major or key accounts that contribute a high level of sales and/or profits.

National Account or Key Account Sales Team: *see* National Account Management.

Need-Satisfaction Presentation: a sales presentation oriented toward discovering and meeting a customer's needs by asking a number of questions.

Negotiation: a conference between two parties that results in the settlement of some matter.

Negotiation Strategy: the general approach a negotiator takes to achieve his or her objectives.

Networking: using one's contacts with other people to achieve a particular goal.

Network of Relationships: interaction between a number of individuals and departments or groups such as between a salesperson and a sales manager, sales and advertising, or sales and production.

New Task: an organizational buying situation in which the buyer has little or no prior experience in dealing with the particular problem or need and will actively seek out information on alternative ways to solve the problem.

Noise: anything in the communication process that detracts from or diminishes the effectiveness of the communication.

O

Objectives: the third step in the personal planning process, in which the salesperson focuses on answering the question of where he or she would like to be at a certain time in the future.

Operative Manager: a first-line manager who spends more time on staffing, directing, and controlling activities than on planning and organizing activities.

Opinion Leader: an individual who influences the purchasing behavior of another consumer through face-to-face communication.

Opinions: *see* Attitudes.

Order Getter: a salesperson who is expected to persuade buyers to purchase a specific brand from among a variety of competing brands.

Order Taker: a salesperson who is expected to take or receive a customer's orders and inform customers about the availability of products.

Organizational Buying: the decision-making process by which formal organizations establish the need for purchased products and services, and identify, evaluate, and choose among alternative brands and suppliers.

Organizational Relationships: the relationships within a company that a salesperson will have with his or her superior, other marketing personnel, and nonmarketing personnel.

Out Supplier: the seller is not the customer's current supplier.

P

Partnering: *see* Strategic Alliances.

Patience-Pays-Off Model: a relationship life cycle in which the first few sales to the buyer by the seller are for relatively small amounts, but after this initial period, the amount of sales to the buyer by the seller increases sharply.

Penetration Model: a relationship life cycle in which the seller cultivates additional business within the buying unit, such as from other departments or people in addition to the original buyer.

Perceived Risk: the belief that negative outcomes may result from engaging in specific types of behavior.

Perception: how individuals collect, process, and interpret information from their environment.

Personality: the sum total of an individual's traits that make that individual unique.

Physical Action Close: behavior by the salesperson that indicates that the sale is a foregone conclusion.

Portfolio Management Concept: a business's product lines that experience various stages of growth, as well as its various potential to established customers and prospects.

Position or Job Description: a description of the job or position title, duties and responsibilities, organizational relationships, and job qualifications for a position.

Postpurchase Evaluation: the fifth step of the consumer's decision-making process in which the customer assesses whether or not he or she has made a good decision as well as whether or not he or she would engage in the same behavior or purchase again.

Preparation Phase: the first stage in a saleperson's career cycle, which often includes extensive training and development activities.

Presentation Pace: the speed with which an attempt is made to move a presentation toward its conclusion.

Presentation Scope: the range of features, benefits, and sales terms covered in one presentation.

Price Discrimination: offering a given customer a price reduction or additional promotional allowance while not offering the same to other customers on a proportionately equal basis.

Problem or Need Recognition: the first step in the consumer's decision-making process in which the problem or need is recognized and is sufficiently important and urgent to warrant action.

Problem-Solution Presentation: a sales presentation based on an in-depth analysis of a specific customer's circumstances, including formal studies of the customer's operations.

Problem-Solving: a method to resolve conflict in which parties to the conflict seek a solution that will satisfy the goals of each.

Problem-Solving Negotiation Strategy: a negotiating tactic that primarily involves discovering ways to increase benefits to both buyer and seller.

Product Life Cycle: the pattern of sales for a product over time.

Product-Market Organization: an organizational sales structure that either divides sales personnel by products and markets or uses product and market managers in staff positions to advise the sales force.

Product Organization: an organizational sales structure in which the sales force is divided by product, particularly when the products are numerous, unrelated, or technical.

Production Era: a stage in the evolution of American business from 1776 to around 1920, which was characterized by an excessive demand for products and services. The salesperson's job was primarily to take orders and thus the salesperson was referred to as an order taker.

Professional: someone participating for gain or livelihood in an activity or field of endeavor often engaged in by amateurs.

Prognosis: the second step in the personal planning process in which the salesperson focuses on assessing where he or she is heading in the near future.

Promotion: the various ways a business addresses customers, including personal selling, advertising, sales promotion, and publicity.

Promotional Mix: the combination of personal selling, advertising, sales promotion, and publicity.

Prospect: a lead judged to possess sufficient potential to warrant further sales effort.

Prospecting: the activity involved in generating names and addresses of people or businesses that may be in the market for the salesperson's products or services.

Proxemics: the study of personal space and the movement of people within it.

Psychological Currency: terms of a sale or contract that are made in exchange for actual dollars.

Purchase Decision: the fourth stage of the consumer's decision-making process in which the consumer has decided to buy the product or service and does so.

R

Receiver: the individual in the communication process who receives or interprets a message or communication that is sent from the sender or source. In a selling situation, the seller and buyer may be both receivers and sources of messages or communications.

Reciprocity: the practice of a buyer giving preference to a supplier who is also a customer of his or her company.

Recycled Model: a relationship life cycle in which sales from a customer may drop for a brief period, but then return to previous levels.

Red, Yellow, and Green Signals: three categories of body language—red signals tell a sales rep to stop the present form of communication; yellow signals reveal customer doubts or boredom; green signals indicate agreement.

Reference Group: any group that has an influence on a person's attitudes, behavior, or decisions.

Referral Approach: an approach method in which the salesperson mentions or refers to the name of someone the customer knows and respects, often someone who has recommended that the salesperson contact the customer.

Relationship Life Cycle: a series of stages or events that are part of the continuing interaction or relationship between the buyer and seller, from the initial sale through future sales over time.

Relationship Management: the planned, goal-oriented interaction between a buyer and a seller designed to render mutually beneficial results and thereby foster subsequent interactions between them.

Resupply Contact: a customer contact in which the contact has extensive experience with the product and the salesperson.

S

Sales Cycle: the period from the moment a contact is initiated with a prospective buyer until the moment when the salesperson knows definitely whether a sale is going to be made and the product or service is going to be installed.

Sales Era: a stage in the evolution of American business from approximately 1920 to 1950 during which the role of the salesperson shifted from an order taker to an order getter.

Sales Leads: the names of persons or organizations that possess some characteristic believed to be an indicator of demand for a product or service.

Sales-Oriented Company: a company focusing on the product and the use of selling and promotion to generate profits and sales volume, particularly in the short term.

Selling Center: a concept similar to a buying center in which representatives from various functional areas in sales are brought together to form a selling team.

Service Selling: selling an intangible product or service, such as life insurance.

Sharp Practices: evasion and indirect misrepresentation that may be just short of fraud, which is illegal.

Single Objection Close: a closing technique in which the salesperson uses an objection raised by the customer as an opportunity to close. After resolving the objection, the salesperson attempts to close to see how close he or she is to achieving a sale.

Social Class: a somewhat permanent and homogeneous group of people with similar behavioral patterns, interests, and life styles.

Source: the individual in the communication process who creates and sends messages. In selling situations, both the

seller and the buyer send and receive messages.

Staff Positions: the jobs of the individuals who serve as support to line personnel, such as a sales trainer who supports the activities of a sales manager.

Standing-Room-Only Close: a closing technique in which the salesperson indicates that a product or service will be available or at a special price for a limited time only in an attempt to get buyers to respond to an attractive offer the seller is making.

Stimulus-Response Presentation: a series of statements about the customer, the salesperson, the salesperson's company, and the product and words and phrases that may act as a stimulus to obtain a positive response from the customer.

Straight Rebuy: an organizational buying situation in which the buyer continues to use the same supplier for a product or service.

Strain: a condition in which the individual may experience actual damage to his or her ability to deal with everyday situations.

Strategic Alliance: a business partnership whereby two companies, one of which is a supplier to the other, join together in a business venture.

Strategic Managers: top-level managers who spend more time planning and organizing than staffing, directing, and controlling operations.

Strategic Marketing Era: a stage in the evolution of American business that has been in effect since about 1980. New emphases are placed on managing customers for profits and not just sales, and on building long-term rather than only short-term relationships with customers.

Strategy: the fourth step of the personal planning process in which the salesperson defines the best way or ways to achieve his or her desired objectives.

Stress: the feelings of frustration, conflict, pressure, anger, inadequacy, guilt, loneliness, or confusion.

Stress Interview: a situation in which an interviewer poses a question or asks the interviewee to do something he or she may not expect. Its purpose is to see how the interviewee manages his or her emotions and maintains his or her poise in times of stress.

Stressors: events external or internal to the individual that cause stress.

Subculture: a distinct social group existing as an identifiable segment within a larger culture.

Subject-oriented Directory: a list of vendors of a particular product or service.

Summary Close: a closing technique in which the salesperson briefly reviews or summarizes the benefits of the product or service and then asks for the order.

Supplementary Sale Contact: a customer contact in which the contact has no experience with the product, but has extensive experience with the salesperson.

Supplier Relationship: a buyer-seller relationship in which the buyer knows the objective he or she wants to attain and the type of product or service needed to achieve the objective, but needs assistance in procuring the specific product or service.

Systems Designer Relationship: a buyer-seller relationship in which the buyer is unaware of ways to perform an activity or function more efficiently, and expects a total solution to the problem once it has been established that a better approach exists.

T

Tactics: the fifth step in the personal planning process in which the salesperson takes specific detailed actions to implement a strategy to accomplish an objective.

Target Market: those individuals or companies who are the most likely customers.

Technical Selling: selling to a buyer who intends to use the seller's products or services to make and sell their own products or services or conduct their operation.

Technology-Oriented Company: a company that focuses on product performance and emphasizes research in order to offer new products or improvements to existing products.

Telemarketing: a system staffed by trained specialists who use telecommunications and information technologies to implement marketing strategies cost-effectively.

Ten-K (10-K) Report: a report providing a detailed description of each firm's business that must be filed with the Securities and Exchange Commission within 90 days of the end of the fiscal year.

Third-Party Method: a method for handling hidden objections in which another customer is used as an example by the salesperson who states that another party had a similar problem and goes on to tell how the problem was resolved.

Threshold: a level of awareness that causes a person to realize that some condition exists.

Tight Lead: people or organizations who intend to buy within a short period of time.

Time Orientation: how long it takes a department to know the results of its actions.

Trade Selling: selling to a buyer who intends to resell the product for a profit

Trade Show: an event where a seller (usually a manufacturer) exhibits products with other sellers. The products are ordinarily not for sale; orders, however, can be placed.

Trial Close: an attempt to determine the prospect's attitude toward the product and the sales presentation.

Two-to-One (2:1) Ratio: if the salesperson doesn't ask twice as many questions compared to statements about the product, he or she may be attempting to overly control the presentation.

Two-Way Communication: the exchange of questions, statements, and other information between the source and the receiver in the communication process. In selling situations, it refers to the exchange between the buyer and seller.

Tying Contract: an attempt by the seller to force the buyer to buy one product in order to obtain another product.

U

Unbundling: breaking down the price of a product into parts, so that each part or component service has a price.

V

Verification Question: a question asked to see whether or not the buyer agrees or disagrees with the salesperson.

W

Walking Away Point: the point in a sales negotiation when it becomes unprofitable to make the sale.

Work Styles: the combination of a people and a task orientation that may be an unequal or equal combination of the two aspects.

Name Index

Subject Index

Photo Credits